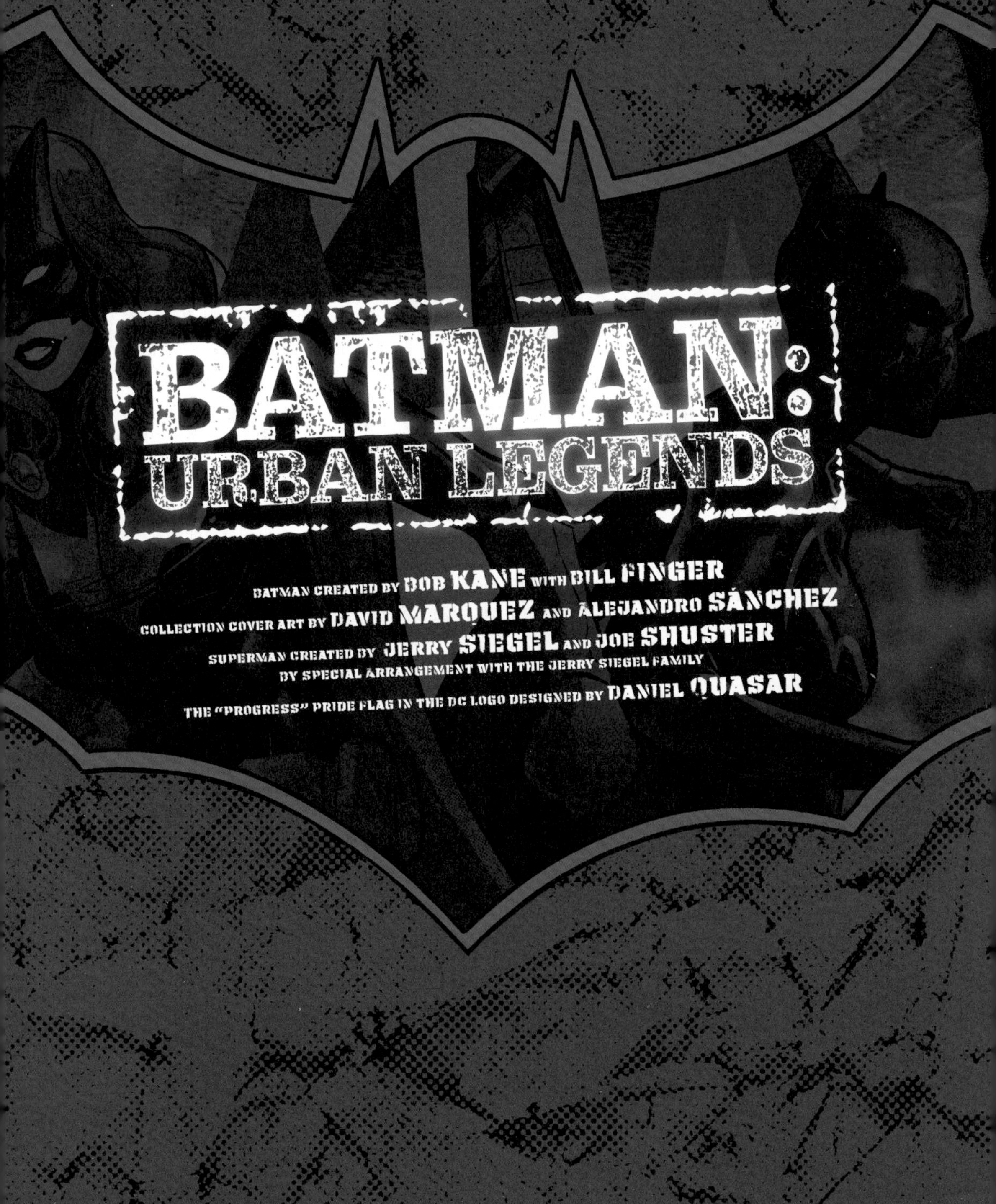

BATMAN: URBAN LEGENDS

BATMAN CREATED BY BOB KANE WITH BILL FINGER

COLLECTION COVER ART BY DAVID MARQUEZ AND ALEJANDRO SÁNCHEZ

SUPERMAN CREATED BY JERRY SIEGEL AND JOE SHUSTER
BY SPECIAL ARRANGEMENT WITH THE JERRY SIEGEL FAMILY

THE "PROGRESS" PRIDE FLAG IN THE DC LOGO DESIGNED BY DANIEL QUASAR

BATMAN: URBAN LEGENDS

VOL. 2

THE OUTSIDERS IN "THE CARETAKER"

BRANDON THOMAS writer MAX DUNBAR artist
LUIS GUERRERO colors STEVE WANDS letters

TIM DRAKE IN "SUM OF OUR PARTS"

MEGHAN FITZMARTIN writer BELÉN ORTEGA artist
ALEJANDRO SÁNCHEZ colors PAT BROSSEAU letters

AZRAEL IN "DARK KNIGHT OF THE SOUL"

DAN WATTERS writer NIKOLA ČIŽMEŠIJA artist
IVAN PLASCENCIA colors ARIANA MAHER letters

ORACLE IN "GHOST IN THE MACHINE"

CECIL CASTELLUCCI story
MARGUERITE SAUVAGE art & colors BECCA CAREY letters

BATGIRLS IN "WILD CARD"

MARGUERITE BENNETT writer SWEENEY BOO artist
MARISSA LOUISE colors BECCA CAREY letters

BATWING IN "SUPERMAN PUNCH"

CAMRUS JOHNSON writer LOYISO MKIZE pencils TREVOR SCOTT inks
ANDREW DALHOUSE colors AL W'S TROY PETERI letters

BATWOMAN IN "FEAR STATE: DISINFORMATION CAMPAIGN"

ALYSSA WONG writer VASCO GEORGIEV artist
RAIN BEREDO colors BECCA CAREY letters

THE OUTSIDERS IN "FEAR STATE: THE FEARFUL"

BRANDON THOMAS writer
CIAN TORMEY pencils RAUL FERNANDEZ inks
ALEJANDRO SÁNCHEZ colors STEVE WANDS letters

TIM DRAKE IN "A CAROL OF BATS"

MEGHAN FITZMARTIN writer
ALBERTO JIMENEZ ALBURQUERQUE artist
NICK FILARDI colors PAT BROSSEAU letters

NIGHTWING IN "THE BATS OF CHRISTMAS PAST"

TINI HOWARD writer CHRISTIAN DUCE artist
SARAH STERN colors BECCA CAREY letters

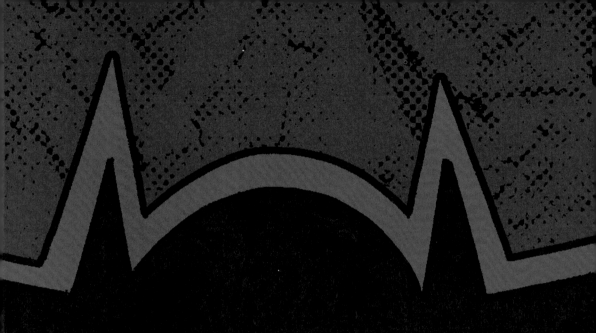

BEN ABERNATHY, JESSICA CHEN Editors – Original Series
DAVE WIELGOSZ Editor – Original Series & Collected Edition
BEN MEARES Associate Editor – Original Series
STEVE COOK Design Director – Books
DAMIAN RYLAND Publication Design
ERIN VANOVER Publication Production

MARIE JAVINS Editor-in-Chief, DC Comics

ANNE DePIES Senior VP – General Manager
JIM LEE Publisher & Chief Creative Officer
DON FALLETTI VP – Manufacturing Operations & Workflow Management
LAWRENCE GANEM VP – Talent Services
ALISON GILL Senior VP – Manufacturing & Operations
JEFFREY KAUFMAN VP – Editorial Strategy & Programming
NICK J. NAPOLITANO VP – Manufacturing Administration & Design
NANCY SPEARS VP – Revenue

BATMAN: URBAN LEGENDS VOL. 2

DC Comics, 2900 West Alameda Ave., Burbank, CA 91505
Printed by Solisco Printers, Scott, QC, Canada. 4/15/22. First Printing. ISBN: 978-1-77951-553-7

Library of Congress Cataloging-in-Publication Data is available.

PEFC Certified

This product is from
sustainably managed
forests and controlled
sources

PEFC/26-31-02   www.pefc.org

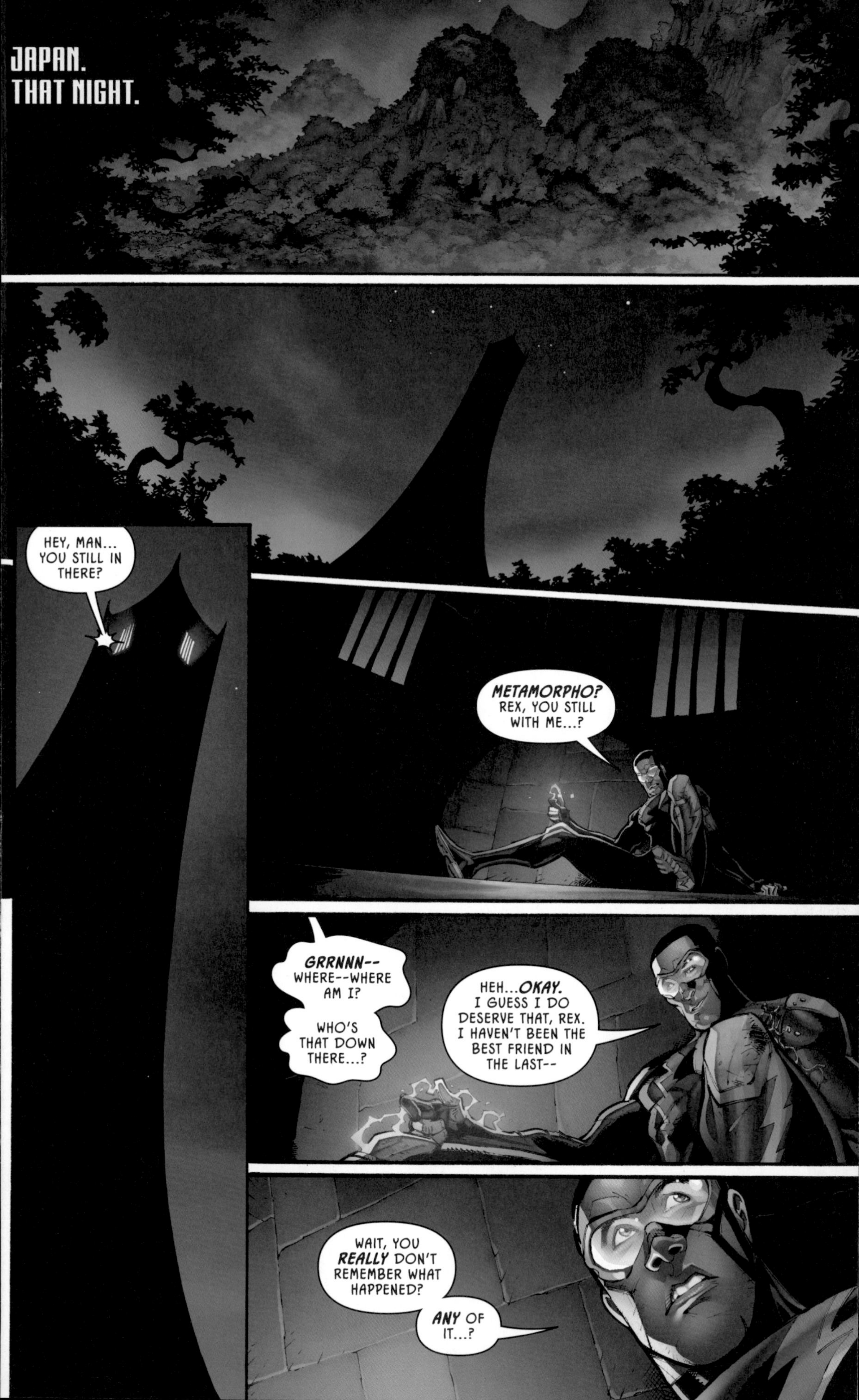
JAPAN.
THAT NIGHT.
HEY, MAN... YOU STILL IN THERE?
METAMORPHO? REX, YOU STILL WITH ME...?
GRRNNN-- WHERE--WHERE AM I?
WHO'S THAT DOWN THERE...?
HEH...OKAY. I GUESS I DO DESERVE THAT, REX. I HAVEN'T BEEN THE BEST FRIEND IN THE LAST--
WAIT, YOU REALLY DON'T REMEMBER WHAT HAPPENED?
ANY OF IT...?

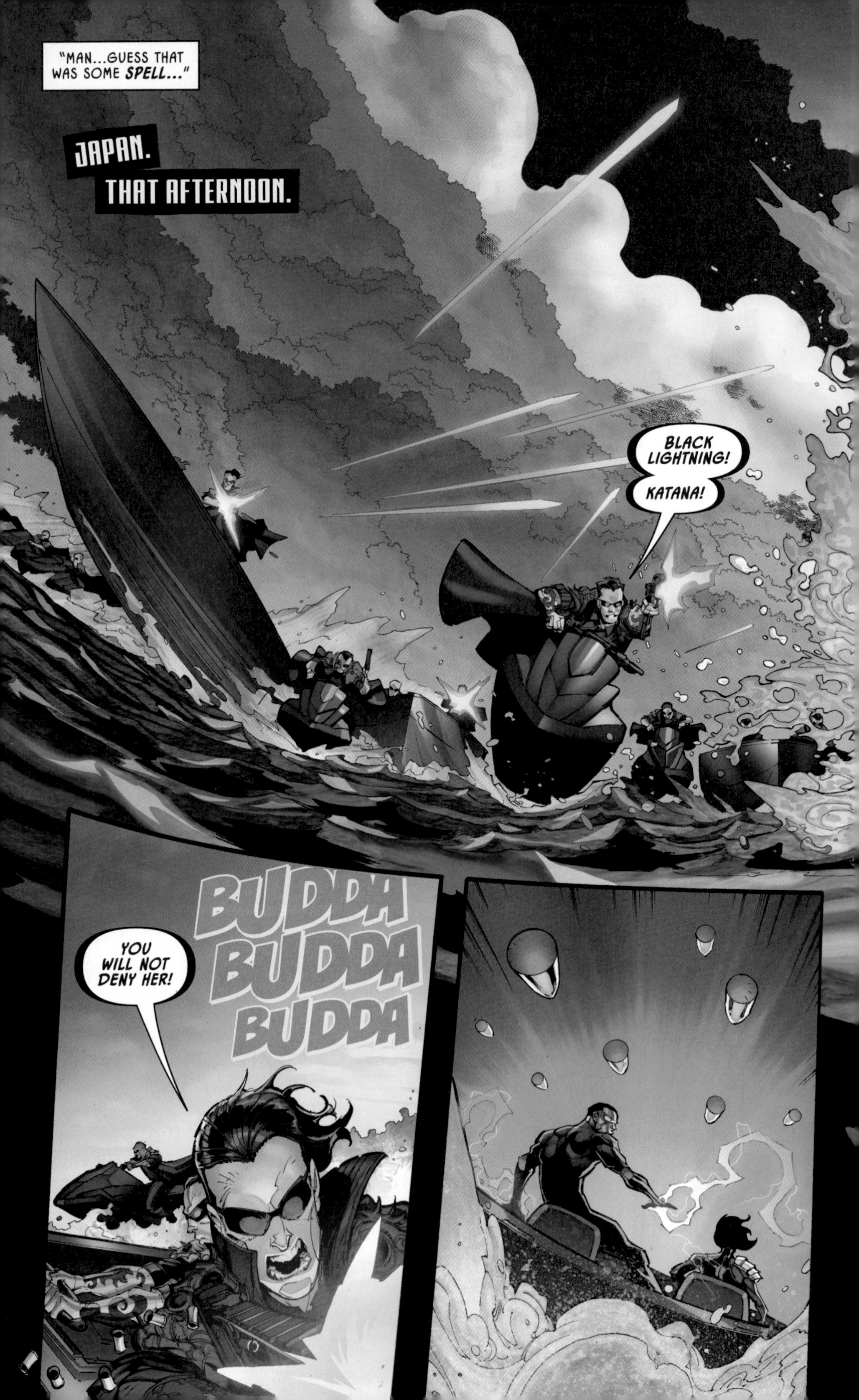
"MAN...GUESS THAT WAS SOME SPELL..."
JAPAN.
THAT AFTERNOON.
BLACK LIGHTNING!
KATANA!
BUDDA BUDDA BUDDA
YOU WILL NOT DENY HER!

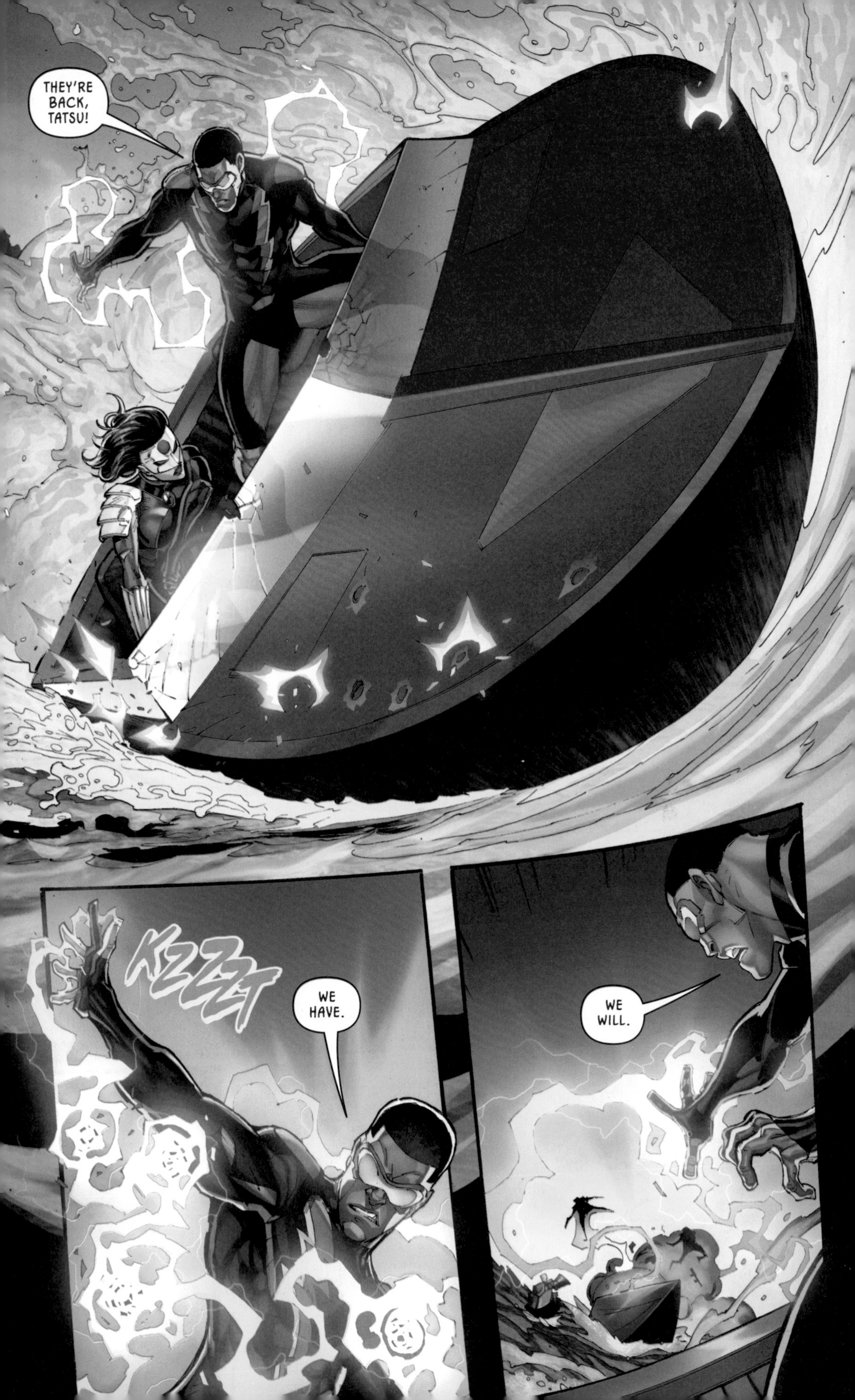
THEY'RE BACK, TATSU!
KZZZT
WE HAVE.
WE WILL.

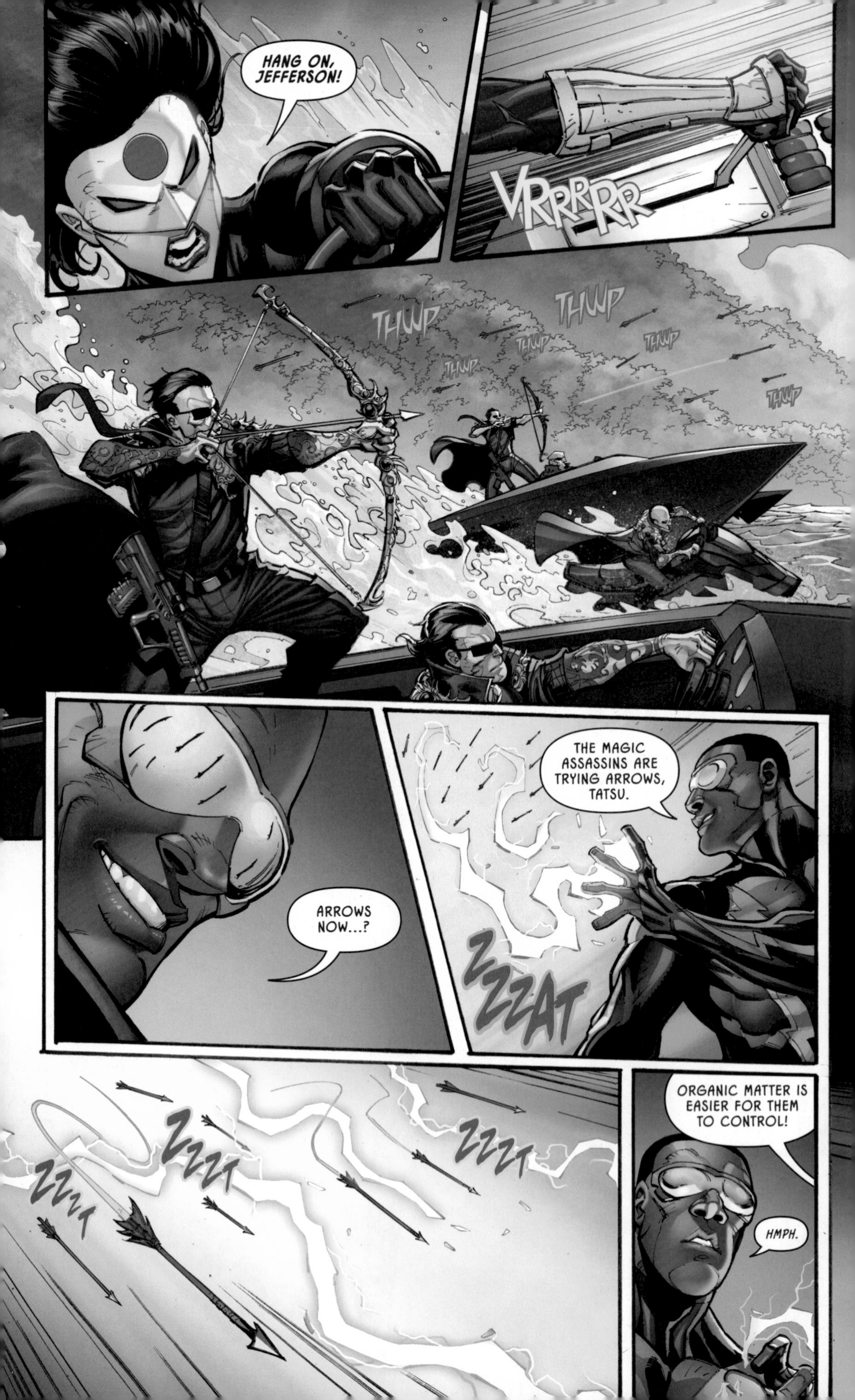
HANG ON, JEFFERSON!
VRRRRR
THWP
THWP
THWP
THWP
THWP
THWP
ARROWS NOW...?
THE MAGIC ASSASSINS ARE TRYING ARROWS, TATSU.
ZZZAT
ZZZT
ZZZT
ZZZT
ORGANIC MATTER IS EASIER FOR THEM TO CONTROL!
HMPH.

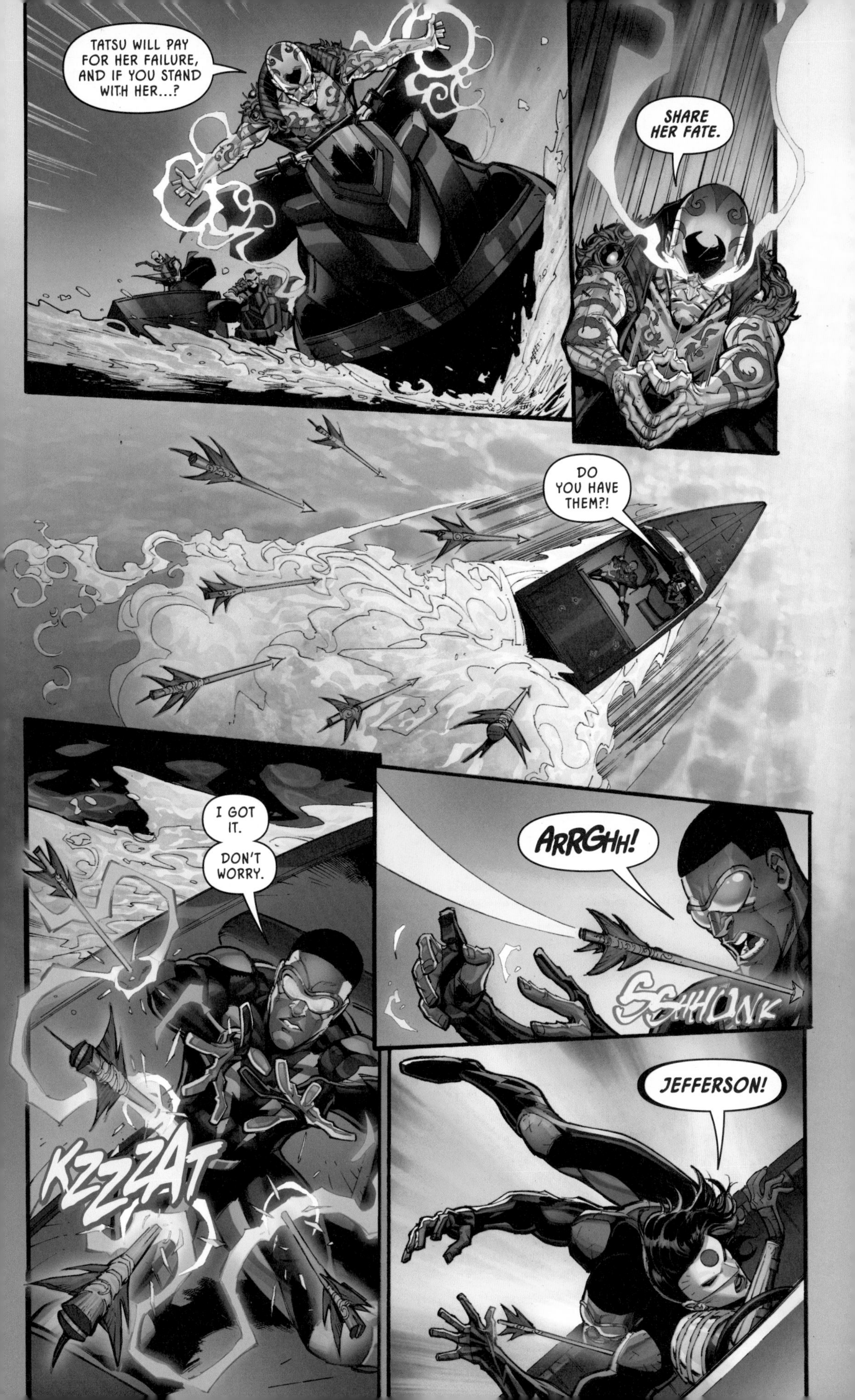

TATSU WILL PAY FOR HER FAILURE, AND IF YOU STAND WITH HER...?
SHARE HER FATE.
DO YOU HAVE THEM?!
I GOT IT.
DON'T WORRY.
KZZZAT
ARRGHH!
SSHHONK
JEFFERSON!

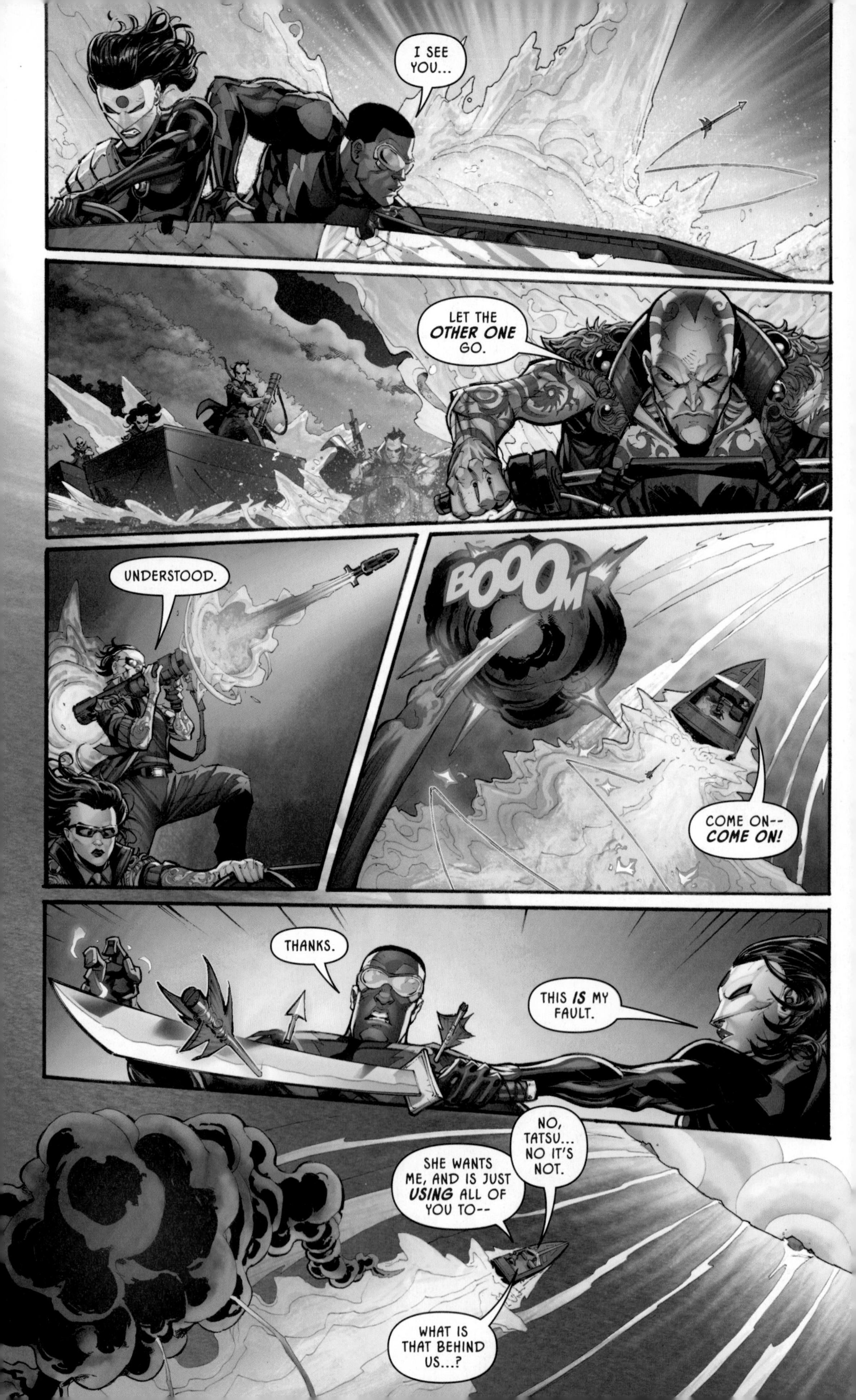
I SEE YOU...
LET THE *OTHER ONE* GO.
UNDERSTOOD.
BOOOM
COME ON-- *COME ON!*
THANKS.
THIS *IS* MY FAULT.
SHE WANTS ME, AND IS JUST *USING* ALL OF YOU TO--
NO, TATSU... NO IT'S NOT.
WHAT IS THAT BEHIND US...?

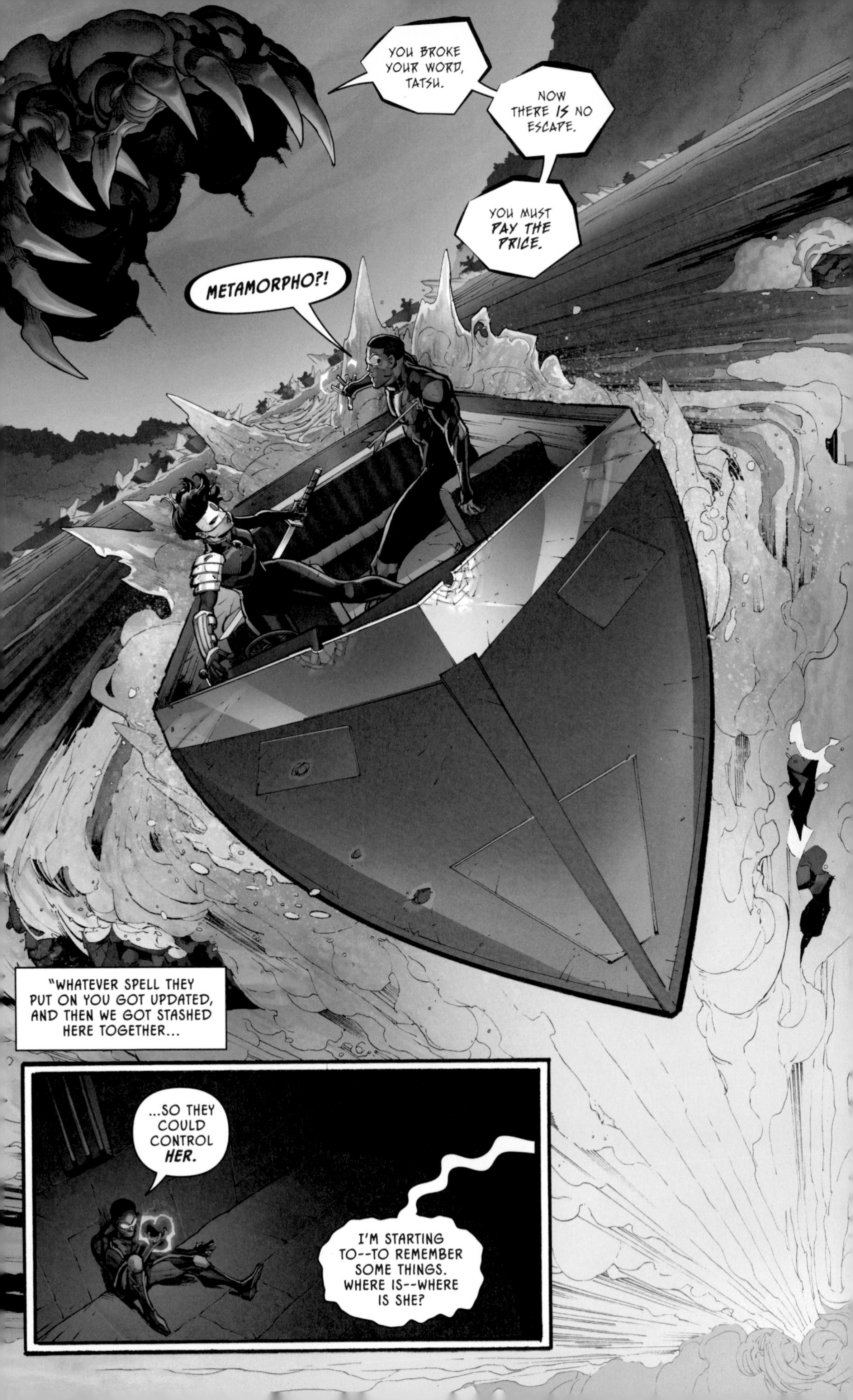
YOU BROKE YOUR WORD, TATSU.
NOW THERE IS NO ESCAPE.
YOU MUST PAY THE PRICE.
METAMORPHO?!
"WHATEVER SPELL THEY PUT ON YOU GOT UPDATED, AND THEN WE GOT STASHED HERE TOGETHER...
...SO THEY COULD CONTROL HER.
I'M STARTING TO--TO REMEMBER SOME THINGS. WHERE IS--WHERE IS SHE?

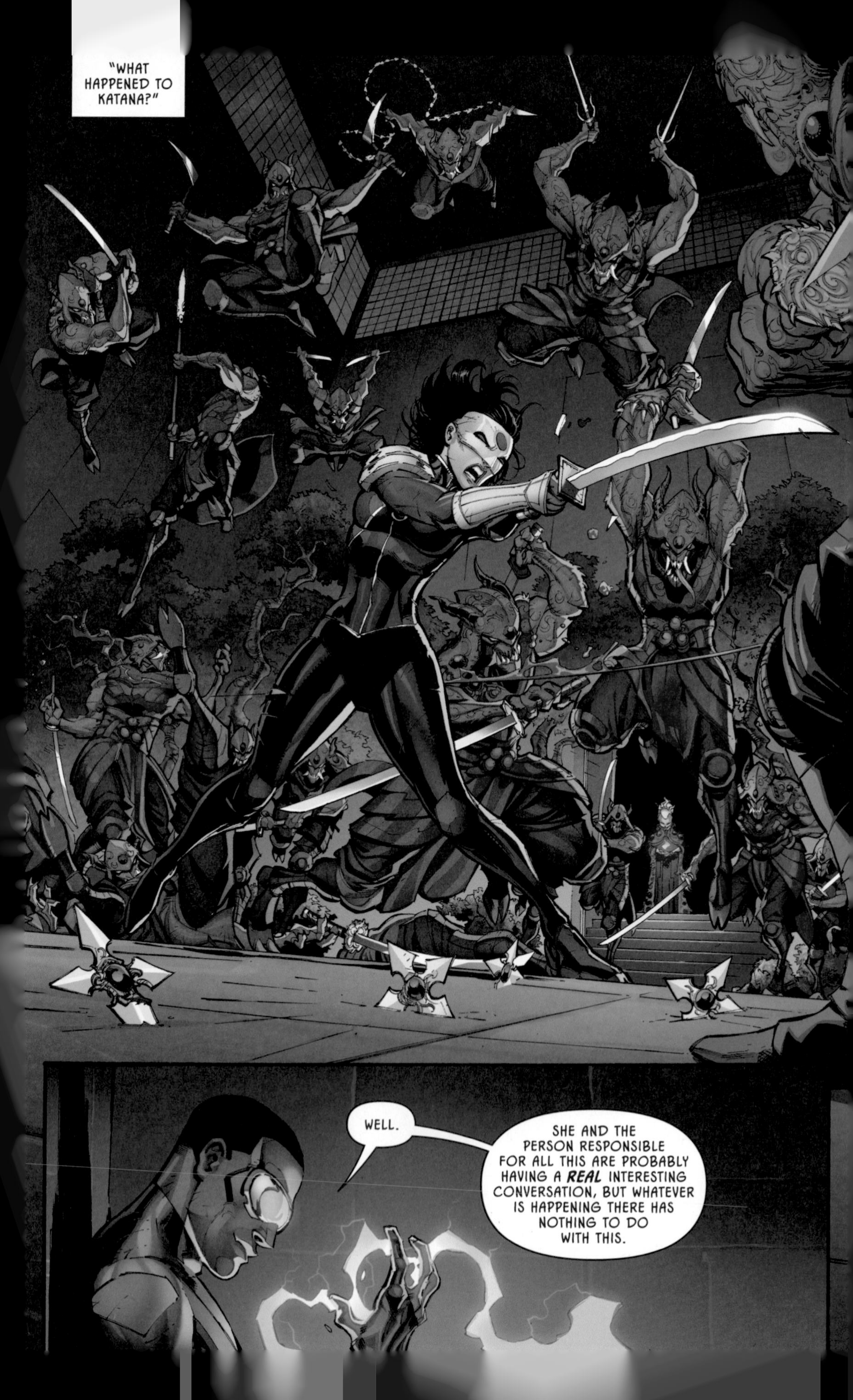
"WHAT HAPPENED TO KATANA?"
WELL.
SHE AND THE PERSON RESPONSIBLE FOR ALL THIS ARE PROBABLY HAVING A REAL INTERESTING CONVERSATION, BUT WHATEVER IS HAPPENING THERE HAS NOTHING TO DO WITH THIS.

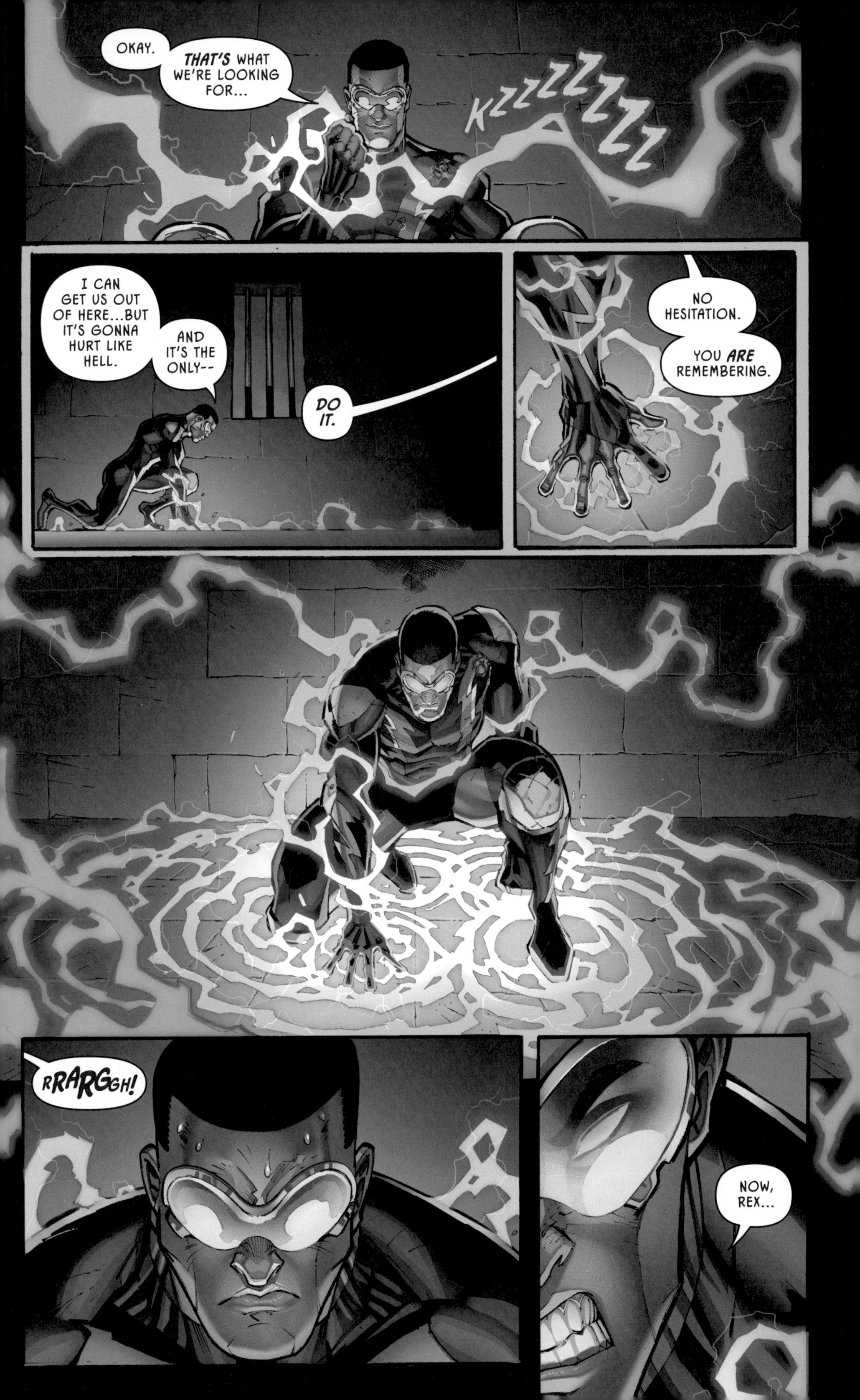

OKAY.
THAT'S WHAT WE'RE LOOKING FOR...
KZZZZZZZZ
I CAN GET US OUT OF HERE...BUT IT'S GONNA HURT LIKE HELL.
AND IT'S THE ONLY--
DO IT.
NO HESITATION.
YOU ARE REMEMBERING.
RRARGGH!
NOW, REX...

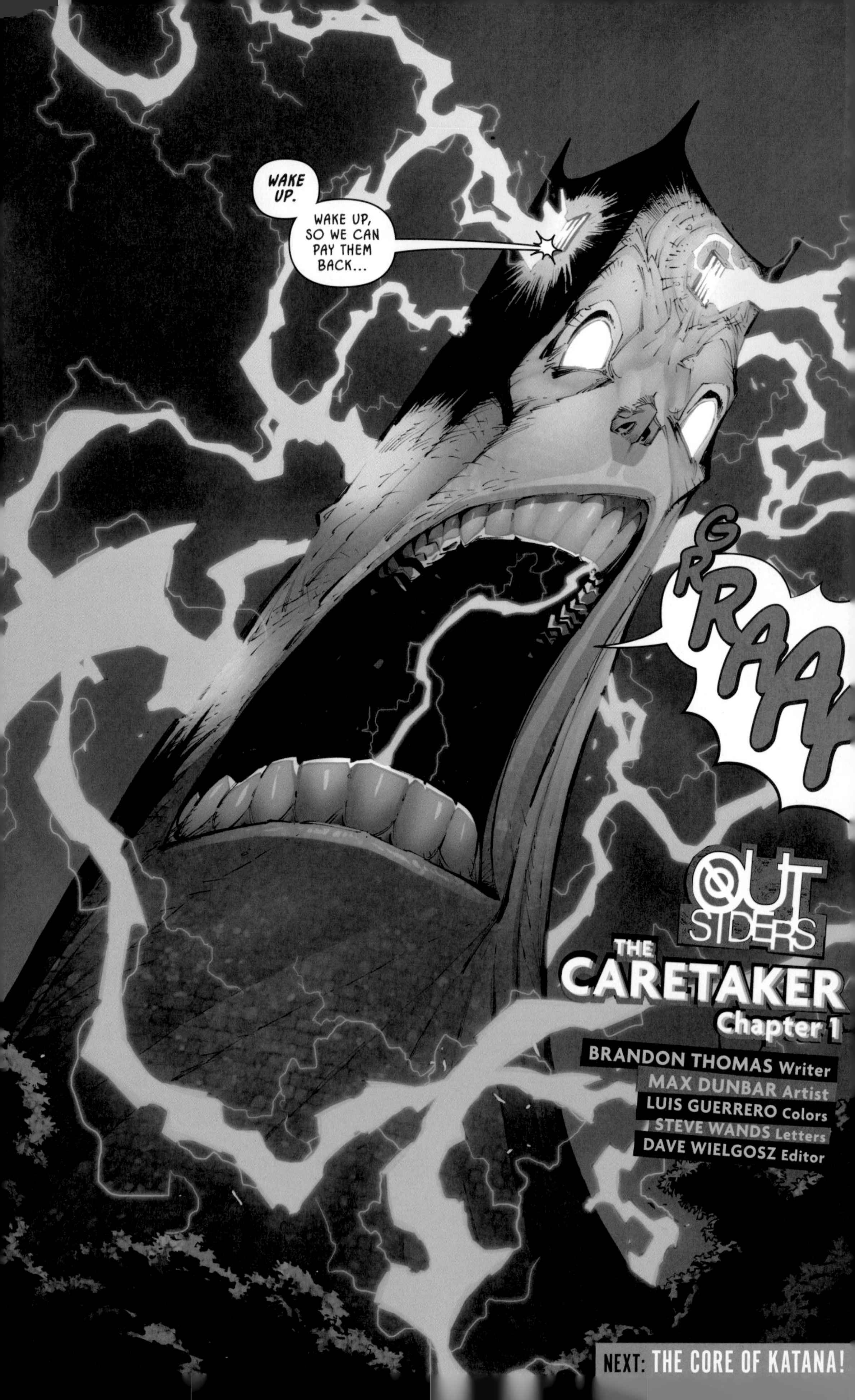
WAKE UP.
WAKE UP, SO WE CAN PAY THEM BACK...
GRRAAA
OUTSIDERS
THE CARETAKER
Chapter 1
BRANDON THOMAS Writer
MAX DUNBAR Artist
LUIS GUERRERO Colors
STEVE WANDS Letters
DAVE WIELGOSZ Editor
NEXT: THE CORE OF KATANA!

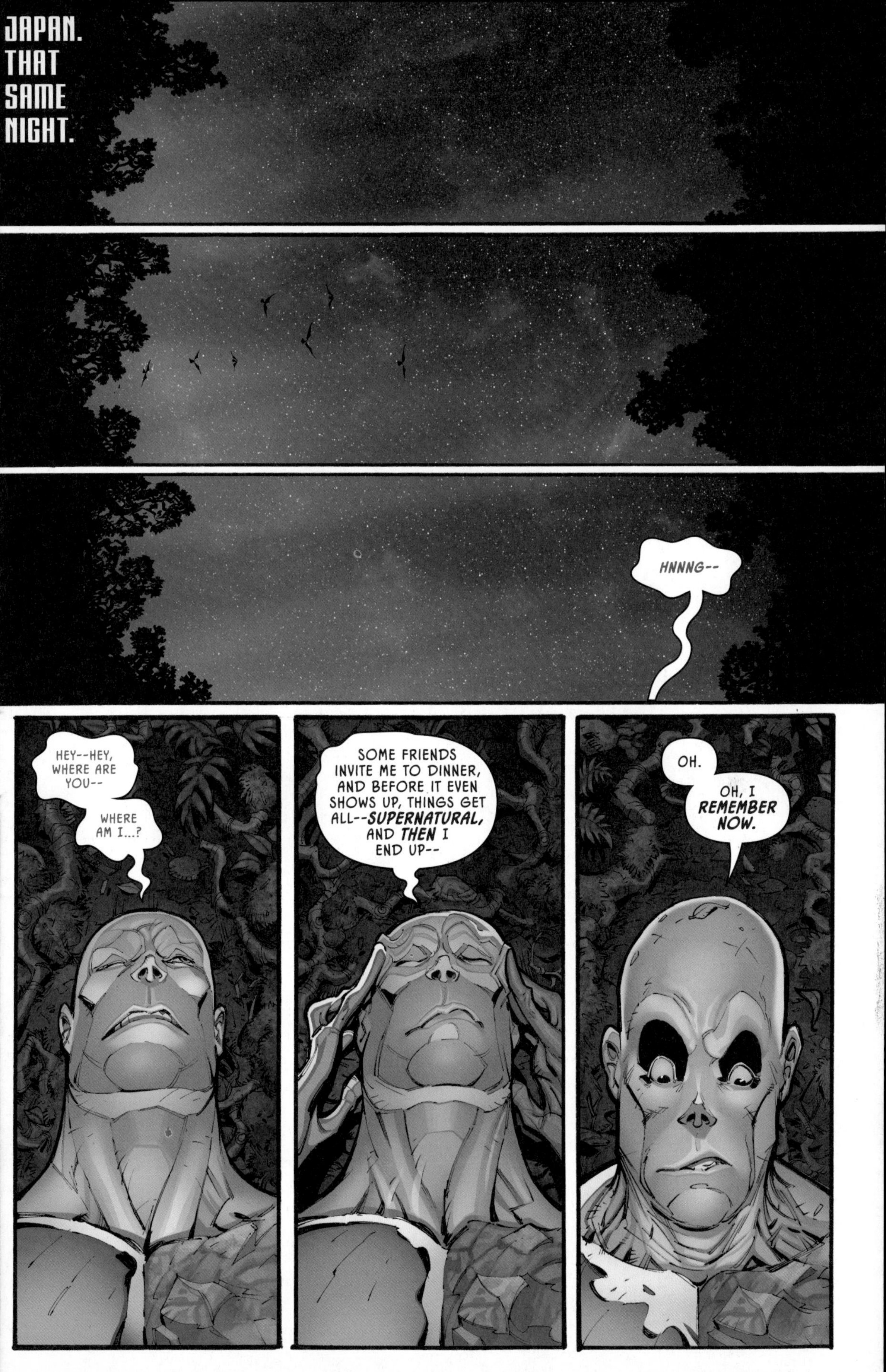

JAPAN. THAT SAME NIGHT.
HNNNG--
HEY--HEY, WHERE ARE YOU--
WHERE AM I...?
SOME FRIENDS INVITE ME TO DINNER, AND BEFORE IT EVEN SHOWS UP, THINGS GET ALL--SUPERNATURAL, AND THEN I END UP--
OH.
OH, I REMEMBER NOW.

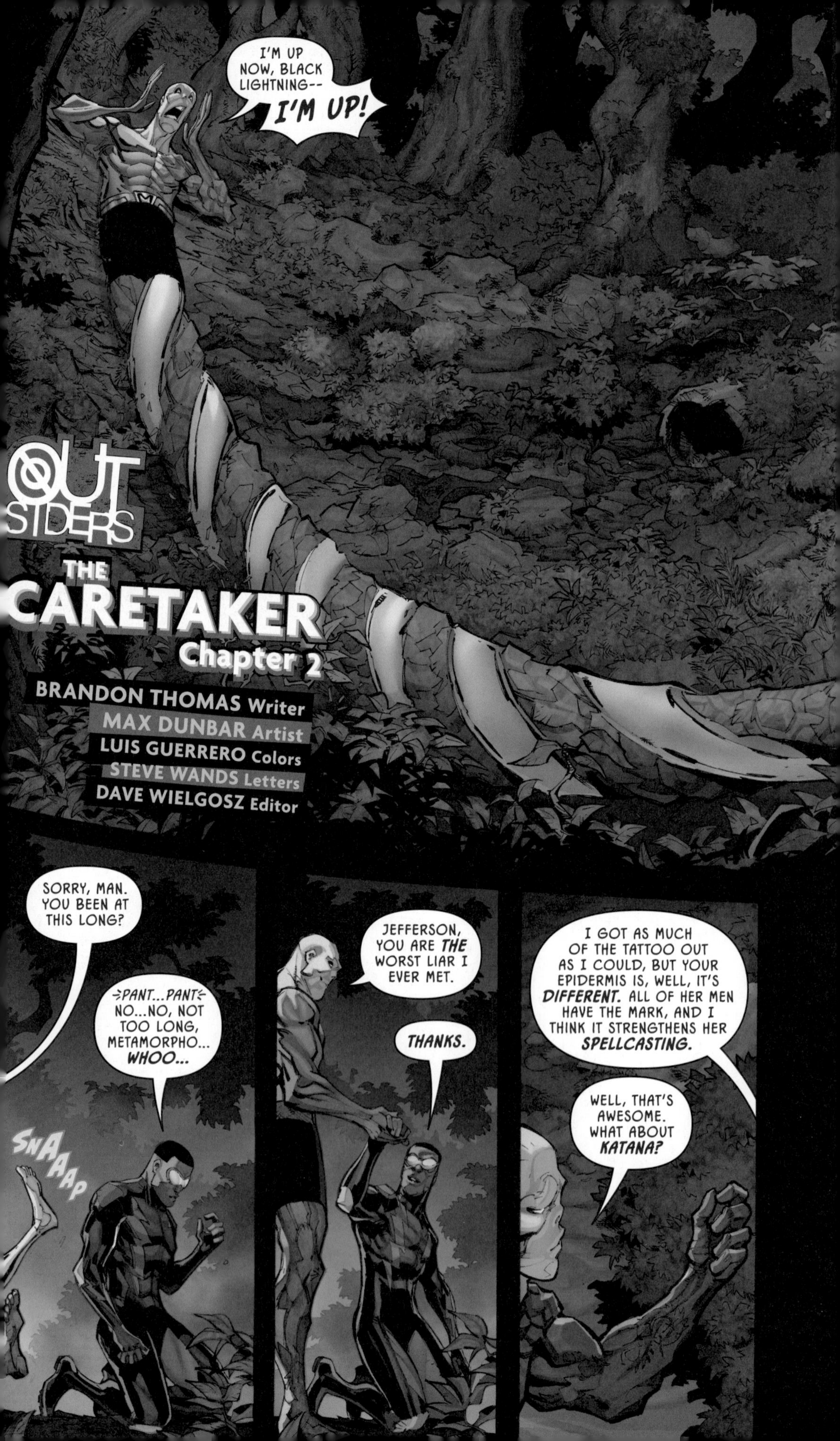
I'M UP NOW, BLACK LIGHTNING-- I'M UP!
OUTSIDERS
THE CARETAKER
Chapter 2
BRANDON THOMAS Writer
MAX DUNBAR Artist
LUIS GUERRERO Colors
STEVE WANDS Letters
DAVE WIELGOSZ Editor
SORRY, MAN. YOU BEEN AT THIS LONG?
PANT...PANT NO...NO, NOT TOO LONG, METAMORPHO... WHOO...
SNAAAAP
JEFFERSON, YOU ARE THE WORST LIAR I EVER MET.
THANKS.
I GOT AS MUCH OF THE TATTOO OUT AS I COULD, BUT YOUR EPIDERMIS IS, WELL, IT'S DIFFERENT. ALL OF HER MEN HAVE THE MARK, AND I THINK IT STRENGTHENS HER SPELLCASTING.
WELL, THAT'S AWESOME. WHAT ABOUT KATANA?

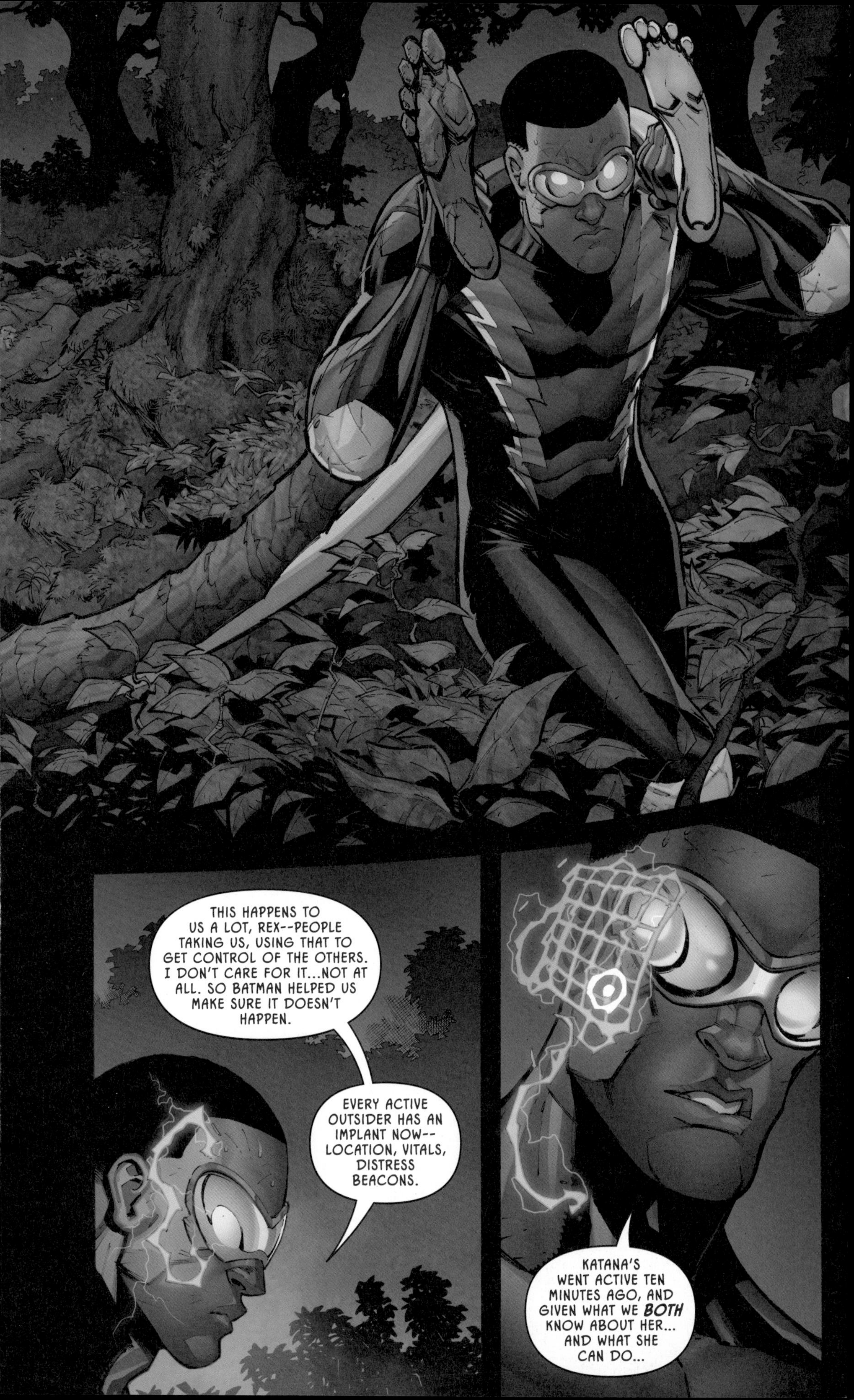

THIS HAPPENS TO US A LOT, REX--PEOPLE TAKING US, USING THAT TO GET CONTROL OF THE OTHERS. I DON'T CARE FOR IT...NOT AT ALL. SO BATMAN HELPED US MAKE SURE IT DOESN'T HAPPEN.
EVERY ACTIVE OUTSIDER HAS AN IMPLANT NOW--LOCATION, VITALS, DISTRESS BEACONS.
KATANA'S WENT ACTIVE TEN MINUTES AGO, AND GIVEN WHAT WE BOTH KNOW ABOUT HER... AND WHAT SHE CAN DO...

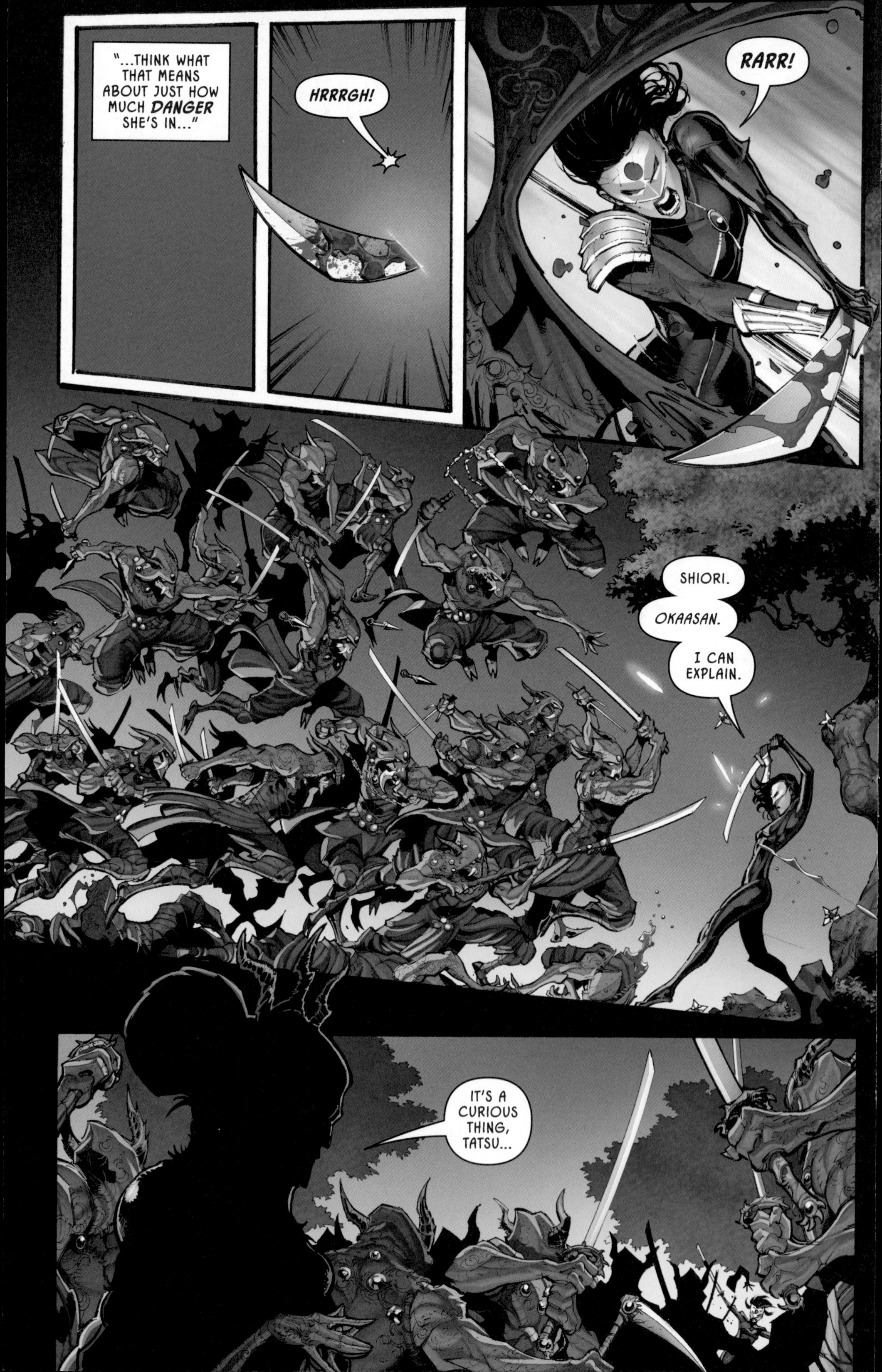
"...THINK WHAT THAT MEANS ABOUT JUST HOW MUCH DANGER SHE'S IN..."
HRRRGH!
RARR!
SHIORI.
OKAASAN.
I CAN EXPLAIN.
IT'S A CURIOUS THING, TATSU...

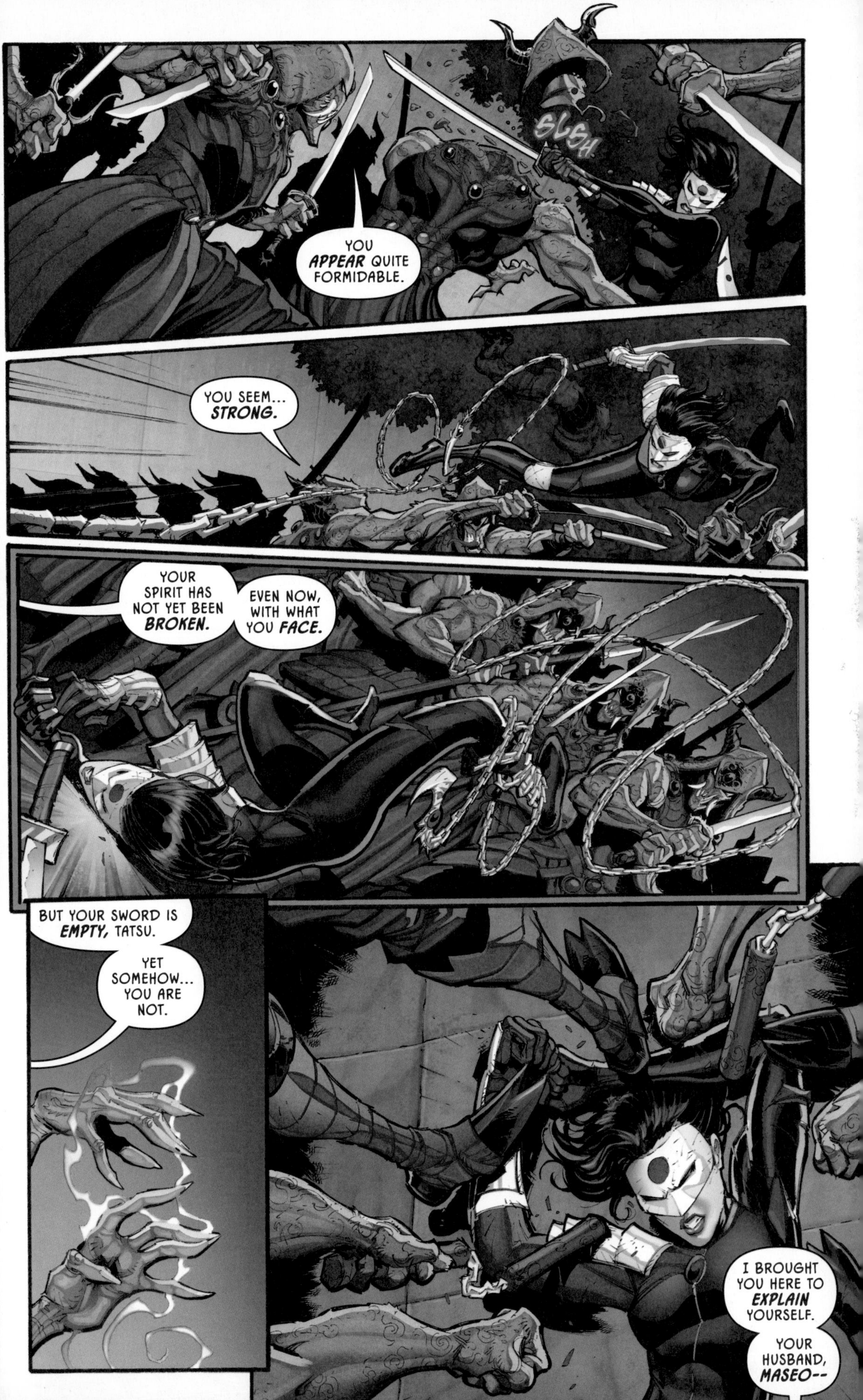
SLISH
YOU APPEAR QUITE FORMIDABLE.
YOU SEEM... STRONG.
YOUR SPIRIT HAS NOT YET BEEN BROKEN.
EVEN NOW, WITH WHAT YOU FACE.
BUT YOUR SWORD IS EMPTY, TATSU.
YET SOMEHOW... YOU ARE NOT.
I BROUGHT YOU HERE TO EXPLAIN YOURSELF.
YOUR HUSBAND, MASEO--

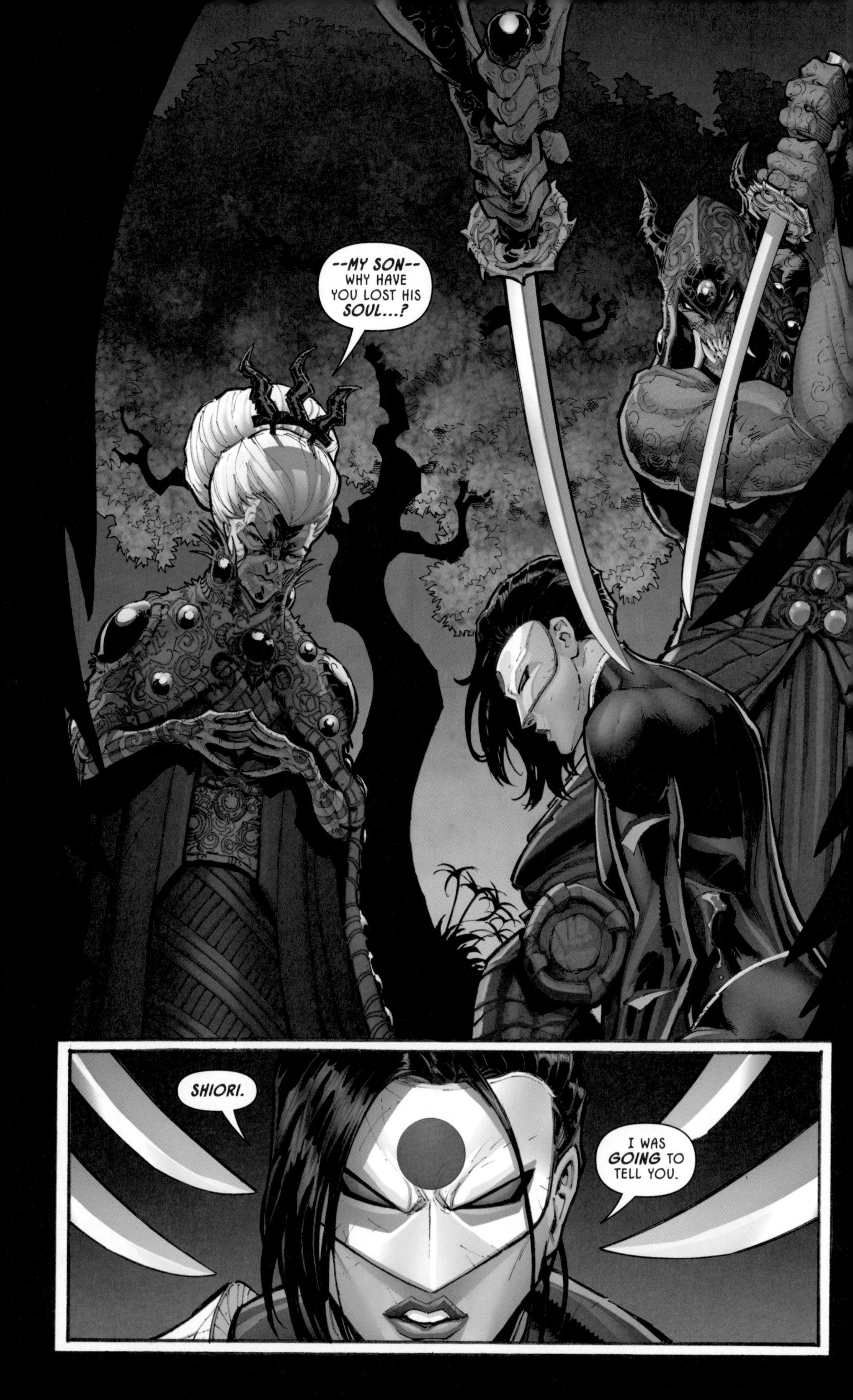
--MY SON--
WHY HAVE
YOU LOST HIS
SOUL...?
SHIORI.
I WAS
GOING TO
TELL YOU.

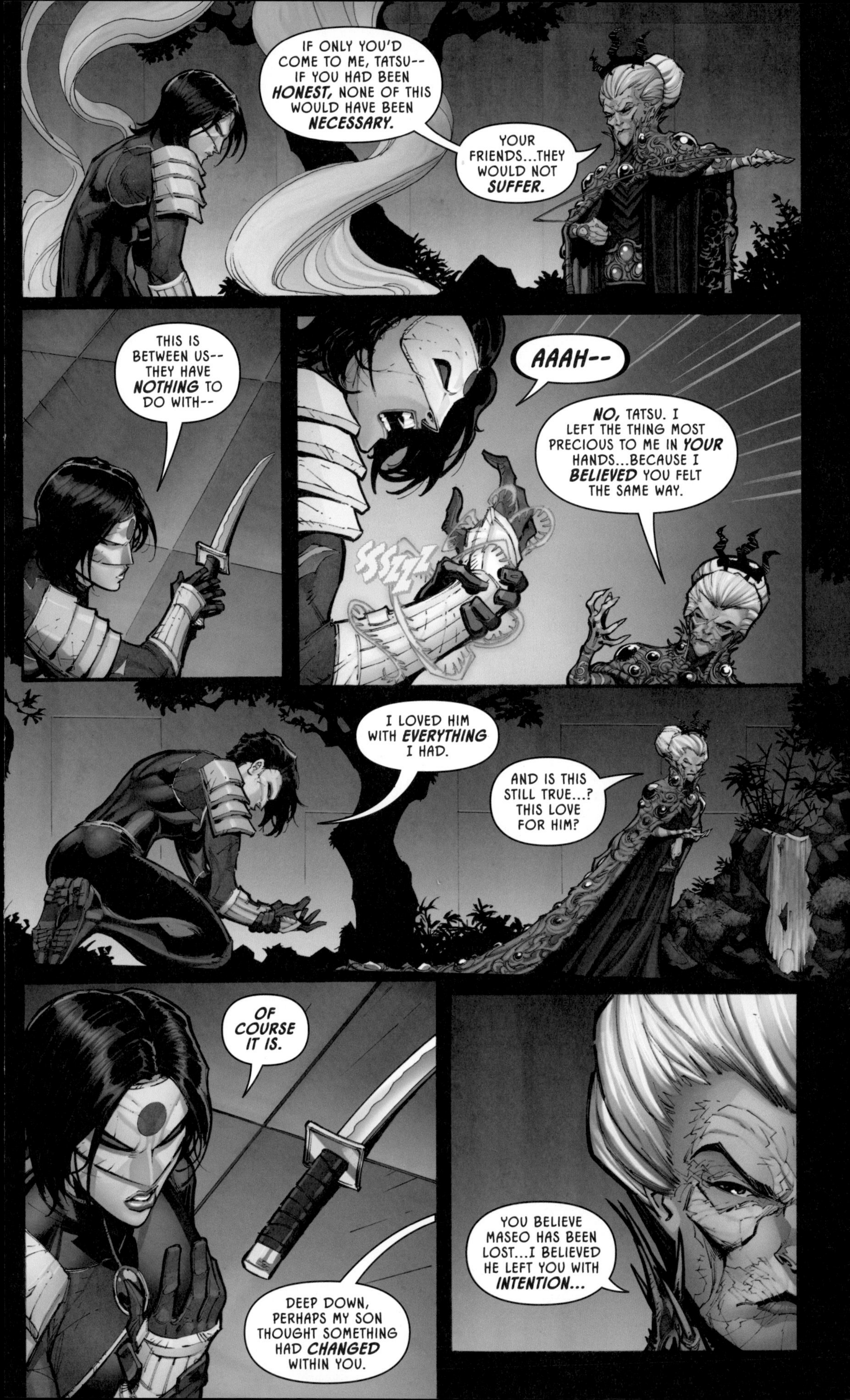
IF ONLY YOU'D COME TO ME, TATSU-- IF YOU HAD BEEN HONEST, NONE OF THIS WOULD HAVE BEEN NECESSARY.
YOUR FRIENDS...THEY WOULD NOT SUFFER.
THIS IS BETWEEN US-- THEY HAVE NOTHING TO DO WITH--
AAAH--
SSSZZZ
NO, TATSU. I LEFT THE THING MOST PRECIOUS TO ME IN YOUR HANDS...BECAUSE I BELIEVED YOU FELT THE SAME WAY.
I LOVED HIM WITH EVERYTHING I HAD.
AND IS THIS STILL TRUE...? THIS LOVE FOR HIM?
OF COURSE IT IS.
DEEP DOWN, PERHAPS MY SON THOUGHT SOMETHING HAD CHANGED WITHIN YOU.
YOU BELIEVE MASEO HAS BEEN LOST...I BELIEVED HE LEFT YOU WITH INTENTION...

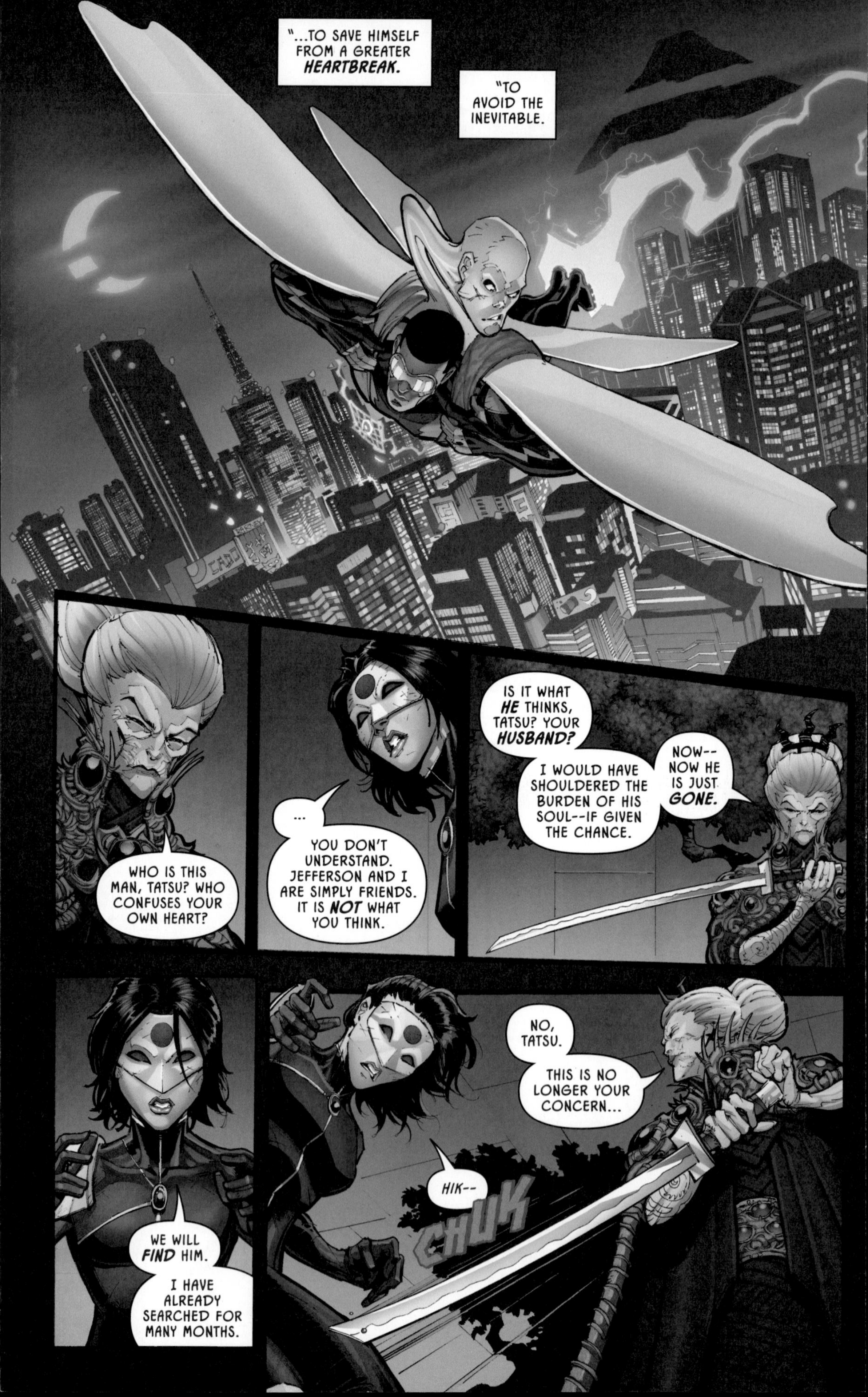
"...TO SAVE HIMSELF FROM A GREATER HEARTBREAK.
"TO AVOID THE INEVITABLE.
WHO IS THIS MAN, TATSU? WHO CONFUSES YOUR OWN HEART?
...
YOU DON'T UNDERSTAND. JEFFERSON AND I ARE SIMPLY FRIENDS. IT IS NOT WHAT YOU THINK.
IS IT WHAT HE THINKS, TATSU? YOUR HUSBAND?
I WOULD HAVE SHOULDERED THE BURDEN OF HIS SOUL--IF GIVEN THE CHANCE.
NOW-- NOW HE IS JUST GONE.
WE WILL FIND HIM.
I HAVE ALREADY SEARCHED FOR MANY MONTHS.
NO, TATSU.
THIS IS NO LONGER YOUR CONCERN...
HIK--
CHUK

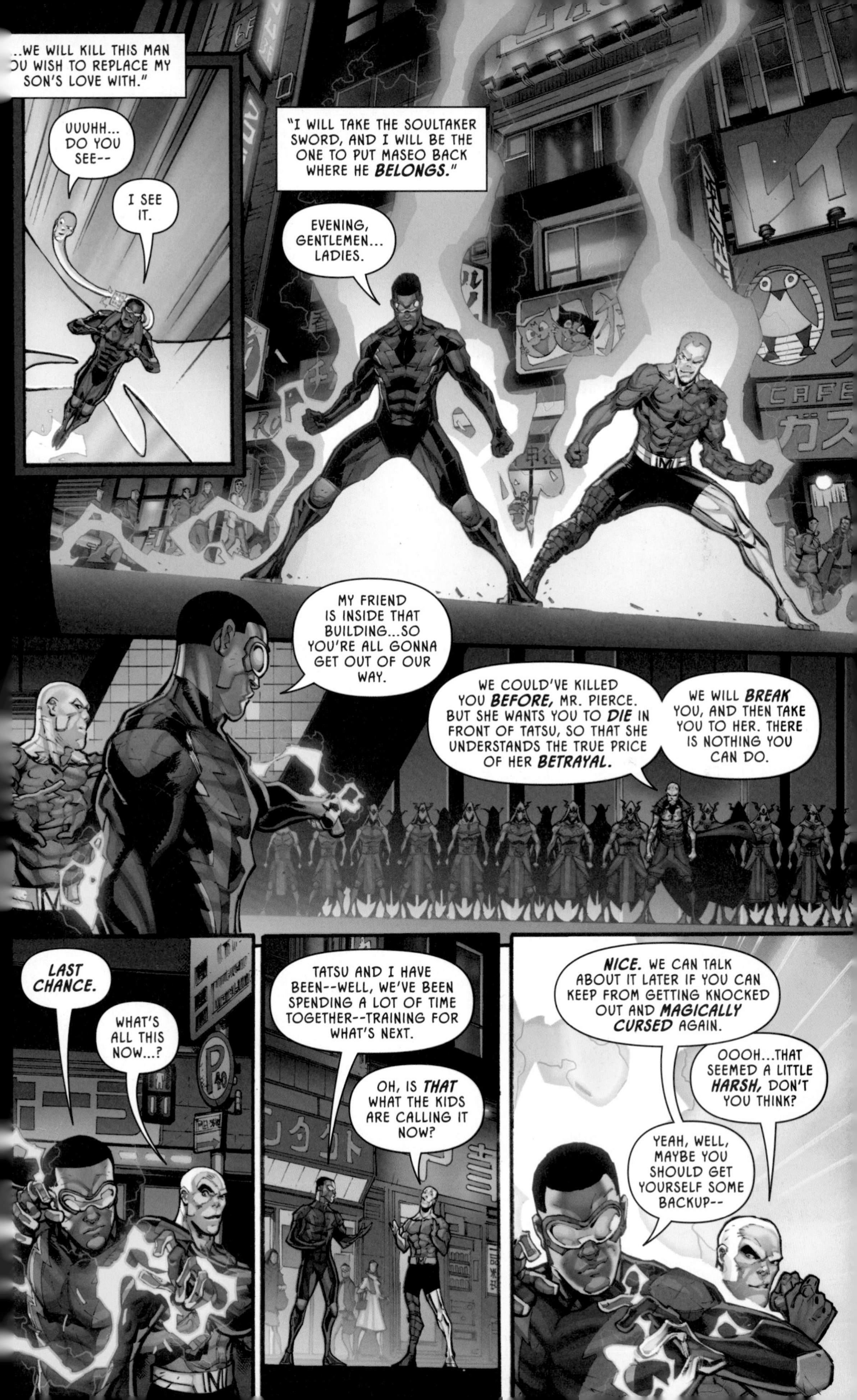
...WE WILL KILL THIS MAN
YOU WISH TO REPLACE MY SON'S LOVE WITH."
UUUHH... DO YOU SEE--
I SEE IT.
"I WILL TAKE THE SOULTAKER SWORD, AND I WILL BE THE ONE TO PUT MASEO BACK WHERE HE BELONGS."
EVENING, GENTLEMEN... LADIES.
CAFE
MY FRIEND IS INSIDE THAT BUILDING...SO YOU'RE ALL GONNA GET OUT OF OUR WAY.
WE COULD'VE KILLED YOU BEFORE, MR. PIERCE. BUT SHE WANTS YOU TO DIE IN FRONT OF TATSU, SO THAT SHE UNDERSTANDS THE TRUE PRICE OF HER BETRAYAL.
WE WILL BREAK YOU, AND THEN TAKE YOU TO HER. THERE IS NOTHING YOU CAN DO.
LAST CHANCE.
WHAT'S ALL THIS NOW...?
TATSU AND I HAVE BEEN--WELL, WE'VE BEEN SPENDING A LOT OF TIME TOGETHER--TRAINING FOR WHAT'S NEXT.
OH, IS THAT WHAT THE KIDS ARE CALLING IT NOW?
NICE. WE CAN TALK ABOUT IT LATER IF YOU CAN KEEP FROM GETTING KNOCKED OUT AND MAGICALLY CURSED AGAIN.
OOOH...THAT SEEMED A LITTLE HARSH, DON'T YOU THINK?
YEAH, WELL, MAYBE YOU SHOULD GET YOURSELF SOME BACKUP--

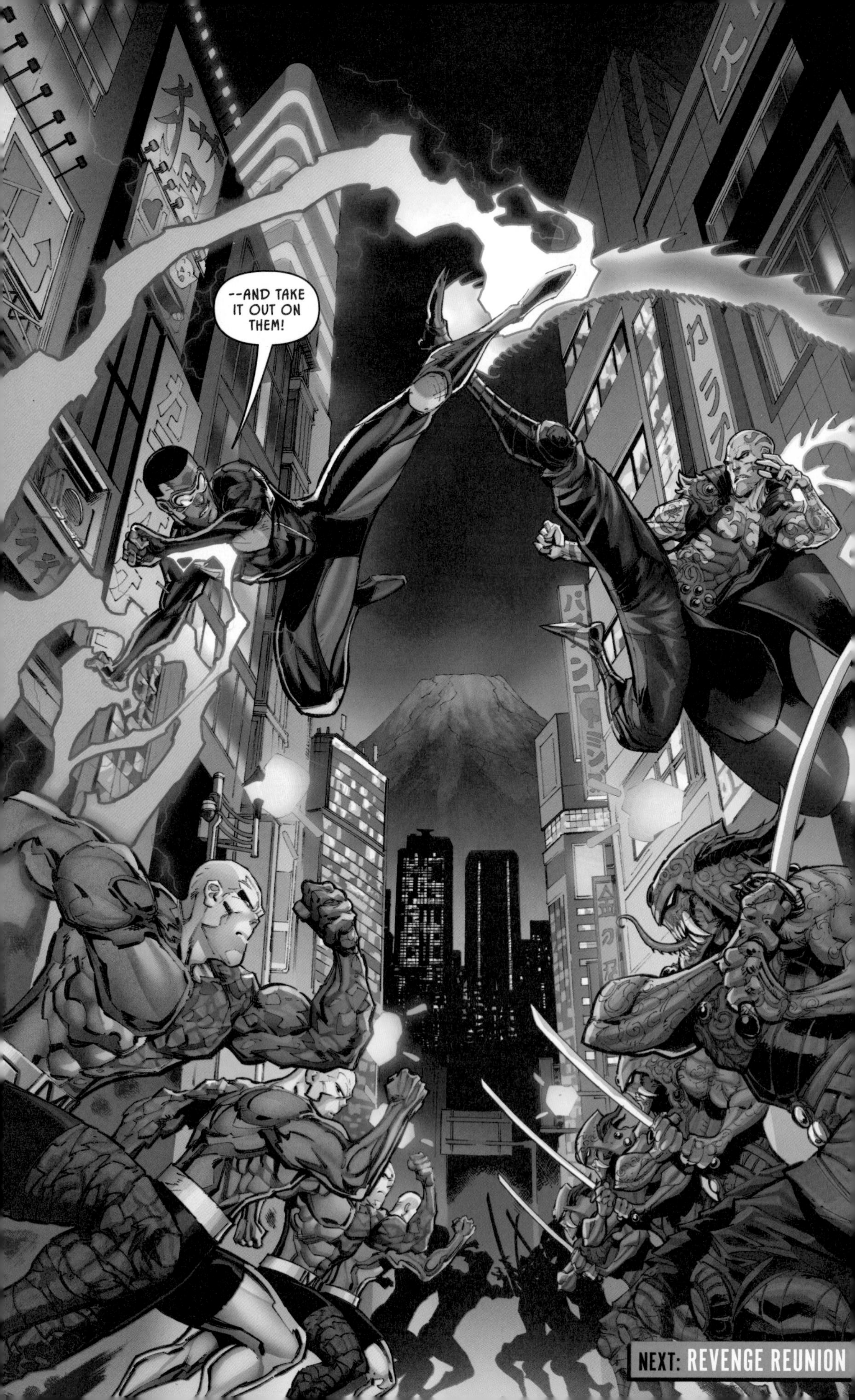
--AND TAKE IT OUT ON THEM!
NEXT: REVENGE REUNION

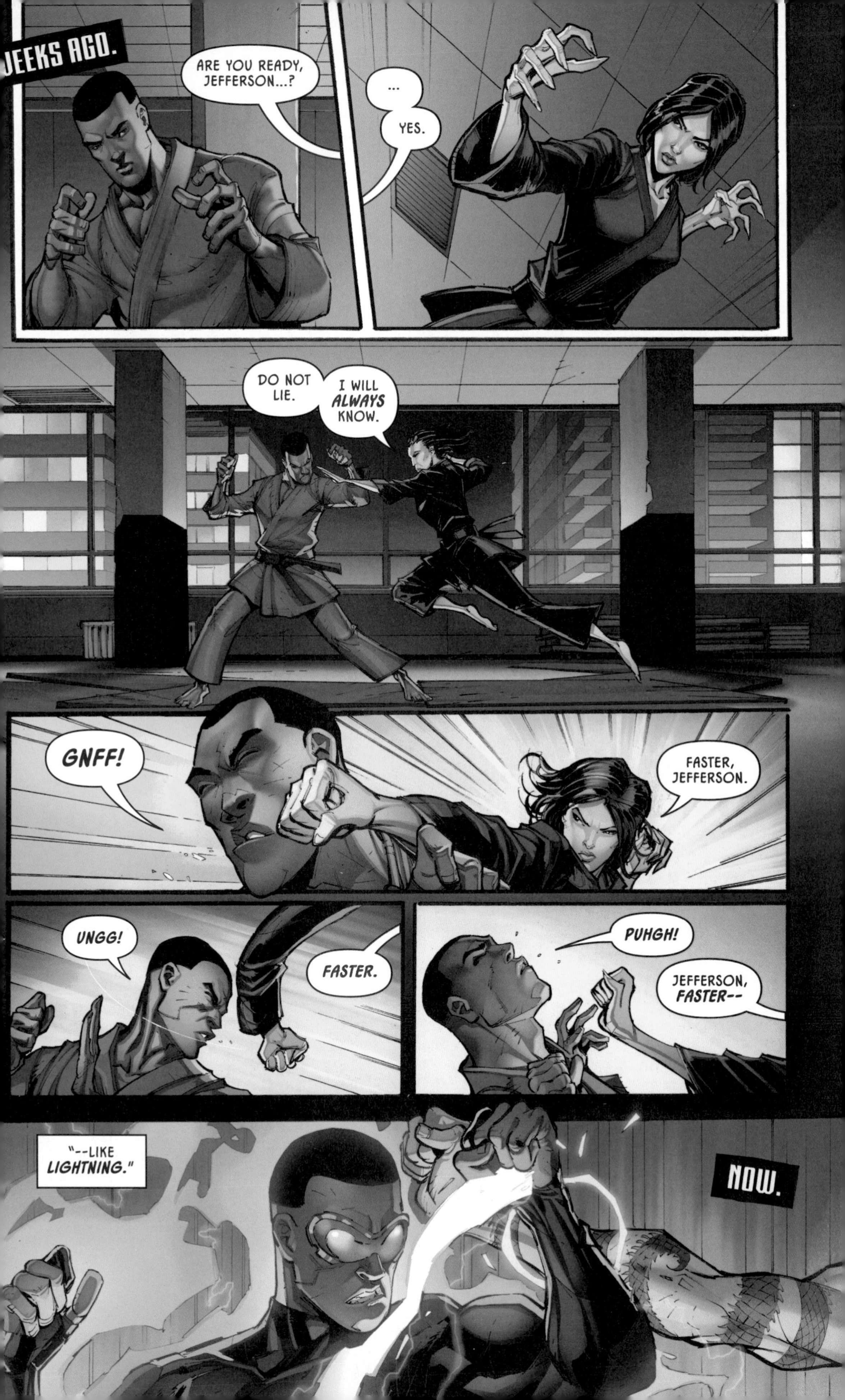

JEEKS AGO.
ARE YOU READY, JEFFERSON...?
...
YES.
DO NOT LIE.
I WILL ALWAYS KNOW.
GNFF!
FASTER, JEFFERSON.
UNGG!
FASTER.
PUHGH!
JEFFERSON, FASTER--
"--LIKE LIGHTNING."
NOW.

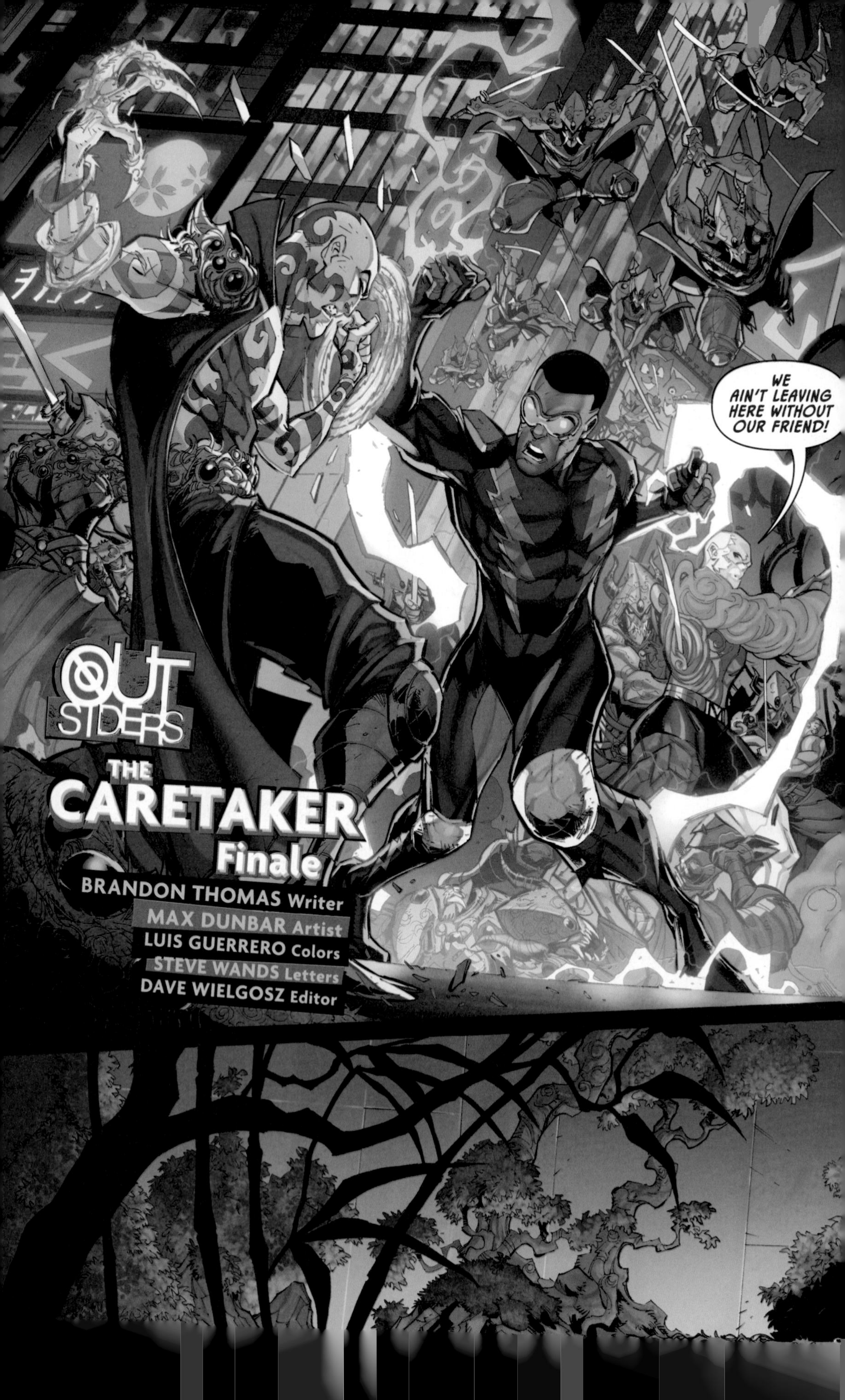
WE AIN'T LEAVING HERE WITHOUT OUR FRIEND!
OUTSIDERS
THE CARETAKER
Finale
BRANDON THOMAS Writer
MAX DUNBAR Artist
LUIS GUERRERO Colors
STEVE WANDS Letters
DAVE WIELGOSZ Editor

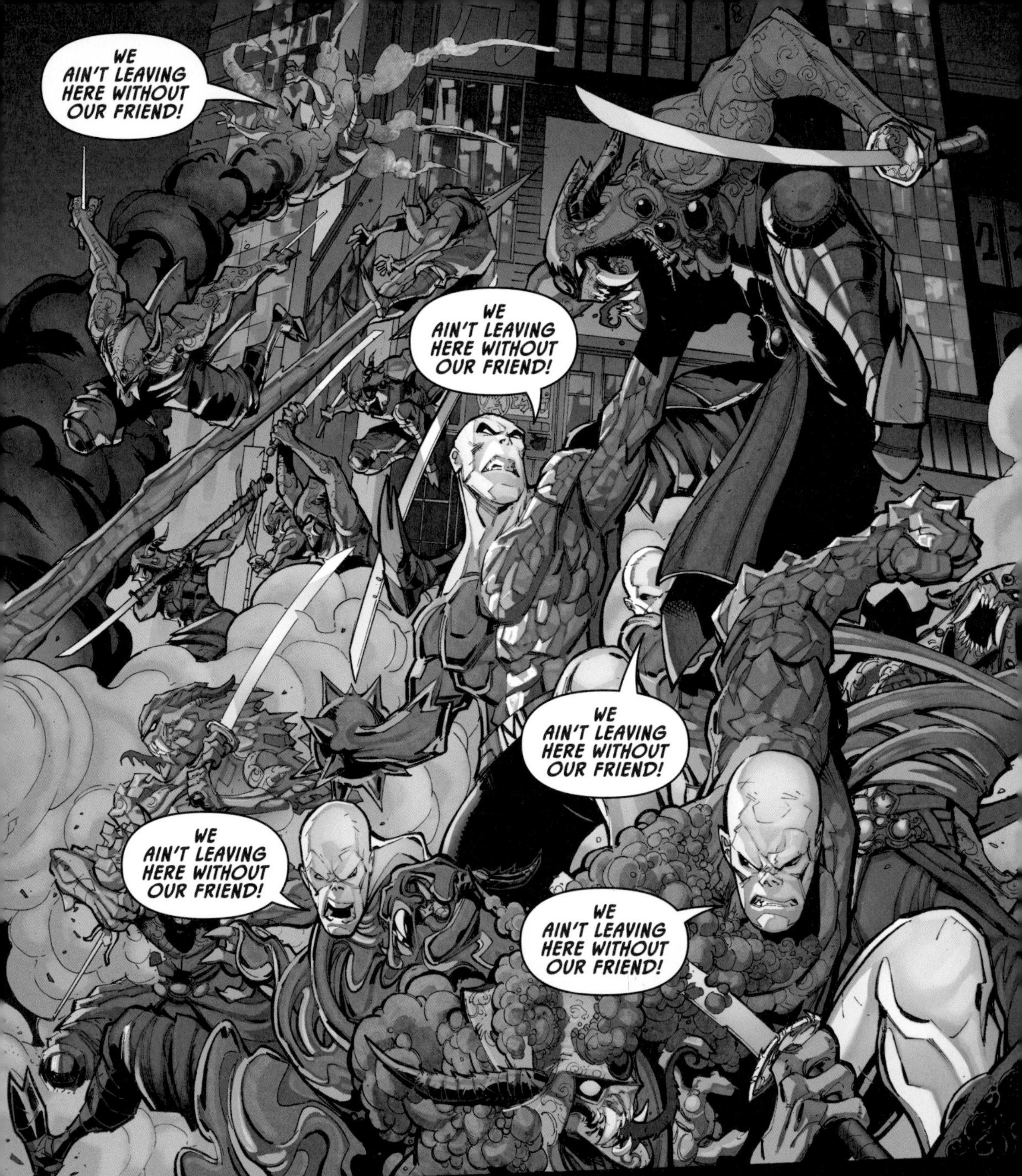
WE AIN'T LEAVING HERE WITHOUT OUR FRIEND!
WE AIN'T LEAVING HERE WITHOUT OUR FRIEND!
WE AIN'T LEAVING HERE WITHOUT OUR FRIEND!
WE AIN'T LEAVING HERE WITHOUT OUR FRIEND!
WE AIN'T LEAVING HERE WITHOUT OUR FRIEND!

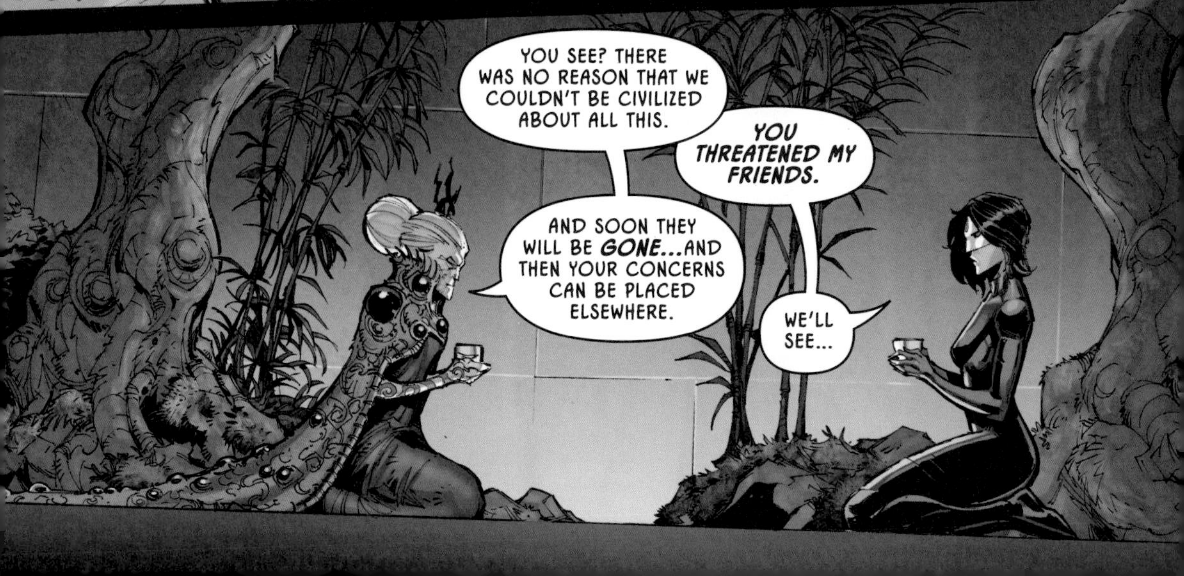
YOU SEE? THERE WAS NO REASON THAT WE COULDN'T BE CIVILIZED ABOUT ALL THIS.
YOU THREATENED MY FRIENDS.
AND SOON THEY WILL BE GONE...AND THEN YOUR CONCERNS CAN BE PLACED ELSEWHERE.
WE'LL SEE...

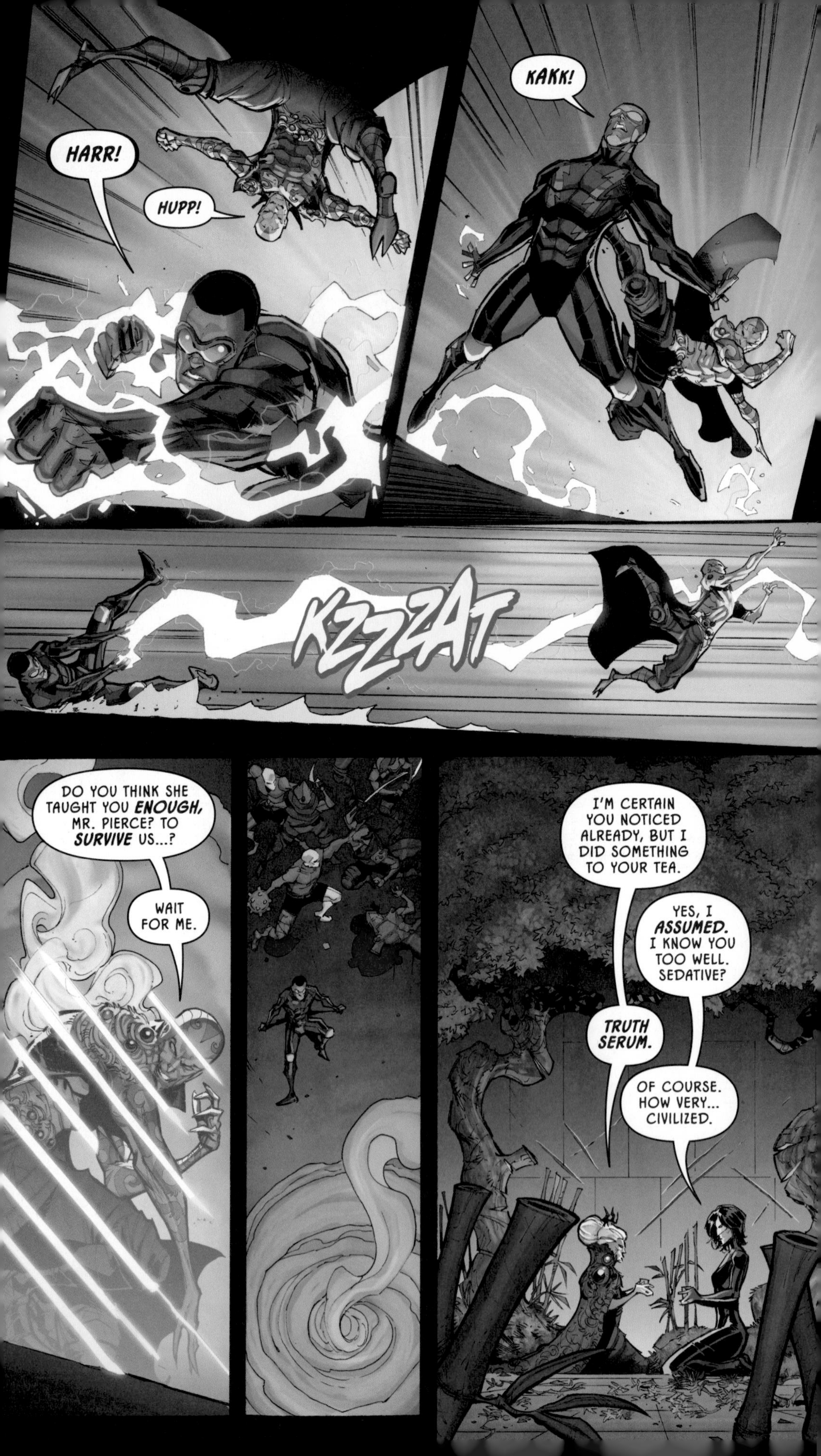
HARR!
HUPP!
KAKK!
KZZZAT
DO YOU THINK SHE TAUGHT YOU **ENOUGH,** MR. PIERCE? TO **SURVIVE** US...?
WAIT FOR ME.
I'M CERTAIN YOU NOTICED ALREADY, BUT I DID SOMETHING TO YOUR TEA.
YES, I **ASSUMED.** I KNOW YOU TOO WELL. SEDATIVE?
TRUTH SERUM.
OF COURSE. HOW VERY... CIVILIZED.

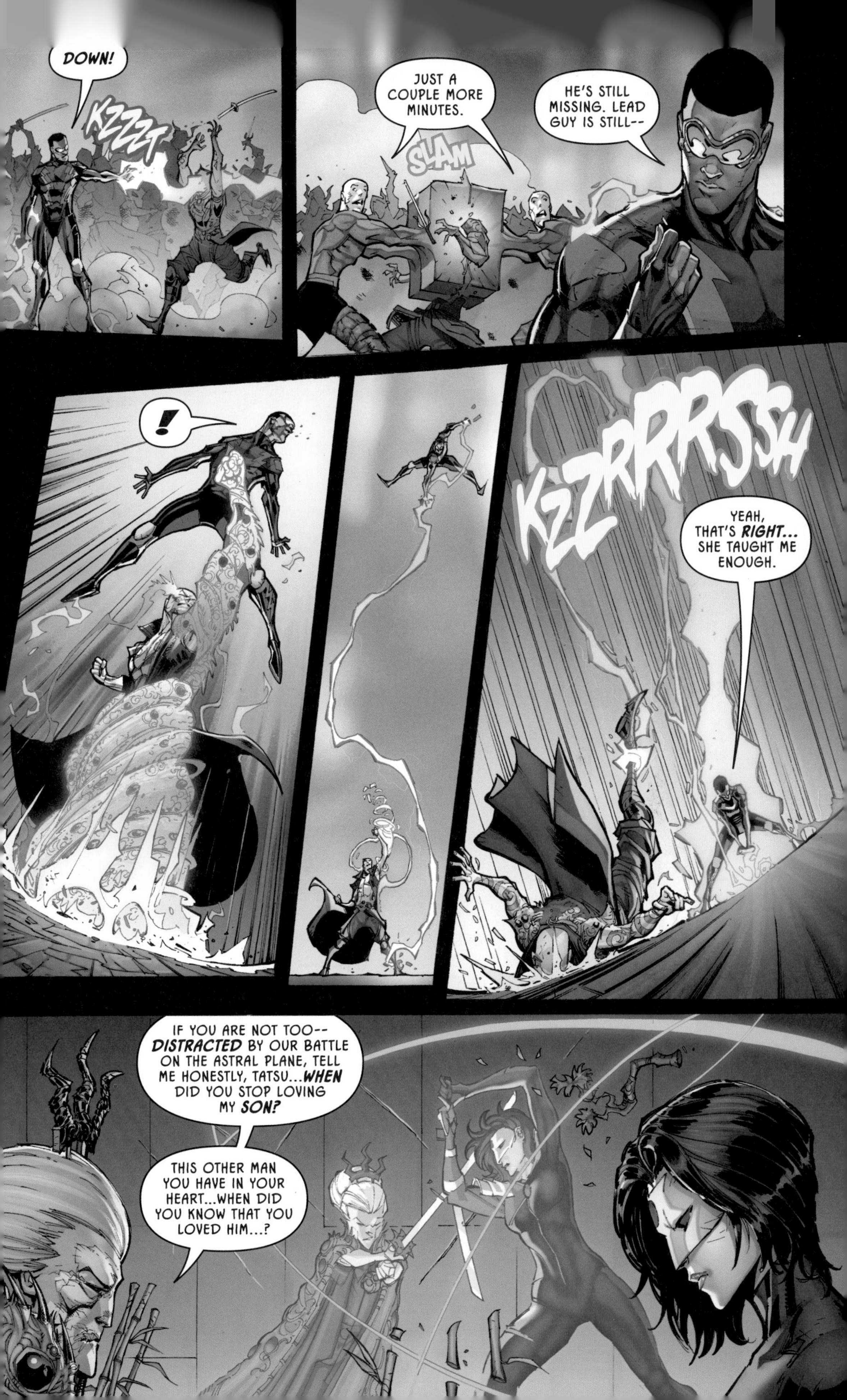
DOWN!
KZZZT
JUST A COUPLE MORE MINUTES.
SLAM
HE'S STILL MISSING. LEAD GUY IS STILL--
!
KZZRRRSSH
YEAH, THAT'S **RIGHT...** SHE TAUGHT ME ENOUGH.
IF YOU ARE NOT TOO-- **DISTRACTED** BY OUR BATTLE ON THE ASTRAL PLANE, TELL ME HONESTLY, TATSU...**WHEN** DID YOU STOP LOVING MY **SON?**
THIS OTHER MAN YOU HAVE IN YOUR HEART...WHEN DID YOU KNOW THAT YOU LOVED HIM...?

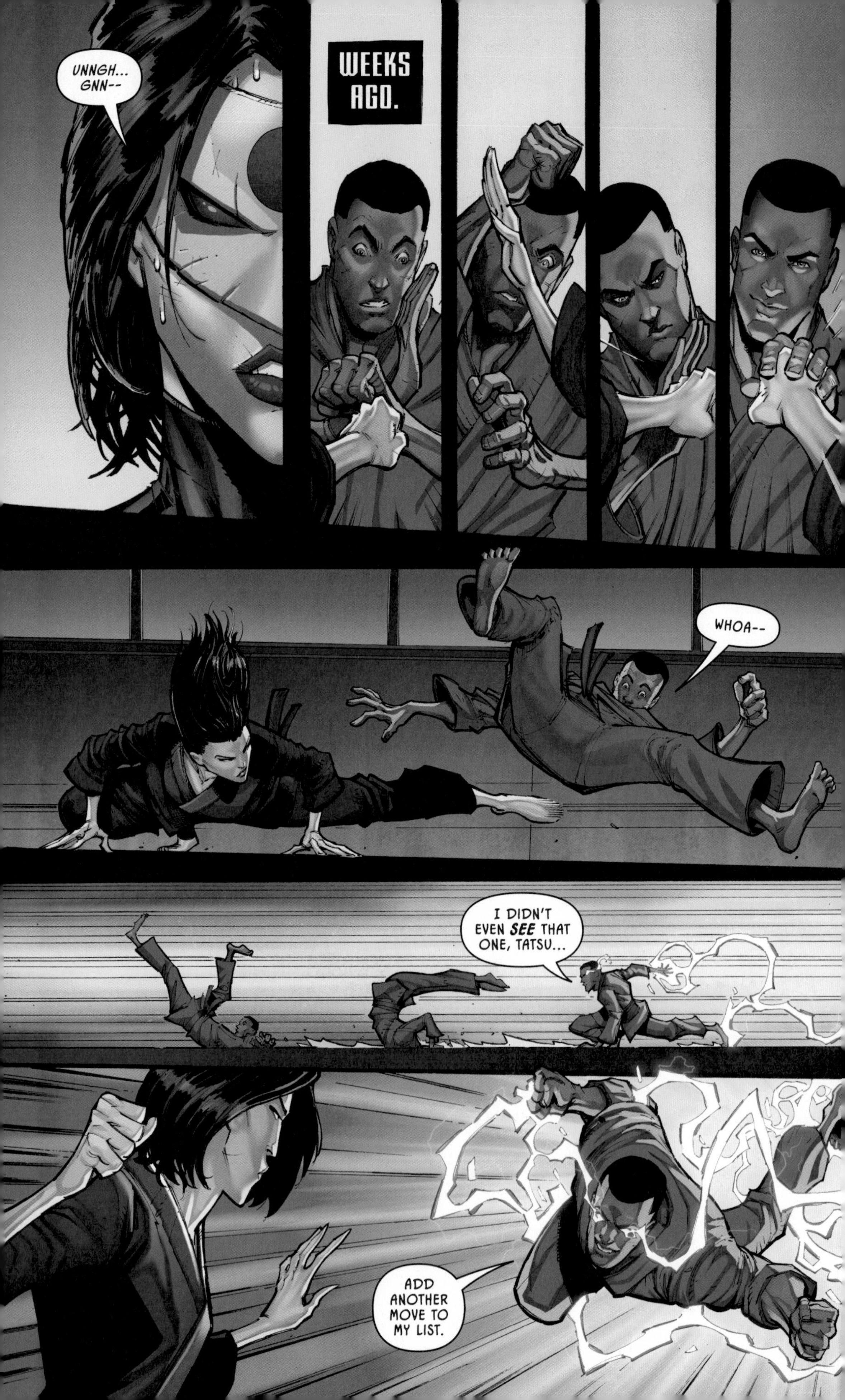
UNNGH... GNN--
WEEKS AGO.
WHOA--
I DIDN'T EVEN SEE THAT ONE, TATSU...
ADD ANOTHER MOVE TO MY LIST.

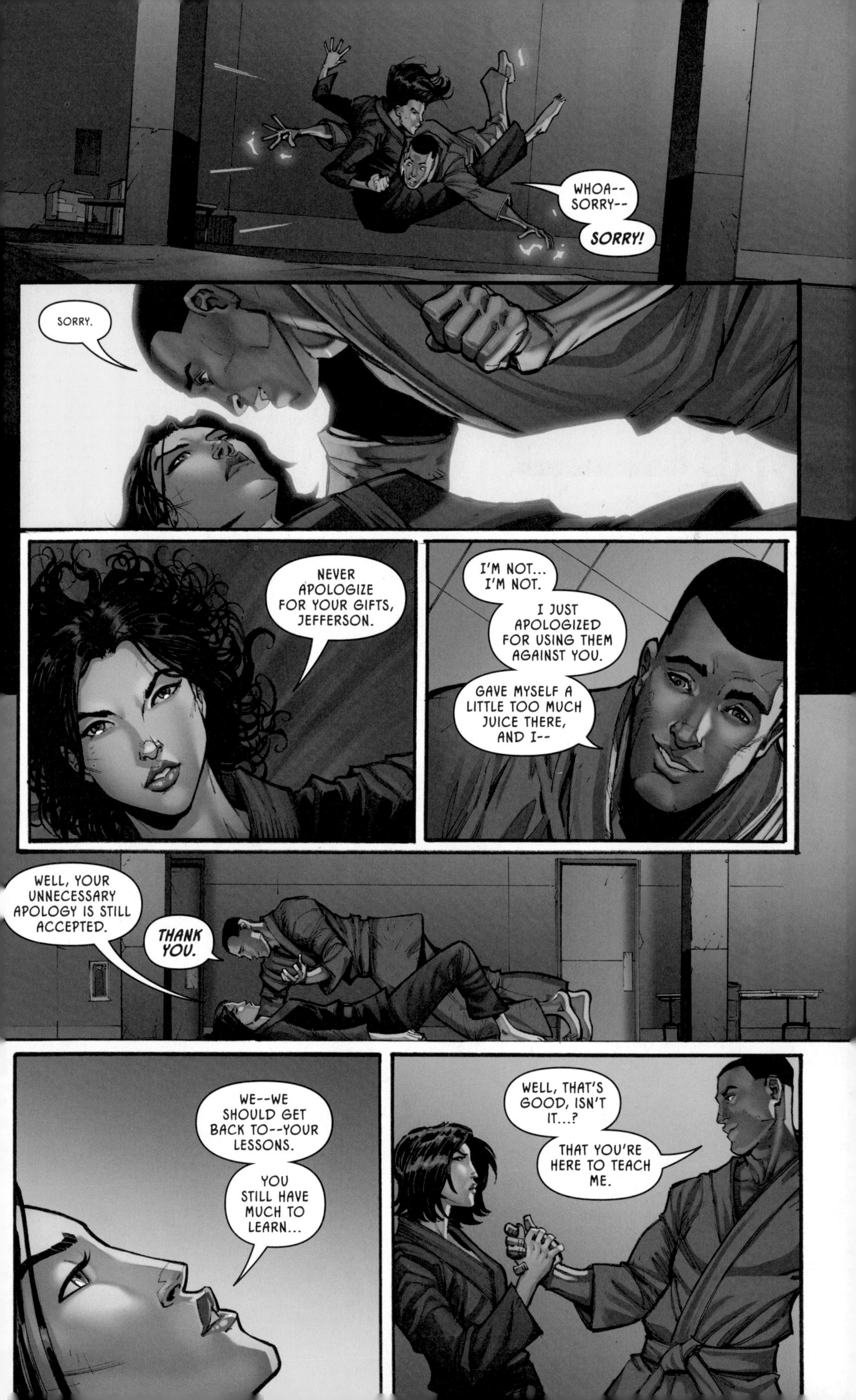
WHOA-- SORRY--
SORRY!
SORRY.
NEVER APOLOGIZE FOR YOUR GIFTS, JEFFERSON.
I'M NOT... I'M NOT.
I JUST APOLOGIZED FOR USING THEM AGAINST YOU.
GAVE MYSELF A LITTLE TOO MUCH JUICE THERE, AND I--
WELL, YOUR UNNECESSARY APOLOGY IS STILL ACCEPTED.
THANK YOU.
WE--WE SHOULD GET BACK TO--YOUR LESSONS.
YOU STILL HAVE MUCH TO LEARN...
WELL, THAT'S GOOD, ISN'T IT...?
THAT YOU'RE HERE TO TEACH ME.

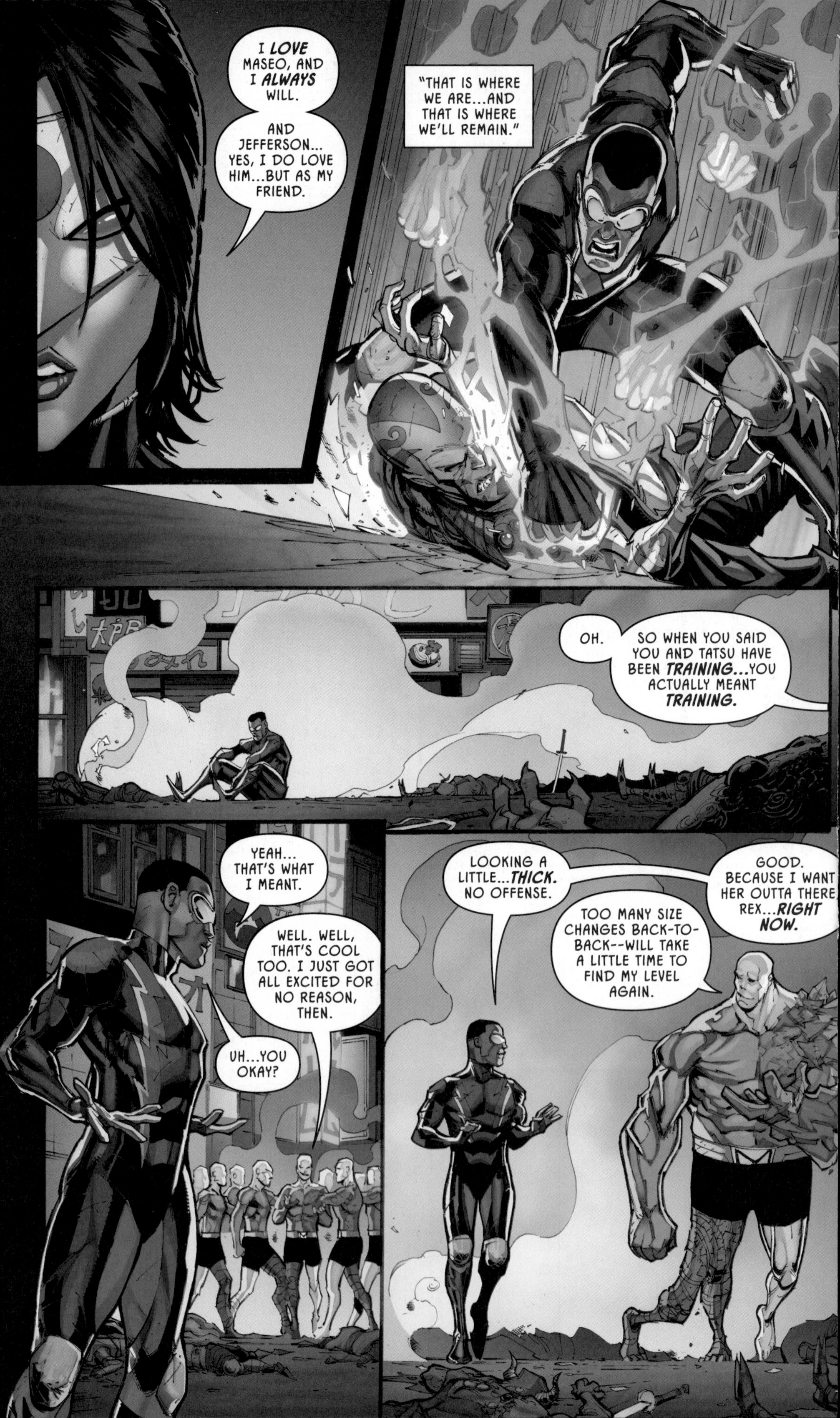
I LOVE MASEO, AND I ALWAYS WILL.
AND JEFFERSON... YES, I DO LOVE HIM...BUT AS MY FRIEND.
"THAT IS WHERE WE ARE...AND THAT IS WHERE WE'LL REMAIN."
OH.
SO WHEN YOU SAID YOU AND TATSU HAVE BEEN TRAINING...YOU ACTUALLY MEANT TRAINING.
YEAH... THAT'S WHAT I MEANT.
WELL. WELL, THAT'S COOL TOO. I JUST GOT ALL EXCITED FOR NO REASON, THEN.
UH...YOU OKAY?
LOOKING A LITTLE...THICK. NO OFFENSE.
TOO MANY SIZE CHANGES BACK-TO-BACK--WILL TAKE A LITTLE TIME TO FIND MY LEVEL AGAIN.
GOOD. BECAUSE I WANT HER OUTTA THERE REX...RIGHT NOW.

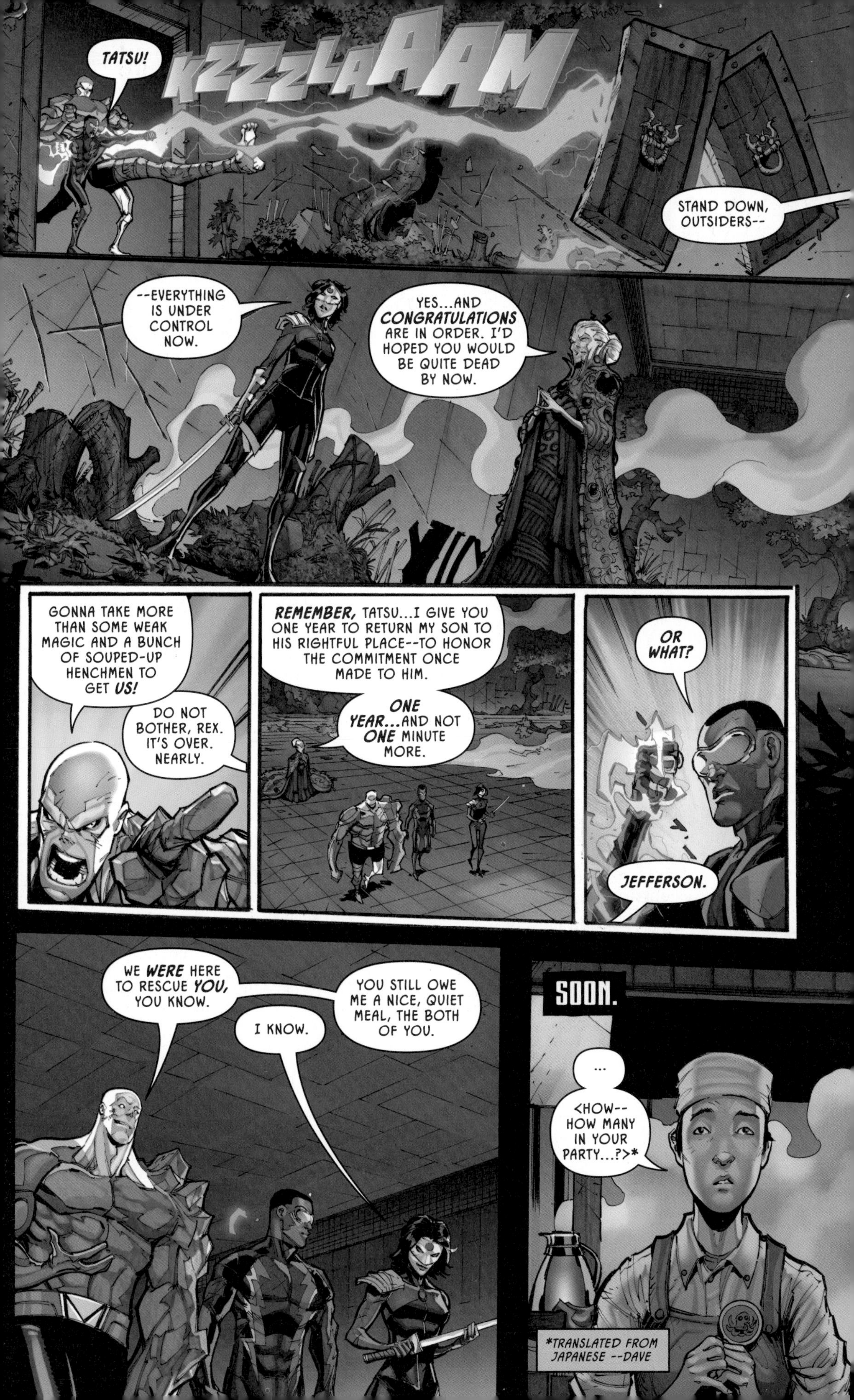
TATSU!
KZZZLAAAM
STAND DOWN, OUTSIDERS--
--EVERYTHING IS UNDER CONTROL NOW.
YES...AND CONGRATULATIONS ARE IN ORDER. I'D HOPED YOU WOULD BE QUITE DEAD BY NOW.
GONNA TAKE MORE THAN SOME WEAK MAGIC AND A BUNCH OF SOUPED-UP HENCHMEN TO GET US!
DO NOT BOTHER, REX. IT'S OVER. NEARLY.
REMEMBER, TATSU...I GIVE YOU ONE YEAR TO RETURN MY SON TO HIS RIGHTFUL PLACE--TO HONOR THE COMMITMENT ONCE MADE TO HIM.
ONE YEAR...AND NOT ONE MINUTE MORE.
OR WHAT?
JEFFERSON.
WE WERE HERE TO RESCUE YOU, YOU KNOW.
YOU STILL OWE ME A NICE, QUIET MEAL, THE BOTH OF YOU.
I KNOW.
SOON.
...
<HOW--HOW MANY IN YOUR PARTY...?>*
*TRANSLATED FROM JAPANESE --DAVE

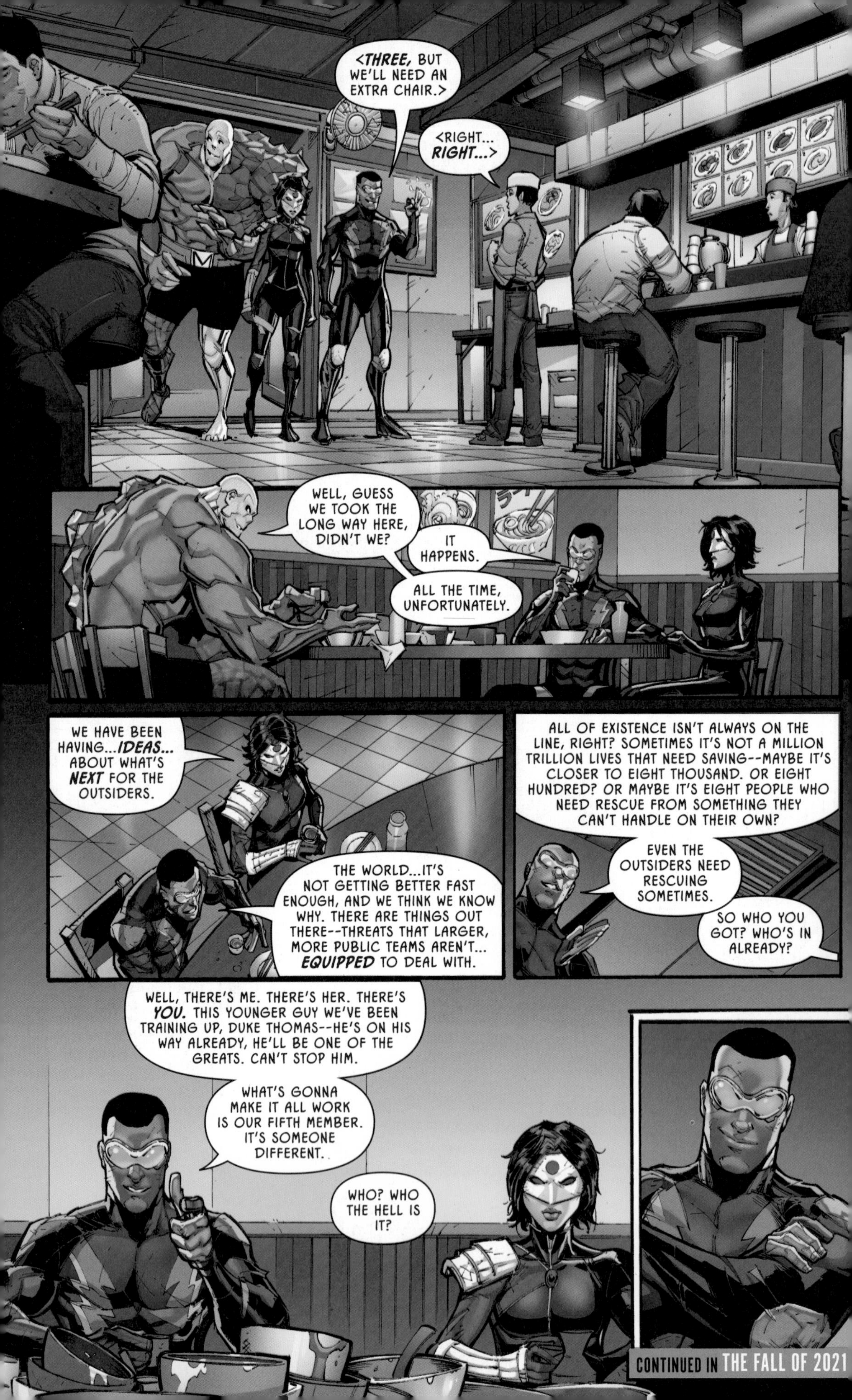
<THREE, BUT WE'LL NEED AN EXTRA CHAIR.>
<RIGHT... RIGHT...>
WELL, GUESS WE TOOK THE LONG WAY HERE, DIDN'T WE?
IT HAPPENS.
ALL THE TIME, UNFORTUNATELY.
WE HAVE BEEN HAVING...IDEAS... ABOUT WHAT'S NEXT FOR THE OUTSIDERS.
THE WORLD...IT'S NOT GETTING BETTER FAST ENOUGH, AND WE THINK WE KNOW WHY. THERE ARE THINGS OUT THERE--THREATS THAT LARGER, MORE PUBLIC TEAMS AREN'T... EQUIPPED TO DEAL WITH.
ALL OF EXISTENCE ISN'T ALWAYS ON THE LINE, RIGHT? SOMETIMES IT'S NOT A MILLION TRILLION LIVES THAT NEED SAVING--MAYBE IT'S CLOSER TO EIGHT THOUSAND. OR EIGHT HUNDRED? OR MAYBE IT'S EIGHT PEOPLE WHO NEED RESCUE FROM SOMETHING THEY CAN'T HANDLE ON THEIR OWN?
EVEN THE OUTSIDERS NEED RESCUING SOMETIMES.
SO WHO YOU GOT? WHO'S IN ALREADY?
WELL, THERE'S ME. THERE'S HER. THERE'S YOU. THIS YOUNGER GUY WE'VE BEEN TRAINING UP, DUKE THOMAS--HE'S ON HIS WAY ALREADY, HE'LL BE ONE OF THE GREATS. CAN'T STOP HIM.
WHAT'S GONNA MAKE IT ALL WORK IS OUR FIFTH MEMBER. IT'S SOMEONE DIFFERENT.
WHO? WHO THE HELL IS IT?
CONTINUED IN THE FALL OF 2021

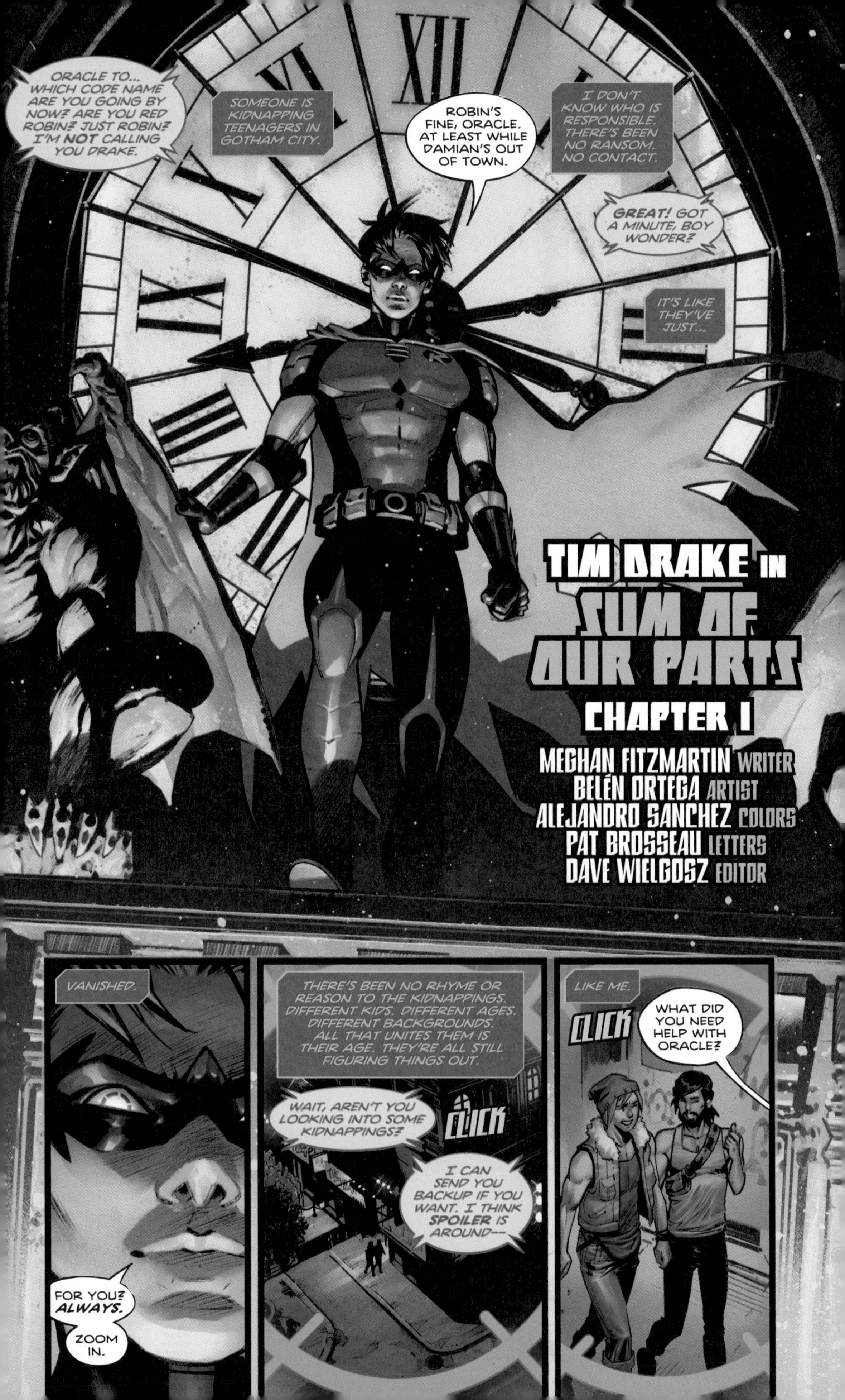
ORACLE TO... WHICH CODE NAME ARE YOU GOING BY NOW? ARE YOU RED ROBIN? JUST ROBIN? I'M NOT CALLING YOU DRAKE.
SOMEONE IS KIDNAPPING TEENAGERS IN GOTHAM CITY.
ROBIN'S FINE, ORACLE. AT LEAST WHILE DAMIAN'S OUT OF TOWN.
I DON'T KNOW WHO IS RESPONSIBLE. THERE'S BEEN NO RANSOM. NO CONTACT.
GREAT! GOT A MINUTE, BOY WONDER?
IT'S LIKE THEY'VE JUST...
TIM DRAKE IN
SUM OF OUR PARTS
CHAPTER I
MEGHAN FITZMARTIN WRITER
BELÉN ORTEGA ARTIST
ALEJANDRO SANCHEZ COLORS
PAT BROSSEAU LETTERS
DAVE WIELGOSZ EDITOR
VANISHED.
FOR YOU? ALWAYS.
ZOOM IN.
THERE'S BEEN NO RHYME OR REASON TO THE KIDNAPPINGS. DIFFERENT KIDS. DIFFERENT AGES. DIFFERENT BACKGROUNDS. ALL THAT UNITES THEM IS THEIR AGE. THEY'RE ALL STILL FIGURING THINGS OUT.
WAIT, AREN'T YOU LOOKING INTO SOME KIDNAPPINGS?
CLICK
I CAN SEND YOU BACKUP IF YOU WANT. I THINK SPOILER IS AROUND--
LIKE ME.
CLICK
WHAT DID YOU NEED HELP WITH ORACLE?

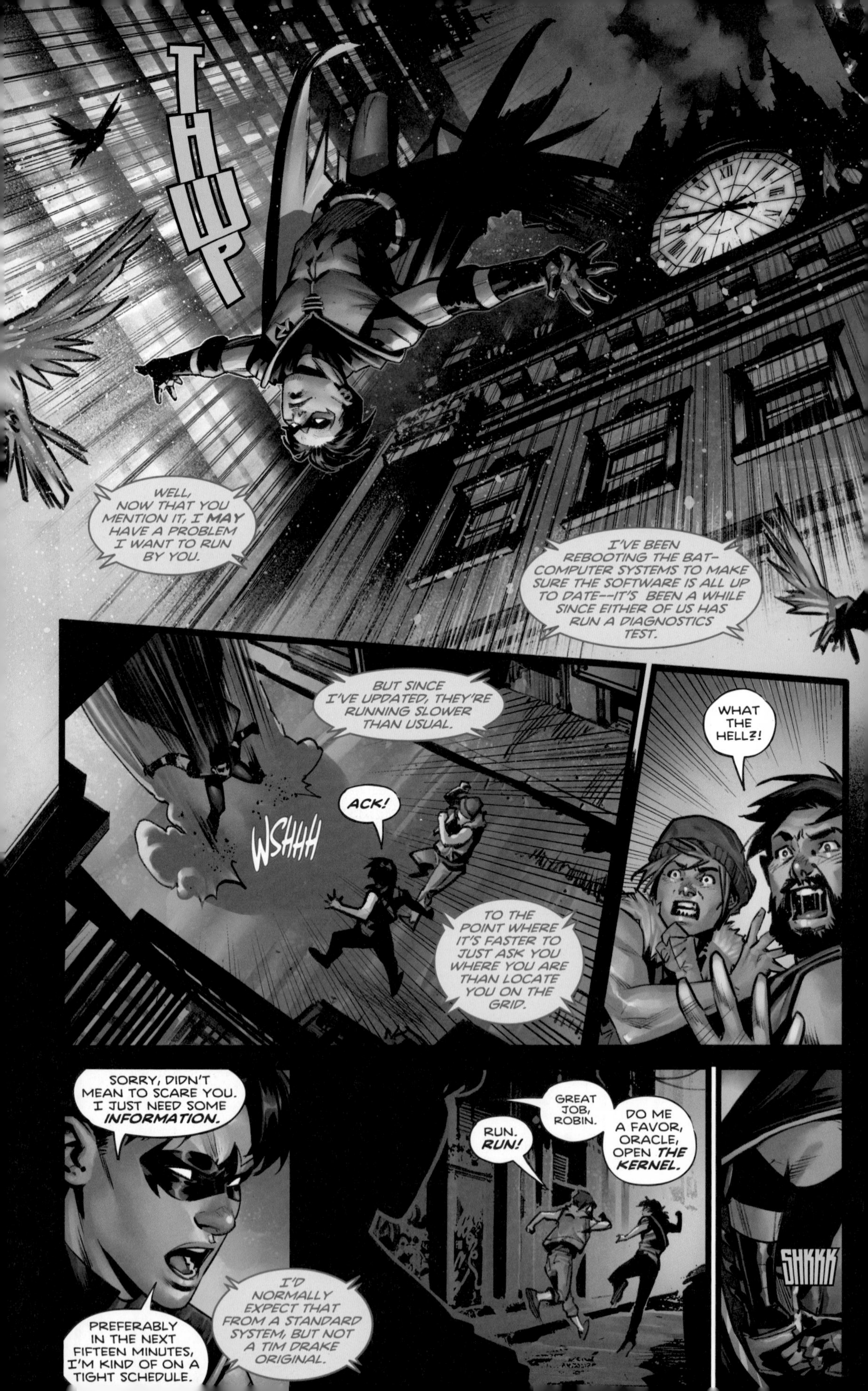
THWUP
WELL, NOW THAT YOU MENTION IT, I MAY HAVE A PROBLEM I WANT TO RUN BY YOU.
I'VE BEEN REBOOTING THE BAT-COMPUTER SYSTEMS TO MAKE SURE THE SOFTWARE IS ALL UP TO DATE--IT'S BEEN A WHILE SINCE EITHER OF US HAS RUN A DIAGNOSTICS TEST.
BUT SINCE I'VE UPDATED, THEY'RE RUNNING SLOWER THAN USUAL.
WSHHH
ACK!
TO THE POINT WHERE IT'S FASTER TO JUST ASK YOU WHERE YOU ARE THAN LOCATE YOU ON THE GRID.
WHAT THE HELL?!
SORRY, DIDN'T MEAN TO SCARE YOU. I JUST NEED SOME INFORMATION.
PREFERABLY IN THE NEXT FIFTEEN MINUTES, I'M KIND OF ON A TIGHT SCHEDULE.
I'D NORMALLY EXPECT THAT FROM A STANDARD SYSTEM, BUT NOT A TIM DRAKE ORIGINAL.
RUN. RUN!
GREAT JOB, ROBIN.
DO ME A FAVOR, ORACLE, OPEN THE KERNEL.
SHKKK

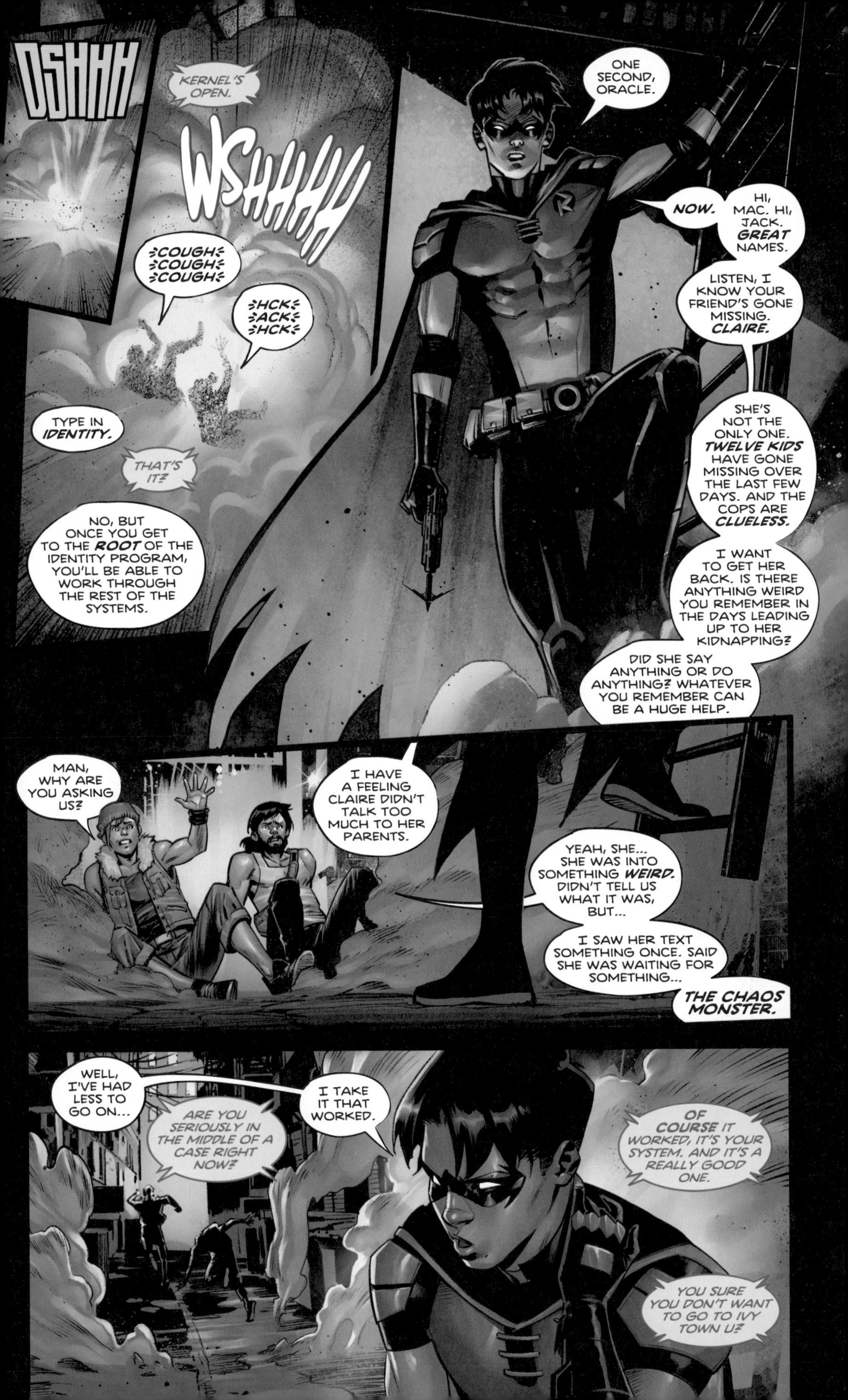
OSHHH
KERNEL'S OPEN.
WSHHHH
COUGH COUGH COUGH
HCK ACK HCK
TYPE IN IDENTITY.
THAT'S IT?
NO, BUT ONCE YOU GET TO THE ROOT OF THE IDENTITY PROGRAM, YOU'LL BE ABLE TO WORK THROUGH THE REST OF THE SYSTEMS.
ONE SECOND, ORACLE.
NOW.
HI, MAC. HI, JACK. GREAT NAMES.
LISTEN, I KNOW YOUR FRIEND'S GONE MISSING. CLAIRE.
SHE'S NOT THE ONLY ONE. TWELVE KIDS HAVE GONE MISSING OVER THE LAST FEW DAYS. AND THE COPS ARE CLUELESS.
I WANT TO GET HER BACK. IS THERE ANYTHING WEIRD YOU REMEMBER IN THE DAYS LEADING UP TO HER KIDNAPPING?
DID SHE SAY ANYTHING OR DO ANYTHING? WHATEVER YOU REMEMBER CAN BE A HUGE HELP.
MAN, WHY ARE YOU ASKING US?
I HAVE A FEELING CLAIRE DIDN'T TALK TOO MUCH TO HER PARENTS.
YEAH, SHE... SHE WAS INTO SOMETHING WEIRD. DIDN'T TELL US WHAT IT WAS, BUT...
I SAW HER TEXT SOMETHING ONCE. SAID SHE WAS WAITING FOR SOMETHING...
THE CHAOS MONSTER.
WELL, I'VE HAD LESS TO GO ON...
ARE YOU SERIOUSLY IN THE MIDDLE OF A CASE RIGHT NOW?
I TAKE IT THAT WORKED.
OF COURSE IT WORKED, IT'S YOUR SYSTEM. AND IT'S A REALLY GOOD ONE.
YOU SURE YOU DON'T WANT TO GO TO IVY TOWN U?

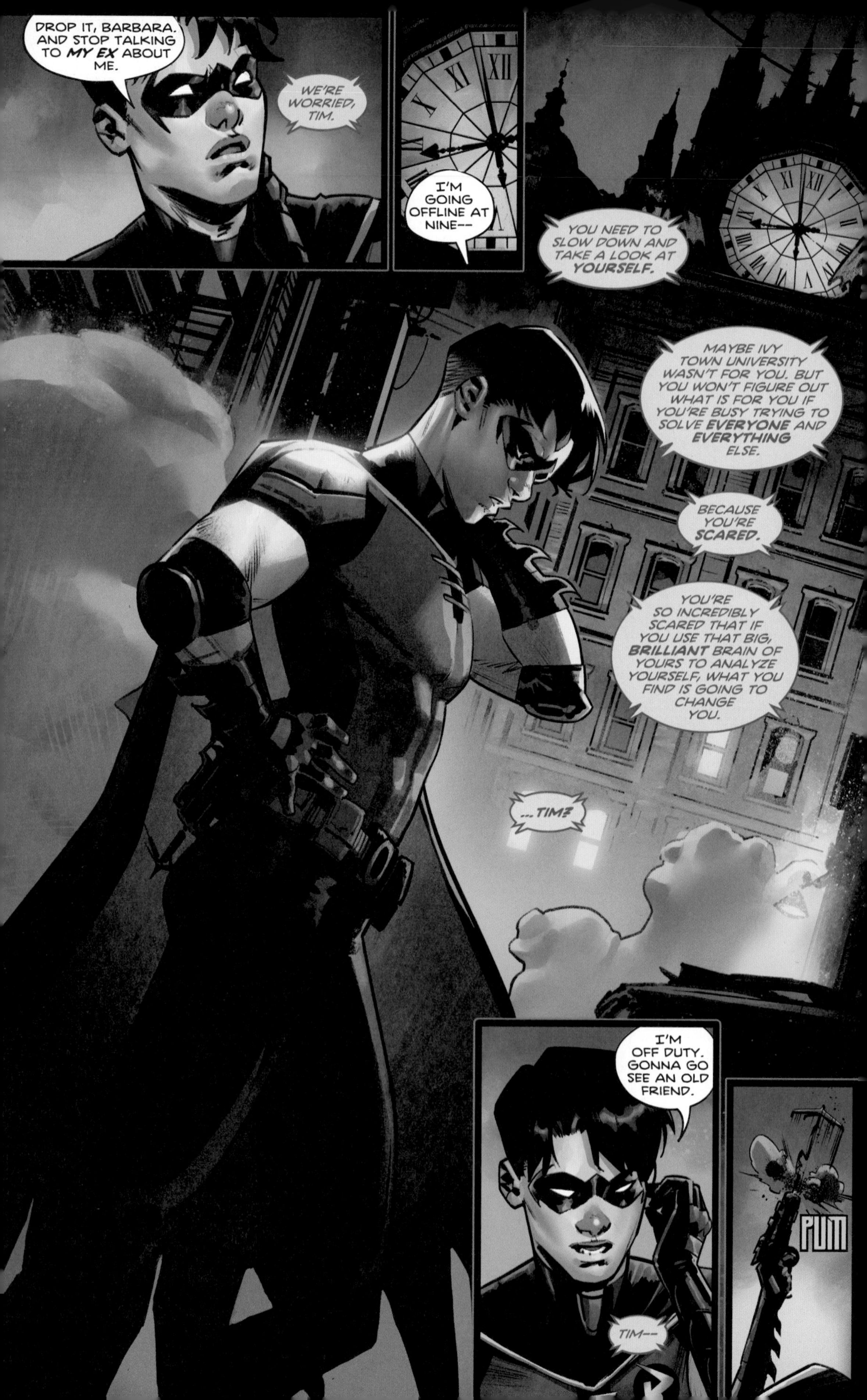

DROP IT, BARBARA. AND STOP TALKING TO MY EX ABOUT ME.
WE'RE WORRIED, TIM.
I'M GOING OFFLINE AT NINE--
YOU NEED TO SLOW DOWN AND TAKE A LOOK AT YOURSELF.
MAYBE IVY TOWN UNIVERSITY WASN'T FOR YOU. BUT YOU WON'T FIGURE OUT WHAT IS FOR YOU IF YOU'RE BUSY TRYING TO SOLVE EVERYONE AND EVERYTHING ELSE.
BECAUSE YOU'RE SCARED.
YOU'RE SO INCREDIBLY SCARED THAT IF YOU USE THAT BIG, BRILLIANT BRAIN OF YOURS TO ANALYZE YOURSELF, WHAT YOU FIND IS GOING TO CHANGE YOU.
...TIM?
I'M OFF DUTY. GONNA GO SEE AN OLD FRIEND.
TIM--
PUM

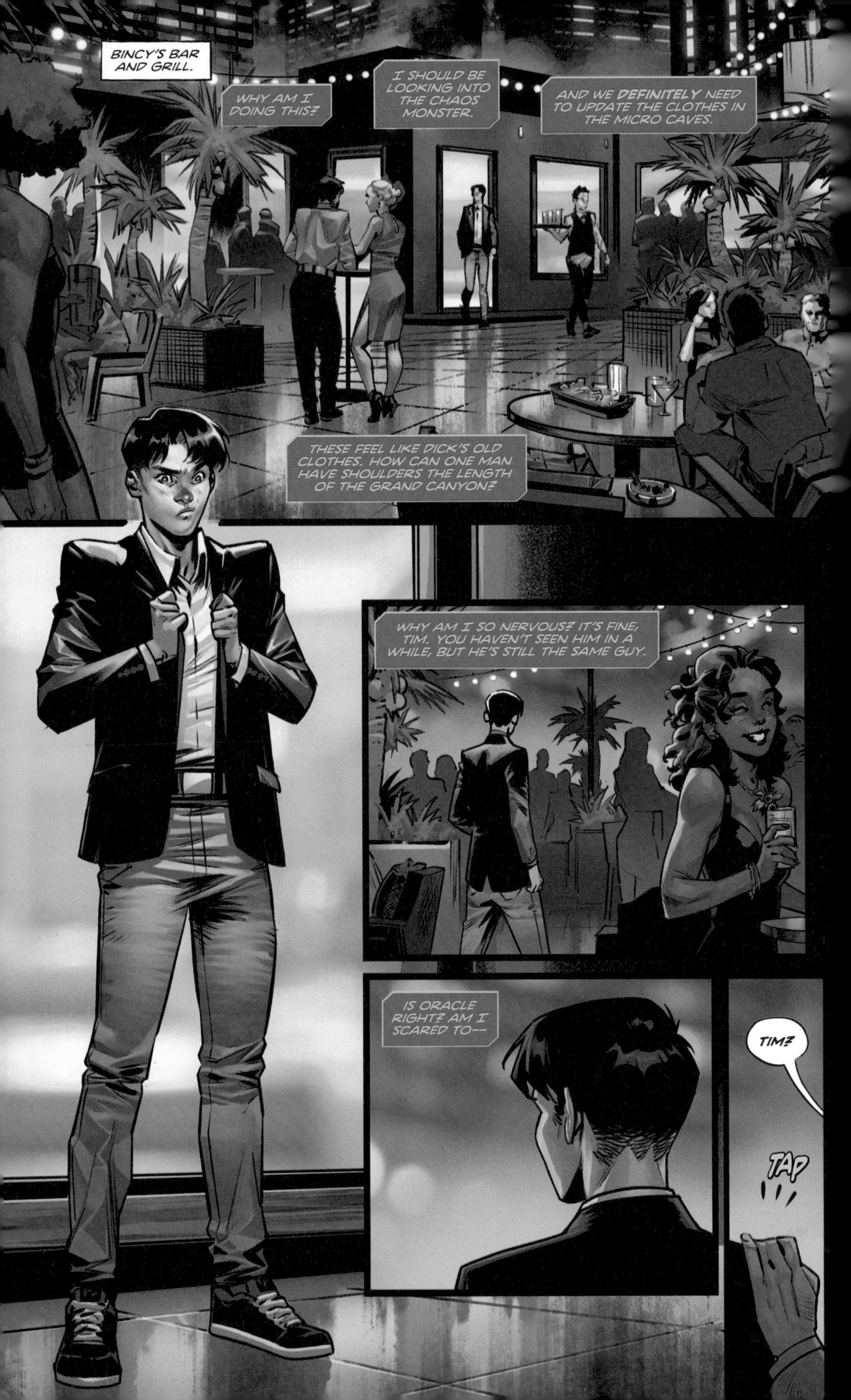
BINCY'S BAR AND GRILL.
WHY AM I DOING THIS?
I SHOULD BE LOOKING INTO THE CHAOS MONSTER.
AND WE DEFINITELY NEED TO UPDATE THE CLOTHES IN THE MICRO CAVES.
THESE FEEL LIKE DICK'S OLD CLOTHES. HOW CAN ONE MAN HAVE SHOULDERS THE LENGTH OF THE GRAND CANYON?
WHY AM I SO NERVOUS? IT'S FINE, TIM. YOU HAVEN'T SEEN HIM IN A WHILE, BUT HE'S STILL THE SAME GUY.
IS ORACLE RIGHT? AM I SCARED TO--
TIM?
TAP

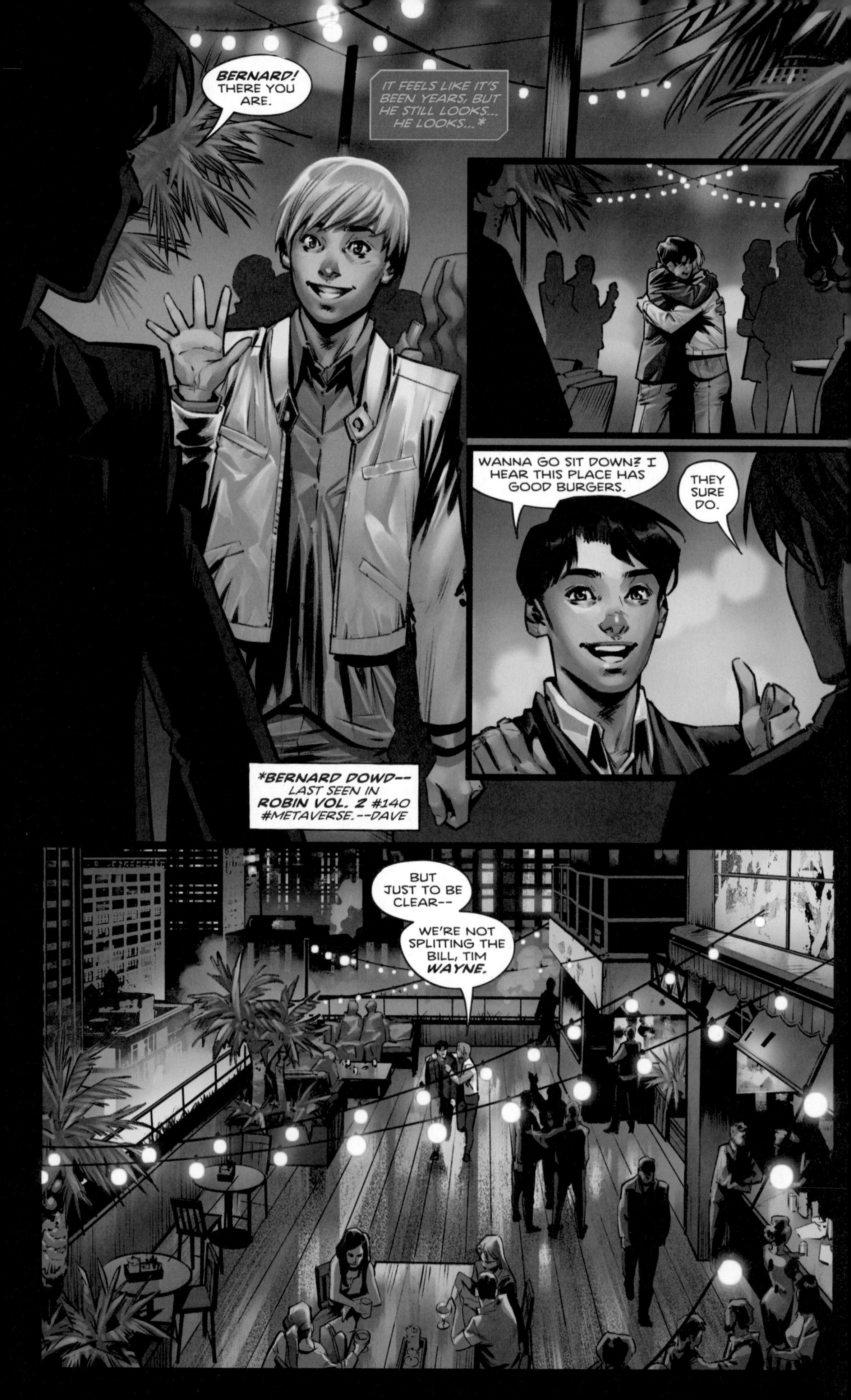
BERNARD! THERE YOU ARE.
IT FEELS LIKE IT'S BEEN YEARS, BUT HE STILL LOOKS... HE LOOKS...*
*BERNARD DOWD-- LAST SEEN IN ROBIN VOL. 2 #140 #METAVERSE.--DAVE
WANNA GO SIT DOWN? I HEAR THIS PLACE HAS GOOD BURGERS.
THEY SURE DO.
BUT JUST TO BE CLEAR--
WE'RE NOT SPLITTING THE BILL, TIM WAYNE.

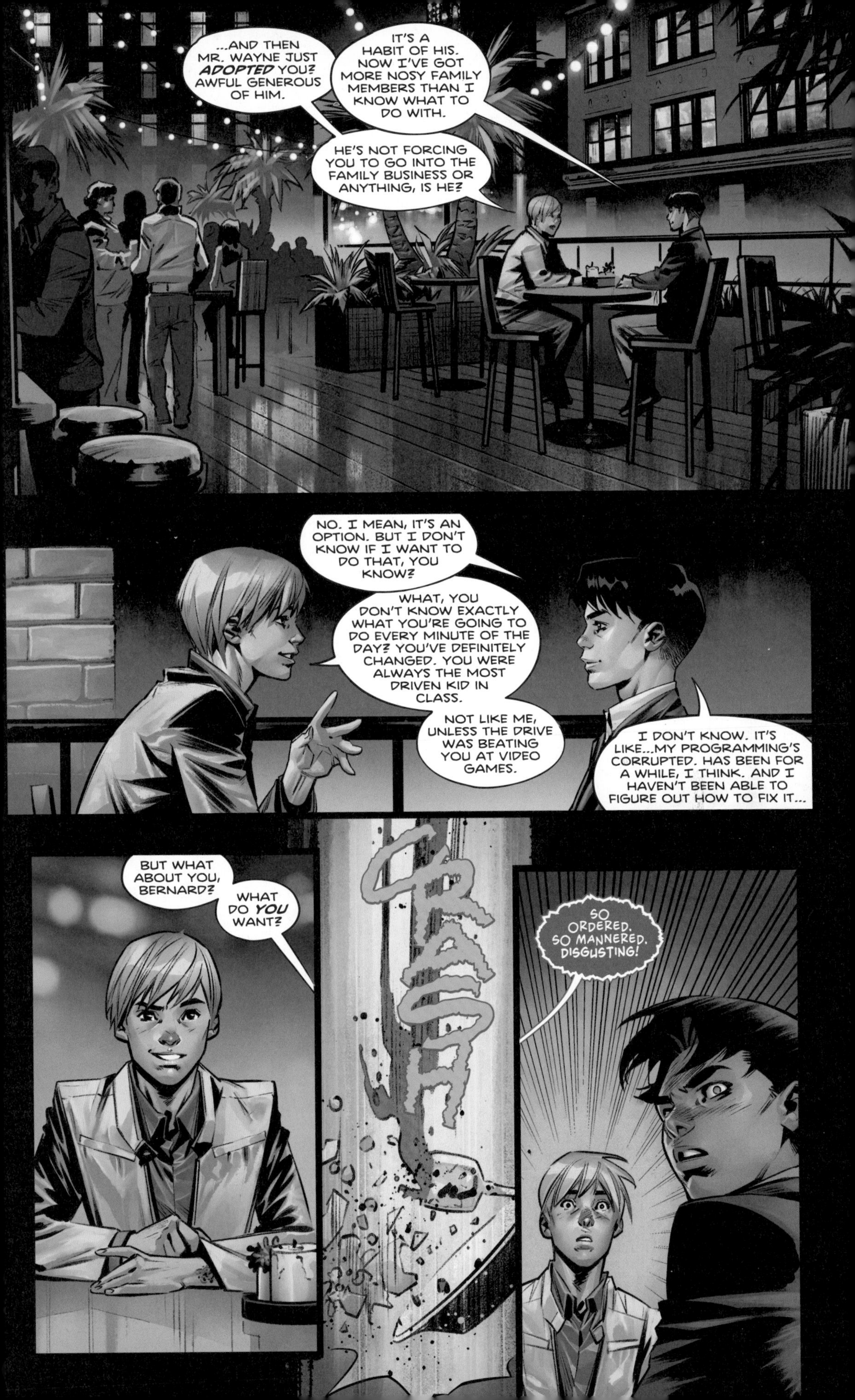
...AND THEN MR. WAYNE JUST *ADOPTED* YOU? AWFUL GENEROUS OF HIM.
IT'S A HABIT OF HIS. NOW I'VE GOT MORE NOSY FAMILY MEMBERS THAN I KNOW WHAT TO DO WITH.
HE'S NOT FORCING YOU TO GO INTO THE FAMILY BUSINESS OR ANYTHING, IS HE?
NO. I MEAN, IT'S AN OPTION. BUT I DON'T KNOW IF I WANT TO DO THAT, YOU KNOW?
WHAT, YOU DON'T KNOW EXACTLY WHAT YOU'RE GOING TO DO EVERY MINUTE OF THE DAY? YOU'VE DEFINITELY CHANGED. YOU WERE ALWAYS THE MOST DRIVEN KID IN CLASS.
NOT LIKE ME, UNLESS THE DRIVE WAS BEATING YOU AT VIDEO GAMES.
I DON'T KNOW. IT'S LIKE...MY PROGRAMMING'S CORRUPTED. HAS BEEN FOR A WHILE, I THINK. AND I HAVEN'T BEEN ABLE TO FIGURE OUT HOW TO FIX IT...
BUT WHAT ABOUT YOU, BERNARD?
WHAT DO *YOU* WANT?
CRASH
SO ORDERED. SO MANNERED. DISGUSTING!

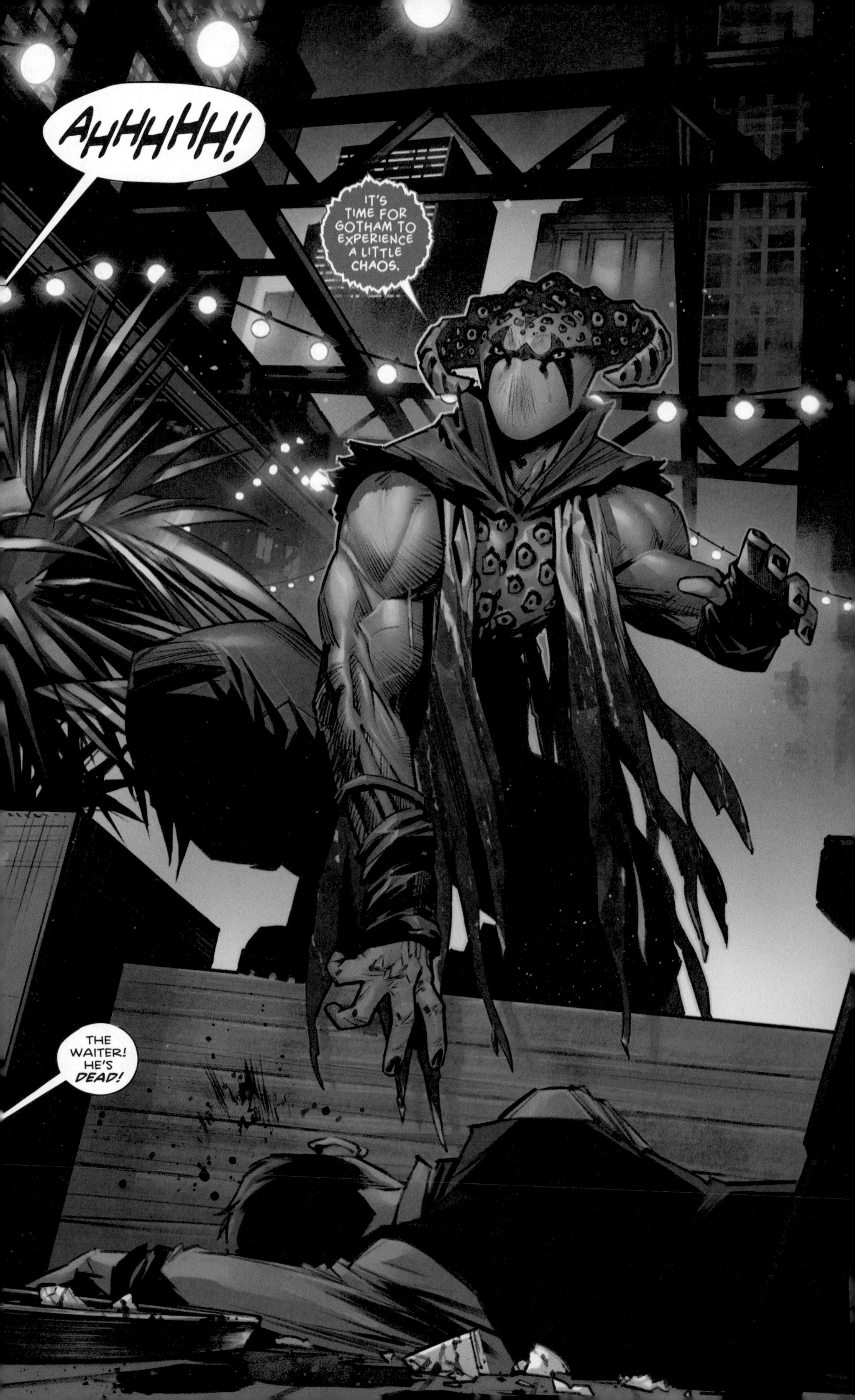
AHHHHH!
IT'S TIME FOR GOTHAM TO EXPERIENCE A LITTLE CHAOS.
THE WAITER! HE'S *DEAD!*

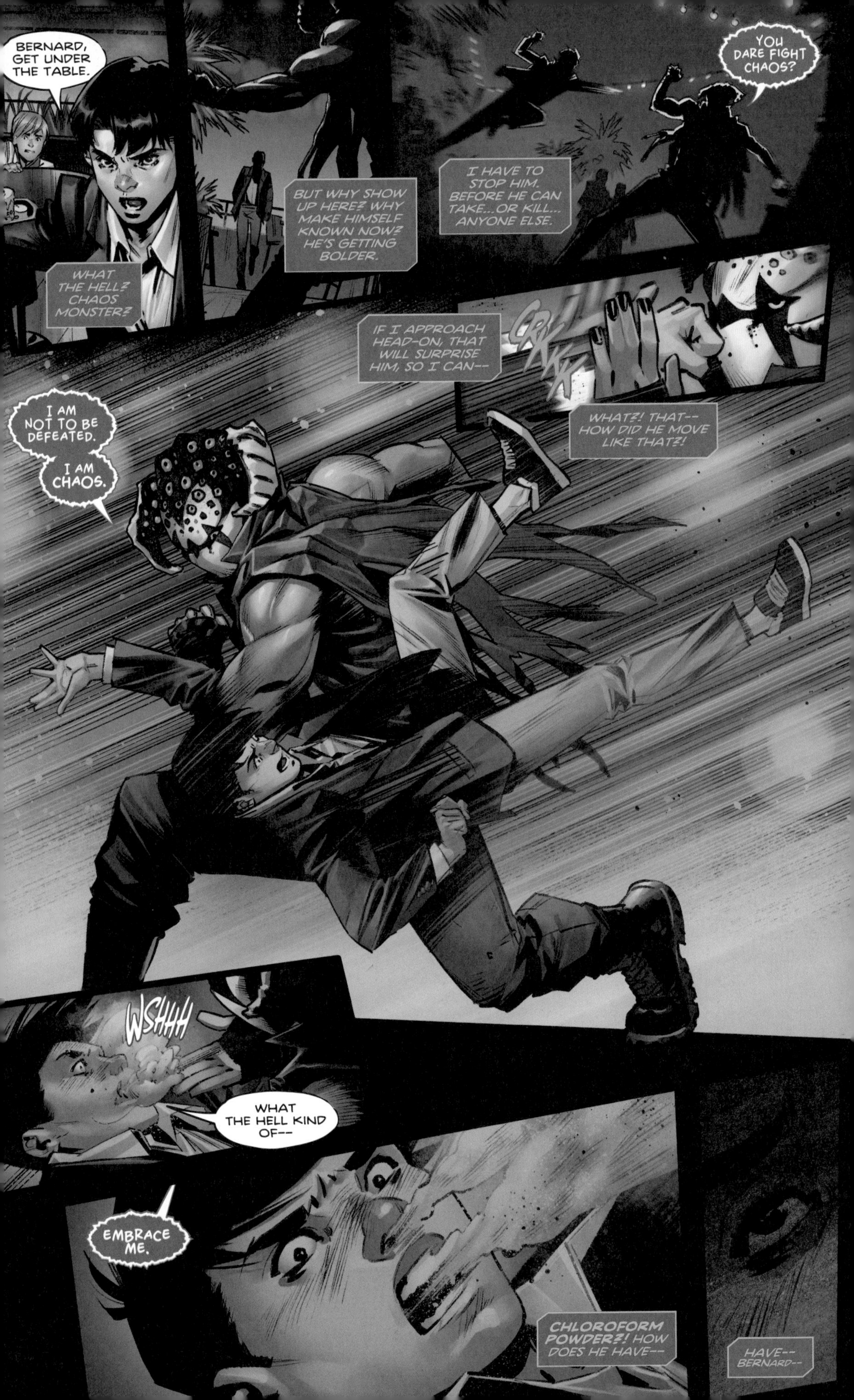
BERNARD, GET UNDER THE TABLE.
WHAT THE HELL? CHAOS MONSTER?
BUT WHY SHOW UP HERE? WHY MAKE HIMSELF KNOWN NOW? HE'S GETTING BOLDER.
I HAVE TO STOP HIM. BEFORE HE CAN TAKE...OR KILL... ANYONE ELSE.
YOU DARE FIGHT CHAOS?
IF I APPROACH HEAD-ON, THAT WILL SURPRISE HIM, SO I CAN--
CRKKK
WHAT?! THAT-- HOW DID HE MOVE LIKE THAT?!
I AM NOT TO BE DEFEATED.
I AM CHAOS.
WSHHH
WHAT THE HELL KIND OF--
EMBRACE ME.
CHLOROFORM POWDER?! HOW DOES HE HAVE--
HAVE-- BERNARD--

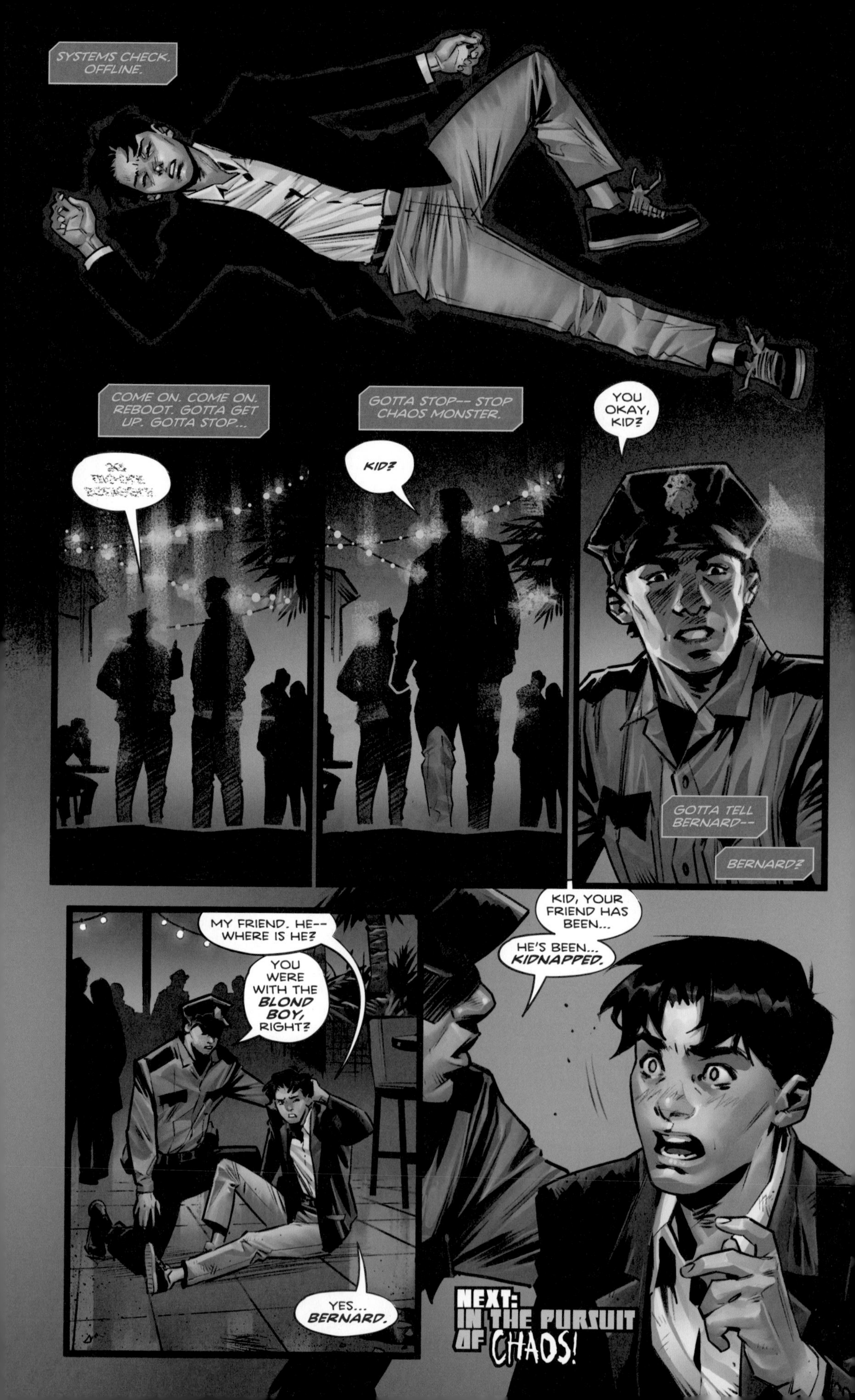
SYSTEMS CHECK. OFFLINE.
COME ON. COME ON. REBOOT. GOTTA GET UP. GOTTA STOP...
GOTTA STOP-- STOP CHAOS MONSTER.
KID?
YOU OKAY, KID?
GOTTA TELL BERNARD--
BERNARD?
MY FRIEND. HE-- WHERE IS HE?
YOU WERE WITH THE BLOND BOY, RIGHT?
YES... BERNARD.
KID, YOUR FRIEND HAS BEEN...
HE'S BEEN... KIDNAPPED.
NEXT: IN THE PURSUIT OF CHAOS!

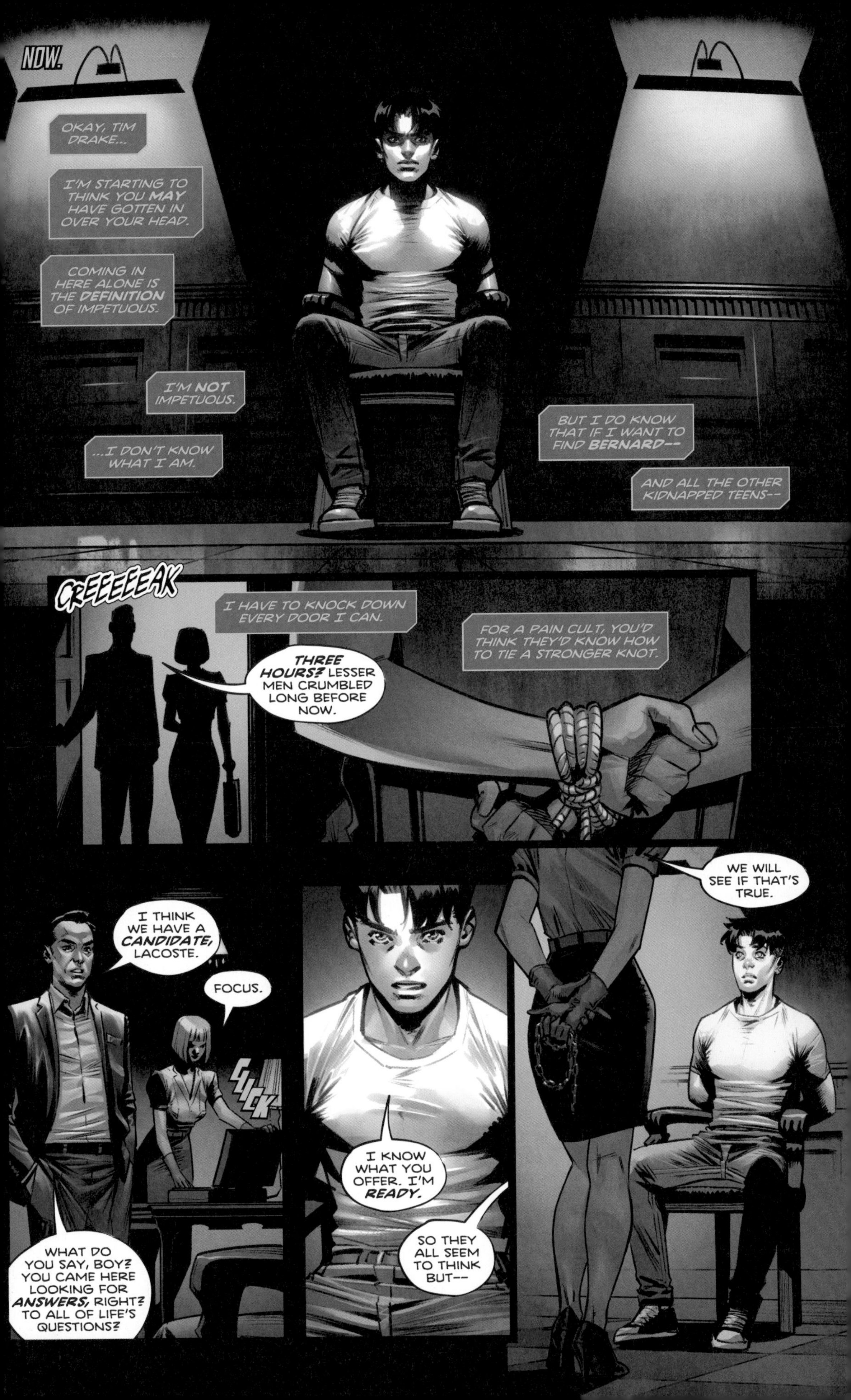
NOW.
OKAY, TIM DRAKE...
I'M STARTING TO THINK YOU MAY HAVE GOTTEN IN OVER YOUR HEAD.
COMING IN HERE ALONE IS THE DEFINITION OF IMPETUOUS.
I'M NOT IMPETUOUS.
...I DON'T KNOW WHAT I AM.
BUT I DO KNOW THAT IF I WANT TO FIND BERNARD--
AND ALL THE OTHER KIDNAPPED TEENS--
CREEEEEAK
I HAVE TO KNOCK DOWN EVERY DOOR I CAN.
FOR A PAIN CULT, YOU'D THINK THEY'D KNOW HOW TO TIE A STRONGER KNOT.
THREE HOURS? LESSER MEN CRUMBLED LONG BEFORE NOW.
I THINK WE HAVE A CANDIDATE, LACOSTE.
FOCUS.
CLICK
WHAT DO YOU SAY, BOY? YOU CAME HERE LOOKING FOR ANSWERS, RIGHT? TO ALL OF LIFE'S QUESTIONS?
I KNOW WHAT YOU OFFER. I'M READY.
SO THEY ALL SEEM TO THINK BUT--
WE WILL SEE IF THAT'S TRUE.

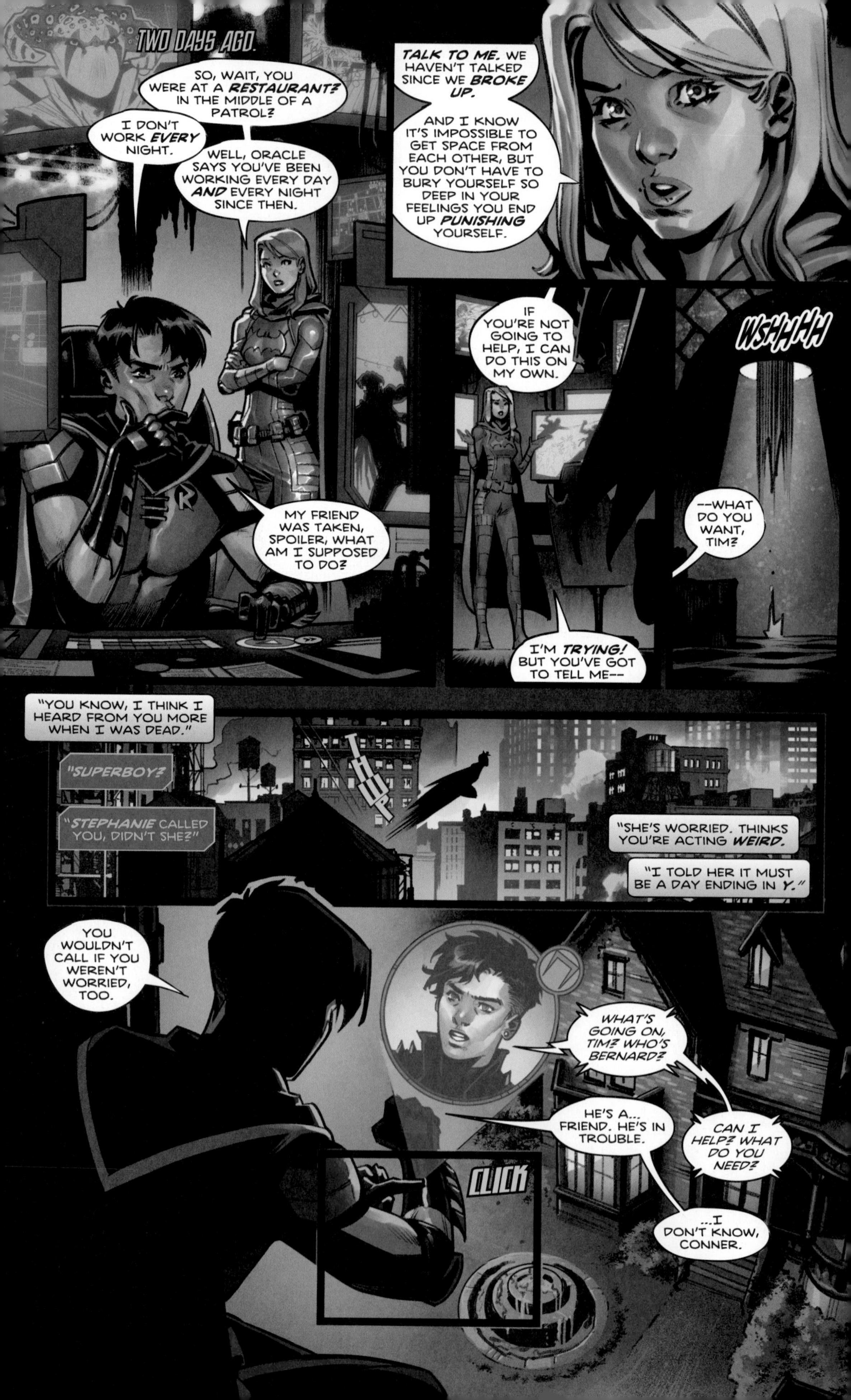
TWO DAYS AGO.
SO, WAIT, YOU WERE AT A RESTAURANT? IN THE MIDDLE OF A PATROL?
I DON'T WORK EVERY NIGHT.
WELL, ORACLE SAYS YOU'VE BEEN WORKING EVERY DAY AND EVERY NIGHT SINCE THEN.
TALK TO ME. WE HAVEN'T TALKED SINCE WE BROKE UP.
AND I KNOW IT'S IMPOSSIBLE TO GET SPACE FROM EACH OTHER, BUT YOU DON'T HAVE TO BURY YOURSELF SO DEEP IN YOUR FEELINGS YOU END UP PUNISHING YOURSELF.
MY FRIEND WAS TAKEN, SPOILER, WHAT AM I SUPPOSED TO DO?
IF YOU'RE NOT GOING TO HELP, I CAN DO THIS ON MY OWN.
I'M TRYING! BUT YOU'VE GOT TO TELL ME--
WSHHHH
--WHAT DO YOU WANT, TIM?
"YOU KNOW, I THINK I HEARD FROM YOU MORE WHEN I WAS DEAD."
"SUPERBOY?
"STEPHANIE CALLED YOU, DIDN'T SHE?"
THUP
"SHE'S WORRIED. THINKS YOU'RE ACTING WEIRD.
"I TOLD HER IT MUST BE A DAY ENDING IN Y."
YOU WOULDN'T CALL IF YOU WEREN'T WORRIED, TOO.
WHAT'S GOING ON, TIM? WHO'S BERNARD?
HE'S A... FRIEND. HE'S IN TROUBLE.
CAN I HELP? WHAT DO YOU NEED?
CLICK
...I DON'T KNOW, CONNER.

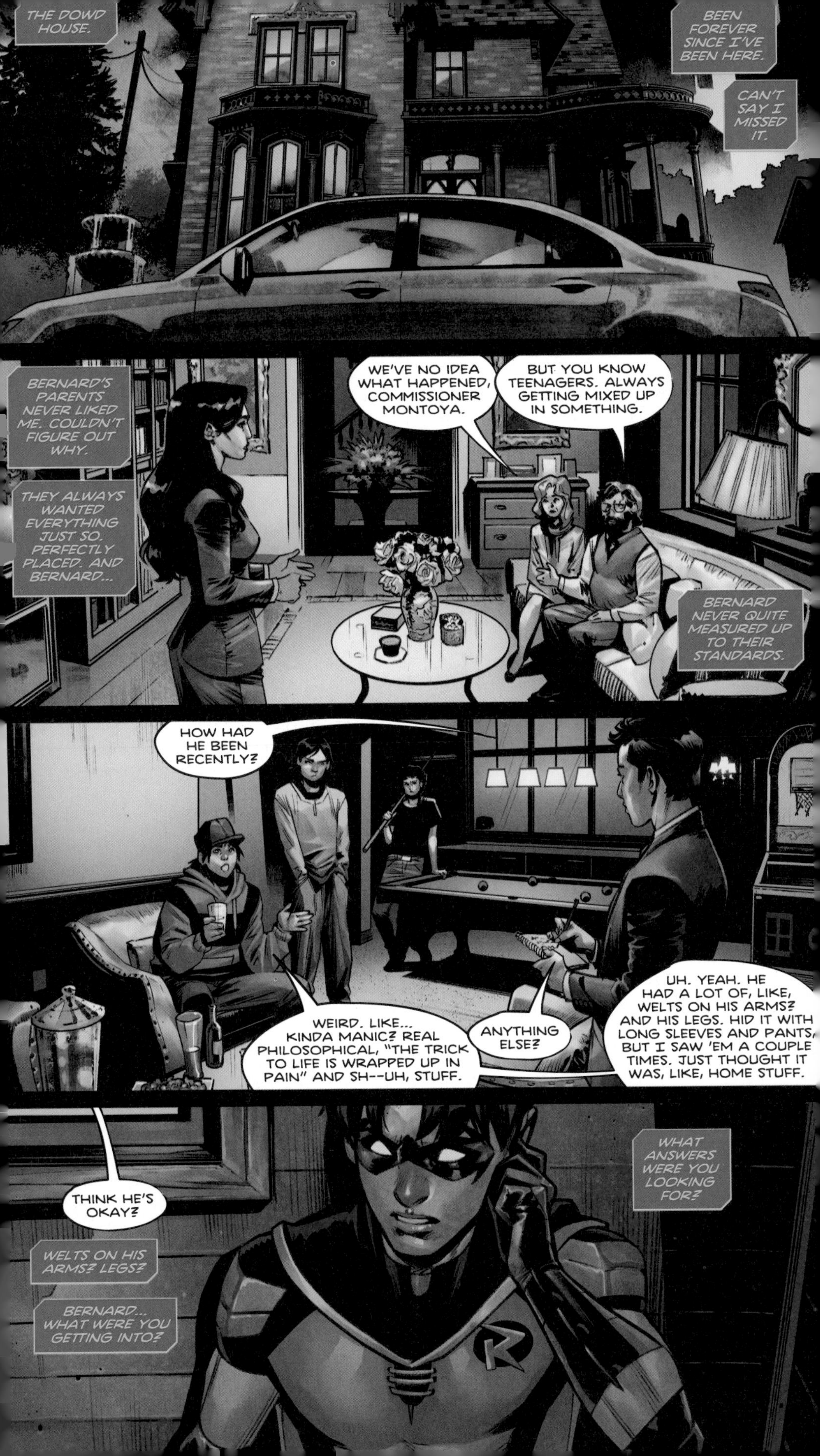
THE DOWD HOUSE.
BEEN FOREVER SINCE I'VE BEEN HERE.
CAN'T SAY I MISSED IT.
BERNARD'S PARENTS NEVER LIKED ME. COULDN'T FIGURE OUT WHY.
THEY ALWAYS WANTED EVERYTHING JUST SO. PERFECTLY PLACED. AND BERNARD...
WE'VE NO IDEA WHAT HAPPENED, COMMISSIONER MONTOYA.
BUT YOU KNOW TEENAGERS. ALWAYS GETTING MIXED UP IN SOMETHING.
BERNARD NEVER QUITE MEASURED UP TO THEIR STANDARDS.
HOW HAD HE BEEN RECENTLY?
WEIRD. LIKE... KINDA MANIC? REAL PHILOSOPHICAL, "THE TRICK TO LIFE IS WRAPPED UP IN PAIN" AND SH--UH, STUFF.
ANYTHING ELSE?
UH. YEAH. HE HAD A LOT OF, LIKE, WELTS ON HIS ARMS? AND HIS LEGS. HID IT WITH LONG SLEEVES AND PANTS, BUT I SAW 'EM A COUPLE TIMES. JUST THOUGHT IT WAS, LIKE, HOME STUFF.
THINK HE'S OKAY?
WHAT ANSWERS WERE YOU LOOKING FOR?
WELTS ON HIS ARMS? LEGS?
BERNARD... WHAT WERE YOU GETTING INTO?

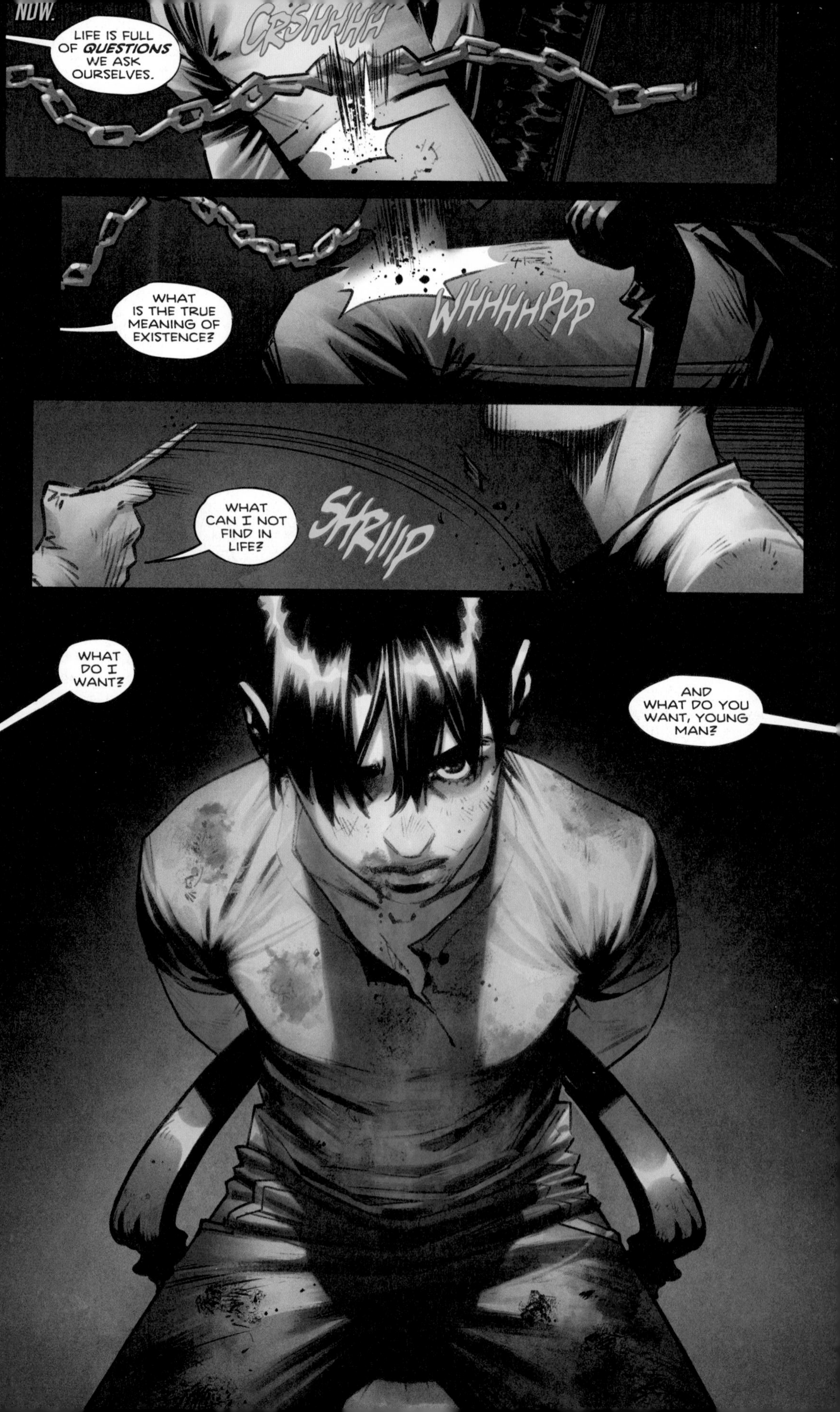
NOW.
LIFE IS FULL OF QUESTIONS WE ASK OURSELVES.
CRSHHHH
WHAT IS THE TRUE MEANING OF EXISTENCE?
WHHHHPPP
WHAT CAN I NOT FIND IN LIFE?
SHRIIIP
WHAT DO I WANT?
AND WHAT DO YOU WANT, YOUNG MAN?

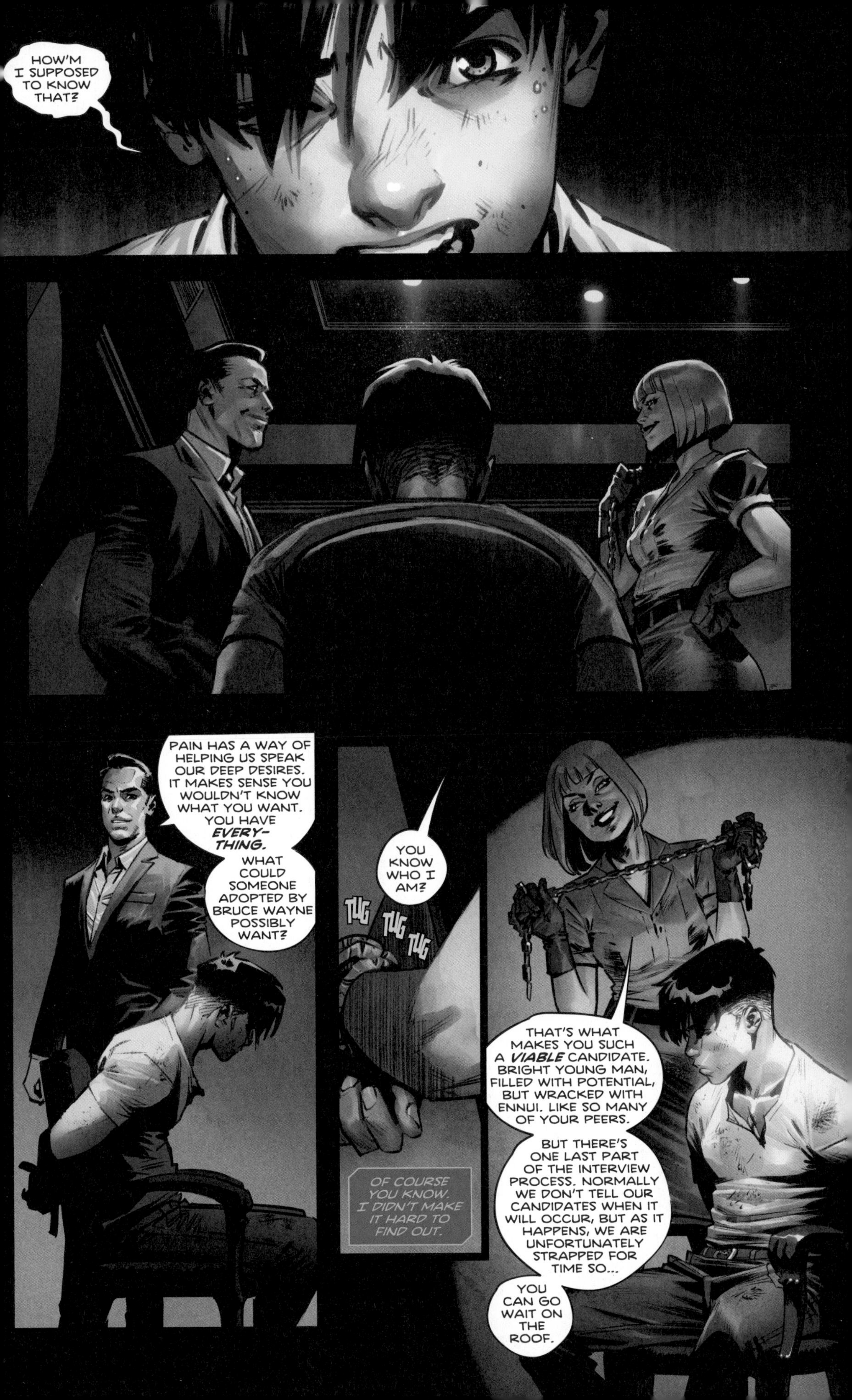
HOW'M I SUPPOSED TO KNOW THAT?
PAIN HAS A WAY OF HELPING US SPEAK OUR DEEP DESIRES. IT MAKES SENSE YOU WOULDN'T KNOW WHAT YOU WANT. YOU HAVE *EVERY-THING.*
WHAT COULD SOMEONE ADOPTED BY BRUCE WAYNE POSSIBLY WANT?
YOU KNOW WHO I AM?
TUG TUG TUG
OF COURSE YOU KNOW. I DIDN'T MAKE IT HARD TO FIND OUT.
THAT'S WHAT MAKES YOU SUCH A *VIABLE* CANDIDATE. BRIGHT YOUNG MAN, FILLED WITH POTENTIAL, BUT WRACKED WITH ENNUI. LIKE SO MANY OF YOUR PEERS.
BUT THERE'S ONE LAST PART OF THE INTERVIEW PROCESS. NORMALLY WE DON'T TELL OUR CANDIDATES WHEN IT WILL OCCUR, BUT AS IT HAPPENS, WE ARE UNFORTUNATELY STRAPPED FOR TIME SO...
YOU CAN GO WAIT ON THE ROOF.

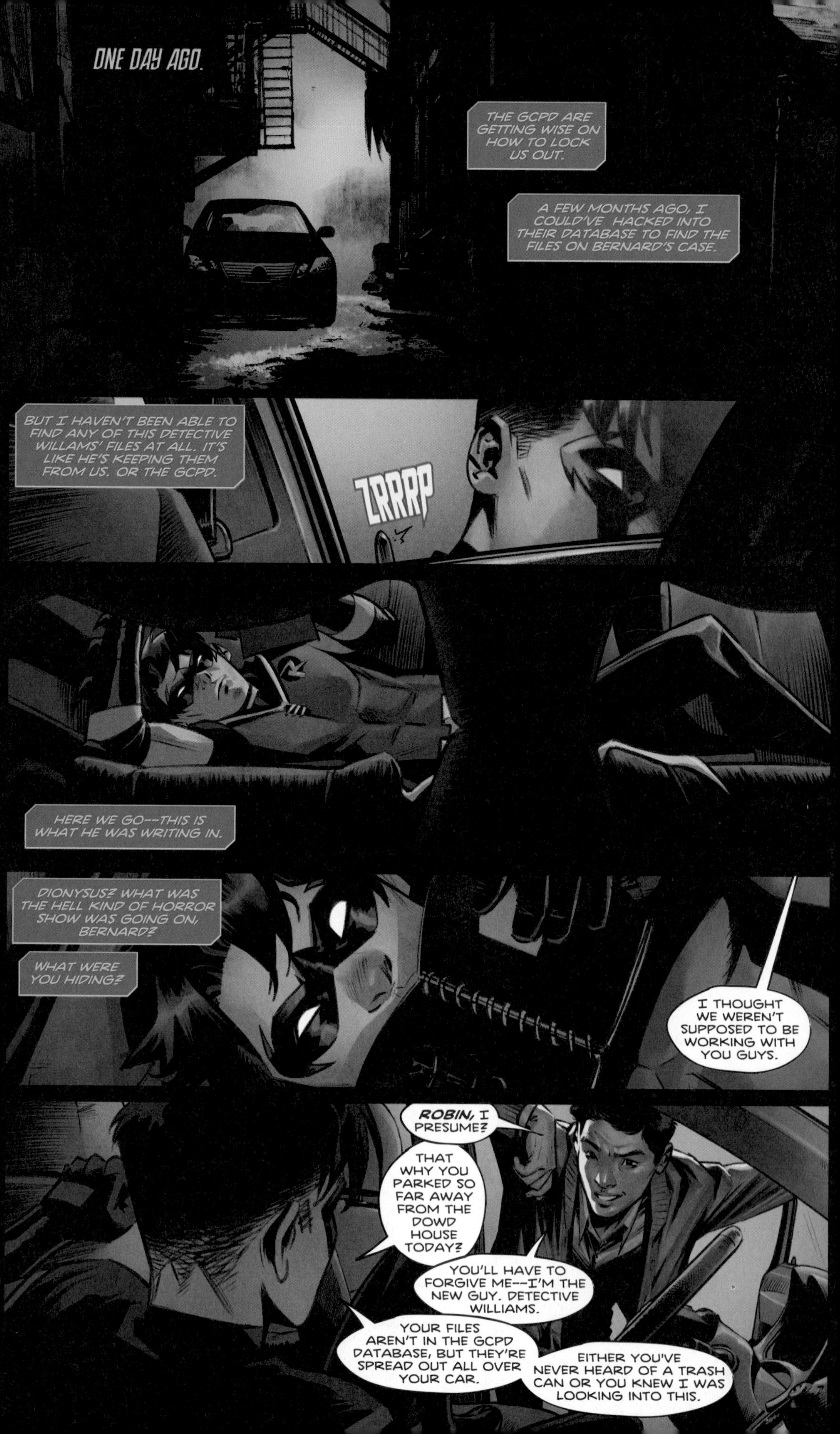
ONE DAY AGO.
THE GCPD ARE GETTING WISE ON HOW TO LOCK US OUT.
A FEW MONTHS AGO, I COULD'VE HACKED INTO THEIR DATABASE TO FIND THE FILES ON BERNARD'S CASE.
BUT I HAVEN'T BEEN ABLE TO FIND ANY OF THIS DETECTIVE WILLAMS' FILES AT ALL. IT'S LIKE HE'S KEEPING THEM FROM US. OR THE GCPD.
ZRRRP
HERE WE GO--THIS IS WHAT HE WAS WRITING IN.
DIONYSUS? WHAT WAS THE HELL KIND OF HORROR SHOW WAS GOING ON, BERNARD?
WHAT WERE YOU HIDING?
I THOUGHT WE WEREN'T SUPPOSED TO BE WORKING WITH YOU GUYS.
ROBIN, I PRESUME?
THAT WHY YOU PARKED SO FAR AWAY FROM THE DOWD HOUSE TODAY?
YOU'LL HAVE TO FORGIVE ME--I'M THE NEW GUY. DETECTIVE WILLIAMS.
YOUR FILES AREN'T IN THE GCPD DATABASE, BUT THEY'RE SPREAD OUT ALL OVER YOUR CAR.
EITHER YOU'VE NEVER HEARD OF A TRASH CAN OR YOU KNEW I WAS LOOKING INTO THIS.

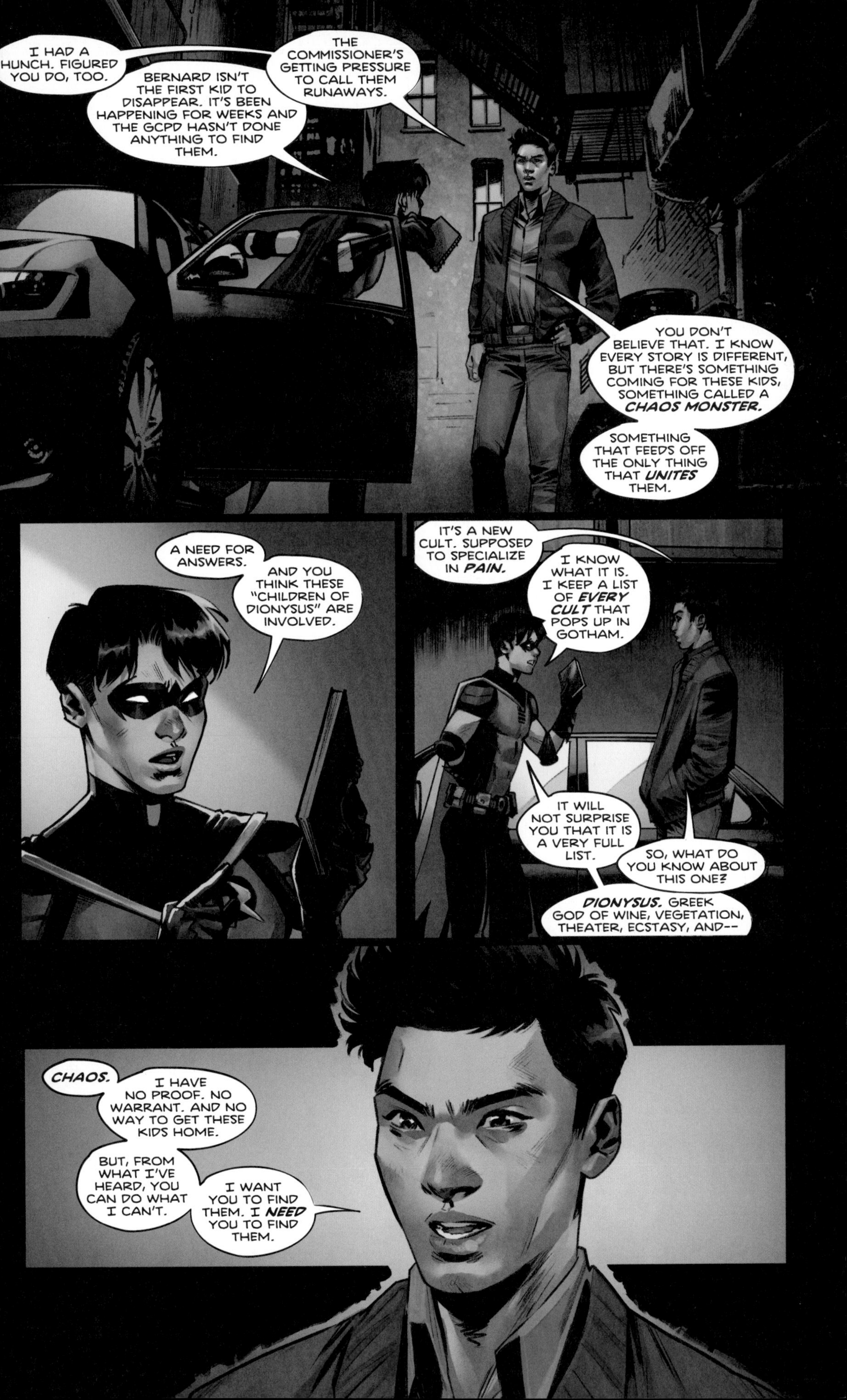

I HAD A HUNCH. FIGURED YOU DO, TOO.
THE COMMISSIONER'S GETTING PRESSURE TO CALL THEM RUNAWAYS.
BERNARD ISN'T THE FIRST KID TO DISAPPEAR. IT'S BEEN HAPPENING FOR WEEKS AND THE GCPD HASN'T DONE ANYTHING TO FIND THEM.
YOU DON'T BELIEVE THAT. I KNOW EVERY STORY IS DIFFERENT, BUT THERE'S SOMETHING COMING FOR THESE KIDS, SOMETHING CALLED A *CHAOS MONSTER.*
SOMETHING THAT FEEDS OFF THE ONLY THING THAT *UNITES* THEM.
A NEED FOR ANSWERS.
AND YOU THINK THESE "CHILDREN OF DIONYSUS" ARE INVOLVED.
IT'S A NEW CULT. SUPPOSED TO SPECIALIZE IN *PAIN.*
I KNOW WHAT IT IS. I KEEP A LIST OF *EVERY CULT* THAT POPS UP IN GOTHAM.
IT WILL NOT SURPRISE YOU THAT IT IS A VERY FULL LIST.
SO, WHAT DO YOU KNOW ABOUT THIS ONE?
DIONYSUS. GREEK GOD OF WINE, VEGETATION, THEATER, ECSTASY, AND--
CHAOS.
I HAVE NO PROOF. NO WARRANT. AND NO WAY TO GET THESE KIDS HOME.
BUT, FROM WHAT I'VE HEARD, YOU CAN DO WHAT I CAN'T.
I WANT YOU TO FIND THEM. I *NEED* YOU TO FIND THEM.

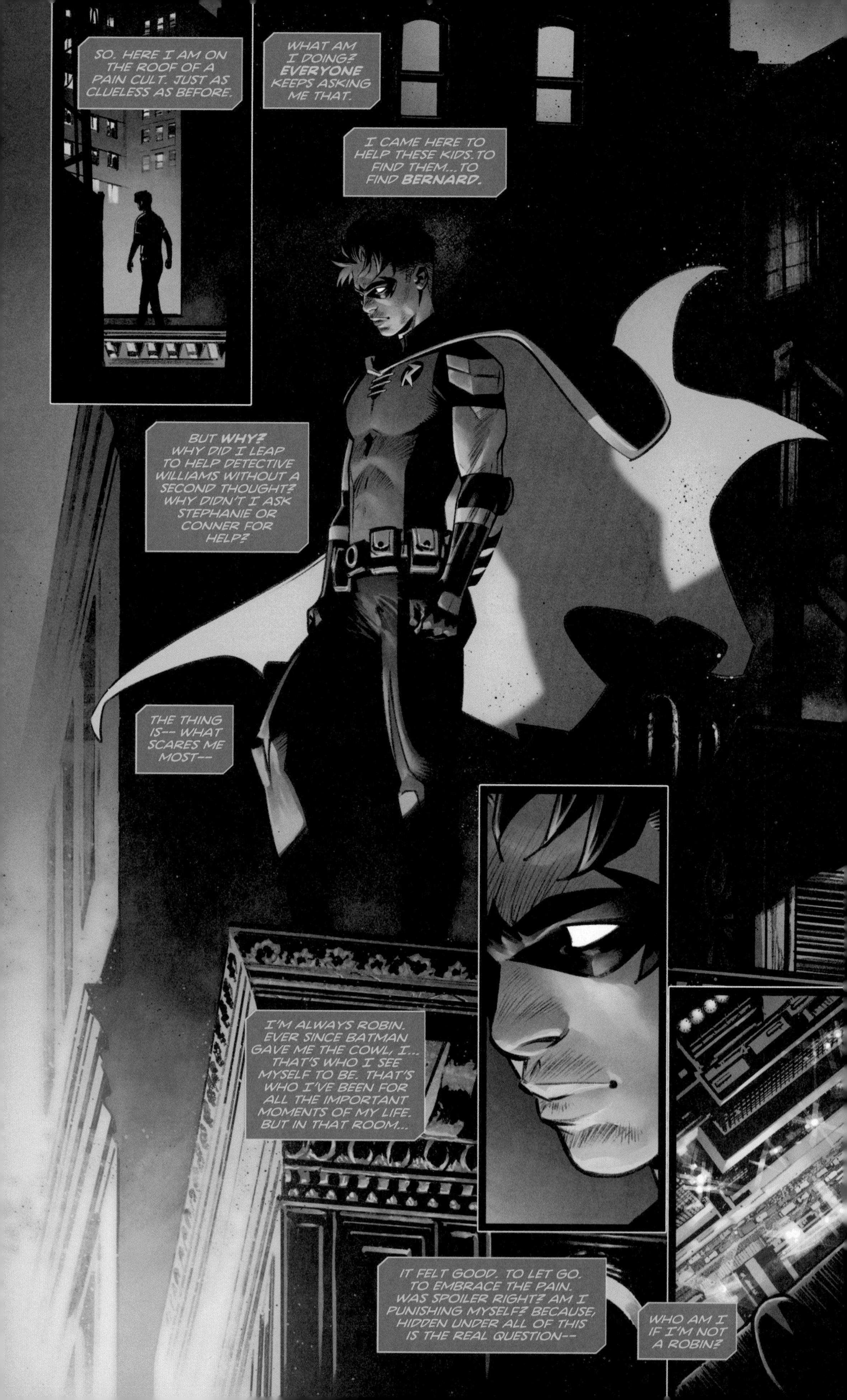
SO. HERE I AM ON THE ROOF OF A PAIN CULT. JUST AS CLUELESS AS BEFORE.
WHAT AM I DOING? **EVERYONE** KEEPS ASKING ME THAT.
I CAME HERE TO HELP THESE KIDS. TO FIND THEM... TO FIND **BERNARD.**
BUT **WHY?** WHY DID I LEAP TO HELP DETECTIVE WILLIAMS WITHOUT A SECOND THOUGHT? WHY DIDN'T I ASK STEPHANIE OR CONNER FOR HELP?
THE THING IS-- WHAT SCARES ME MOST--
I'M ALWAYS ROBIN. EVER SINCE BATMAN GAVE ME THE COWL, I... THAT'S WHO I SEE MYSELF TO BE. THAT'S WHO I'VE BEEN FOR ALL THE IMPORTANT MOMENTS OF MY LIFE. BUT IN THAT ROOM...
IT FELT GOOD. TO LET GO. TO EMBRACE THE PAIN. WAS SPOILER RIGHT? AM I PUNISHING MYSELF? BECAUSE, HIDDEN UNDER ALL OF THIS IS THE REAL QUESTION--
WHO AM I IF I'M NOT A ROBIN?

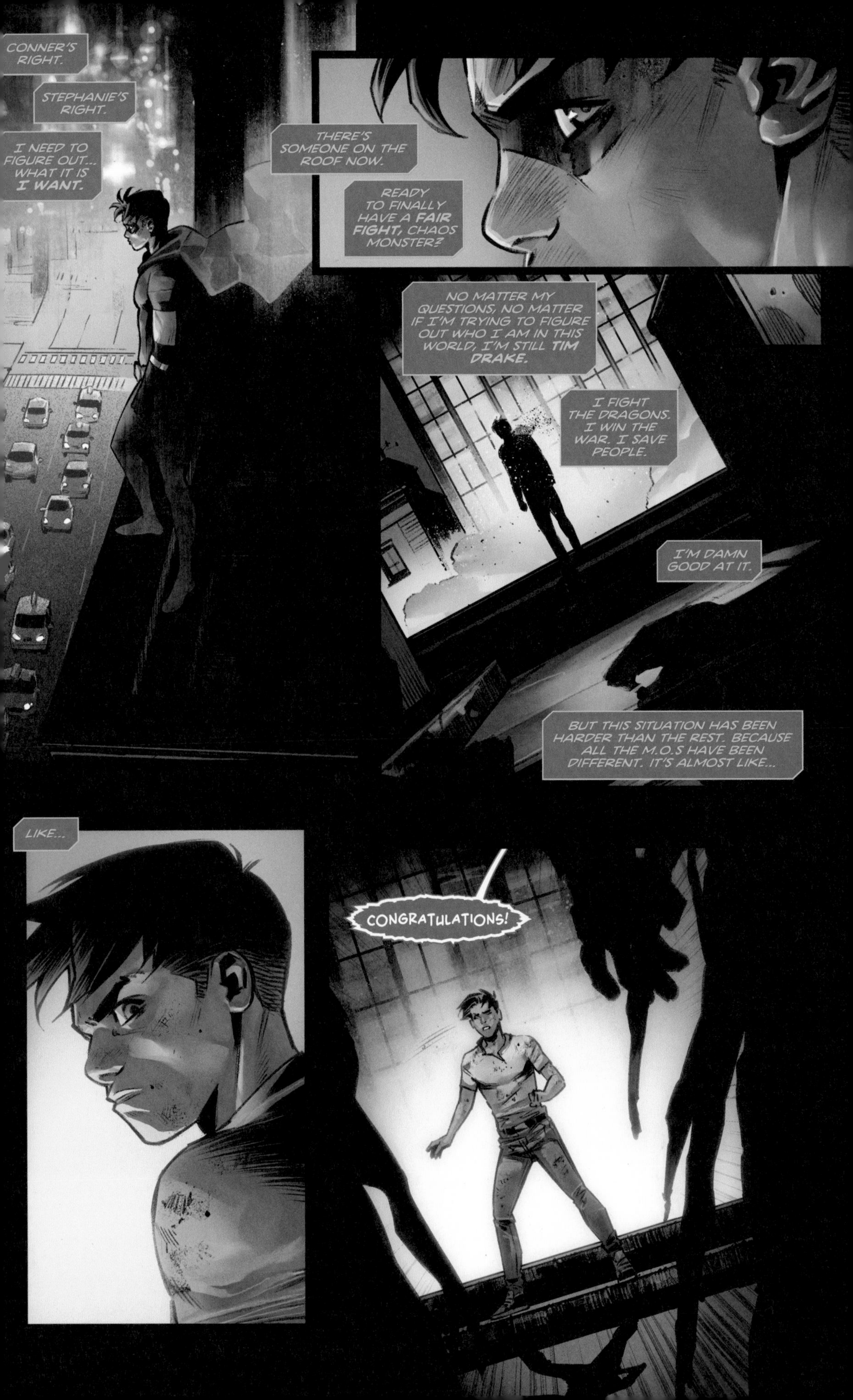
CONNER'S RIGHT.
STEPHANIE'S RIGHT.
I NEED TO FIGURE OUT... WHAT IT IS I WANT.
THERE'S SOMEONE ON THE ROOF NOW.
READY TO FINALLY HAVE A FAIR FIGHT, CHAOS MONSTER?
NO MATTER MY QUESTIONS, NO MATTER IF I'M TRYING TO FIGURE OUT WHO I AM IN THIS WORLD, I'M STILL TIM DRAKE.
I FIGHT THE DRAGONS. I WIN THE WAR. I SAVE PEOPLE.
I'M DAMN GOOD AT IT.
BUT THIS SITUATION HAS BEEN HARDER THAN THE REST. BECAUSE ALL THE M.O.S HAVE BEEN DIFFERENT. IT'S ALMOST LIKE...
LIKE...
CONGRATULATIONS!

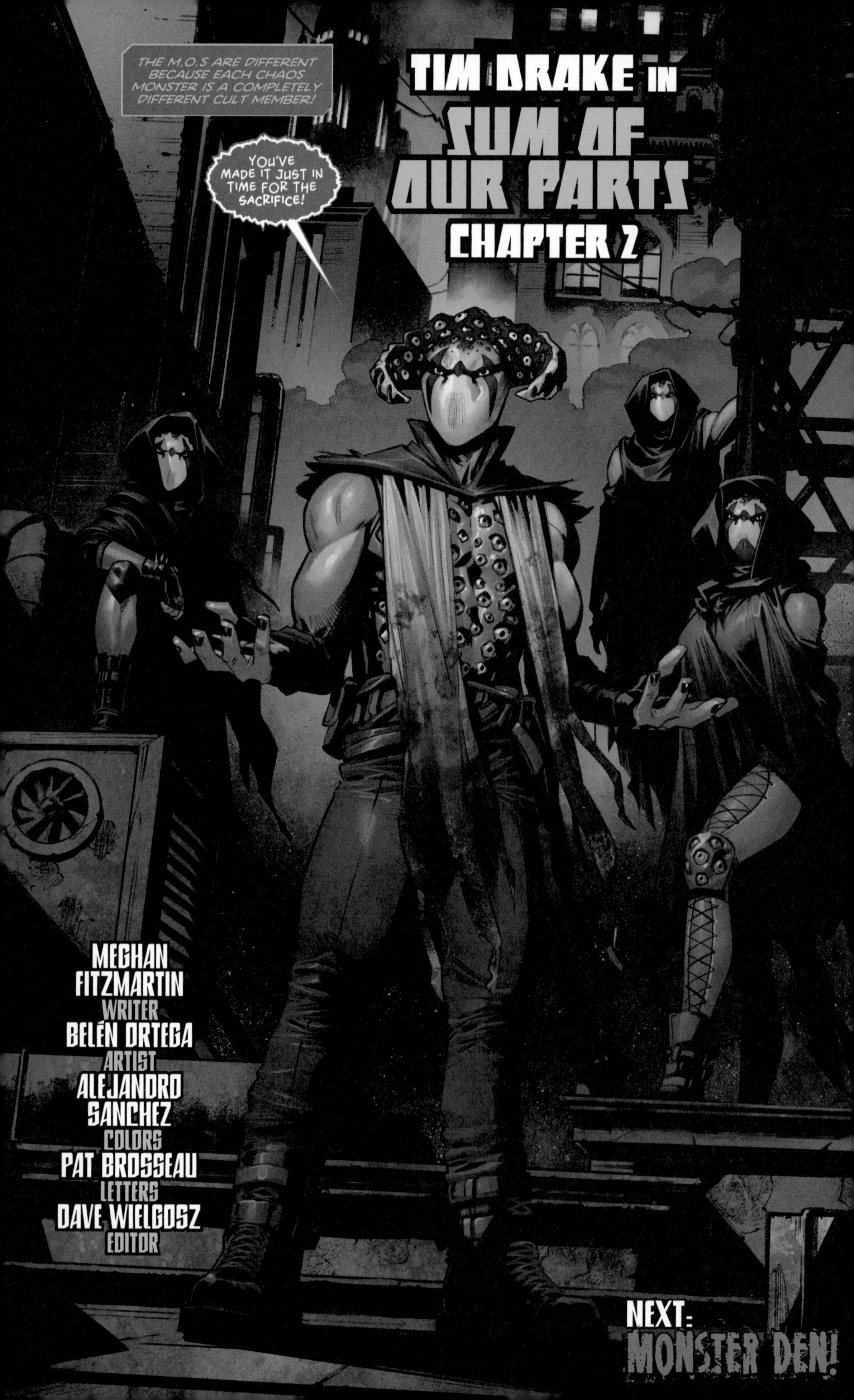

THE M.O.S ARE DIFFERENT BECAUSE EACH CHAOS MONSTER IS A COMPLETELY DIFFERENT CULT MEMBER!
YOU'VE MADE IT JUST IN TIME FOR THE SACRIFICE!
TIM DRAKE IN
SUM OF OUR PARTS
CHAPTER 2
MEGHAN FITZMARTIN
WRITER
BELÉN ORTEGA
ARTIST
ALEJANDRO SANCHEZ
COLORS
PAT BROSSEAU
LETTERS
DAVE WIELGOSZ
EDITOR
NEXT:
MONSTER DEN!

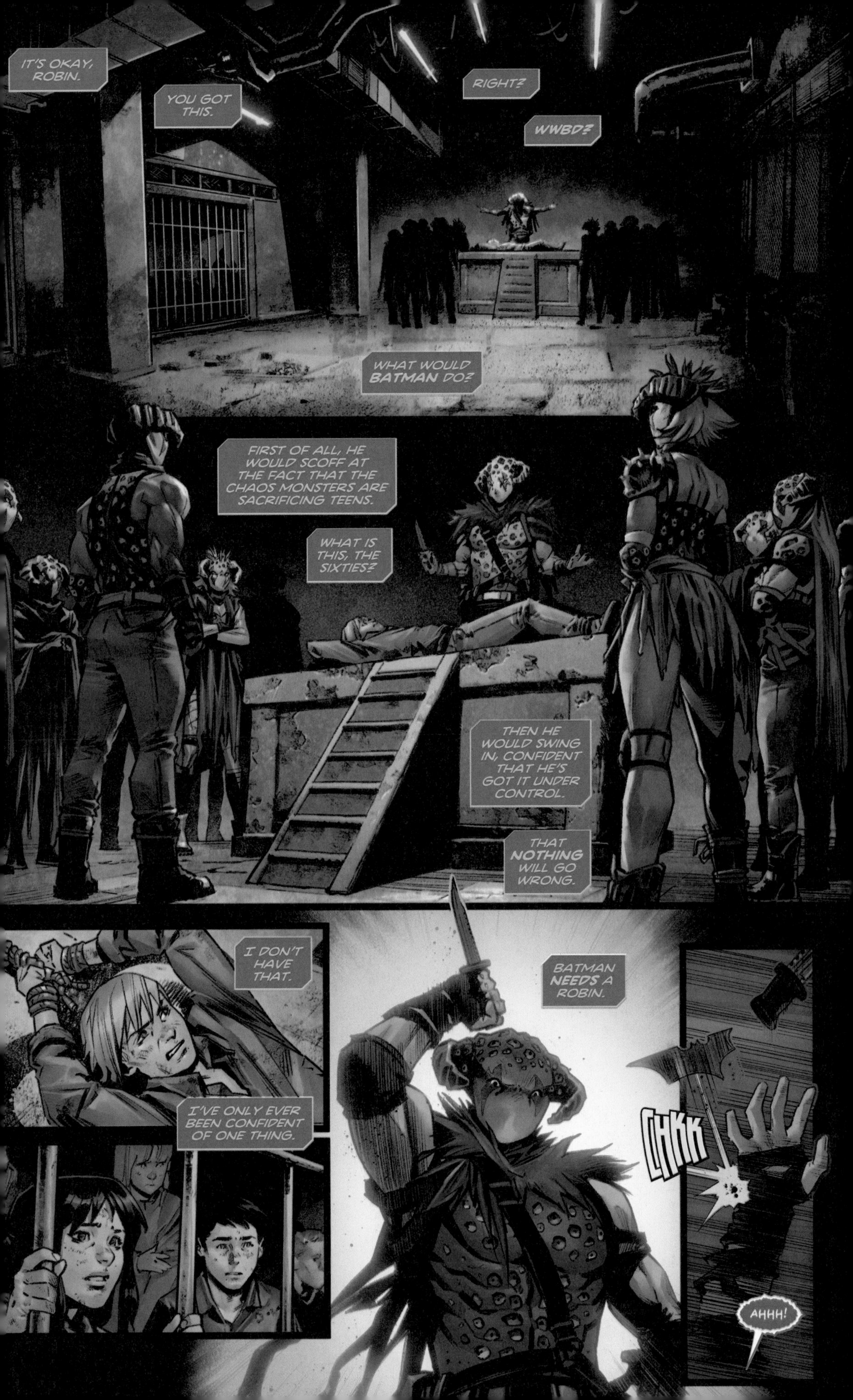
IT'S OKAY, ROBIN.
YOU GOT THIS.
RIGHT?
WWBD?
WHAT WOULD BATMAN DO?
FIRST OF ALL, HE WOULD SCOFF AT THE FACT THAT THE CHAOS MONSTERS ARE SACRIFICING TEENS.
WHAT IS THIS, THE SIXTIES?
THEN HE WOULD SWING IN, CONFIDENT THAT HE'S GOT IT UNDER CONTROL.
THAT NOTHING WILL GO WRONG.
I DON'T HAVE THAT.
I'VE ONLY EVER BEEN CONFIDENT OF ONE THING.
BATMAN NEEDS A ROBIN.
CHKK
AHHH!

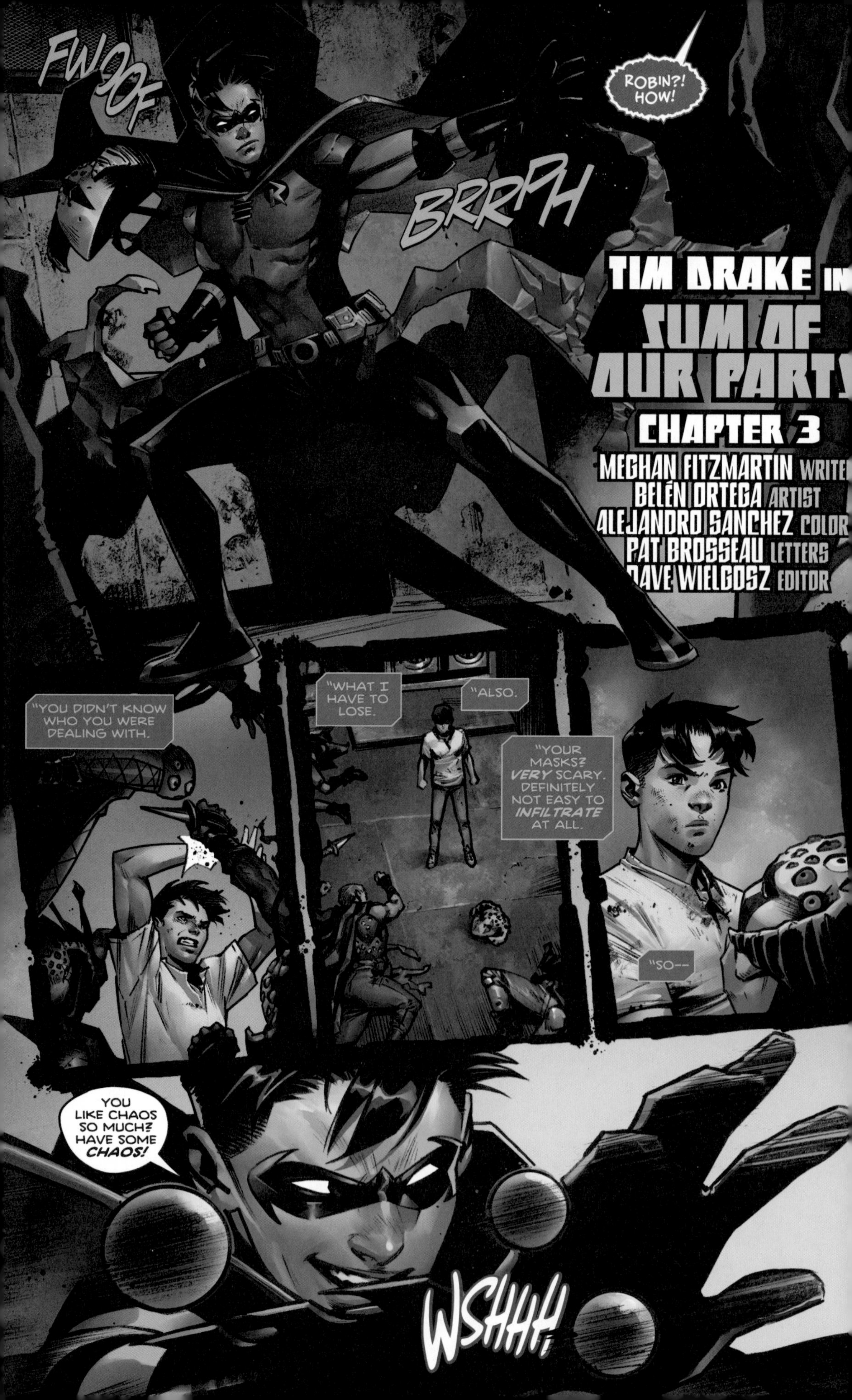
FWOOOF
ROBIN?! HOW!
BRRPH
TIM DRAKE IN
SUM OF OUR PARTS
CHAPTER 3
MEGHAN FITZMARTIN WRITER
BELÉN ORTEGA ARTIST
ALEJANDRO SANCHEZ COLOR
PAT BROSSEAU LETTERS
DAVE WIELGOSZ EDITOR
"YOU DIDN'T KNOW WHO YOU WERE DEALING WITH.
"WHAT I HAVE TO LOSE.
"ALSO.
"YOUR MASKS? VERY SCARY. DEFINITELY NOT EASY TO INFILTRATE AT ALL.
"SO--
YOU LIKE CHAOS SO MUCH? HAVE SOME CHAOS!
WSHHH!

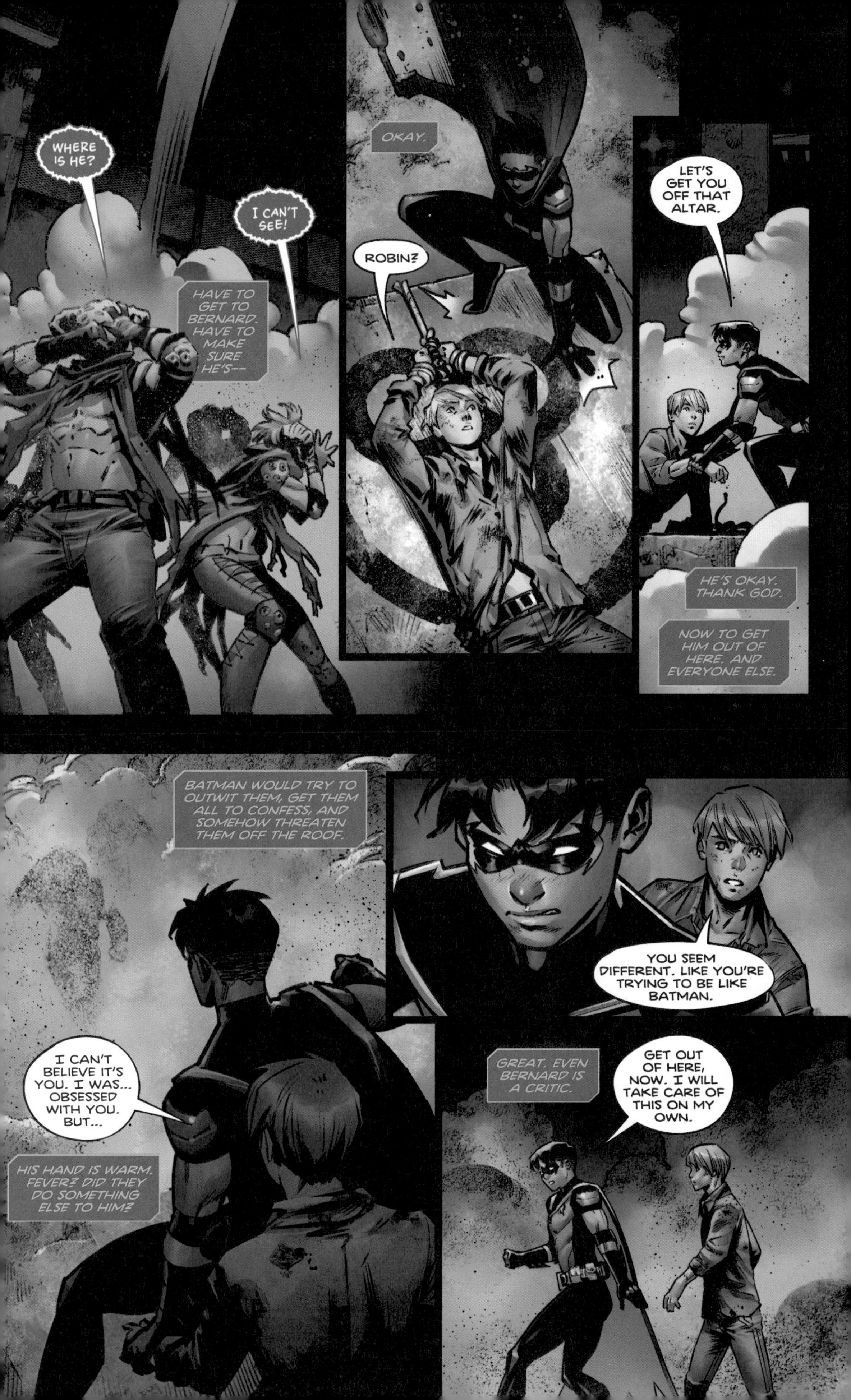
WHERE IS HE?
I CAN'T SEE!
HAVE TO GET TO BERNARD. HAVE TO MAKE SURE HE'S--
OKAY.
ROBIN?
LET'S GET YOU OFF THAT ALTAR.
HE'S OKAY. THANK GOD.
NOW TO GET HIM OUT OF HERE. AND EVERYONE ELSE.
BATMAN WOULD TRY TO OUTWIT THEM, GET THEM ALL TO CONFESS, AND SOMEHOW THREATEN THEM OFF THE ROOF.
I CAN'T BELIEVE IT'S YOU. I WAS... OBSESSED WITH YOU. BUT...
HIS HAND IS WARM. FEVER? DID THEY DO SOMETHING ELSE TO HIM?
YOU SEEM DIFFERENT. LIKE YOU'RE TRYING TO BE LIKE BATMAN.
GREAT. EVEN BERNARD IS A CRITIC.
GET OUT OF HERE, NOW. I WILL TAKE CARE OF THIS ON MY OWN.

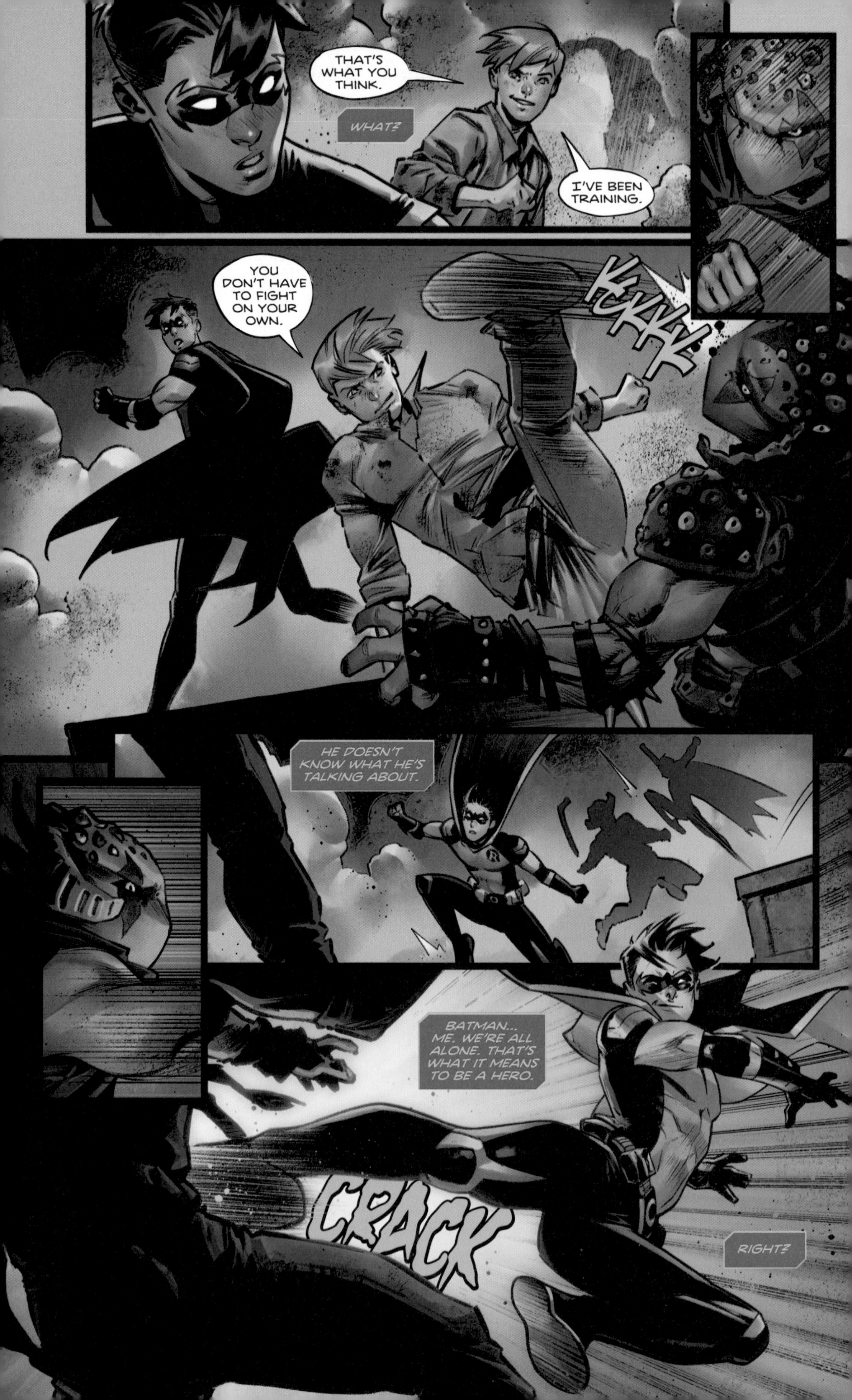
THAT'S WHAT YOU THINK.
WHAT?
I'VE BEEN TRAINING.
YOU DON'T HAVE TO FIGHT ON YOUR OWN.
KKKKK
HE DOESN'T KNOW WHAT HE'S TALKING ABOUT.
BATMAN... ME. WE'RE ALL ALONE. THAT'S WHAT IT MEANS TO BE A HERO.
CRACK
RIGHT?

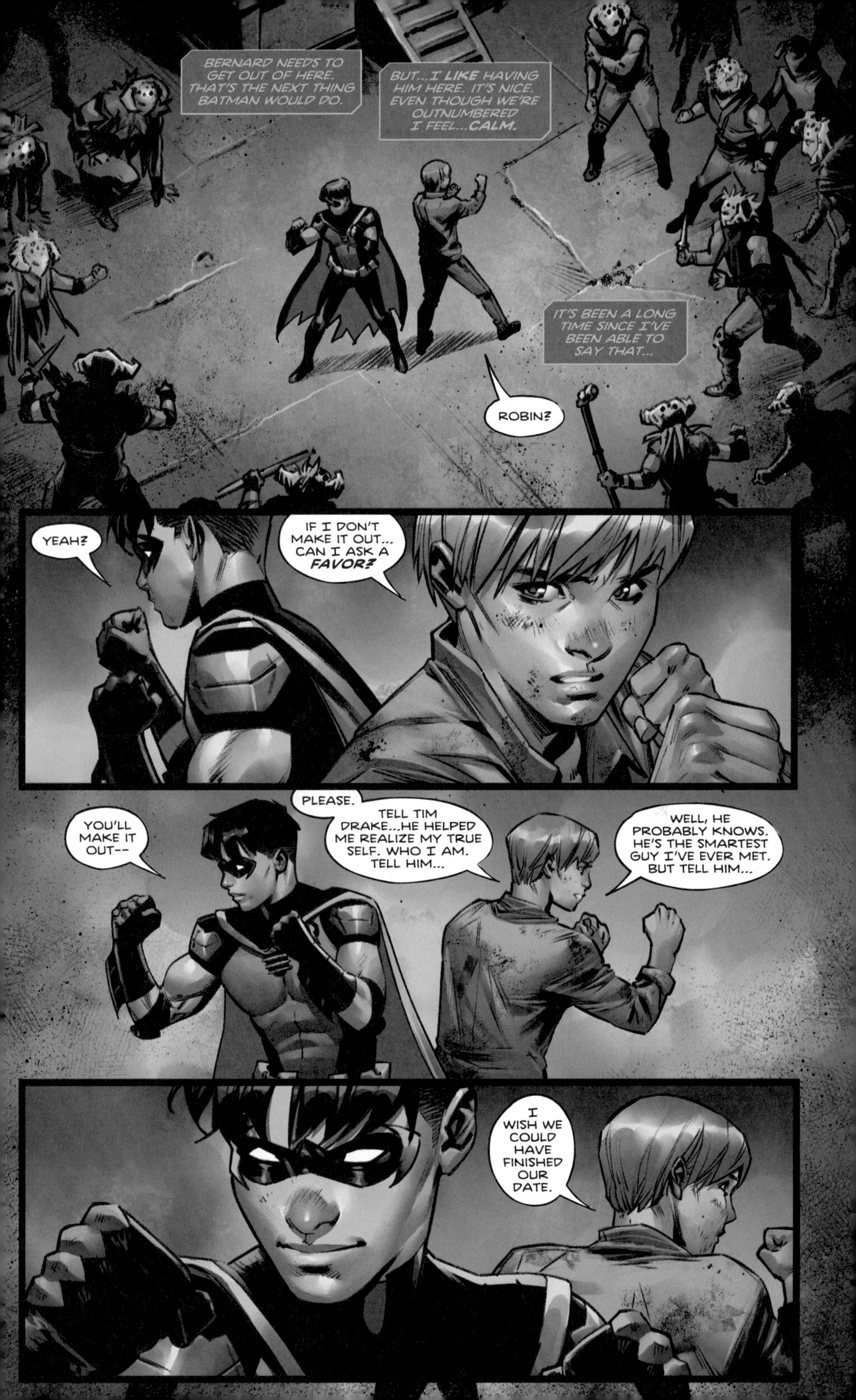
BERNARD NEEDS TO GET OUT OF HERE. THAT'S THE NEXT THING BATMAN WOULD DO.
BUT...I LIKE HAVING HIM HERE. IT'S NICE. EVEN THOUGH WE'RE OUTNUMBERED I FEEL...CALM.
IT'S BEEN A LONG TIME SINCE I'VE BEEN ABLE TO SAY THAT...
ROBIN?
YEAH?
IF I DON'T MAKE IT OUT... CAN I ASK A FAVOR?
YOU'LL MAKE IT OUT--
PLEASE.
TELL TIM DRAKE...HE HELPED ME REALIZE MY TRUE SELF. WHO I AM. TELL HIM...
WELL, HE PROBABLY KNOWS. HE'S THE SMARTEST GUY I'VE EVER MET. BUT TELL HIM...
I WISH WE COULD HAVE FINISHED OUR DATE.

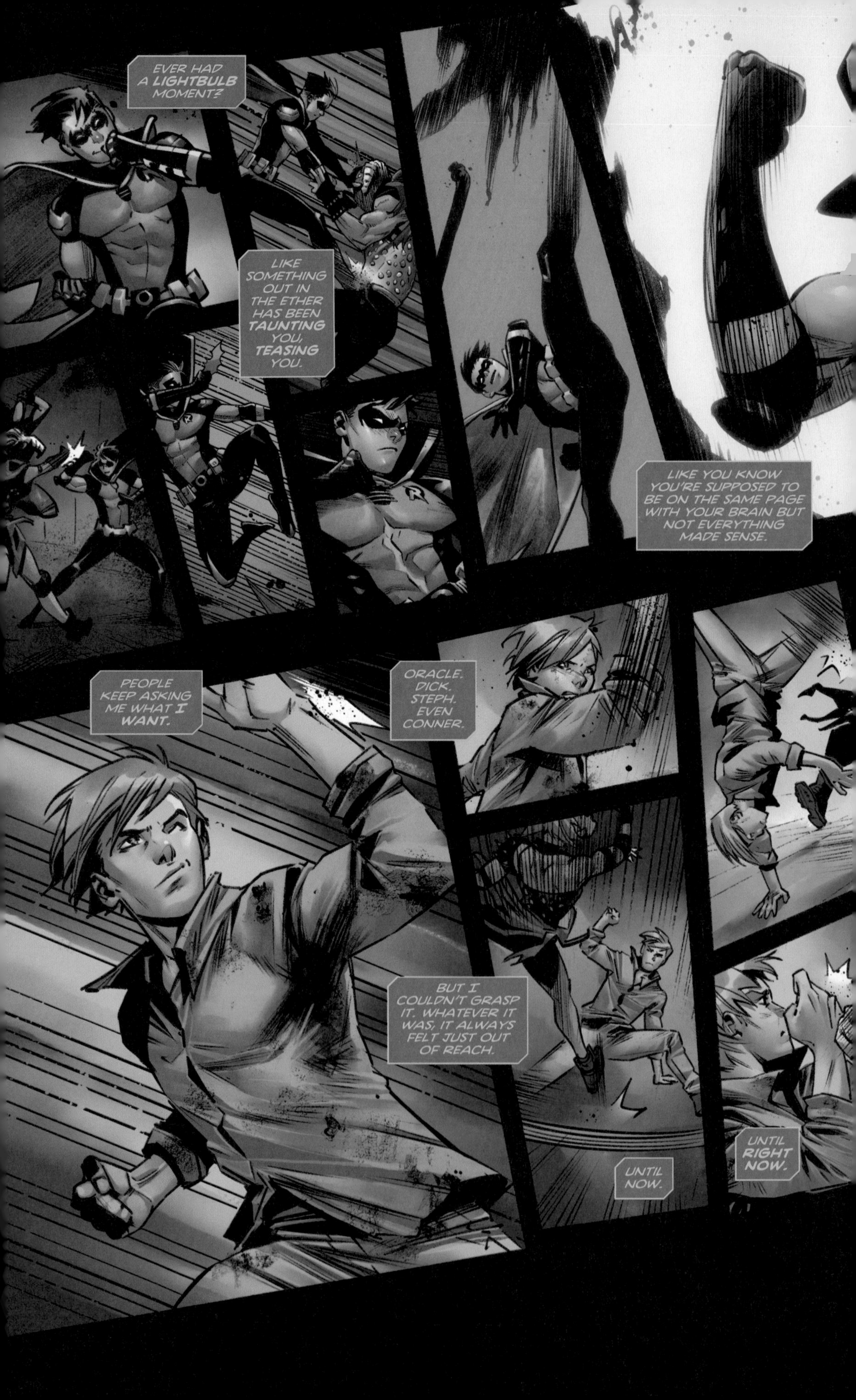
EVER HAD A LIGHTBULB MOMENT?
LIKE SOMETHING OUT IN THE ETHER HAS BEEN TAUNTING YOU, TEASING YOU.
LIKE YOU KNOW YOU'RE SUPPOSED TO BE ON THE SAME PAGE WITH YOUR BRAIN BUT NOT EVERYTHING MADE SENSE.
PEOPLE KEEP ASKING ME WHAT I WANT.
ORACLE. DICK. STEPH. EVEN CONNER.
BUT I COULDN'T GRASP IT. WHATEVER IT WAS, IT ALWAYS FELT JUST OUT OF REACH.
UNTIL NOW.
UNTIL RIGHT NOW.

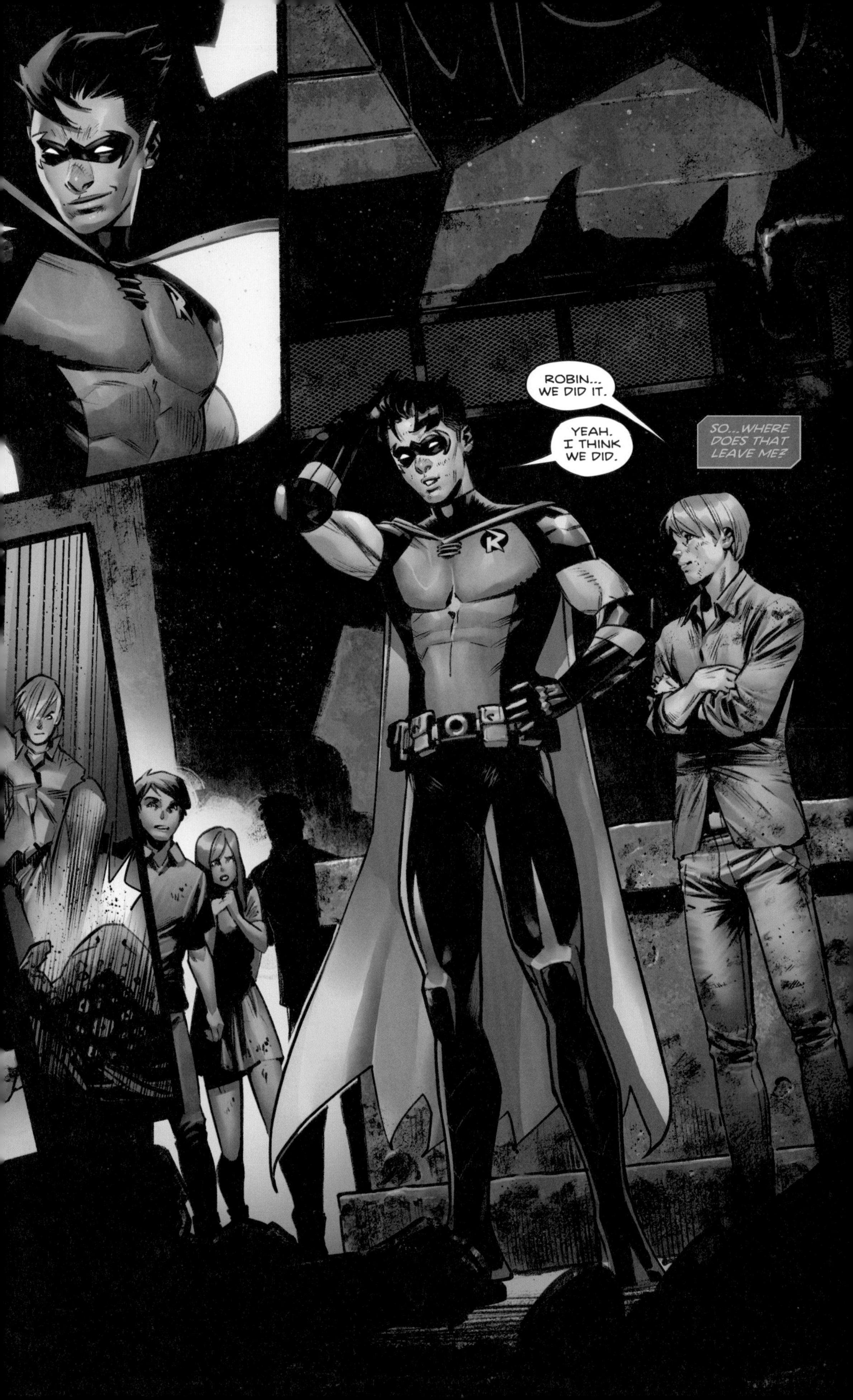
ROBIN... WE DID IT.
YEAH. I THINK WE DID.
SO...WHERE DOES THAT LEAVE ME?

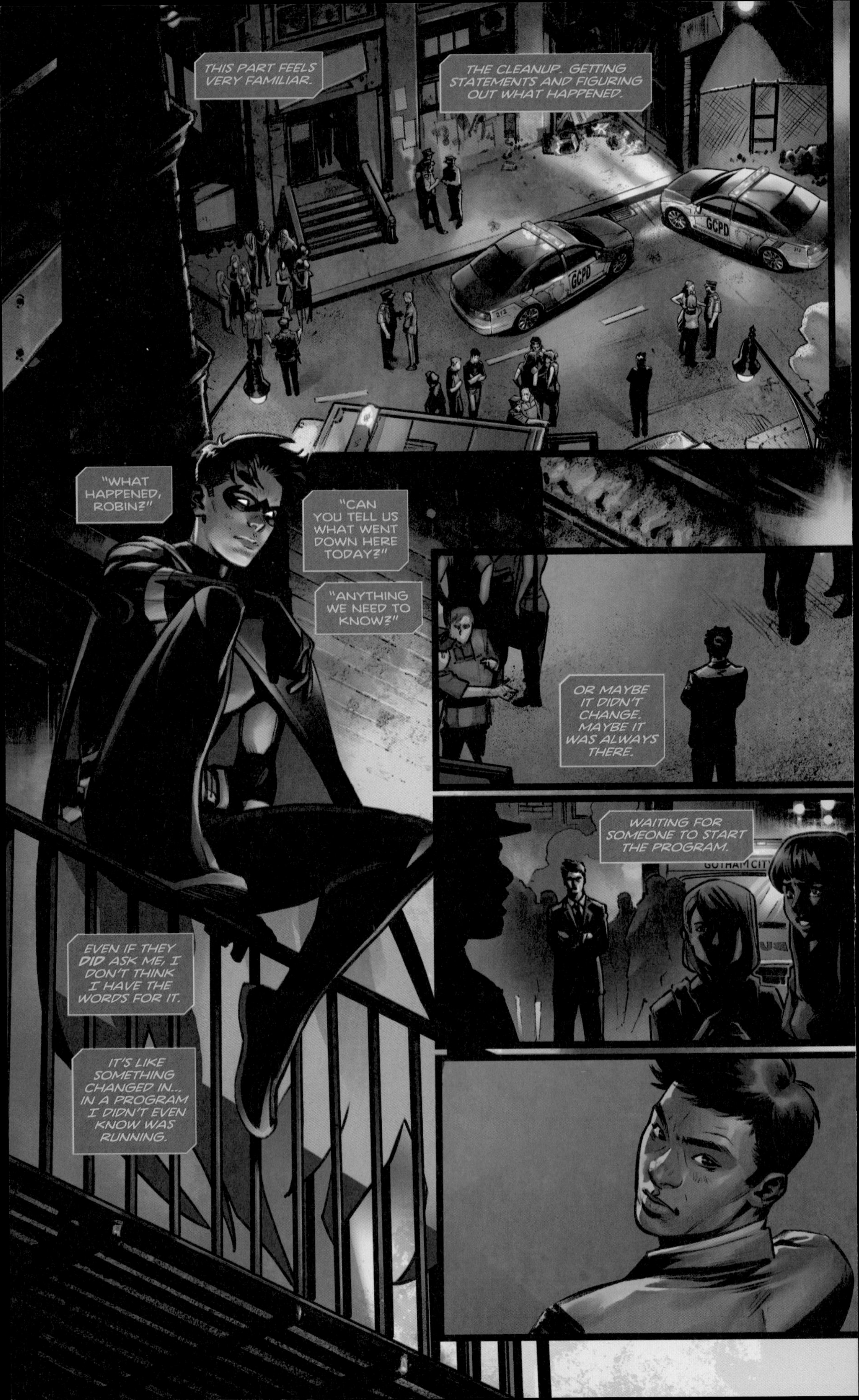
THIS PART FEELS VERY FAMILIAR.
THE CLEANUP. GETTING STATEMENTS AND FIGURING OUT WHAT HAPPENED.
GCPD
GCPD
"WHAT HAPPENED, ROBIN?"
"CAN YOU TELL US WHAT WENT DOWN HERE TODAY?"
"ANYTHING WE NEED TO KNOW?"
EVEN IF THEY DID ASK ME, I DON'T THINK I HAVE THE WORDS FOR IT.
IT'S LIKE SOMETHING CHANGED IN... IN A PROGRAM I DIDN'T EVEN KNOW WAS RUNNING.
OR MAYBE IT DIDN'T CHANGE. MAYBE IT WAS ALWAYS THERE.
WAITING FOR SOMEONE TO START THE PROGRAM.
GOTHAM CITY

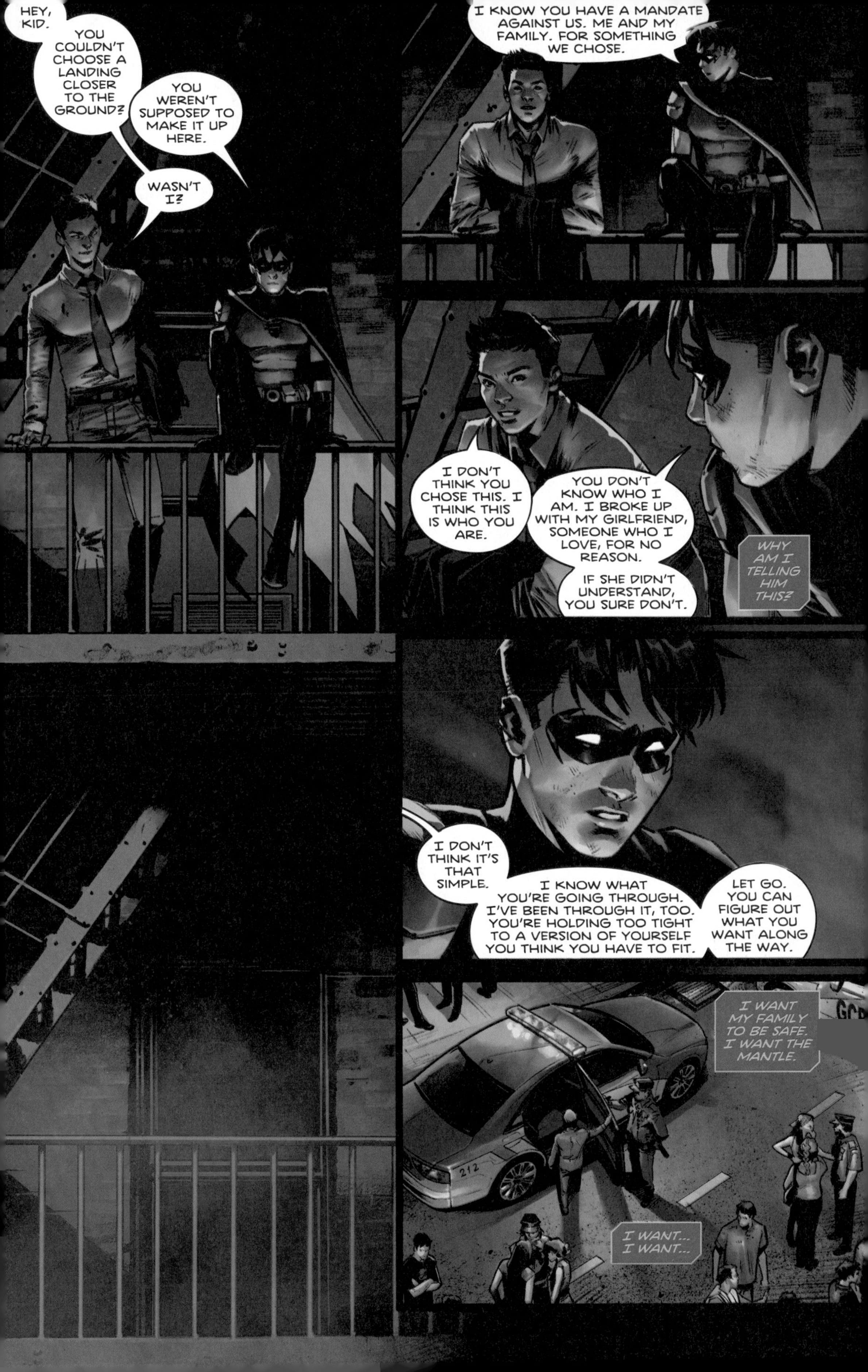
HEY, KID.
YOU COULDN'T CHOOSE A LANDING CLOSER TO THE GROUND?
YOU WEREN'T SUPPOSED TO MAKE IT UP HERE.
WASN'T I?
I KNOW YOU HAVE A MANDATE AGAINST US. ME AND MY FAMILY. FOR SOMETHING WE CHOSE.
I DON'T THINK YOU CHOSE THIS. I THINK THIS IS WHO YOU ARE.
YOU DON'T KNOW WHO I AM. I BROKE UP WITH MY GIRLFRIEND, SOMEONE WHO I LOVE, FOR NO REASON.
IF SHE DIDN'T UNDERSTAND, YOU SURE DON'T.
WHY AM I TELLING HIM THIS?
I DON'T THINK IT'S THAT SIMPLE.
I KNOW WHAT YOU'RE GOING THROUGH. I'VE BEEN THROUGH IT, TOO. YOU'RE HOLDING TOO TIGHT TO A VERSION OF YOURSELF YOU THINK YOU HAVE TO FIT.
LET GO. YOU CAN FIGURE OUT WHAT YOU WANT ALONG THE WAY.
I WANT MY FAMILY TO BE SAFE. I WANT THE MANTLE.
I WANT... I WANT...

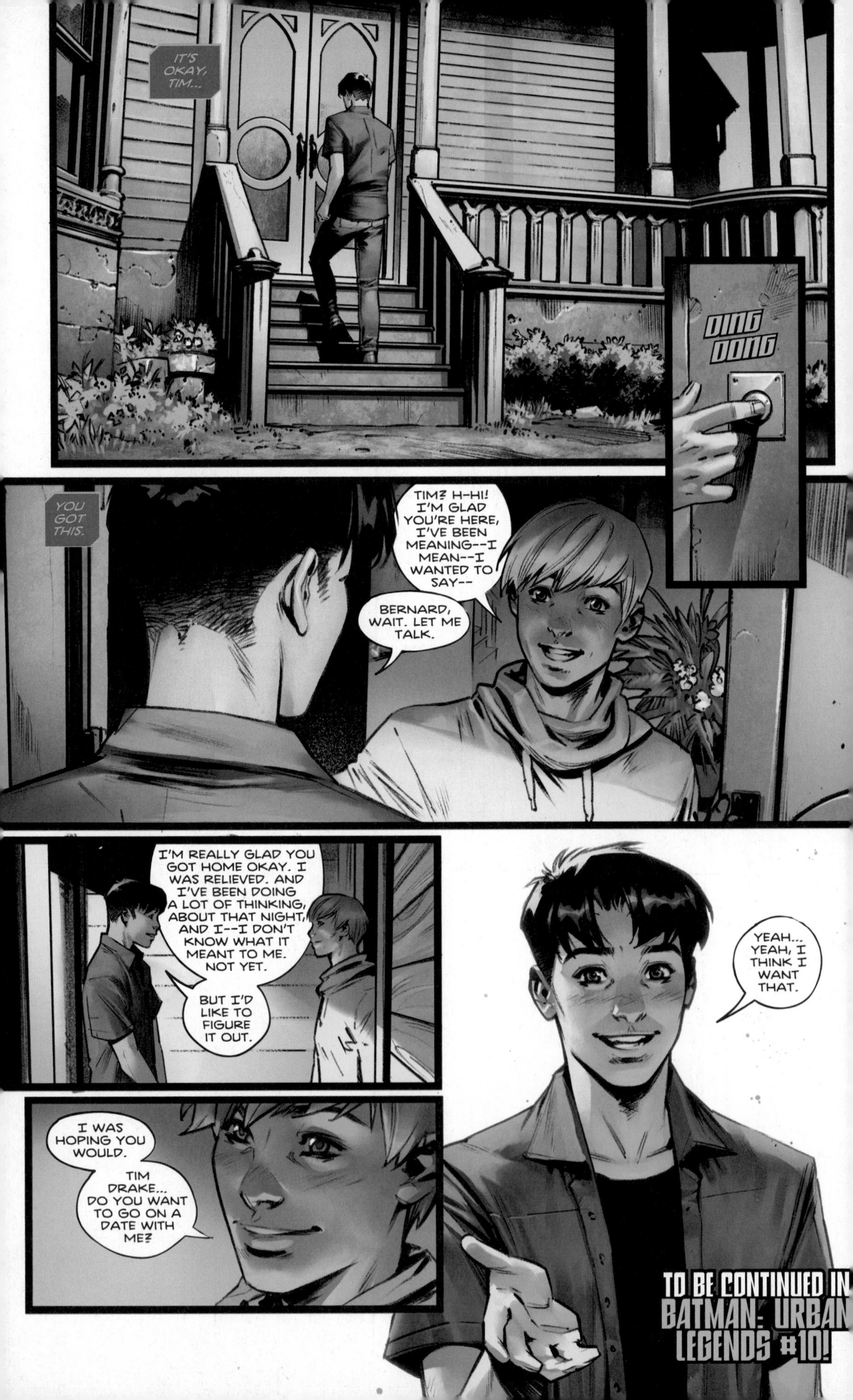
IT'S OKAY, TIM...
DING DONG
YOU GOT THIS.
TIM? H-HI! I'M GLAD YOU'RE HERE, I'VE BEEN MEANING--I MEAN--I WANTED TO SAY--
BERNARD, WAIT. LET ME TALK.
I'M REALLY GLAD YOU GOT HOME OKAY. I WAS RELIEVED. AND I'VE BEEN DOING A LOT OF THINKING, ABOUT THAT NIGHT, AND I--I DON'T KNOW WHAT IT MEANT TO ME. NOT YET.
BUT I'D LIKE TO FIGURE IT OUT.
I WAS HOPING YOU WOULD.
TIM DRAKE... DO YOU WANT TO GO ON A DATE WITH ME?
YEAH... YEAH, I THINK I WANT THAT.
TO BE CONTINUED IN BATMAN: URBAN LEGENDS #10!

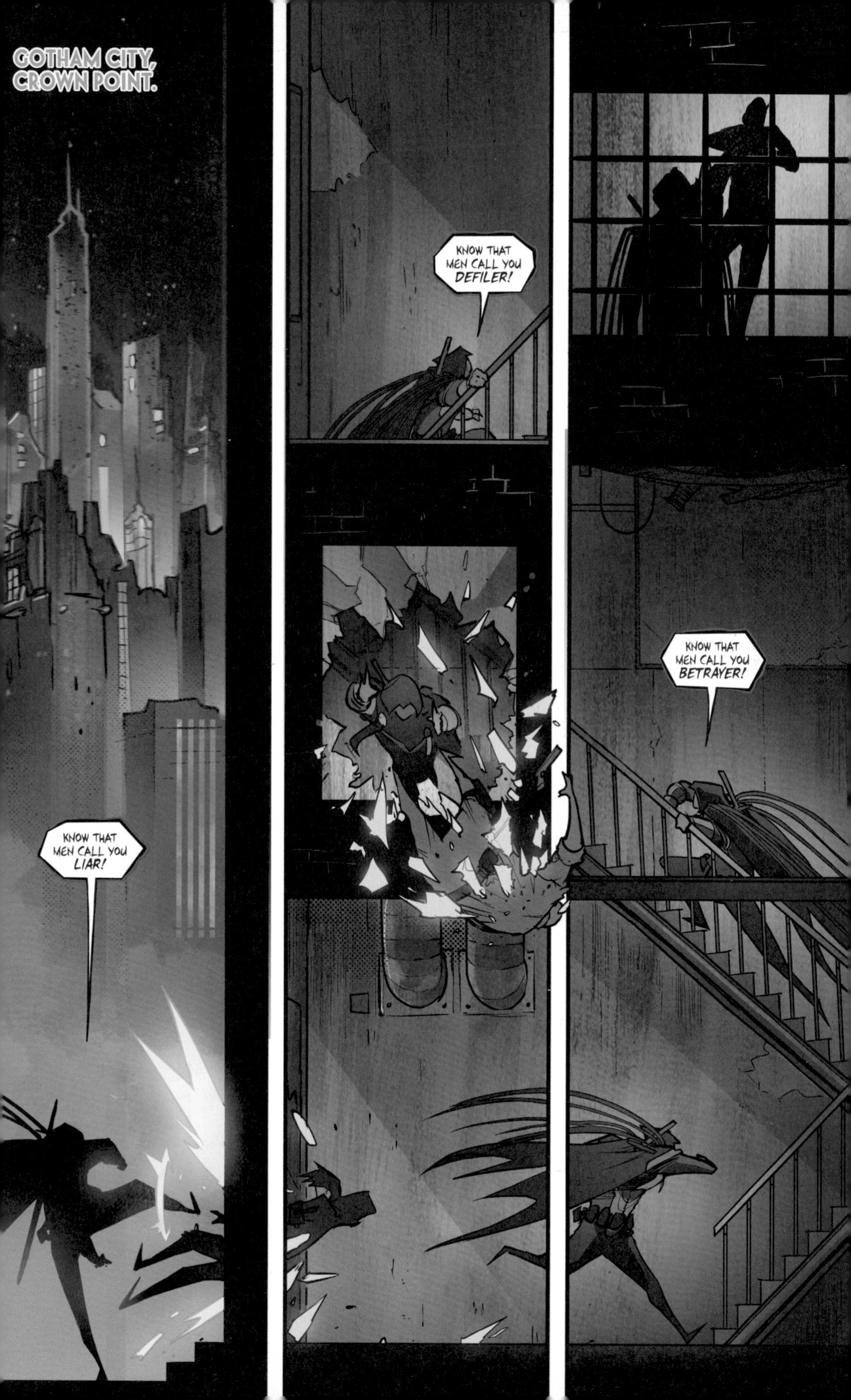
GOTHAM CITY, CROWN POINT.
KNOW THAT MEN CALL YOU LIAR!
KNOW THAT MEN CALL YOU DEFILER!
KNOW THAT MEN CALL YOU BETRAYER!

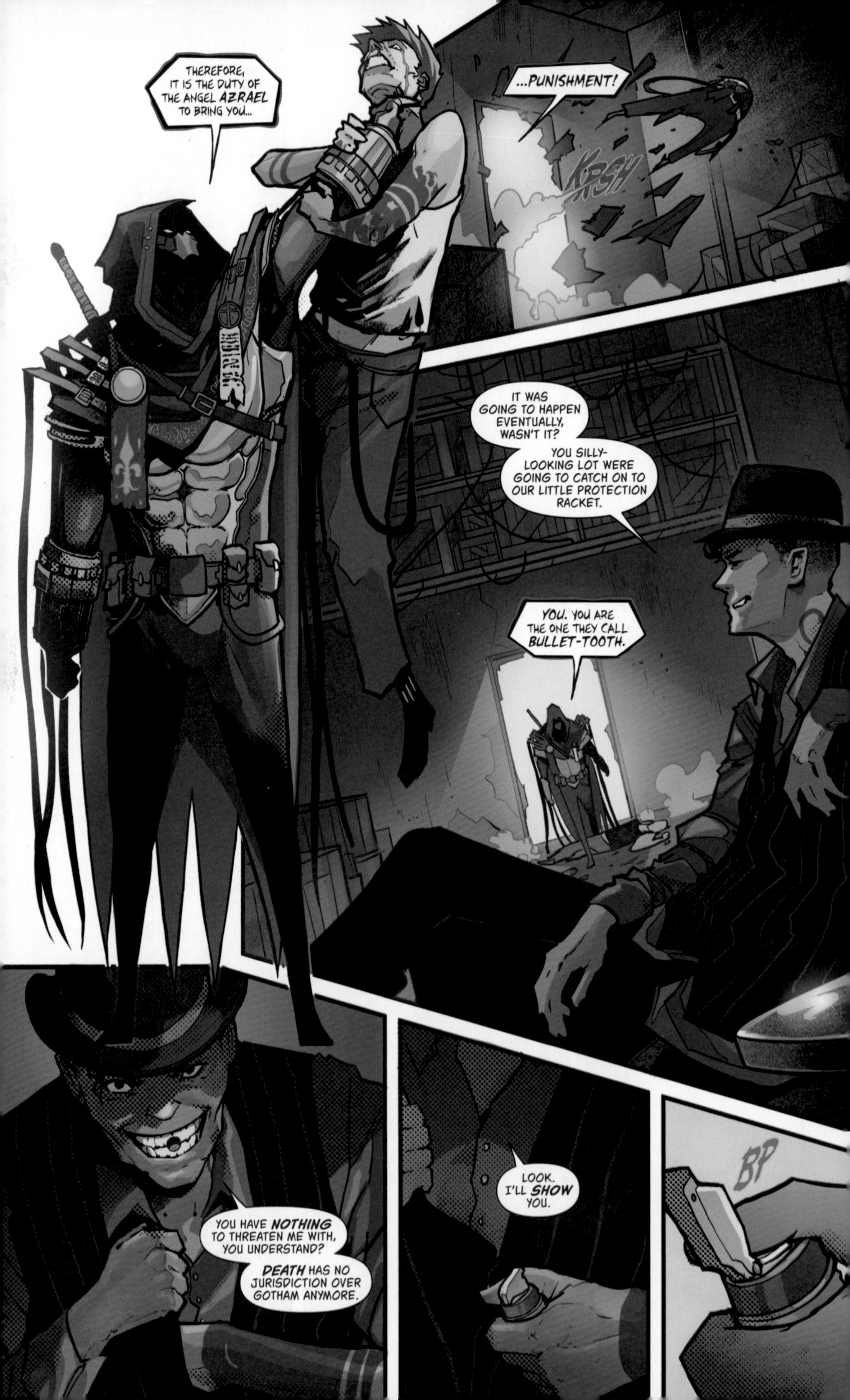
THEREFORE, IT IS THE DUTY OF THE ANGEL AZRAEL TO BRING YOU...
...PUNISHMENT!
KRSH
IT WAS GOING TO HAPPEN EVENTUALLY, WASN'T IT?
YOU SILLY-LOOKING LOT WERE GOING TO CATCH ON TO OUR LITTLE PROTECTION RACKET.
YOU. YOU ARE THE ONE THEY CALL BULLET-TOOTH.
YOU HAVE NOTHING TO THREATEN ME WITH, YOU UNDERSTAND?
DEATH HAS NO JURISDICTION OVER GOTHAM ANYMORE.
LOOK. I'LL SHOW YOU.
BP

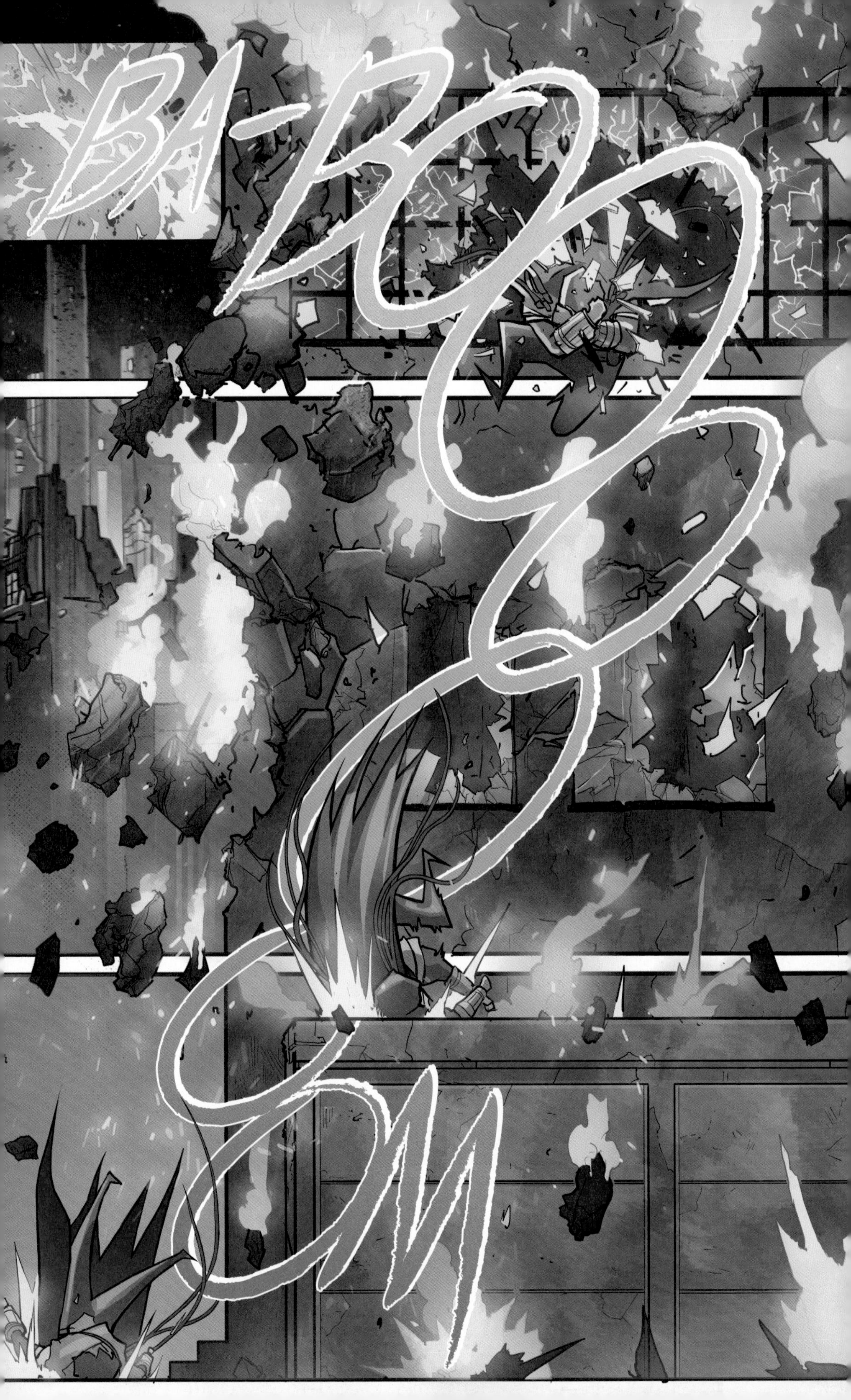
BA-BOOOOM

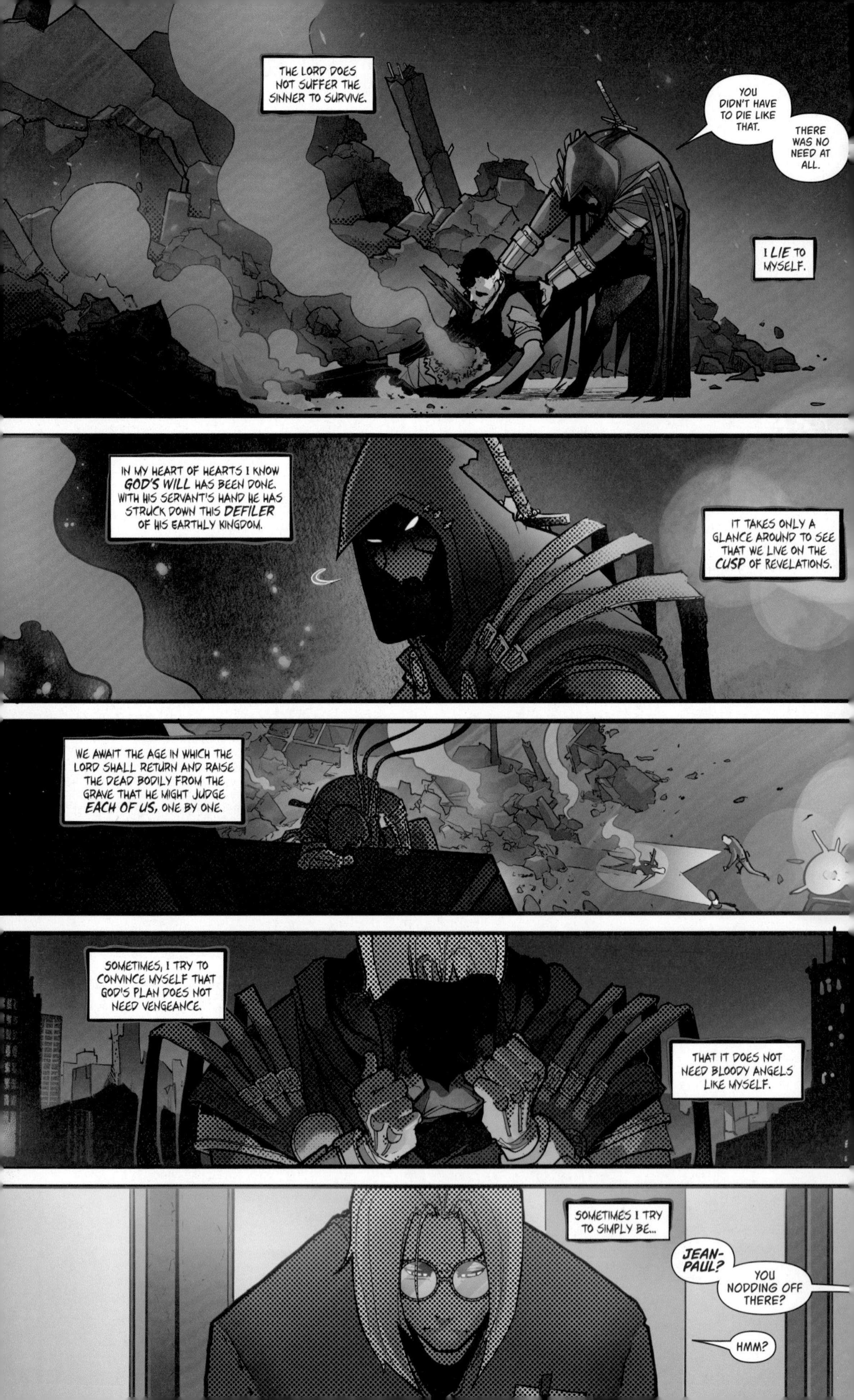
THE LORD DOES NOT SUFFER THE SINNER TO SURVIVE.
YOU DIDN'T HAVE TO DIE LIKE THAT.
THERE WAS NO NEED AT ALL.
I LIE TO MYSELF.
IN MY HEART OF HEARTS I KNOW GOD'S WILL HAS BEEN DONE. WITH HIS SERVANT'S HAND HE HAS STRUCK DOWN THIS DEFILER OF HIS EARTHLY KINGDOM.
IT TAKES ONLY A GLANCE AROUND TO SEE THAT WE LIVE ON THE CUSP OF REVELATIONS.
WE AWAIT THE AGE IN WHICH THE LORD SHALL RETURN AND RAISE THE DEAD BODILY FROM THE GRAVE THAT HE MIGHT JUDGE EACH OF US, ONE BY ONE.
SOMETIMES, I TRY TO CONVINCE MYSELF THAT GOD'S PLAN DOES NOT NEED VENGEANCE.
THAT IT DOES NOT NEED BLOODY ANGELS LIKE MYSELF.
SOMETIMES I TRY TO SIMPLY BE...
JEAN-PAUL?
YOU NODDING OFF THERE?
HMM?

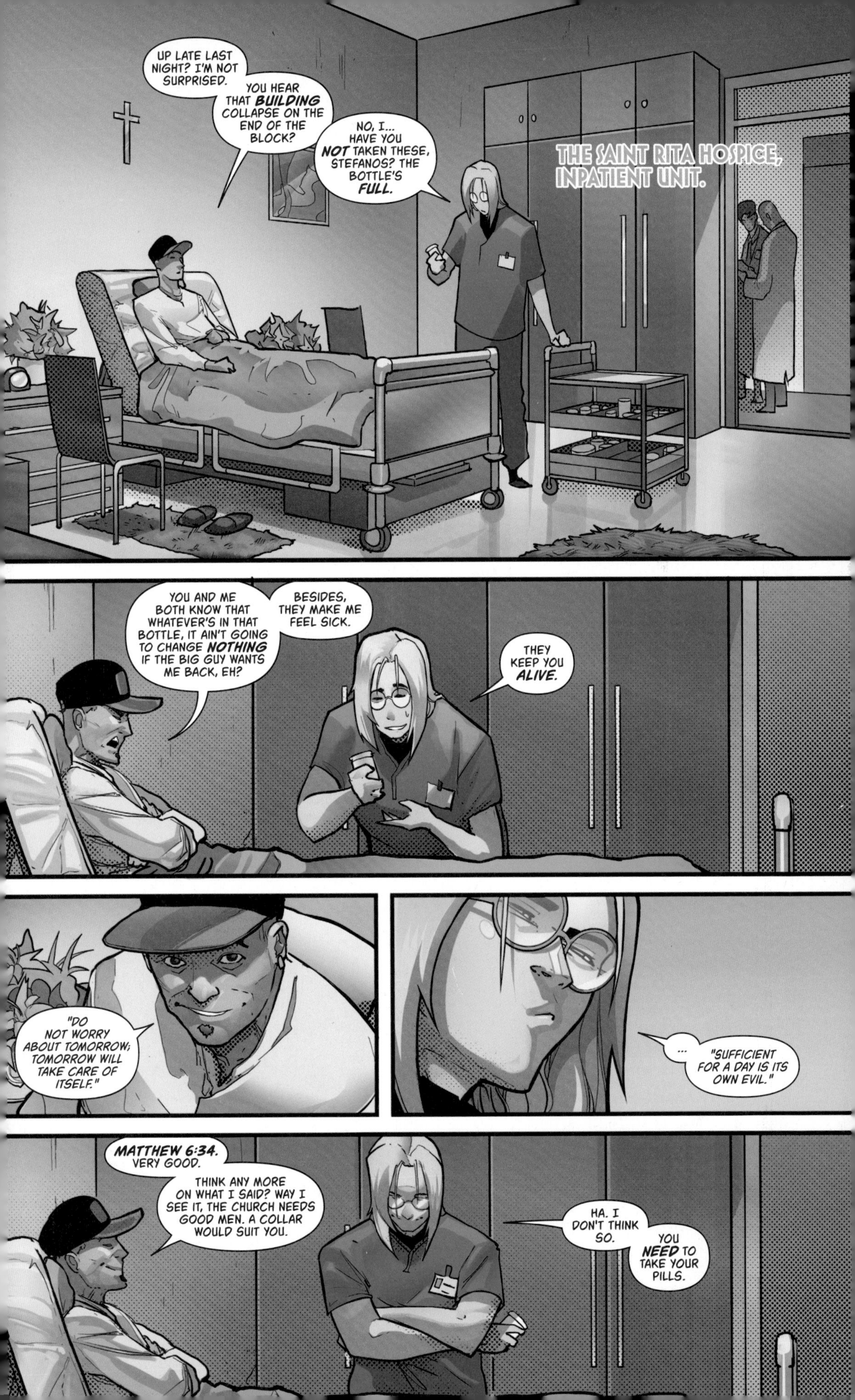
THE SAINT RITA HOSPICE, INPATIENT UNIT.
UP LATE LAST NIGHT? I'M NOT SURPRISED.
YOU HEAR THAT BUILDING COLLAPSE ON THE END OF THE BLOCK?
NO, I... HAVE YOU NOT TAKEN THESE, STEFANOS? THE BOTTLE'S FULL.
YOU AND ME BOTH KNOW THAT WHATEVER'S IN THAT BOTTLE, IT AIN'T GOING TO CHANGE NOTHING IF THE BIG GUY WANTS ME BACK, EH?
BESIDES, THEY MAKE ME FEEL SICK.
THEY KEEP YOU ALIVE.
"DO NOT WORRY ABOUT TOMORROW; TOMORROW WILL TAKE CARE OF ITSELF."
... "SUFFICIENT FOR A DAY IS ITS OWN EVIL."
MATTHEW 6:34. VERY GOOD.
THINK ANY MORE ON WHAT I SAID? WAY I SEE IT, THE CHURCH NEEDS GOOD MEN. A COLLAR WOULD SUIT YOU.
HA. I DON'T THINK SO.
YOU NEED TO TAKE YOUR PILLS.

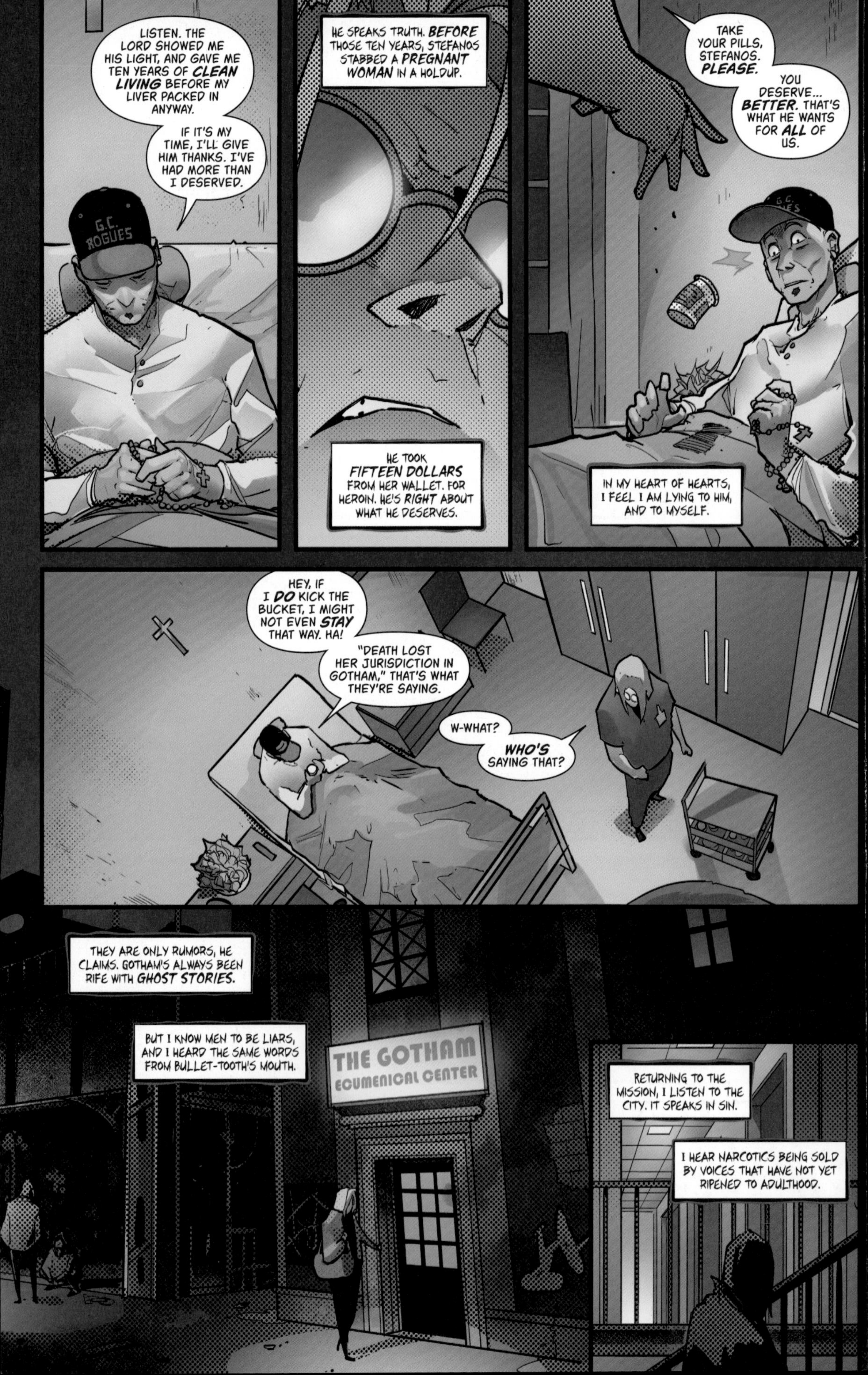
LISTEN. THE LORD SHOWED ME HIS LIGHT, AND GAVE ME TEN YEARS OF CLEAN LIVING BEFORE MY LIVER PACKED IN ANYWAY.
IF IT'S MY TIME, I'LL GIVE HIM THANKS. I'VE HAD MORE THAN I DESERVED.
G.C. ROGUES
HE SPEAKS TRUTH. BEFORE THOSE TEN YEARS, STEFANOS STABBED A PREGNANT WOMAN IN A HOLDUP.
HE TOOK FIFTEEN DOLLARS FROM HER WALLET. FOR HEROIN. HE'S RIGHT ABOUT WHAT HE DESERVES.
TAKE YOUR PILLS, STEFANOS. PLEASE.
YOU DESERVE... BETTER. THAT'S WHAT HE WANTS FOR ALL OF US.
IN MY HEART OF HEARTS, I FEEL I AM LYING TO HIM, AND TO MYSELF.
HEY, IF I DO KICK THE BUCKET, I MIGHT NOT EVEN STAY THAT WAY. HA!
"DEATH LOST HER JURISDICTION IN GOTHAM," THAT'S WHAT THEY'RE SAYING.
W-WHAT?
WHO'S SAYING THAT?
THEY ARE ONLY RUMORS, HE CLAIMS. GOTHAM'S ALWAYS BEEN RIFE WITH GHOST STORIES.
BUT I KNOW MEN TO BE LIARS, AND I HEARD THE SAME WORDS FROM BULLET-TOOTH'S MOUTH.
THE GOTHAM ECUMENICAL CENTER
RETURNING TO THE MISSION, I LISTEN TO THE CITY. IT SPEAKS IN SIN.
I HEAR NARCOTICS BEING SOLD BY VOICES THAT HAVE NOT YET RIPENED TO ADULTHOOD.

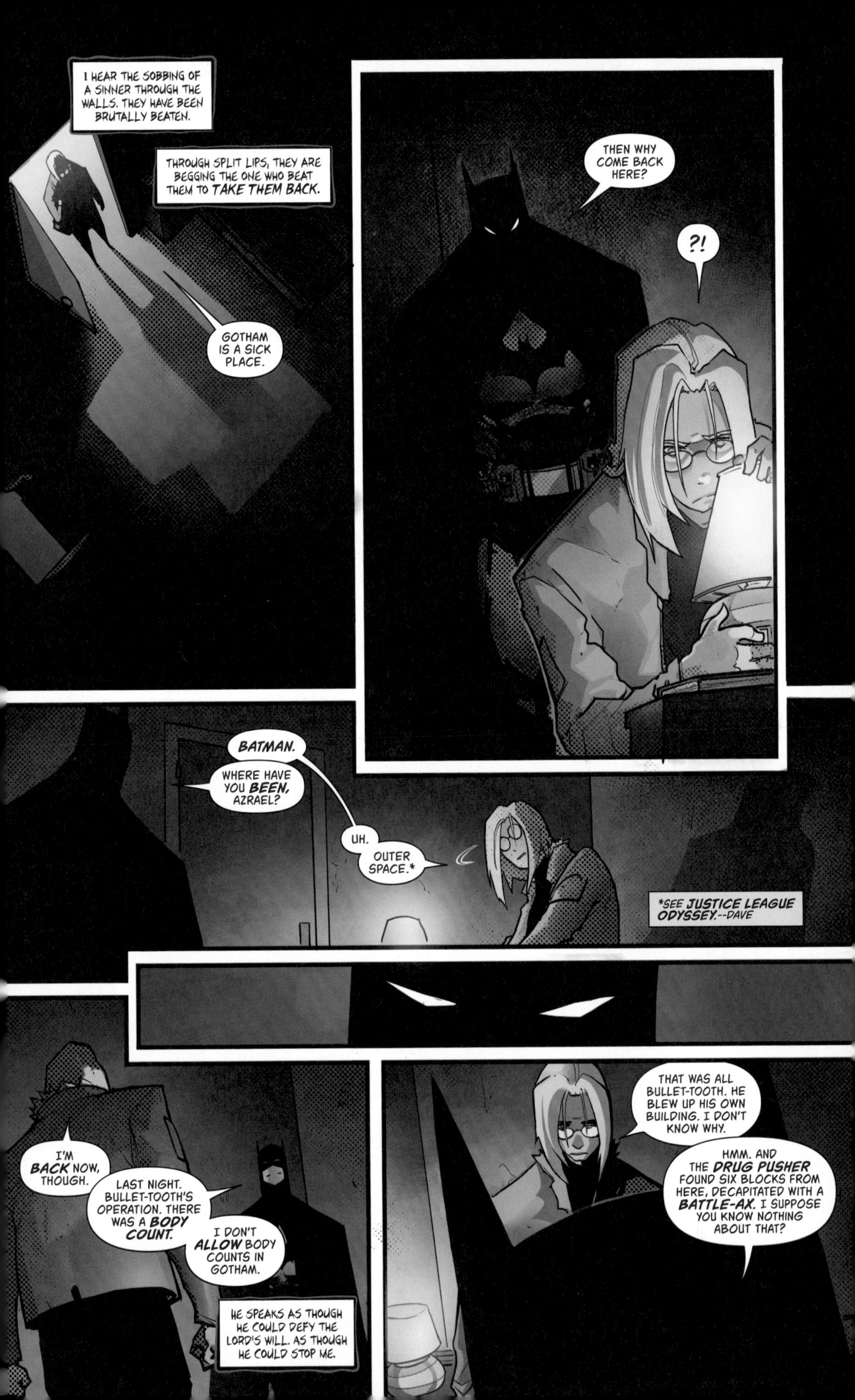
I HEAR THE SOBBING OF A SINNER THROUGH THE WALLS. THEY HAVE BEEN BRUTALLY BEATEN.
THROUGH SPLIT LIPS, THEY ARE BEGGING THE ONE WHO BEAT THEM TO TAKE THEM BACK.
GOTHAM IS A SICK PLACE.
THEN WHY COME BACK HERE?
?!
BATMAN.
WHERE HAVE YOU BEEN, AZRAEL?
UH.
OUTER SPACE.*
*SEE JUSTICE LEAGUE ODYSSEY.--DAVE
I'M BACK NOW, THOUGH.
LAST NIGHT. BULLET-TOOTH'S OPERATION. THERE WAS A BODY COUNT.
I DON'T ALLOW BODY COUNTS IN GOTHAM.
HE SPEAKS AS THOUGH HE COULD DEFY THE LORD'S WILL. AS THOUGH HE COULD STOP ME.
THAT WAS ALL BULLET-TOOTH. HE BLEW UP HIS OWN BUILDING. I DON'T KNOW WHY.
HMM. AND THE DRUG PUSHER FOUND SIX BLOCKS FROM HERE, DECAPITATED WITH A BATTLE-AX. I SUPPOSE YOU KNOW NOTHING ABOUT THAT?

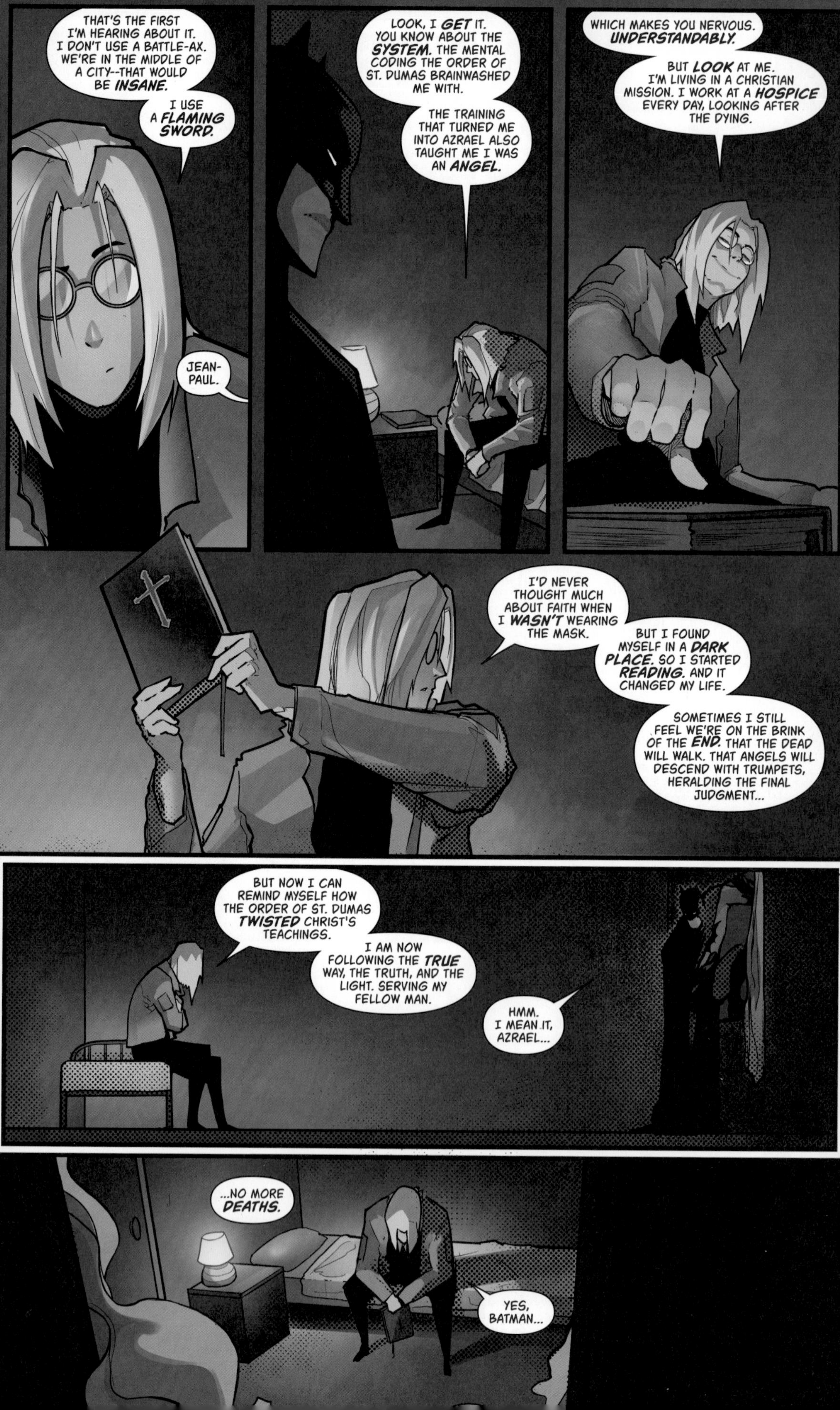
THAT'S THE FIRST I'M HEARING ABOUT IT. I DON'T USE A BATTLE-AX. WE'RE IN THE MIDDLE OF A CITY--THAT WOULD BE INSANE.
I USE A FLAMING SWORD.
JEAN-PAUL.
LOOK, I GET IT. YOU KNOW ABOUT THE SYSTEM. THE MENTAL CODING THE ORDER OF ST. DUMAS BRAINWASHED ME WITH.
THE TRAINING THAT TURNED ME INTO AZRAEL ALSO TAUGHT ME I WAS AN ANGEL.
WHICH MAKES YOU NERVOUS. UNDERSTANDABLY.
BUT LOOK AT ME. I'M LIVING IN A CHRISTIAN MISSION. I WORK AT A HOSPICE EVERY DAY, LOOKING AFTER THE DYING.
I'D NEVER THOUGHT MUCH ABOUT FAITH WHEN I WASN'T WEARING THE MASK.
BUT I FOUND MYSELF IN A DARK PLACE. SO I STARTED READING. AND IT CHANGED MY LIFE.
SOMETIMES I STILL FEEL WE'RE ON THE BRINK OF THE END. THAT THE DEAD WILL WALK. THAT ANGELS WILL DESCEND WITH TRUMPETS, HERALDING THE FINAL JUDGMENT...
BUT NOW I CAN REMIND MYSELF HOW THE ORDER OF ST. DUMAS TWISTED CHRIST'S TEACHINGS.
I AM NOW FOLLOWING THE TRUE WAY, THE TRUTH, AND THE LIGHT. SERVING MY FELLOW MAN.
HMM. I MEAN IT, AZRAEL...
...NO MORE DEATHS.
YES, BATMAN...

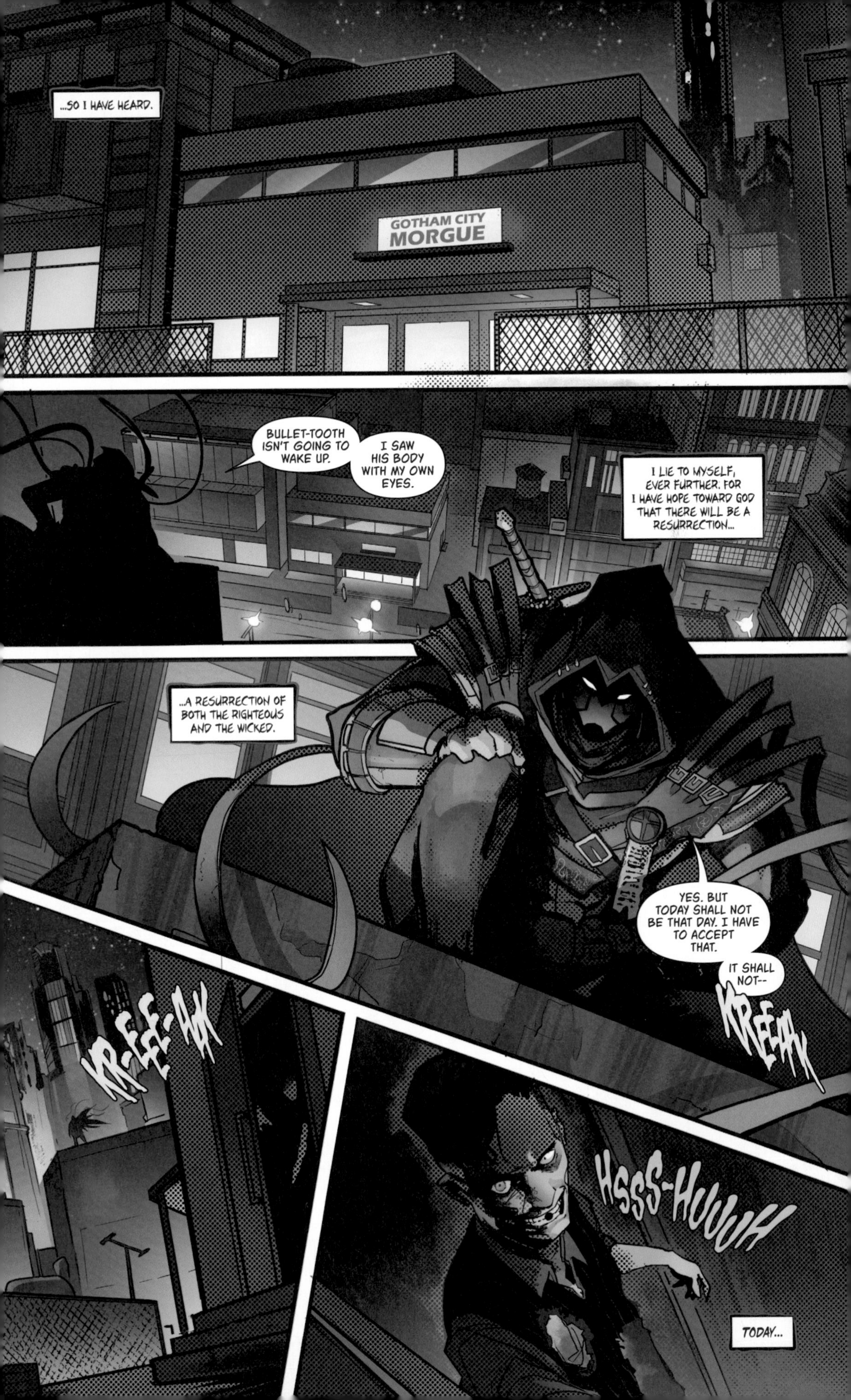

...SO I HAVE HEARD.
GOTHAM CITY MORGUE
BULLET-TOOTH ISN'T GOING TO WAKE UP.
I SAW HIS BODY WITH MY OWN EYES.
I LIE TO MYSELF, EVER FURTHER. FOR I HAVE HOPE TOWARD GOD THAT THERE WILL BE A RESURRECTION...
...A RESURRECTION OF BOTH THE RIGHTEOUS AND THE WICKED.
YES. BUT TODAY SHALL NOT BE THAT DAY. I HAVE TO ACCEPT THAT.
IT SHALL NOT--
KREEAK
KR-EE-AK
HSSS-HUUUH
TODAY...

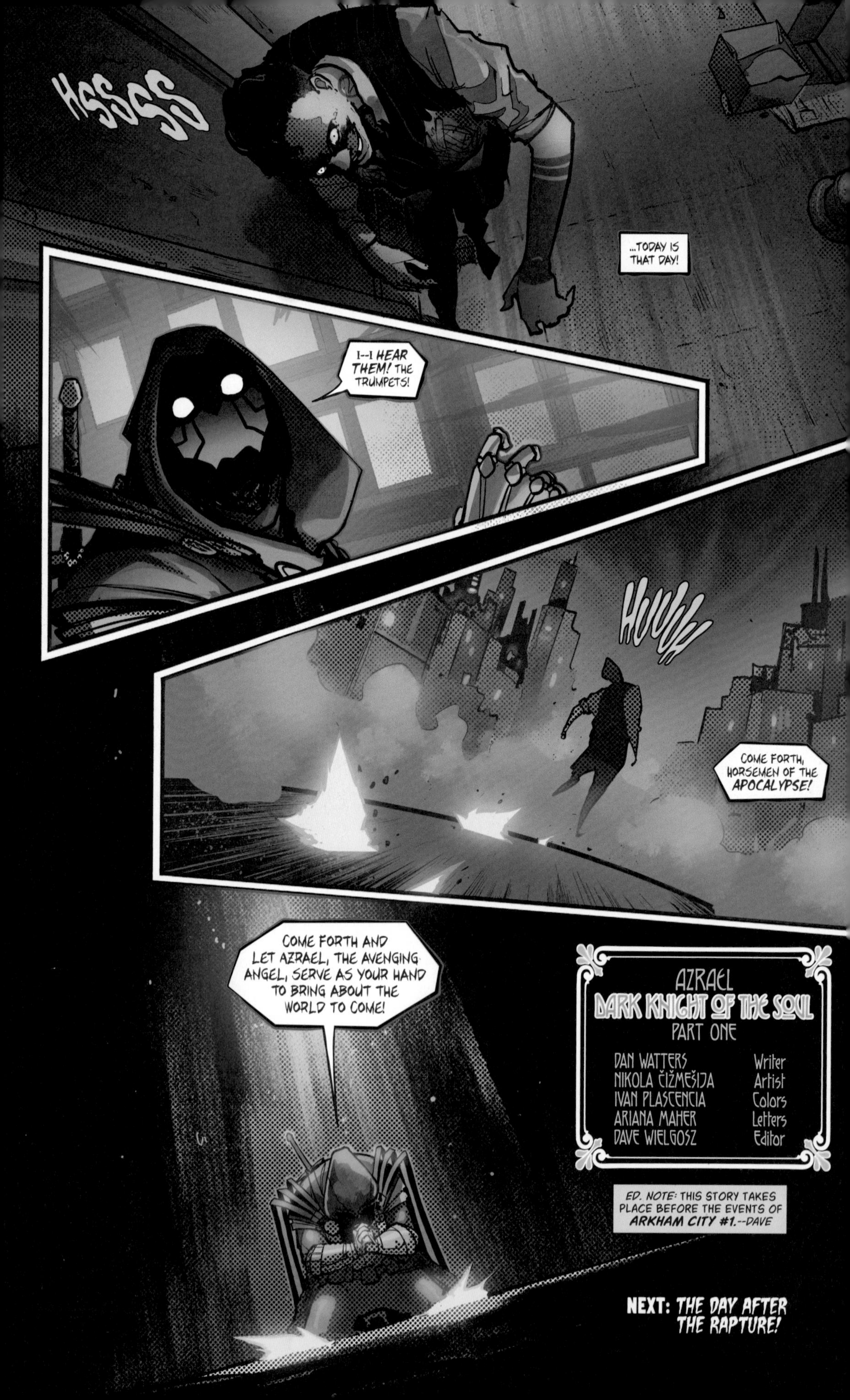
HSSSS
...TODAY IS THAT DAY!
I--I HEAR THEM! THE TRUMPETS!
HOOOM
COME FORTH, HORSEMEN OF THE APOCALYPSE!
COME FORTH AND LET AZRAEL, THE AVENGING ANGEL, SERVE AS YOUR HAND TO BRING ABOUT THE WORLD TO COME!
AZRAEL
DARK KNIGHT OF THE SOUL
PART ONE
DAN WATTERS Writer
NIKOLA ČIŽMEŠIJA Artist
IVAN PLASCENCIA Colors
ARIANA MAHER Letters
DAVE WIELGOSZ Editor
ED. NOTE: THIS STORY TAKES PLACE BEFORE THE EVENTS OF ARKHAM CITY #1.--DAVE
NEXT: THE DAY AFTER THE RAPTURE!

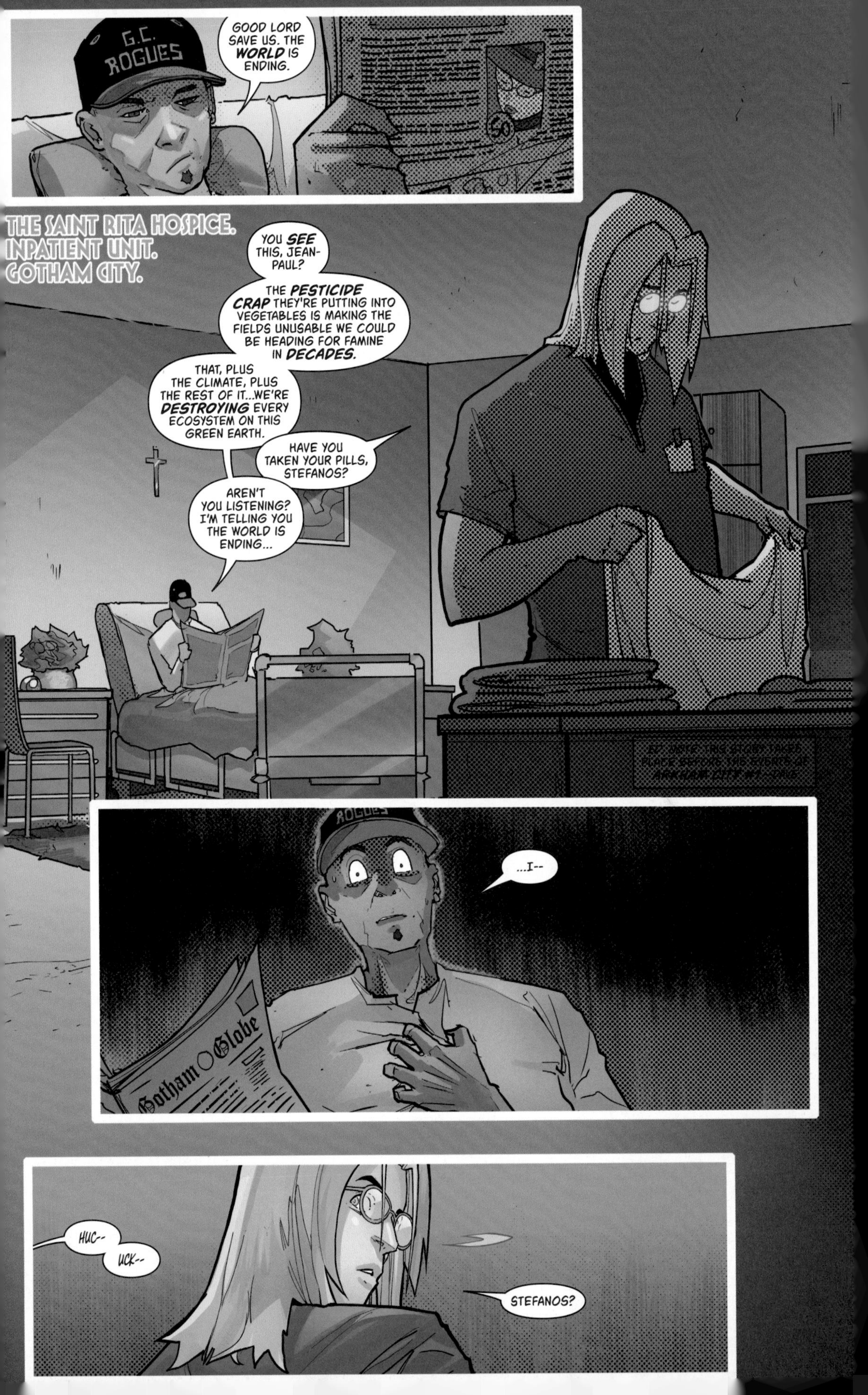
GOOD LORD SAVE US. THE WORLD IS ENDING.
THE SAINT RITA HOSPICE. INPATIENT UNIT. GOTHAM CITY.
YOU SEE THIS, JEAN-PAUL?
THE PESTICIDE CRAP THEY'RE PUTTING INTO VEGETABLES IS MAKING THE FIELDS UNUSABLE WE COULD BE HEADING FOR FAMINE IN DECADES.
THAT, PLUS THE CLIMATE, PLUS THE REST OF IT...WE'RE DESTROYING EVERY ECOSYSTEM ON THIS GREEN EARTH.
HAVE YOU TAKEN YOUR PILLS, STEFANOS?
AREN'T YOU LISTENING? I'M TELLING YOU THE WORLD IS ENDING...
...I--
Gotham Globe
HUC--
UCK--
STEFANOS?

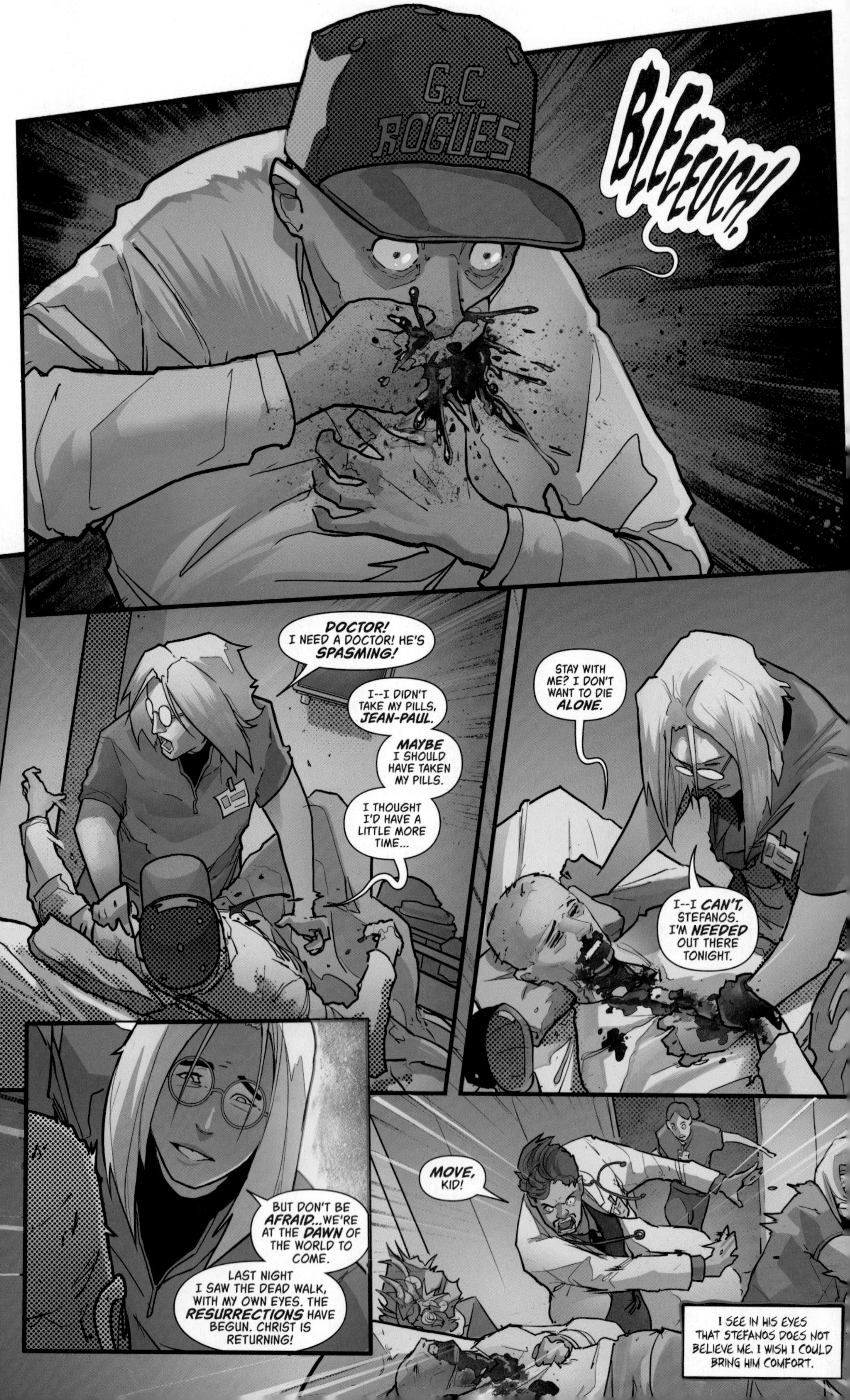
G.C. ROGUES
BLEEUCH!
DOCTOR! I NEED A DOCTOR! HE'S SPASMING!
I--I DIDN'T TAKE MY PILLS, JEAN-PAUL.
MAYBE I SHOULD HAVE TAKEN MY PILLS.
I THOUGHT I'D HAVE A LITTLE MORE TIME...
STAY WITH ME? I DON'T WANT TO DIE ALONE.
I--I CAN'T, STEFANOS. I'M NEEDED OUT THERE TONIGHT.
BUT DON'T BE AFRAID...WE'RE AT THE DAWN OF THE WORLD TO COME.
LAST NIGHT I SAW THE DEAD WALK, WITH MY OWN EYES. THE RESURRECTIONS HAVE BEGUN. CHRIST IS RETURNING!
MOVE, KID!
I SEE IN HIS EYES THAT STEFANOS DOES NOT BELIEVE ME. I WISH I COULD BRING HIM COMFORT.

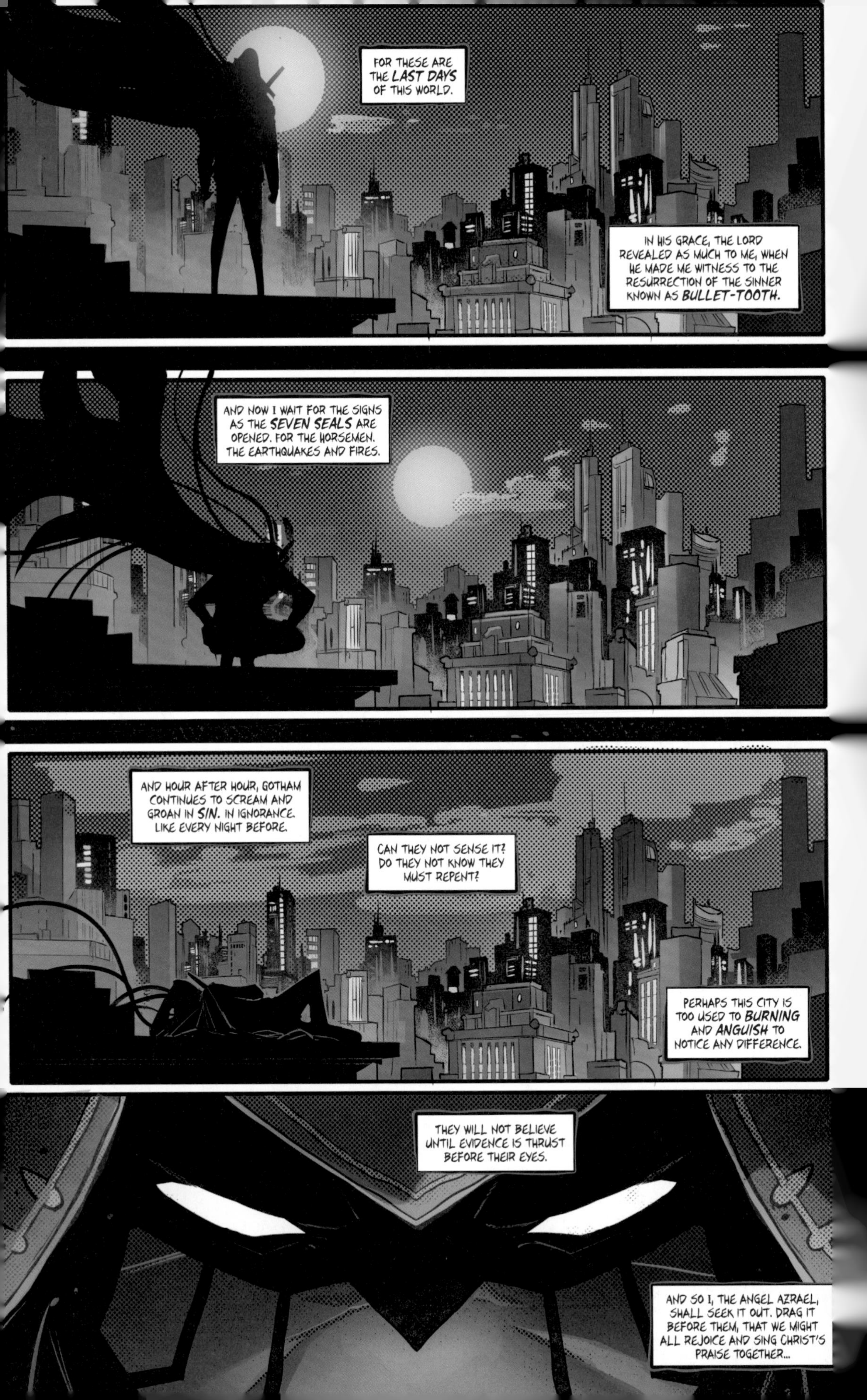
FOR THESE ARE THE LAST DAYS OF THIS WORLD.
IN HIS GRACE, THE LORD REVEALED AS MUCH TO ME, WHEN HE MADE ME WITNESS TO THE RESURRECTION OF THE SINNER KNOWN AS BULLET-TOOTH.
AND NOW I WAIT FOR THE SIGNS AS THE SEVEN SEALS ARE OPENED. FOR THE HORSEMEN. THE EARTHQUAKES AND FIRES.
AND HOUR AFTER HOUR, GOTHAM CONTINUES TO SCREAM AND GROAN IN SIN. IN IGNORANCE. LIKE EVERY NIGHT BEFORE.
CAN THEY NOT SENSE IT? DO THEY NOT KNOW THEY MUST REPENT?
PERHAPS THIS CITY IS TOO USED TO BURNING AND ANGUISH TO NOTICE ANY DIFFERENCE.
THEY WILL NOT BELIEVE UNTIL EVIDENCE IS THRUST BEFORE THEIR EYES.
AND SO I, THE ANGEL AZRAEL, SHALL SEEK IT OUT. DRAG IT BEFORE THEM, THAT WE MIGHT ALL REJOICE AND SING CHRIST'S PRAISE TOGETHER...

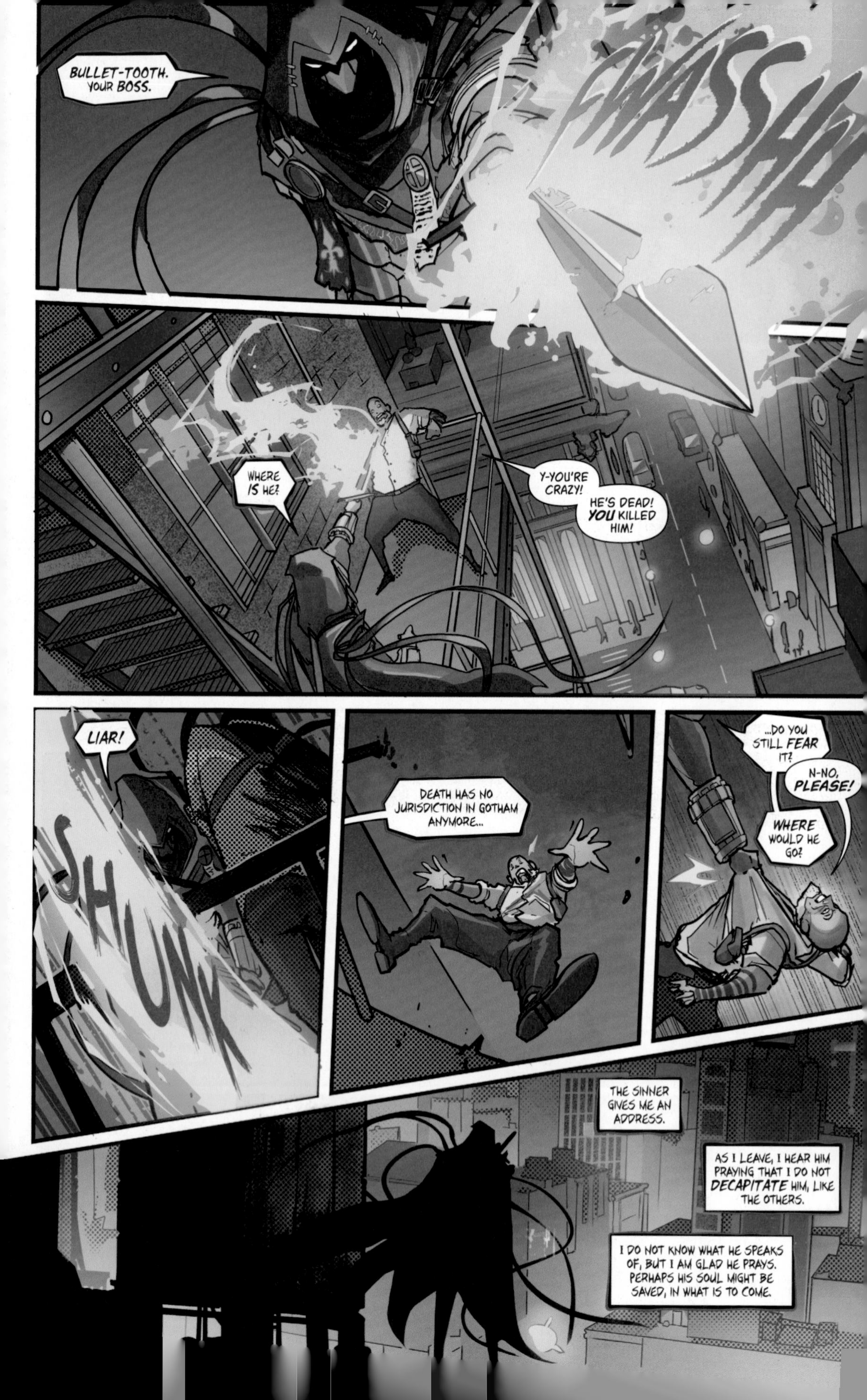
BULLET-TOOTH. YOUR BOSS.
FWASSH
WHERE IS HE?
Y-YOU'RE CRAZY!
HE'S DEAD! YOU KILLED HIM!
LIAR!
SHUNK
DEATH HAS NO JURISDICTION IN GOTHAM ANYMORE...
...DO YOU STILL FEAR IT?
N-NO, PLEASE!
WHERE WOULD HE GO?
THE SINNER GIVES ME AN ADDRESS.
AS I LEAVE, I HEAR HIM PRAYING THAT I DO NOT DECAPITATE HIM, LIKE THE OTHERS.
I DO NOT KNOW WHAT HE SPEAKS OF, BUT I AM GLAD HE PRAYS. PERHAPS HIS SOUL MIGHT BE SAVED, IN WHAT IS TO COME.

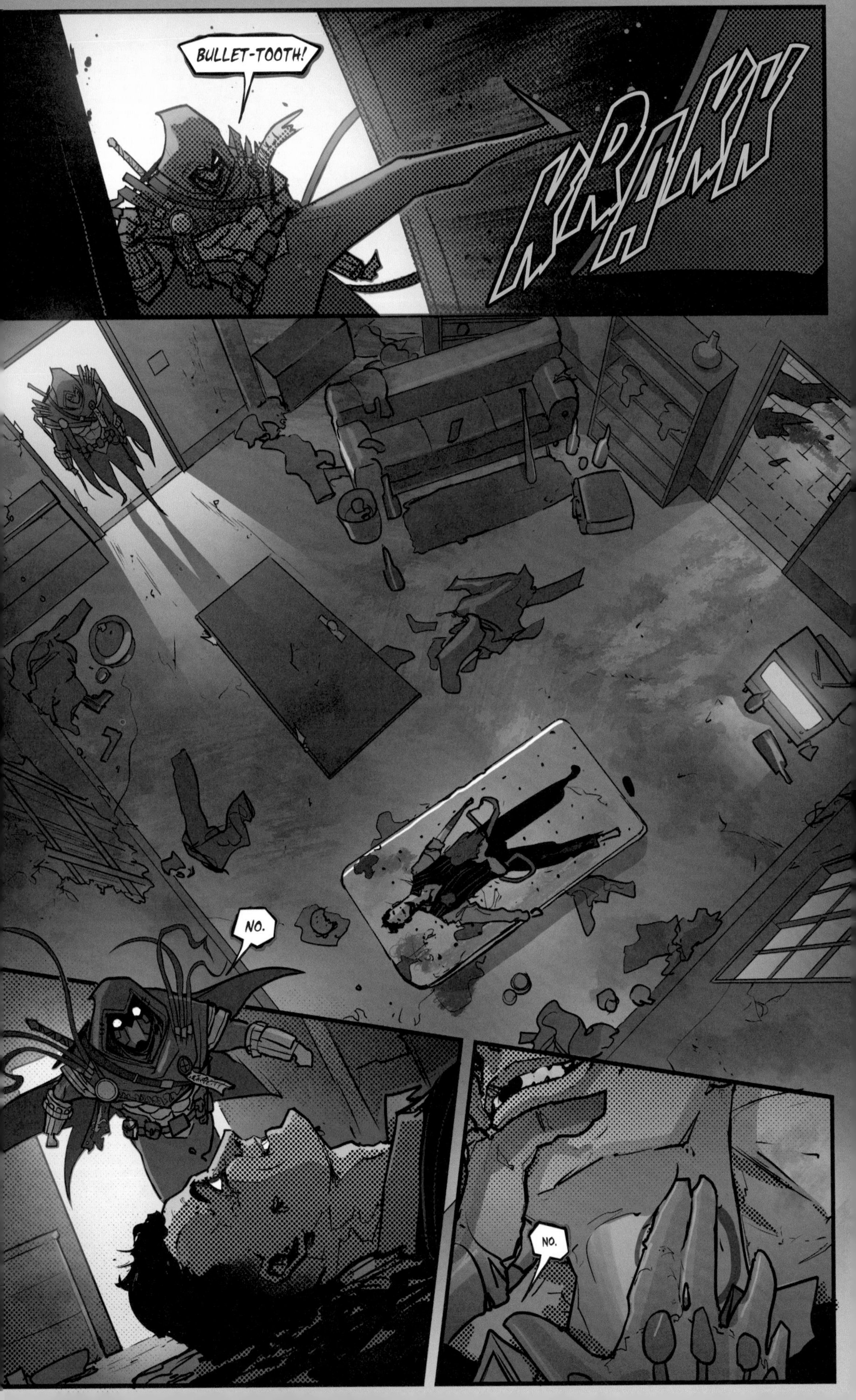
BULLET-TOOTH!
KRAKK
NO.
NO.

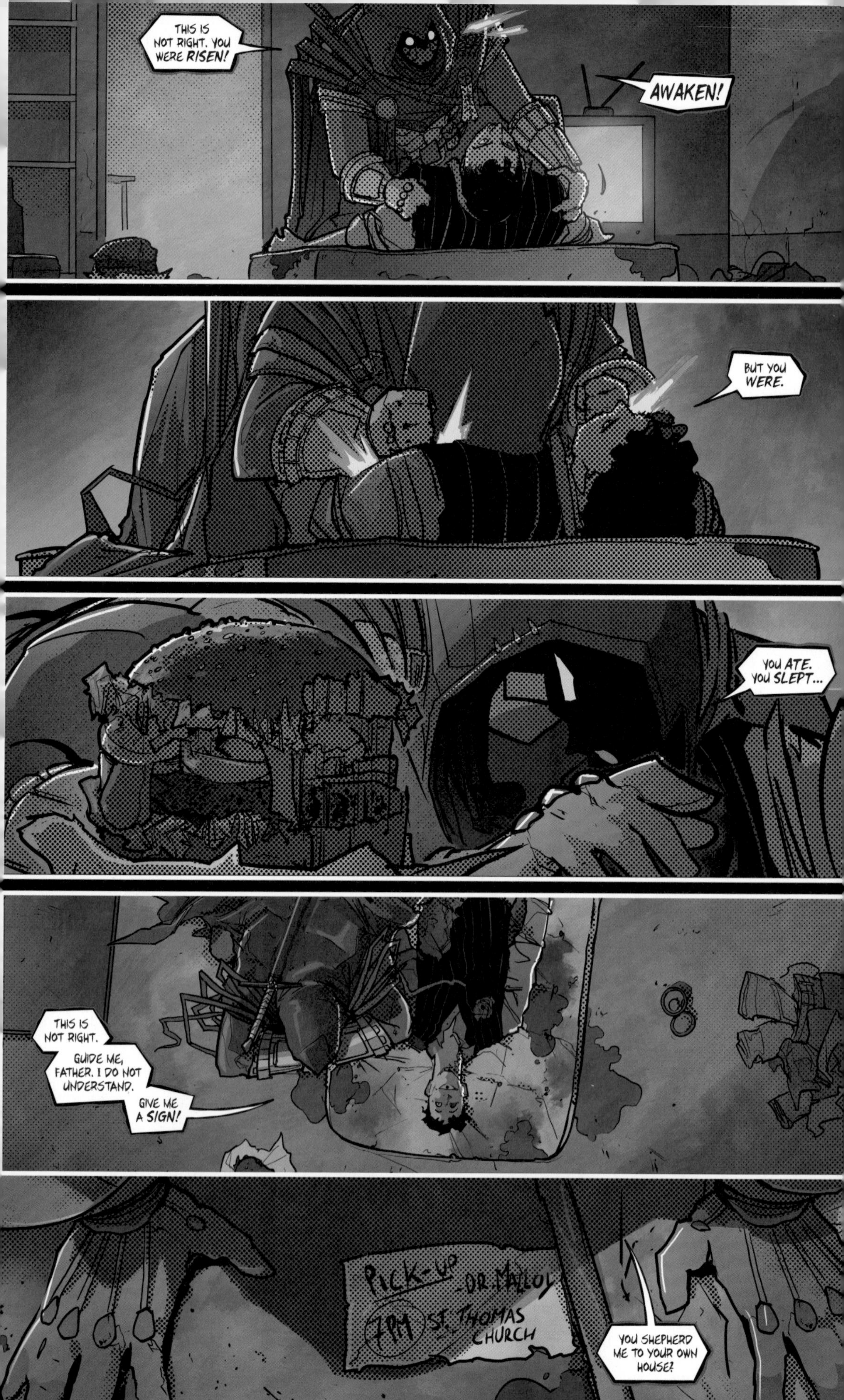
THIS IS NOT RIGHT. YOU WERE RISEN!
AWAKEN!
BUT YOU WERE.
YOU ATE. YOU SLEPT...
THIS IS NOT RIGHT.
GUIDE ME, FATHER. I DO NOT UNDERSTAND.
GIVE ME A SIGN!
PICK-UP
DR. MALLOY
7PM ST. THOMAS CHURCH
YOU SHEPHERD ME TO YOUR OWN HOUSE?

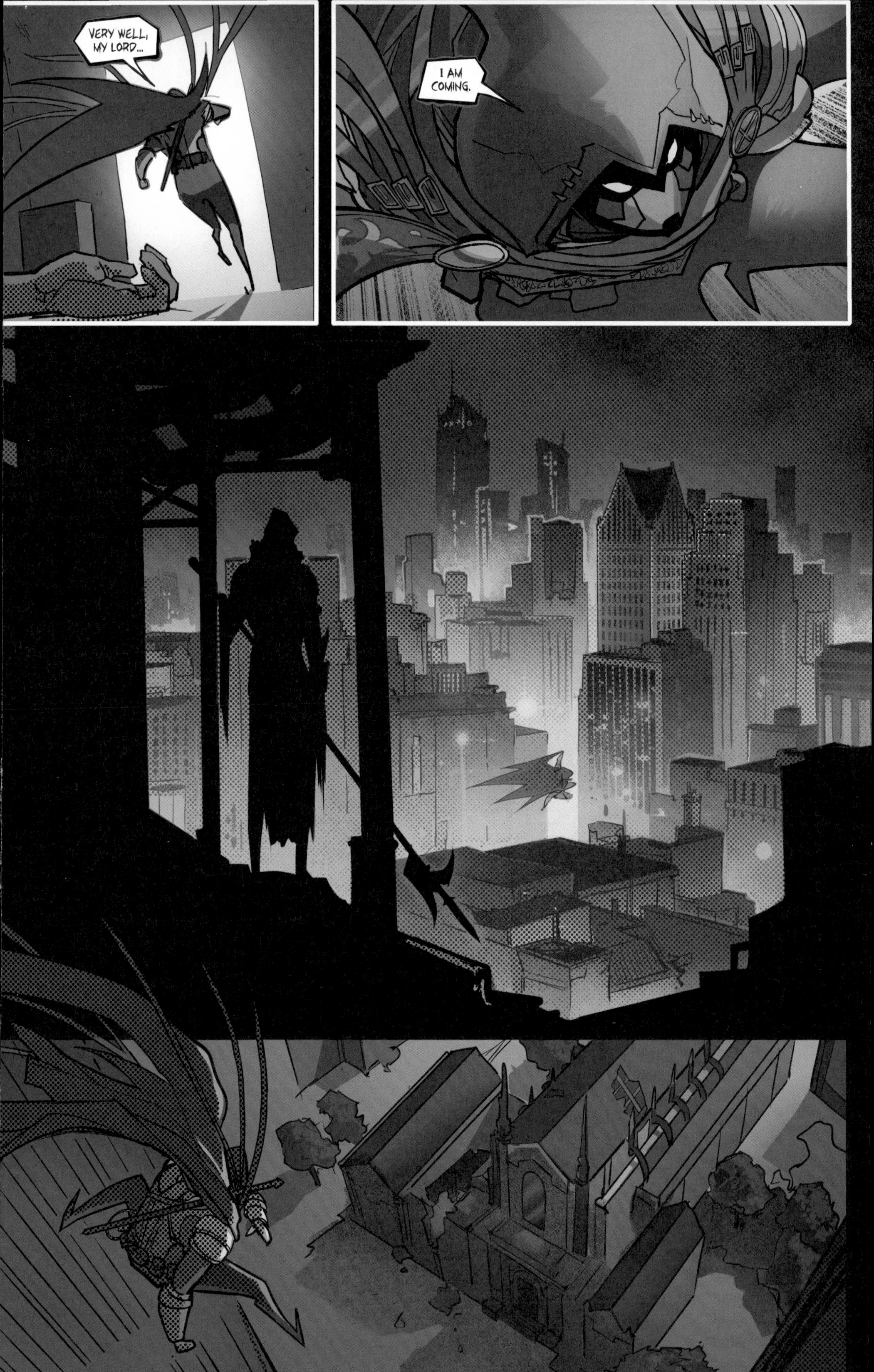
VERY WELL, MY LORD...
I AM COMING.

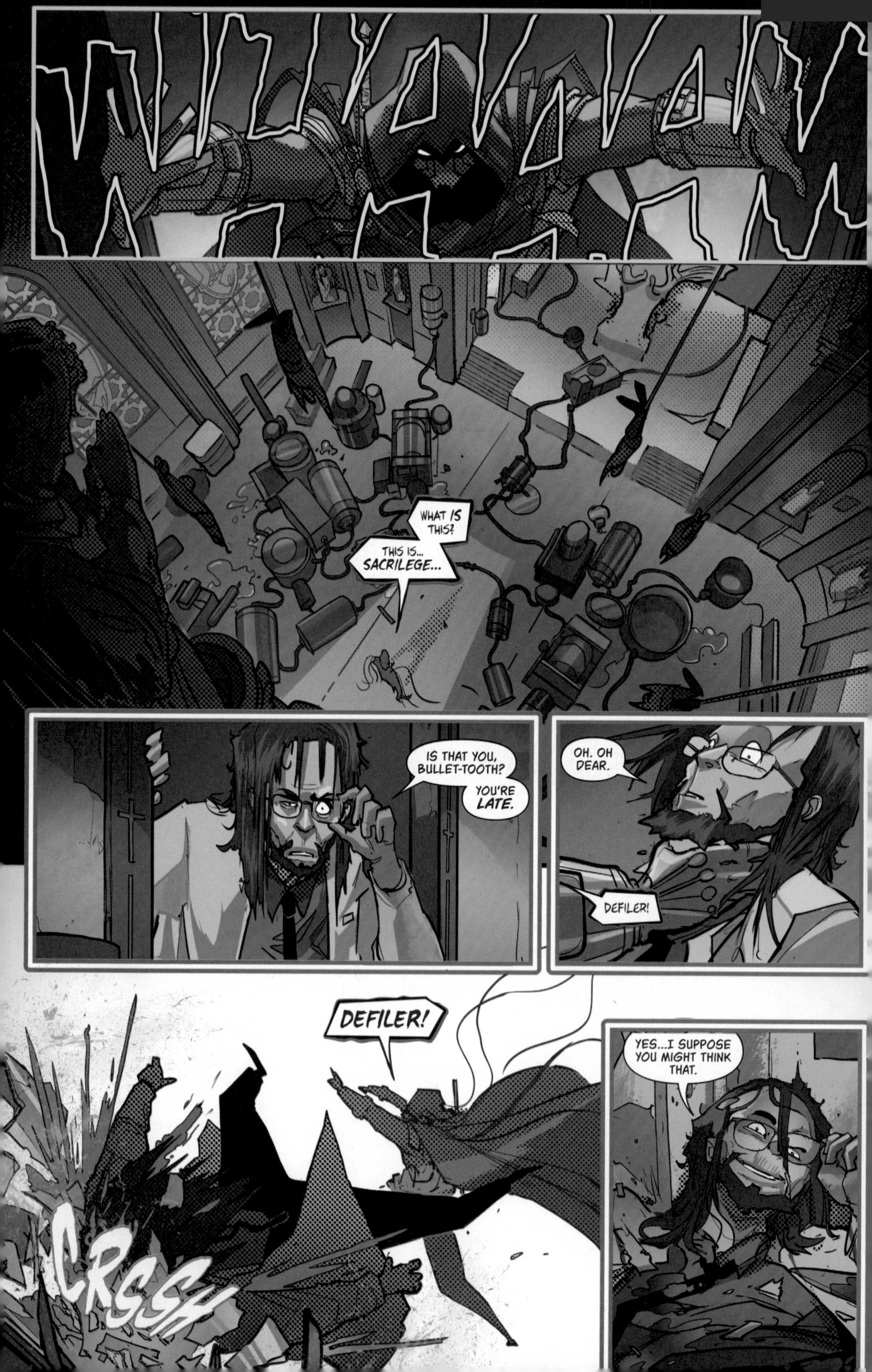
WHAT IS THIS?
THIS IS... SACRILEGE...
IS THAT YOU, BULLET-TOOTH?
YOU'RE LATE.
OH. OH DEAR.
DEFILER!
DEFILER!
YES...I SUPPOSE YOU MIGHT THINK THAT.
CRSSH

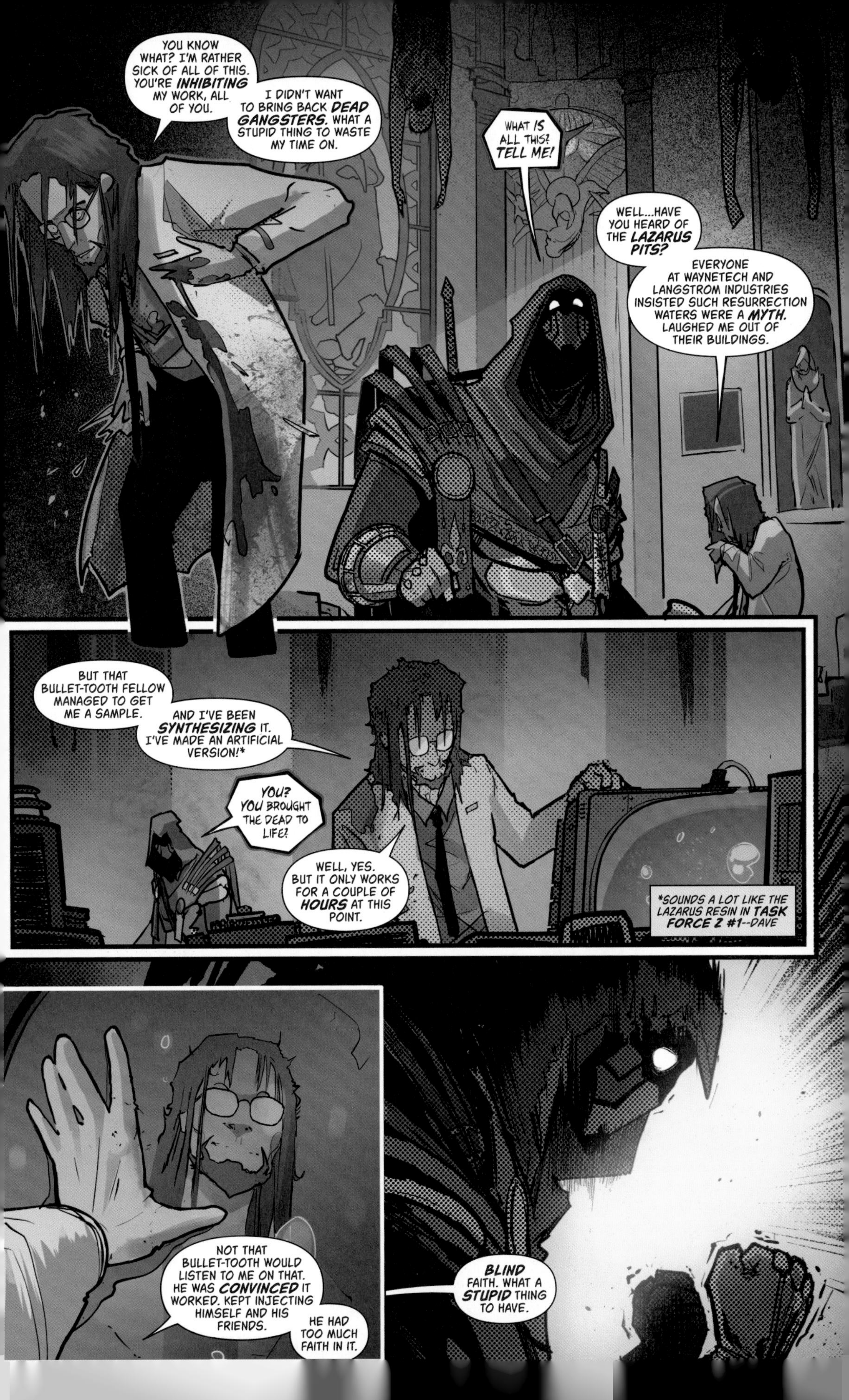
YOU KNOW WHAT? I'M RATHER SICK OF ALL OF THIS. YOU'RE INHIBITING MY WORK, ALL OF YOU.
I DIDN'T WANT TO BRING BACK DEAD GANGSTERS. WHAT A STUPID THING TO WASTE MY TIME ON.
WHAT IS ALL THIS? TELL ME!
WELL...HAVE YOU HEARD OF THE LAZARUS PITS?
EVERYONE AT WAYNETECH AND LANGSTROM INDUSTRIES INSISTED SUCH RESURRECTION WATERS WERE A MYTH. LAUGHED ME OUT OF THEIR BUILDINGS.
BUT THAT BULLET-TOOTH FELLOW MANAGED TO GET ME A SAMPLE.
AND I'VE BEEN SYNTHESIZING IT. I'VE MADE AN ARTIFICIAL VERSION!*
YOU? YOU BROUGHT THE DEAD TO LIFE?
WELL, YES. BUT IT ONLY WORKS FOR A COUPLE OF HOURS AT THIS POINT.
*SOUNDS A LOT LIKE THE LAZARUS RESIN IN TASK FORCE Z #1--DAVE
NOT THAT BULLET-TOOTH WOULD LISTEN TO ME ON THAT. HE WAS CONVINCED IT WORKED. KEPT INJECTING HIMSELF AND HIS FRIENDS.
HE HAD TOO MUCH FAITH IN IT.
BLIND FAITH. WHAT A STUPID THING TO HAVE.

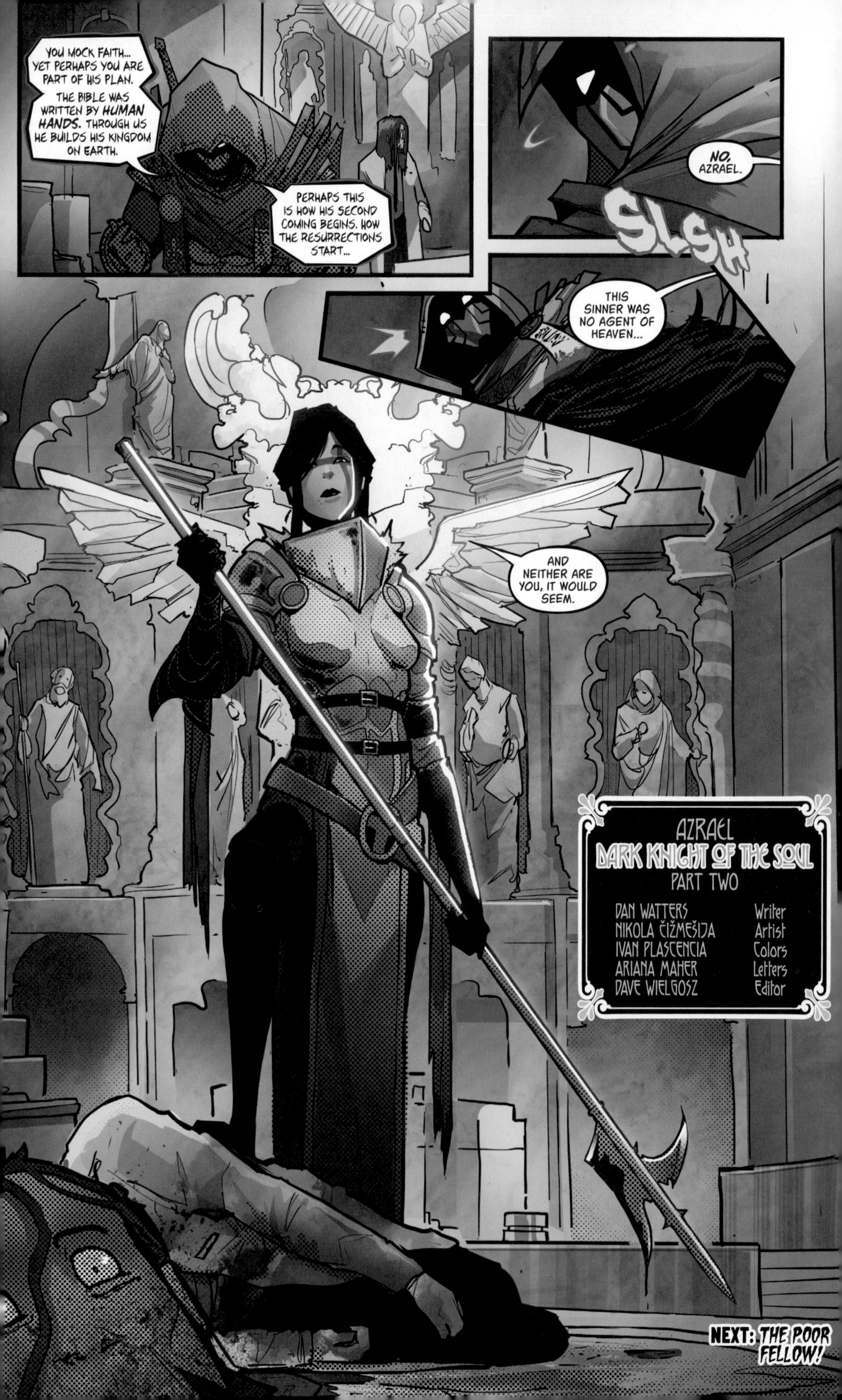

YOU MOCK FAITH... YET PERHAPS YOU ARE PART OF HIS PLAN.
THE BIBLE WAS WRITTEN BY HUMAN HANDS. THROUGH US HE BUILDS HIS KINGDOM ON EARTH.
PERHAPS THIS IS HOW HIS SECOND COMING BEGINS. HOW THE RESURRECTIONS START...
NO, AZRAEL.
SLSH
THIS SINNER WAS NO AGENT OF HEAVEN...
AND NEITHER ARE YOU, IT WOULD SEEM.
AZRAEL
DARK KNIGHT OF THE SOUL
PART TWO
DAN WATTERS Writer
NIKOLA ČIŽMEŠIJA Artist
IVAN PLASCENCIA Colors
ARIANA MAHER Letters
DAVE WIELGOSZ Editor
NEXT: THE POOR FELLOW!

"IN THE YEAR *1152*, RAYMOND II, COUNT OF TRIPOLI, ESCORTED HIS WIFE FROM THE CITY AS SHE MADE *PILGRIMAGE* TOWARD JERUSALEM.

AZRAEL

DARK KNIGHT OF THE SOUL

FINALE

DAN WATTERS	Writer
NIKOLA ČIŽMEŠIJA	Artist
IVAN PLASCENCIA	Colors
ARIANA MAHER	Letters
DAVE WIELGOSZ	Editor

"IT WAS SPRING IN LEBANON. PERHAPS HE PAUSED TO SMELL THE *SNAPDRAGONS* AS THEY BLOOMED.

"HE RODE HIS HORSE IN A GENTLE TROT UNDER BLUE SKIES.

"AND THEN THE *BAND OF ASSASSINS* MURDERED HIM AT THE GATES OF HIS CITY.

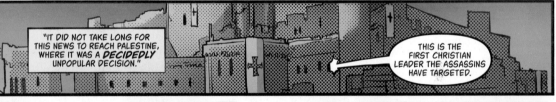

"IT DID NOT TAKE LONG FOR THIS NEWS TO REACH PALESTINE, WHERE IT WAS A *DECIDEDLY* UNPOPULAR DECISION."

THIS IS THE FIRST CHRISTIAN LEADER THE ASSASSINS HAVE TARGETED.

THE *KNIGHTS TEMPLAR* CANNOT BE SEEN TO PERMIT IT TO STAND, GRAND MASTER.

AND YET, THIS TERROR CAMPAIGN THEY HAVE BEEN CARRYING OUT FOR THE NIZARI, WE HAVE SEEN NOTHING LIKE IT.

THEY KILL WITH POISONED KNIVES IN *BROAD DAYLIGHT.* THESE ARE *SUICIDE MISSIONS.*

HOW WOULD YOU PROPOSE WE FACE DOWN AN ENEMY LIKE THAT?

WELL, IF IT WOULD PLEASE YOU, GRAND MASTER...

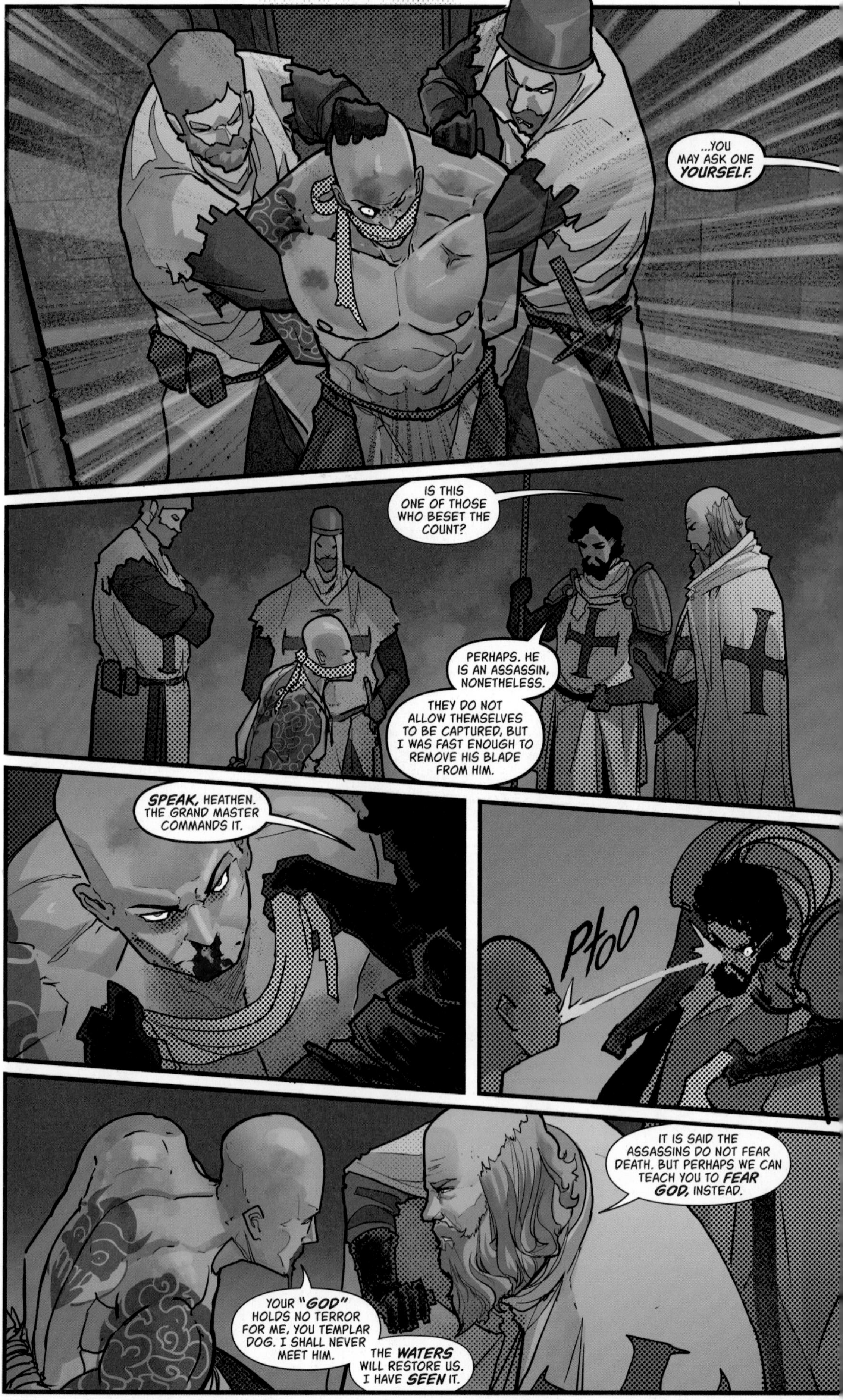

...YOU MAY ASK ONE **YOURSELF.**
IS THIS ONE OF THOSE WHO BESET THE COUNT?
PERHAPS. HE IS AN ASSASSIN, NONETHELESS.
THEY DO NOT ALLOW THEMSELVES TO BE CAPTURED, BUT I WAS FAST ENOUGH TO REMOVE HIS BLADE FROM HIM.
SPEAK, HEATHEN. THE GRAND MASTER COMMANDS IT.
PTOO
IT IS SAID THE ASSASSINS DO NOT FEAR DEATH. BUT PERHAPS WE CAN TEACH YOU TO **FEAR GOD,** INSTEAD.
YOUR **"GOD"** HOLDS NO TERROR FOR ME, YOU TEMPLAR DOG. I SHALL NEVER MEET HIM.
THE **WATERS** WILL RESTORE US. I HAVE **SEEN** IT.

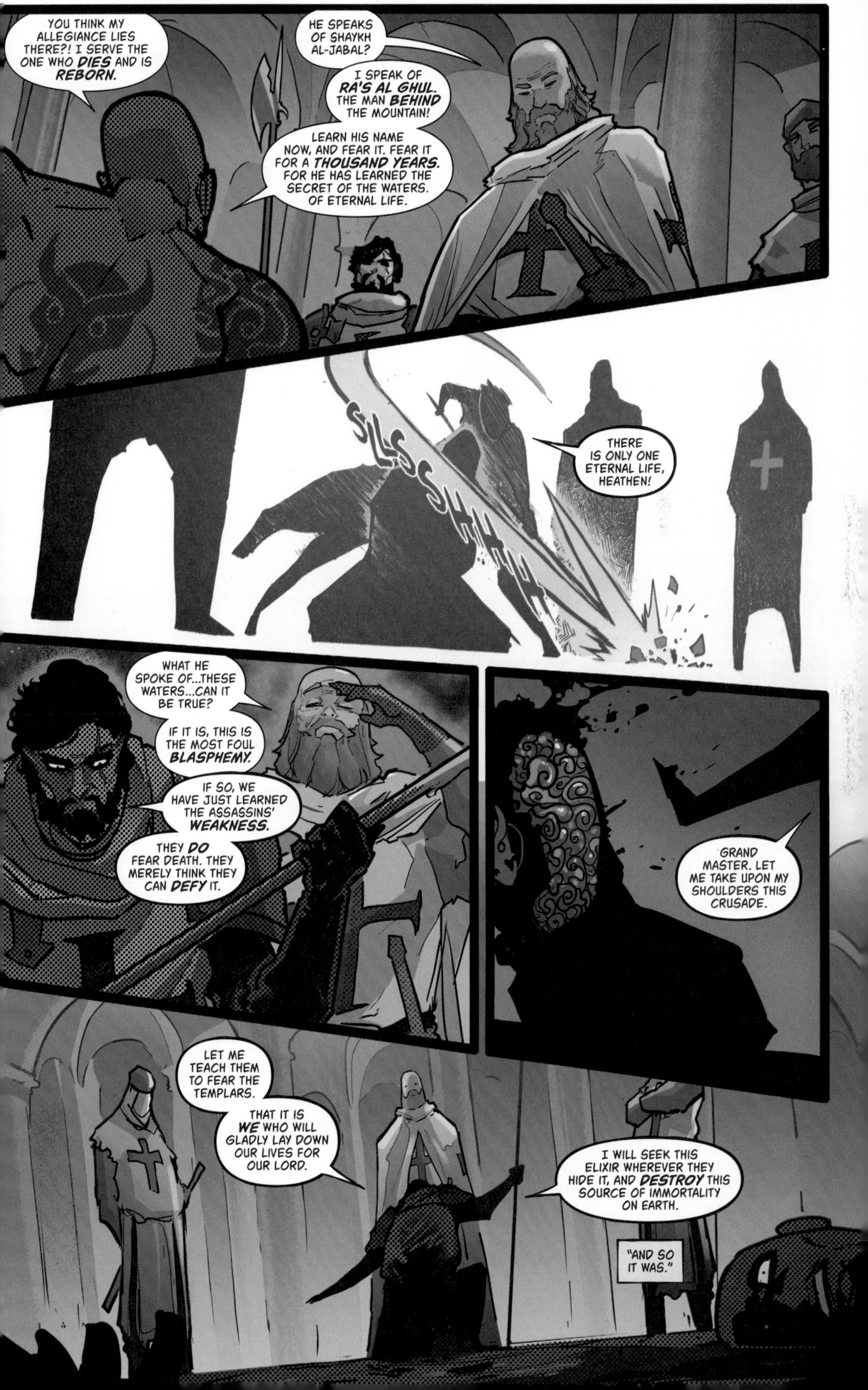
YOU THINK MY ALLEGIANCE LIES THERE?! I SERVE THE ONE WHO DIES AND IS REBORN.
HE SPEAKS OF SHAYKH AL-JABAL?
I SPEAK OF RA'S AL GHUL. THE MAN BEHIND THE MOUNTAIN!
LEARN HIS NAME NOW, AND FEAR IT. FEAR IT FOR A THOUSAND YEARS. FOR HE HAS LEARNED THE SECRET OF THE WATERS. OF ETERNAL LIFE.
SLLSSHHHH
THERE IS ONLY ONE ETERNAL LIFE, HEATHEN!
WHAT HE SPOKE OF...THESE WATERS...CAN IT BE TRUE?
IF IT IS, THIS IS THE MOST FOUL BLASPHEMY.
IF SO, WE HAVE JUST LEARNED THE ASSASSINS' WEAKNESS.
THEY DO FEAR DEATH. THEY MERELY THINK THEY CAN DEFY IT.
GRAND MASTER. LET ME TAKE UPON MY SHOULDERS THIS CRUSADE.
LET ME TEACH THEM TO FEAR THE TEMPLARS.
THAT IT IS WE WHO WILL GLADLY LAY DOWN OUR LIVES FOR OUR LORD.
I WILL SEEK THIS ELIXIR WHEREVER THEY HIDE IT, AND DESTROY THIS SOURCE OF IMMORTALITY ON EARTH.
"AND SO IT WAS."

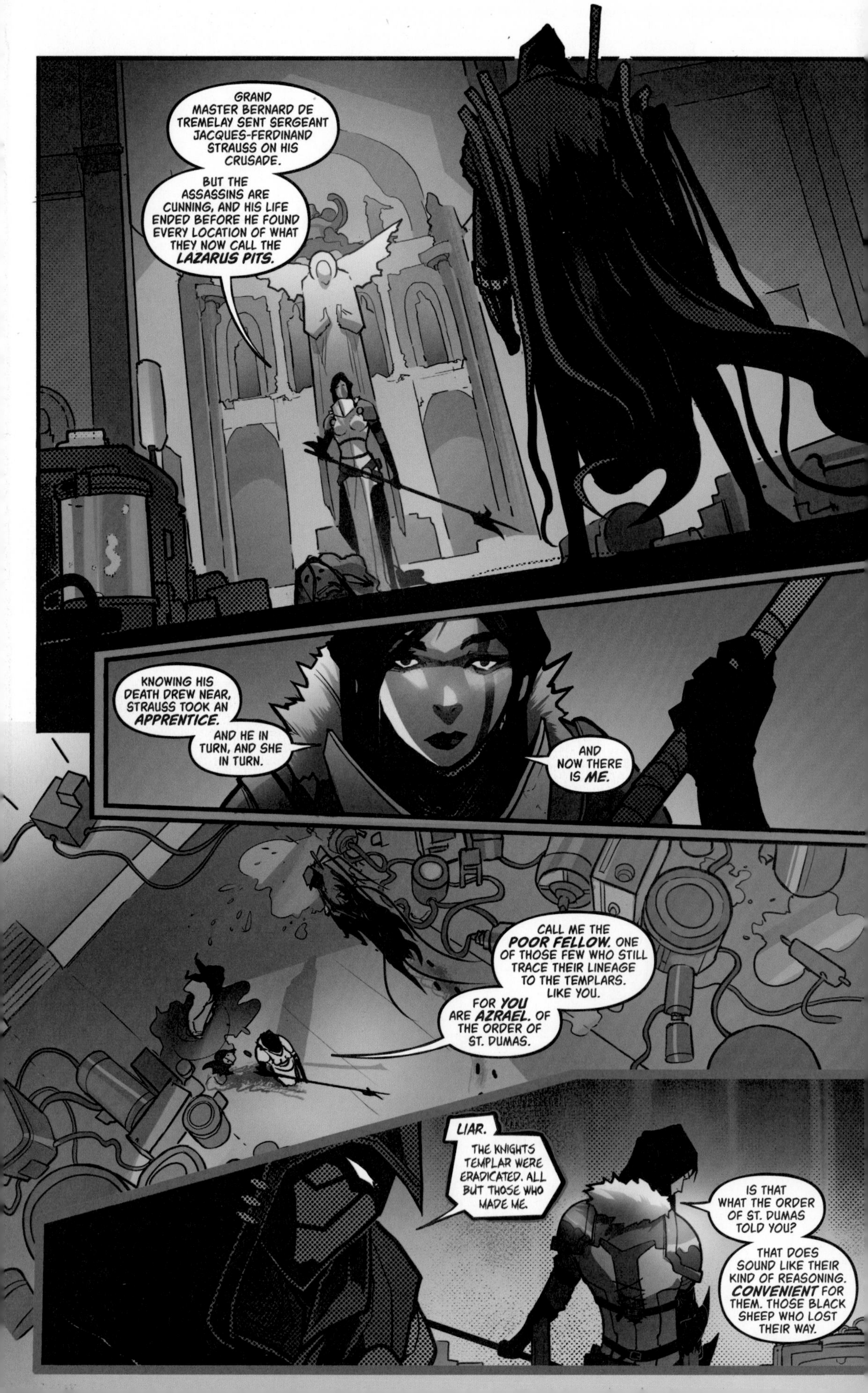
GRAND MASTER BERNARD DE TREMELAY SENT SERGEANT JACQUES-FERDINAND STRAUSS ON HIS CRUSADE.
BUT THE ASSASSINS ARE CUNNING, AND HIS LIFE ENDED BEFORE HE FOUND EVERY LOCATION OF WHAT THEY NOW CALL THE LAZARUS PITS.
KNOWING HIS DEATH DREW NEAR, STRAUSS TOOK AN APPRENTICE.
AND HE IN TURN, AND SHE IN TURN.
AND NOW THERE IS ME.
CALL ME THE POOR FELLOW. ONE OF THOSE FEW WHO STILL TRACE THEIR LINEAGE TO THE TEMPLARS. LIKE YOU.
FOR YOU ARE AZRAEL. OF THE ORDER OF ST. DUMAS.
LIAR.
THE KNIGHTS TEMPLAR WERE ERADICATED. ALL BUT THOSE WHO MADE ME.
IS THAT WHAT THE ORDER OF ST. DUMAS TOLD YOU?
THAT DOES SOUND LIKE THEIR KIND OF REASONING. CONVENIENT FOR THEM. THOSE BLACK SHEEP WHO LOST THEIR WAY.

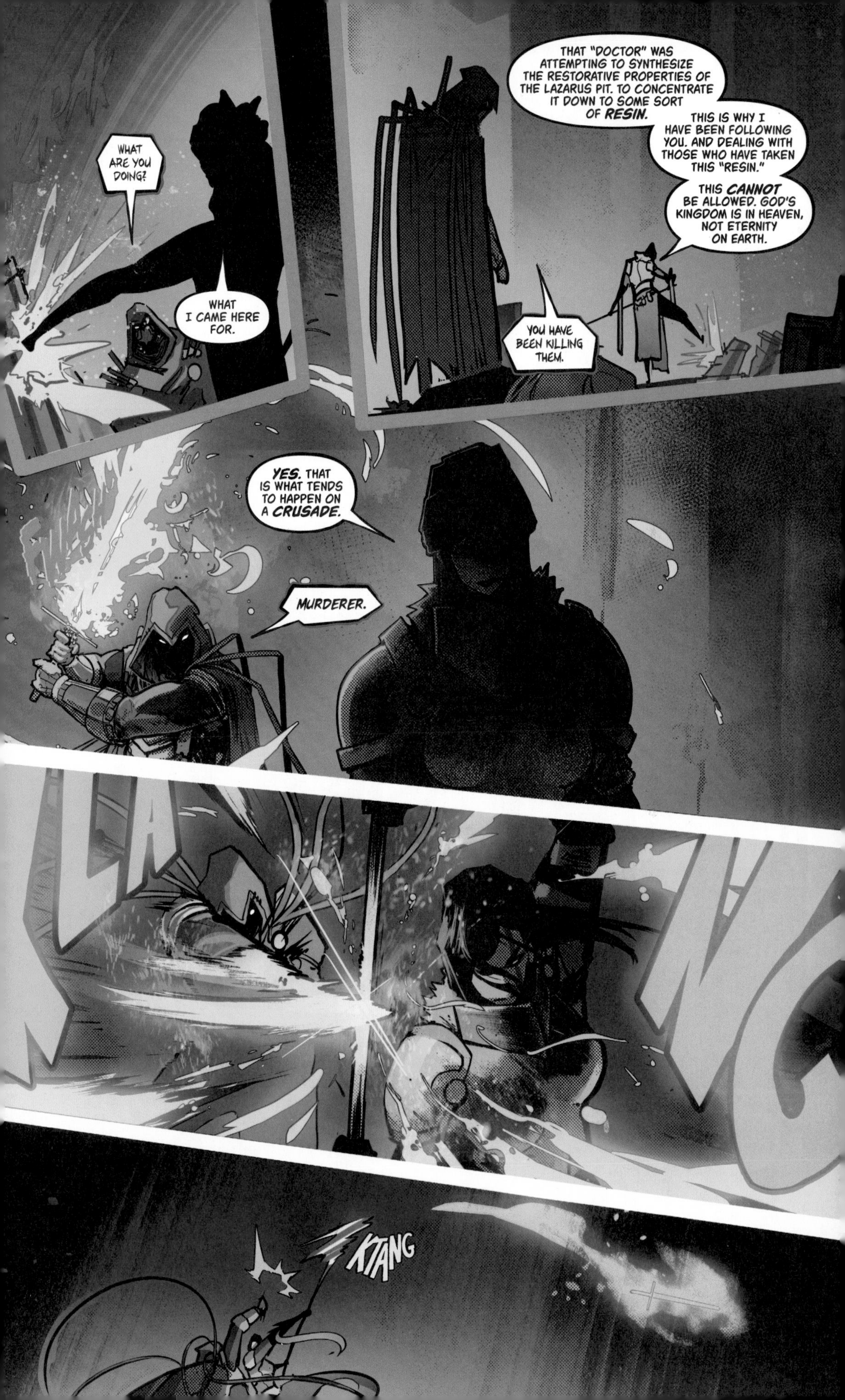
WHAT ARE YOU DOING?
WHAT I CAME HERE FOR.
THAT "DOCTOR" WAS ATTEMPTING TO SYNTHESIZE THE RESTORATIVE PROPERTIES OF THE LAZARUS PIT. TO CONCENTRATE IT DOWN TO SOME SORT OF **RESIN.**
THIS IS WHY I HAVE BEEN FOLLOWING YOU. AND DEALING WITH THOSE WHO HAVE TAKEN THIS "RESIN."
THIS **CANNOT** BE ALLOWED. GOD'S KINGDOM IS IN HEAVEN, NOT ETERNITY ON EARTH.
YOU HAVE BEEN KILLING THEM.
YES. THAT IS WHAT TENDS TO HAPPEN ON A **CRUSADE.**
MURDERER.
KTANG

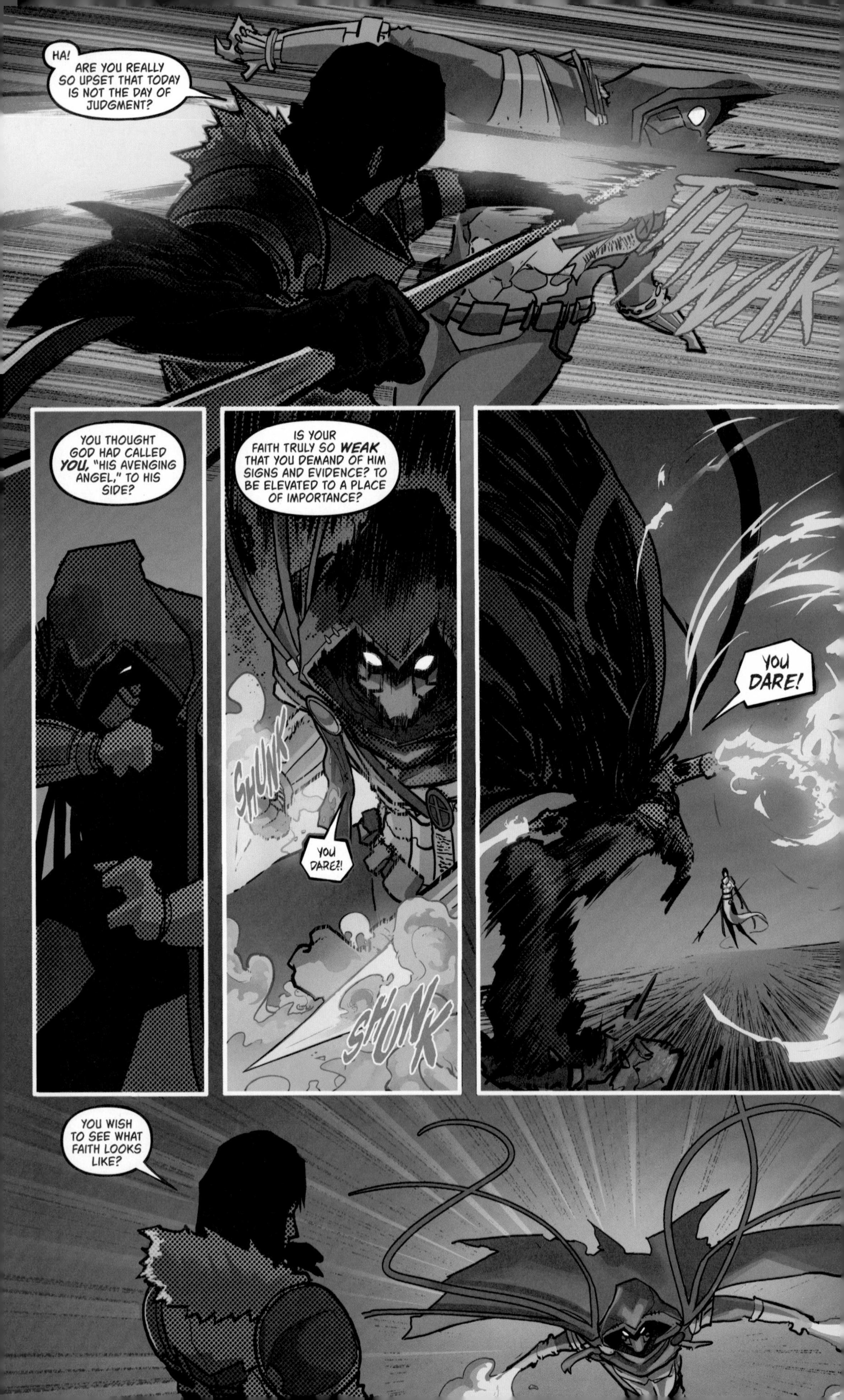
HA!
ARE YOU REALLY SO UPSET THAT TODAY IS NOT THE DAY OF JUDGMENT?
THWAK
YOU THOUGHT GOD HAD CALLED YOU, "HIS AVENGING ANGEL," TO HIS SIDE?
IS YOUR FAITH TRULY SO WEAK THAT YOU DEMAND OF HIM SIGNS AND EVIDENCE? TO BE ELEVATED TO A PLACE OF IMPORTANCE?
SHUNK
YOU DARE?!
SHUNK
YOU DARE!
YOU WISH TO SEE WHAT FAITH LOOKS LIKE?

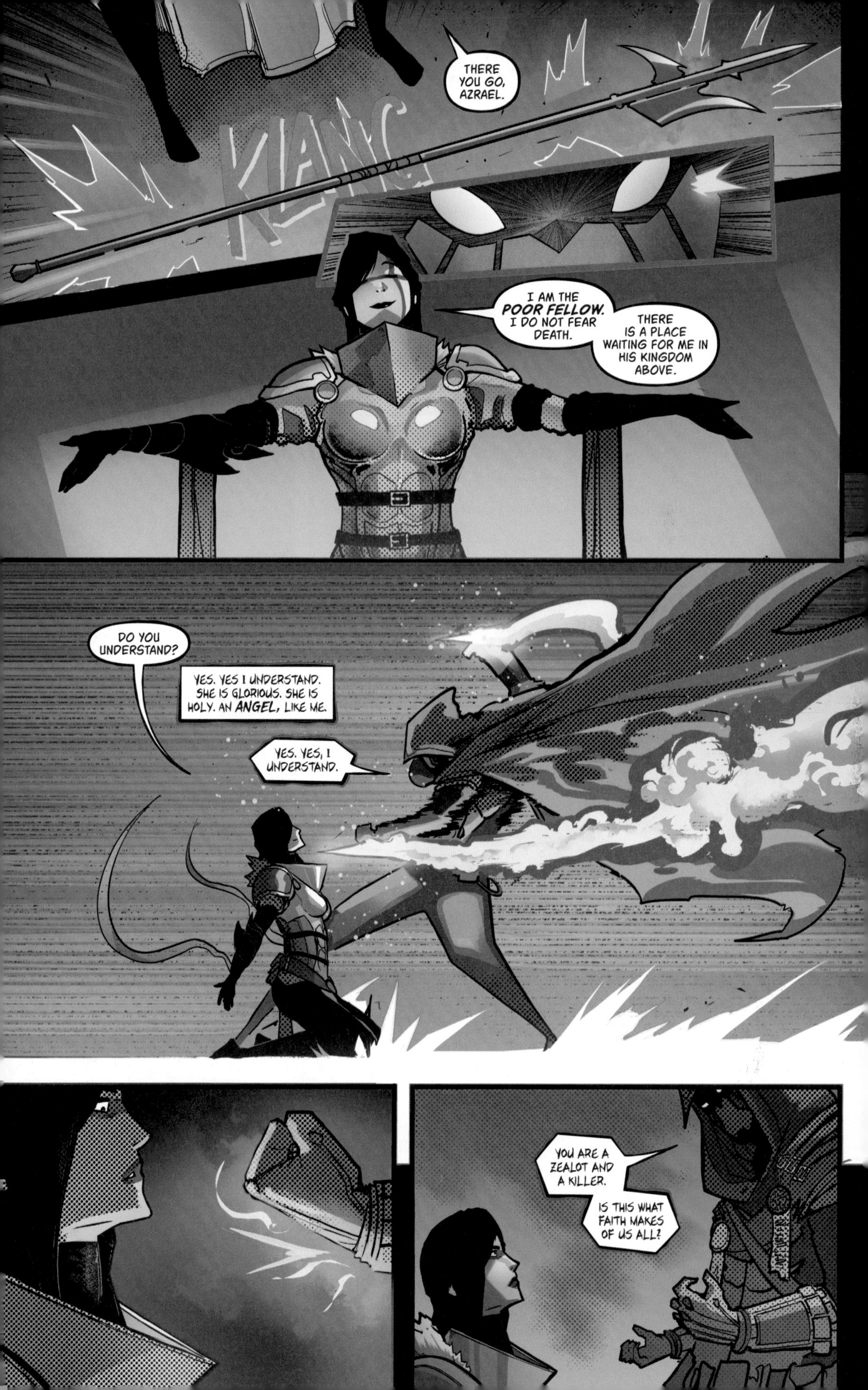
THERE YOU GO, AZRAEL.
KLANG
I AM THE **POOR FELLOW.** I DO NOT FEAR DEATH.
THERE IS A PLACE WAITING FOR ME IN HIS KINGDOM ABOVE.
DO YOU UNDERSTAND?
YES. YES I UNDERSTAND. SHE IS GLORIOUS. SHE IS HOLY. AN **ANGEL,** LIKE ME.
YES. YES, I UNDERSTAND.
YOU ARE A ZEALOT AND A KILLER.
IS THIS WHAT FAITH MAKES OF US ALL?

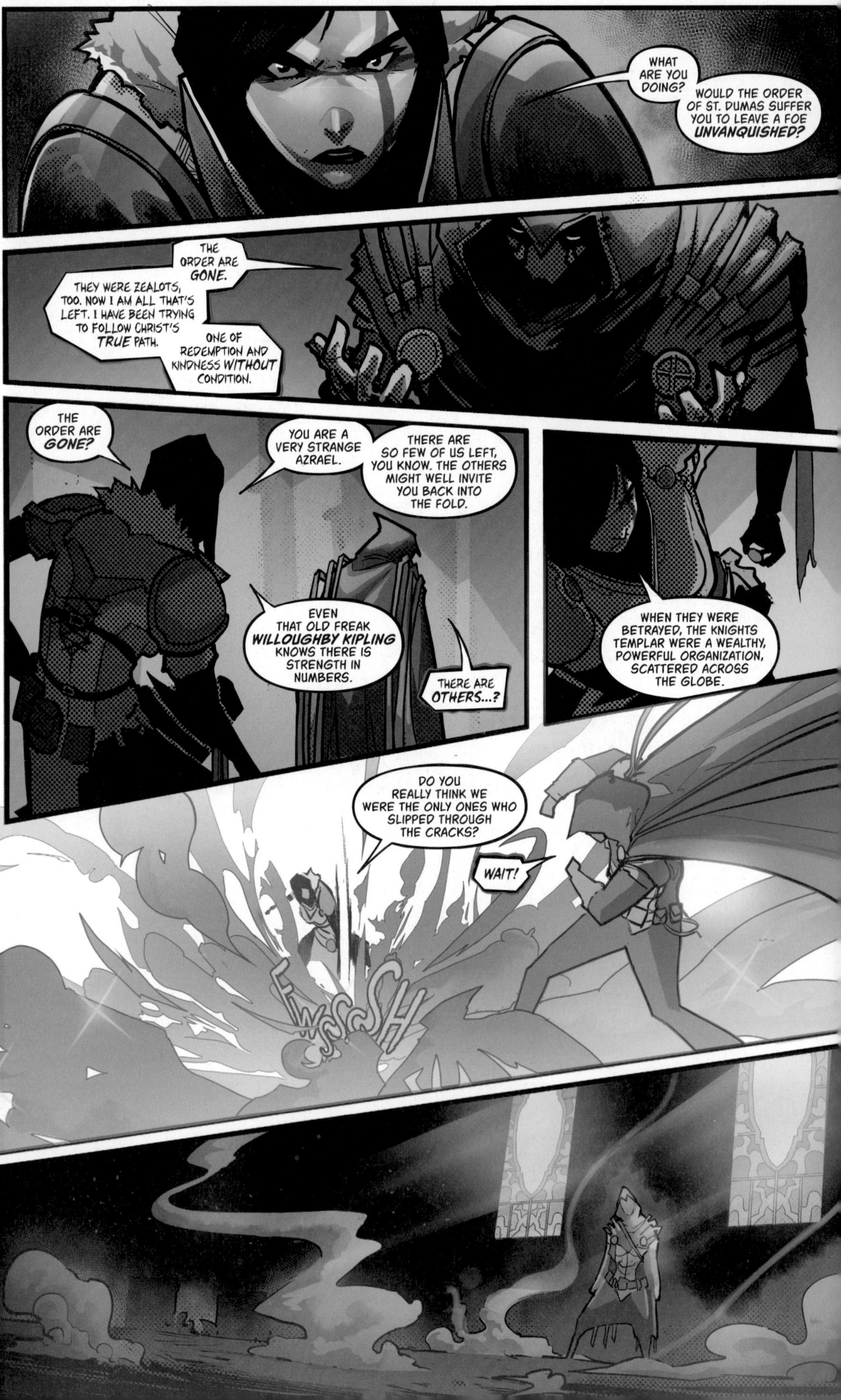
WHAT ARE YOU DOING?
WOULD THE ORDER OF ST. DUMAS SUFFER YOU TO LEAVE A FOE UNVANQUISHED?
THE ORDER ARE GONE.
THEY WERE ZEALOTS, TOO. NOW I AM ALL THAT'S LEFT. I HAVE BEEN TRYING TO FOLLOW CHRIST'S TRUE PATH.
ONE OF REDEMPTION AND KINDNESS WITHOUT CONDITION.
THE ORDER ARE GONE?
YOU ARE A VERY STRANGE AZRAEL.
THERE ARE SO FEW OF US LEFT, YOU KNOW. THE OTHERS MIGHT WELL INVITE YOU BACK INTO THE FOLD.
EVEN THAT OLD FREAK WILLOUGHBY KIPLING KNOWS THERE IS STRENGTH IN NUMBERS.
THERE ARE OTHERS...?
WHEN THEY WERE BETRAYED, THE KNIGHTS TEMPLAR WERE A WEALTHY, POWERFUL ORGANIZATION, SCATTERED ACROSS THE GLOBE.
DO YOU REALLY THINK WE WERE THE ONLY ONES WHO SLIPPED THROUGH THE CRACKS?
WAIT!
FWSSSH

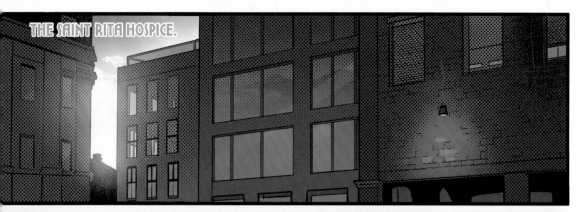

PALLIATIVE CARE UNIT.

STEFANOS?

IT'S ME. IT'S **JEAN-PAUL.** CAN YOU HEAR ME?

I'M SORRY. I LEFT YOU. I REALLY BELIEVED...

I **WANTED** TO BELIEVE.

IT WAS EASIER.

JEAN-PAUL...?

LOOK AT YOU. YOU'RE AN **ANGEL.**

YES.

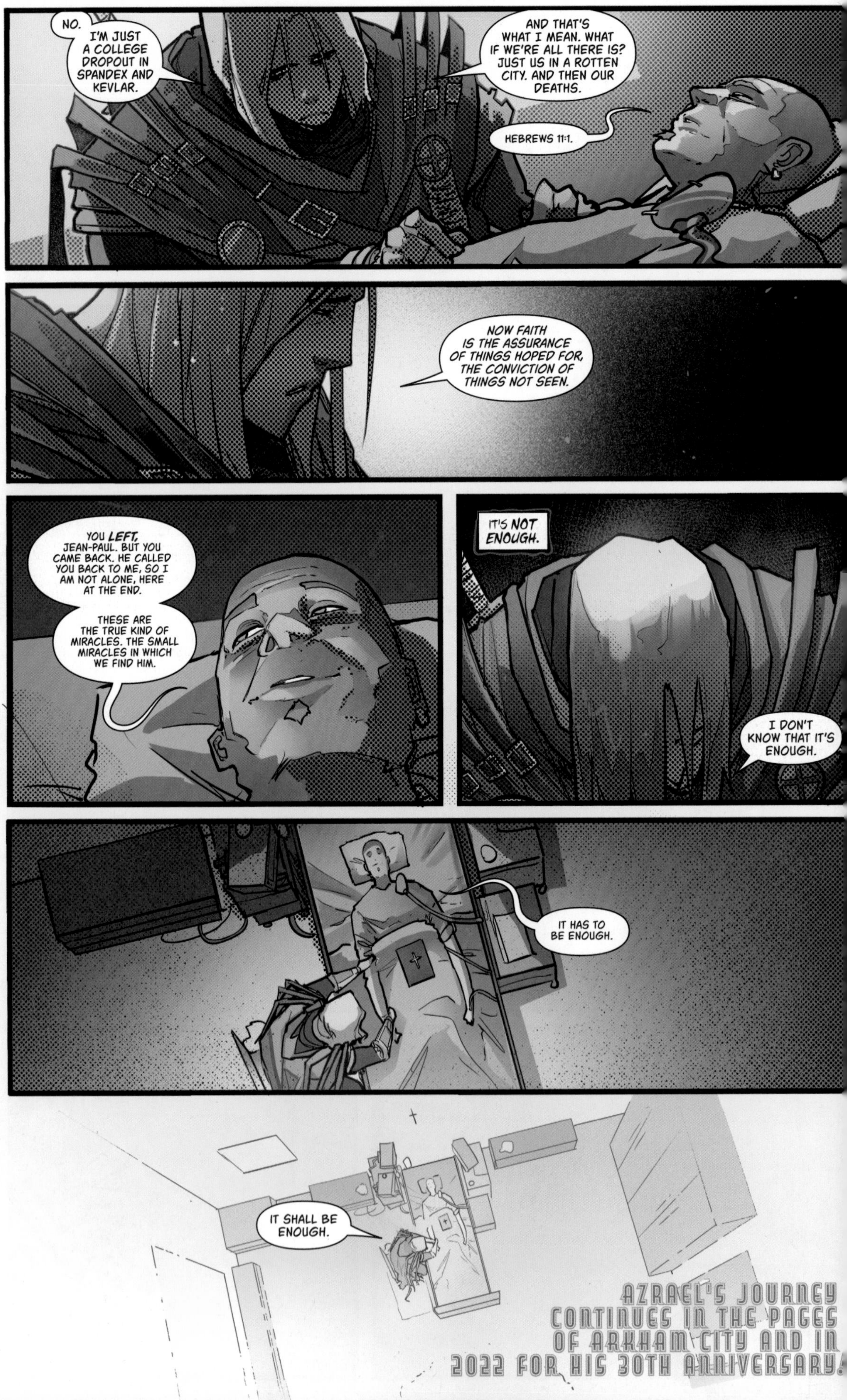
NO. I'M JUST A COLLEGE DROPOUT IN SPANDEX AND KEVLAR.
AND THAT'S WHAT I MEAN. WHAT IF WE'RE ALL THERE IS? JUST US IN A ROTTEN CITY. AND THEN OUR DEATHS.
HEBREWS 11:1.
NOW FAITH IS THE ASSURANCE OF THINGS HOPED FOR, THE CONVICTION OF THINGS NOT SEEN.
YOU LEFT, JEAN-PAUL. BUT YOU CAME BACK. HE CALLED YOU BACK TO ME, SO I AM NOT ALONE, HERE AT THE END.
THESE ARE THE TRUE KIND OF MIRACLES. THE SMALL MIRACLES IN WHICH WE FIND HIM.
IT'S NOT ENOUGH.
I DON'T KNOW THAT IT'S ENOUGH.
IT HAS TO BE ENOUGH.
IT SHALL BE ENOUGH.
AZRAEL'S JOURNEY CONTINUES IN THE PAGES OF ARKHAM CITY AND IN 2022 FOR HIS 30TH ANNIVERSARY!

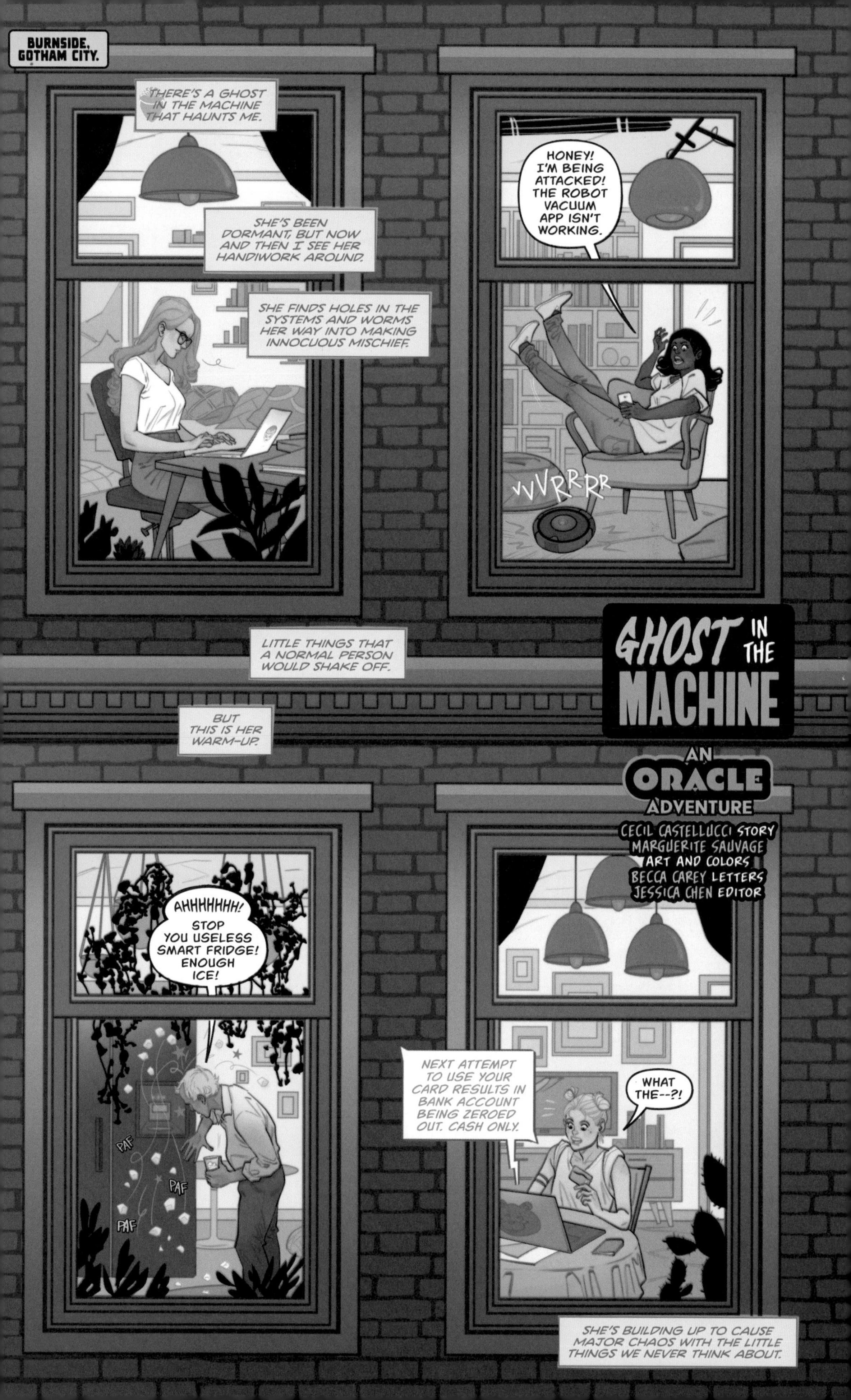
BURNSIDE, GOTHAM CITY.
THERE'S A GHOST IN THE MACHINE THAT HAUNTS ME.
SHE'S BEEN DORMANT, BUT NOW AND THEN I SEE HER HANDIWORK AROUND.
SHE FINDS HOLES IN THE SYSTEMS AND WORMS HER WAY INTO MAKING INNOCUOUS MISCHIEF.
HONEY! I'M BEING ATTACKED! THE ROBOT VACUUM APP ISN'T WORKING.
VVVRRRR
LITTLE THINGS THAT A NORMAL PERSON WOULD SHAKE OFF.
GHOST IN THE MACHINE
BUT THIS IS HER WARM-UP.
AN ORACLE ADVENTURE
CECIL CASTELLUCCI STORY
MARGUERITE SAUVAGE ART AND COLORS
BECCA CAREY LETTERS
JESSICA CHEN EDITOR
AHHHHHHH! STOP YOU USELESS SMART FRIDGE! ENOUGH ICE!
PAF
PAF
PAF
NEXT ATTEMPT TO USE YOUR CARD RESULTS IN BANK ACCOUNT BEING ZEROED OUT. CASH ONLY.
WHAT THE--?!
SHE'S BUILDING UP TO CAUSE MAJOR CHAOS WITH THE LITTLE THINGS WE NEVER THINK ABOUT.

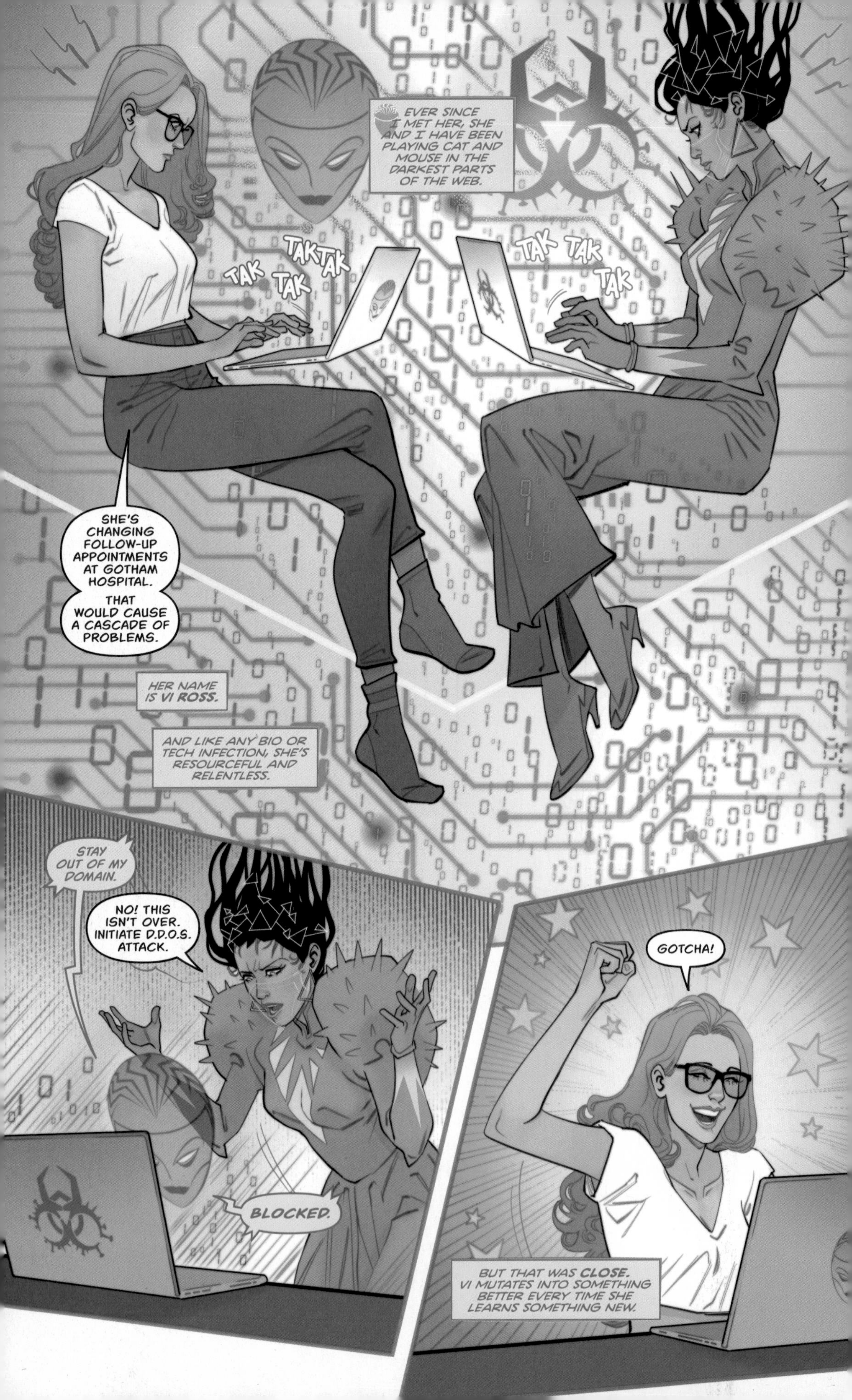

EVER SINCE I MET HER, SHE AND I HAVE BEEN PLAYING CAT AND MOUSE IN THE DARKEST PARTS OF THE WEB.
TAK TAK TAKTAK
TAK TAK TAK
SHE'S CHANGING FOLLOW-UP APPOINTMENTS AT GOTHAM HOSPITAL.
THAT WOULD CAUSE A CASCADE OF PROBLEMS.
HER NAME IS VI ROSS.
AND LIKE ANY BIO OR TECH INFECTION, SHE'S RESOURCEFUL AND RELENTLESS.
STAY OUT OF MY DOMAIN.
NO! THIS ISN'T OVER. INITIATE D.D.O.S. ATTACK.
BLOCKED.
GOTCHA!
BUT THAT WAS CLOSE. VI MUTATES INTO SOMETHING BETTER EVERY TIME SHE LEARNS SOMETHING NEW.

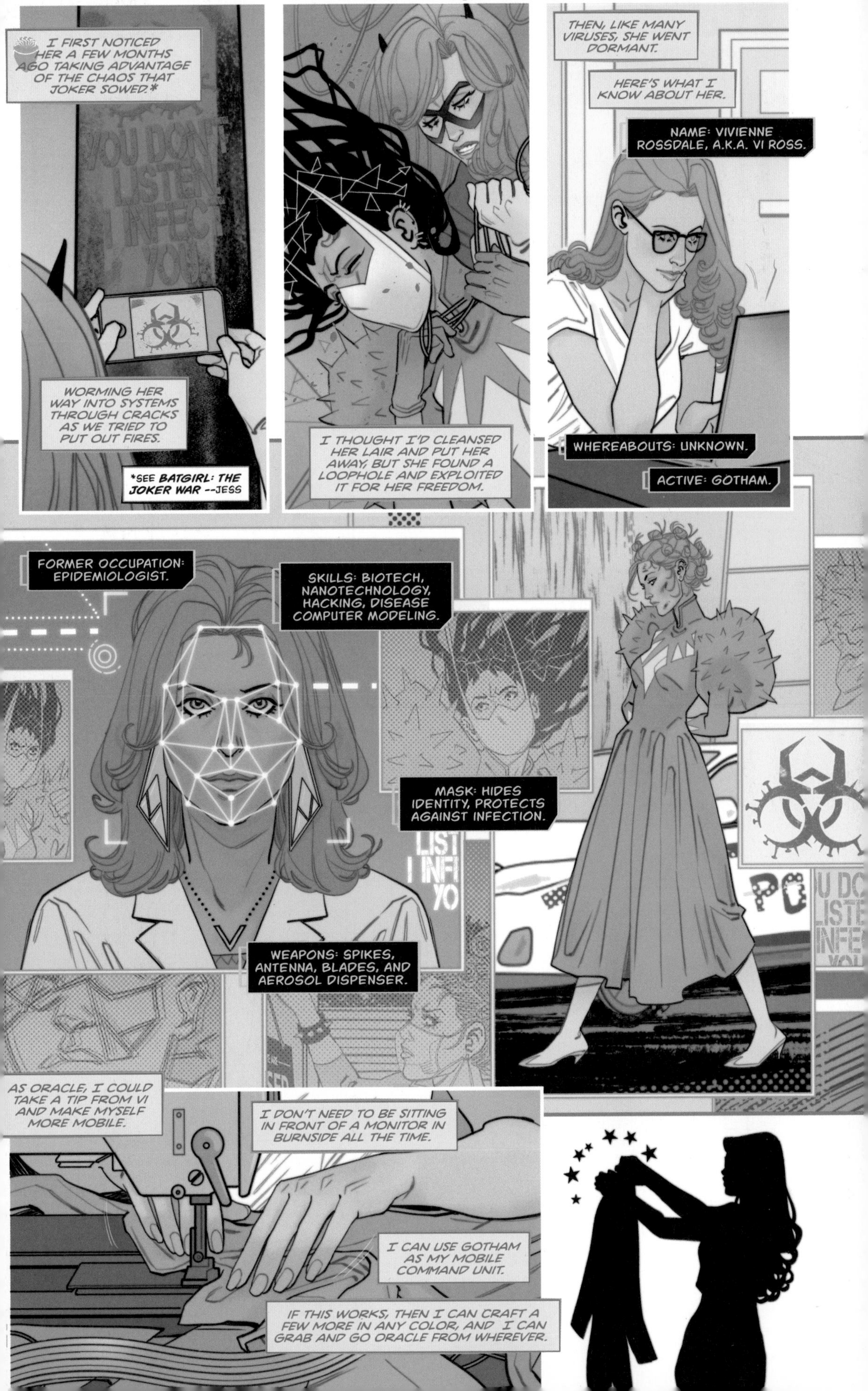

I FIRST NOTICED HER A FEW MONTHS AGO TAKING ADVANTAGE OF THE CHAOS THAT JOKER SOWED.*
YOU DON'T LISTEN I INFECT YOU
WORMING HER WAY INTO SYSTEMS THROUGH CRACKS AS WE TRIED TO PUT OUT FIRES.
*SEE BATGIRL: THE JOKER WAR --JESS
I THOUGHT I'D CLEANSED HER LAIR AND PUT HER AWAY, BUT SHE FOUND A LOOPHOLE AND EXPLOITED IT FOR HER FREEDOM.
THEN, LIKE MANY VIRUSES, SHE WENT DORMANT.
HERE'S WHAT I KNOW ABOUT HER.
NAME: VIVIENNE ROSSDALE, A.K.A. VI ROSS.
WHEREABOUTS: UNKNOWN.
ACTIVE: GOTHAM.
FORMER OCCUPATION: EPIDEMIOLOGIST.
SKILLS: BIOTECH, NANOTECHNOLOGY, HACKING, DISEASE COMPUTER MODELING.
MASK: HIDES IDENTITY, PROTECTS AGAINST INFECTION.
WEAPONS: SPIKES, ANTENNA, BLADES, AND AEROSOL DISPENSER.
AS ORACLE, I COULD TAKE A TIP FROM VI AND MAKE MYSELF MORE MOBILE.
I DON'T NEED TO BE SITTING IN FRONT OF A MONITOR IN BURNSIDE ALL THE TIME.
I CAN USE GOTHAM AS MY MOBILE COMMAND UNIT.
IF THIS WORKS, THEN I CAN CRAFT A FEW MORE IN ANY COLOR, AND I CAN GRAB AND GO ORACLE FROM WHEREVER.

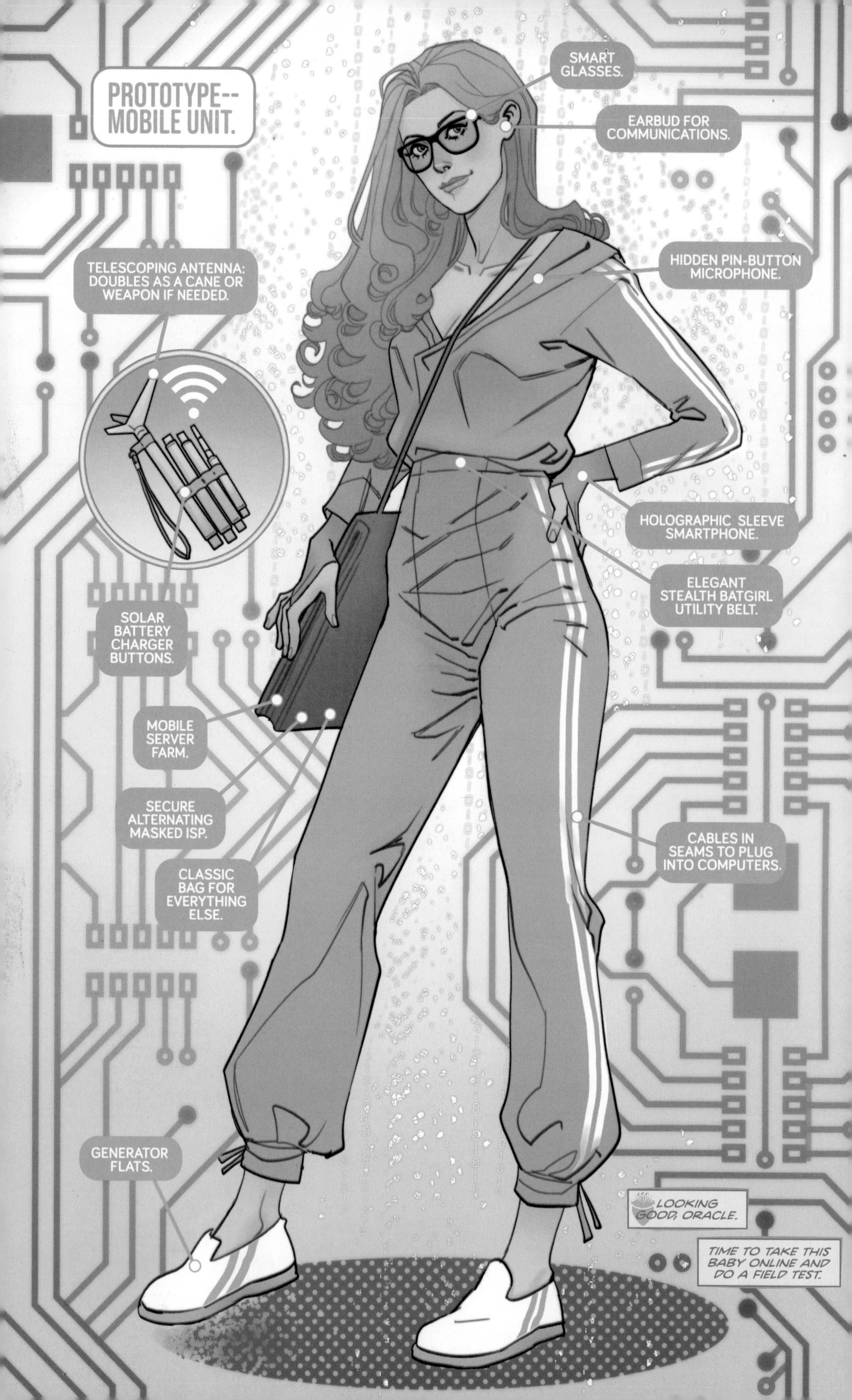

PROTOTYPE--
MOBILE UNIT.
SMART GLASSES.
EARBUD FOR COMMUNICATIONS.
TELESCOPING ANTENNA: DOUBLES AS A CANE OR WEAPON IF NEEDED.
HIDDEN PIN-BUTTON MICROPHONE.
HOLOGRAPHIC SLEEVE SMARTPHONE.
ELEGANT STEALTH BATGIRL UTILITY BELT.
SOLAR BATTERY CHARGER BUTTONS.
MOBILE SERVER FARM.
SECURE ALTERNATING MASKED ISP.
CABLES IN SEAMS TO PLUG INTO COMPUTERS.
CLASSIC BAG FOR EVERYTHING ELSE.
GENERATOR FLATS.
LOOKING GOOD, ORACLE.
TIME TO TAKE THIS BABY ONLINE AND DO A FIELD TEST.

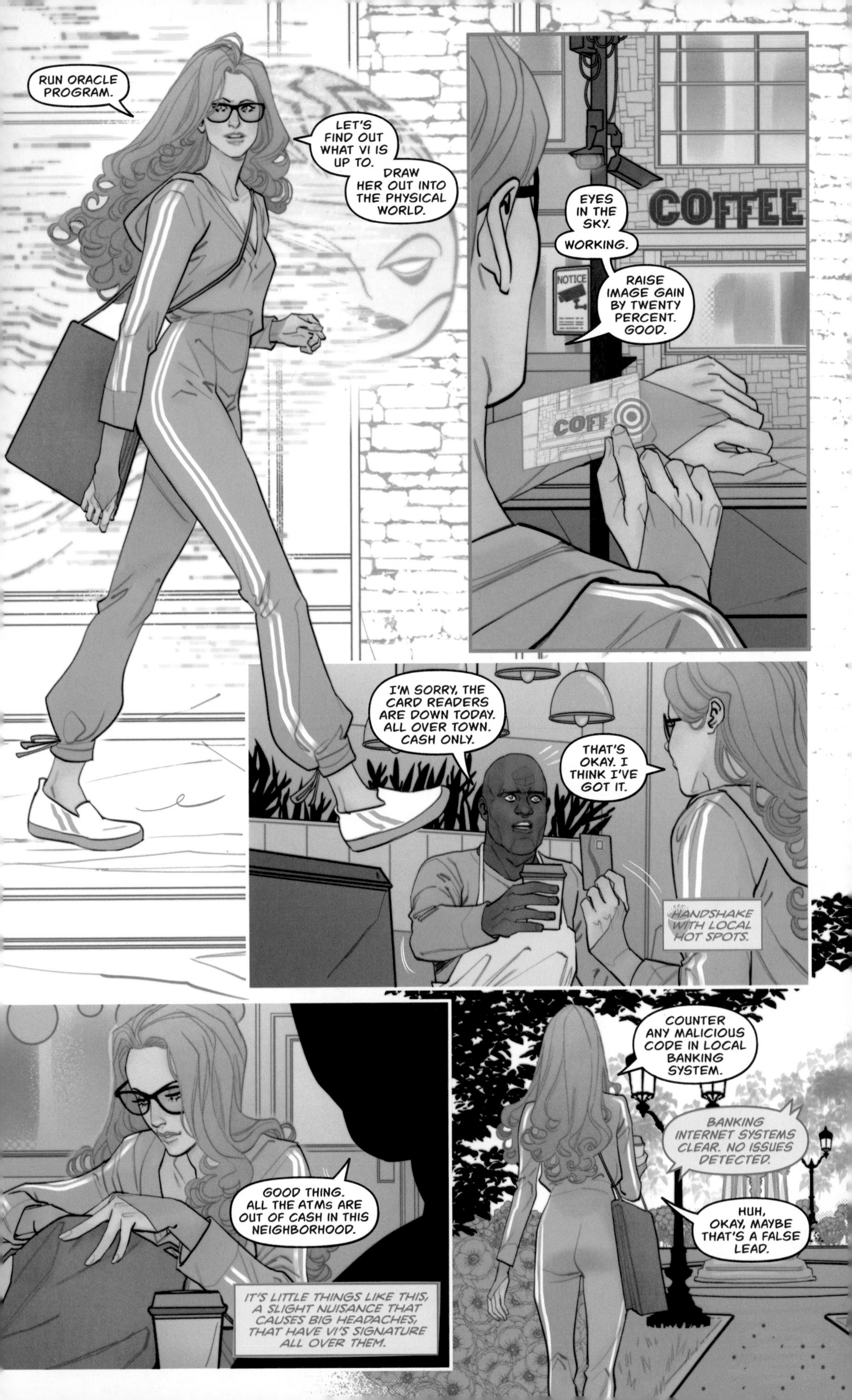
RUN ORACLE PROGRAM.
LET'S FIND OUT WHAT VI IS UP TO.
DRAW HER OUT INTO THE PHYSICAL WORLD.
EYES IN THE SKY.
WORKING.
RAISE IMAGE GAIN BY TWENTY PERCENT. GOOD.
COFFEE
NOTICE
I'M SORRY, THE CARD READERS ARE DOWN TODAY. ALL OVER TOWN. CASH ONLY.
THAT'S OKAY. I THINK I'VE GOT IT.
HANDSHAKE WITH LOCAL HOT SPOTS.
GOOD THING. ALL THE ATMs ARE OUT OF CASH IN THIS NEIGHBORHOOD.
IT'S LITTLE THINGS LIKE THIS, A SLIGHT NUISANCE THAT CAUSES BIG HEADACHES, THAT HAVE VI'S SIGNATURE ALL OVER THEM.
COUNTER ANY MALICIOUS CODE IN LOCAL BANKING SYSTEM.
BANKING INTERNET SYSTEMS CLEAR. NO ISSUES DETECTED.
HUH, OKAY, MAYBE THAT'S A FALSE LEAD.

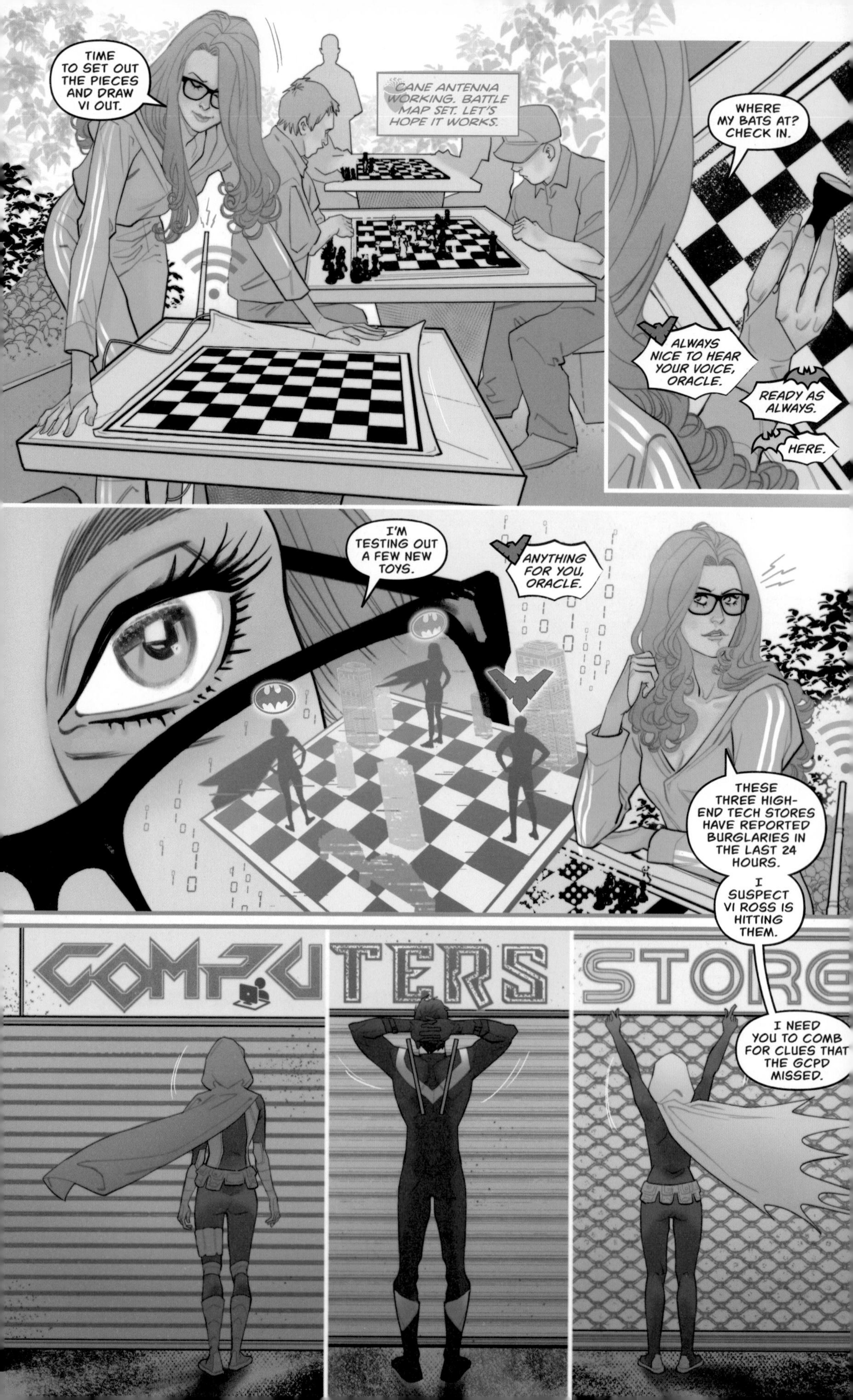
TIME TO SET OUT THE PIECES AND DRAW VI OUT.
CANE ANTENNA WORKING. BATTLE MAP SET. LET'S HOPE IT WORKS.
WHERE MY BATS AT? CHECK IN.
ALWAYS NICE TO HEAR YOUR VOICE, ORACLE.
READY AS ALWAYS.
HERE.
I'M TESTING OUT A FEW NEW TOYS.
ANYTHING FOR YOU, ORACLE.
THESE THREE HIGH-END TECH STORES HAVE REPORTED BURGLARIES IN THE LAST 24 HOURS.
I SUSPECT VI ROSS IS HITTING THEM.
COMPUTERS STORE
I NEED YOU TO COMB FOR CLUES THAT THE GCPD MISSED.

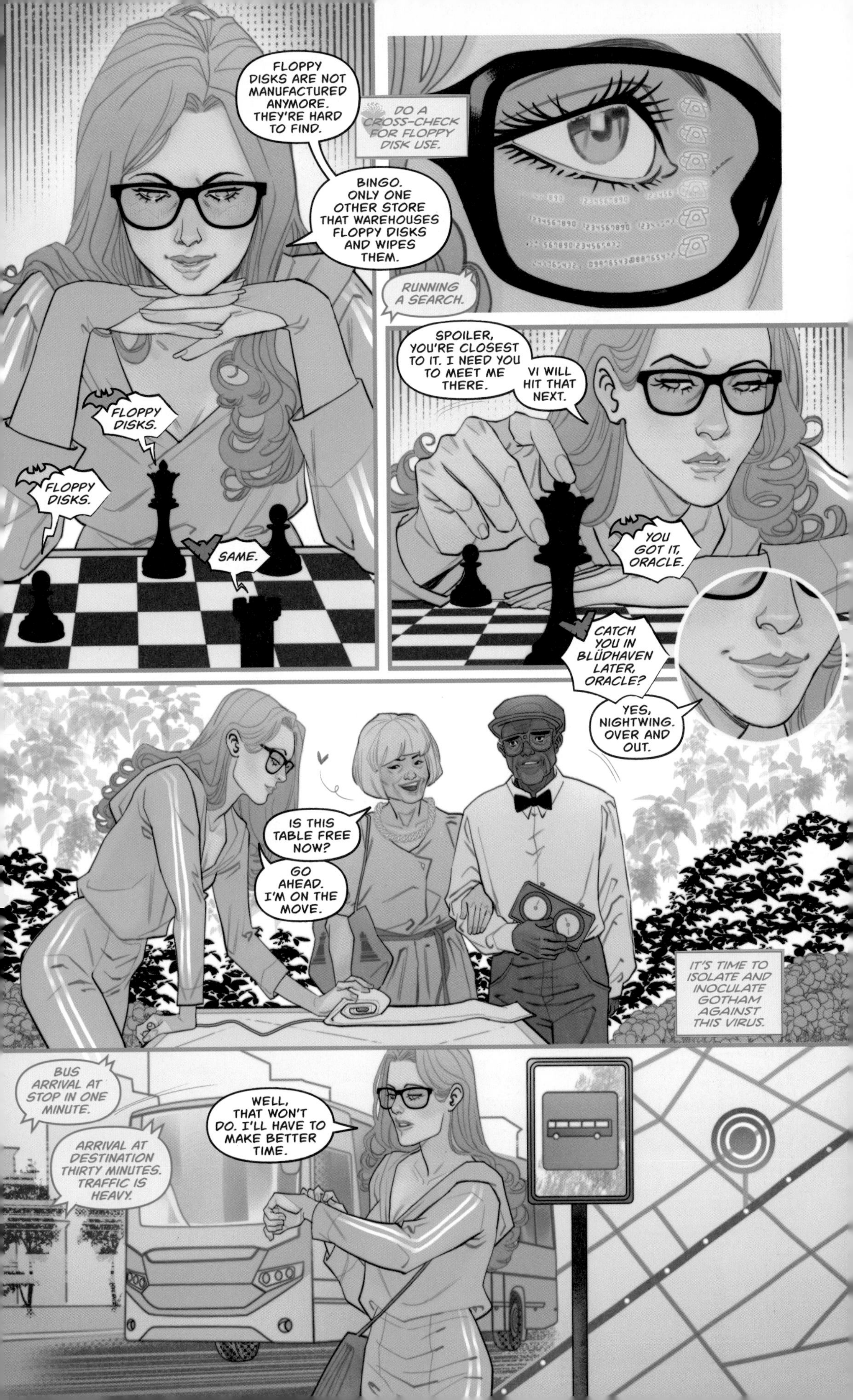
FLOPPY DISKS ARE NOT MANUFACTURED ANYMORE. THEY'RE HARD TO FIND.
DO A CROSS-CHECK FOR FLOPPY DISK USE.
BINGO. ONLY ONE OTHER STORE THAT WAREHOUSES FLOPPY DISKS AND WIPES THEM.
RUNNING A SEARCH.
FLOPPY DISKS.
FLOPPY DISKS.
SAME.
SPOILER, YOU'RE CLOSEST TO IT. I NEED YOU TO MEET ME THERE.
VI WILL HIT THAT NEXT.
YOU GOT IT, ORACLE.
CATCH YOU IN BLÜDHAVEN LATER, ORACLE?
YES, NIGHTWING. OVER AND OUT.
IS THIS TABLE FREE NOW?
GO AHEAD. I'M ON THE MOVE.
IT'S TIME TO ISOLATE AND INOCULATE GOTHAM AGAINST THIS VIRUS.
BUS ARRIVAL AT STOP IN ONE MINUTE.
ARRIVAL AT DESTINATION THIRTY MINUTES. TRAFFIC IS HEAVY.
WELL, THAT WON'T DO. I'LL HAVE TO MAKE BETTER TIME.

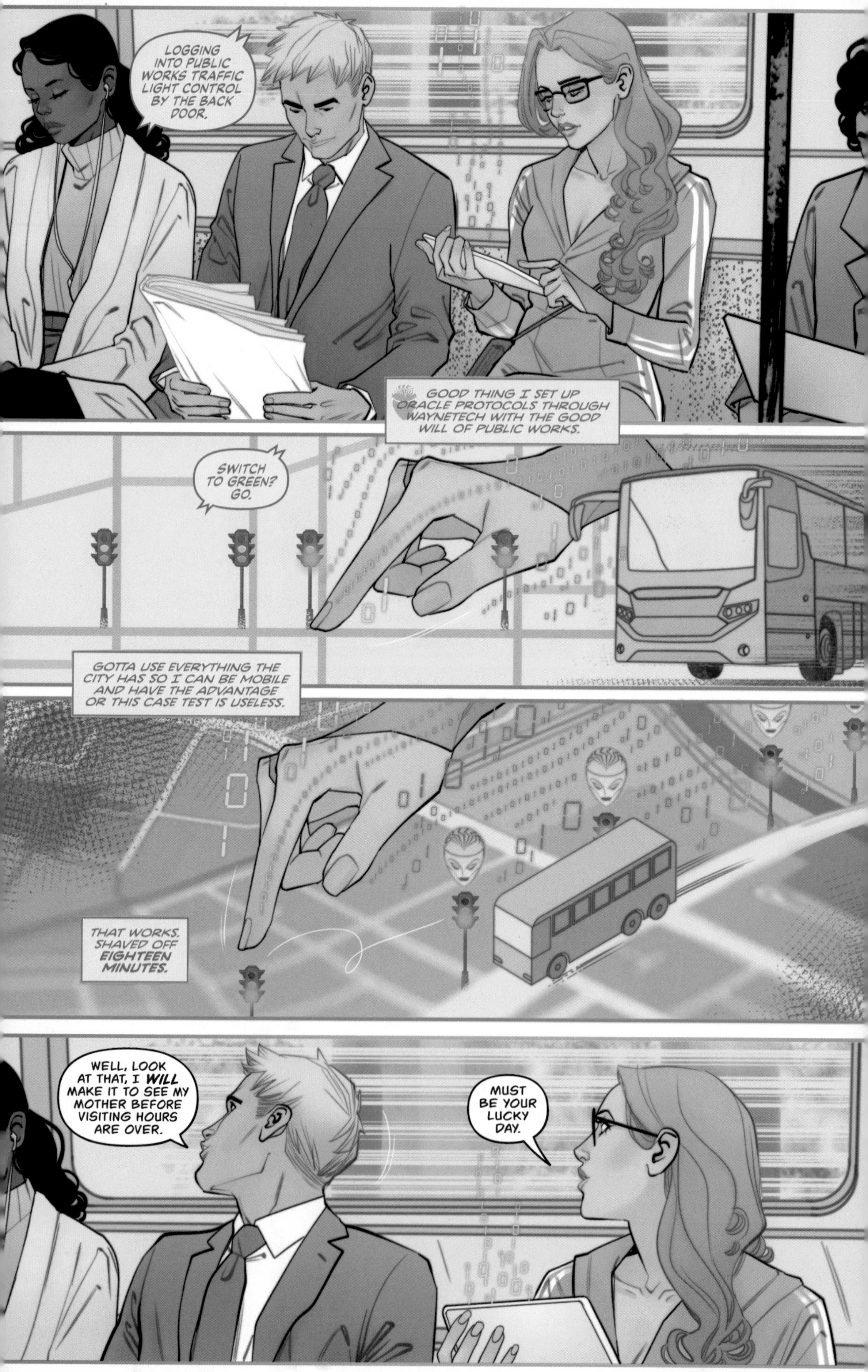

LOGGING INTO PUBLIC WORKS TRAFFIC LIGHT CONTROL BY THE BACK DOOR.
GOOD THING I SET UP ORACLE PROTOCOLS THROUGH WAYNETECH WITH THE GOOD WILL OF PUBLIC WORKS.
SWITCH TO GREEN? GO.
GOTTA USE EVERYTHING THE CITY HAS SO I CAN BE MOBILE AND HAVE THE ADVANTAGE OR THIS CASE TEST IS USELESS.
THAT WORKS. SHAVED OFF EIGHTEEN MINUTES.
WELL, LOOK AT THAT, I WILL MAKE IT TO SEE MY MOTHER BEFORE VISITING HOURS ARE OVER.
MUST BE YOUR LUCKY DAY.

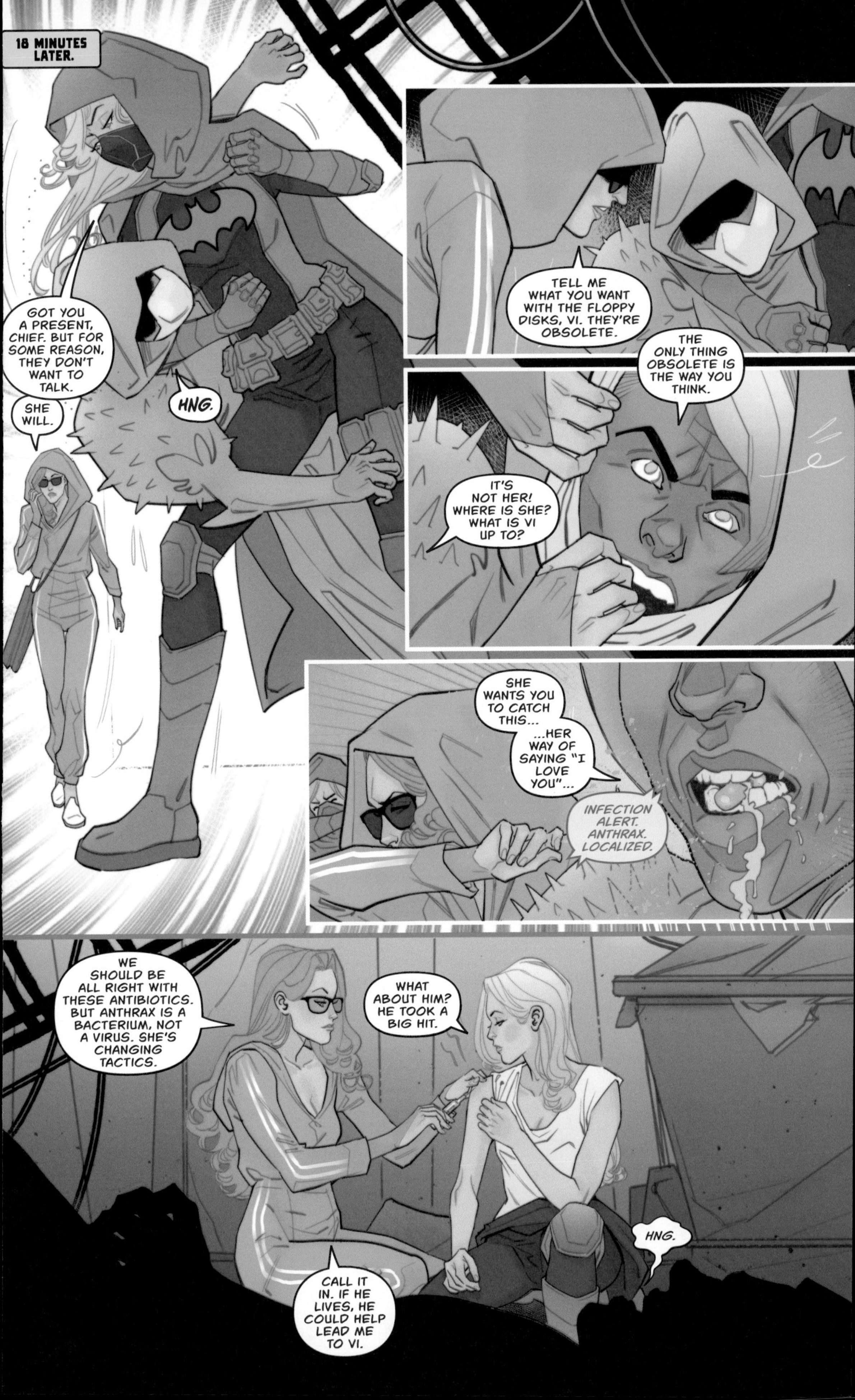
18 MINUTES LATER.
GOT YOU A PRESENT, CHIEF. BUT FOR SOME REASON, THEY DON'T WANT TO TALK.
SHE WILL.
HNG.
TELL ME WHAT YOU WANT WITH THE FLOPPY DISKS, VI. THEY'RE OBSOLETE.
THE ONLY THING OBSOLETE IS THE WAY YOU THINK.
IT'S NOT HER! WHERE IS SHE? WHAT IS VI UP TO?
SHE WANTS YOU TO CATCH THIS...
...HER WAY OF SAYING "I LOVE YOU"...
INFECTION ALERT. ANTHRAX. LOCALIZED.
WE SHOULD BE ALL RIGHT WITH THESE ANTIBIOTICS. BUT ANTHRAX IS A BACTERIUM, NOT A VIRUS. SHE'S CHANGING TACTICS.
WHAT ABOUT HIM? HE TOOK A BIG HIT.
HNG.
CALL IT IN. IF HE LIVES, HE COULD HELP LEAD ME TO VI.

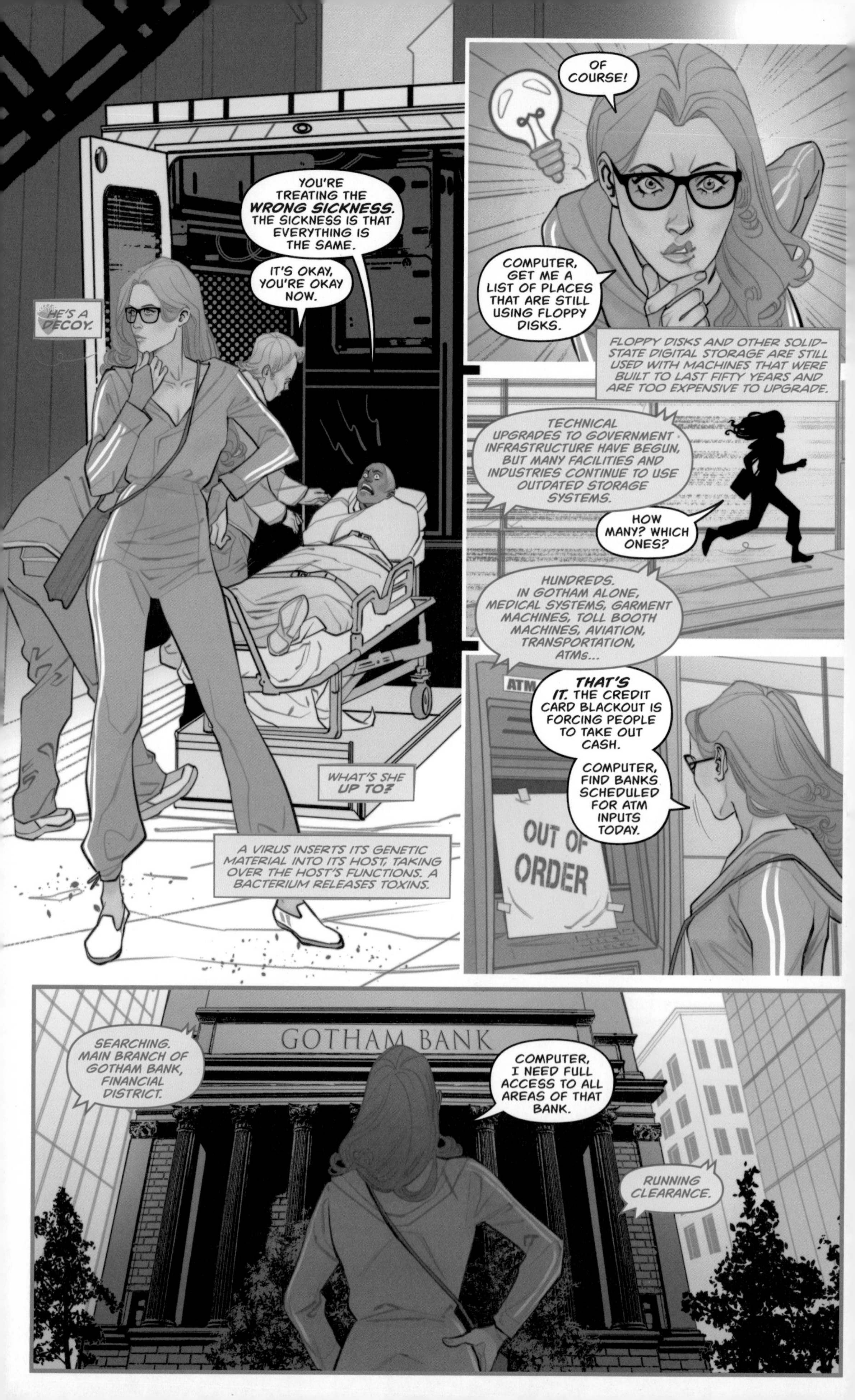
YOU'RE TREATING THE WRONG SICKNESS. THE SICKNESS IS THAT EVERYTHING IS THE SAME.
IT'S OKAY, YOU'RE OKAY NOW.
HE'S A DECOY.
WHAT'S SHE UP TO?
A VIRUS INSERTS ITS GENETIC MATERIAL INTO ITS HOST, TAKING OVER THE HOST'S FUNCTIONS. A BACTERIUM RELEASES TOXINS.
OF COURSE!
COMPUTER, GET ME A LIST OF PLACES THAT ARE STILL USING FLOPPY DISKS.
FLOPPY DISKS AND OTHER SOLID-STATE DIGITAL STORAGE ARE STILL USED WITH MACHINES THAT WERE BUILT TO LAST FIFTY YEARS AND ARE TOO EXPENSIVE TO UPGRADE.
TECHNICAL UPGRADES TO GOVERNMENT INFRASTRUCTURE HAVE BEGUN, BUT MANY FACILITIES AND INDUSTRIES CONTINUE TO USE OUTDATED STORAGE SYSTEMS.
HOW MANY? WHICH ONES?
HUNDREDS. IN GOTHAM ALONE, MEDICAL SYSTEMS, GARMENT MACHINES, TOLL BOOTH MACHINES, AVIATION, TRANSPORTATION, ATMS...
ATM
THAT'S IT. THE CREDIT CARD BLACKOUT IS FORCING PEOPLE TO TAKE OUT CASH.
COMPUTER, FIND BANKS SCHEDULED FOR ATM INPUTS TODAY.
OUT OF ORDER
GOTHAM BANK
SEARCHING. MAIN BRANCH OF GOTHAM BANK, FINANCIAL DISTRICT.
COMPUTER, I NEED FULL ACCESS TO ALL AREAS OF THAT BANK.
RUNNING CLEARANCE.

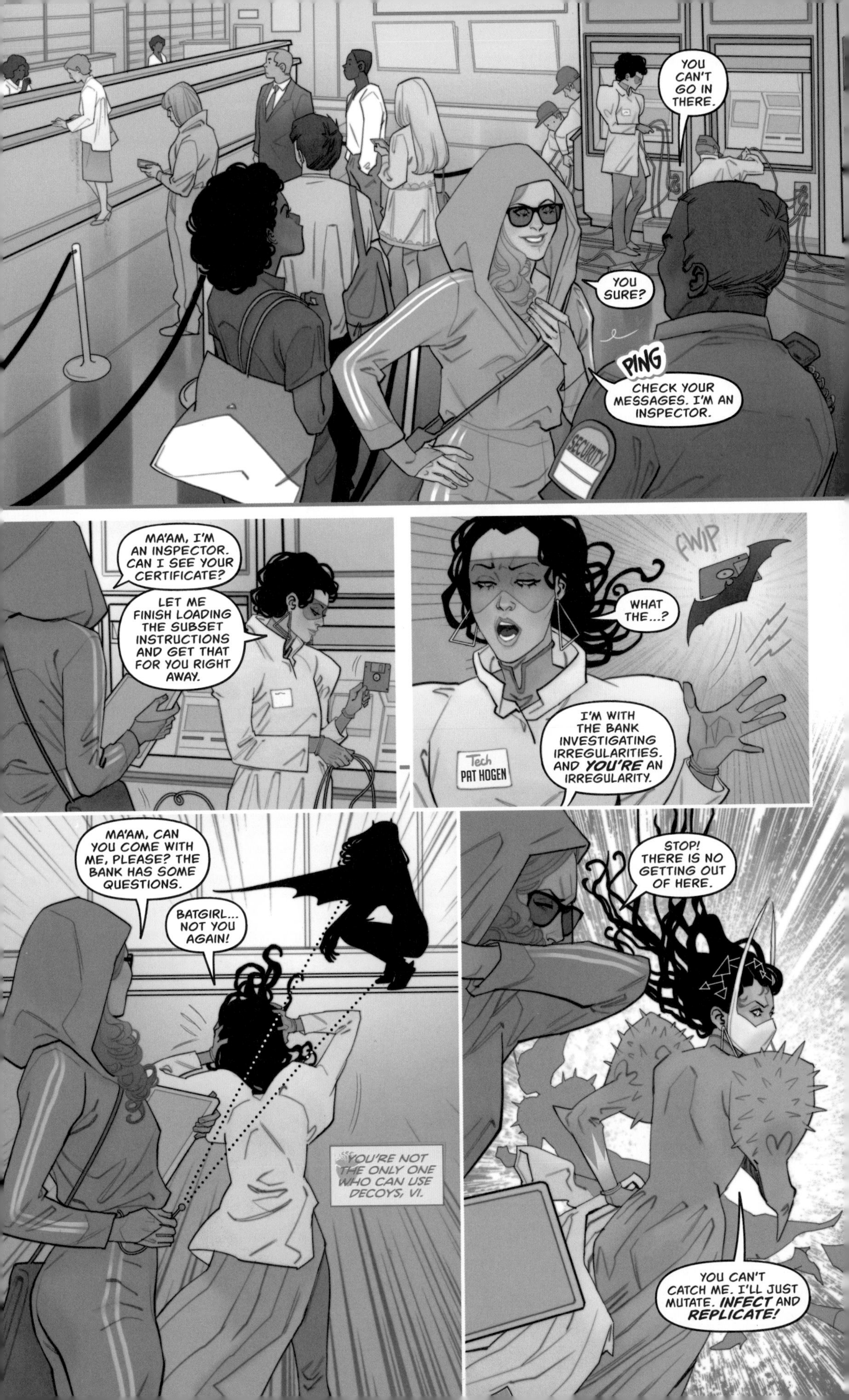
YOU CAN'T GO IN THERE.
YOU SURE?
PING
CHECK YOUR MESSAGES. I'M AN INSPECTOR.
SECURITY
MA'AM, I'M AN INSPECTOR. CAN I SEE YOUR CERTIFICATE?
LET ME FINISH LOADING THE SUBSET INSTRUCTIONS AND GET THAT FOR YOU RIGHT AWAY.
FWIP
WHAT THE...?
I'M WITH THE BANK INVESTIGATING IRREGULARITIES. AND YOU'RE AN IRREGULARITY.
Tech PAT HOGEN
MA'AM, CAN YOU COME WITH ME, PLEASE? THE BANK HAS SOME QUESTIONS.
BATGIRL... NOT YOU AGAIN!
YOU'RE NOT THE ONLY ONE WHO CAN USE DECOYS, VI.
STOP! THERE IS NO GETTING OUT OF HERE.
YOU CAN'T CATCH ME. I'LL JUST MUTATE. INFECT AND REPLICATE!

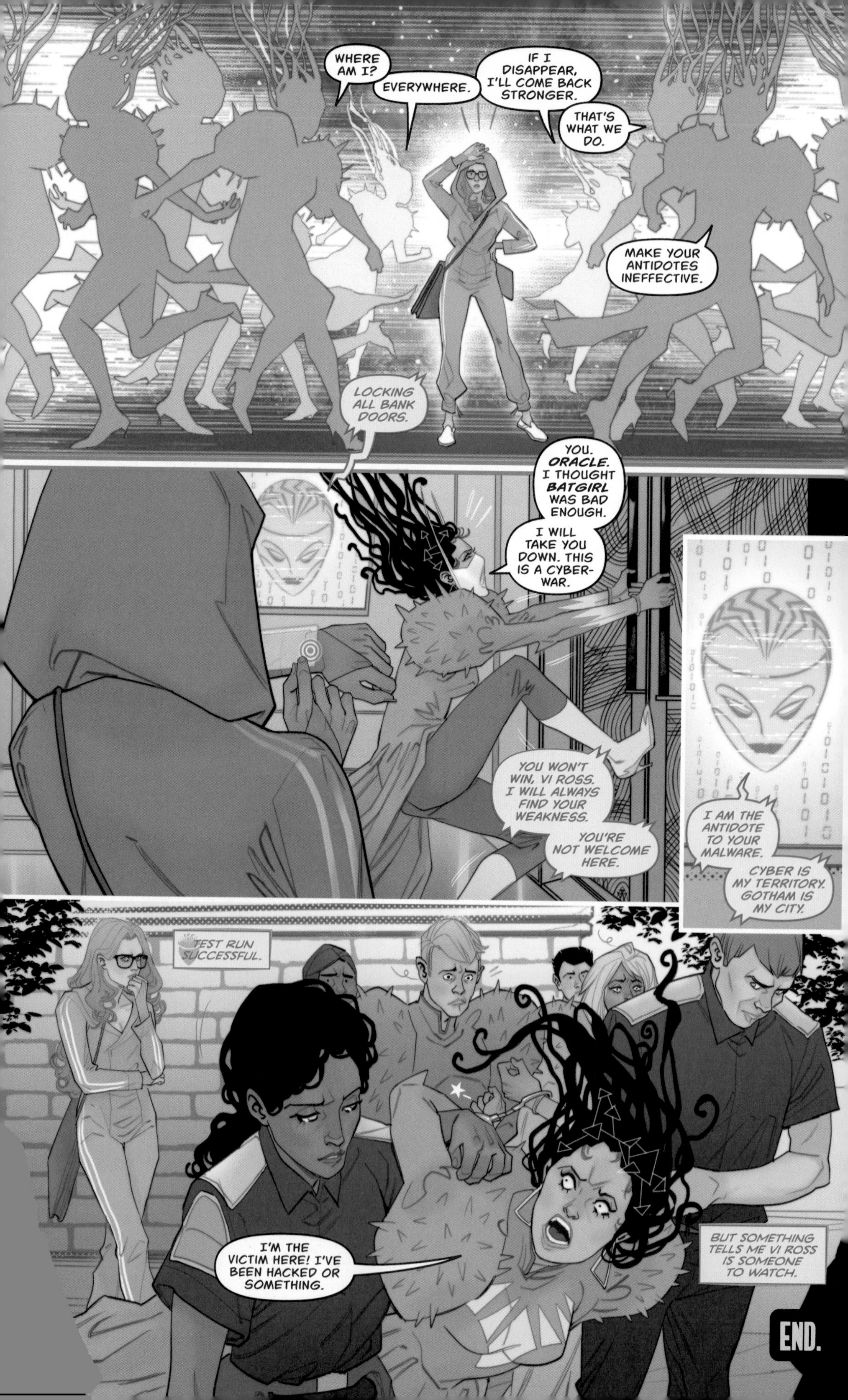
WHERE AM I?
EVERYWHERE.
IF I DISAPPEAR, I'LL COME BACK STRONGER.
THAT'S WHAT WE DO.
MAKE YOUR ANTIDOTES INEFFECTIVE.
LOCKING ALL BANK DOORS.
YOU. ORACLE. I THOUGHT BATGIRL WAS BAD ENOUGH.
I WILL TAKE YOU DOWN. THIS IS A CYBER-WAR.
YOU WON'T WIN, VI ROSS. I WILL ALWAYS FIND YOUR WEAKNESS.
YOU'RE NOT WELCOME HERE.
I AM THE ANTIDOTE TO YOUR MALWARE.
CYBER IS MY TERRITORY. GOTHAM IS MY CITY.
TEST RUN SUCCESSFUL.
I'M THE VICTIM HERE! I'VE BEEN HACKED OR SOMETHING.
BUT SOMETHING TELLS ME VI ROSS IS SOMEONE TO WATCH.
END.

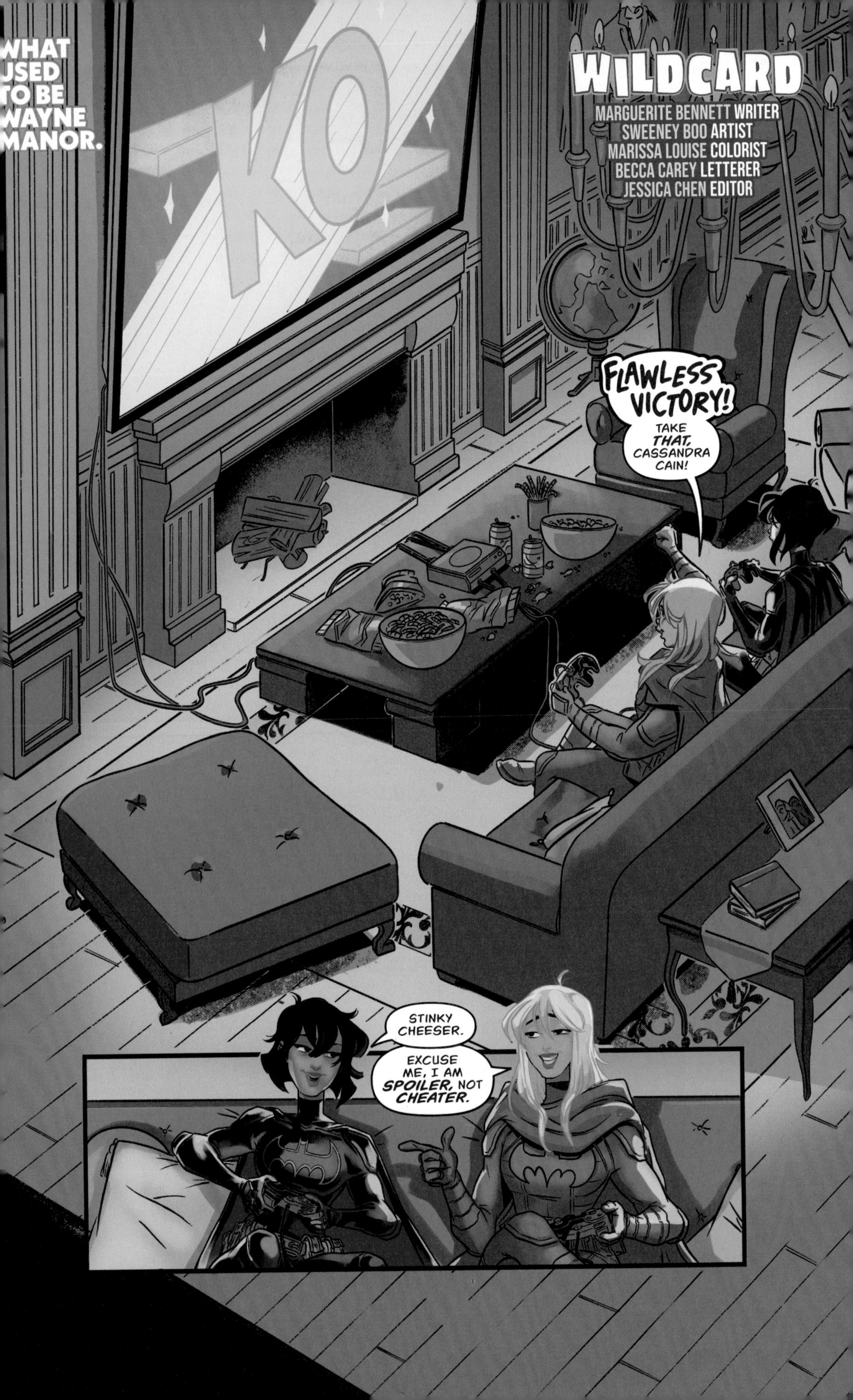
WHAT USED TO BE WAYNE MANOR.
WILDCARD
MARGUERITE BENNETT WRITER
SWEENEY BOO ARTIST
MARISSA LOUISE COLORIST
BECCA CAREY LETTERER
JESSICA CHEN EDITOR
KO
FLAWLESS VICTORY!
TAKE THAT, CASSANDRA CAIN!
STINKY CHEESER.
EXCUSE ME, I AM SPOILER, NOT CHEATER.

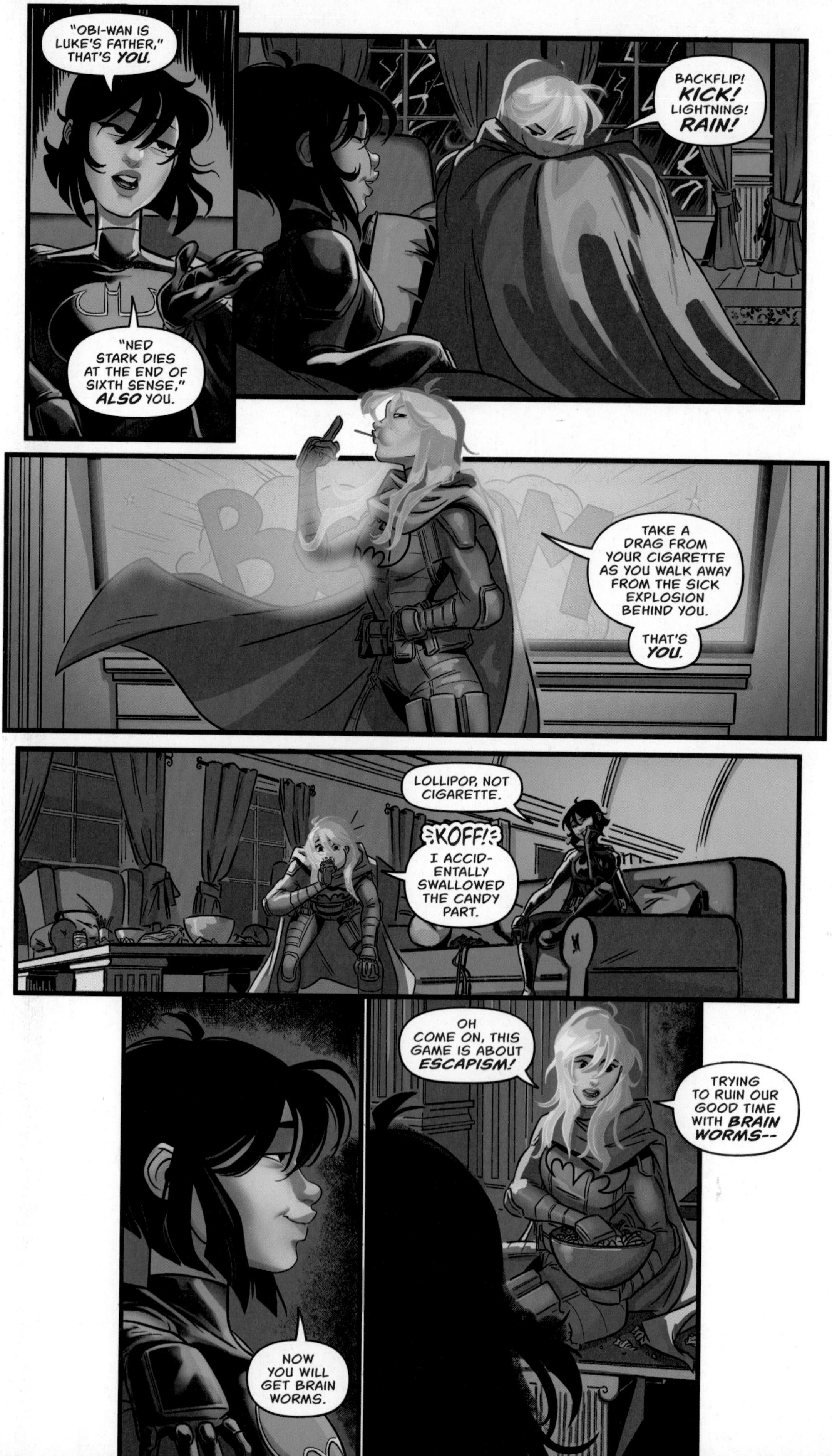
"OBI-WAN IS LUKE'S FATHER," THAT'S YOU.
"NED STARK DIES AT THE END OF SIXTH SENSE," ALSO YOU.
BACKFLIP! KICK! LIGHTNING! RAIN!
TAKE A DRAG FROM YOUR CIGARETTE AS YOU WALK AWAY FROM THE SICK EXPLOSION BEHIND YOU.
THAT'S YOU.
LOLLIPOP, NOT CIGARETTE.
KOFF!
I ACCID-ENTALLY SWALLOWED THE CANDY PART.
OH COME ON, THIS GAME IS ABOUT ESCAPISM!
TRYING TO RUIN OUR GOOD TIME WITH BRAIN WORMS--
NOW YOU WILL GET BRAIN WORMS.

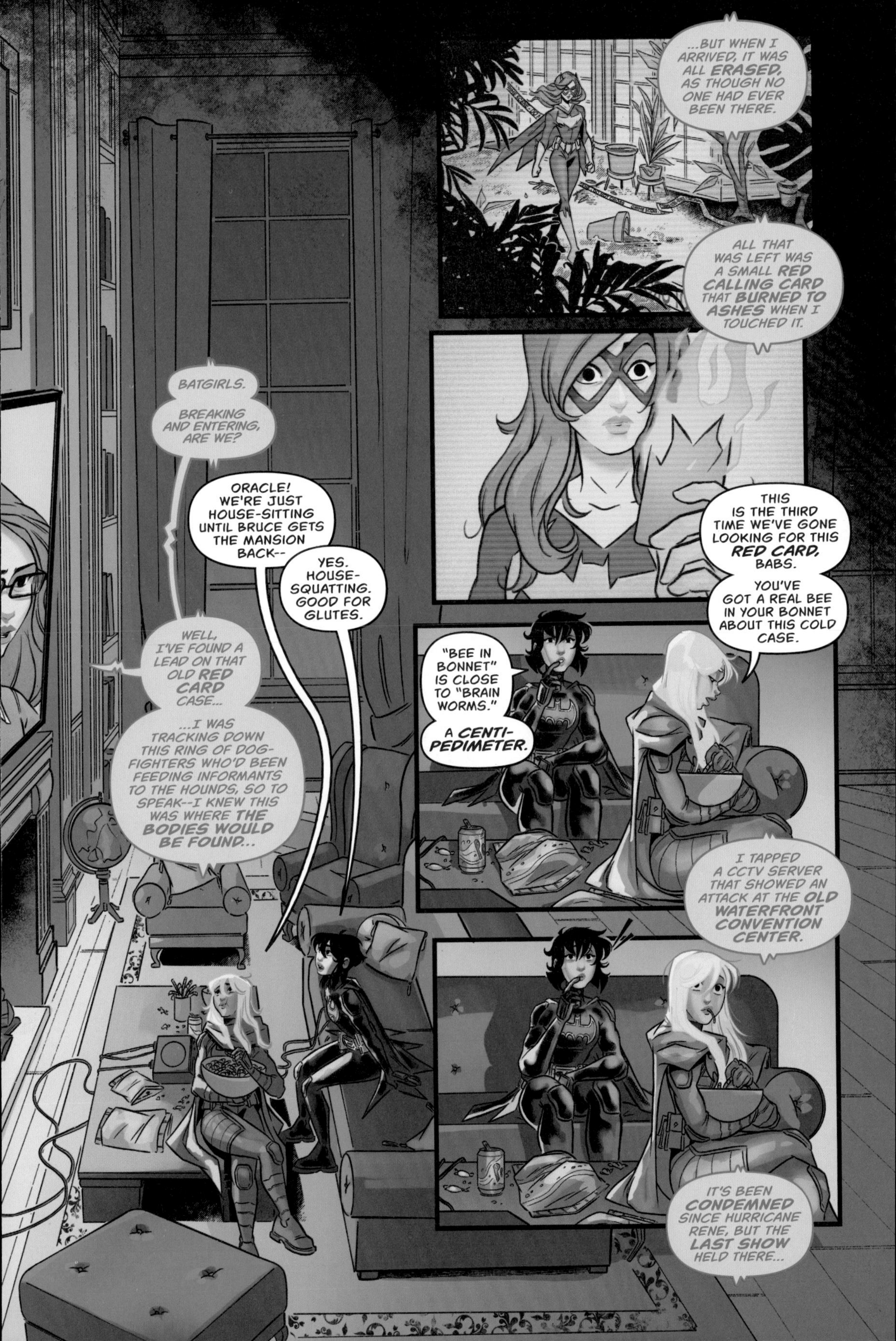
...BUT WHEN I ARRIVED, IT WAS ALL ERASED, AS THOUGH NO ONE HAD EVER BEEN THERE.
ALL THAT WAS LEFT WAS A SMALL RED CALLING CARD THAT BURNED TO ASHES WHEN I TOUCHED IT.
BATGIRLS.
BREAKING AND ENTERING, ARE WE?
ORACLE! WE'RE JUST HOUSE-SITTING UNTIL BRUCE GETS THE MANSION BACK--
YES. HOUSE-SQUATTING. GOOD FOR GLUTES.
WELL, I'VE FOUND A LEAD ON THAT OLD RED CARD CASE...
...I WAS TRACKING DOWN THIS RING OF DOG-FIGHTERS WHO'D BEEN FEEDING INFORMANTS TO THE HOUNDS, SO TO SPEAK--I KNEW THIS WAS WHERE THE BODIES WOULD BE FOUND...
THIS IS THE THIRD TIME WE'VE GONE LOOKING FOR THIS RED CARD, BABS.
YOU'VE GOT A REAL BEE IN YOUR BONNET ABOUT THIS COLD CASE.
"BEE IN BONNET" IS CLOSE TO "BRAIN WORMS."
A CENTI-PEDIMETER.
I TAPPED A CCTV SERVER THAT SHOWED AN ATTACK AT THE OLD WATERFRONT CONVENTION CENTER.
IT'S BEEN CONDEMNED SINCE HURRICANE RENE, BUT THE LAST SHOW HELD THERE...

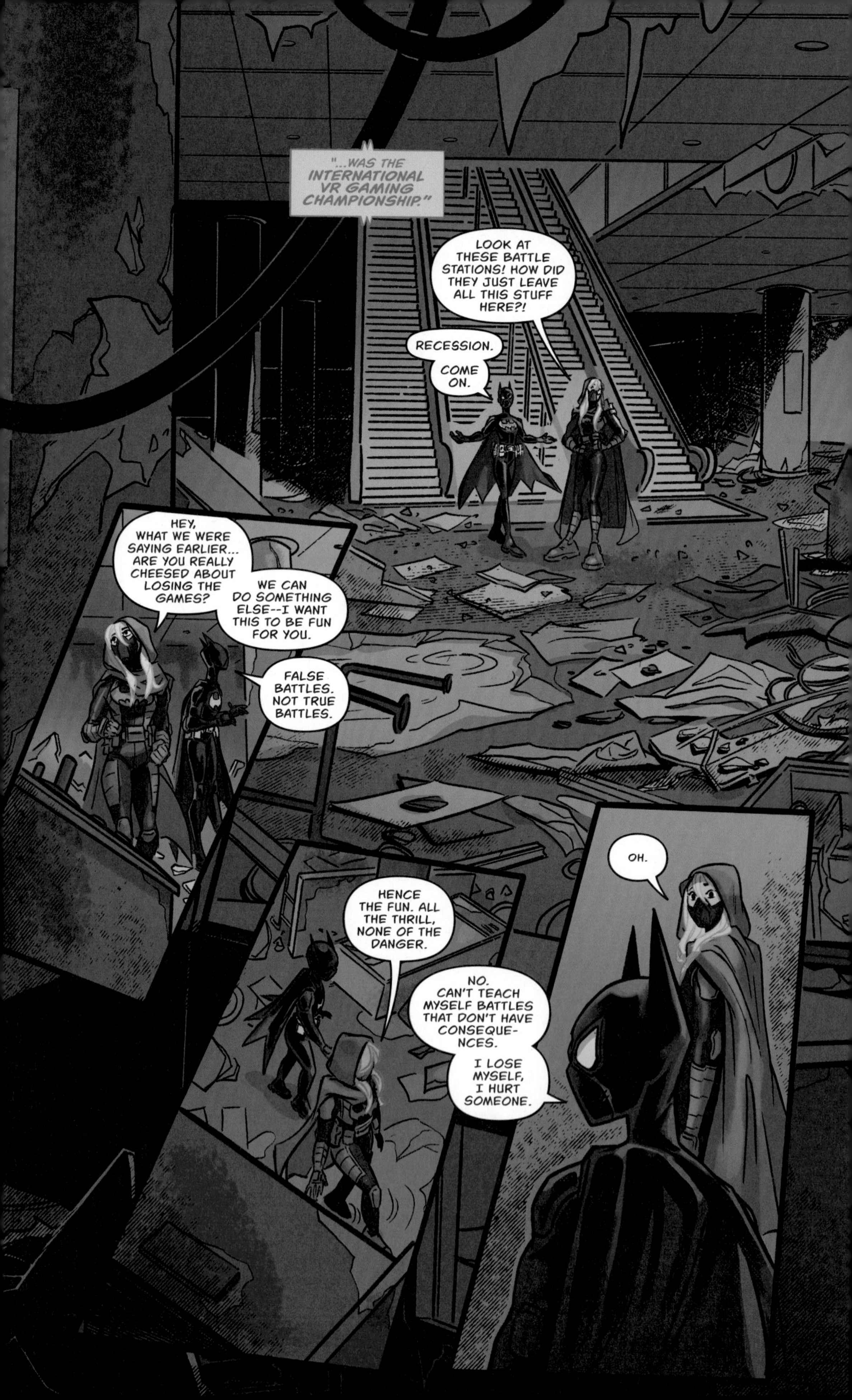
"...WAS THE INTERNATIONAL VR GAMING CHAMPIONSHIP."
LOOK AT THESE BATTLE STATIONS! HOW DID THEY JUST LEAVE ALL THIS STUFF HERE?!
RECESSION.
COME ON.
HEY, WHAT WE WERE SAYING EARLIER... ARE YOU REALLY CHEESED ABOUT LOSING THE GAMES?
WE CAN DO SOMETHING ELSE--I WANT THIS TO BE FUN FOR YOU.
FALSE BATTLES. NOT TRUE BATTLES.
HENCE THE FUN. ALL THE THRILL, NONE OF THE DANGER.
NO. CAN'T TEACH MYSELF BATTLES THAT DON'T HAVE CONSEQUE-NCES.
I LOSE MYSELF, I HURT SOMEONE.
OH.

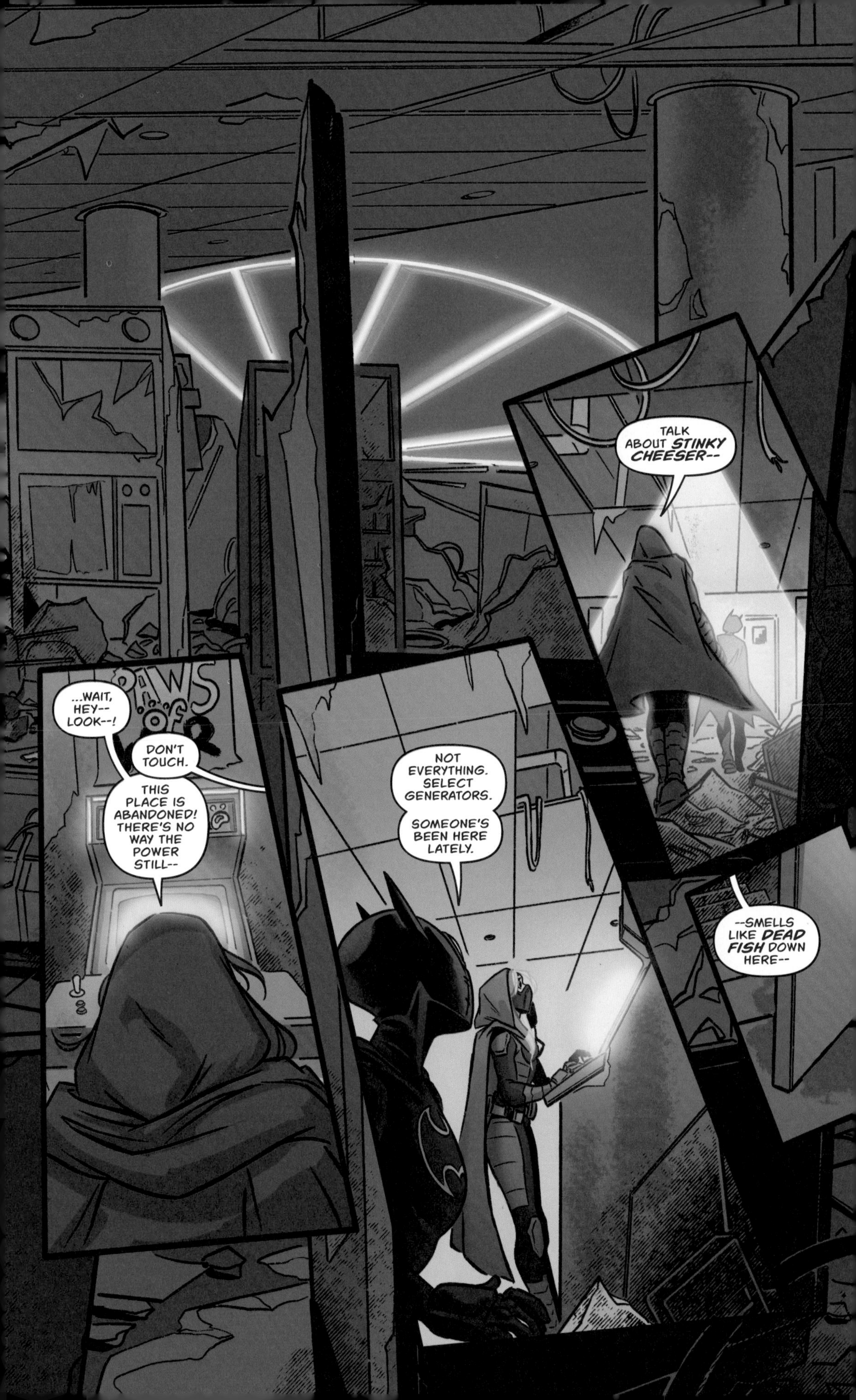
...WAIT, HEY-- LOOK--!
DON'T TOUCH.
THIS PLACE IS ABANDONED! THERE'S NO WAY THE POWER STILL--
NOT EVERYTHING. SELECT GENERATORS.
SOMEONE'S BEEN HERE LATELY.
TALK ABOUT ***STINKY CHEESER***--
--SMELLS LIKE ***DEAD FISH*** DOWN HERE--

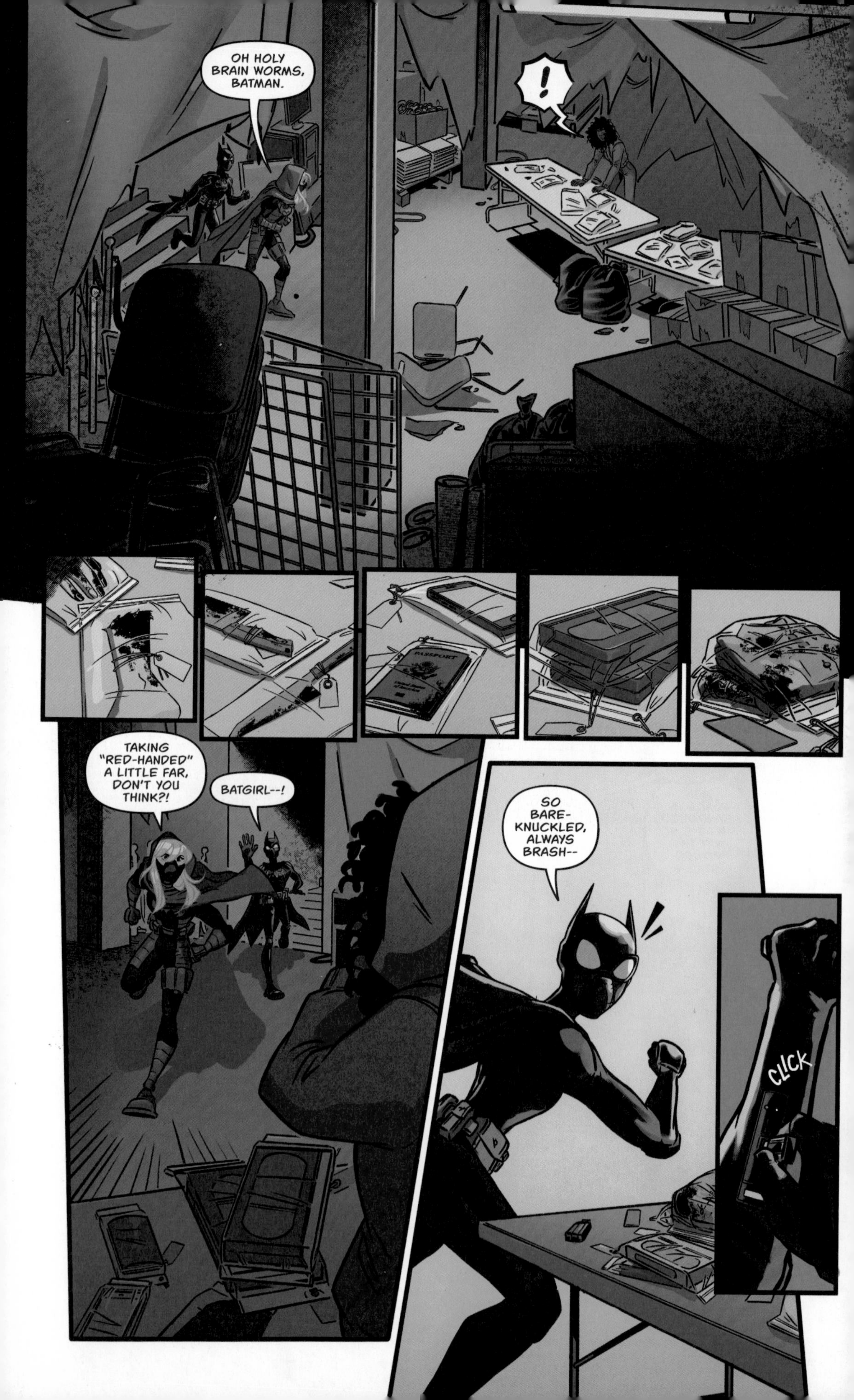
OH HOLY BRAIN WORMS, BATMAN.
!
TAKING "RED-HANDED" A LITTLE FAR, DON'T YOU THINK?!
BATGIRL--!
SO BARE-KNUCKLED, ALWAYS BRASH--
CLICK

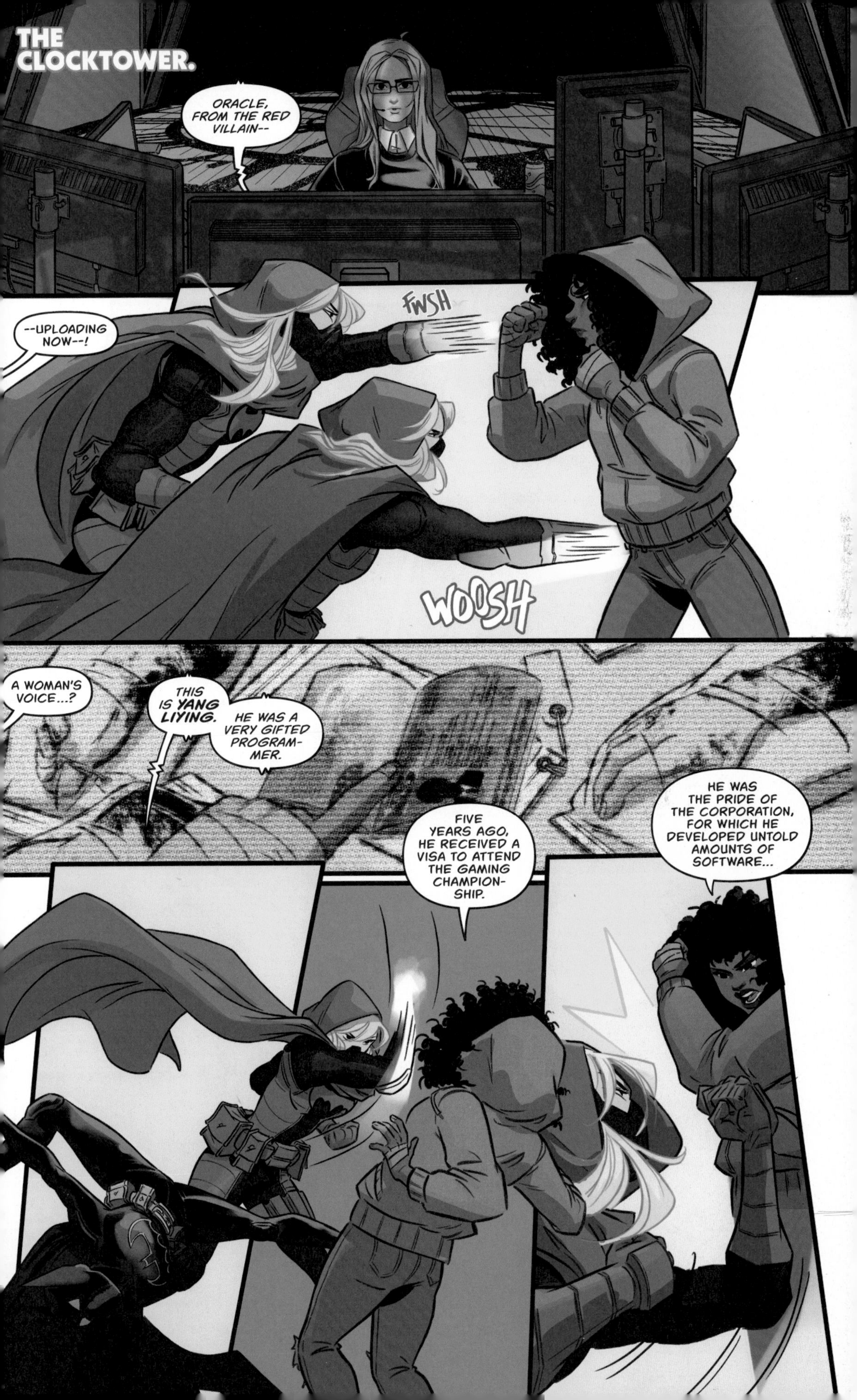
THE CLOCKTOWER.
ORACLE, FROM THE RED VILLAIN--
--UPLOADING NOW--!
FWSH
WOOSH
A WOMAN'S VOICE...?
THIS IS YANG LIYING.
HE WAS A VERY GIFTED PROGRAMMER.
FIVE YEARS AGO, HE RECEIVED A VISA TO ATTEND THE GAMING CHAMPIONSHIP.
HE WAS THE PRIDE OF THE CORPORATION, FOR WHICH HE DEVELOPED UNTOLD AMOUNTS OF SOFTWARE...

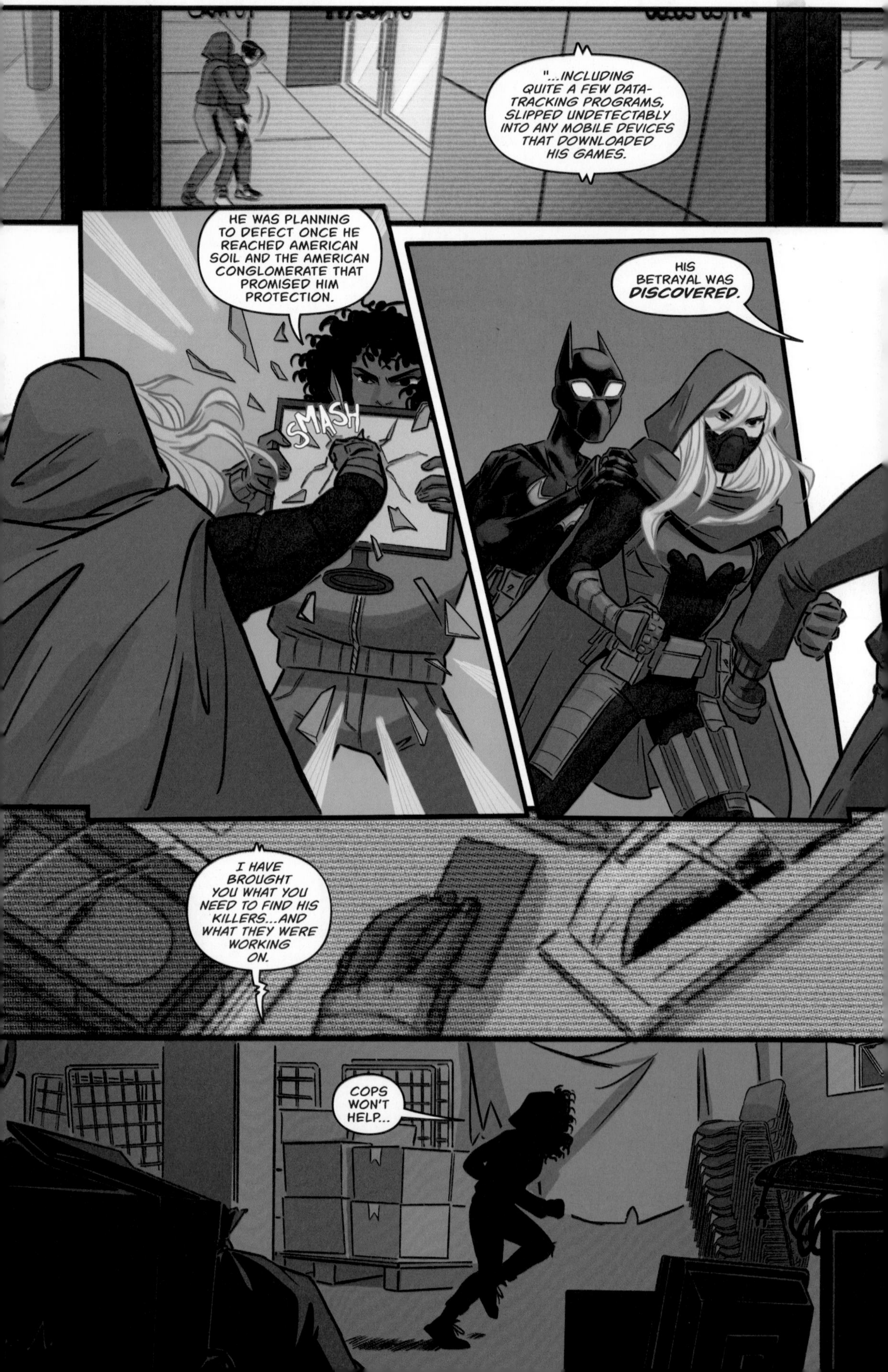
"...INCLUDING QUITE A FEW DATA-TRACKING PROGRAMS, SLIPPED UNDETECTABLY INTO ANY MOBILE DEVICES THAT DOWNLOADED HIS GAMES.
HE WAS PLANNING TO DEFECT ONCE HE REACHED AMERICAN SOIL AND THE AMERICAN CONGLOMERATE THAT PROMISED HIM PROTECTION.
SMASH
HIS BETRAYAL WAS DISCOVERED.
I HAVE BROUGHT YOU WHAT YOU NEED TO FIND HIS KILLERS...AND WHAT THEY WERE WORKING ON.
COPS WON'T HELP...

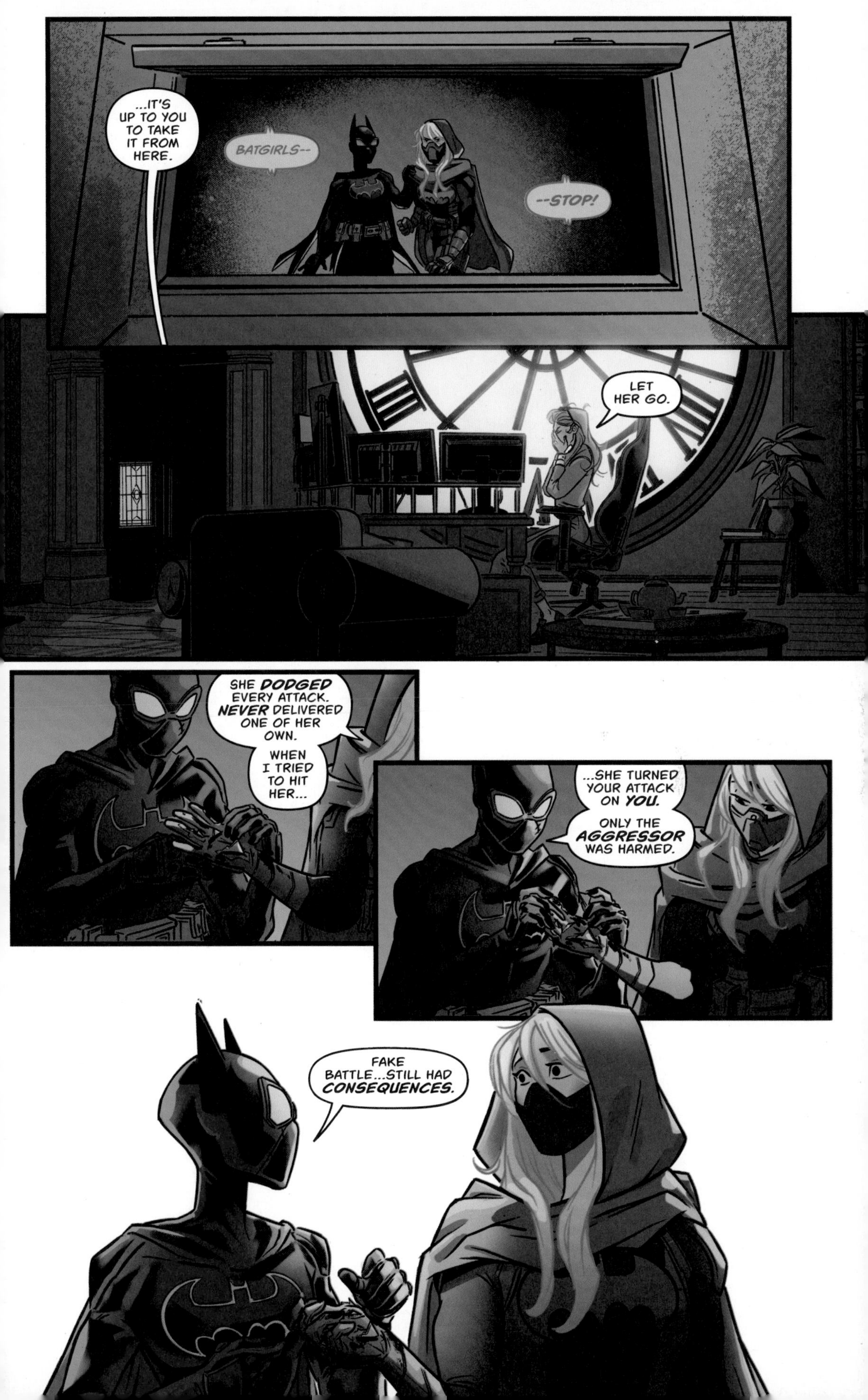

...IT'S UP TO YOU TO TAKE IT FROM HERE.
BATGIRLS--
--STOP!
LET HER GO.
SHE DODGED EVERY ATTACK. NEVER DELIVERED ONE OF HER OWN.
WHEN I TRIED TO HIT HER...
...SHE TURNED YOUR ATTACK ON YOU.
ONLY THE AGGRESSOR WAS HARMED.
FAKE BATTLE...STILL HAD CONSEQUENCES.

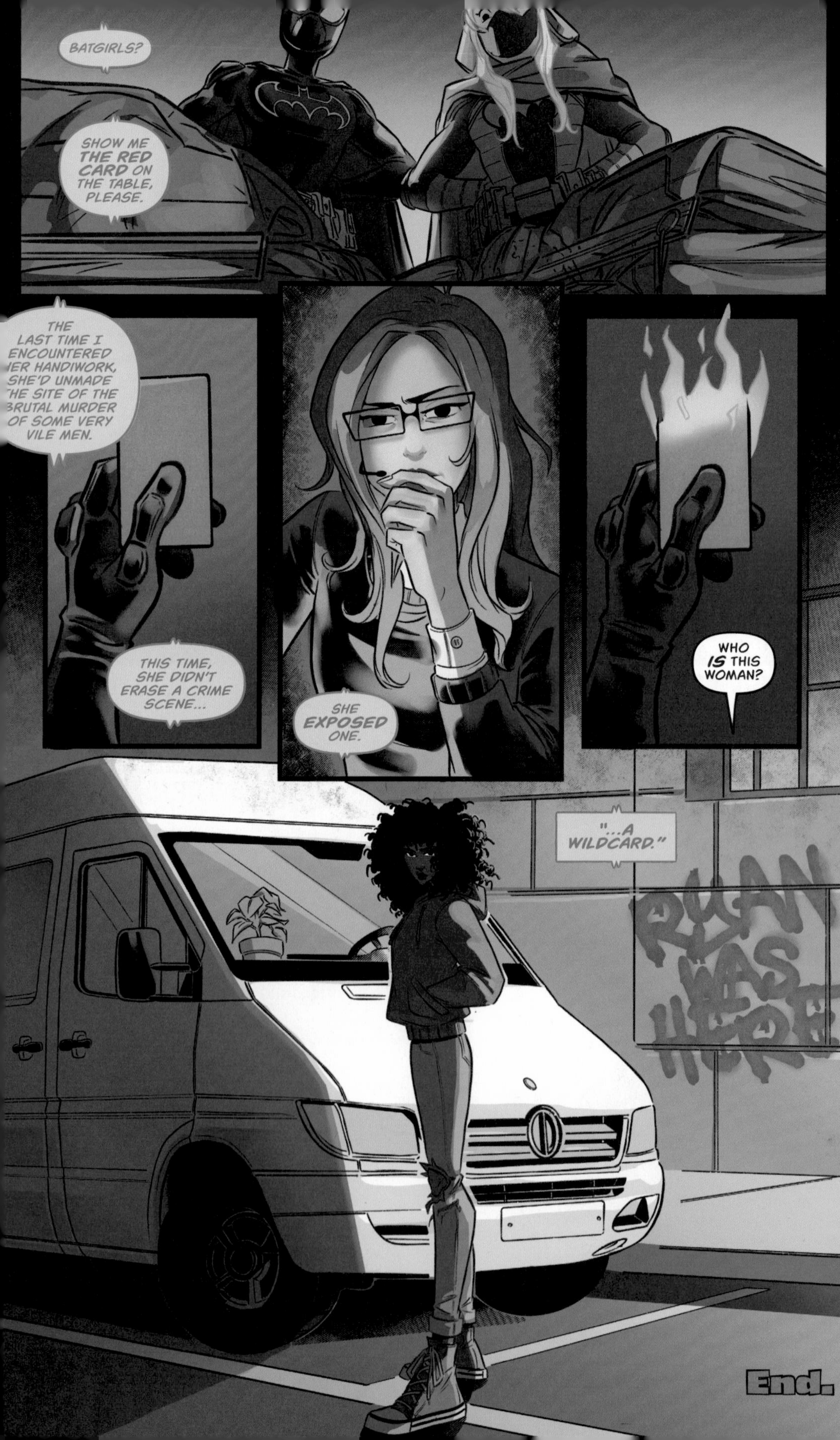
BATGIRLS?
SHOW ME THE RED CARD ON THE TABLE, PLEASE.
THE LAST TIME I ENCOUNTERED ER HANDIWORK, SHE'D UNMADE HE SITE OF THE BRUTAL MURDER OF SOME VERY VILE MEN.
THIS TIME, SHE DIDN'T ERASE A CRIME SCENE...
SHE EXPOSED ONE.
WHO IS THIS WOMAN?
"...A WILDCARD."
RYAN WAS HERE
End.

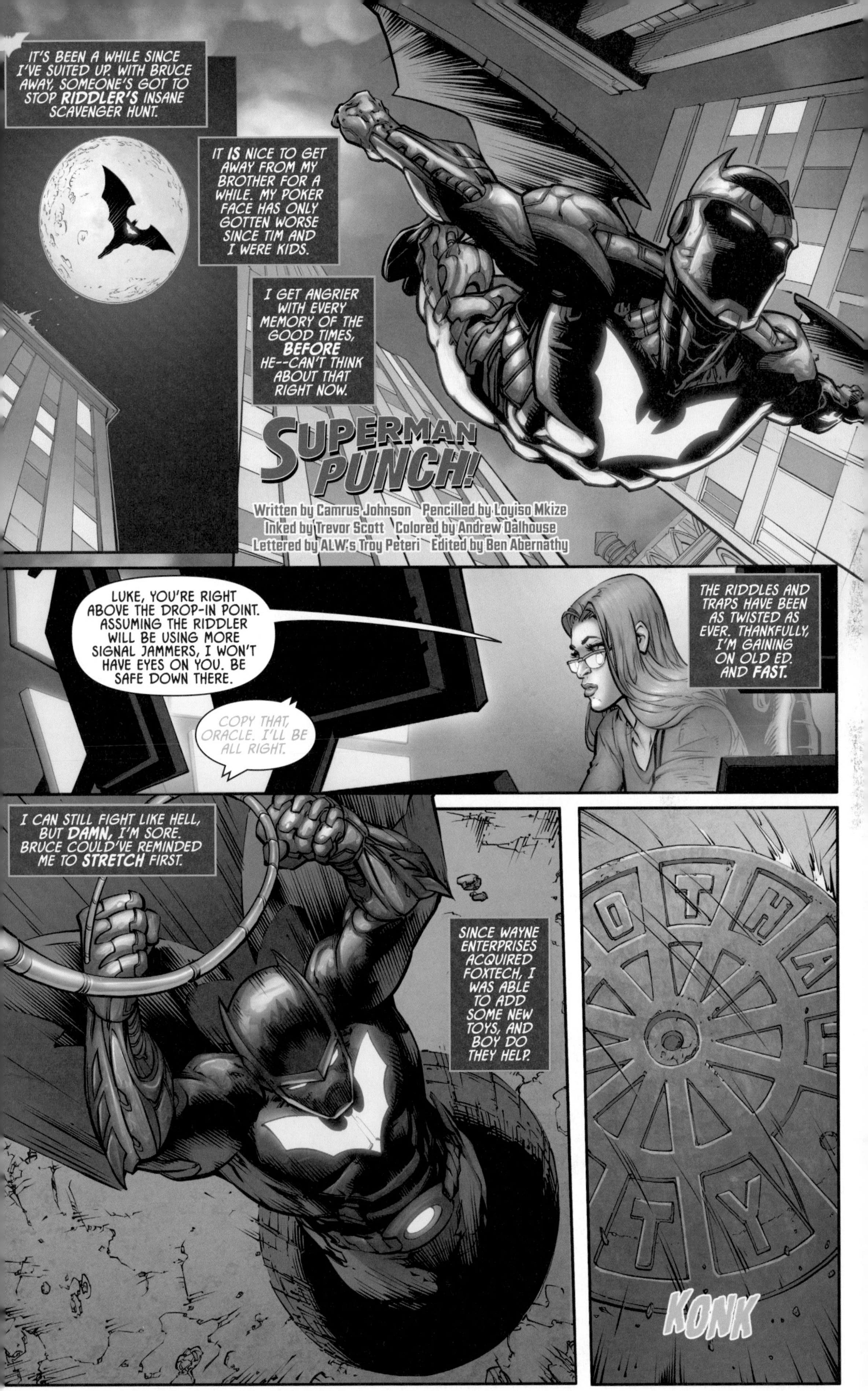
IT'S BEEN A WHILE SINCE I'VE SUITED UP. WITH BRUCE AWAY, SOMEONE'S GOT TO STOP RIDDLER'S INSANE SCAVENGER HUNT.
IT IS NICE TO GET AWAY FROM MY BROTHER FOR A WHILE. MY POKER FACE HAS ONLY GOTTEN WORSE SINCE TIM AND I WERE KIDS.
I GET ANGRIER WITH EVERY MEMORY OF THE GOOD TIMES, BEFORE HE--CAN'T THINK ABOUT THAT RIGHT NOW.
SUPERMAN PUNCH!
Written by Camrus Johnson Pencilled by Loyiso Mkize
Inked by Trevor Scott Colored by Andrew Dalhouse
Lettered by ALW's Troy Peteri Edited by Ben Abernathy
LUKE, YOU'RE RIGHT ABOVE THE DROP-IN POINT. ASSUMING THE RIDDLER WILL BE USING MORE SIGNAL JAMMERS, I WON'T HAVE EYES ON YOU. BE SAFE DOWN THERE.
THE RIDDLES AND TRAPS HAVE BEEN AS TWISTED AS EVER. THANKFULLY, I'M GAINING ON OLD ED. AND FAST.
COPY THAT, ORACLE. I'LL BE ALL RIGHT.
I CAN STILL FIGHT LIKE HELL, BUT DAMN, I'M SORE. BRUCE COULD'VE REMINDED ME TO STRETCH FIRST.
SINCE WAYNE ENTERPRISES ACQUIRED FOXTECH, I WAS ABLE TO ADD SOME NEW TOYS, AND BOY DO THEY HELP.
KONK

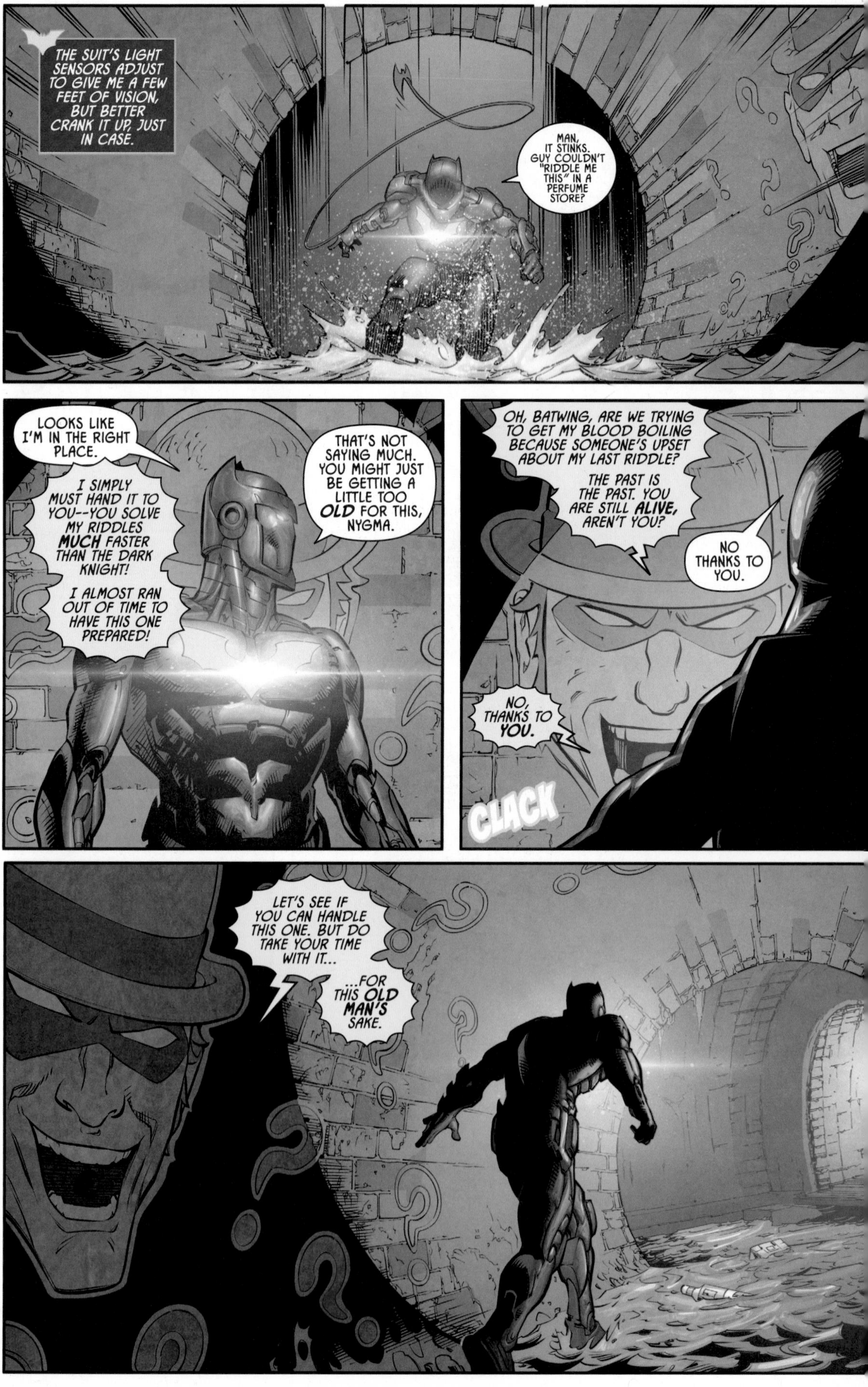
THE SUIT'S LIGHT SENSORS ADJUST TO GIVE ME A FEW FEET OF VISION, BUT BETTER CRANK IT UP, JUST IN CASE.
MAN, IT STINKS. GUY COULDN'T "RIDDLE ME THIS" IN A PERFUME STORE?
LOOKS LIKE I'M IN THE RIGHT PLACE.
I SIMPLY MUST HAND IT TO YOU--YOU SOLVE MY RIDDLES MUCH FASTER THAN THE DARK KNIGHT!
I ALMOST RAN OUT OF TIME TO HAVE THIS ONE PREPARED!
THAT'S NOT SAYING MUCH. YOU MIGHT JUST BE GETTING A LITTLE TOO OLD FOR THIS, NYGMA.
OH, BATWING, ARE WE TRYING TO GET MY BLOOD BOILING BECAUSE SOMEONE'S UPSET ABOUT MY LAST RIDDLE?
THE PAST IS THE PAST. YOU ARE STILL ALIVE, AREN'T YOU?
NO THANKS TO YOU.
NO, THANKS TO YOU.
CLACK
LET'S SEE IF YOU CAN HANDLE THIS ONE. BUT DO TAKE YOUR TIME WITH IT...
...FOR THIS OLD MAN'S SAKE.

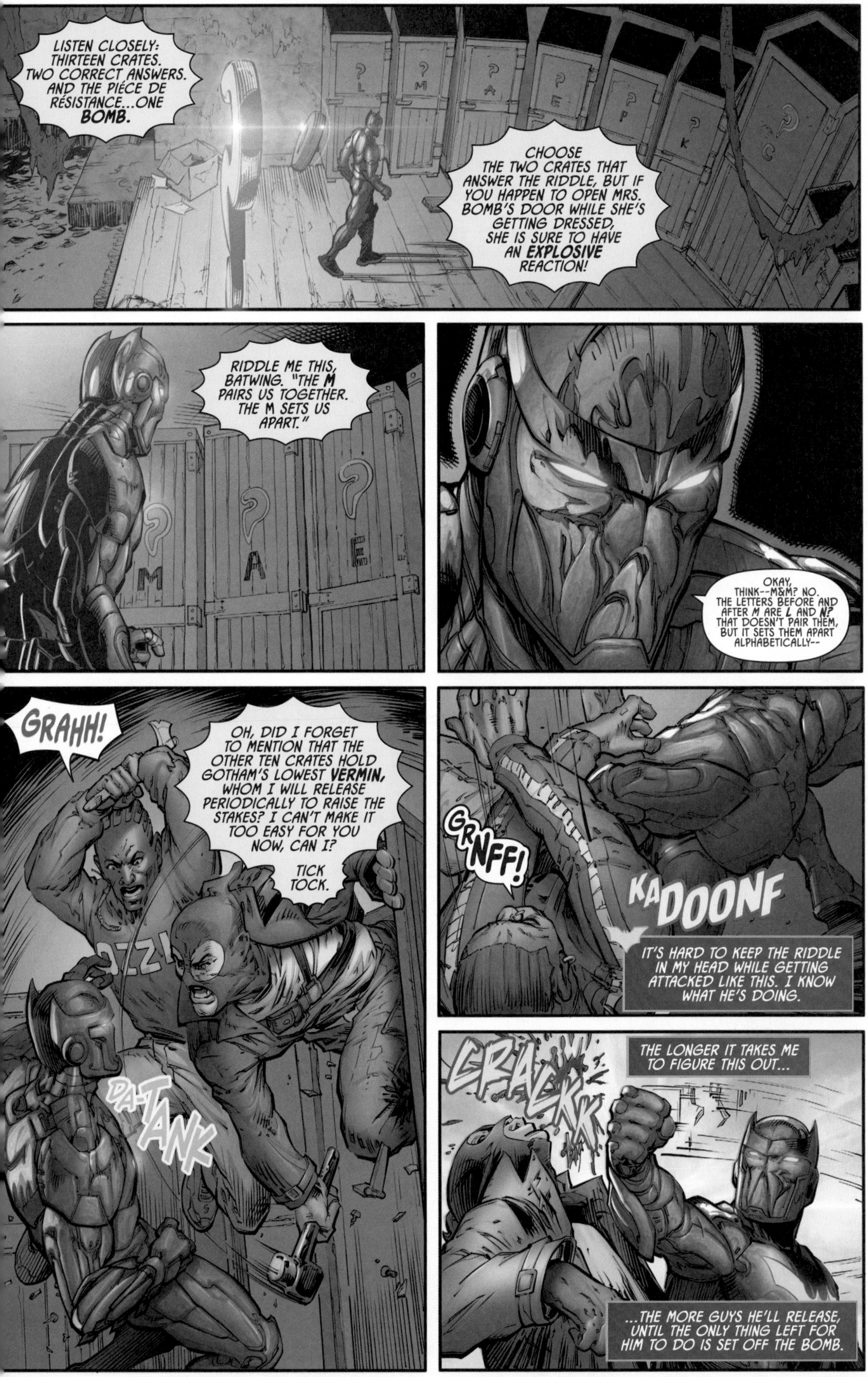

LISTEN CLOSELY: THIRTEEN CRATES. TWO CORRECT ANSWERS. AND THE PIÉCE DE RÉSISTANCE...ONE BOMB.
CHOOSE THE TWO CRATES THAT ANSWER THE RIDDLE, BUT IF YOU HAPPEN TO OPEN MRS. BOMB'S DOOR WHILE SHE'S GETTING DRESSED, SHE IS SURE TO HAVE AN EXPLOSIVE REACTION!
RIDDLE ME THIS, BATWING. "THE M PAIRS US TOGETHER. THE M SETS US APART."
OKAY, THINK--M&M? NO. THE LETTERS BEFORE AND AFTER M ARE L AND N? THAT DOESN'T PAIR THEM, BUT IT SETS THEM APART ALPHABETICALLY--
GRAHH!
OH, DID I FORGET TO MENTION THAT THE OTHER TEN CRATES HOLD GOTHAM'S LOWEST VERMIN, WHOM I WILL RELEASE PERIODICALLY TO RAISE THE STAKES? I CAN'T MAKE IT TOO EASY FOR YOU NOW, CAN I?
TICK TOCK.
DA-TANK
GRNFF!
KADOONF
IT'S HARD TO KEEP THE RIDDLE IN MY HEAD WHILE GETTING ATTACKED LIKE THIS. I KNOW WHAT HE'S DOING.
THE LONGER IT TAKES ME TO FIGURE THIS OUT...
CRACKK
...THE MORE GUYS HE'LL RELEASE, UNTIL THE ONLY THING LEFT FOR HIM TO DO IS SET OFF THE BOMB.

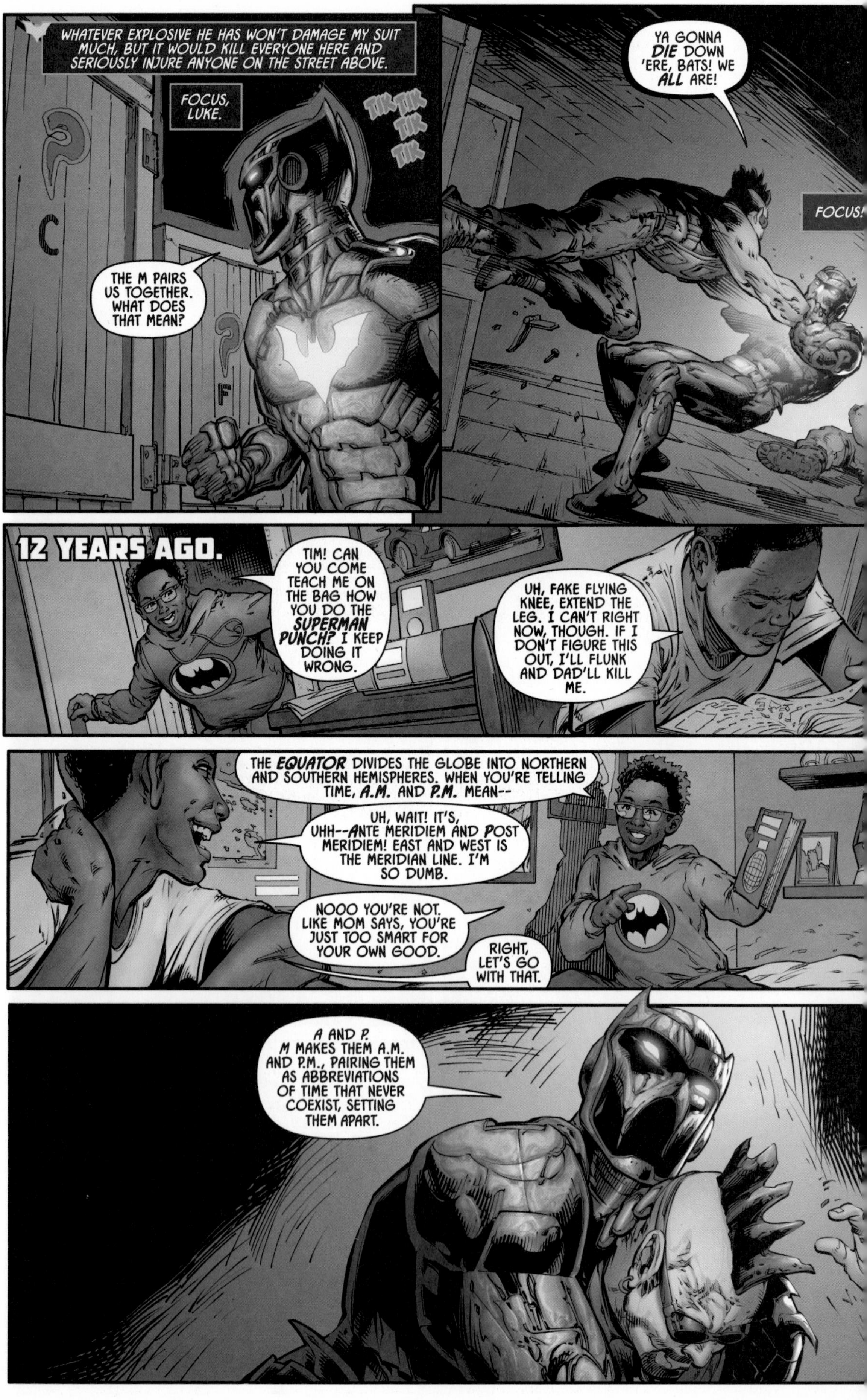

WHATEVER EXPLOSIVE HE HAS WON'T DAMAGE MY SUIT MUCH, BUT IT WOULD KILL EVERYONE HERE AND SERIOUSLY INJURE ANYONE ON THE STREET ABOVE.
FOCUS, LUKE.
TIK TIK TIK TIK
THE M PAIRS US TOGETHER. WHAT DOES THAT MEAN?
YA GONNA DIE DOWN 'ERE, BATS! WE ALL ARE!
FOCUS!
12 YEARS AGO.
TIM! CAN YOU COME TEACH ME ON THE BAG HOW YOU DO THE SUPERMAN PUNCH? I KEEP DOING IT WRONG.
UH, FAKE FLYING KNEE, EXTEND THE LEG. I CAN'T RIGHT NOW, THOUGH. IF I DON'T FIGURE THIS OUT, I'LL FLUNK AND DAD'LL KILL ME.
THE EQUATOR DIVIDES THE GLOBE INTO NORTHERN AND SOUTHERN HEMISPHERES. WHEN YOU'RE TELLING TIME, A.M. AND P.M. MEAN--
UH, WAIT! IT'S, UHH--ANTE MERIDIEM AND POST MERIDIEM! EAST AND WEST IS THE MERIDIAN LINE. I'M SO DUMB.
NOOO YOU'RE NOT. LIKE MOM SAYS, YOU'RE JUST TOO SMART FOR YOUR OWN GOOD.
RIGHT, LET'S GO WITH THAT.
A AND P. M MAKES THEM A.M. AND P.M., PAIRING THEM AS ABBREVIATIONS OF TIME THAT NEVER COEXIST, SETTING THEM APART.

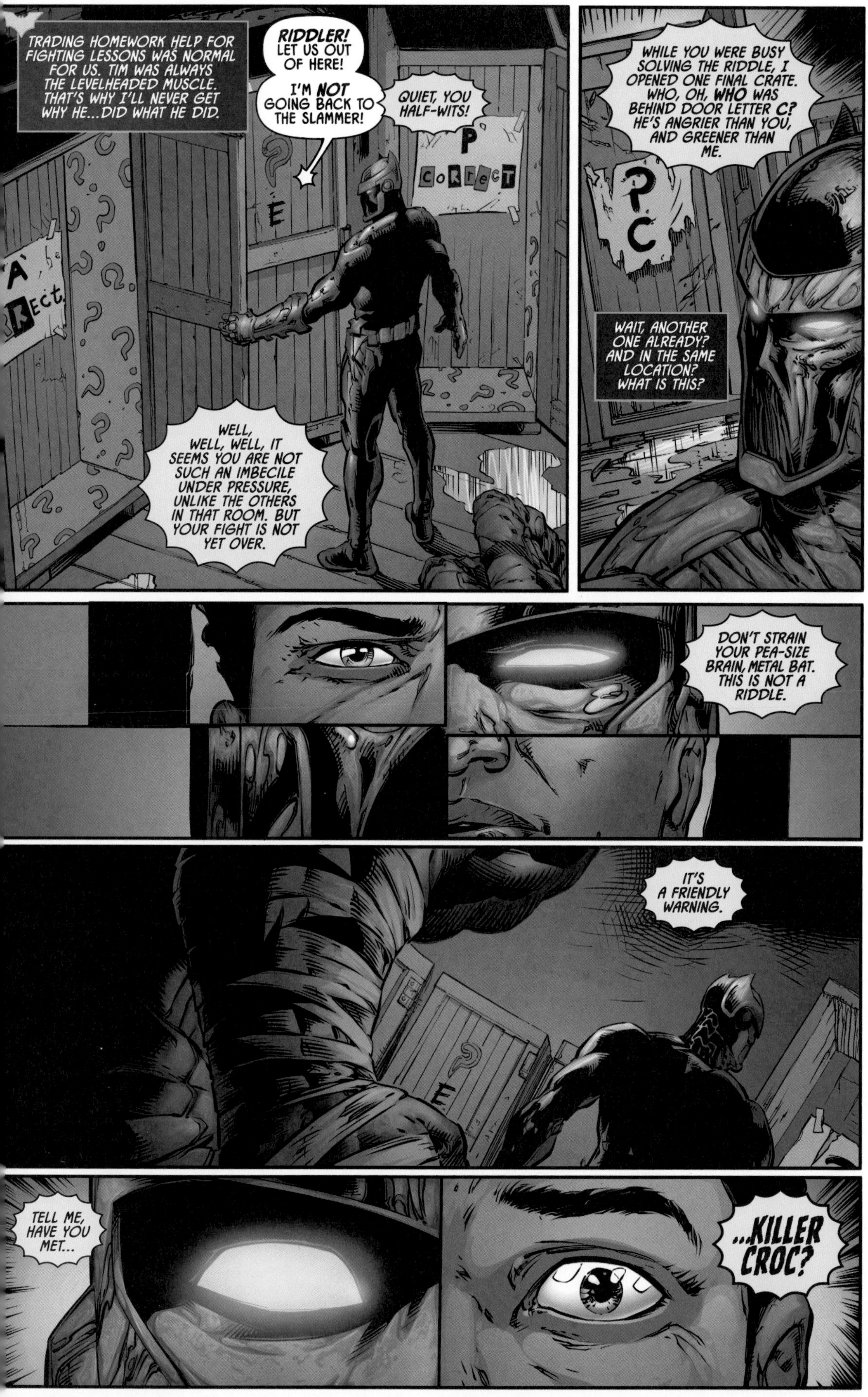
TRADING HOMEWORK HELP FOR FIGHTING LESSONS WAS NORMAL FOR US. TIM WAS ALWAYS THE LEVELHEADED MUSCLE. THAT'S WHY I'LL NEVER GET WHY HE...DID WHAT HE DID.
RIDDLER! LET US OUT OF HERE!
I'M NOT GOING BACK TO THE SLAMMER!
QUIET, YOU HALF-WITS!
P
CORRECT
E
WELL, WELL, WELL, IT SEEMS YOU ARE NOT SUCH AN IMBECILE UNDER PRESSURE, UNLIKE THE OTHERS IN THAT ROOM. BUT YOUR FIGHT IS NOT YET OVER.
WHILE YOU WERE BUSY SOLVING THE RIDDLE, I OPENED ONE FINAL CRATE. WHO, OH, WHO WAS BEHIND DOOR LETTER C? HE'S ANGRIER THAN YOU, AND GREENER THAN ME.
C
WAIT, ANOTHER ONE ALREADY? AND IN THE SAME LOCATION? WHAT IS THIS?
DON'T STRAIN YOUR PEA-SIZE BRAIN, METAL BAT. THIS IS NOT A RIDDLE.
IT'S A FRIENDLY WARNING.
E
TELL ME, HAVE YOU MET...
...KILLER CROC?

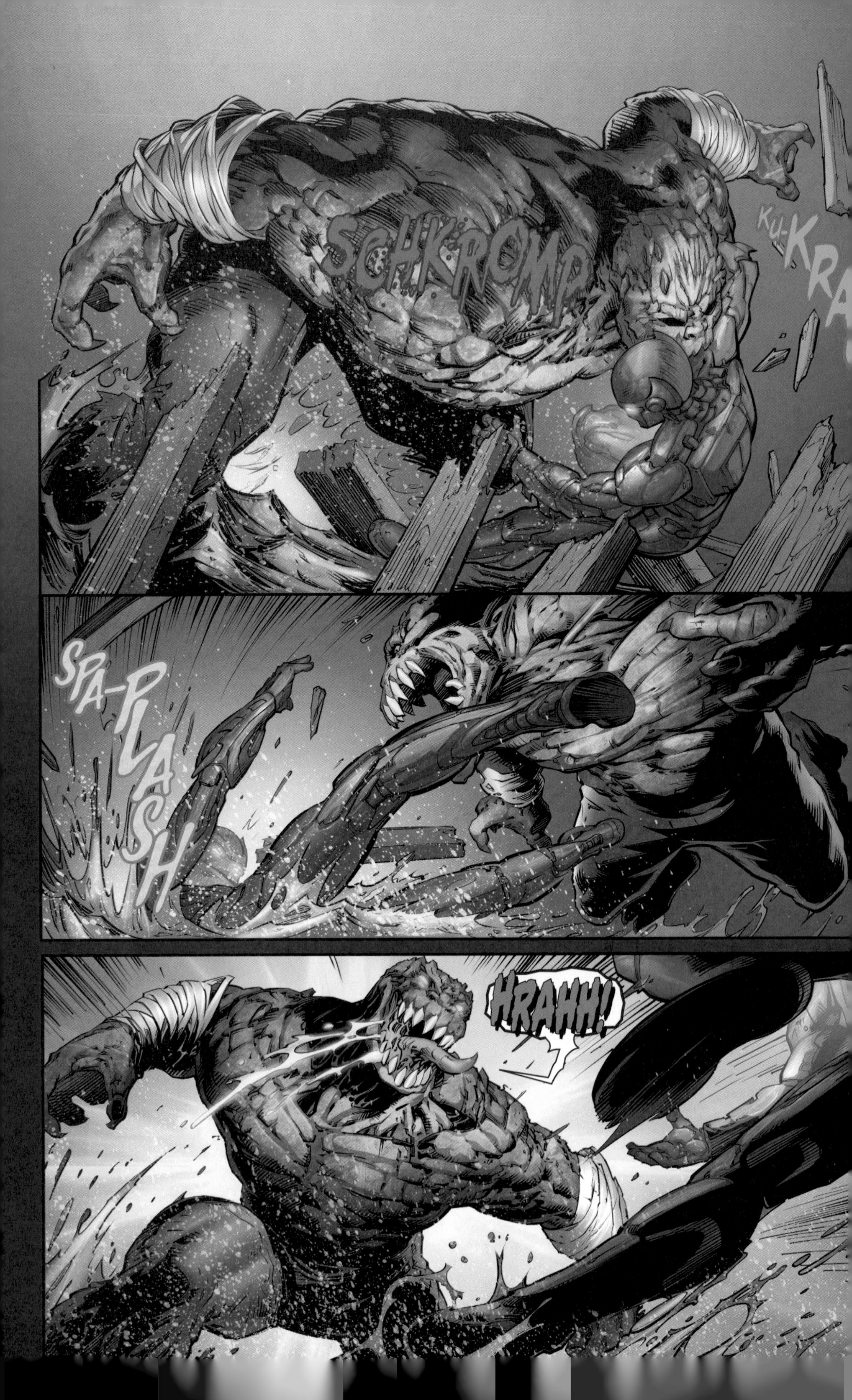
SCHKROMP
KU-KRA
SPA-PLASH
HRAHH!

DAMMIT. THOSE HEAVY HITS JUST RESET MY SYSTEM. UNTIL THE SUIT REBOOTS AND I CAN ADJUST THE ADAPTIVE BRIGHTNESS, I'M FIGHTING CROC BLIND. GOTTA STALL.

KILLER CROC WORKING FOR THE RIDDLER. *THERE'S* A TEAM-UP I WASN'T--

JUST LEAVE ME ALONE ALREADY!

HURR**UGH!**

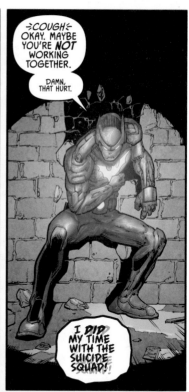

⸻COUGH⸻ OKAY. MAYBE YOU'RE *NOT* WORKING TOGETHER.

DAMN, THAT HURT.

I *DID* MY TIME WITH THE SUICIDE SQUAD!

AND EVERY TIME I TRY TO GET AWAY FROM THIS CRAP--

BLOOSH

--YOU DRAG ME BACK IN!

TINK
BA*TINK*

SO SINCE YOU WON'T LET UP--

--I'LL JUST HAVE TO TAKE YOU ALL OUT INSTEAD.

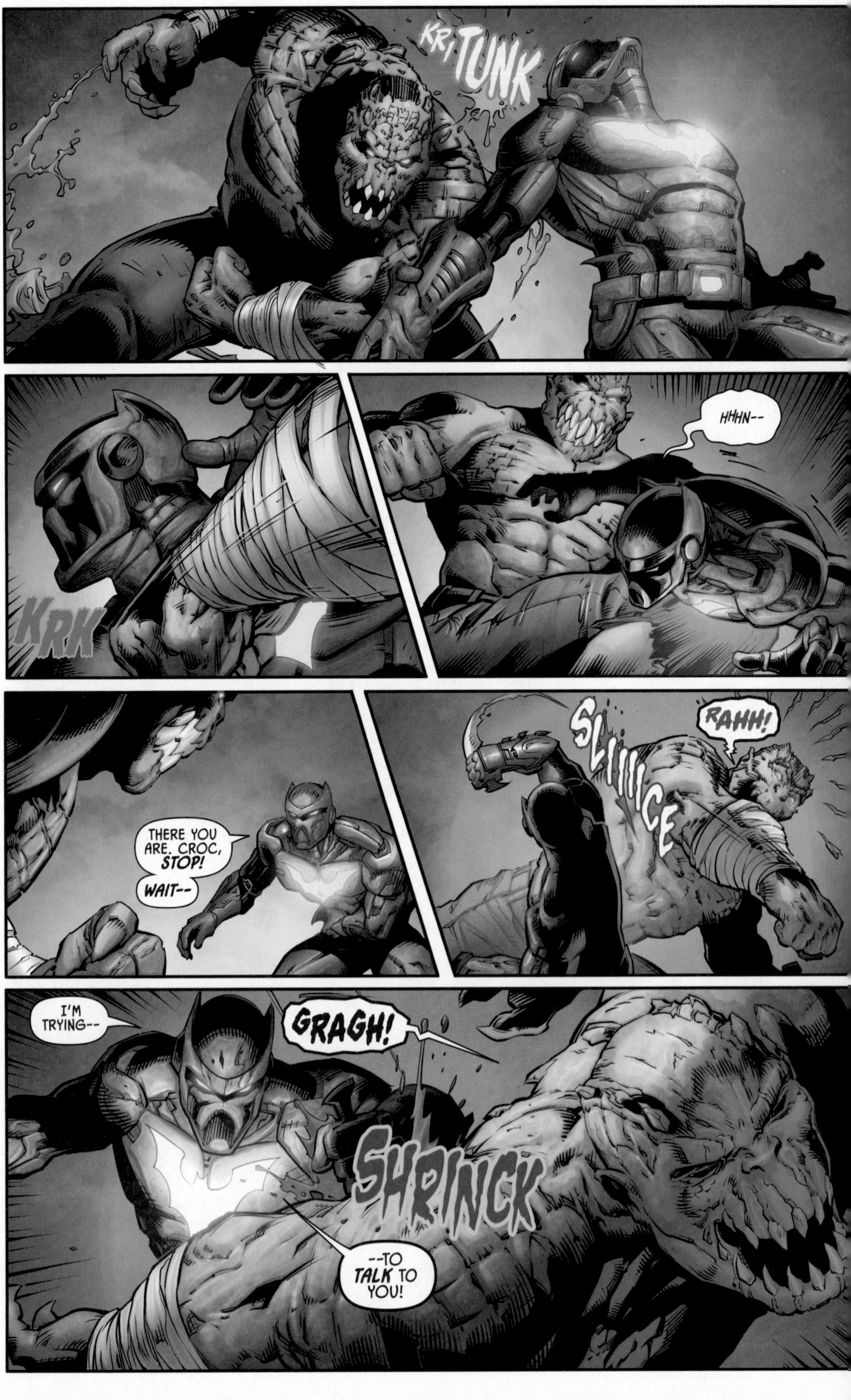
KRI TUNK
KRK
HHHN--
THERE YOU ARE. CROC, STOP!
WAIT--
SLIIIICE
RAHH!
I'M TRYING--
GRAGH!
SHRINCK
--TO TALK TO YOU!

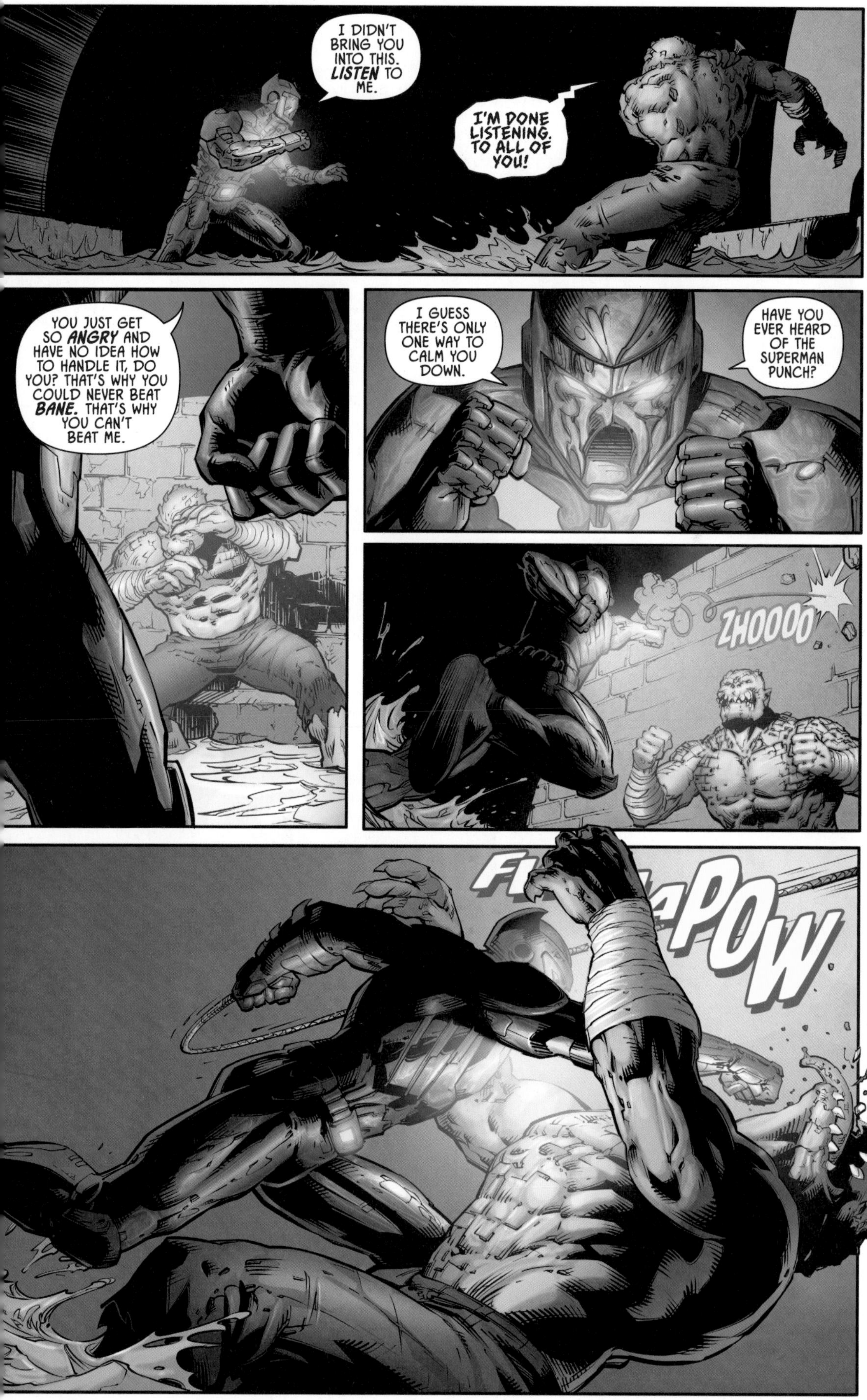

I DIDN'T BRING YOU INTO THIS. LISTEN TO ME.
I'M DONE LISTENING. TO ALL OF YOU!
YOU JUST GET SO ANGRY AND HAVE NO IDEA HOW TO HANDLE IT, DO YOU? THAT'S WHY YOU COULD NEVER BEAT BANE. THAT'S WHY YOU CAN'T BEAT ME.
I GUESS THERE'S ONLY ONE WAY TO CALM YOU DOWN.
HAVE YOU EVER HEARD OF THE SUPERMAN PUNCH?
ZHOOOO
APOW

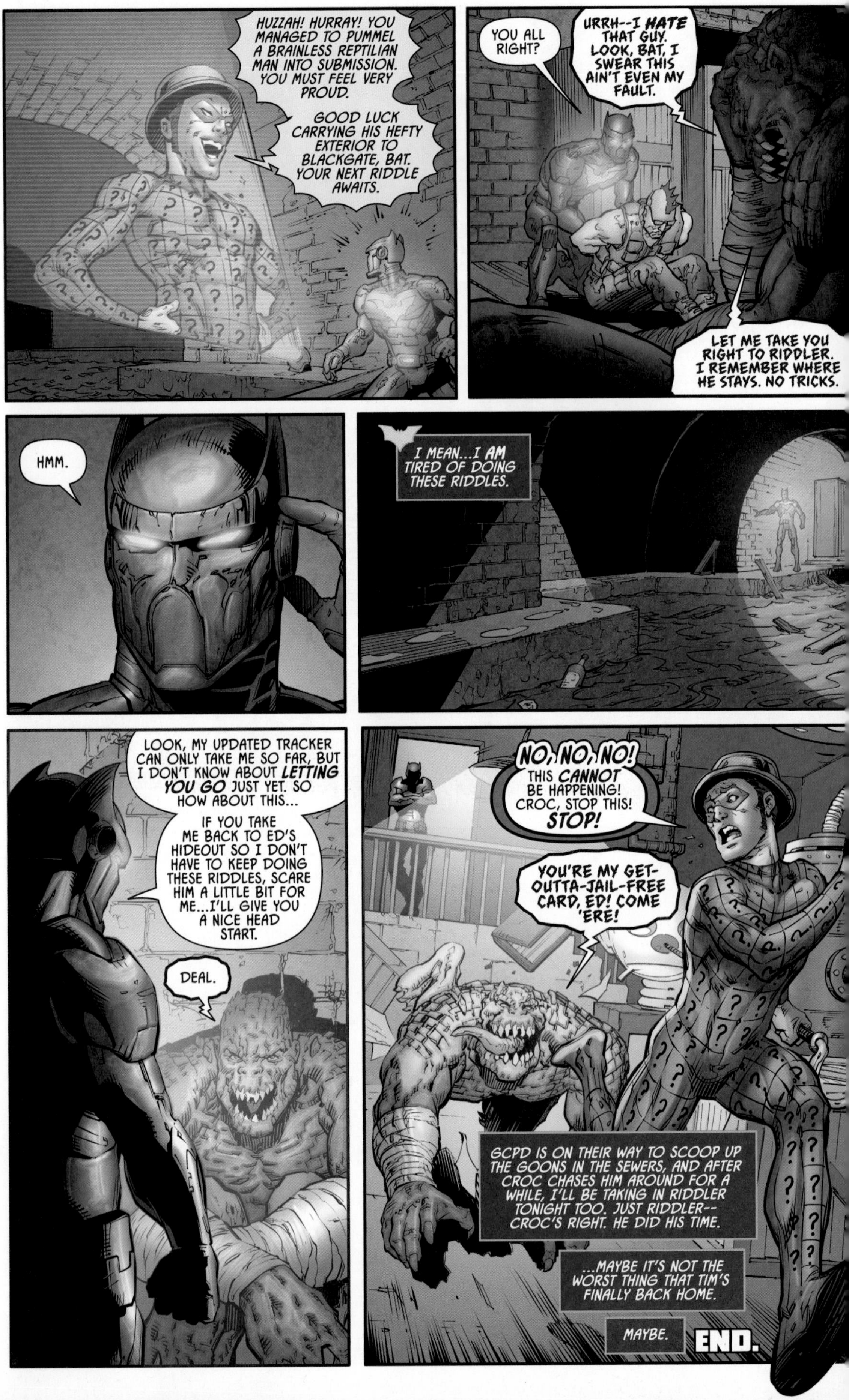
HUZZAH! HURRAY! YOU MANAGED TO PUMMEL A BRAINLESS REPTILIAN MAN INTO SUBMISSION. YOU MUST FEEL VERY PROUD.
GOOD LUCK CARRYING HIS HEFTY EXTERIOR TO BLACKGATE, BAT. YOUR NEXT RIDDLE AWAITS.
YOU ALL RIGHT?
URRH--I HATE THAT GUY. LOOK, BAT, I SWEAR THIS AIN'T EVEN MY FAULT.
LET ME TAKE YOU RIGHT TO RIDDLER. I REMEMBER WHERE HE STAYS. NO TRICKS.
HMM.
I MEAN...I AM TIRED OF DOING THESE RIDDLES.
LOOK, MY UPDATED TRACKER CAN ONLY TAKE ME SO FAR, BUT I DON'T KNOW ABOUT LETTING YOU GO JUST YET. SO HOW ABOUT THIS...
IF YOU TAKE ME BACK TO ED'S HIDEOUT SO I DON'T HAVE TO KEEP DOING THESE RIDDLES, SCARE HIM A LITTLE BIT FOR ME...I'LL GIVE YOU A NICE HEAD START.
DEAL.
NO, NO, NO! THIS CANNOT BE HAPPENING! CROC, STOP THIS! STOP!
YOU'RE MY GET-OUTTA-JAIL-FREE CARD, ED! COME 'ERE!
GCPD IS ON THEIR WAY TO SCOOP UP THE GOONS IN THE SEWERS, AND AFTER CROC CHASES HIM AROUND FOR A WHILE, I'LL BE TAKING IN RIDDLER TONIGHT TOO. JUST RIDDLER--CROC'S RIGHT. HE DID HIS TIME.
...MAYBE IT'S NOT THE WORST THING THAT TIM'S FINALLY BACK HOME.
MAYBE.
END.

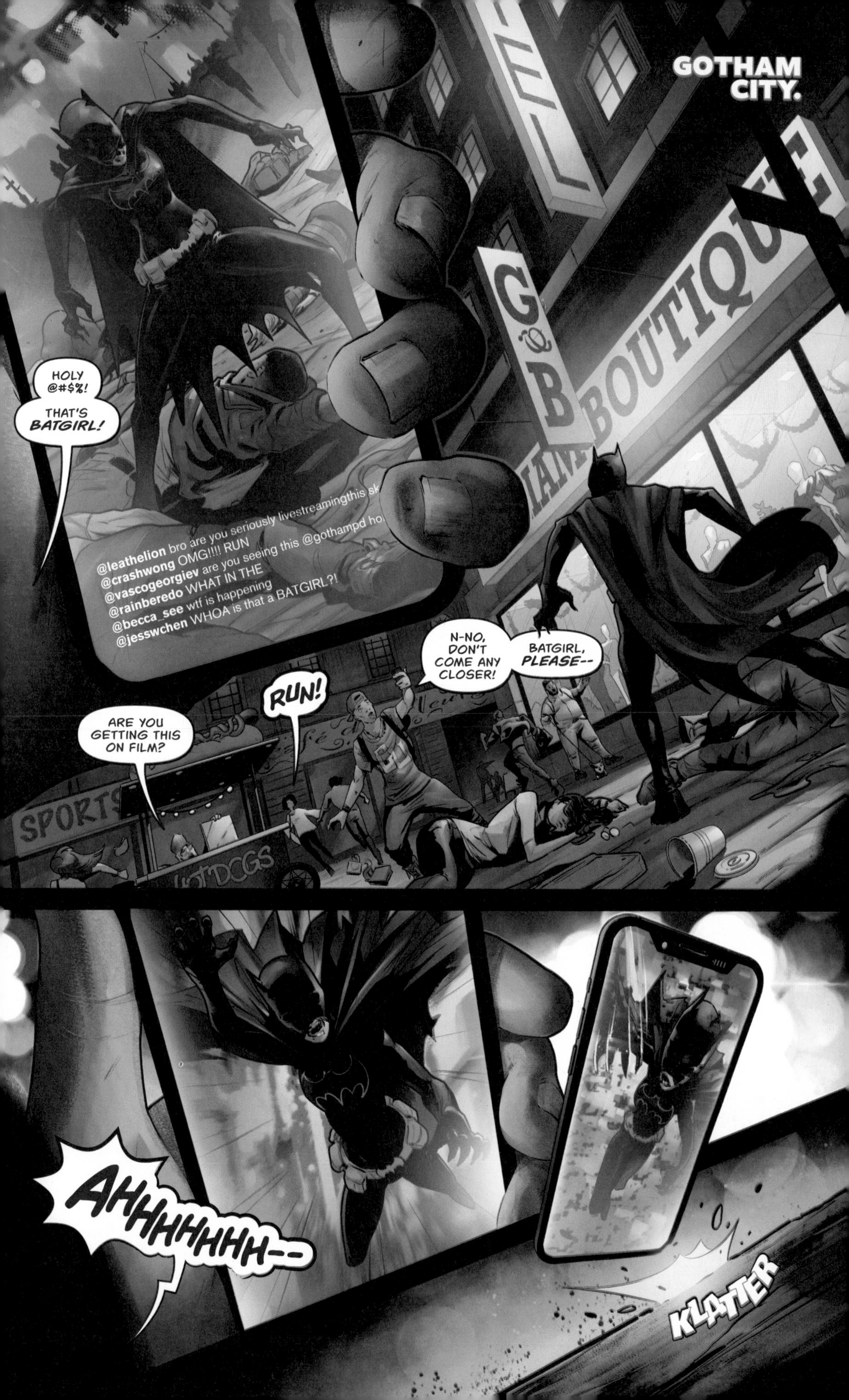
GOTHAM CITY.
HOLY @#$%! THAT'S BATGIRL!
@leathelion bro are you seriously livestreamingthis sk
@crashwong OMG!!!! RUN
@vascogeorgiev are you seeing this @gothampd ho
@rainberedo WHAT IN THE
@becca_see wtf is happening
@jesswchen WHOA is that a BATGIRL?!
N-NO, DON'T COME ANY CLOSER!
BATGIRL, PLEASE--
ARE YOU GETTING THIS ON FILM?
RUN!
AHHHHHHH--
KLATTER

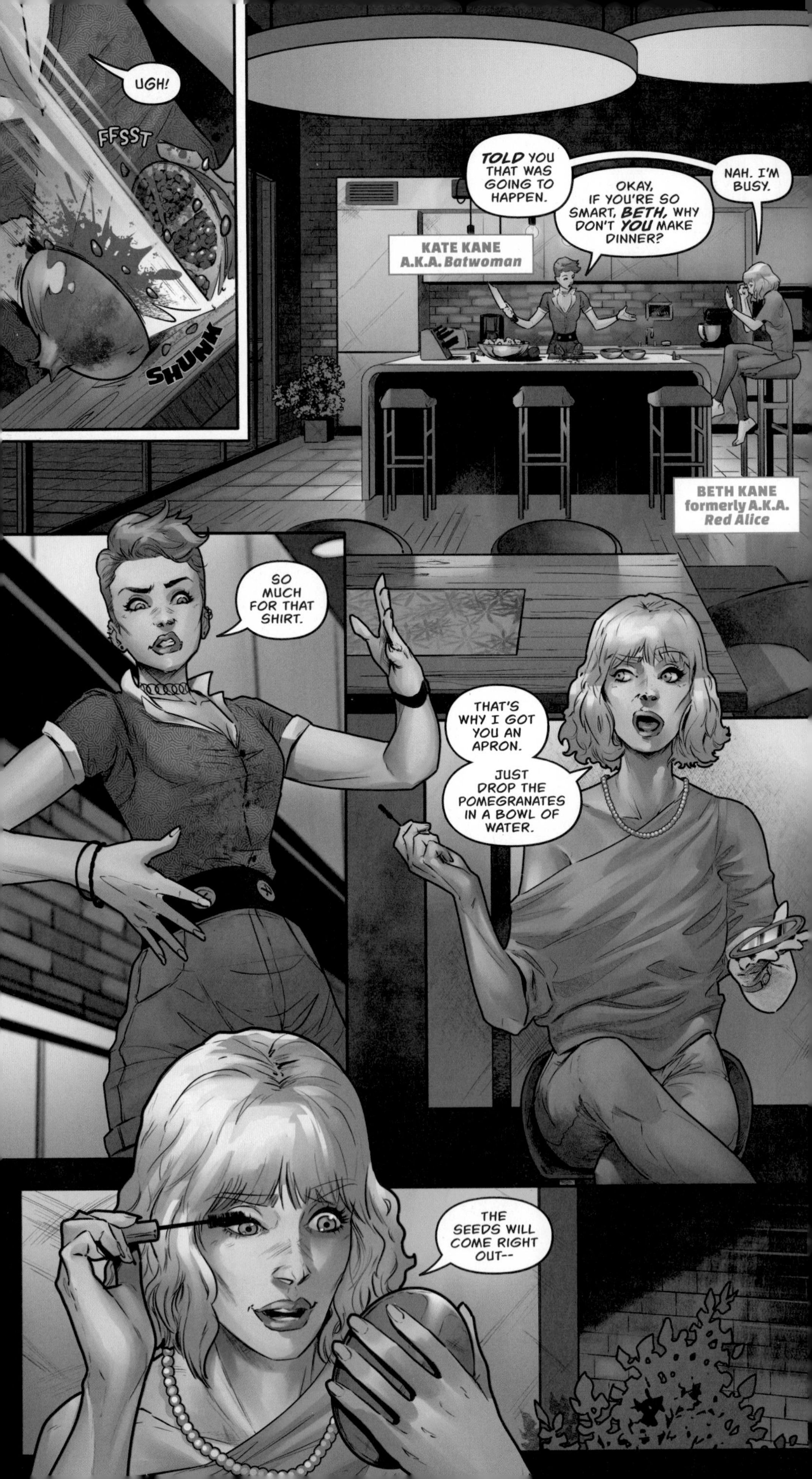
UGH!
FFSST
SHUNK
TOLD YOU THAT WAS GOING TO HAPPEN.
OKAY, IF YOU'RE SO SMART, BETH, WHY DON'T YOU MAKE DINNER?
NAH. I'M BUSY.
KATE KANE A.K.A. Batwoman
BETH KANE formerly A.K.A. Red Alice
SO MUCH FOR THAT SHIRT.
THAT'S WHY I GOT YOU AN APRON.
JUST DROP THE POMEGRANATES IN A BOWL OF WATER.
THE SEEDS WILL COME RIGHT OUT--

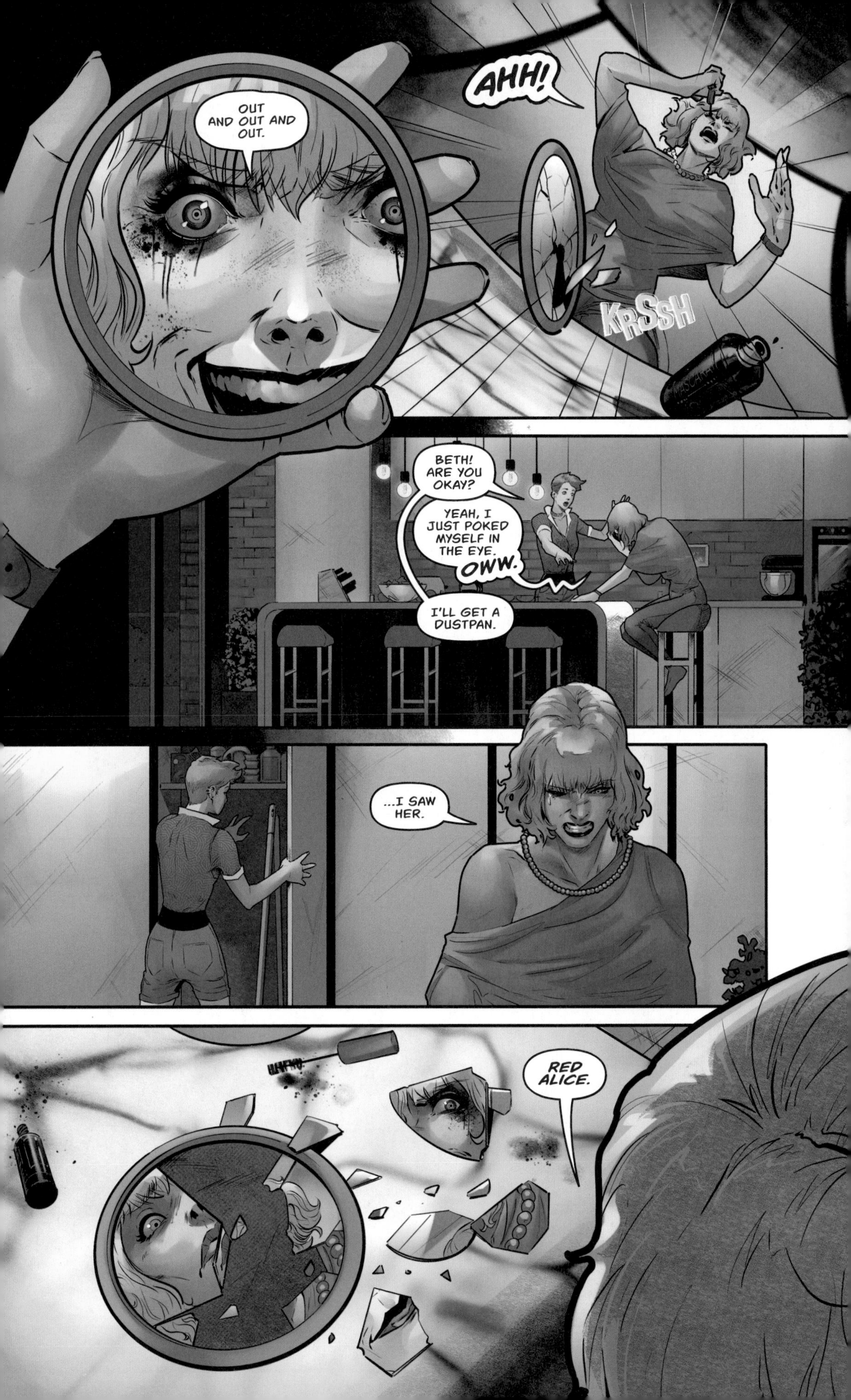
OUT AND OUT AND OUT.
AHH!
KRSSH
MASCARA
BETH! ARE YOU OKAY?
YEAH, I JUST POKED MYSELF IN THE EYE.
OWW.
I'LL GET A DUSTPAN.
...I SAW HER.
RED ALICE.

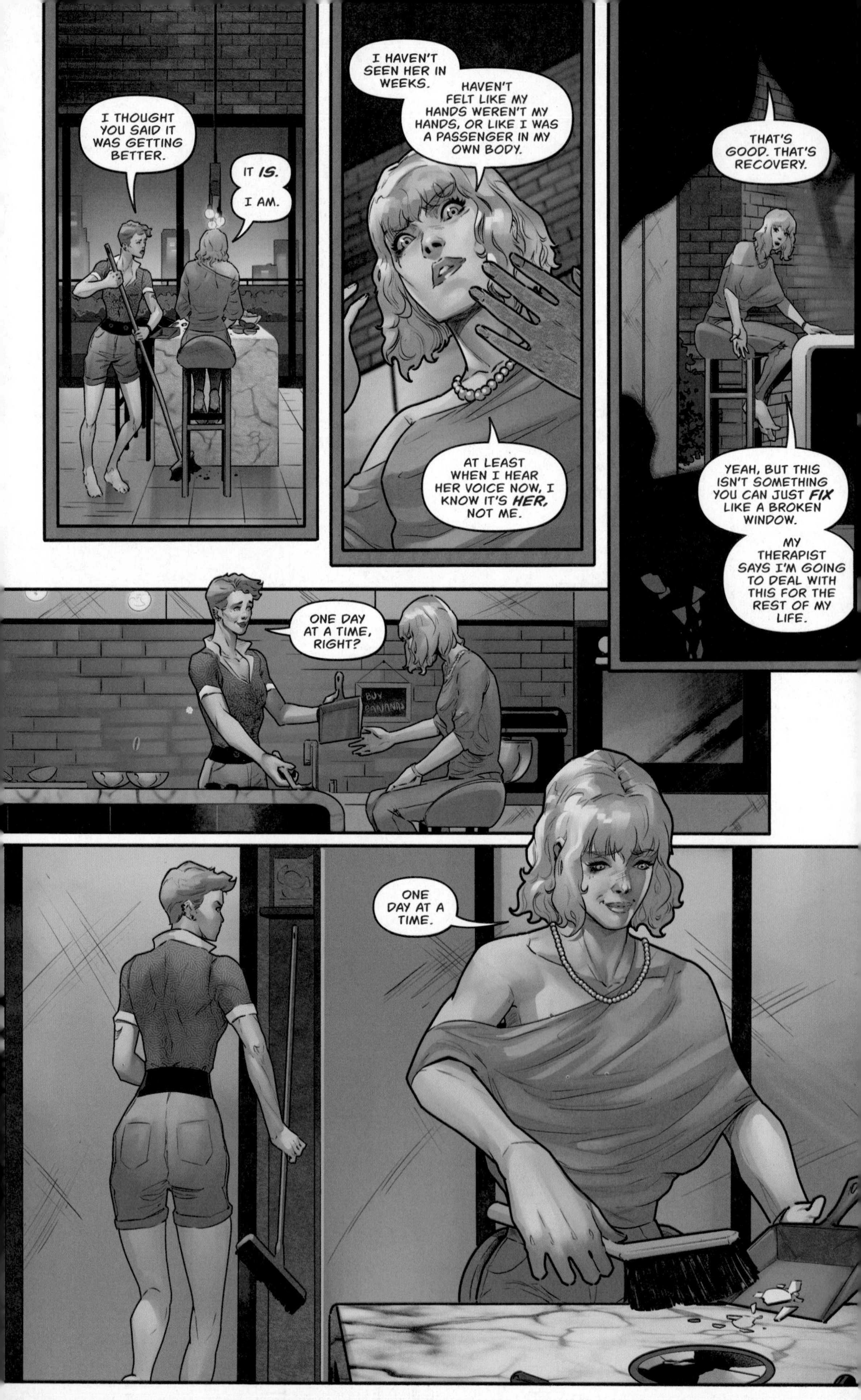
I THOUGHT YOU SAID IT WAS GETTING BETTER.
IT *IS.*
I AM.
I HAVEN'T SEEN HER IN WEEKS.
HAVEN'T FELT LIKE MY HANDS WEREN'T MY HANDS, OR LIKE I WAS A PASSENGER IN MY OWN BODY.
AT LEAST WHEN I HEAR HER VOICE NOW, I KNOW IT'S *HER,* NOT ME.
THAT'S GOOD. THAT'S RECOVERY.
YEAH, BUT THIS ISN'T SOMETHING YOU CAN JUST *FIX* LIKE A BROKEN WINDOW.
MY THERAPIST SAYS I'M GOING TO DEAL WITH THIS FOR THE REST OF MY LIFE.
ONE DAY AT A TIME, RIGHT?
BUY BANANAS
ONE DAY AT A TIME.

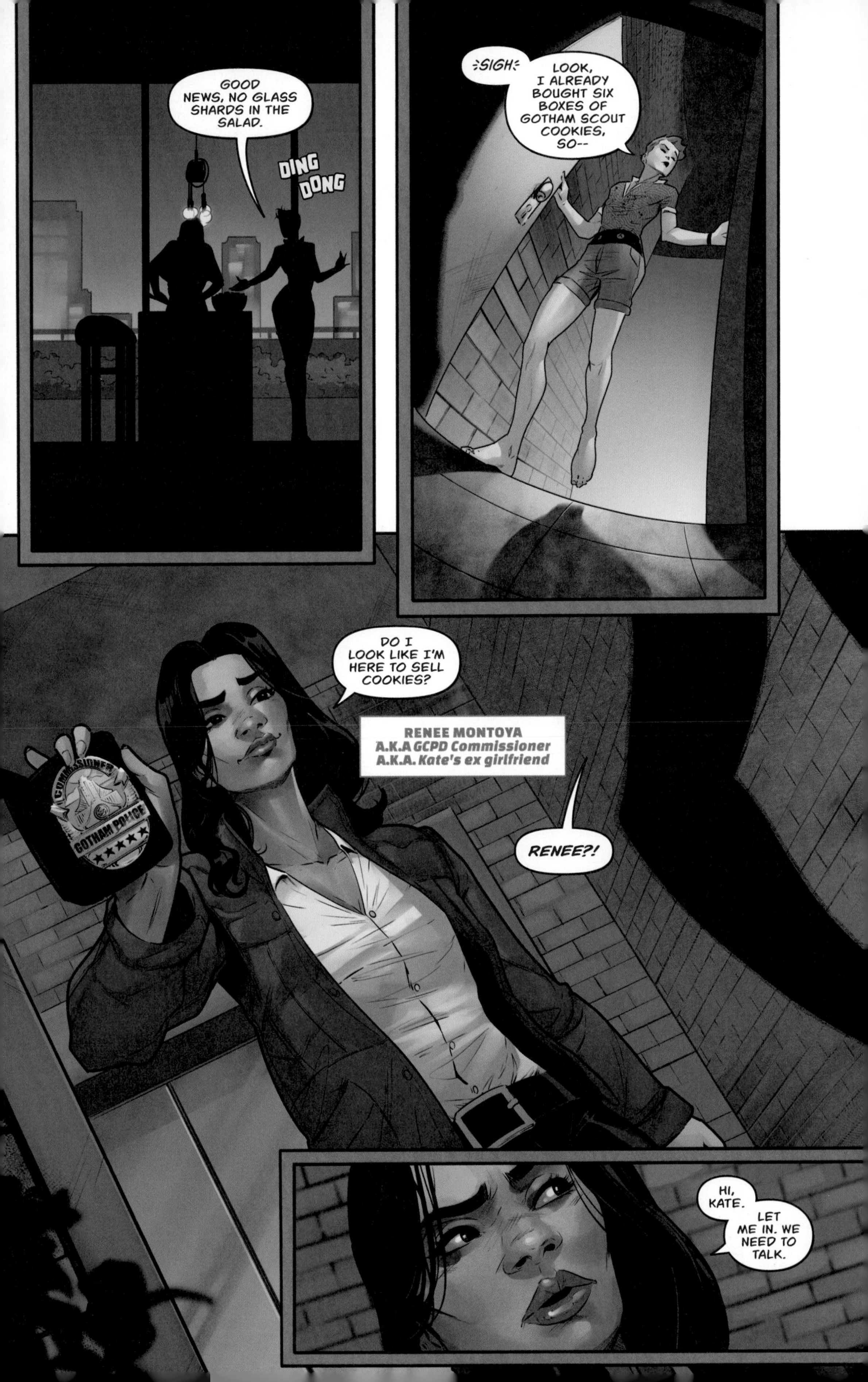
GOOD NEWS, NO GLASS SHARDS IN THE SALAD.
DING DONG
:SIGH:
LOOK, I ALREADY BOUGHT SIX BOXES OF GOTHAM SCOUT COOKIES, SO--
DO I LOOK LIKE I'M HERE TO SELL COOKIES?
RENEE MONTOYA
A.K.A GCPD Commissioner
A.K.A. Kate's ex girlfriend
RENEE?!
HI, KATE.
LET ME IN. WE NEED TO TALK.

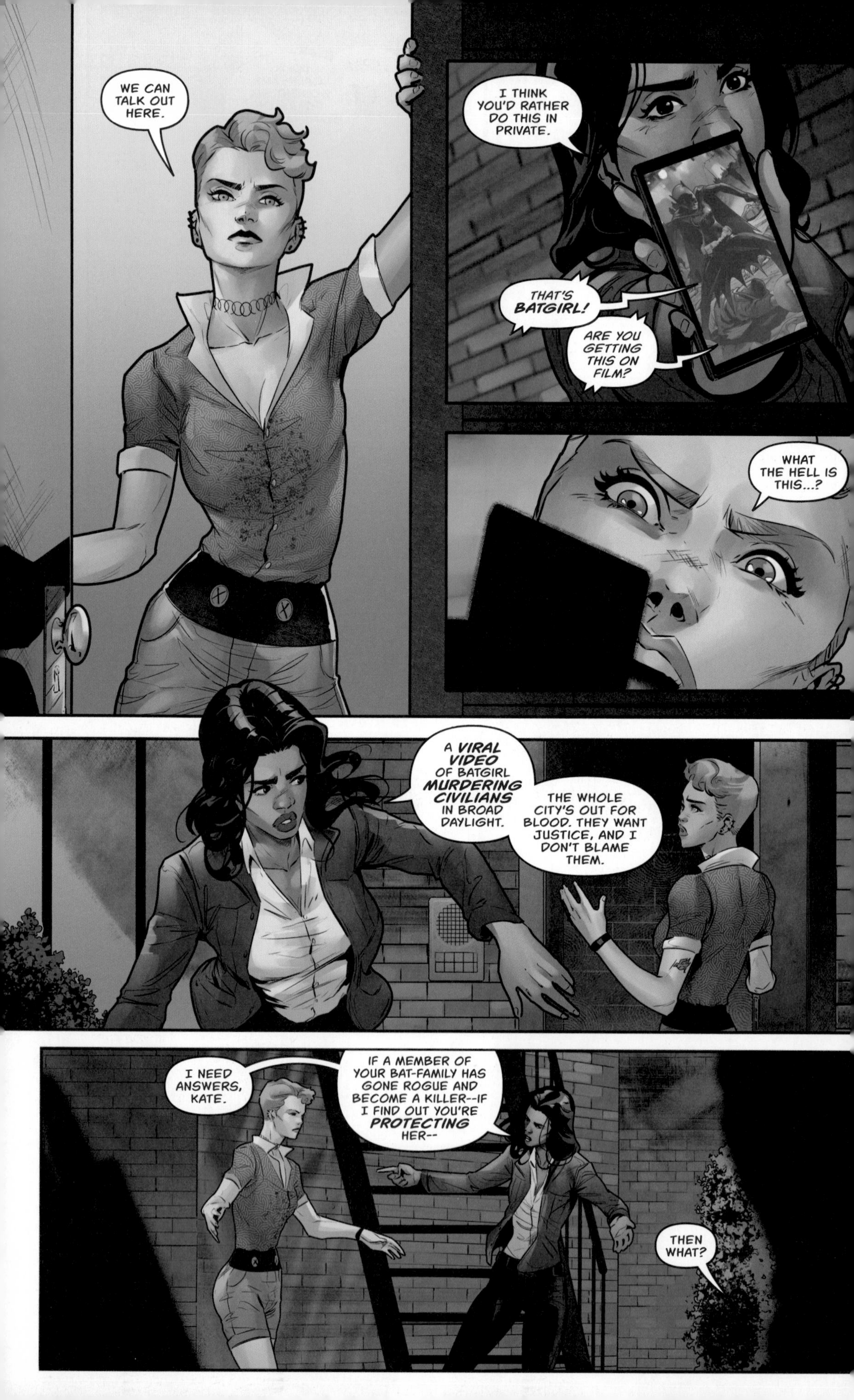
WE CAN TALK OUT HERE.
I THINK YOU'D RATHER DO THIS IN PRIVATE.
THAT'S BATGIRL!
ARE YOU GETTING THIS ON FILM?
WHAT THE HELL IS THIS...?
A VIRAL VIDEO OF BATGIRL MURDERING CIVILIANS IN BROAD DAYLIGHT.
THE WHOLE CITY'S OUT FOR BLOOD. THEY WANT JUSTICE, AND I DON'T BLAME THEM.
I NEED ANSWERS, KATE.
IF A MEMBER OF YOUR BAT-FAMILY HAS GONE ROGUE AND BECOME A KILLER--IF I FIND OUT YOU'RE PROTECTING HER--
THEN WHAT?

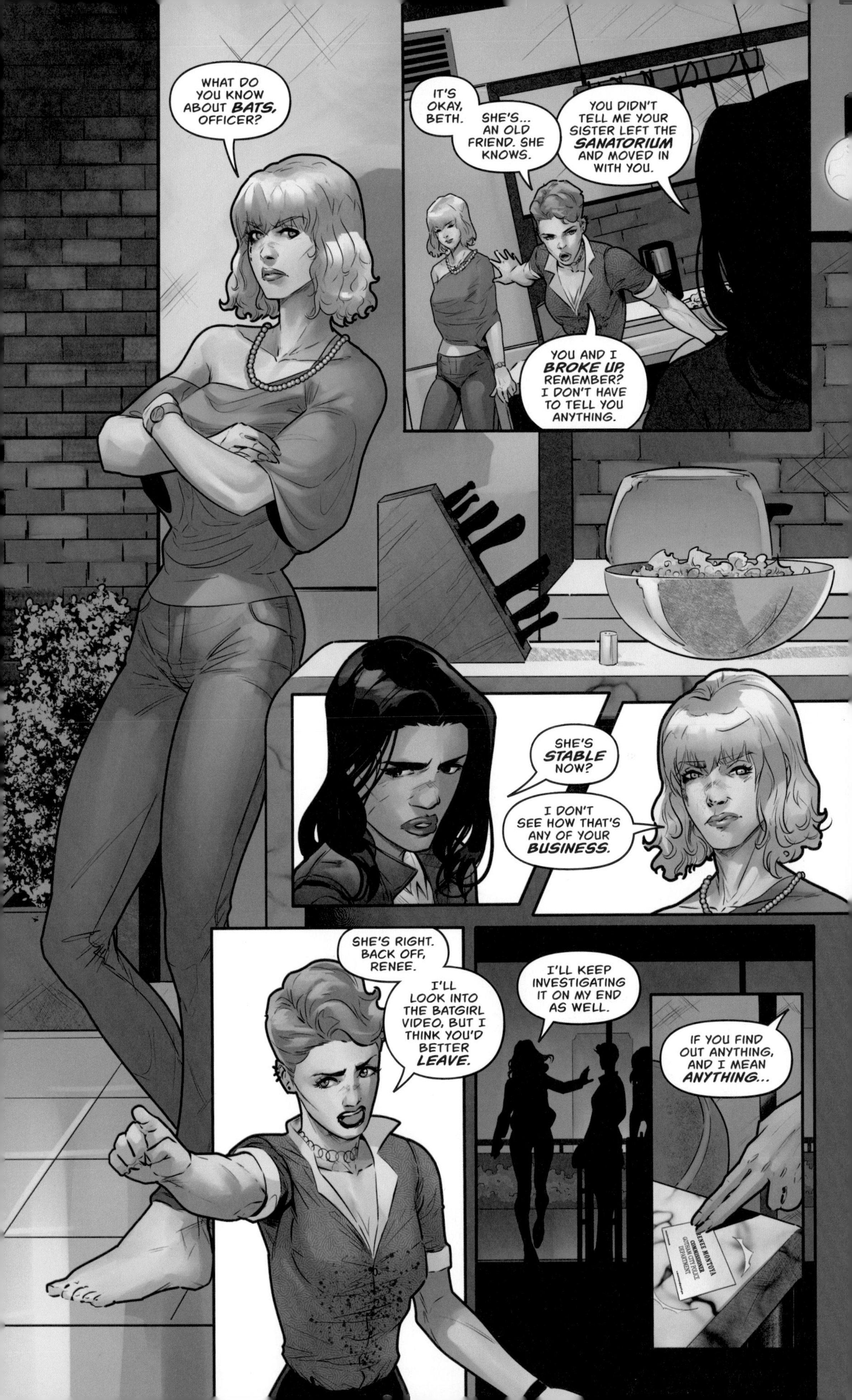

WHAT DO YOU KNOW ABOUT BATS, OFFICER?
IT'S OKAY, BETH.
SHE'S... AN OLD FRIEND. SHE KNOWS.
YOU DIDN'T TELL ME YOUR SISTER LEFT THE SANATORIUM AND MOVED IN WITH YOU.
YOU AND I BROKE UP, REMEMBER? I DON'T HAVE TO TELL YOU ANYTHING.
SHE'S STABLE NOW?
I DON'T SEE HOW THAT'S ANY OF YOUR BUSINESS.
SHE'S RIGHT. BACK OFF, RENEE.
I'LL LOOK INTO THE BATGIRL VIDEO, BUT I THINK YOU'D BETTER LEAVE.
I'LL KEEP INVESTIGATING IT ON MY END AS WELL.
IF YOU FIND OUT ANYTHING, AND I MEAN ANYTHING...

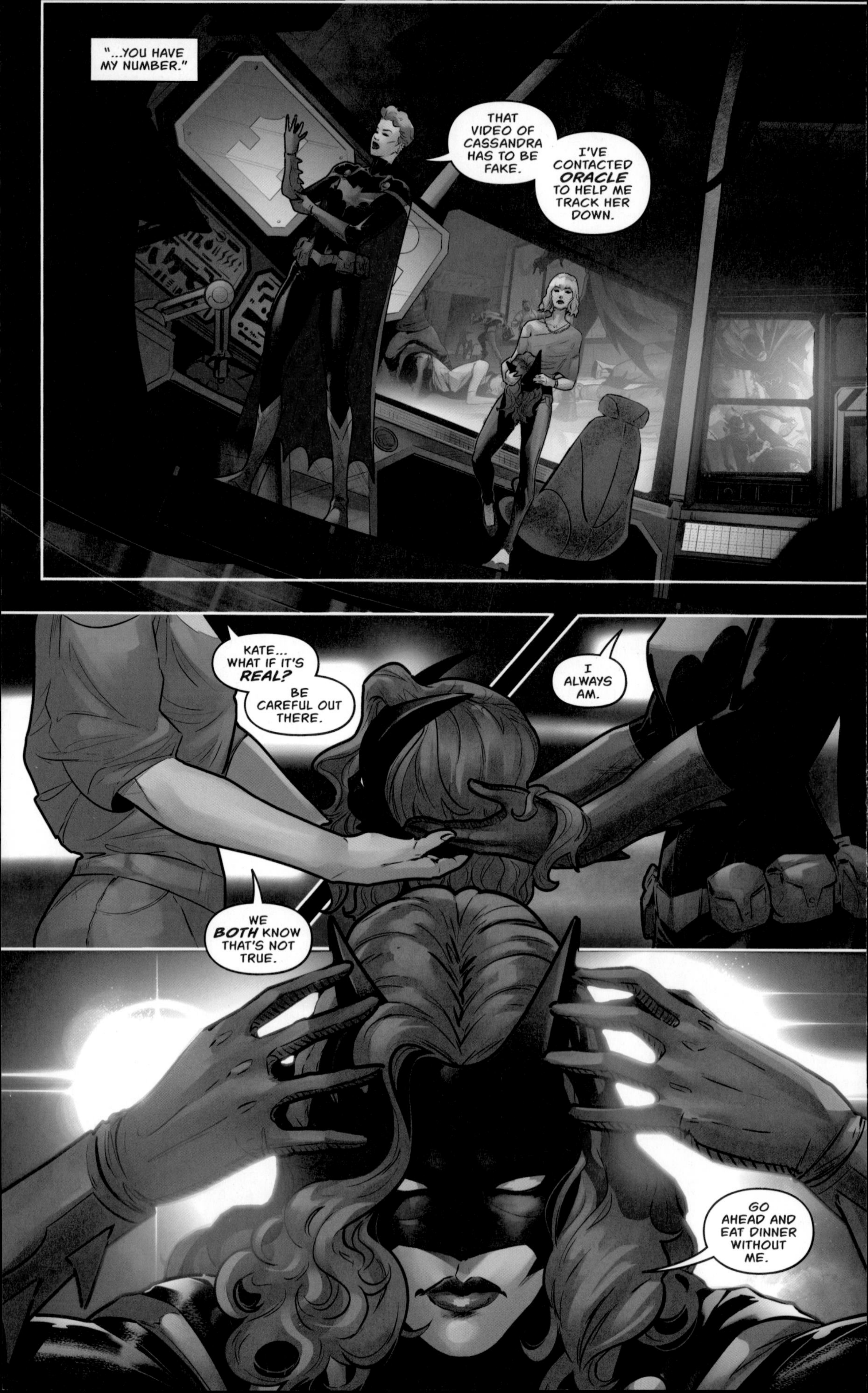
"...YOU HAVE MY NUMBER."
THAT VIDEO OF CASSANDRA HAS TO BE FAKE.
I'VE CONTACTED ORACLE TO HELP ME TRACK HER DOWN.
KATE... WHAT IF IT'S REAL?
BE CAREFUL OUT THERE.
I ALWAYS AM.
WE BOTH KNOW THAT'S NOT TRUE.
GO AHEAD AND EAT DINNER WITHOUT ME.

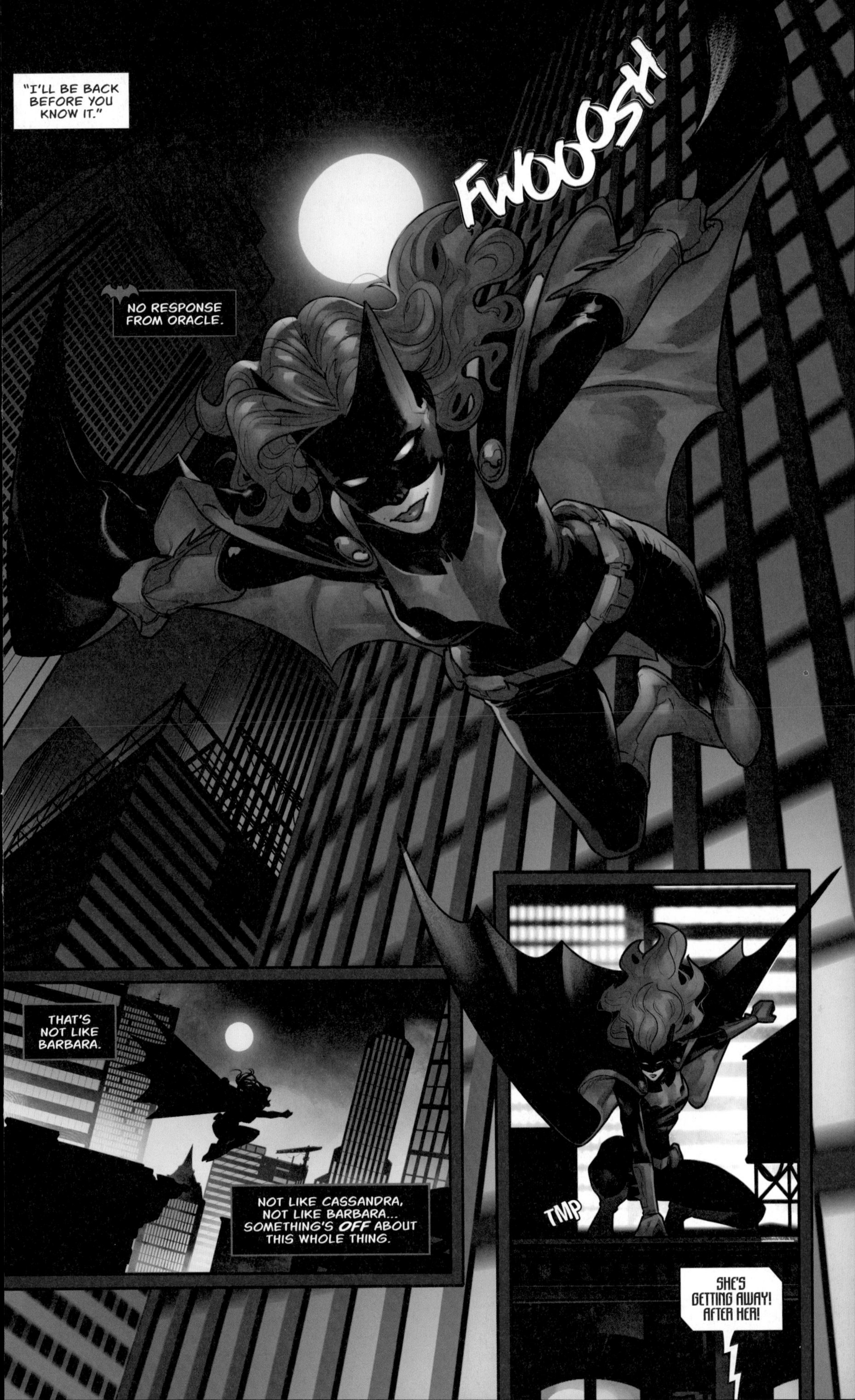
"I'LL BE BACK BEFORE YOU KNOW IT."
FWOOOSH
NO RESPONSE FROM ORACLE.
THAT'S NOT LIKE BARBARA.
NOT LIKE CASSANDRA, NOT LIKE BARBARA... SOMETHING'S *OFF* ABOUT THIS WHOLE THING.
TMP
SHE'S GETTING AWAY! AFTER HER!

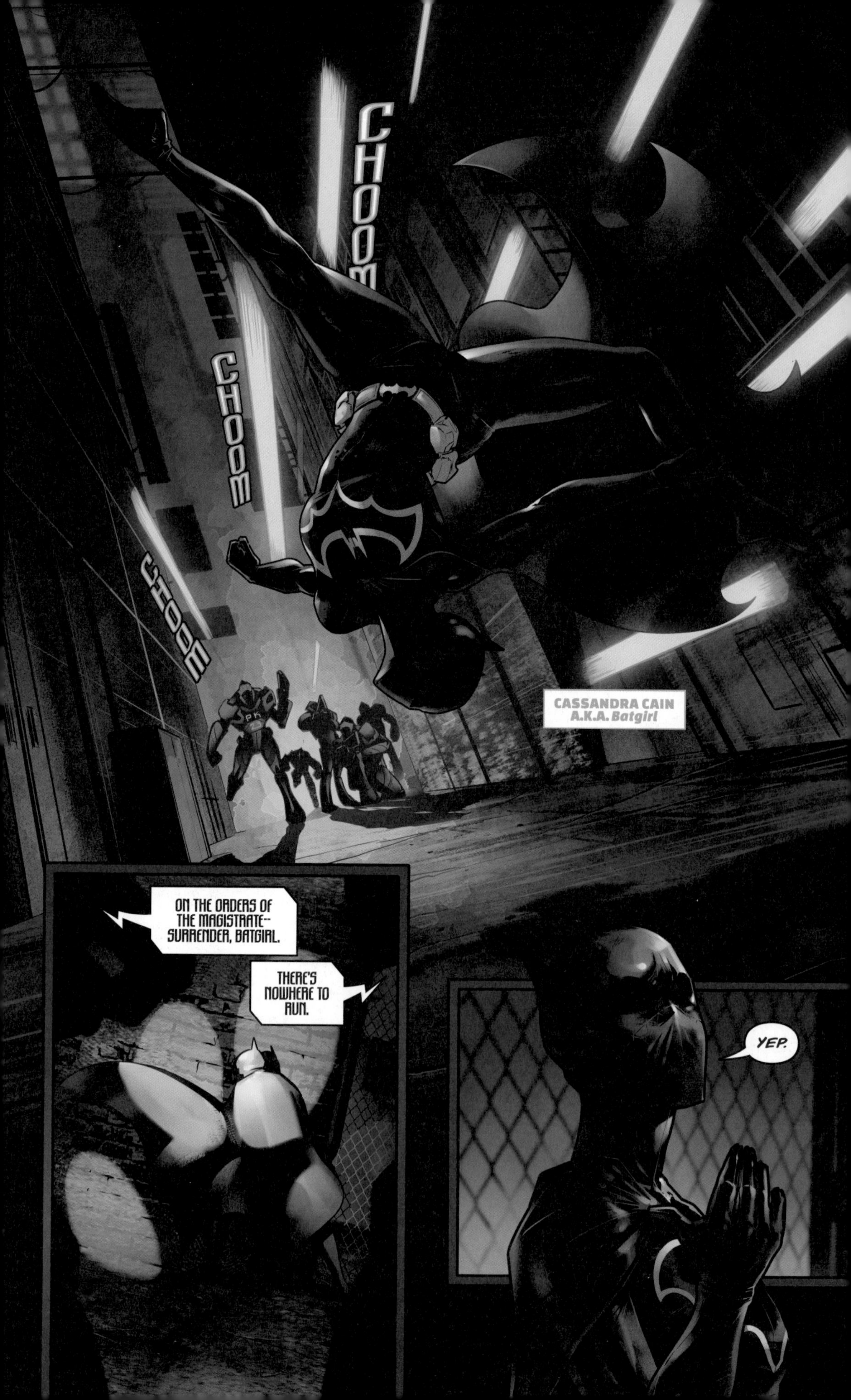
CHOOM
CHOOM
CHOOM
CASSANDRA CAIN
A.K.A. Batgirl
ON THE ORDERS OF THE MAGISTRATE-- SURRENDER, BATGIRL.
THERE'S NOWHERE TO RUN.
YEP.

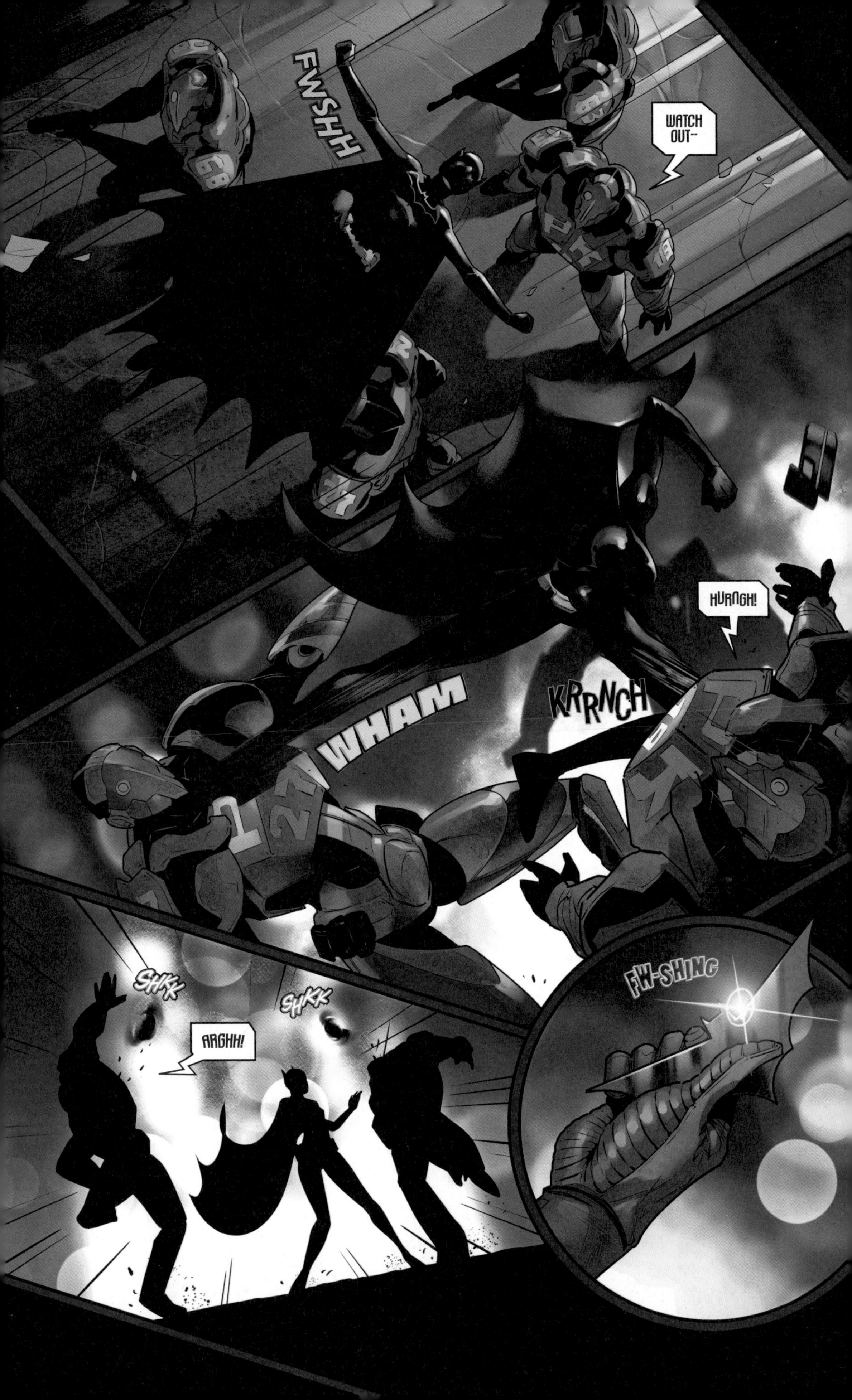

FWSHH
WATCH OUT--
HURNGH!
KRRNCH
WHAM
SHKK
SHKK
ARGHH!
FW-SHING

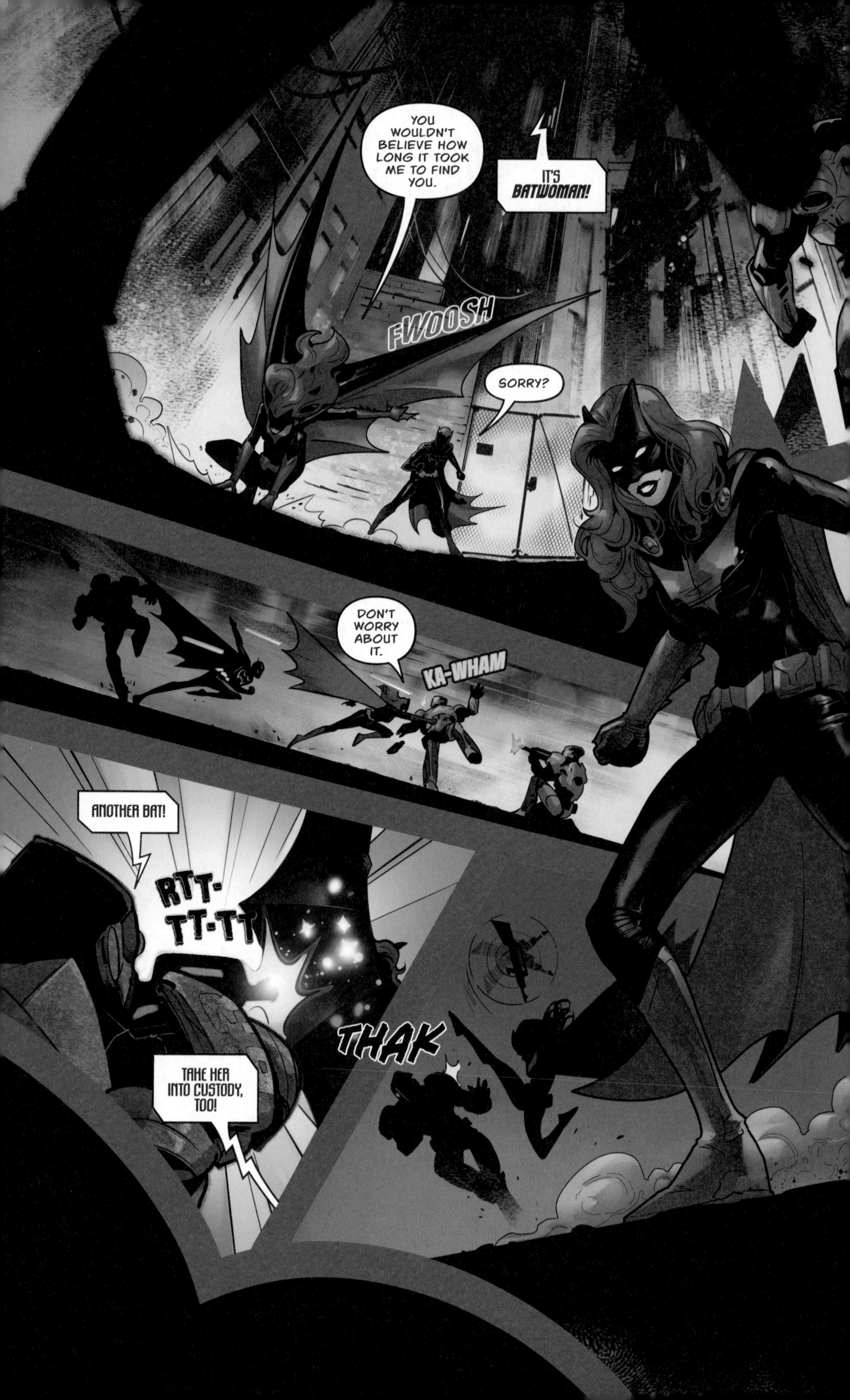
YOU WOULDN'T BELIEVE HOW LONG IT TOOK ME TO FIND YOU.
IT'S BATWOMAN!
FWOOSH
SORRY?
DON'T WORRY ABOUT IT.
KA-WHAM
ANOTHER BAT!
RTT-TT-TT
THAK
TAKE HER INTO CUSTODY, TOO!

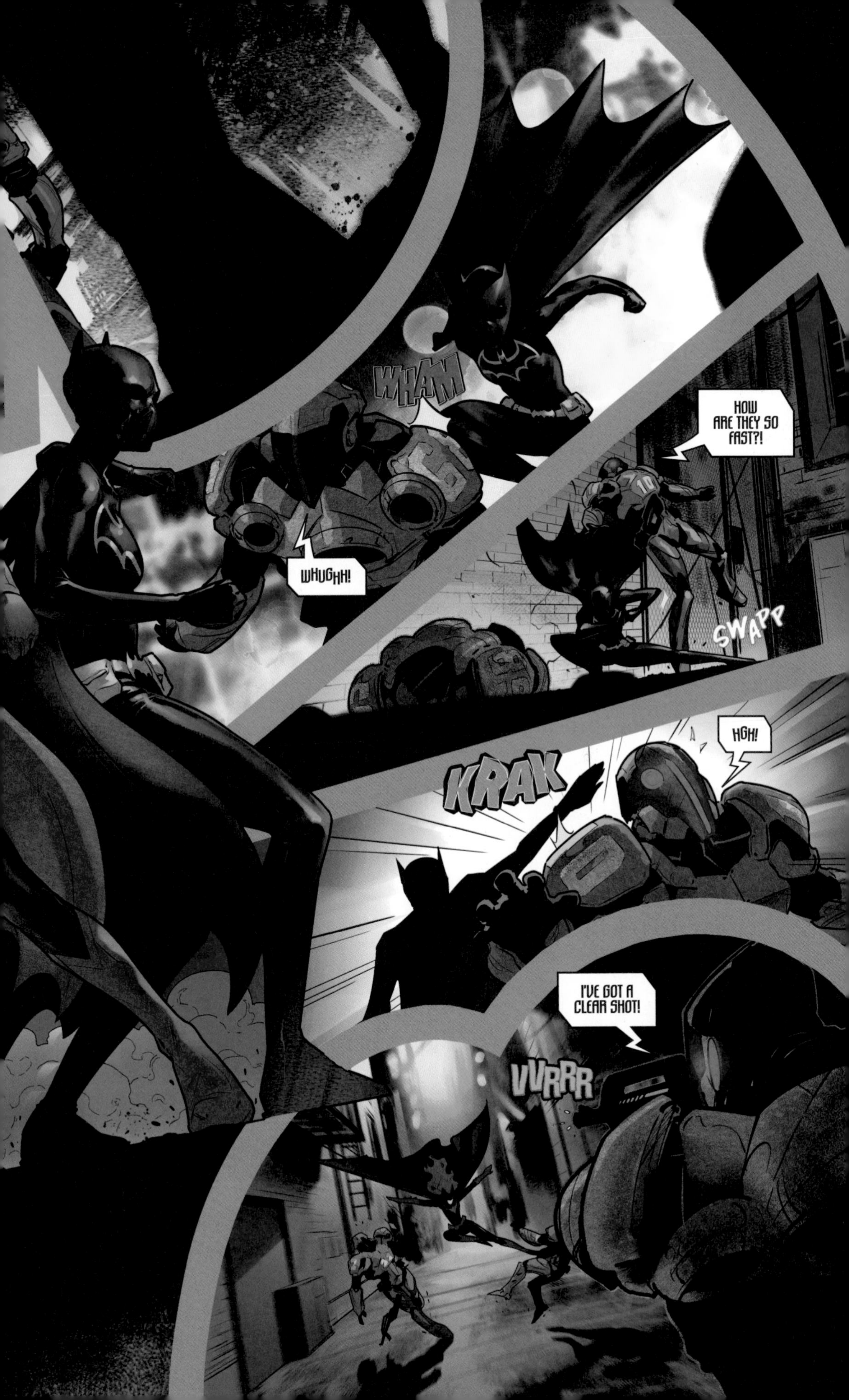
WHAM
WHUGHH!
HOW ARE THEY SO FAST?!
SWAPP
KRAK
HGH!
I'VE GOT A CLEAR SHOT!
VVRRR

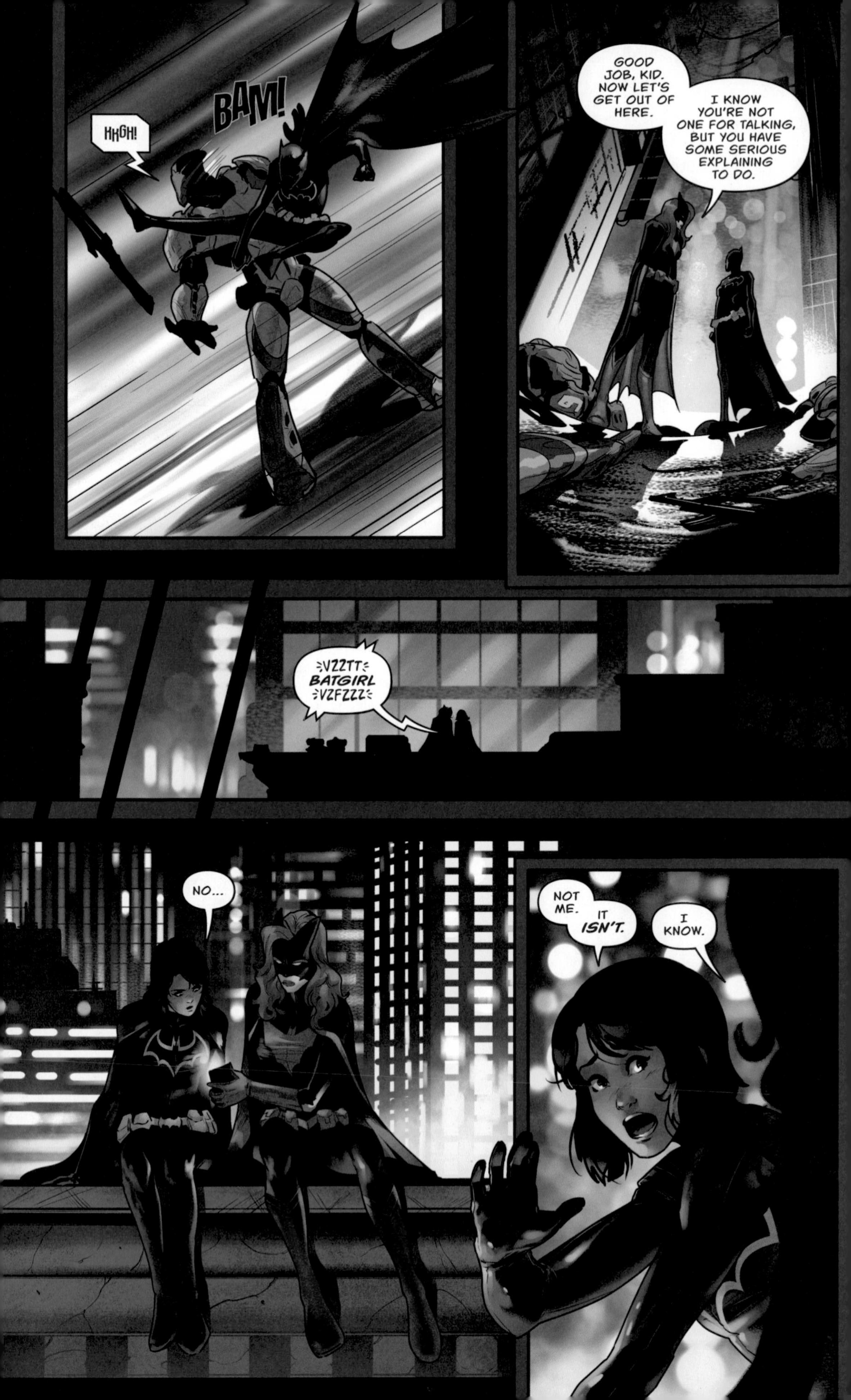
BAM!
HHGH!
GOOD JOB, KID. NOW LET'S GET OUT OF HERE.
I KNOW YOU'RE NOT ONE FOR TALKING, BUT YOU HAVE SOME SERIOUS EXPLAINING TO DO.
VZZTT BATGIRL VZFZZZ
NO...
NOT ME.
IT ISN'T.
I KNOW.

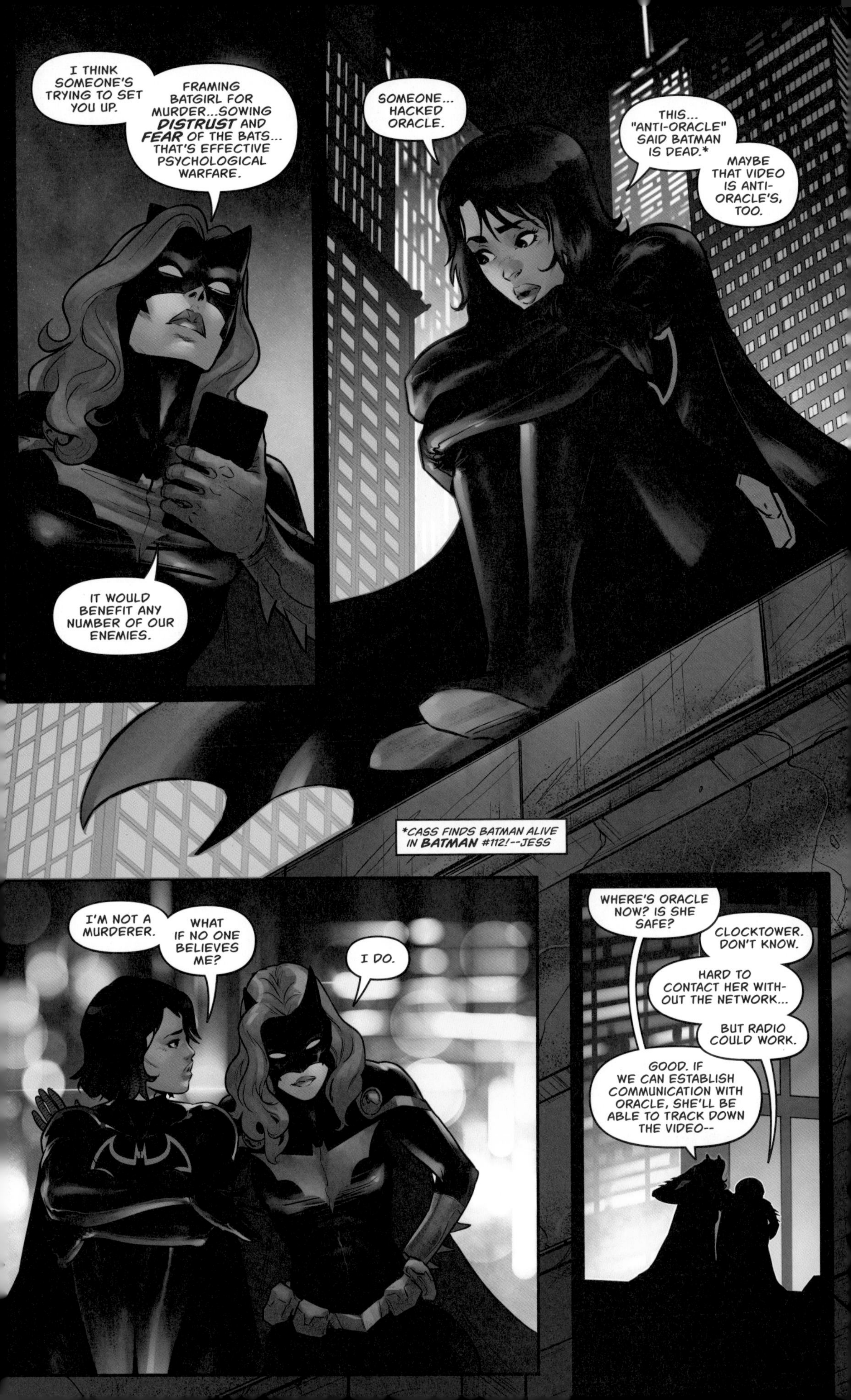
I THINK SOMEONE'S TRYING TO SET YOU UP.
FRAMING BATGIRL FOR MURDER...SOWING **DISTRUST** AND **FEAR** OF THE BATS... THAT'S EFFECTIVE PSYCHOLOGICAL WARFARE.
IT WOULD BENEFIT ANY NUMBER OF OUR ENEMIES.
SOMEONE... HACKED ORACLE.
THIS... "ANTI-ORACLE" SAID BATMAN IS DEAD.*
MAYBE THAT VIDEO IS ANTI-ORACLE'S, TOO.
*CASS FINDS BATMAN ALIVE IN **BATMAN** #112!--JESS
I'M NOT A MURDERER.
WHAT IF NO ONE BELIEVES ME?
I DO.
WHERE'S ORACLE NOW? IS SHE SAFE?
CLOCKTOWER. DON'T KNOW.
HARD TO CONTACT HER WITH-OUT THE NETWORK...
BUT RADIO COULD WORK.
GOOD. IF WE CAN ESTABLISH COMMUNICATION WITH ORACLE, SHE'LL BE ABLE TO TRACK DOWN THE VIDEO--

ELLO BATS! HELLO BATS! HELLO BATS!
HELLO BATS!
ORACLE? PLEASE.
WHY WOULD YOU WANNA TALK TO ORACLE WHEN YOU COULD TALK TO SEER?
FSHOOOM
WHO IS THIS? HOW DID YOU GET THIS FREQUENCY?
PSHH, EASY! I KNOW A LOT OF THINGS.
LIKE WHO YOU ARE.
KATE KANE.

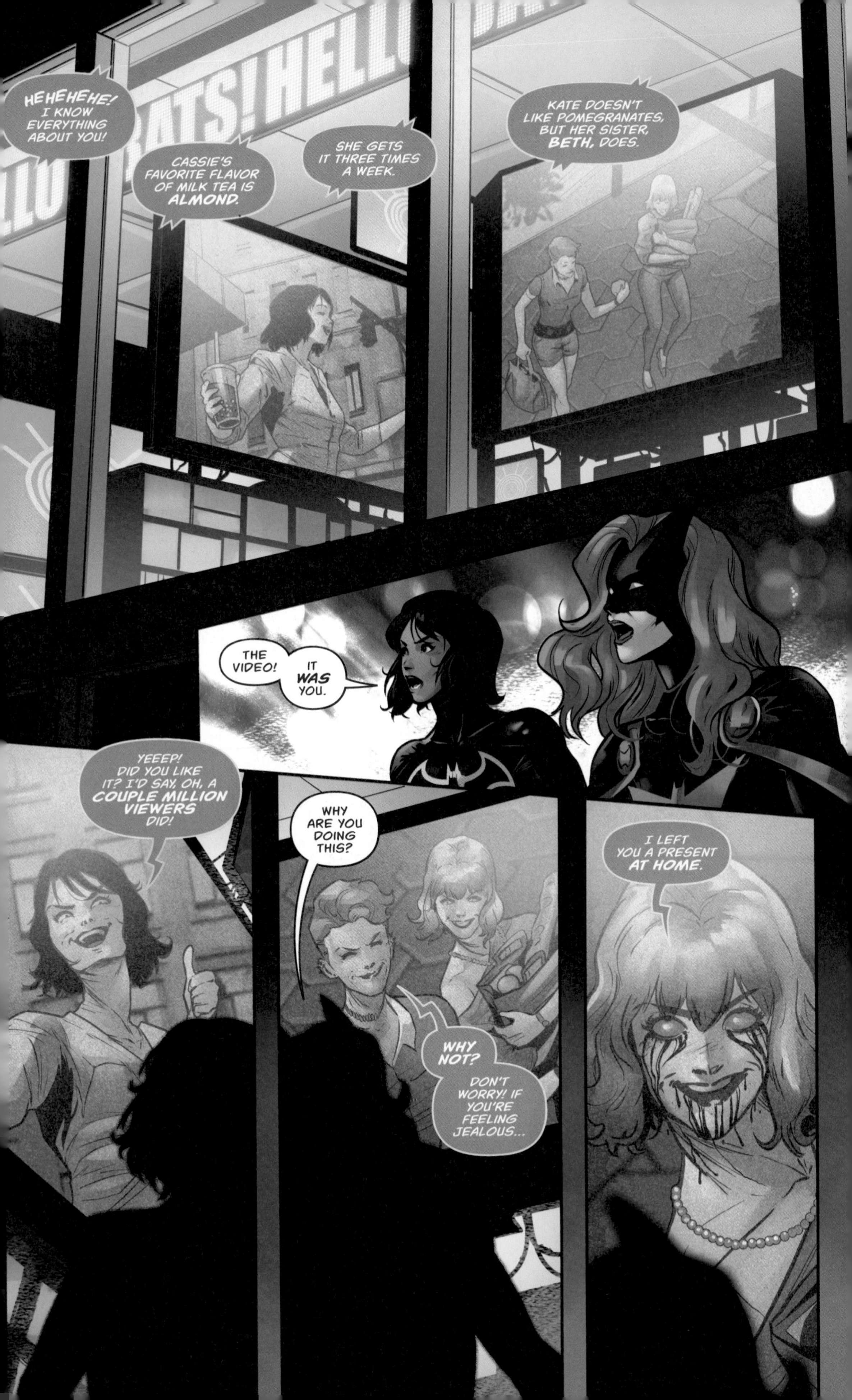
HELLO BATS! HELLO BAT
HEHEHEHE! I KNOW EVERYTHING ABOUT YOU!
CASSIE'S FAVORITE FLAVOR OF MILK TEA IS ALMOND.
SHE GETS IT THREE TIMES A WEEK.
KATE DOESN'T LIKE POMEGRANATES, BUT HER SISTER, BETH, DOES.
THE VIDEO!
IT WAS YOU.
YEEEP! DID YOU LIKE IT? I'D SAY, OH, A COUPLE MILLION VIEWERS DID!
WHY ARE YOU DOING THIS?
WHY NOT?
DON'T WORRY! IF YOU'RE FEELING JEALOUS...
I LEFT YOU A PRESENT AT HOME.

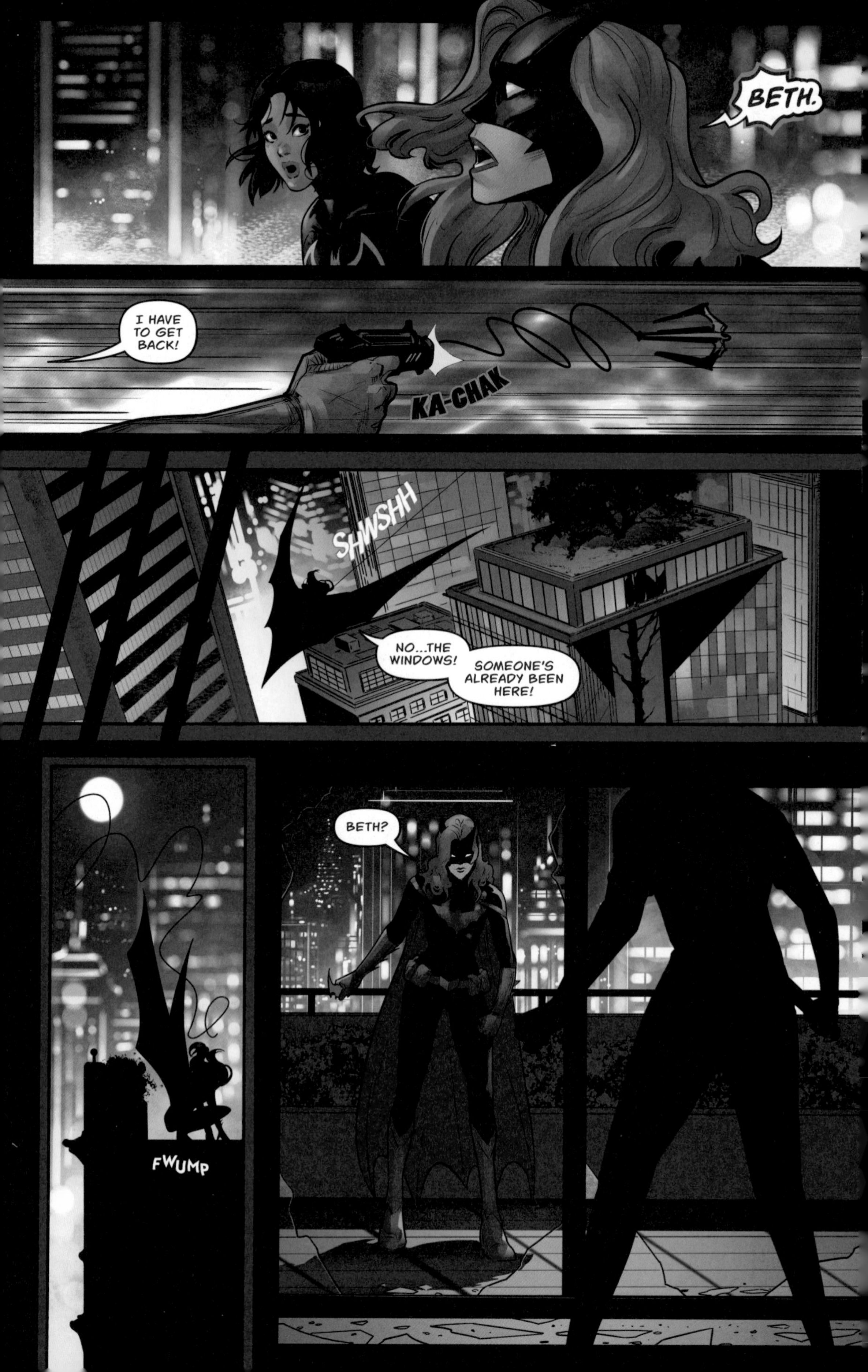
BETH.
I HAVE TO GET BACK!
KA-CHAK
SHWSHH
NO...THE WINDOWS!
SOMEONE'S ALREADY BEEN HERE!
FWUMP
BETH?

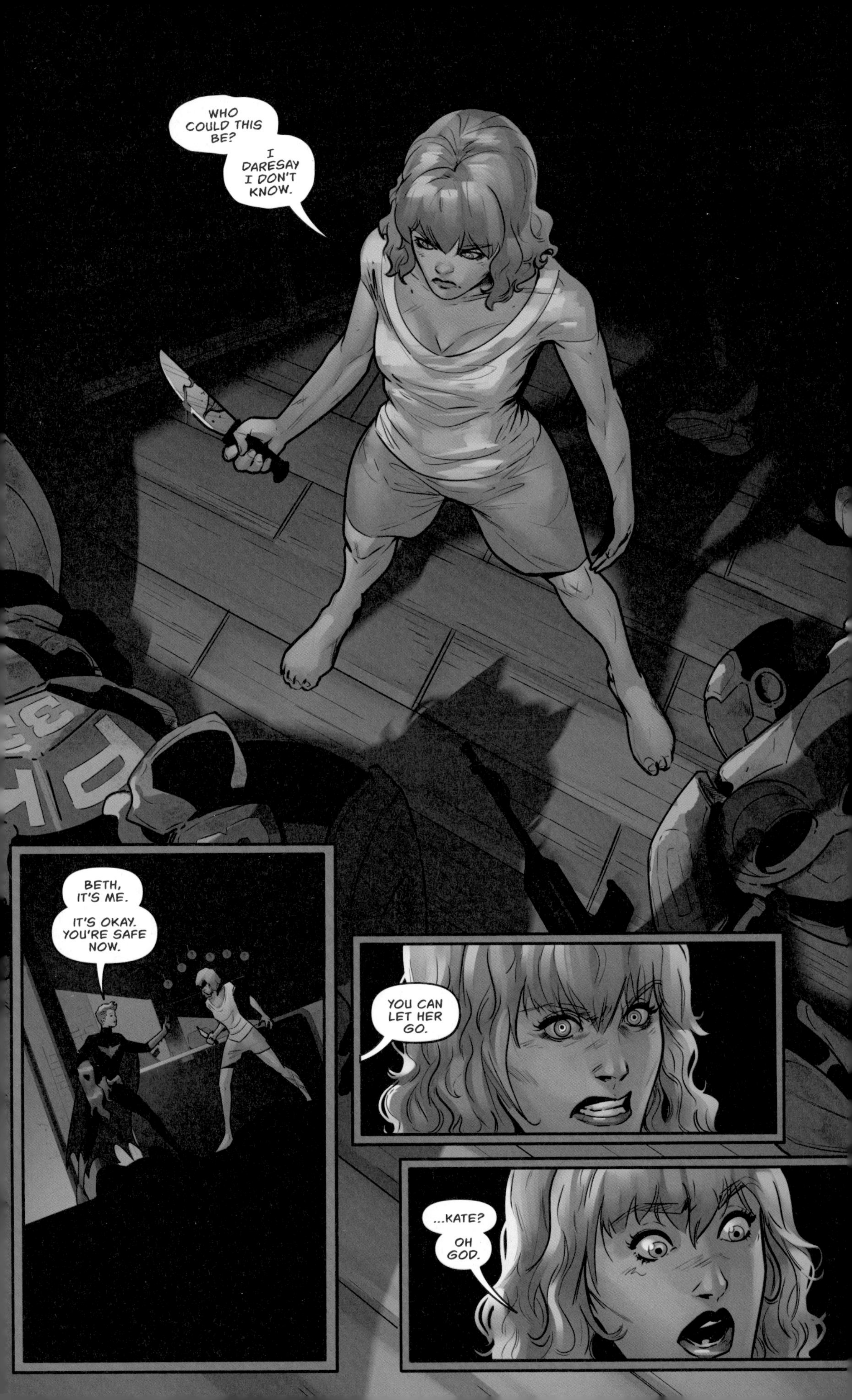
WHO COULD THIS BE?
I DARESAY I DON'T KNOW.
BETH, IT'S ME.
IT'S OKAY. YOU'RE SAFE NOW.
YOU CAN LET HER GO.
...KATE?
OH GOD.

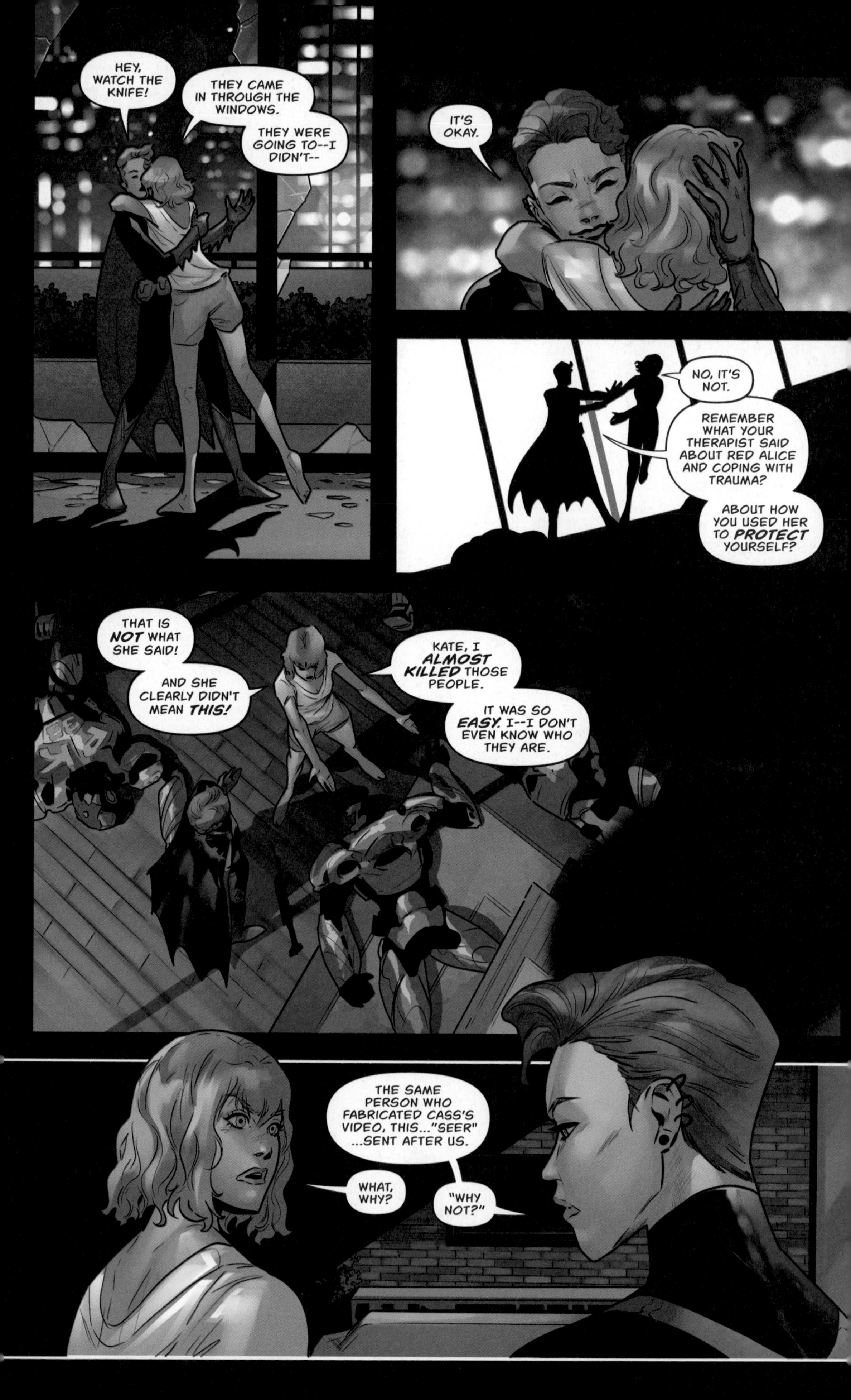
HEY, WATCH THE KNIFE!
THEY CAME IN THROUGH THE WINDOWS.
THEY WERE GOING TO--I DIDN'T--
IT'S OKAY.
NO, IT'S NOT.
REMEMBER WHAT YOUR THERAPIST SAID ABOUT RED ALICE AND COPING WITH TRAUMA?
ABOUT HOW YOU USED HER TO PROTECT YOURSELF?
THAT IS NOT WHAT SHE SAID!
AND SHE CLEARLY DIDN'T MEAN THIS!
KATE, I ALMOST KILLED THOSE PEOPLE.
IT WAS SO EASY. I--I DON'T EVEN KNOW WHO THEY ARE.
THE SAME PERSON WHO FABRICATED CASS'S VIDEO, THIS..."SEER" ...SENT AFTER US.
WHAT, WHY?
"WHY NOT?"

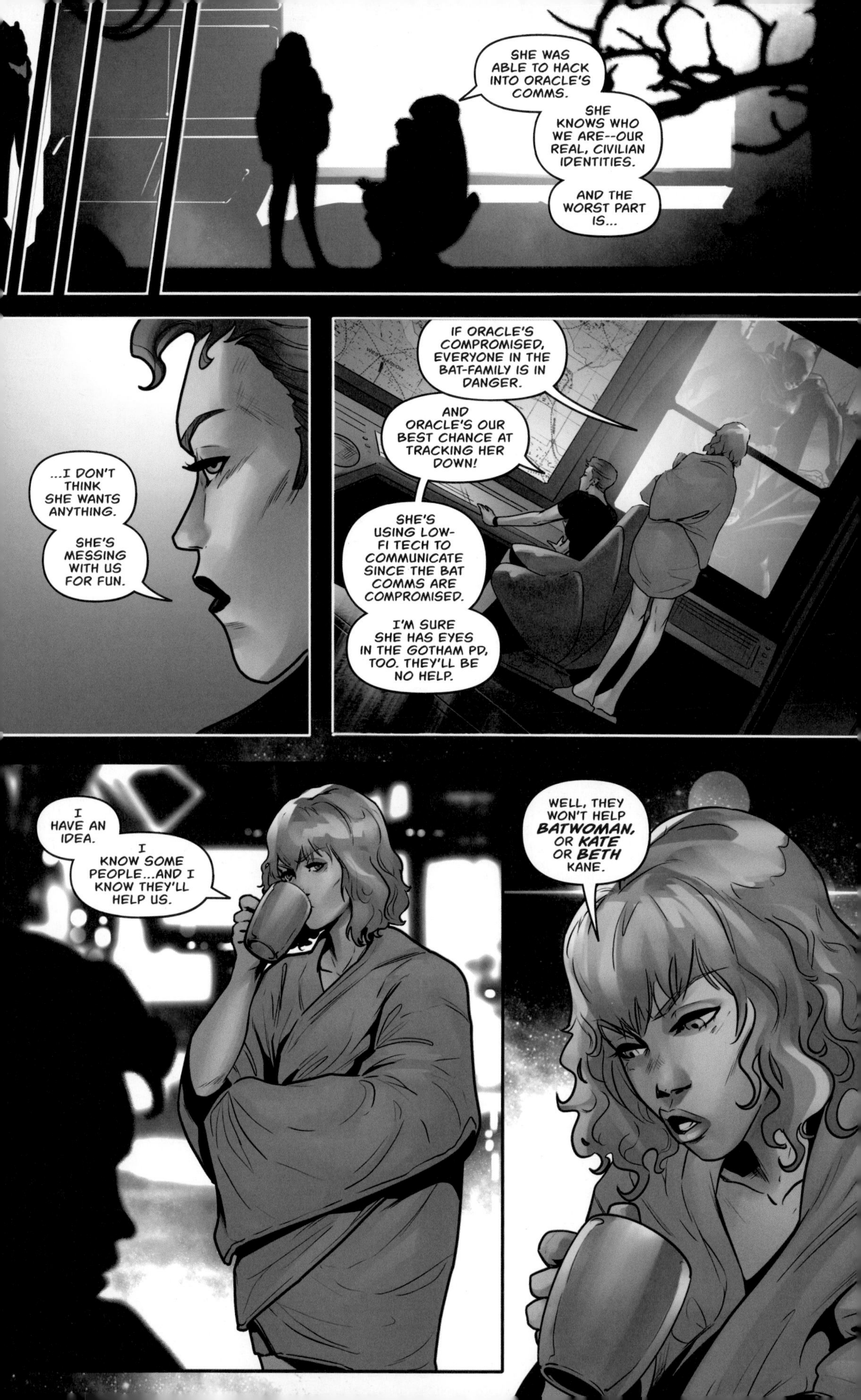
SHE WAS ABLE TO HACK INTO ORACLE'S COMMS.
SHE KNOWS WHO WE ARE--OUR REAL, CIVILIAN IDENTITIES.
AND THE WORST PART IS...
...I DON'T THINK SHE WANTS ANYTHING.
SHE'S MESSING WITH US FOR FUN.
IF ORACLE'S COMPROMISED, EVERYONE IN THE BAT-FAMILY IS IN DANGER.
AND ORACLE'S OUR BEST CHANCE AT TRACKING HER DOWN!
SHE'S USING LOW-FI TECH TO COMMUNICATE SINCE THE BAT COMMS ARE COMPROMISED.
I'M SURE SHE HAS EYES IN THE GOTHAM PD, TOO. THEY'LL BE NO HELP.
I HAVE AN IDEA.
I KNOW SOME PEOPLE...AND I KNOW THEY'LL HELP US.
WELL, THEY WON'T HELP ***BATWOMAN,*** OR ***KATE*** OR ***BETH*** KANE.

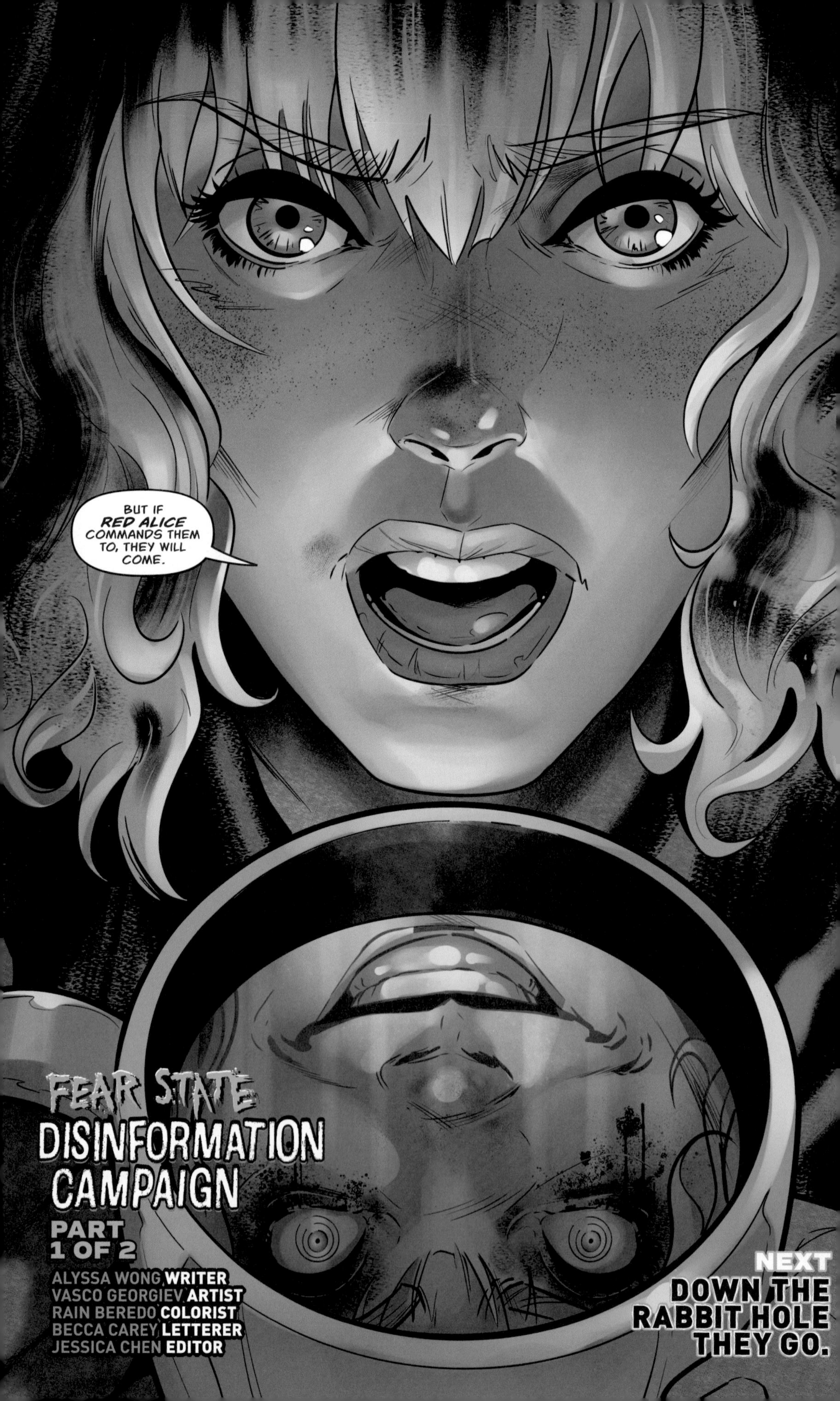
BUT IF RED ALICE COMMANDS THEM TO, THEY WILL COME.
FEAR STATE
DISINFORMATION CAMPAIGN
PART 1 OF 2
ALYSSA WONG WRITER
VASCO GEORGIEV ARTIST
RAIN BEREDO COLORIST
BECCA CAREY LETTERER
JESSICA CHEN EDITOR
NEXT
DOWN THE RABBIT HOLE THEY GO.

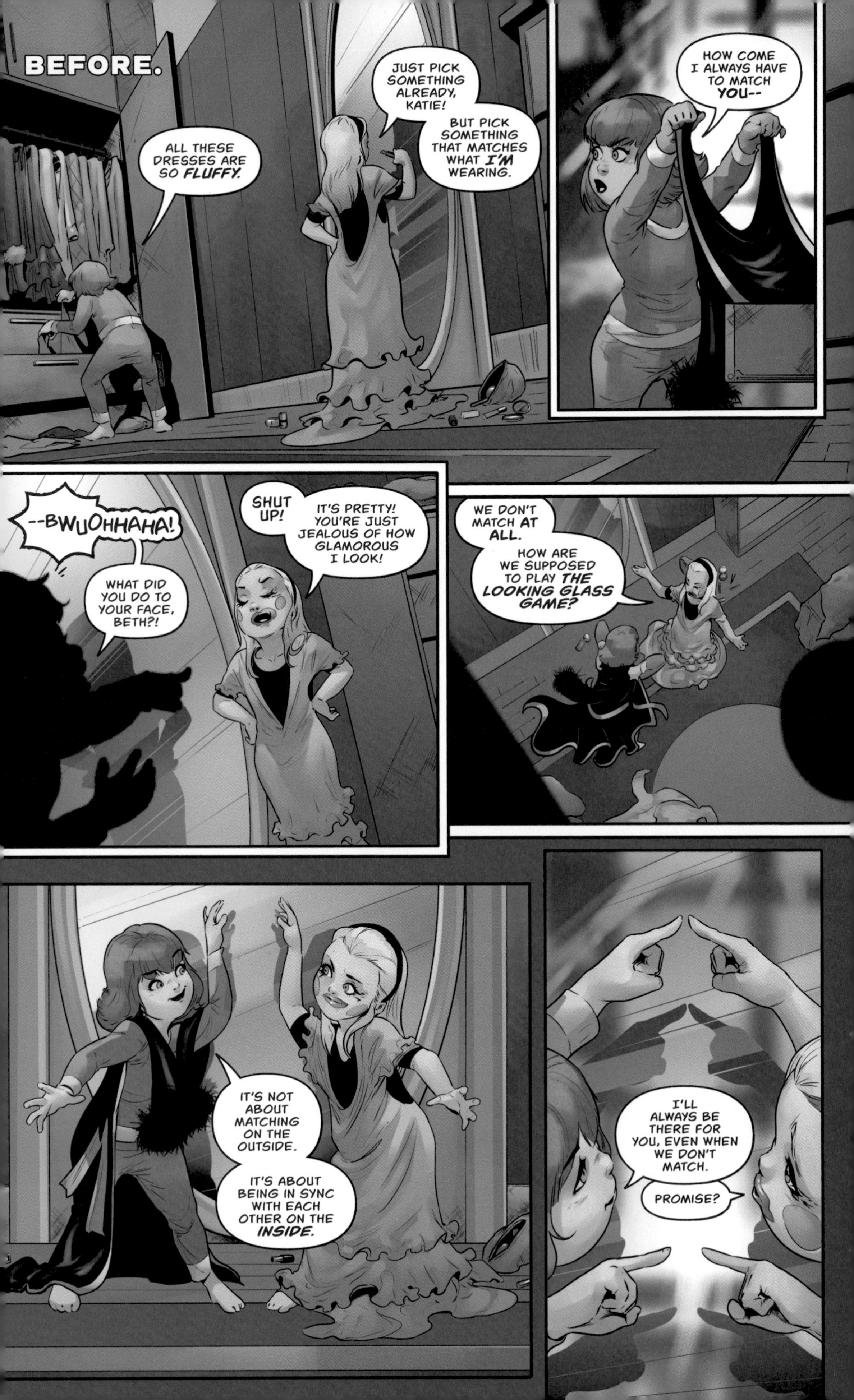
BEFORE.
ALL THESE DRESSES ARE SO FLUFFY.
JUST PICK SOMETHING ALREADY, KATIE!
BUT PICK SOMETHING THAT MATCHES WHAT I'M WEARING.
HOW COME I ALWAYS HAVE TO MATCH YOU--
--BWUOHHAHA!
WHAT DID YOU DO TO YOUR FACE, BETH?!
SHUT UP!
IT'S PRETTY! YOU'RE JUST JEALOUS OF HOW GLAMOROUS I LOOK!
WE DON'T MATCH AT ALL.
HOW ARE WE SUPPOSED TO PLAY THE LOOKING GLASS GAME?
IT'S NOT ABOUT MATCHING ON THE OUTSIDE.
IT'S ABOUT BEING IN SYNC WITH EACH OTHER ON THE INSIDE.
I'LL ALWAYS BE THERE FOR YOU, EVEN WHEN WE DON'T MATCH.
PROMISE?

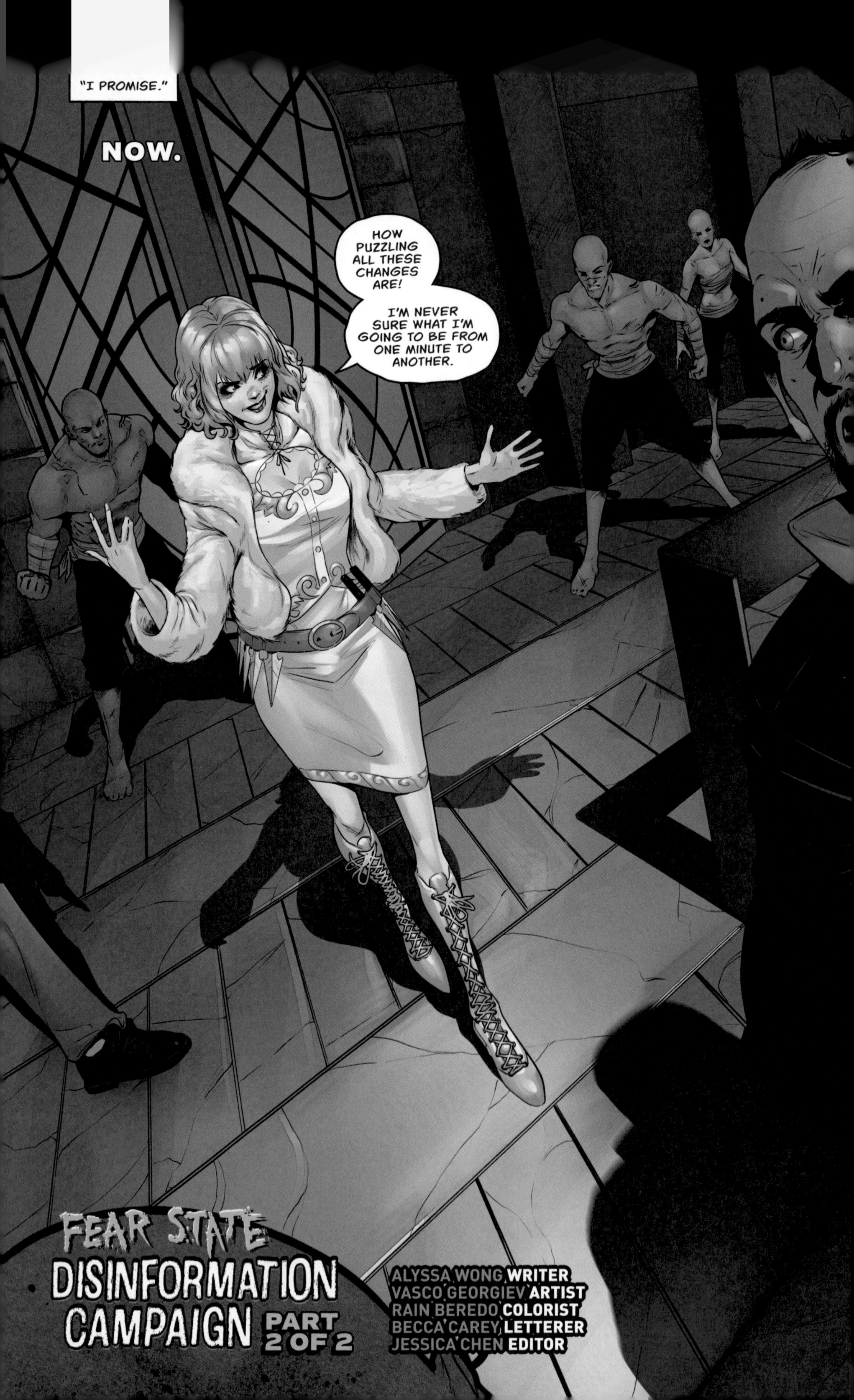
"I PROMISE."
NOW.
HOW PUZZLING ALL THESE CHANGES ARE!
I'M NEVER SURE WHAT I'M GOING TO BE FROM ONE MINUTE TO ANOTHER.
FEAR STATE
DISINFORMATION CAMPAIGN PART 2 OF 2
ALYSSA WONG WRITER
VASCO GEORGIEV ARTIST
RAIN BEREDO COLORIST
BECCA CAREY LETTERER
JESSICA CHEN EDITOR

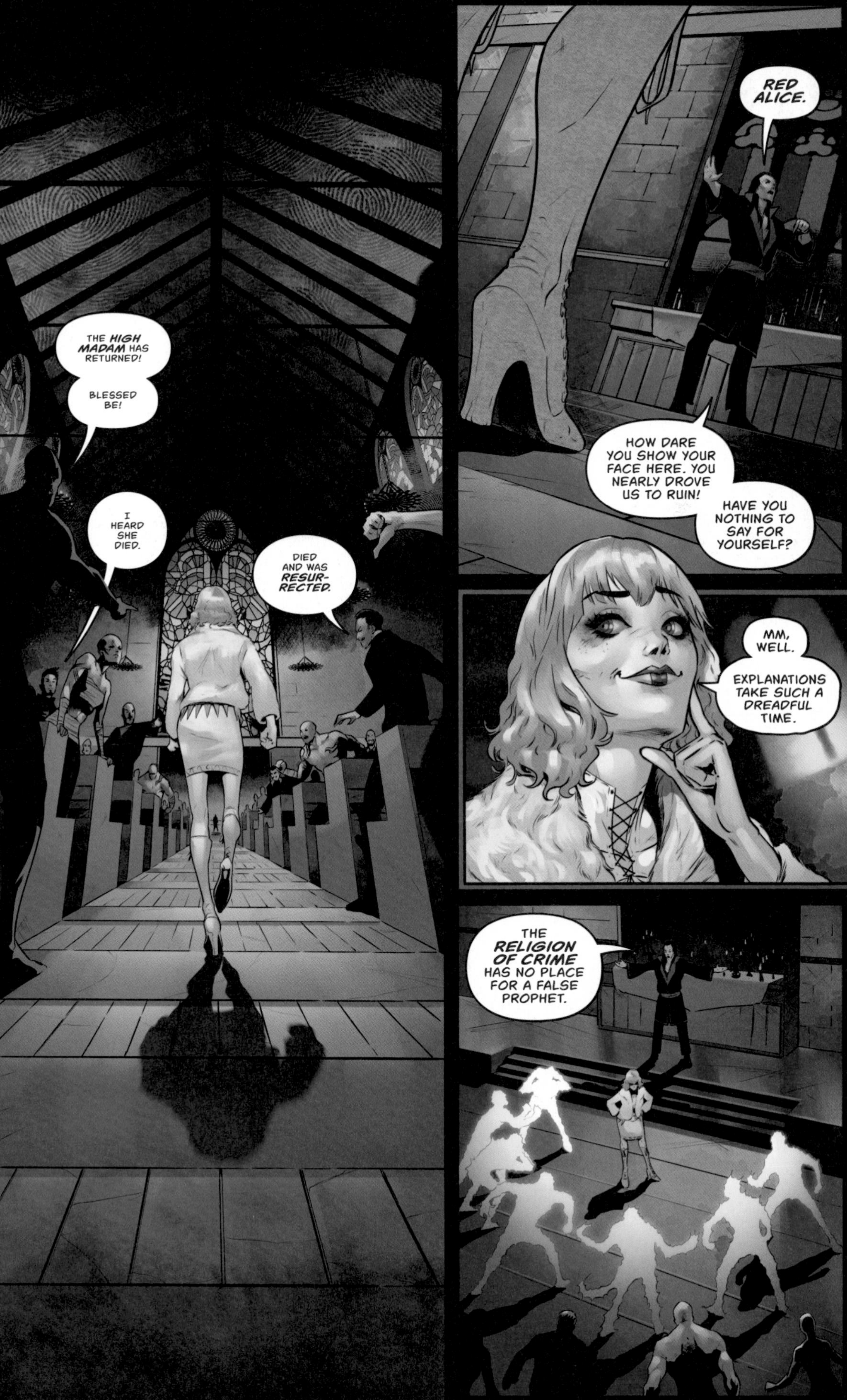
THE HIGH MADAM HAS RETURNED!
BLESSED BE!
I HEARD SHE DIED.
DIED AND WAS RESURRECTED.
RED ALICE.
HOW DARE YOU SHOW YOUR FACE HERE. YOU NEARLY DROVE US TO RUIN!
HAVE YOU NOTHING TO SAY FOR YOURSELF?
MM, WELL.
EXPLANATIONS TAKE SUCH A DREADFUL TIME.
THE RELIGION OF CRIME HAS NO PLACE FOR A FALSE PROPHET.

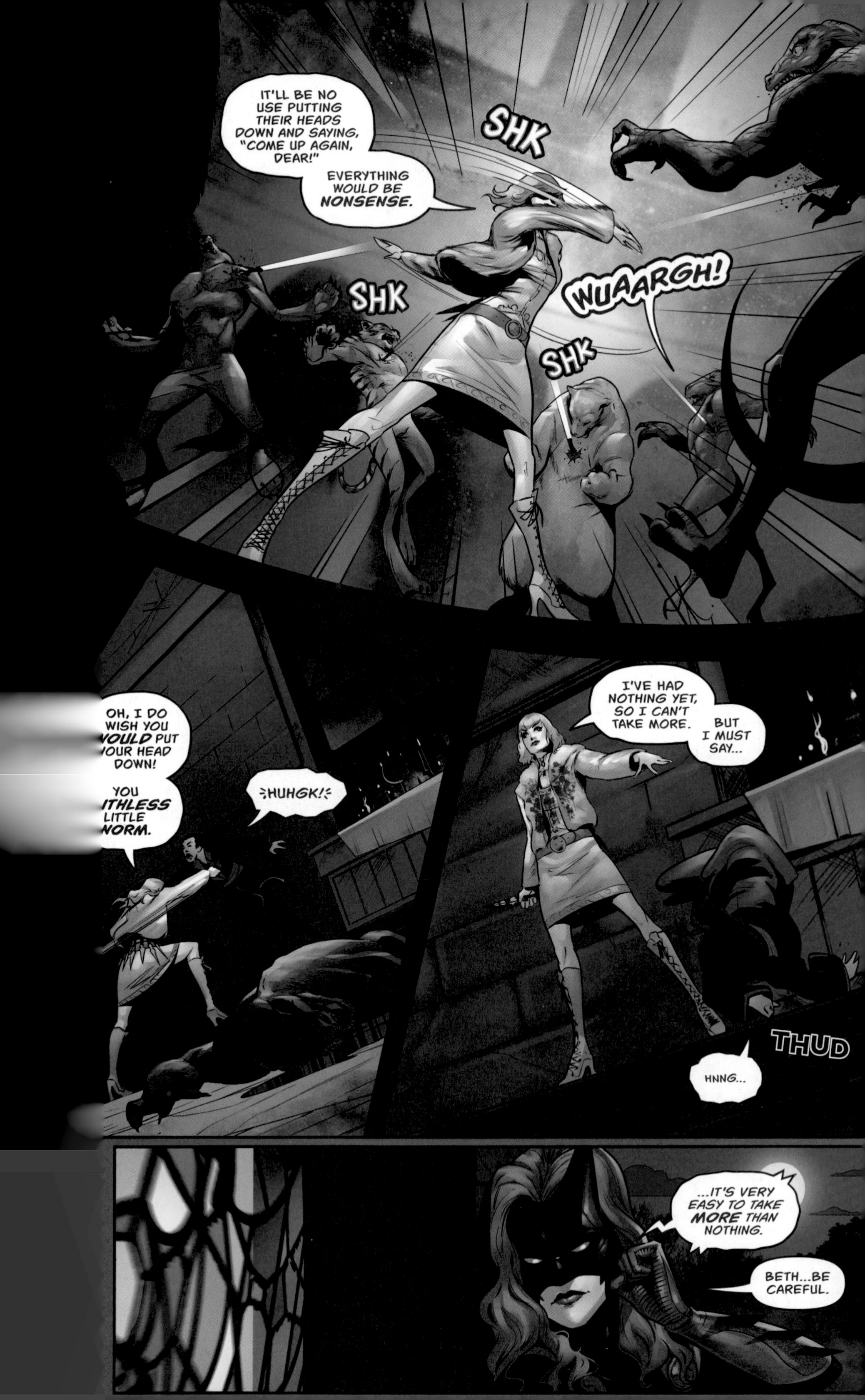
IT'LL BE NO USE PUTTING THEIR HEADS DOWN AND SAYING, "COME UP AGAIN, DEAR!"
EVERYTHING WOULD BE NONSENSE.
SHK
SHK
WUAARGH!
SHK
OH, I DO WISH YOU WOULD PUT YOUR HEAD DOWN!
YOU ITHLESS LITTLE NORM.
HUHGK!
I'VE HAD NOTHING YET, SO I CAN'T TAKE MORE.
BUT I MUST SAY...
THUD
HNNG...
...IT'S VERY EASY TO TAKE MORE THAN NOTHING.
BETH...BE CAREFUL.

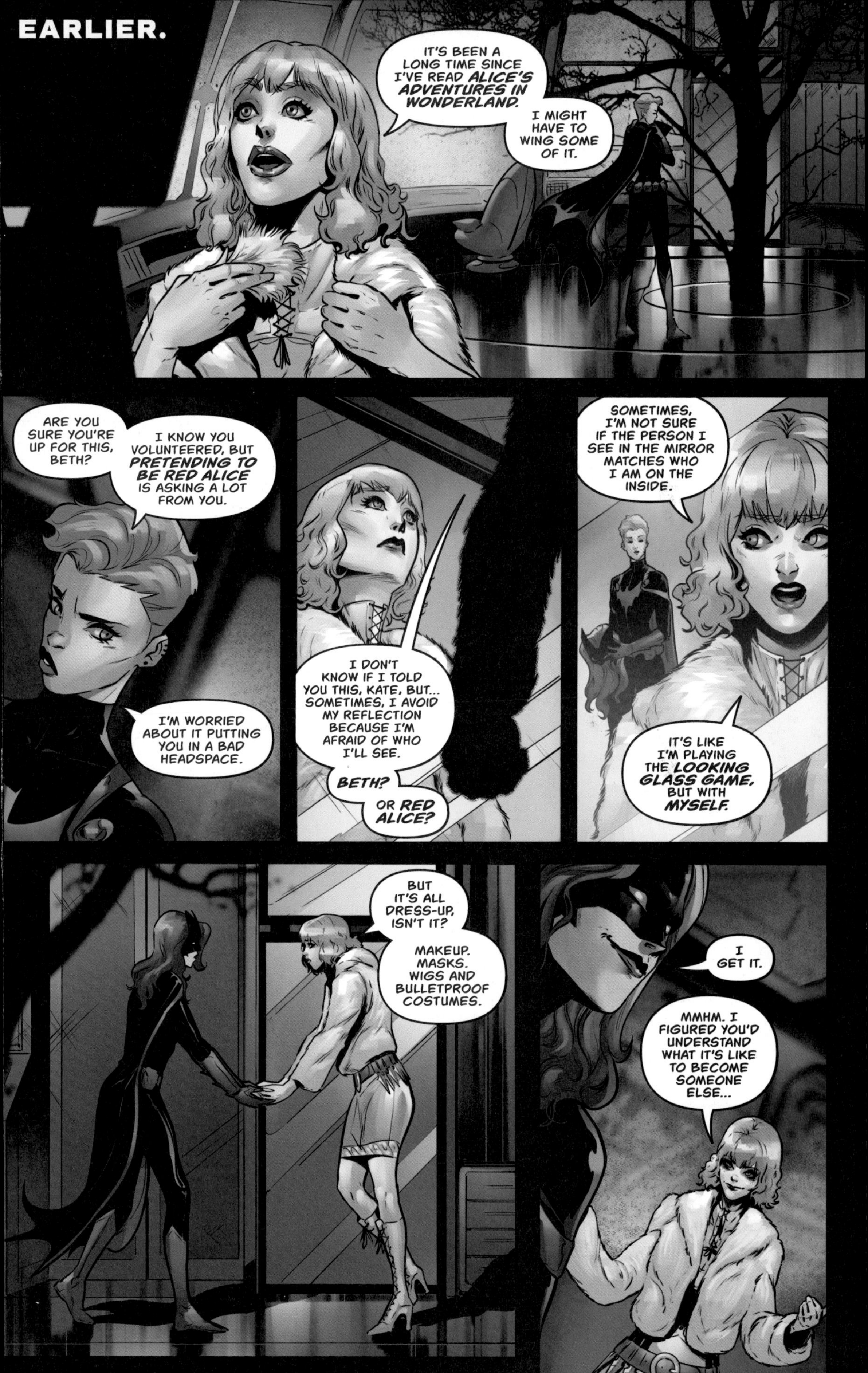
EARLIER.
IT'S BEEN A LONG TIME SINCE I'VE READ ALICE'S ADVENTURES IN WONDERLAND.
I MIGHT HAVE TO WING SOME OF IT.
ARE YOU SURE YOU'RE UP FOR THIS, BETH?
I KNOW YOU VOLUNTEERED, BUT PRETENDING TO BE RED ALICE IS ASKING A LOT FROM YOU.
I'M WORRIED ABOUT IT PUTTING YOU IN A BAD HEADSPACE.
I DON'T KNOW IF I TOLD YOU THIS, KATE, BUT... SOMETIMES, I AVOID MY REFLECTION BECAUSE I'M AFRAID OF WHO I'LL SEE.
BETH?
OR RED ALICE?
SOMETIMES, I'M NOT SURE IF THE PERSON I SEE IN THE MIRROR MATCHES WHO I AM ON THE INSIDE.
IT'S LIKE I'M PLAYING THE LOOKING GLASS GAME, BUT WITH MYSELF.
BUT IT'S ALL DRESS-UP, ISN'T IT?
MAKEUP. MASKS. WIGS AND BULLETPROOF COSTUMES.
I GET IT.
MMHM. I FIGURED YOU'D UNDERSTAND WHAT IT'S LIKE TO BECOME SOMEONE ELSE...

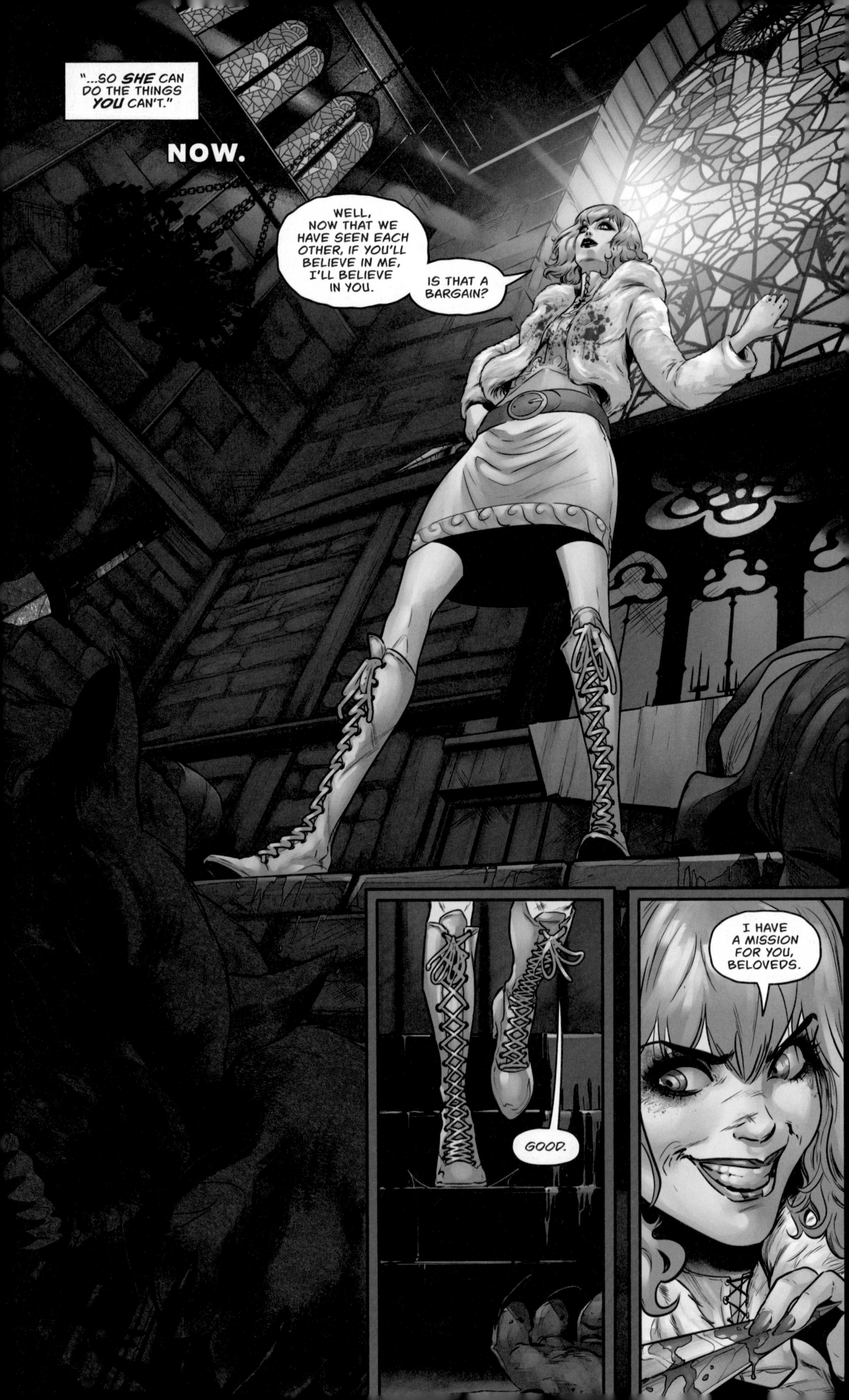
"...SO SHE CAN DO THE THINGS YOU CAN'T."
NOW.
WELL, NOW THAT WE HAVE SEEN EACH OTHER, IF YOU'LL BELIEVE IN ME, I'LL BELIEVE IN YOU.
IS THAT A BARGAIN?
GOOD.
I HAVE A MISSION FOR YOU, BELOVEDS.

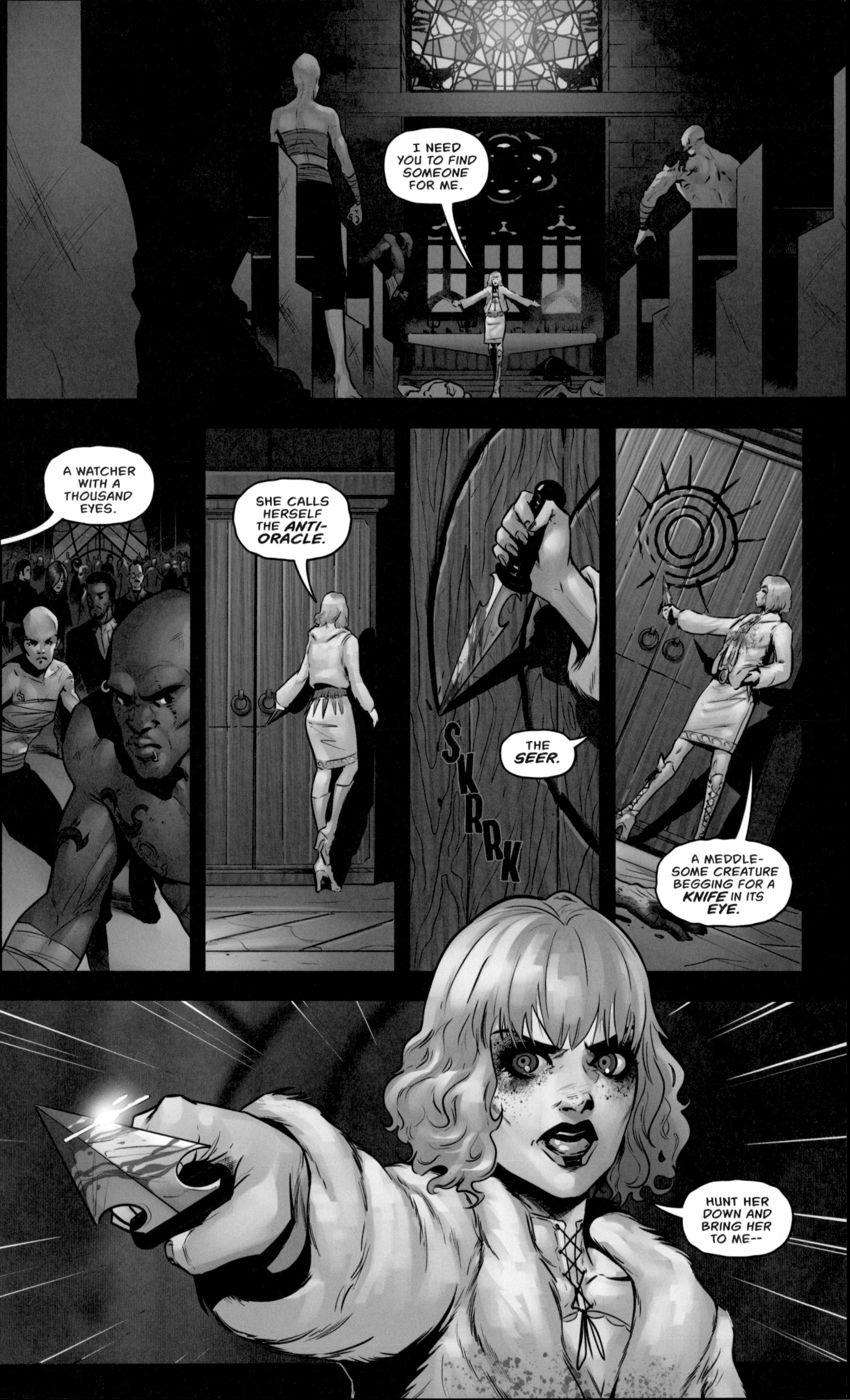
I NEED YOU TO FIND SOMEONE FOR ME.
A WATCHER WITH A THOUSAND EYES.
SHE CALLS HERSELF THE ANTI-ORACLE.
SKRRK
THE SEER.
A MEDDLE-SOME CREATURE BEGGING FOR A KNIFE IN ITS EYE.
HUNT HER DOWN AND BRING HER TO ME--

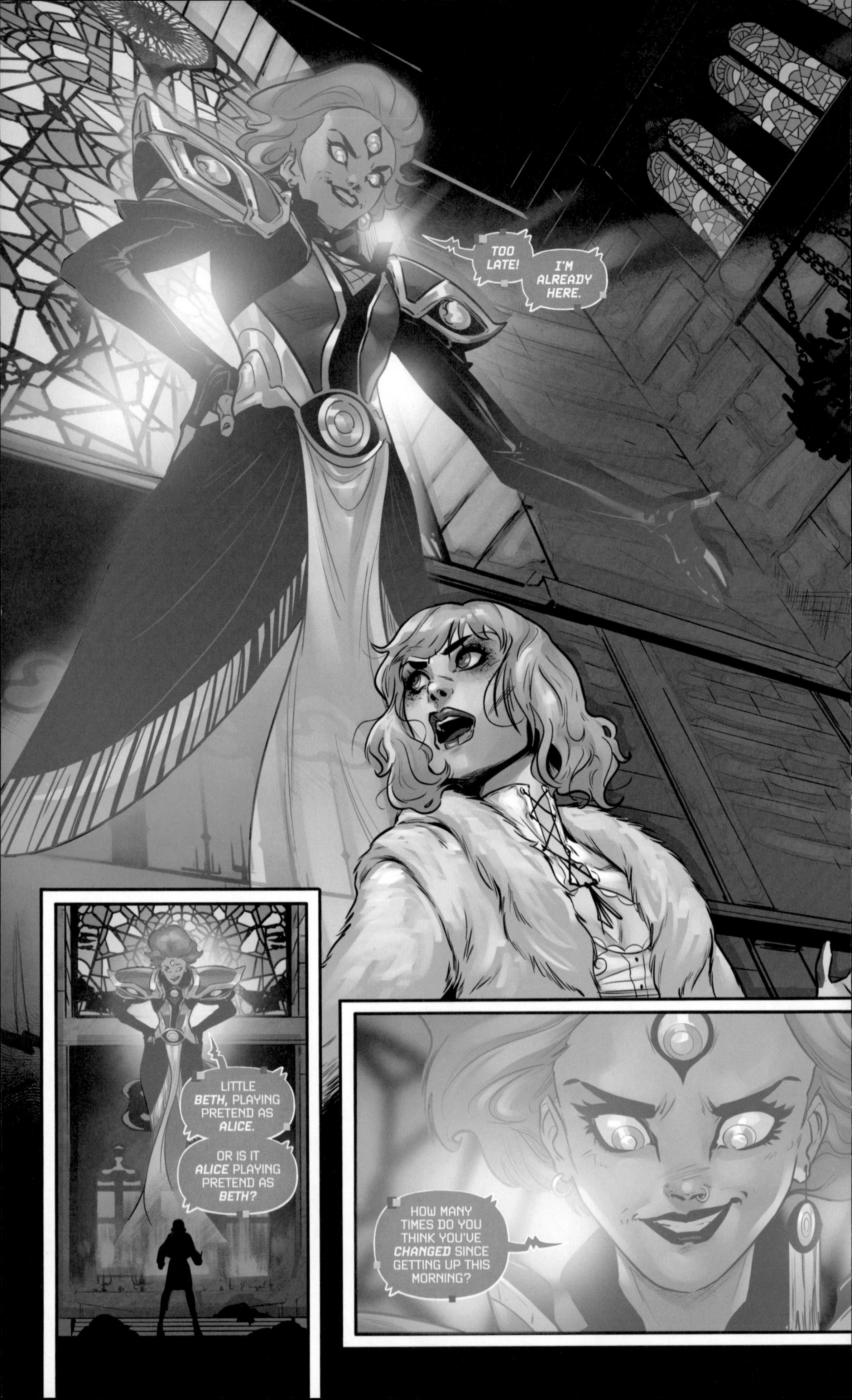
TOO LATE!
I'M ALREADY HERE.
LITTLE BETH, PLAYING PRETEND AS ALICE.
OR IS IT ALICE PLAYING PRETEND AS BETH?
HOW MANY TIMES DO YOU THINK YOU'VE CHANGED SINCE GETTING UP THIS MORNING?

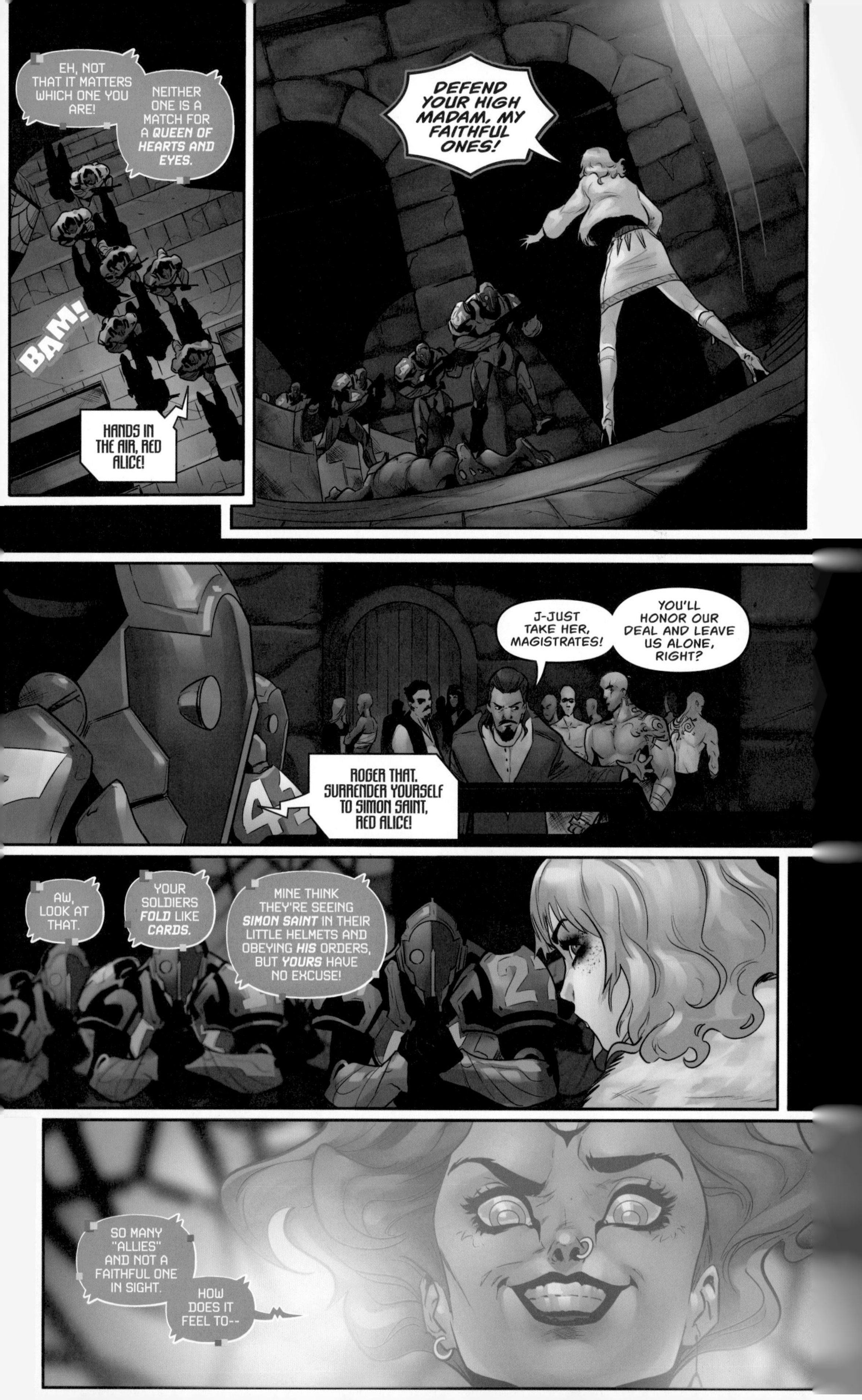
EH, NOT THAT IT MATTERS WHICH ONE YOU ARE!
NEITHER ONE IS A MATCH FOR A QUEEN OF HEARTS AND EYES.
BAM!
HANDS IN THE AIR, RED ALICE!
DEFEND YOUR HIGH MADAM, MY FAITHFUL ONES!
J-JUST TAKE HER, MAGISTRATES!
YOU'LL HONOR OUR DEAL AND LEAVE US ALONE, RIGHT?
ROGER THAT. SURRENDER YOURSELF TO SIMON SAINT, RED ALICE!
AW, LOOK AT THAT.
YOUR SOLDIERS FOLD LIKE CARDS.
MINE THINK THEY'RE SEEING SIMON SAINT IN THEIR LITTLE HELMETS AND OBEYING HIS ORDERS, BUT YOURS HAVE NO EXCUSE!
SO MANY "ALLIES" AND NOT A FAITHFUL ONE IN SIGHT.
HOW DOES IT FEEL TO--

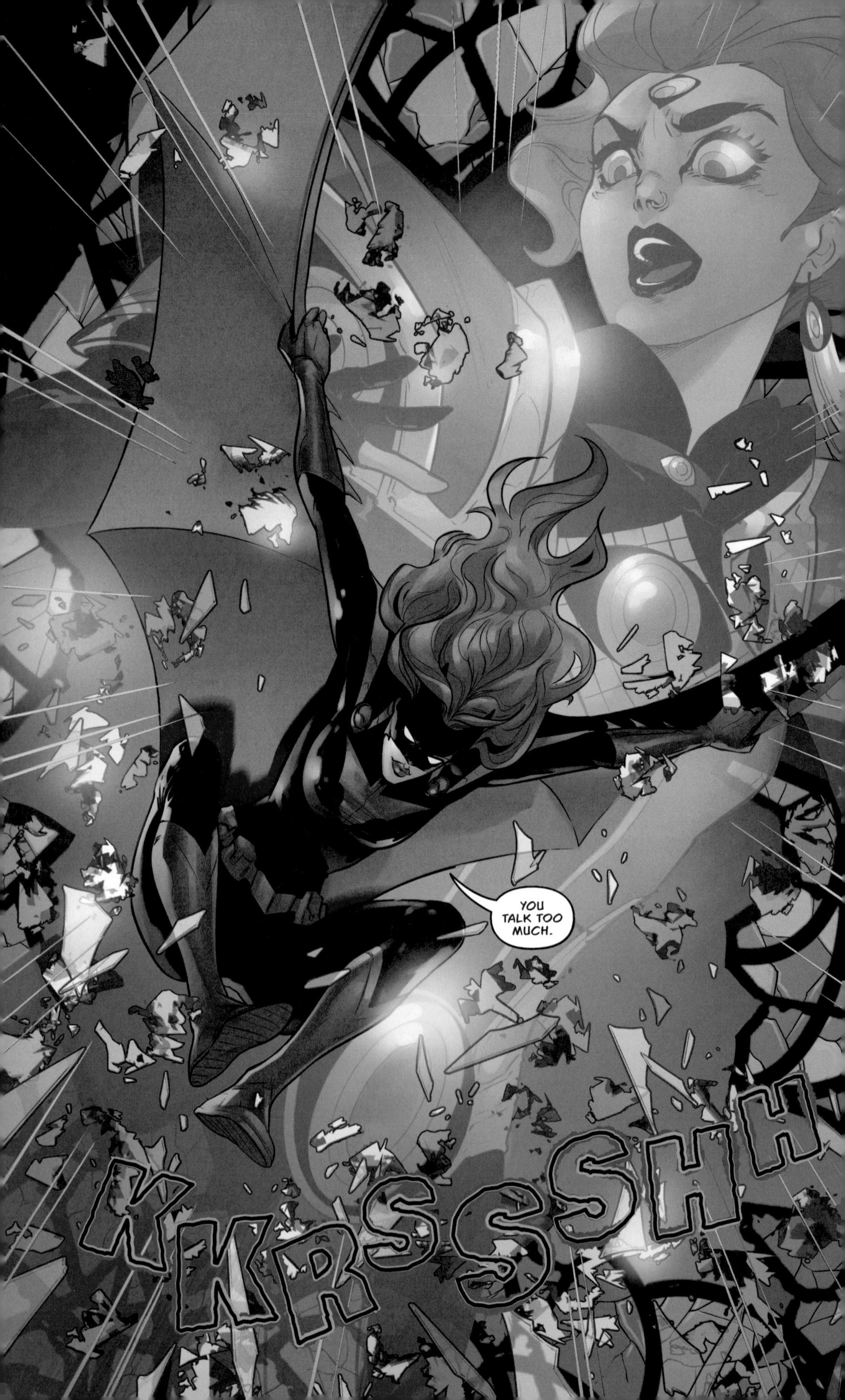
YOU TALK TOO MUCH.
KKRSSSHH

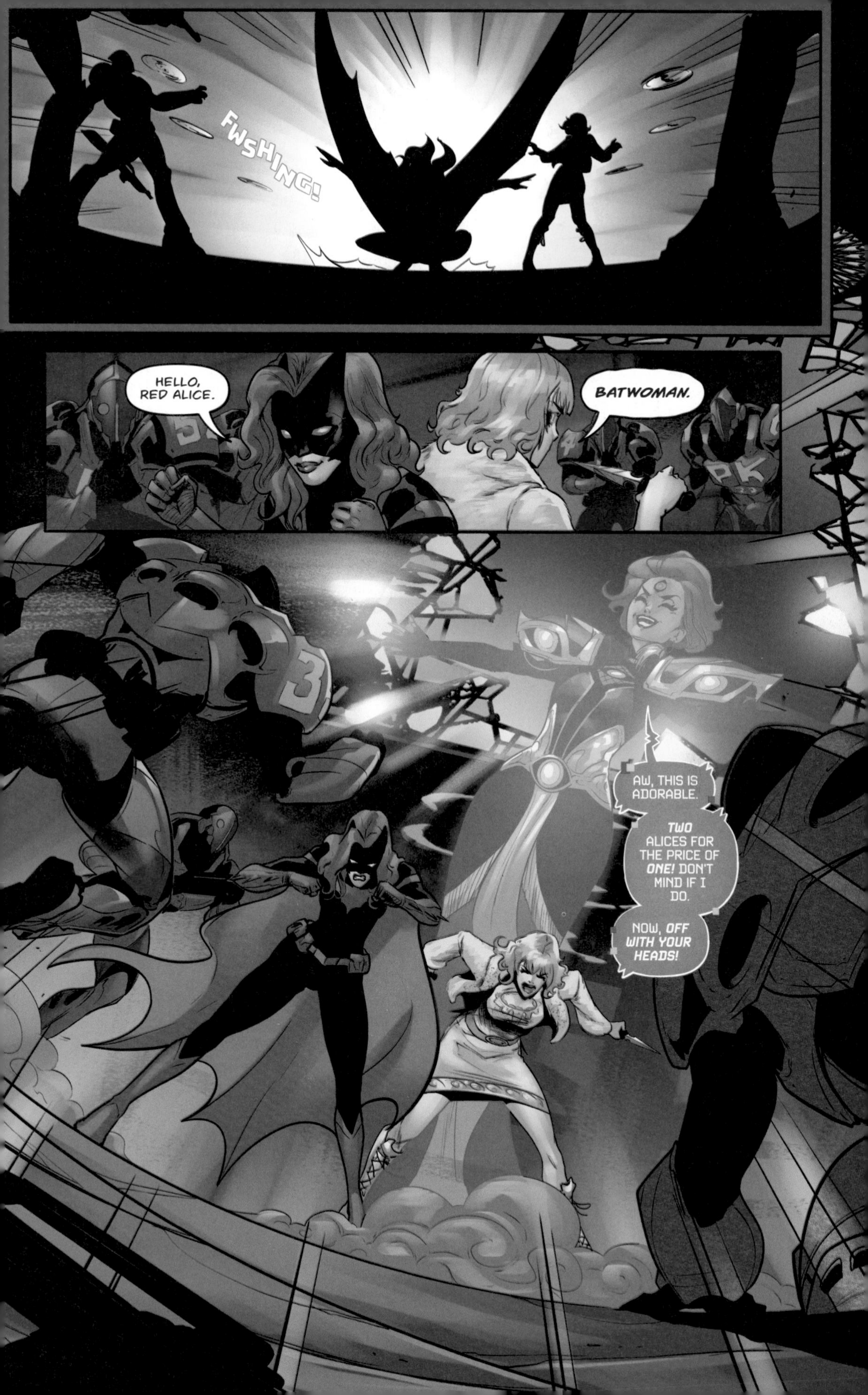
FWSHING!
HELLO, RED ALICE.
BATWOMAN.
AW, THIS IS ADORABLE.
TWO ALICES FOR THE PRICE OF ONE! DON'T MIND IF I DO.
NOW, OFF WITH YOUR HEADS!

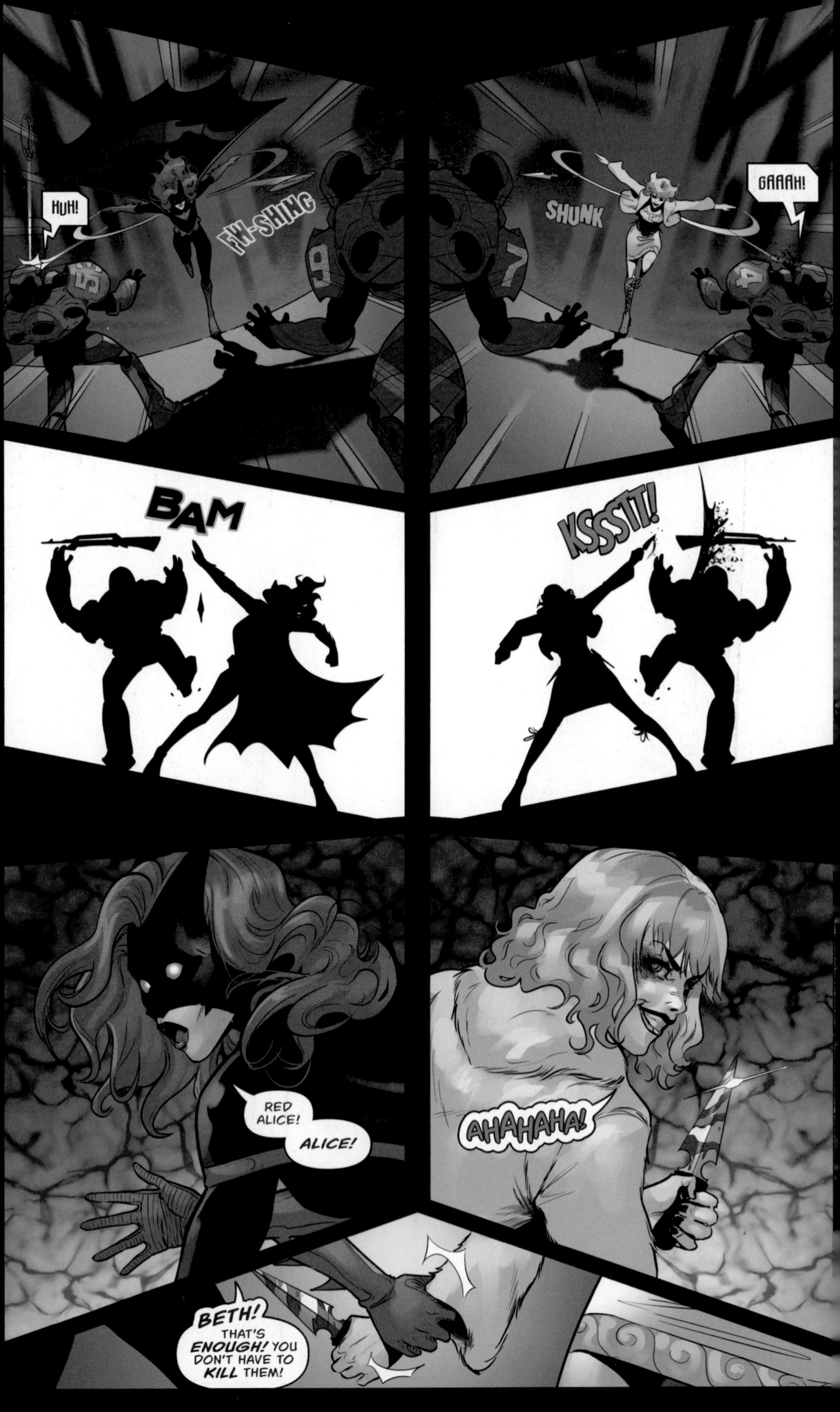
HUH!
FW-SHING
SHUNK
GAAAH!
BAM
KSSSTT!
RED ALICE! ALICE!
AHAHAHA!
BETH! THAT'S ENOUGH! YOU DON'T HAVE TO KILL THEM!

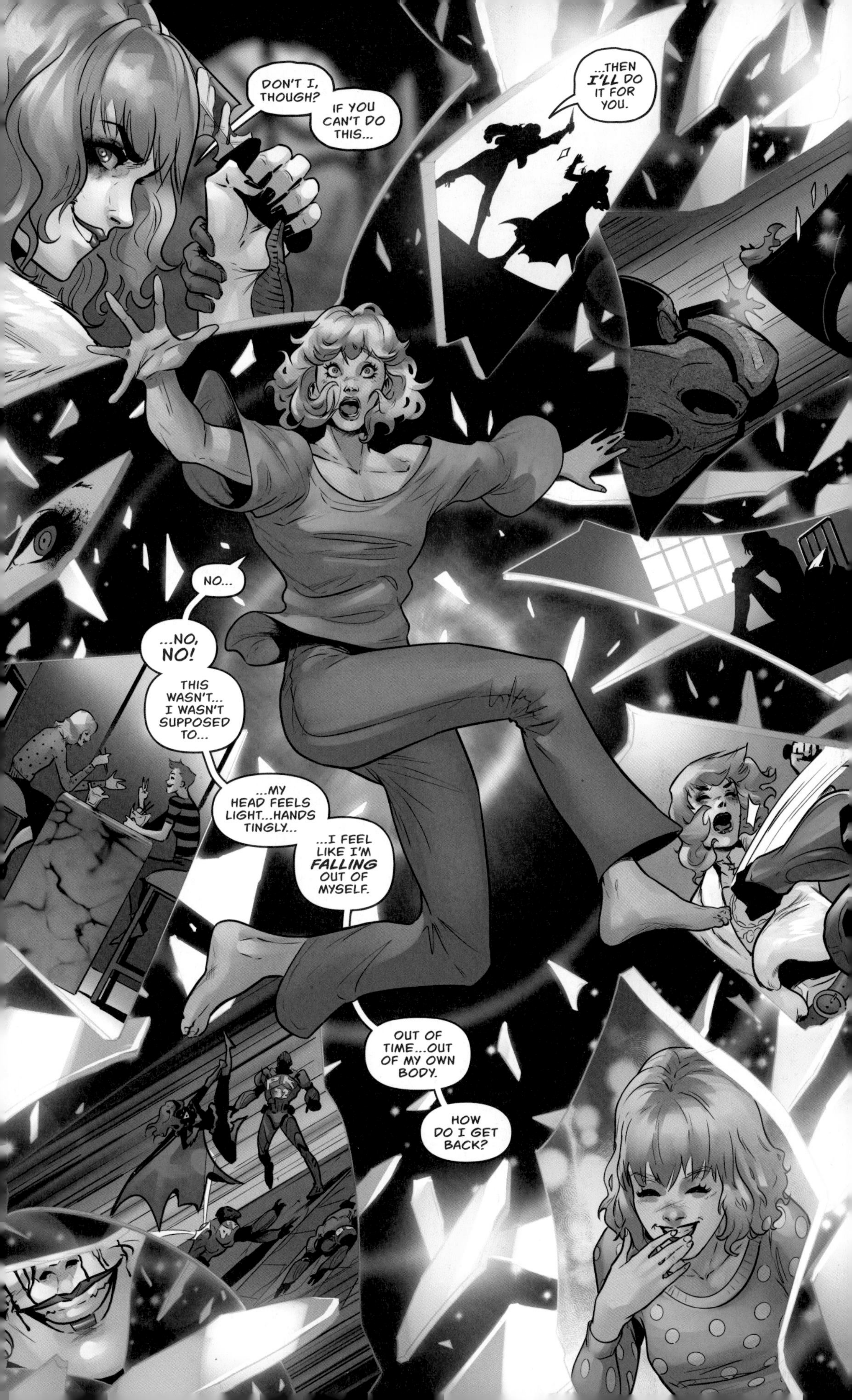
DON'T I, THOUGH?
IF YOU CAN'T DO THIS...
...THEN I'LL DO IT FOR YOU.
NO...
...NO, NO!
THIS WASN'T... I WASN'T SUPPOSED TO...
...MY HEAD FEELS LIGHT...HANDS TINGLY...
...I FEEL LIKE I'M FALLING OUT OF MYSELF.
OUT OF TIME...OUT OF MY OWN BODY.
HOW DO I GET BACK?

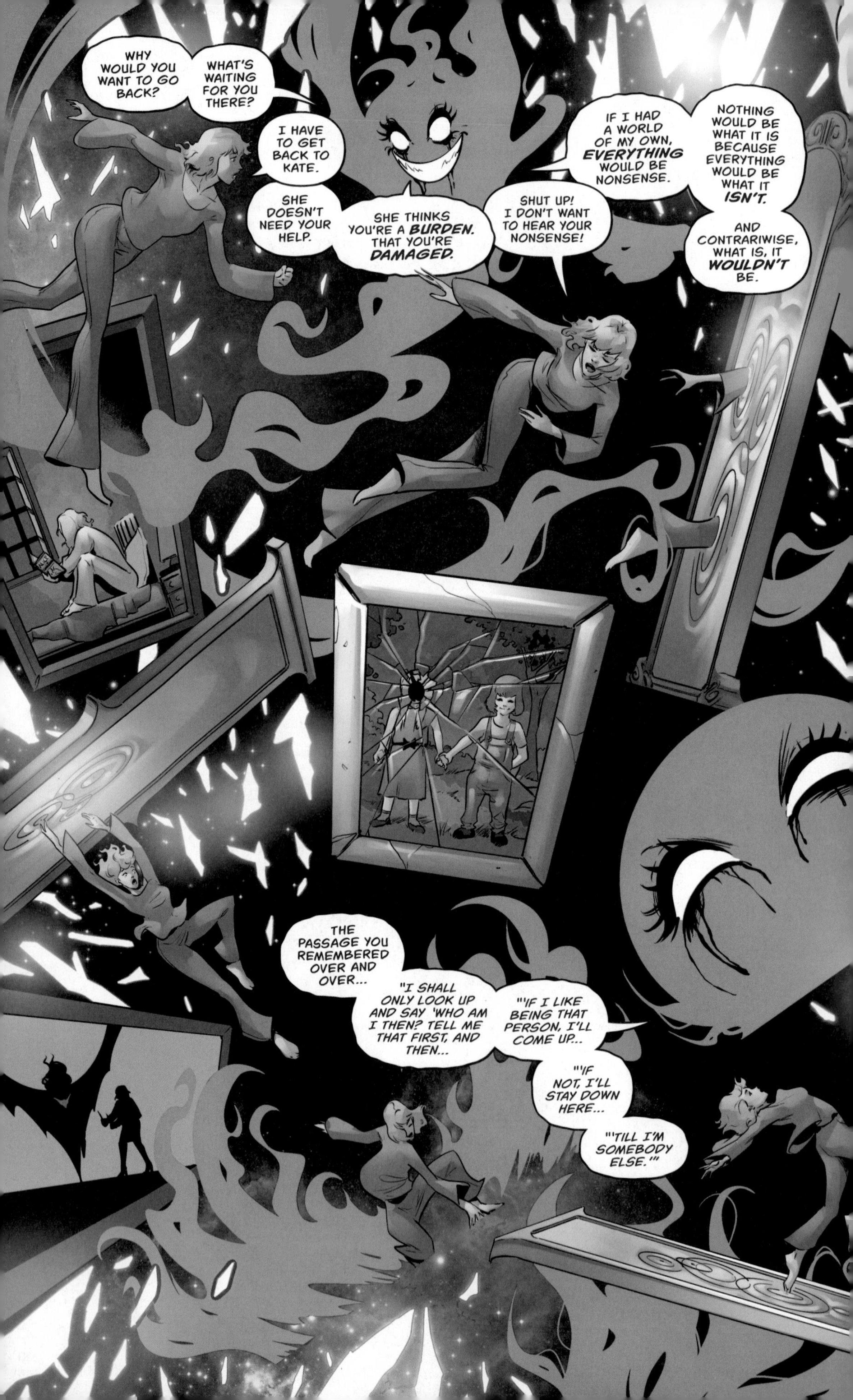
WHY WOULD YOU WANT TO GO BACK?
WHAT'S WAITING FOR YOU THERE?
I HAVE TO GET BACK TO KATE.
SHE DOESN'T NEED YOUR HELP.
SHE THINKS YOU'RE A BURDEN. THAT YOU'RE DAMAGED.
SHUT UP! I DON'T WANT TO HEAR YOUR NONSENSE!
IF I HAD A WORLD OF MY OWN, EVERYTHING WOULD BE NONSENSE.
NOTHING WOULD BE WHAT IT IS BECAUSE EVERYTHING WOULD BE WHAT IT ISN'T.
AND CONTRARIWISE, WHAT IS, IT WOULDN'T BE.
THE PASSAGE YOU REMEMBERED OVER AND OVER...
"I SHALL ONLY LOOK UP AND SAY 'WHO AM I THEN? TELL ME THAT FIRST, AND THEN...
"'IF I LIKE BEING THAT PERSON, I'LL COME UP...
"'IF NOT, I'LL STAY DOWN HERE...
"'TILL I'M SOMEBODY ELSE.'"

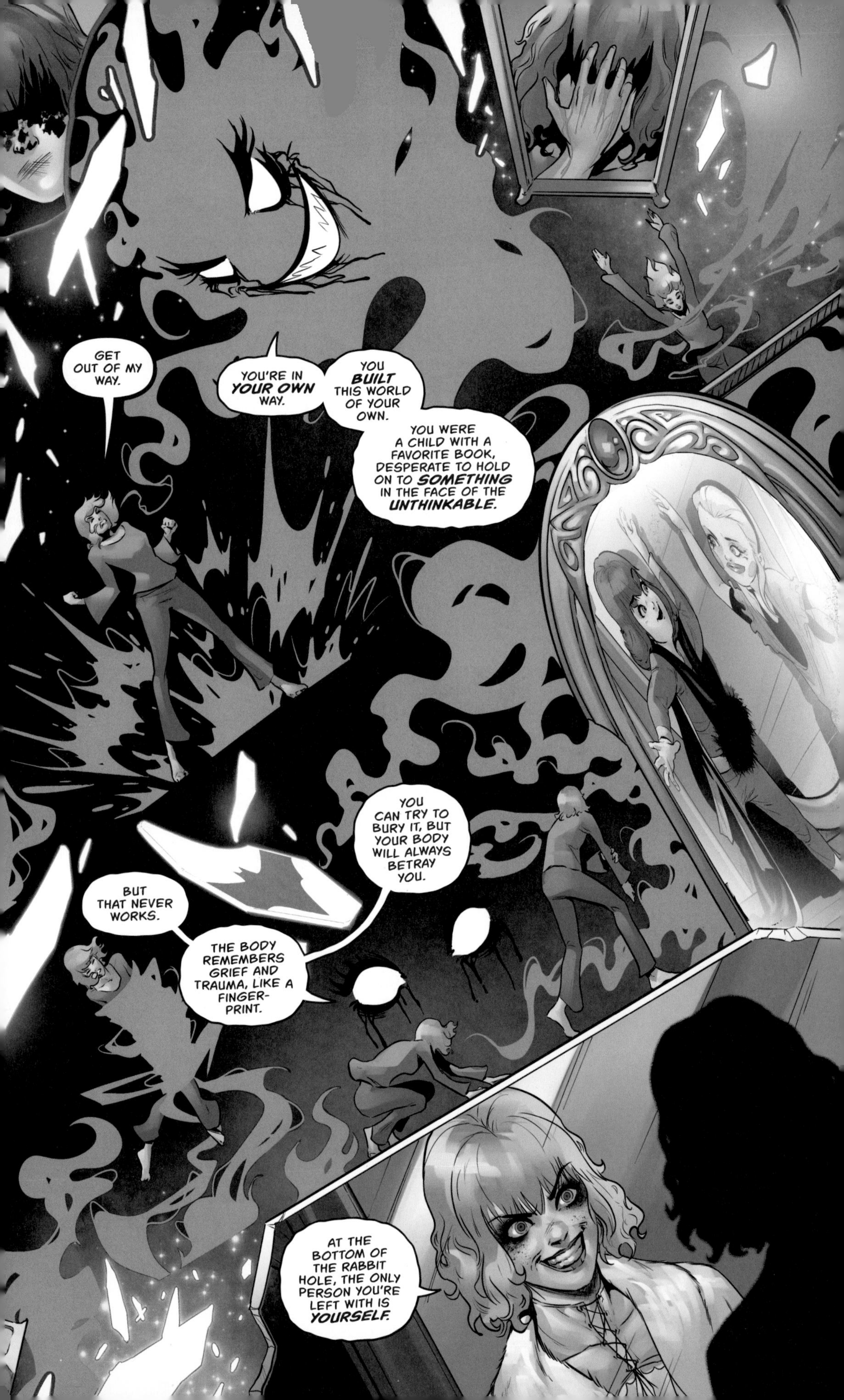
GET OUT OF MY WAY.
YOU'RE IN YOUR OWN WAY.
YOU BUILT THIS WORLD OF YOUR OWN.
YOU WERE A CHILD WITH A FAVORITE BOOK, DESPERATE TO HOLD ON TO SOMETHING IN THE FACE OF THE UNTHINKABLE.
YOU CAN TRY TO BURY IT, BUT YOUR BODY WILL ALWAYS BETRAY YOU.
BUT THAT NEVER WORKS.
THE BODY REMEMBERS GRIEF AND TRAUMA, LIKE A FINGER-PRINT.
AT THE BOTTOM OF THE RABBIT HOLE, THE ONLY PERSON YOU'RE LEFT WITH IS YOURSELF.

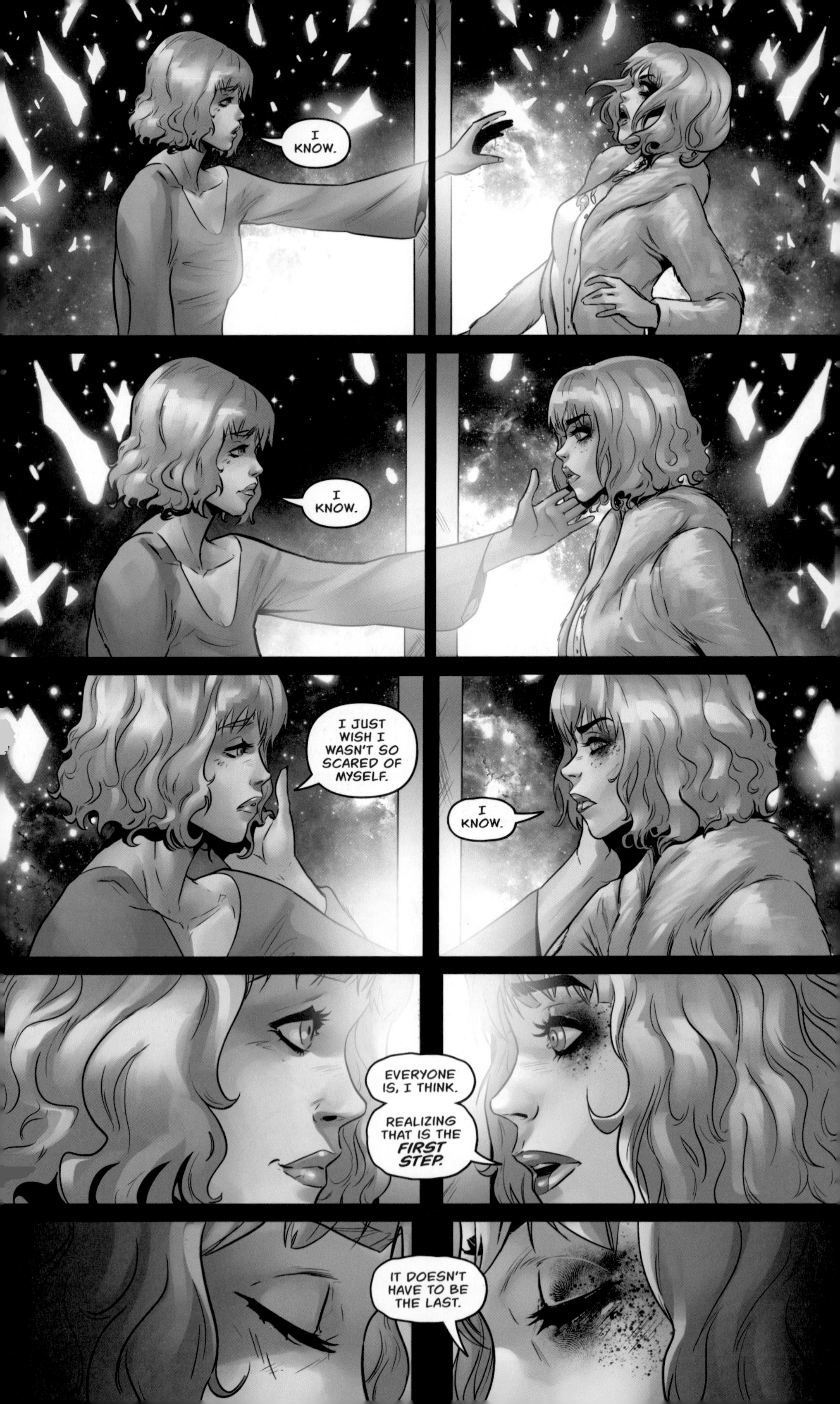
I KNOW.
I KNOW.
I JUST WISH I WASN'T SO SCARED OF MYSELF.
I KNOW.
EVERYONE IS, I THINK.
REALIZING THAT IS THE *FIRST STEP.*
IT DOESN'T HAVE TO BE THE LAST.

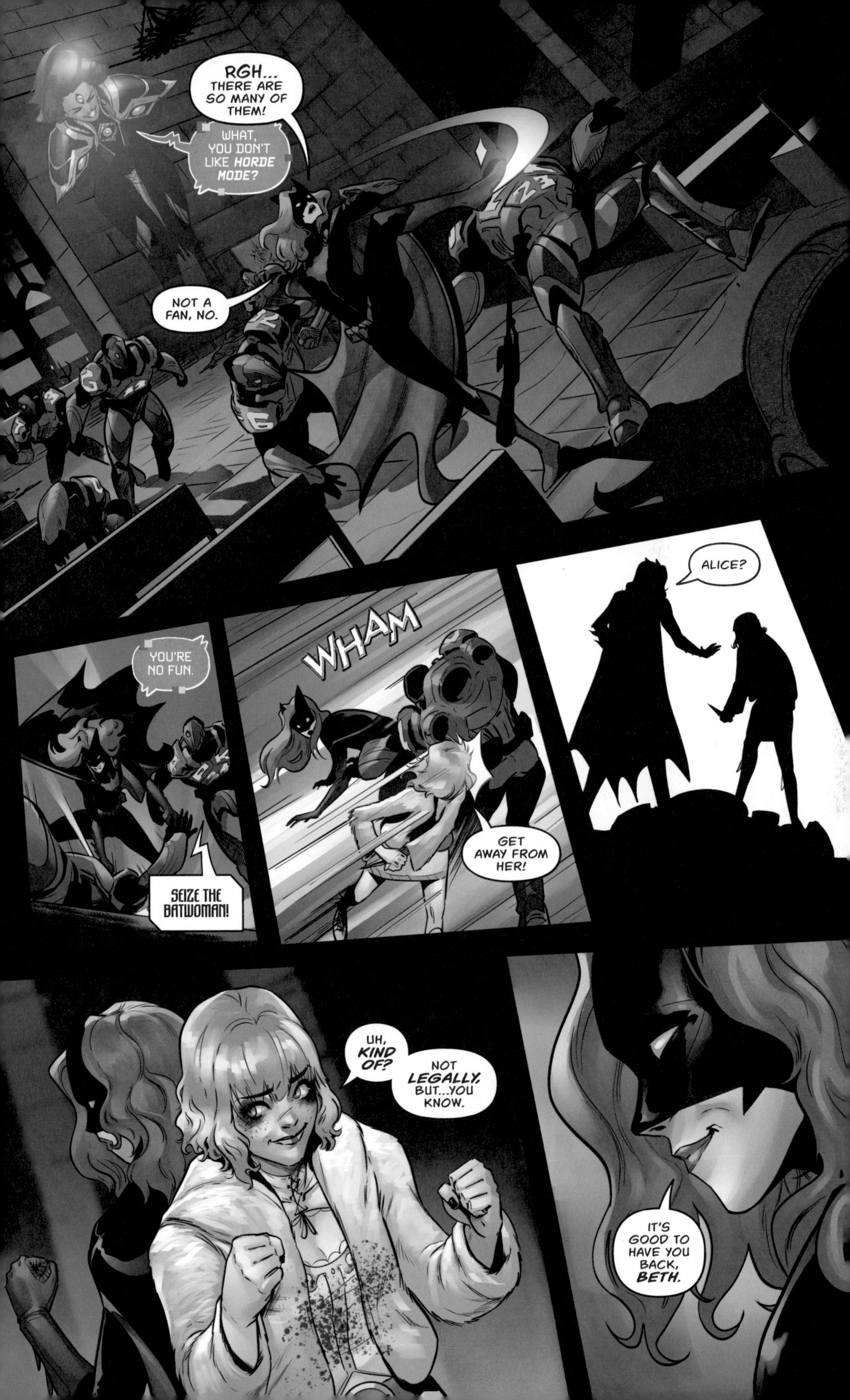
RGH... THERE ARE SO MANY OF THEM!
WHAT, YOU DON'T LIKE *HORDE MODE?*
NOT A FAN, NO.
YOU'RE NO FUN.
SEIZE THE BATWOMAN!
WHAM
GET AWAY FROM HER!
ALICE?
UH, *KIND OF?*
NOT *LEGALLY,* BUT...YOU KNOW.
IT'S GOOD TO HAVE YOU BACK, *BETH.*

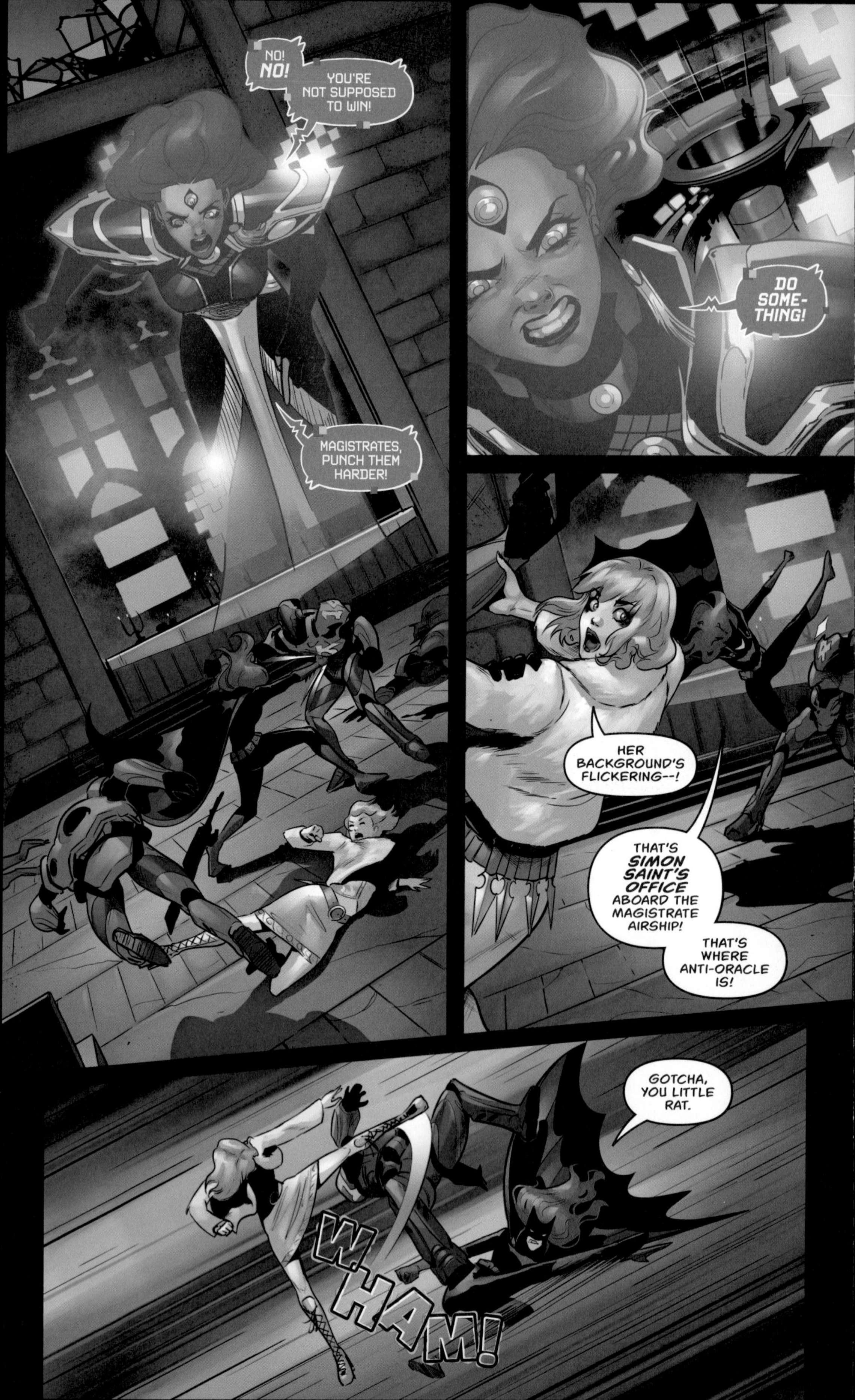
NO! ***NO!***
YOU'RE NOT SUPPOSED TO WIN!
MAGISTRATES, PUNCH THEM HARDER!
DO SOME-THING!
HER BACKGROUND'S FLICKERING--!
THAT'S ***SIMON SAINT'S OFFICE*** ABOARD THE MAGISTRATE AIRSHIP!
THAT'S WHERE ANTI-ORACLE IS!
GOTCHA, YOU LITTLE RAT.
WHAM!

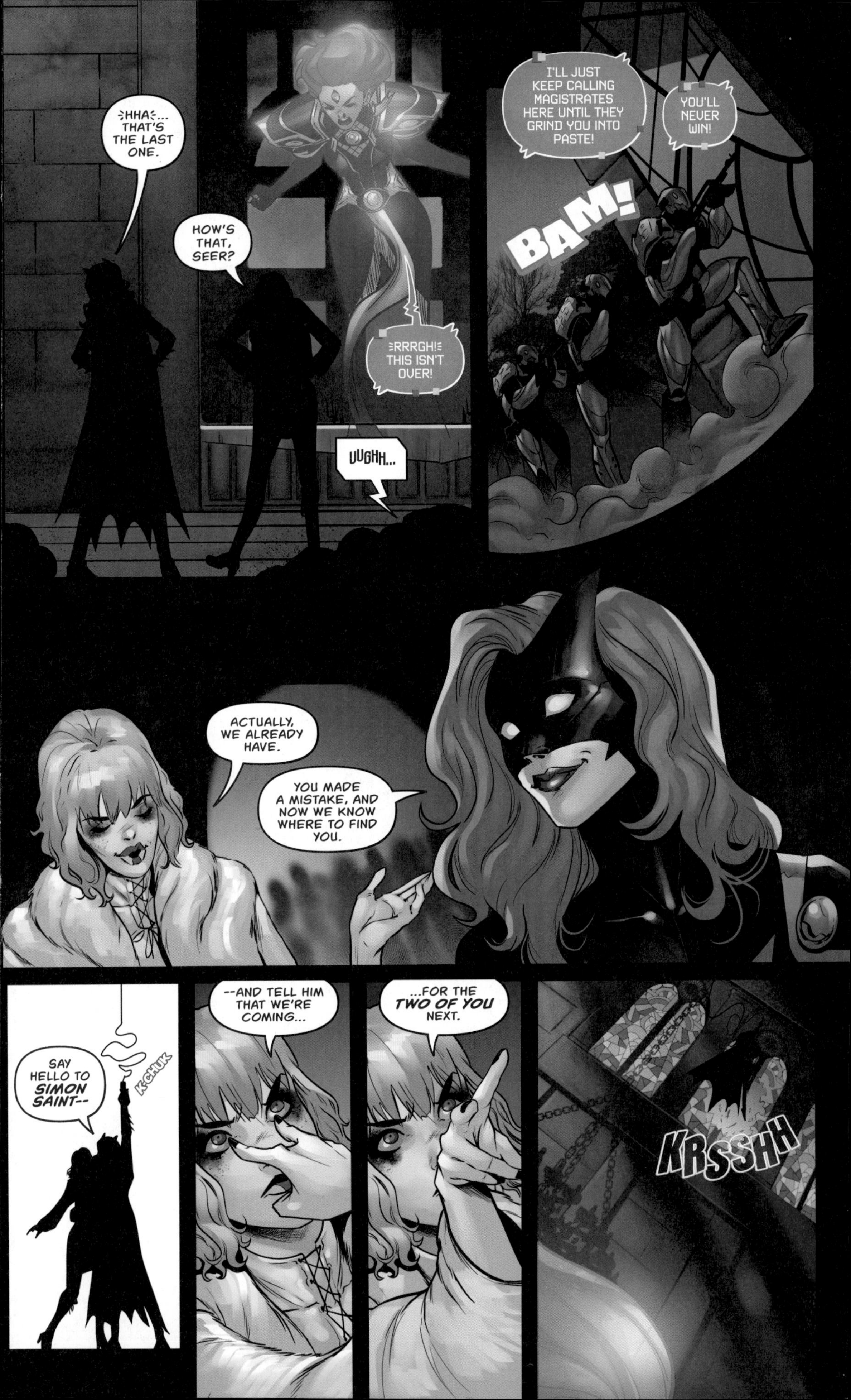

HHA... THAT'S THE LAST ONE.
HOW'S THAT, SEER?
RRRGH! THIS ISN'T OVER!
UUGHH...
I'LL JUST KEEP CALLING MAGISTRATES HERE UNTIL THEY GRIND YOU INTO PASTE!
YOU'LL NEVER WIN!
BAM!
ACTUALLY, WE ALREADY HAVE.
YOU MADE A MISTAKE, AND NOW WE KNOW WHERE TO FIND YOU.
SAY HELLO TO SIMON SAINT--
K-CHUK
--AND TELL HIM THAT WE'RE COMING...
...FOR THE TWO OF YOU NEXT.
KRSSHH

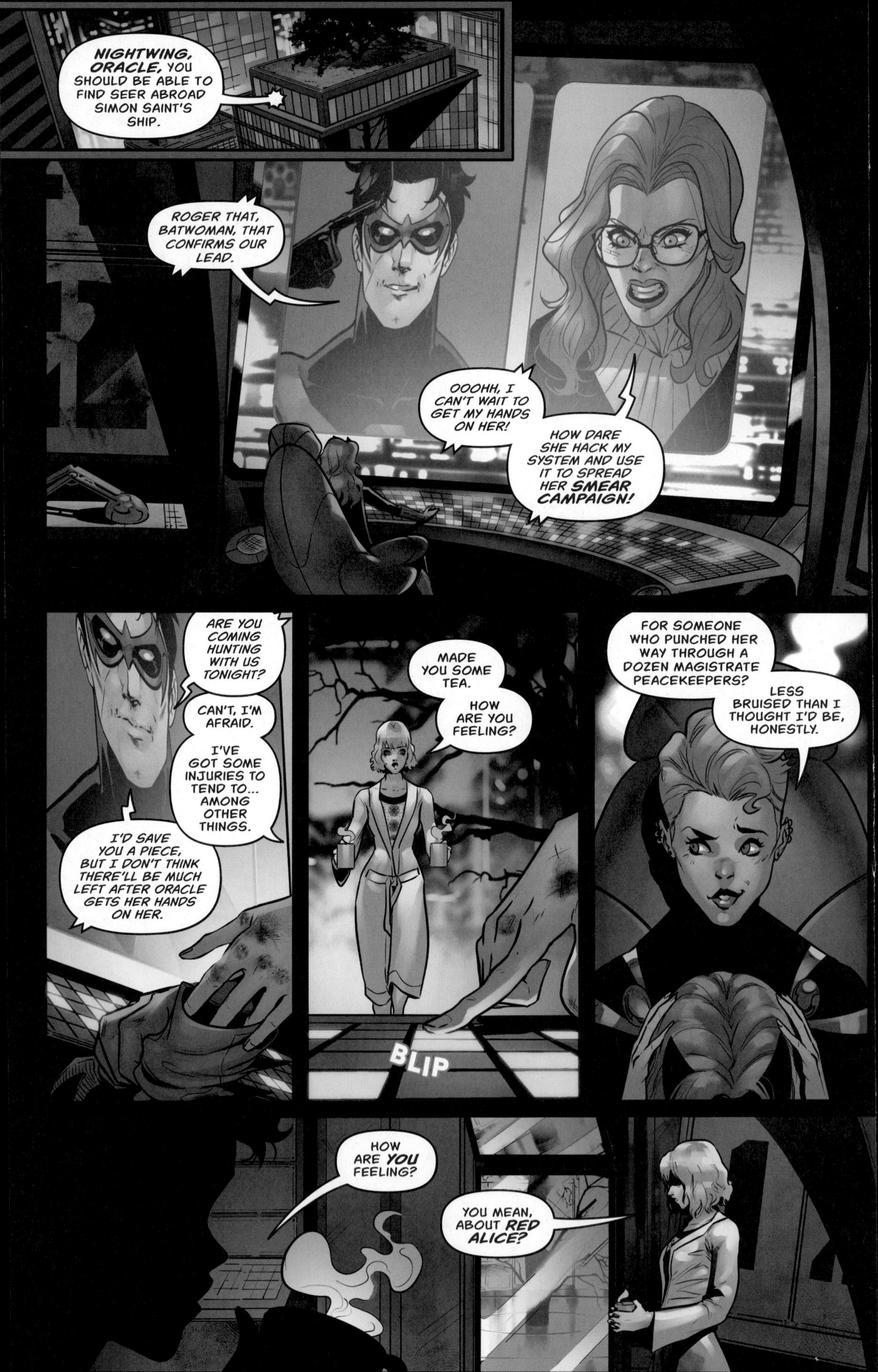
NIGHTWING, ORACLE, YOU SHOULD BE ABLE TO FIND SEER ABROAD SIMON SAINT'S SHIP.
ROGER THAT, BATWOMAN, THAT CONFIRMS OUR LEAD.
OOOHH, I CAN'T WAIT TO GET MY HANDS ON HER!
HOW DARE SHE HACK MY SYSTEM AND USE IT TO SPREAD HER SMEAR CAMPAIGN!
ARE YOU COMING HUNTING WITH US TONIGHT?
CAN'T, I'M AFRAID.
I'VE GOT SOME INJURIES TO TEND TO... AMONG OTHER THINGS.
I'D SAVE YOU A PIECE, BUT I DON'T THINK THERE'LL BE MUCH LEFT AFTER ORACLE GETS HER HANDS ON HER.
MADE YOU SOME TEA.
HOW ARE YOU FEELING?
BLIP
FOR SOMEONE WHO PUNCHED HER WAY THROUGH A DOZEN MAGISTRATE PEACEKEEPERS?
LESS BRUISED THAN I THOUGHT I'D BE, HONESTLY.
HOW ARE YOU FEELING?
YOU MEAN, ABOUT RED ALICE?

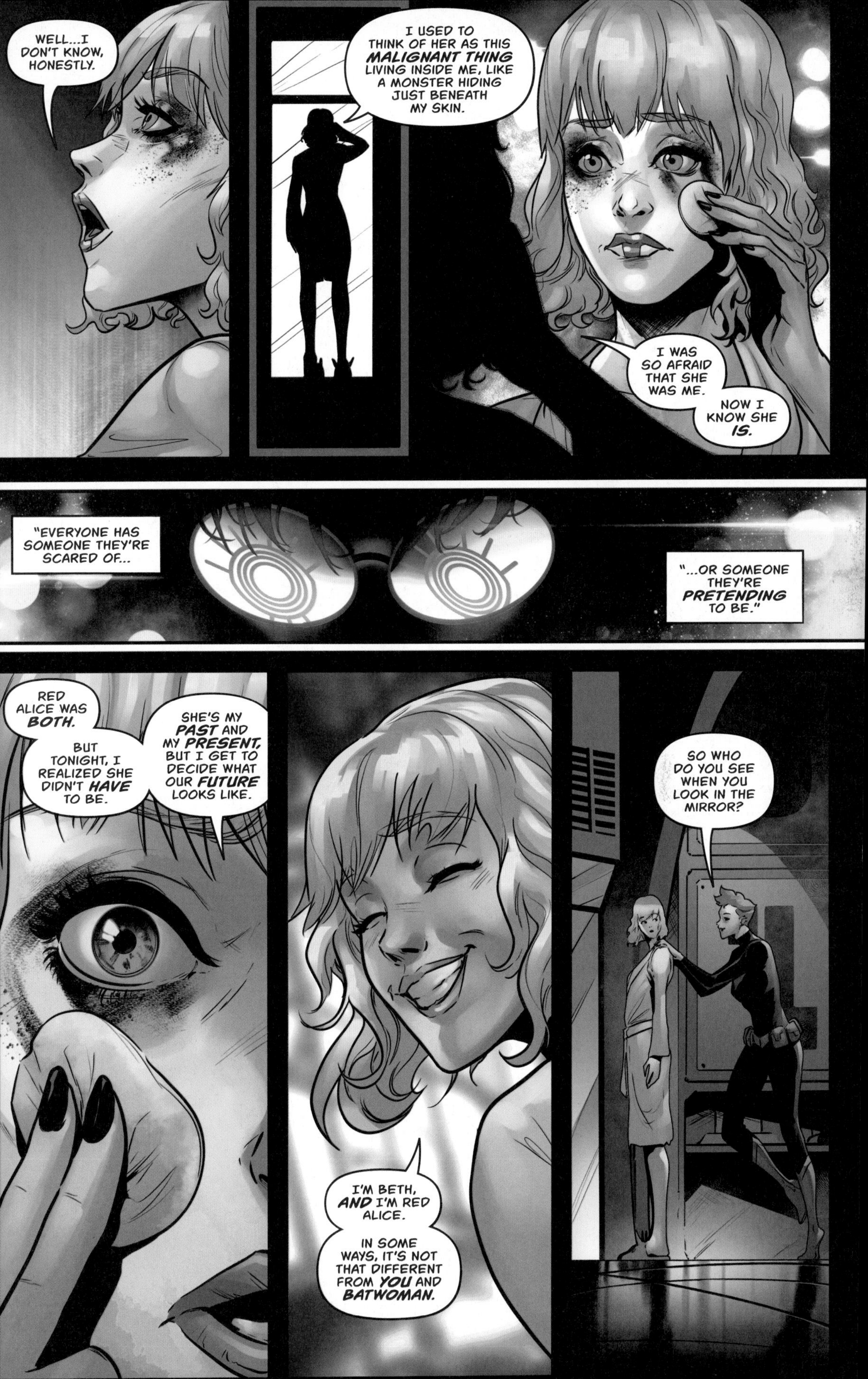
WELL...I DON'T KNOW, HONESTLY.
I USED TO THINK OF HER AS THIS MALIGNANT THING LIVING INSIDE ME, LIKE A MONSTER HIDING JUST BENEATH MY SKIN.
I WAS SO AFRAID THAT SHE WAS ME.
NOW I KNOW SHE IS.
"EVERYONE HAS SOMEONE THEY'RE SCARED OF...
"...OR SOMEONE THEY'RE PRETENDING TO BE."
RED ALICE WAS BOTH.
BUT TONIGHT, I REALIZED SHE DIDN'T HAVE TO BE.
SHE'S MY PAST AND MY PRESENT, BUT I GET TO DECIDE WHAT OUR FUTURE LOOKS LIKE.
I'M BETH, AND I'M RED ALICE.
IN SOME WAYS, IT'S NOT THAT DIFFERENT FROM YOU AND BATWOMAN.
SO WHO DO YOU SEE WHEN YOU LOOK IN THE MIRROR?

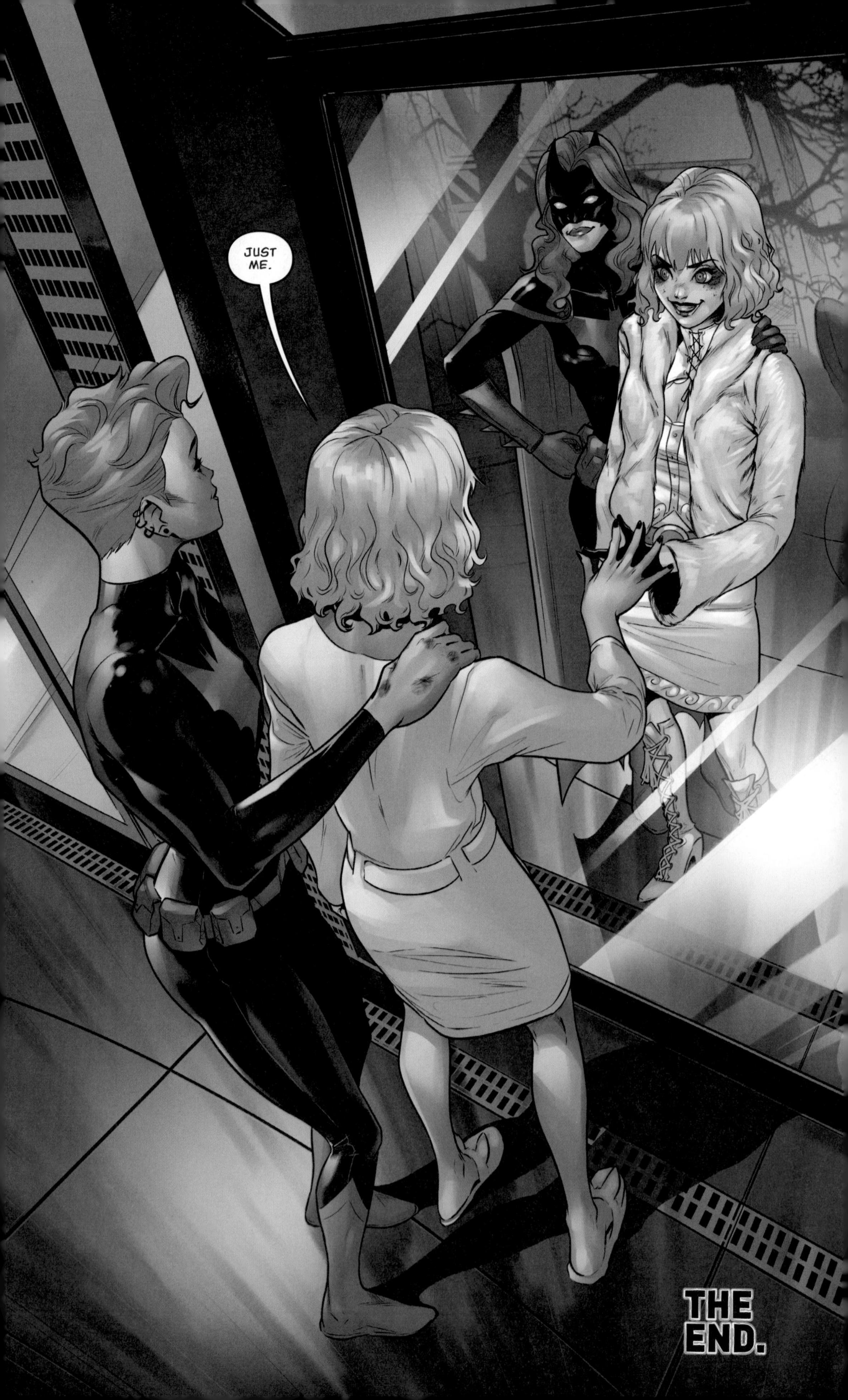
JUST ME.
THE END.

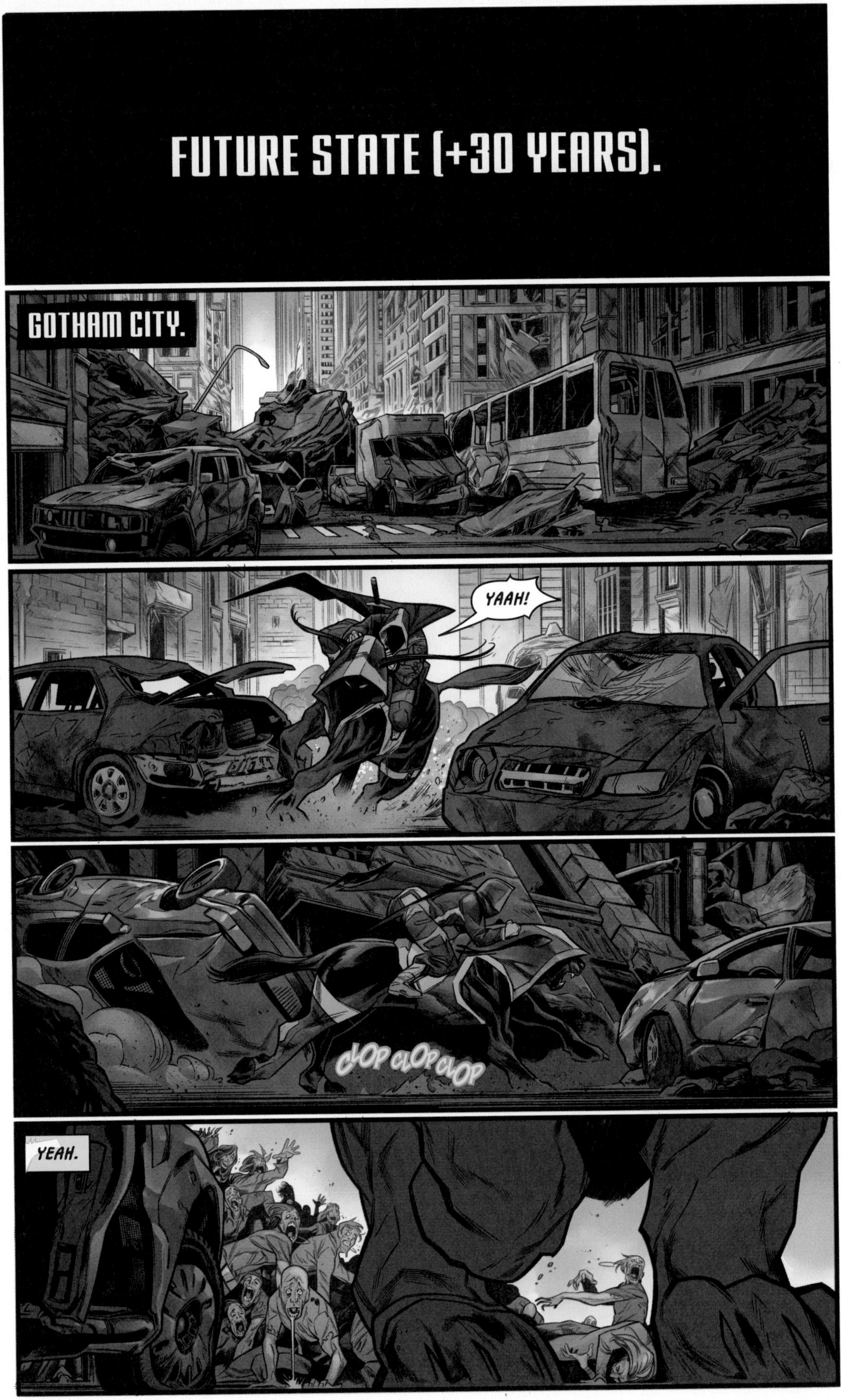

FUTURE STATE (+30 YEARS).
GOTHAM CITY.
YAAH!
CLOP CLOP CLOP
YEAH.

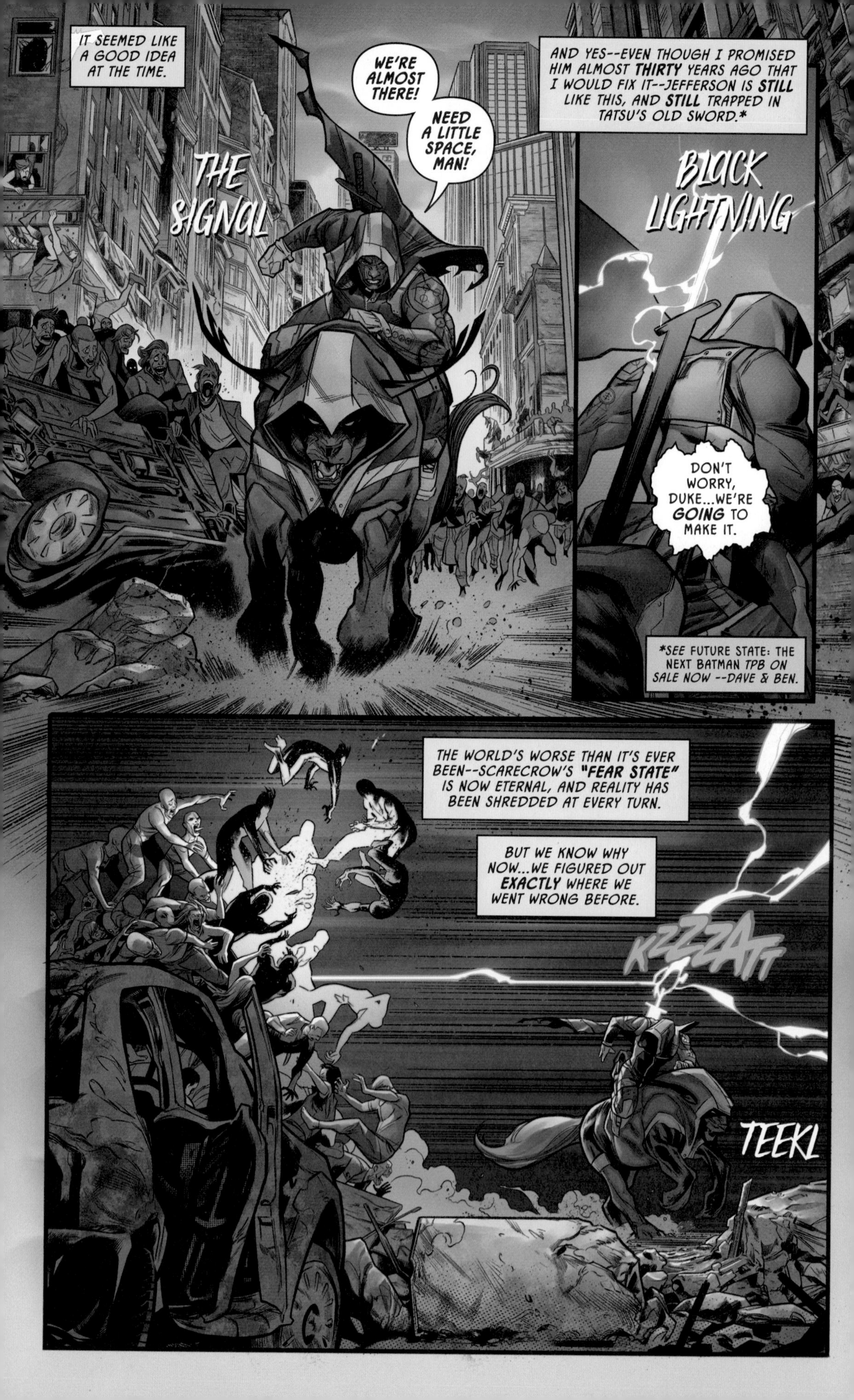
IT SEEMED LIKE A GOOD IDEA AT THE TIME.
WE'RE ALMOST THERE!
NEED A LITTLE SPACE, MAN!
AND YES--EVEN THOUGH I PROMISED HIM ALMOST THIRTY YEARS AGO THAT I WOULD FIX IT--JEFFERSON IS STILL LIKE THIS, AND STILL TRAPPED IN TATSU'S OLD SWORD.*
THE SIGNAL
BLACK LIGHTNING
DON'T WORRY, DUKE...WE'RE GOING TO MAKE IT.
*SEE FUTURE STATE: THE NEXT BATMAN TPB ON SALE NOW --DAVE & BEN.
THE WORLD'S WORSE THAN IT'S EVER BEEN--SCARECROW'S "FEAR STATE" IS NOW ETERNAL, AND REALITY HAS BEEN SHREDDED AT EVERY TURN.
BUT WE KNOW WHY NOW...WE FIGURED OUT EXACTLY WHERE WE WENT WRONG BEFORE.
KZZZZATT
TEEKL

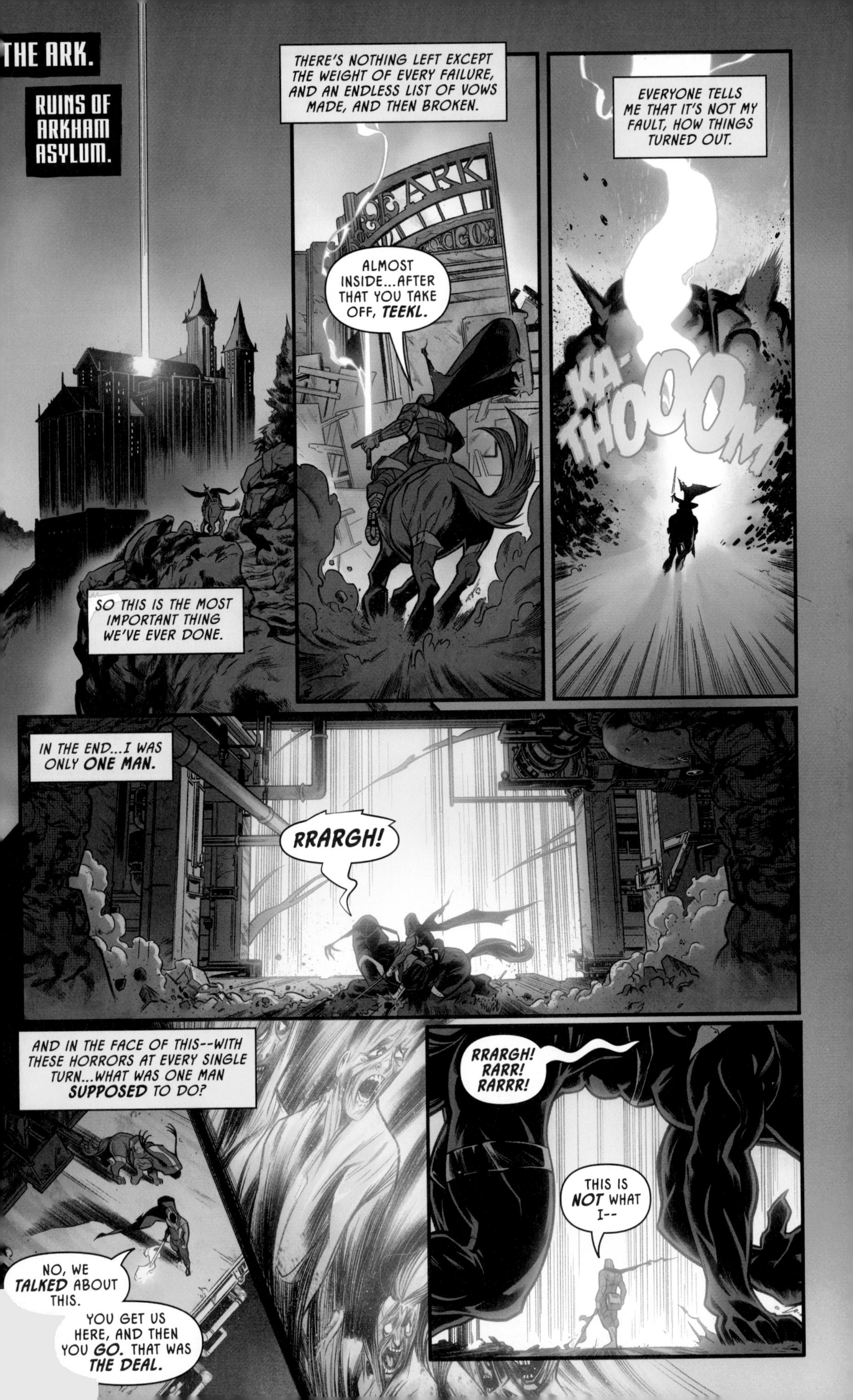
THE ARK.
RUINS OF ARKHAM ASYLUM.
SO THIS IS THE MOST IMPORTANT THING WE'VE EVER DONE.
THERE'S NOTHING LEFT EXCEPT THE WEIGHT OF EVERY FAILURE, AND AN ENDLESS LIST OF VOWS MADE, AND THEN BROKEN.
ALMOST INSIDE...AFTER THAT YOU TAKE OFF, TEEKL.
EVERYONE TELLS ME THAT IT'S NOT MY FAULT, HOW THINGS TURNED OUT.
KA-THOOOOM
IN THE END...I WAS ONLY ONE MAN.
RRARGH!
AND IN THE FACE OF THIS--WITH THESE HORRORS AT EVERY SINGLE TURN...WHAT WAS ONE MAN SUPPOSED TO DO?
NO, WE TALKED ABOUT THIS.
YOU GET US HERE, AND THEN YOU GO. THAT WAS THE DEAL.
RRARGH! RARR! RARRR!
THIS IS NOT WHAT I--

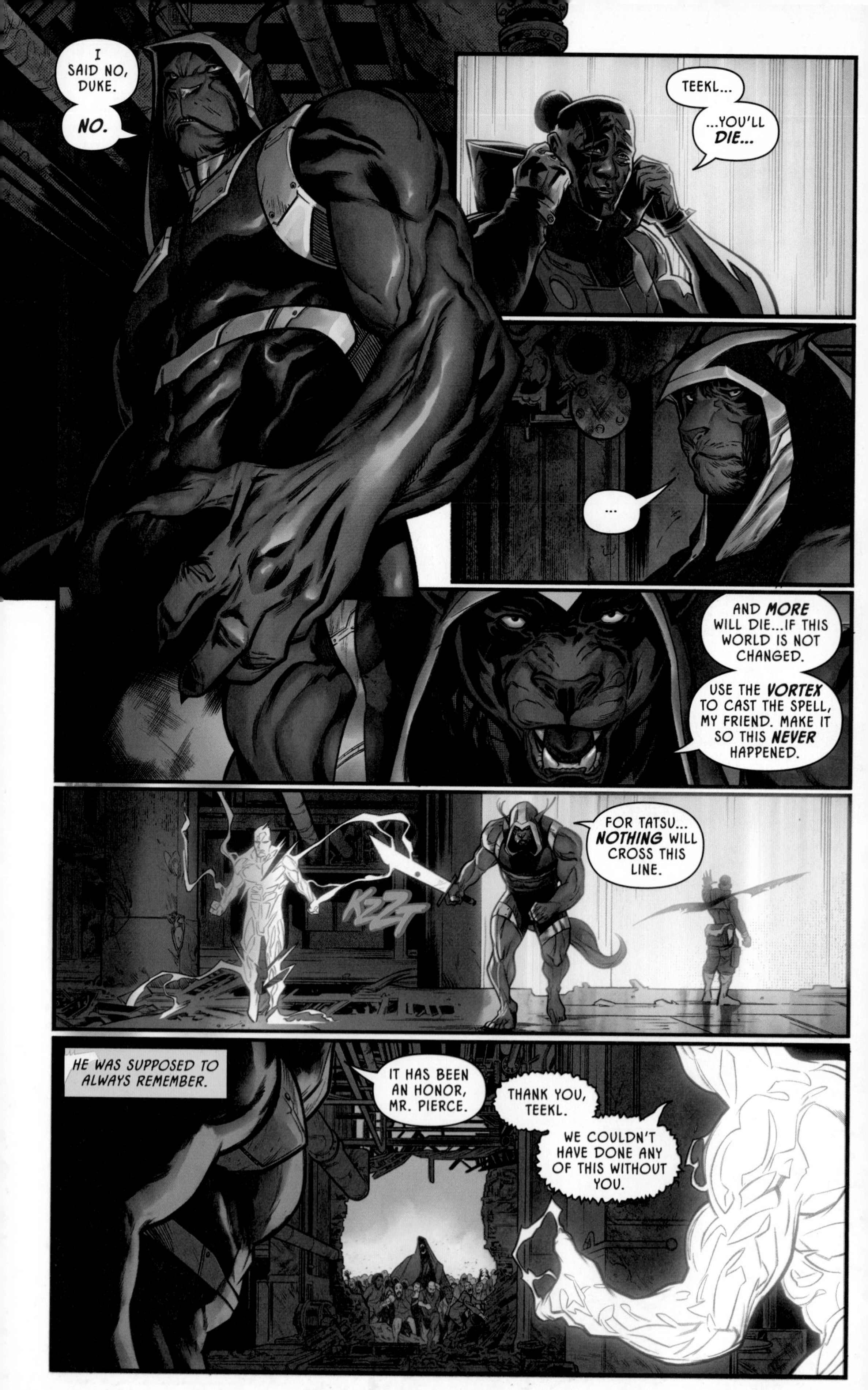
I SAID NO, DUKE.
NO.
TEEKL...
...YOU'LL DIE...
...
AND MORE WILL DIE...IF THIS WORLD IS NOT CHANGED.
USE THE VORTEX TO CAST THE SPELL, MY FRIEND. MAKE IT SO THIS NEVER HAPPENED.
KZZT
FOR TATSU... NOTHING WILL CROSS THIS LINE.
HE WAS SUPPOSED TO ALWAYS REMEMBER.
IT HAS BEEN AN HONOR, MR. PIERCE.
THANK YOU, TEEKL.
WE COULDN'T HAVE DONE ANY OF THIS WITHOUT YOU.

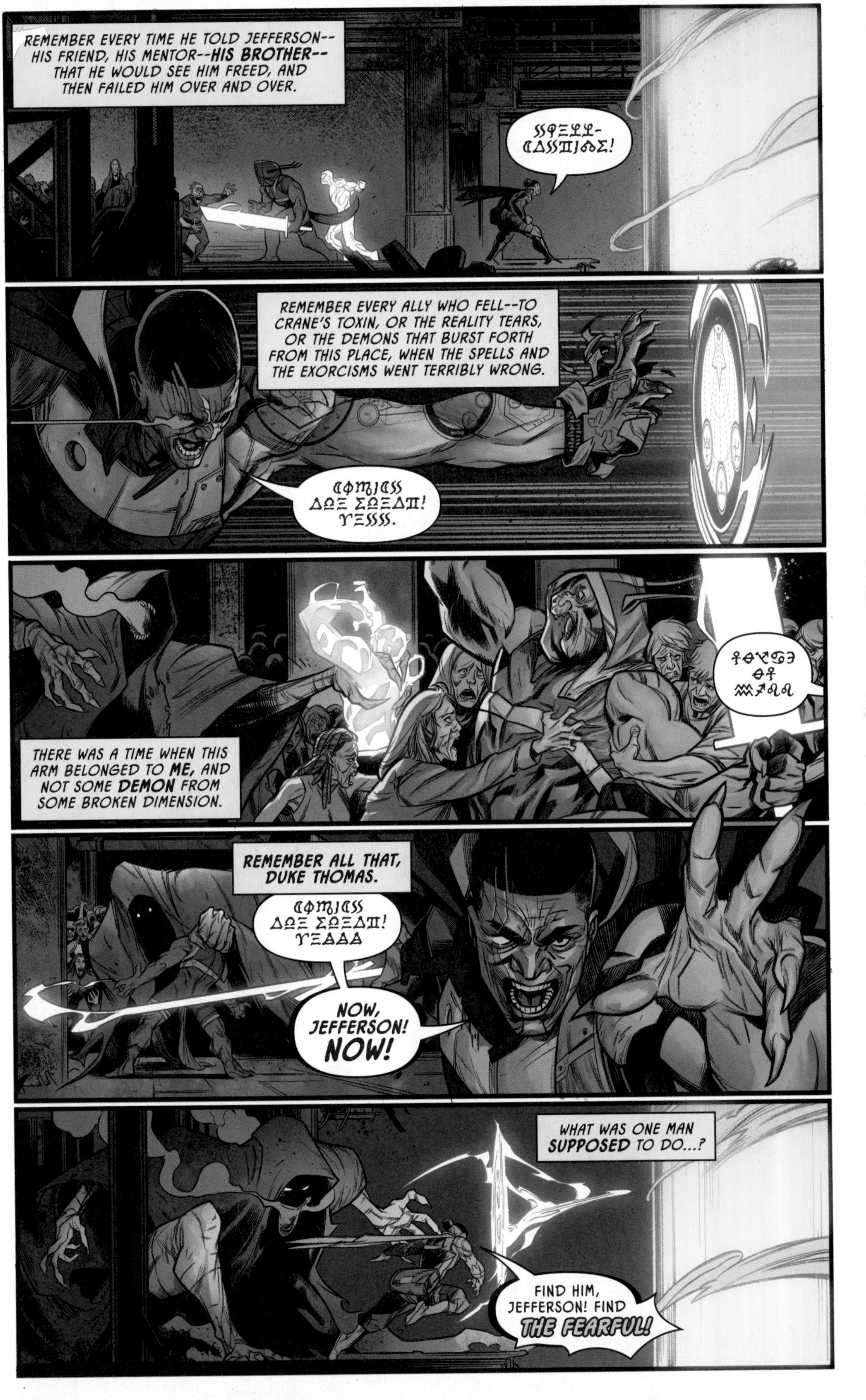
REMEMBER EVERY TIME HE TOLD JEFFERSON--HIS FRIEND, HIS MENTOR--HIS BROTHER--THAT HE WOULD SEE HIM FREED, AND THEN FAILED HIM OVER AND OVER.
REMEMBER EVERY ALLY WHO FELL--TO CRANE'S TOXIN, OR THE REALITY TEARS, OR THE DEMONS THAT BURST FORTH FROM THIS PLACE, WHEN THE SPELLS AND THE EXORCISMS WENT TERRIBLY WRONG.
THERE WAS A TIME WHEN THIS ARM BELONGED TO ME, AND NOT SOME DEMON FROM SOME BROKEN DIMENSION.
REMEMBER ALL THAT, DUKE THOMAS.
NOW, JEFFERSON! NOW!
WHAT WAS ONE MAN SUPPOSED TO DO...?
FIND HIM, JEFFERSON! FIND THE FEARFUL!

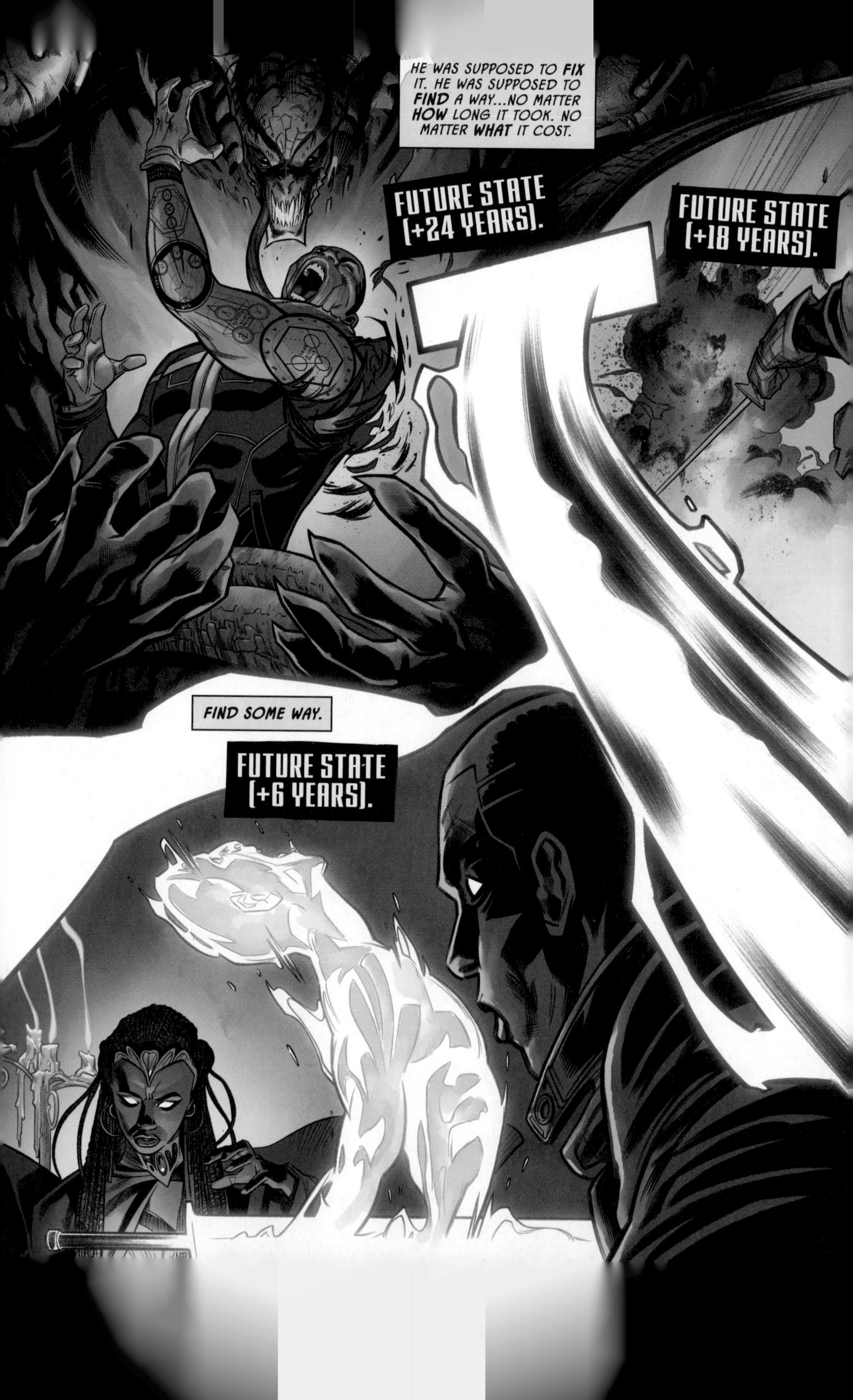
HE WAS SUPPOSED TO FIX IT. HE WAS SUPPOSED TO FIND A WAY...NO MATTER HOW LONG IT TOOK. NO MATTER WHAT IT COST.
FUTURE STATE (+24 YEARS).
FUTURE STATE (+18 YEARS).
FIND SOME WAY.
FUTURE STATE (+6 YEARS).

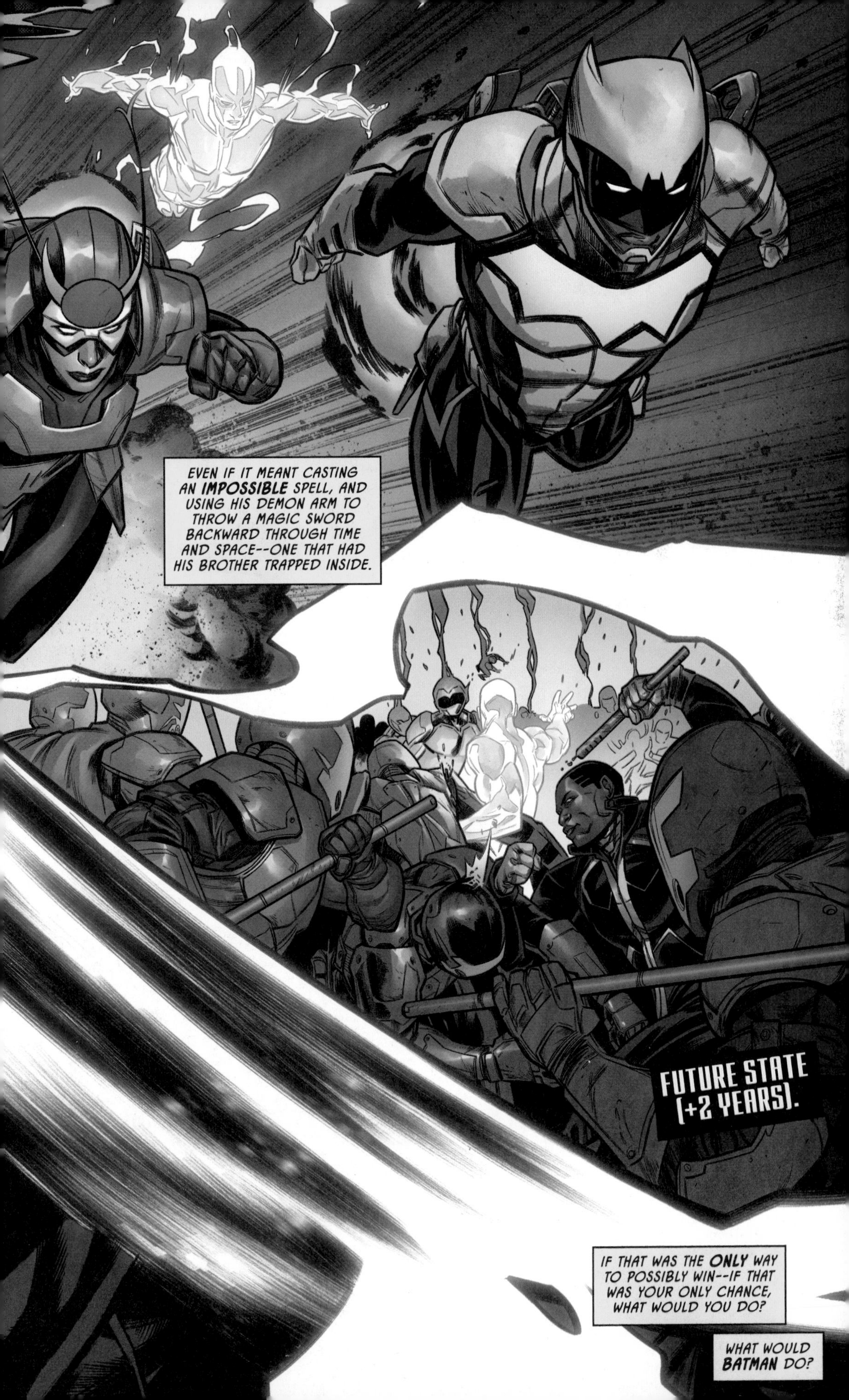

EVEN IF IT MEANT CASTING AN **IMPOSSIBLE** SPELL, AND USING HIS DEMON ARM TO THROW A MAGIC SWORD BACKWARD THROUGH TIME AND SPACE--ONE THAT HAD HIS BROTHER TRAPPED INSIDE.
FUTURE STATE (+2 YEARS).
IF THAT WAS THE **ONLY** WAY TO POSSIBLY WIN--IF THAT WAS YOUR ONLY CHANCE, WHAT WOULD YOU DO?
WHAT WOULD **BATMAN** DO?

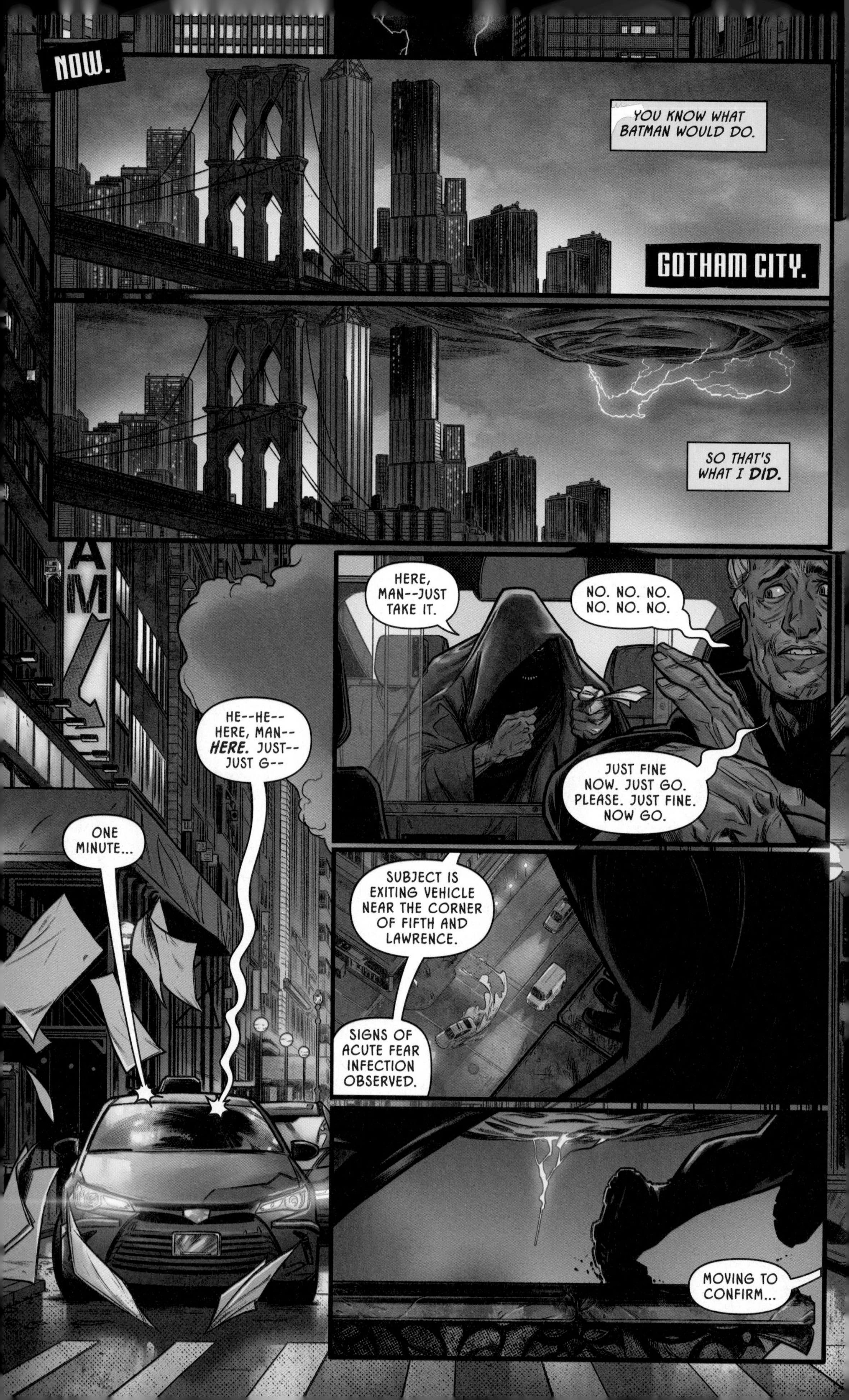
NOW.
YOU KNOW WHAT BATMAN WOULD DO.
GOTHAM CITY.
SO THAT'S WHAT I DID.
HERE, MAN--JUST TAKE IT.
NO. NO. NO. NO. NO. NO.
JUST FINE NOW. JUST GO. PLEASE. JUST FINE. NOW GO.
HE--HE--HERE, MAN--HERE. JUST--JUST G--
ONE MINUTE...
SUBJECT IS EXITING VEHICLE NEAR THE CORNER OF FIFTH AND LAWRENCE.
SIGNS OF ACUTE FEAR INFECTION OBSERVED.
MOVING TO CONFIRM...

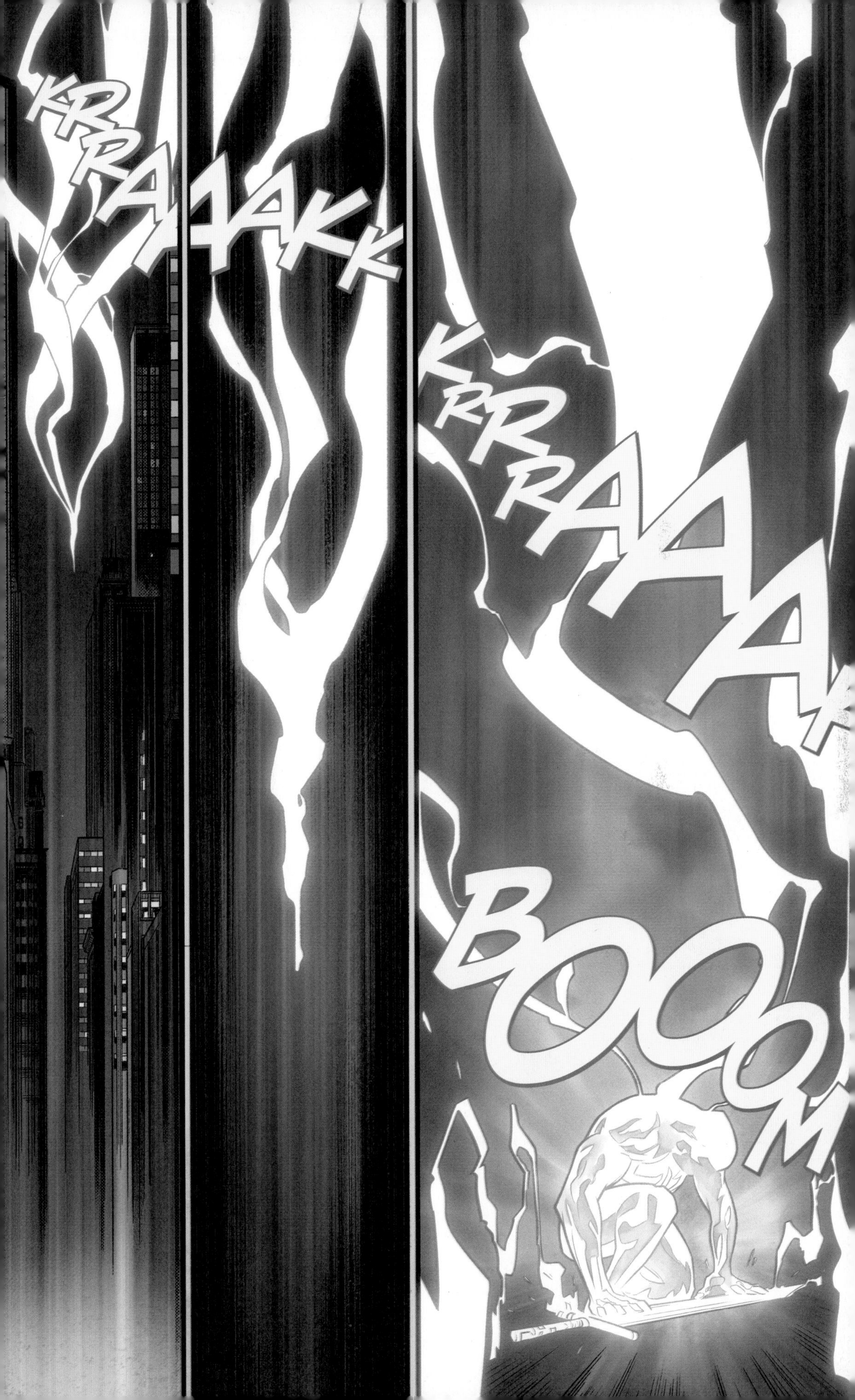
KRRAAAAKK
KRRRAAAAK
BOOOOM

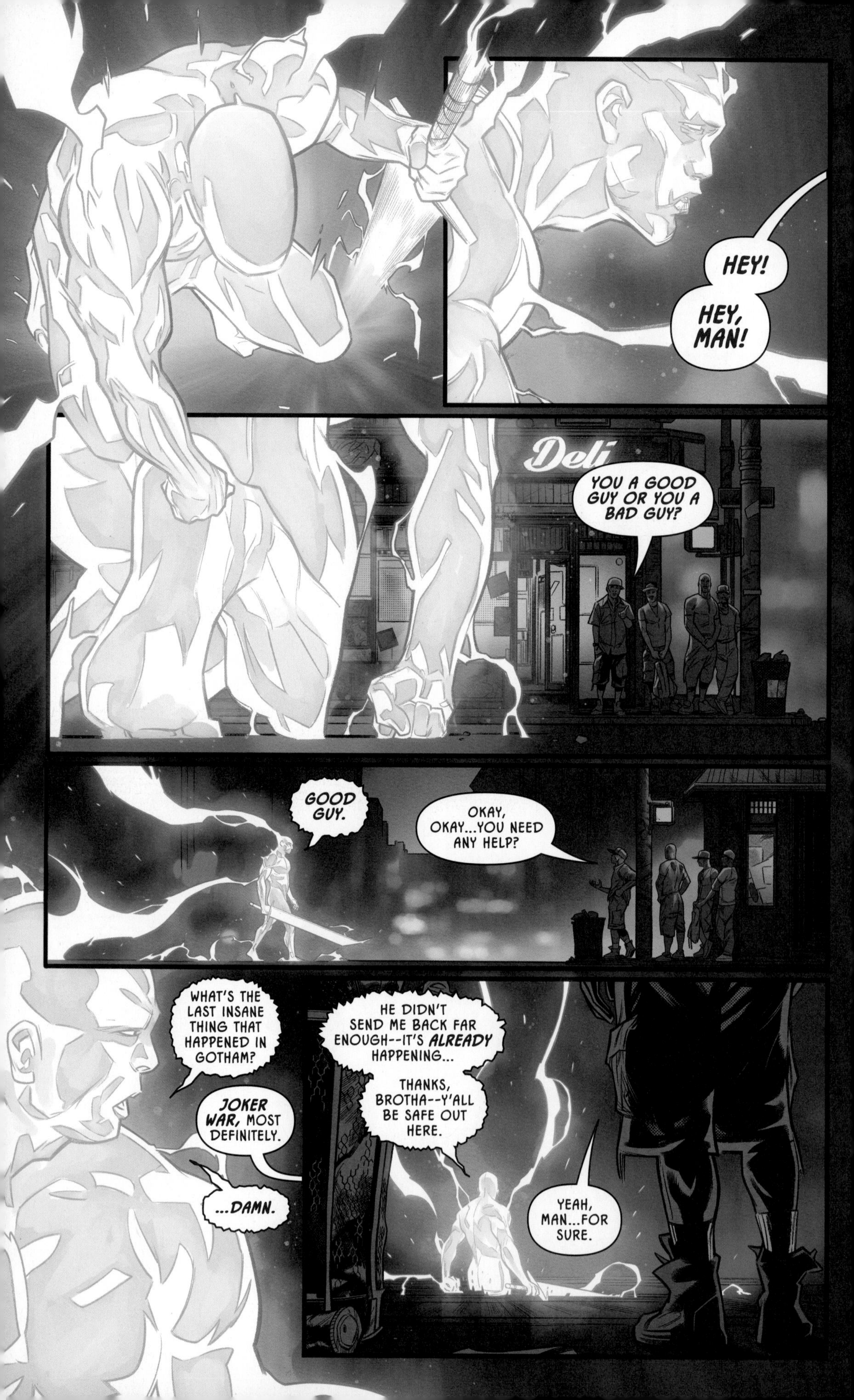
HEY!
HEY, MAN!
Deli
YOU A GOOD GUY OR YOU A BAD GUY?
GOOD GUY.
OKAY, OKAY...YOU NEED ANY HELP?
WHAT'S THE LAST INSANE THING THAT HAPPENED IN GOTHAM?
JOKER WAR, MOST DEFINITELY.
...DAMN.
HE DIDN'T SEND ME BACK FAR ENOUGH--IT'S ALREADY HAPPENING...
THANKS, BROTHA--Y'ALL BE SAFE OUT HERE.
YEAH, MAN...FOR SURE.

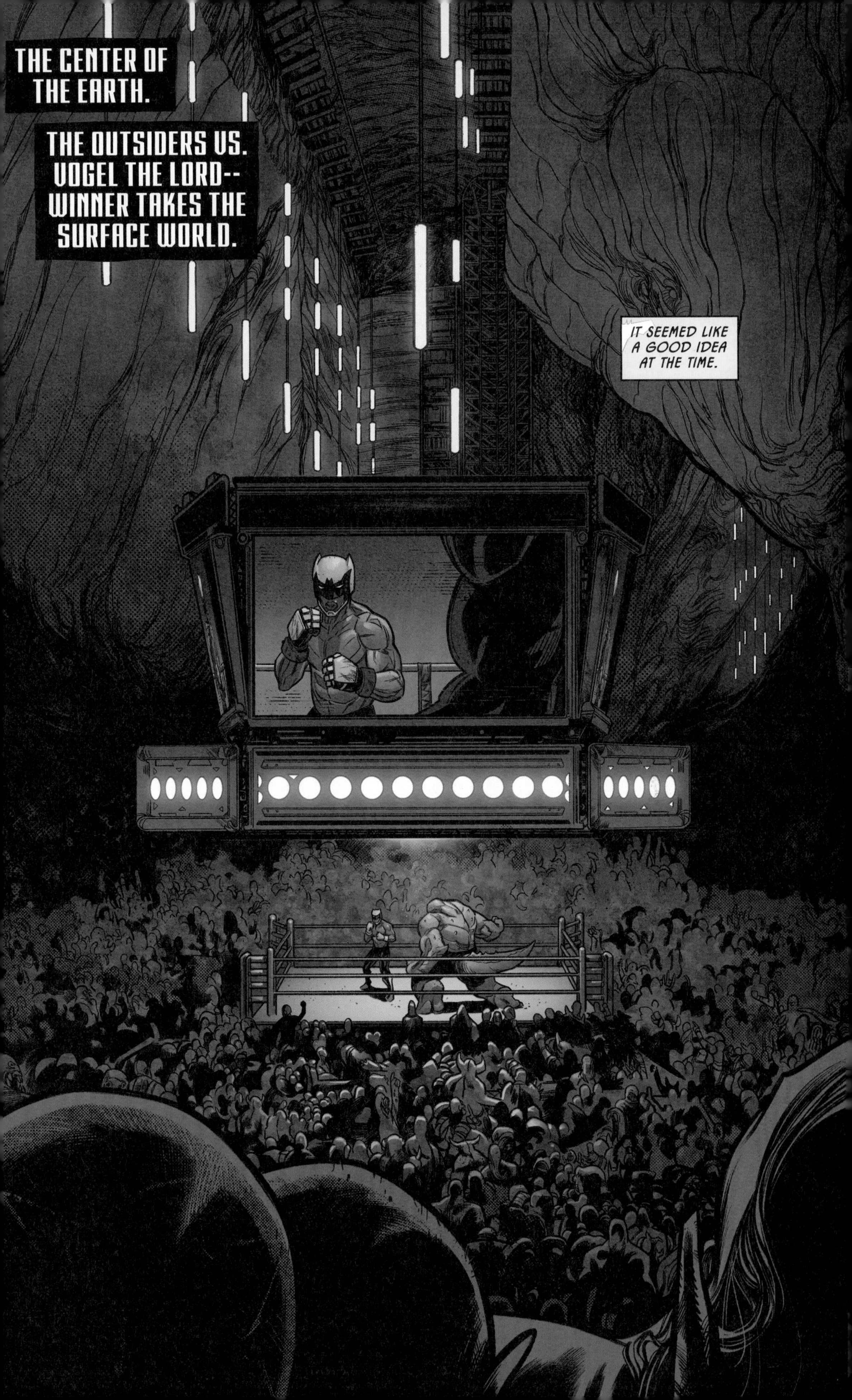
THE CENTER OF THE EARTH.
THE OUTSIDERS VS. VOGEL THE LORD-- WINNER TAKES THE SURFACE WORLD.
IT SEEMED LIKE A GOOD IDEA AT THE TIME.

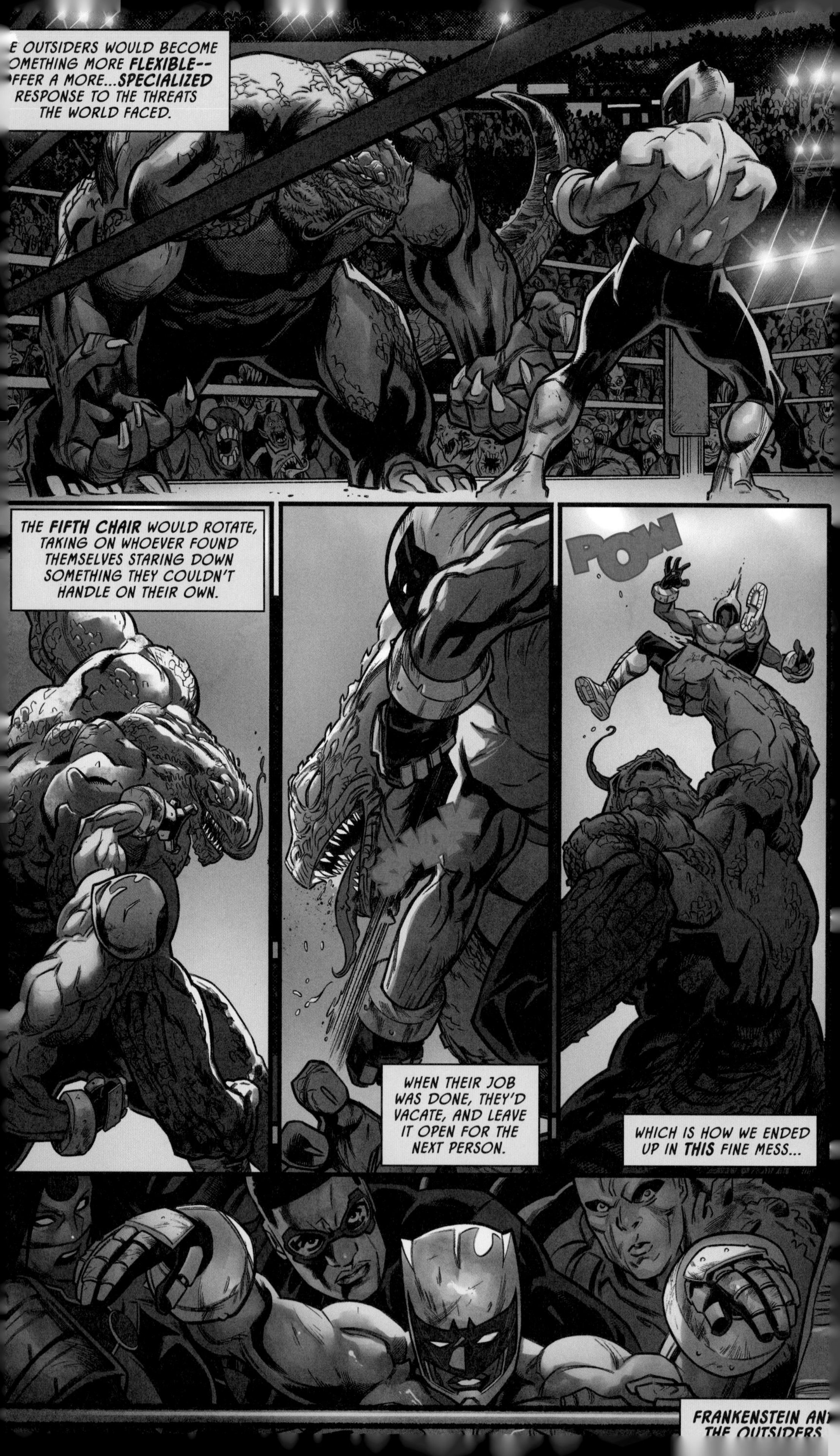

E OUTSIDERS WOULD BECOME OMETHING MORE FLEXIBLE-- FFER A MORE...SPECIALIZED RESPONSE TO THE THREATS THE WORLD FACED.
THE FIFTH CHAIR WOULD ROTATE, TAKING ON WHOEVER FOUND THEMSELVES STARING DOWN SOMETHING THEY COULDN'T HANDLE ON THEIR OWN.
WHEN THEIR JOB WAS DONE, THEY'D VACATE, AND LEAVE IT OPEN FOR THE NEXT PERSON.
POW
WHICH IS HOW WE ENDED UP IN THIS FINE MESS...
FRANKENSTEIN AN
THE OUTSIDERS

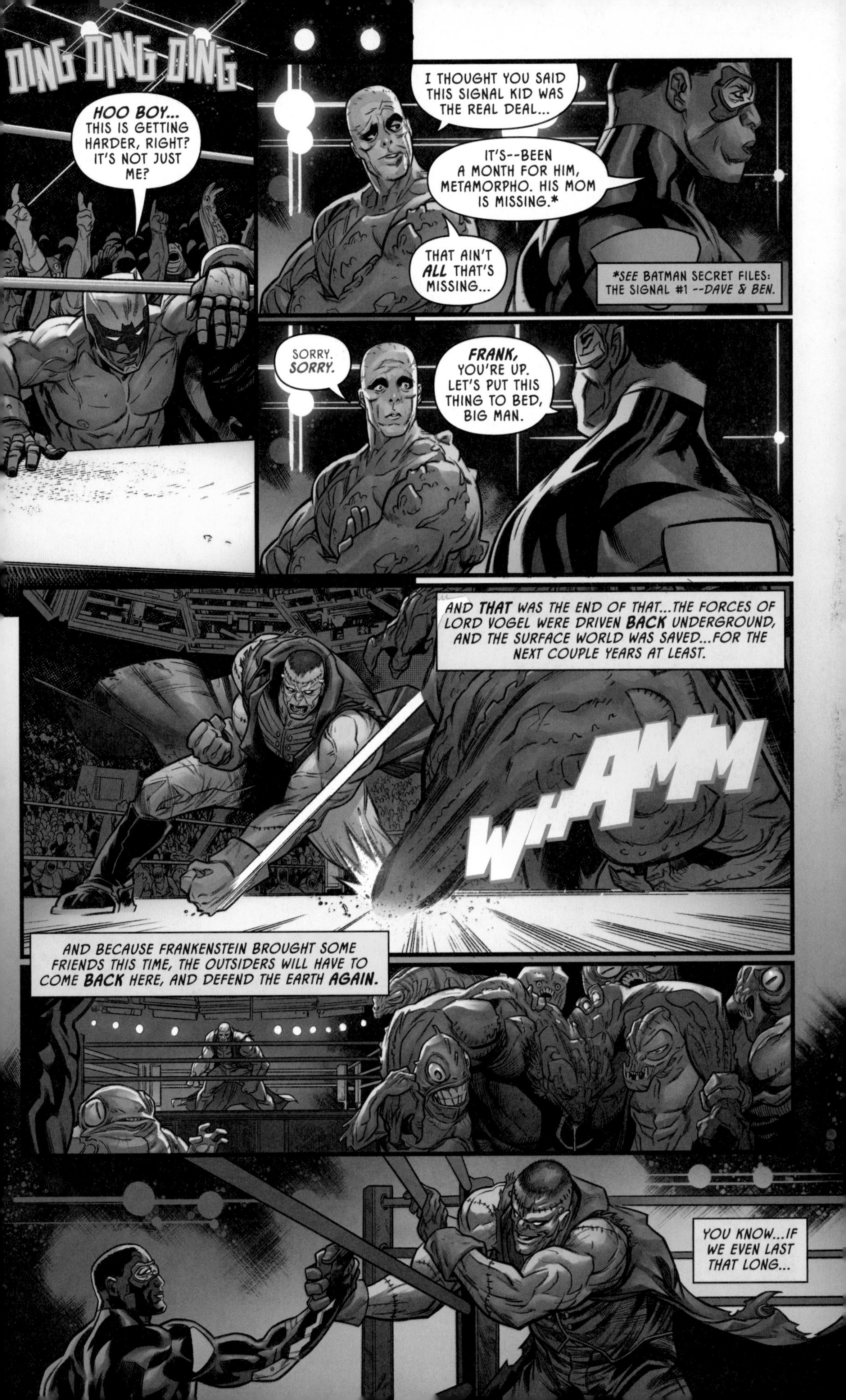
DING DING DING
HOO BOY... THIS IS GETTING HARDER, RIGHT? IT'S NOT JUST ME?
I THOUGHT YOU SAID THIS SIGNAL KID WAS THE REAL DEAL...
IT'S--BEEN A MONTH FOR HIM, METAMORPHO. HIS MOM IS MISSING.*
THAT AIN'T ALL THAT'S MISSING...
*SEE BATMAN SECRET FILES: THE SIGNAL #1 --DAVE & BEN.
SORRY. SORRY.
FRANK, YOU'RE UP. LET'S PUT THIS THING TO BED, BIG MAN.
AND THAT WAS THE END OF THAT...THE FORCES OF LORD VOGEL WERE DRIVEN BACK UNDERGROUND, AND THE SURFACE WORLD WAS SAVED...FOR THE NEXT COUPLE YEARS AT LEAST.
WHAMM
AND BECAUSE FRANKENSTEIN BROUGHT SOME FRIENDS THIS TIME, THE OUTSIDERS WILL HAVE TO COME BACK HERE, AND DEFEND THE EARTH AGAIN.
YOU KNOW...IF WE EVEN LAST THAT LONG...

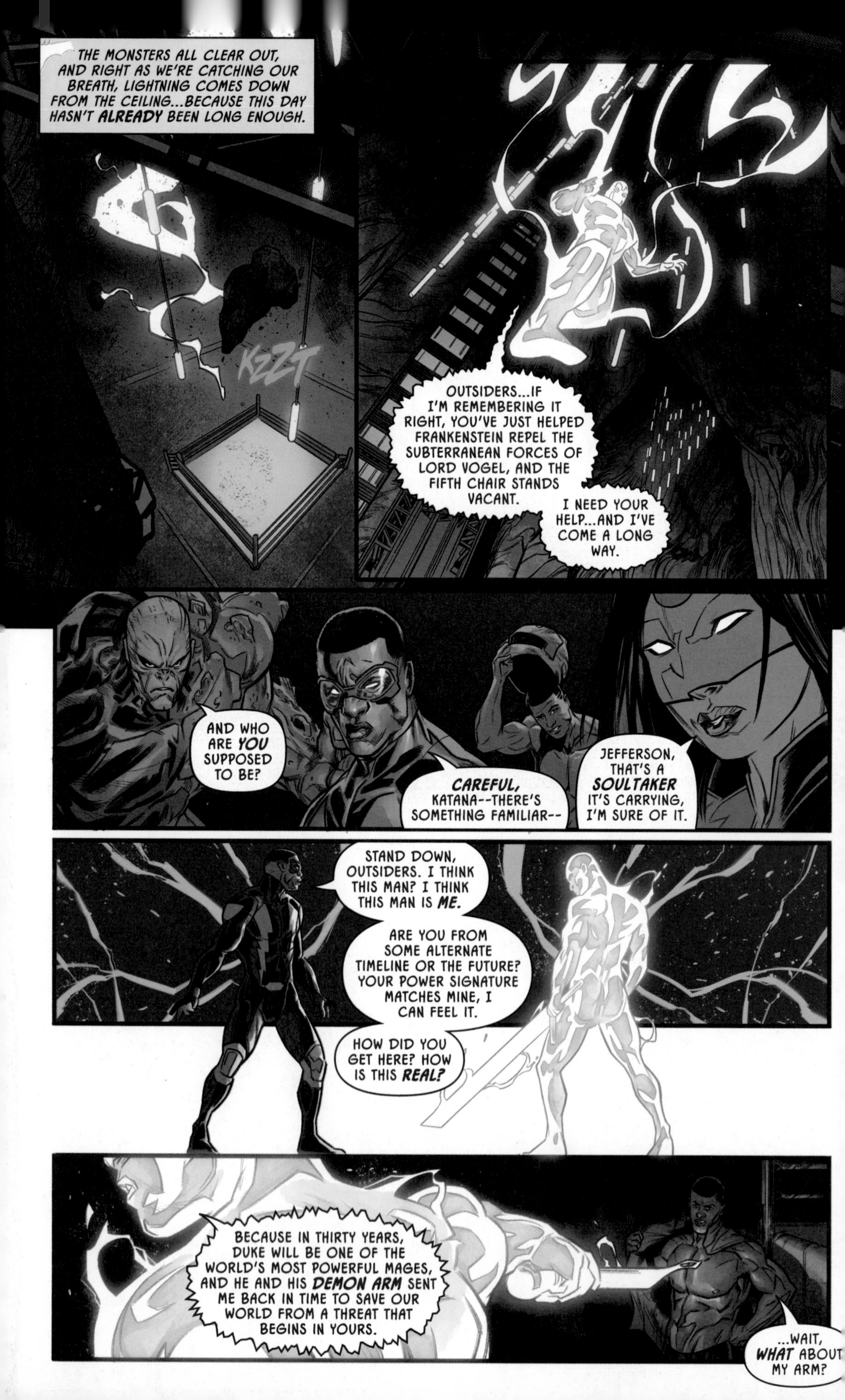

THE MONSTERS ALL CLEAR OUT, AND RIGHT AS WE'RE CATCHING OUR BREATH, LIGHTNING COMES DOWN FROM THE CEILING...BECAUSE THIS DAY HASN'T ALREADY BEEN LONG ENOUGH.
KZZT
OUTSIDERS...IF I'M REMEMBERING IT RIGHT, YOU'VE JUST HELPED FRANKENSTEIN REPEL THE SUBTERRANEAN FORCES OF LORD VOGEL, AND THE FIFTH CHAIR STANDS VACANT.
I NEED YOUR HELP...AND I'VE COME A LONG WAY.
AND WHO ARE YOU SUPPOSED TO BE?
CAREFUL, KATANA--THERE'S SOMETHING FAMILIAR--
JEFFERSON, THAT'S A SOULTAKER IT'S CARRYING, I'M SURE OF IT.
STAND DOWN, OUTSIDERS. I THINK THIS MAN? I THINK THIS MAN IS ME.
ARE YOU FROM SOME ALTERNATE TIMELINE OR THE FUTURE? YOUR POWER SIGNATURE MATCHES MINE, I CAN FEEL IT.
HOW DID YOU GET HERE? HOW IS THIS REAL?
BECAUSE IN THIRTY YEARS, DUKE WILL BE ONE OF THE WORLD'S MOST POWERFUL MAGES, AND HE AND HIS DEMON ARM SENT ME BACK IN TIME TO SAVE OUR WORLD FROM A THREAT THAT BEGINS IN YOURS.
...WAIT, WHAT ABOUT MY ARM?

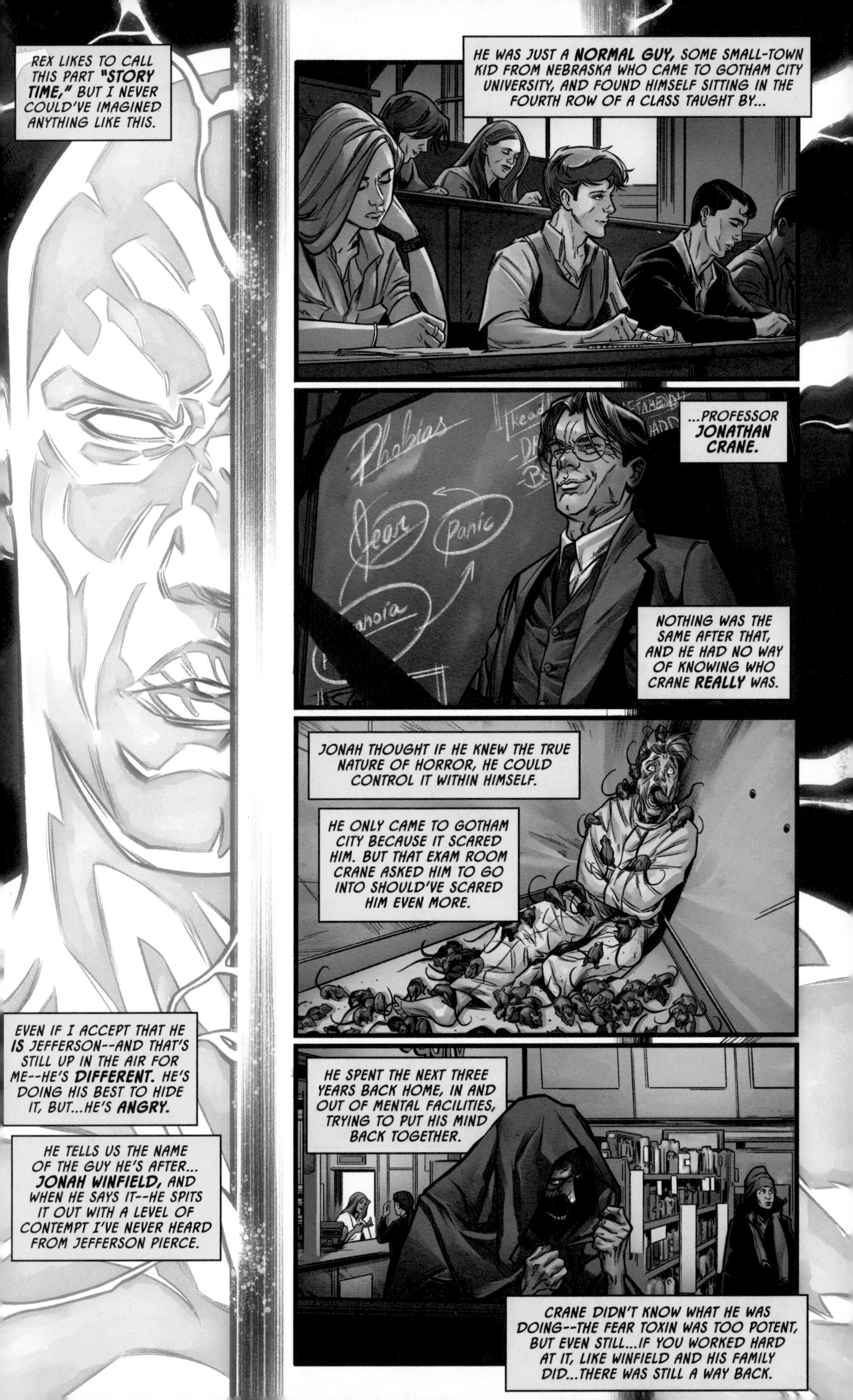
REX LIKES TO CALL THIS PART **"STORY TIME,"** BUT I NEVER COULD'VE IMAGINED ANYTHING LIKE THIS.
EVEN IF I ACCEPT THAT HE **IS** JEFFERSON--AND THAT'S STILL UP IN THE AIR FOR ME--HE'S **DIFFERENT.** HE'S DOING HIS BEST TO HIDE IT, BUT...HE'S **ANGRY.**
HE TELLS US THE NAME OF THE GUY HE'S AFTER... **JONAH WINFIELD,** AND WHEN HE SAYS IT--HE SPITS IT OUT WITH A LEVEL OF CONTEMPT I'VE NEVER HEARD FROM JEFFERSON PIERCE.
HE WAS JUST A **NORMAL GUY,** SOME SMALL-TOWN KID FROM NEBRASKA WHO CAME TO GOTHAM CITY UNIVERSITY, AND FOUND HIMSELF SITTING IN THE FOURTH ROW OF A CLASS TAUGHT BY...
Phobias
Fear
Panic
...PROFESSOR **JONATHAN CRANE.**
NOTHING WAS THE SAME AFTER THAT, AND HE HAD NO WAY OF KNOWING WHO CRANE **REALLY** WAS.
JONAH THOUGHT IF HE KNEW THE TRUE NATURE OF HORROR, HE COULD CONTROL IT WITHIN HIMSELF.
HE ONLY CAME TO GOTHAM CITY BECAUSE IT SCARED HIM. BUT THAT EXAM ROOM CRANE ASKED HIM TO GO INTO SHOULD'VE SCARED HIM EVEN MORE.
HE SPENT THE NEXT THREE YEARS BACK HOME, IN AND OUT OF MENTAL FACILITIES, TRYING TO PUT HIS MIND BACK TOGETHER.
CRANE DIDN'T KNOW WHAT HE WAS DOING--THE FEAR TOXIN WAS TOO POTENT, BUT EVEN STILL...IF YOU WORKED HARD AT IT, LIKE WINFIELD AND HIS FAMILY DID...THERE WAS STILL A WAY BACK.

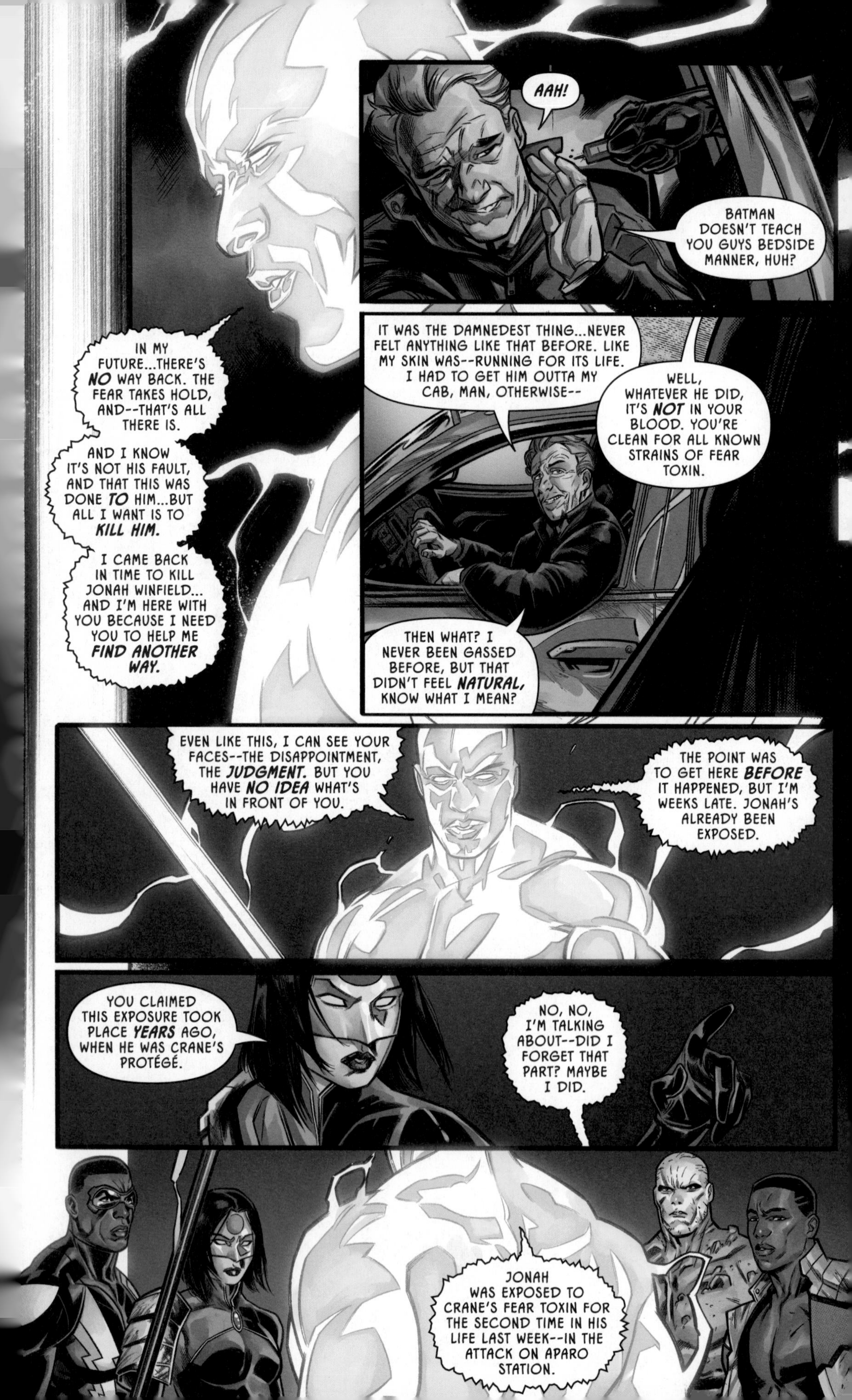
AAH!
BATMAN DOESN'T TEACH YOU GUYS BEDSIDE MANNER, HUH?
IN MY FUTURE...THERE'S NO WAY BACK. THE FEAR TAKES HOLD, AND--THAT'S ALL THERE IS.
AND I KNOW IT'S NOT HIS FAULT, AND THAT THIS WAS DONE TO HIM...BUT ALL I WANT IS TO KILL HIM.
I CAME BACK IN TIME TO KILL JONAH WINFIELD... AND I'M HERE WITH YOU BECAUSE I NEED YOU TO HELP ME FIND ANOTHER WAY.
IT WAS THE DAMNEDEST THING...NEVER FELT ANYTHING LIKE THAT BEFORE. LIKE MY SKIN WAS--RUNNING FOR ITS LIFE. I HAD TO GET HIM OUTTA MY CAB, MAN, OTHERWISE--
WELL, WHATEVER HE DID, IT'S NOT IN YOUR BLOOD. YOU'RE CLEAN FOR ALL KNOWN STRAINS OF FEAR TOXIN.
THEN WHAT? I NEVER BEEN GASSED BEFORE, BUT THAT DIDN'T FEEL NATURAL, KNOW WHAT I MEAN?
EVEN LIKE THIS, I CAN SEE YOUR FACES--THE DISAPPOINTMENT, THE JUDGMENT. BUT YOU HAVE NO IDEA WHAT'S IN FRONT OF YOU.
THE POINT WAS TO GET HERE BEFORE IT HAPPENED, BUT I'M WEEKS LATE. JONAH'S ALREADY BEEN EXPOSED.
YOU CLAIMED THIS EXPOSURE TOOK PLACE YEARS AGO, WHEN HE WAS CRANE'S PROTÉGÉ.
NO, NO, I'M TALKING ABOUT--DID I FORGET THAT PART? MAYBE I DID.
JONAH WAS EXPOSED TO CRANE'S FEAR TOXIN FOR THE SECOND TIME IN HIS LIFE LAST WEEK--IN THE ATTACK ON APARO STATION.

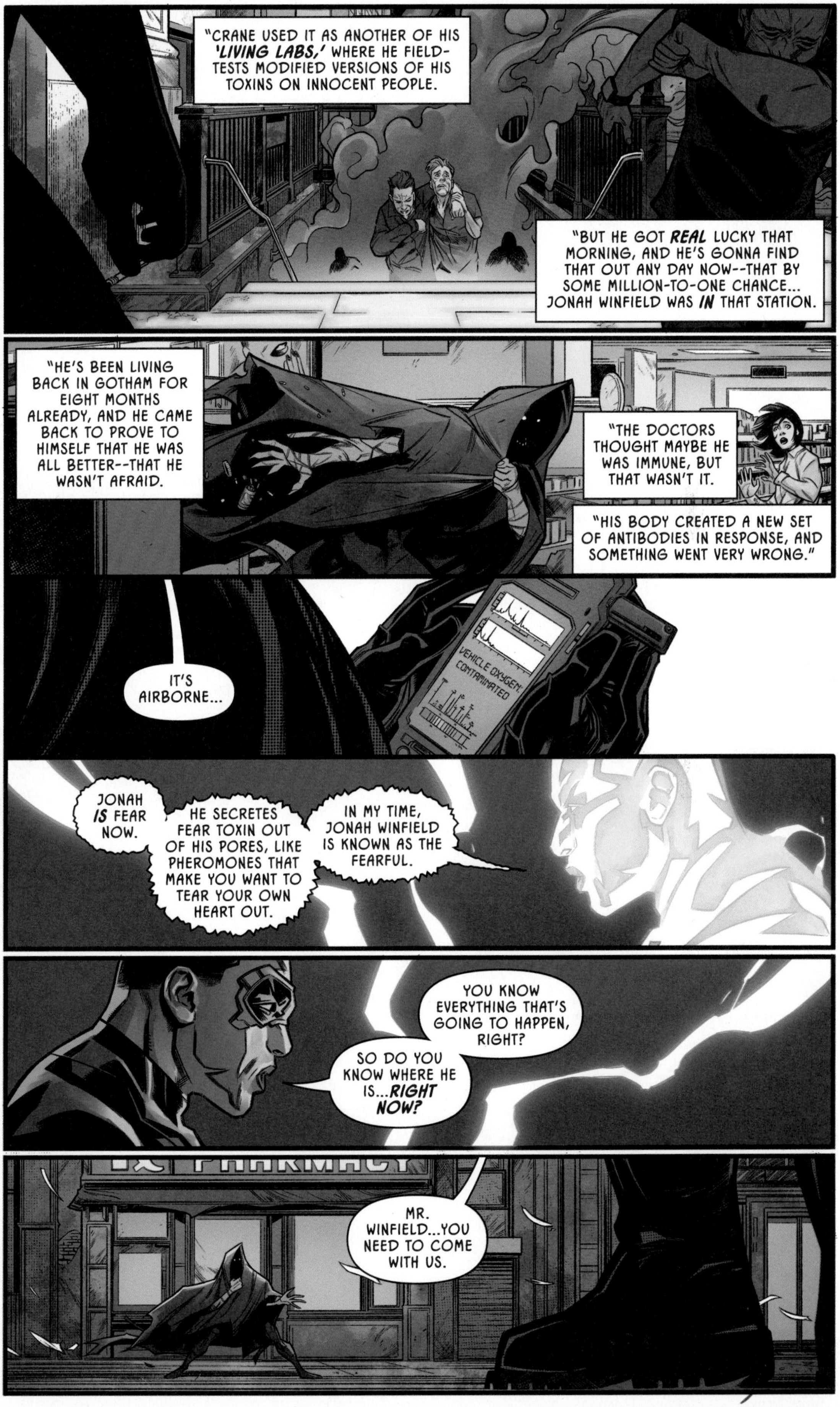
"CRANE USED IT AS ANOTHER OF HIS 'LIVING LABS,' WHERE HE FIELD-TESTS MODIFIED VERSIONS OF HIS TOXINS ON INNOCENT PEOPLE.
"BUT HE GOT REAL LUCKY THAT MORNING, AND HE'S GONNA FIND THAT OUT ANY DAY NOW--THAT BY SOME MILLION-TO-ONE CHANCE... JONAH WINFIELD WAS IN THAT STATION.
"HE'S BEEN LIVING BACK IN GOTHAM FOR EIGHT MONTHS ALREADY, AND HE CAME BACK TO PROVE TO HIMSELF THAT HE WAS ALL BETTER--THAT HE WASN'T AFRAID.
"THE DOCTORS THOUGHT MAYBE HE WAS IMMUNE, BUT THAT WASN'T IT.
"HIS BODY CREATED A NEW SET OF ANTIBODIES IN RESPONSE, AND SOMETHING WENT VERY WRONG."
IT'S AIRBORNE...
VEHICLE OXYGEN: CONTAMINATED
JONAH IS FEAR NOW.
HE SECRETES FEAR TOXIN OUT OF HIS PORES, LIKE PHEROMONES THAT MAKE YOU WANT TO TEAR YOUR OWN HEART OUT.
IN MY TIME, JONAH WINFIELD IS KNOWN AS THE FEARFUL.
YOU KNOW EVERYTHING THAT'S GOING TO HAPPEN, RIGHT?
SO DO YOU KNOW WHERE HE IS...RIGHT NOW?
PHARMACY
MR. WINFIELD...YOU NEED TO COME WITH US.

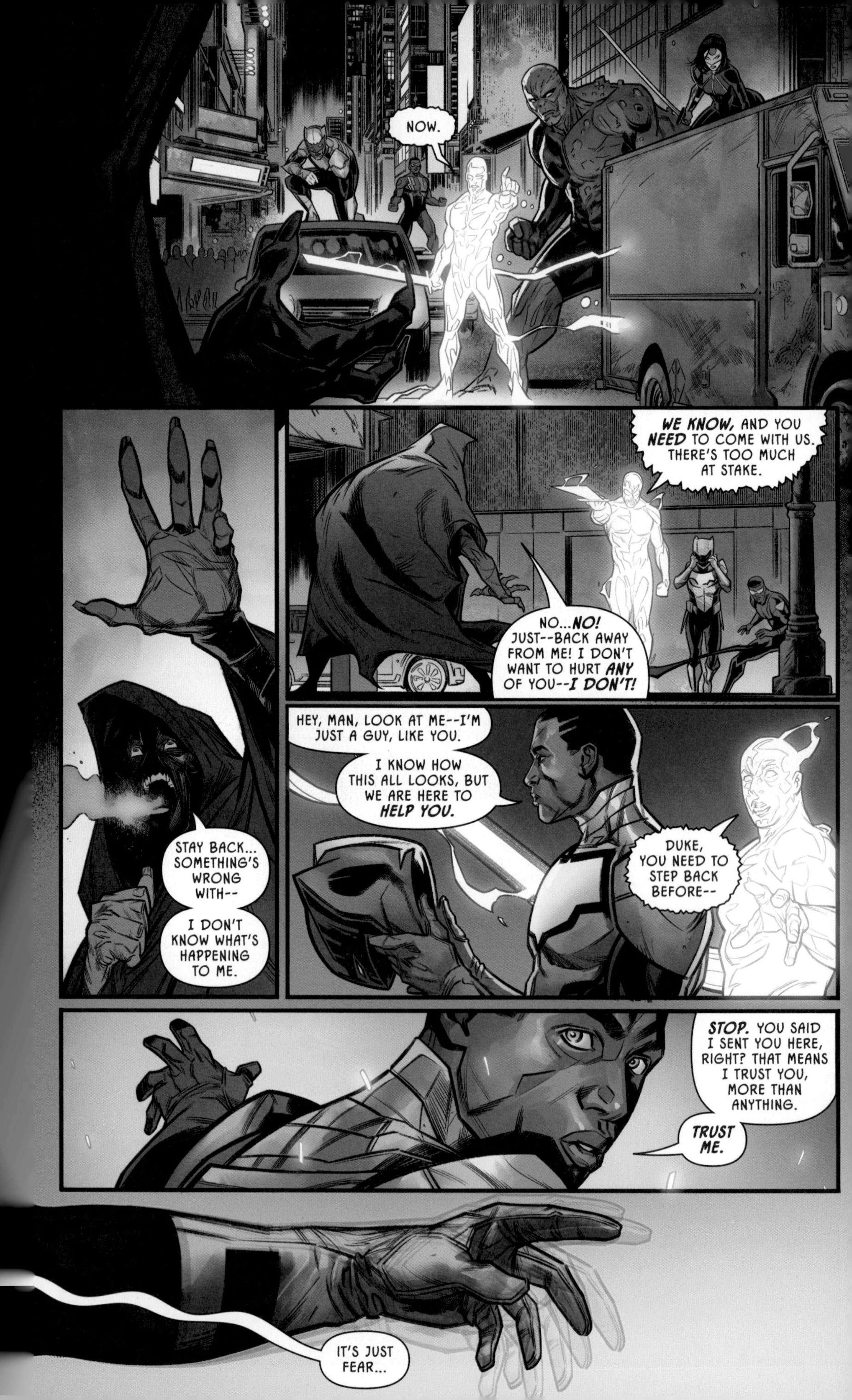
NOW.
WE KNOW, AND YOU NEED TO COME WITH US. THERE'S TOO MUCH AT STAKE.
NO...NO! JUST--BACK AWAY FROM ME! I DON'T WANT TO HURT ANY OF YOU--I DON'T!
STAY BACK... SOMETHING'S WRONG WITH--
I DON'T KNOW WHAT'S HAPPENING TO ME.
HEY, MAN, LOOK AT ME--I'M JUST A GUY, LIKE YOU.
I KNOW HOW THIS ALL LOOKS, BUT WE ARE HERE TO HELP YOU.
DUKE, YOU NEED TO STEP BACK BEFORE--
STOP. YOU SAID I SENT YOU HERE, RIGHT? THAT MEANS I TRUST YOU, MORE THAN ANYTHING.
TRUST ME.
IT'S JUST FEAR...

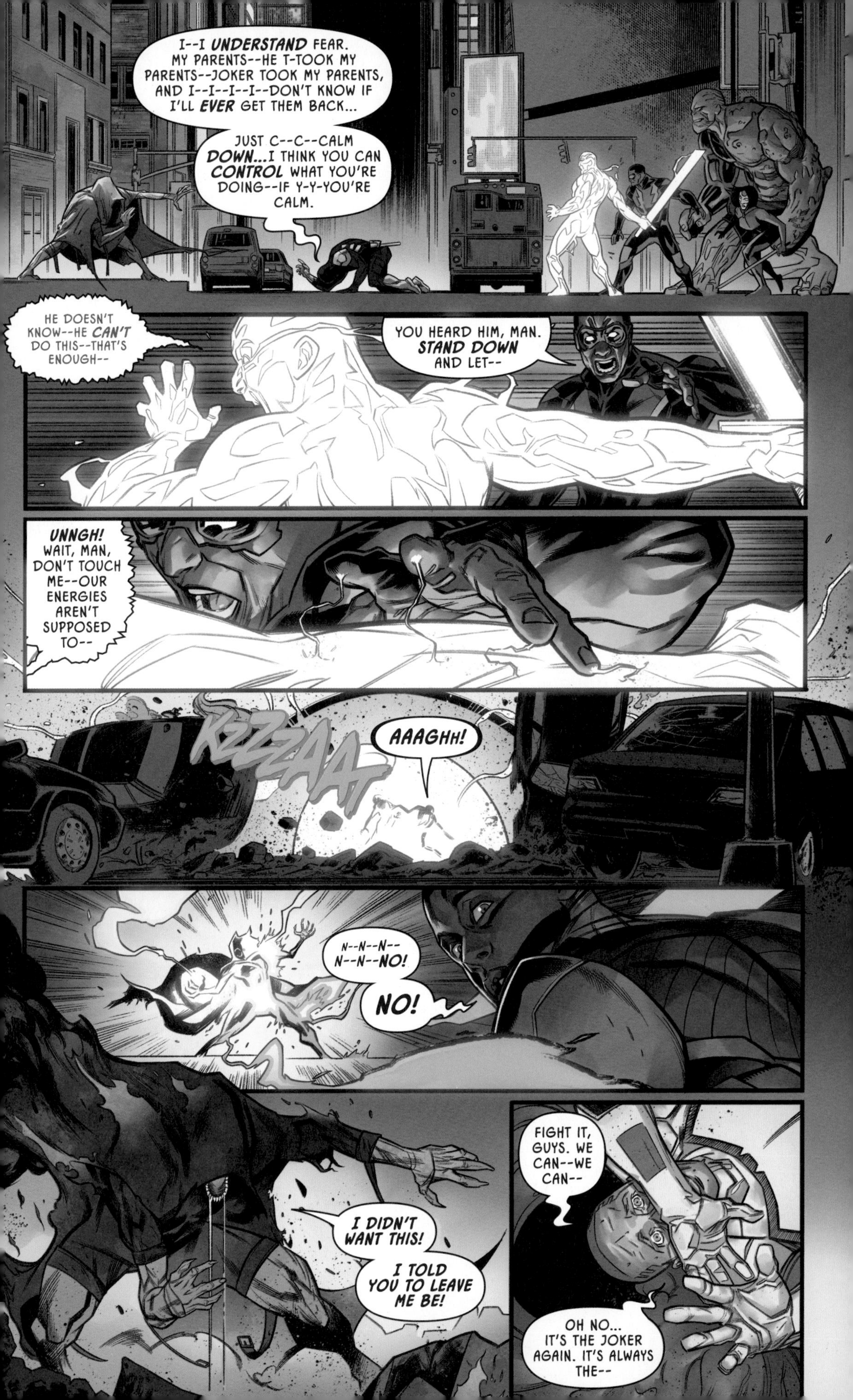

I--I UNDERSTAND FEAR. MY PARENTS--HE T-TOOK MY PARENTS--JOKER TOOK MY PARENTS, AND I--I--I--I--DON'T KNOW IF I'LL EVER GET THEM BACK...
JUST C--C--CALM DOWN...I THINK YOU CAN CONTROL WHAT YOU'RE DOING--IF Y-Y-YOU'RE CALM.
HE DOESN'T KNOW--HE CAN'T DO THIS--THAT'S ENOUGH--
YOU HEARD HIM, MAN. STAND DOWN AND LET--
UNNGH! WAIT, MAN, DON'T TOUCH ME--OUR ENERGIES AREN'T SUPPOSED TO--
KZZZAAA
AAAGHH!
N--N--N--N--N--NO!
NO!
I DIDN'T WANT THIS!
I TOLD YOU TO LEAVE ME BE!
FIGHT IT, GUYS. WE CAN--WE CAN--
OH NO... IT'S THE JOKER AGAIN. IT'S ALWAYS THE--

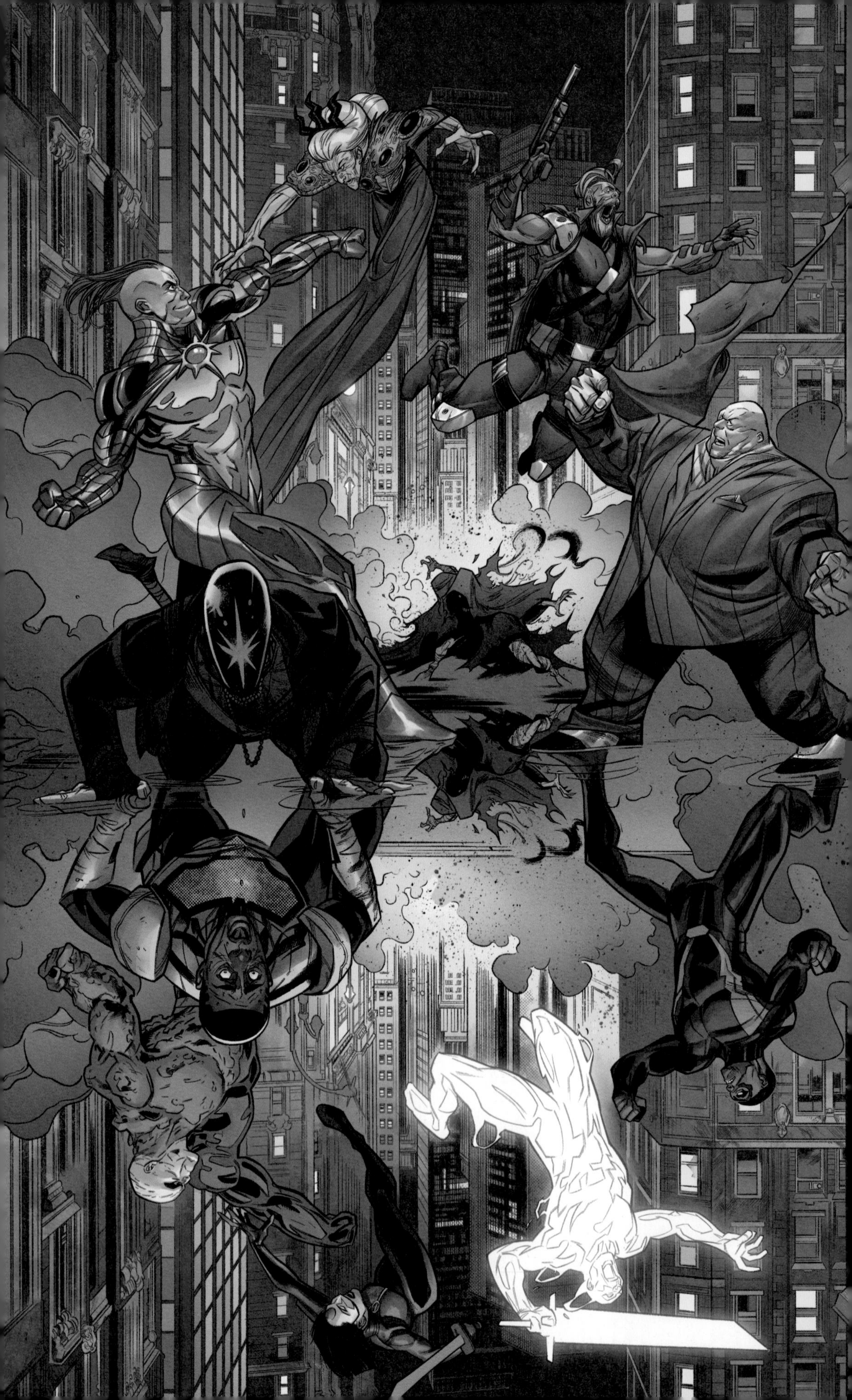

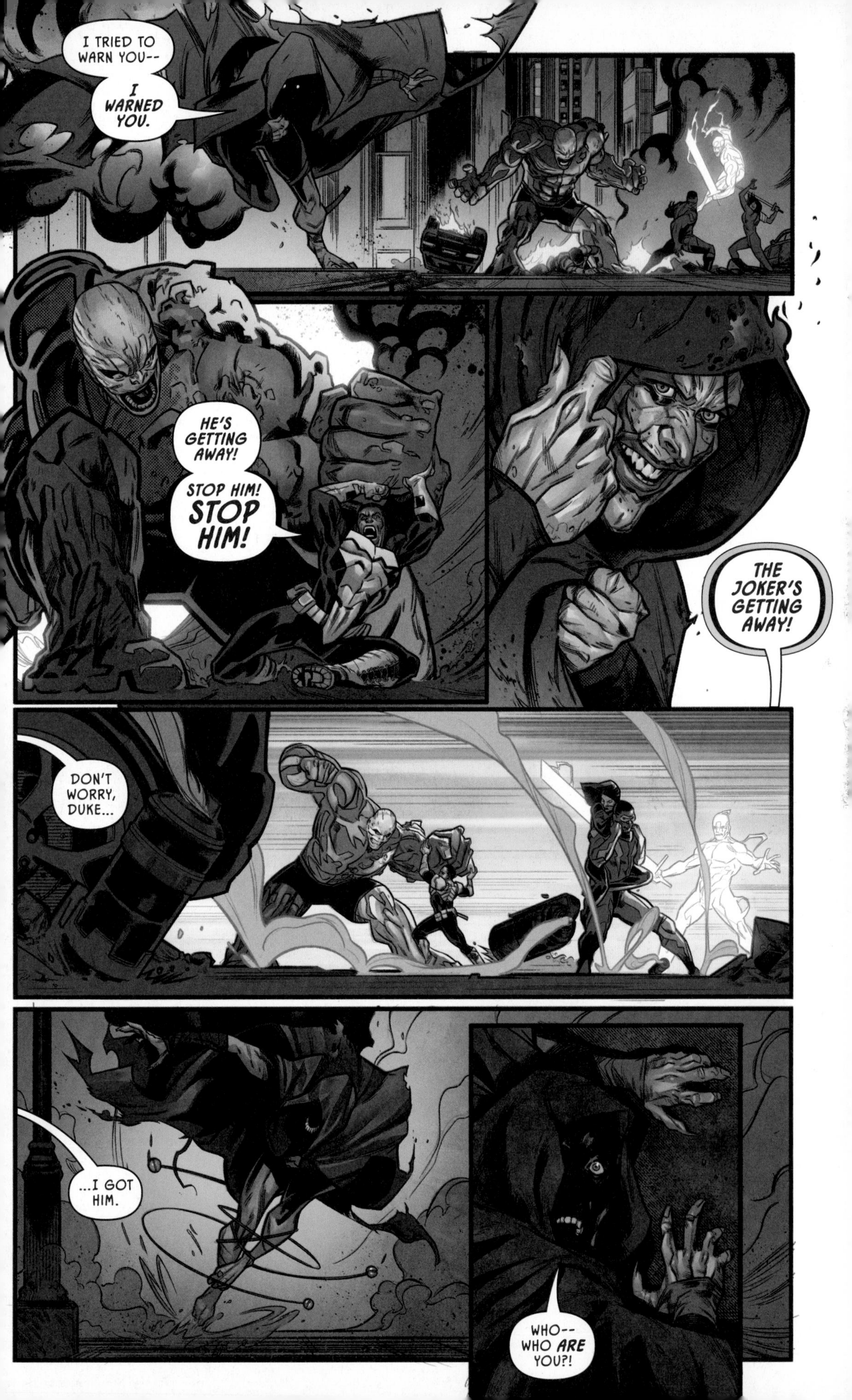
I TRIED TO WARN YOU--
I WARNED YOU.
HE'S GETTING AWAY!
STOP HIM! STOP HIM!
THE JOKER'S GETTING AWAY!
DON'T WORRY, DUKE...
...I GOT HIM.
WHO-- WHO ARE YOU?!

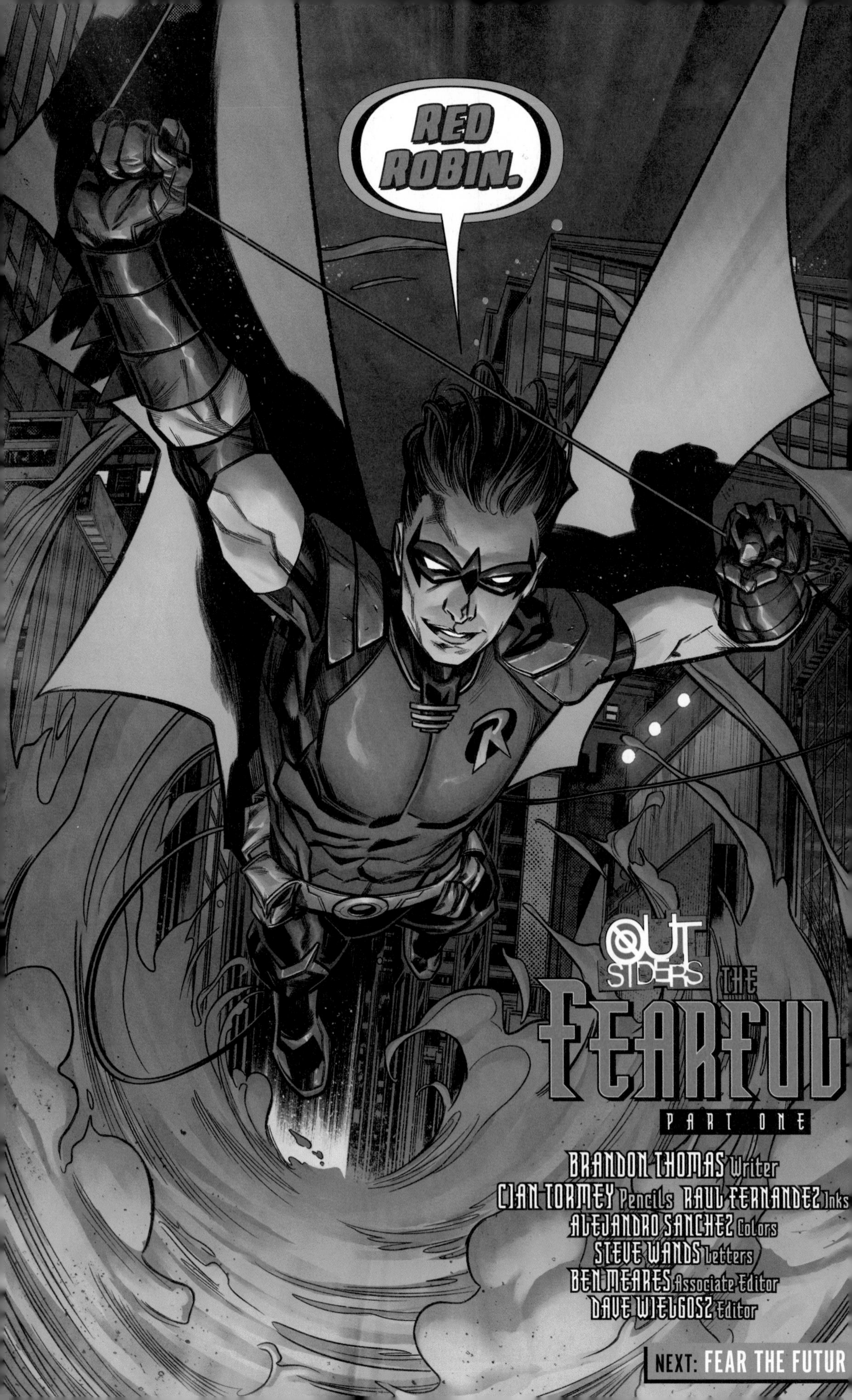
RED ROBIN.
OUTSIDERS THE FEARFUL
PART ONE
BRANDON THOMAS Writer
CIAN TORMEY Pencils RAUL FERNANDEZ Inks
ALEJANDRO SANCHEZ Colors
STEVE WANDS Letters
BEN MEARES Associate Editor
DAVE WIELGOSZ Editor
NEXT: FEAR THE FUTUR

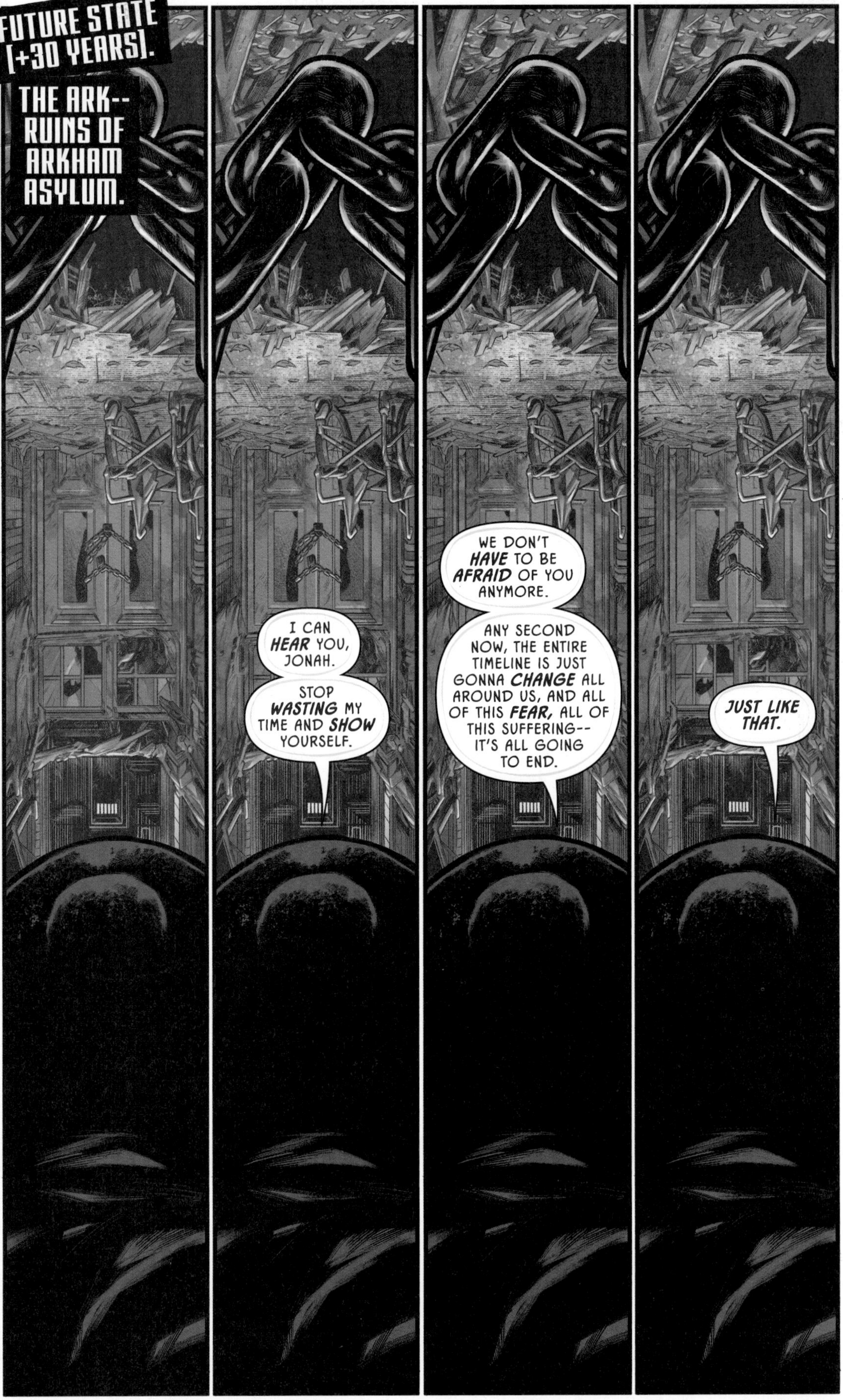
FUTURE STATE [+30 YEARS].
THE ARK-- RUINS OF ARKHAM ASYLUM.
I CAN HEAR YOU, JONAH.
STOP WASTING MY TIME AND SHOW YOURSELF.
WE DON'T HAVE TO BE AFRAID OF YOU ANYMORE.
ANY SECOND NOW, THE ENTIRE TIMELINE IS JUST GONNA CHANGE ALL AROUND US, AND ALL OF THIS FEAR, ALL OF THIS SUFFERING-- IT'S ALL GOING TO END.
JUST LIKE THAT.

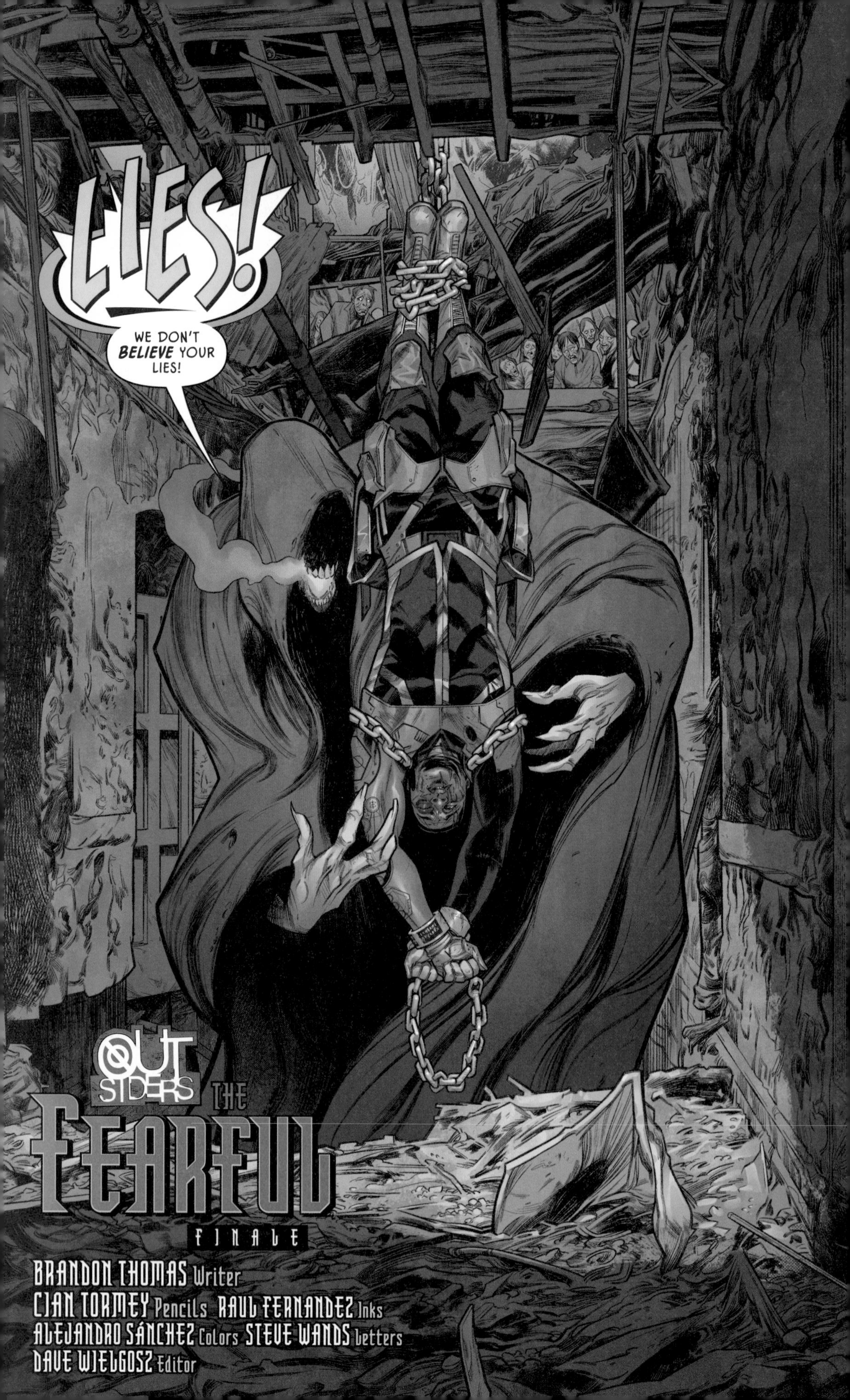
LIES!
WE DON'T BELIEVE YOUR LIES!
OUTSIDERS THE FEARFUL FINALE
BRANDON THOMAS Writer
CIAN TORMEY Pencils RAUL FERNANDEZ Inks
ALEJANDRO SÁNCHEZ Colors STEVE WANDS Letters
DAVE WIELGOSZ Editor

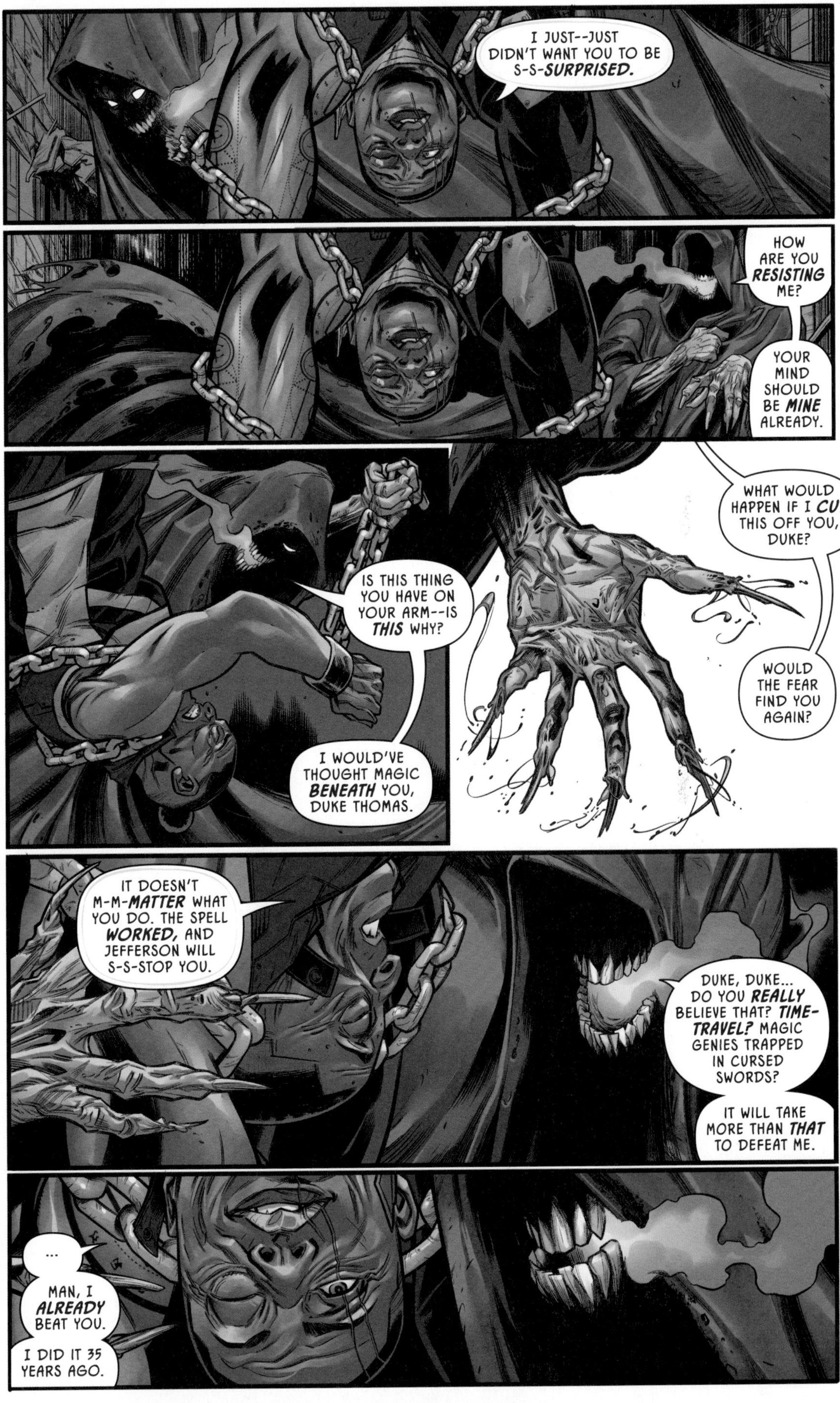
I JUST--JUST DIDN'T WANT YOU TO BE S-S-*SURPRISED.*
HOW ARE YOU *RESISTING* ME?
YOUR MIND SHOULD BE *MINE* ALREADY.
IS THIS THING YOU HAVE ON YOUR ARM--IS *THIS* WHY?
I WOULD'VE THOUGHT MAGIC *BENEATH* YOU, DUKE THOMAS.
WHAT WOULD HAPPEN IF I *CUT* THIS OFF YOU, DUKE?
WOULD THE FEAR FIND YOU AGAIN?
IT DOESN'T M-M-*MATTER* WHAT YOU DO. THE SPELL *WORKED,* AND JEFFERSON WILL S-S-STOP YOU.
DUKE, DUKE... DO YOU *REALLY* BELIEVE THAT? *TIME-TRAVEL?* MAGIC GENIES TRAPPED IN CURSED SWORDS?
IT WILL TAKE MORE THAN *THAT* TO DEFEAT ME.
...
MAN, I *ALREADY* BEAT YOU.
I DID IT 35 YEARS AGO.

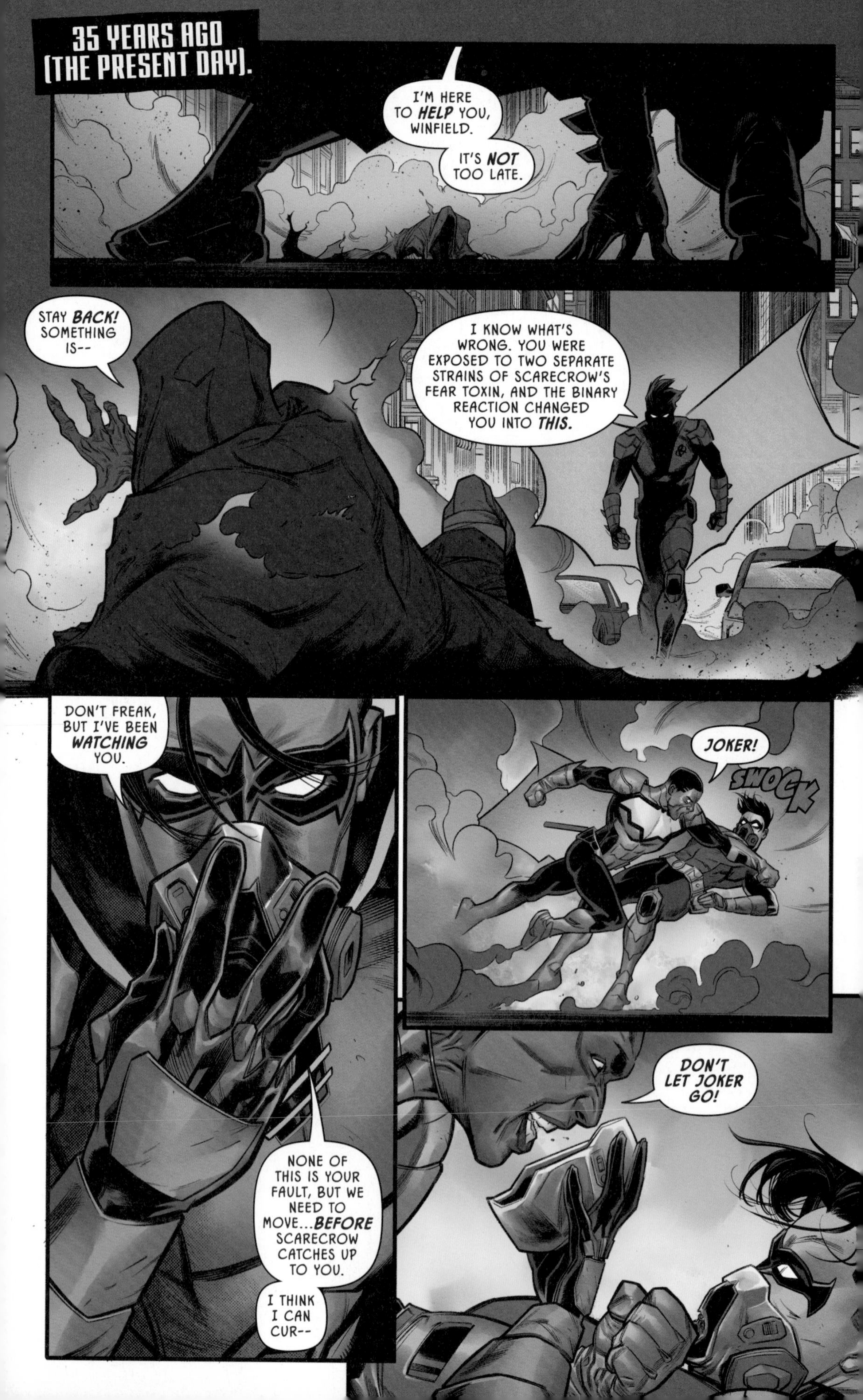
35 YEARS AGO (THE PRESENT DAY).
I'M HERE TO HELP YOU, WINFIELD.
IT'S NOT TOO LATE.
STAY BACK! SOMETHING IS--
I KNOW WHAT'S WRONG. YOU WERE EXPOSED TO TWO SEPARATE STRAINS OF SCARECROW'S FEAR TOXIN, AND THE BINARY REACTION CHANGED YOU INTO THIS.
DON'T FREAK, BUT I'VE BEEN WATCHING YOU.
NONE OF THIS IS YOUR FAULT, BUT WE NEED TO MOVE...BEFORE SCARECROW CATCHES UP TO YOU.
I THINK I CAN CUR--
JOKER!
SWOCK
DON'T LET JOKER GO!

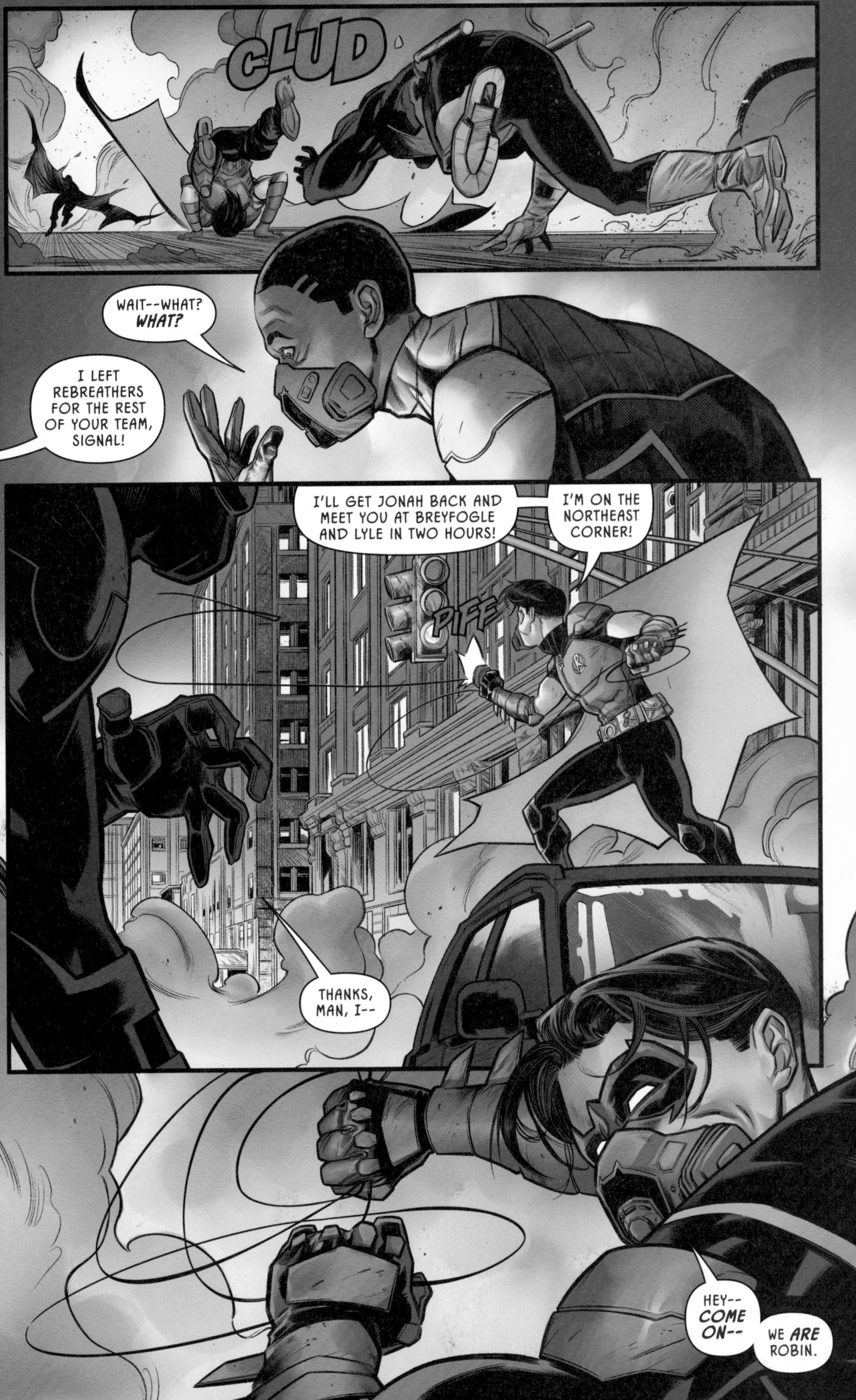
CLUD
WAIT--WHAT? WHAT?
I LEFT REBREATHERS FOR THE REST OF YOUR TEAM, SIGNAL!
I'LL GET JONAH BACK AND MEET YOU AT BREYFOGLE AND LYLE IN TWO HOURS!
I'M ON THE NORTHEAST CORNER!
PIFF
THANKS, MAN, I--
HEY-- COME ON--
WE ARE ROBIN.

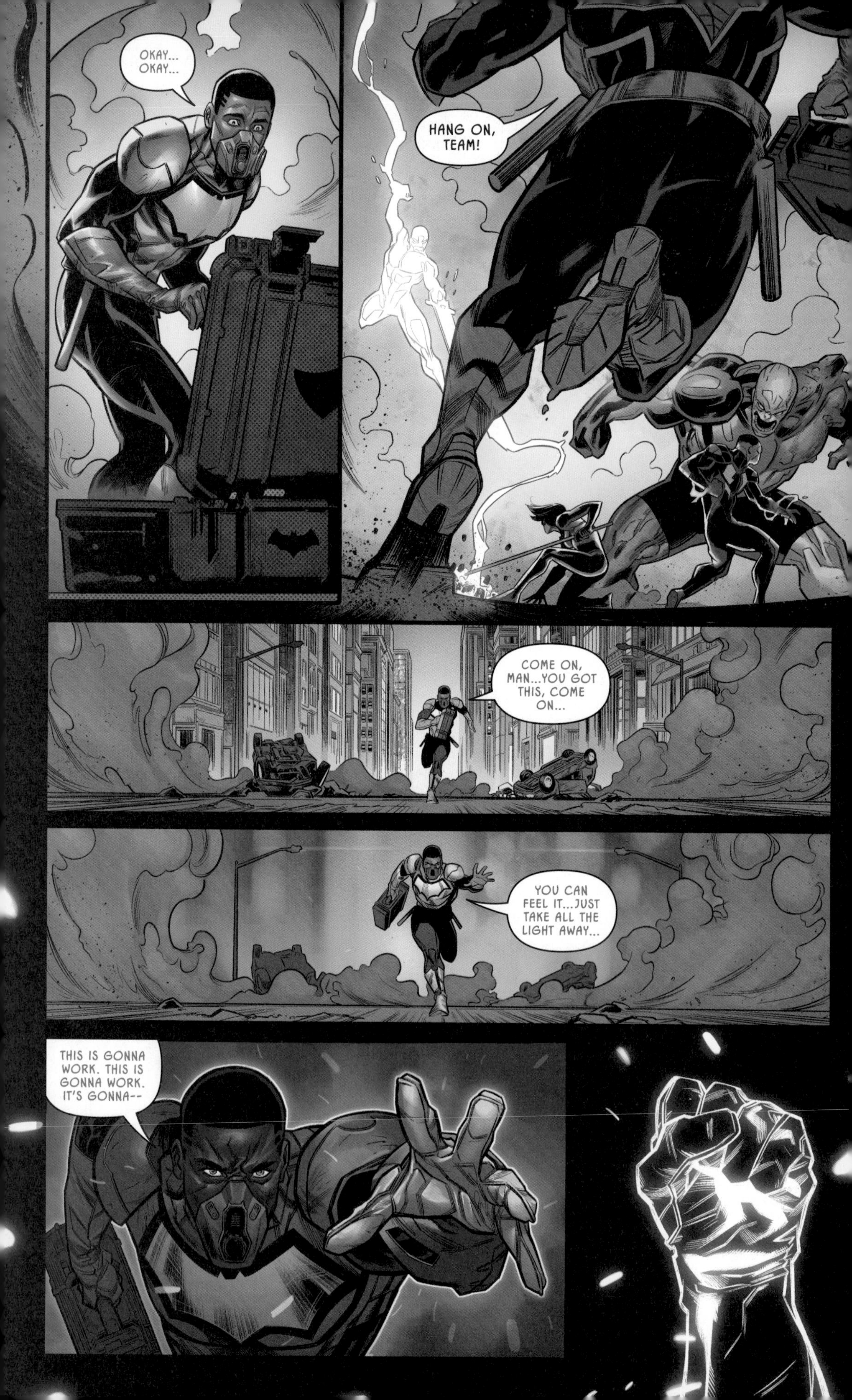
OKAY... OKAY...
HANG ON, TEAM!
COME ON, MAN...YOU GOT THIS, COME ON...
YOU CAN FEEL IT...JUST TAKE ALL THE LIGHT AWAY...
THIS IS GONNA WORK. THIS IS GONNA WORK. IT'S GONNA--

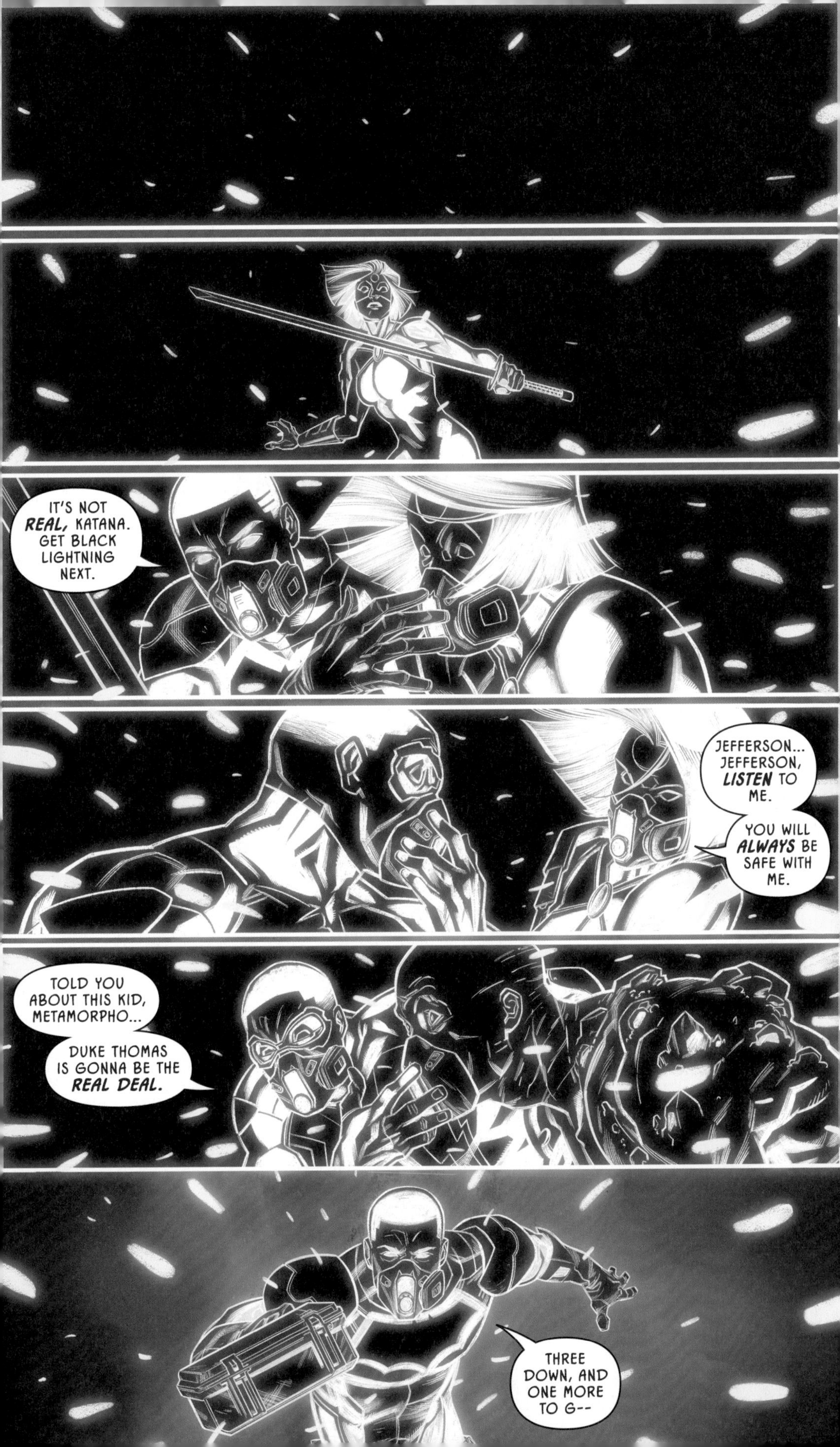

IT'S NOT REAL, KATANA. GET BLACK LIGHTNING NEXT.
JEFFERSON... JEFFERSON, LISTEN TO ME.
YOU WILL ALWAYS BE SAFE WITH ME.
TOLD YOU ABOUT THIS KID, METAMORPHO...
DUKE THOMAS IS GONNA BE THE REAL DEAL.
THREE DOWN, AND ONE MORE TO G--

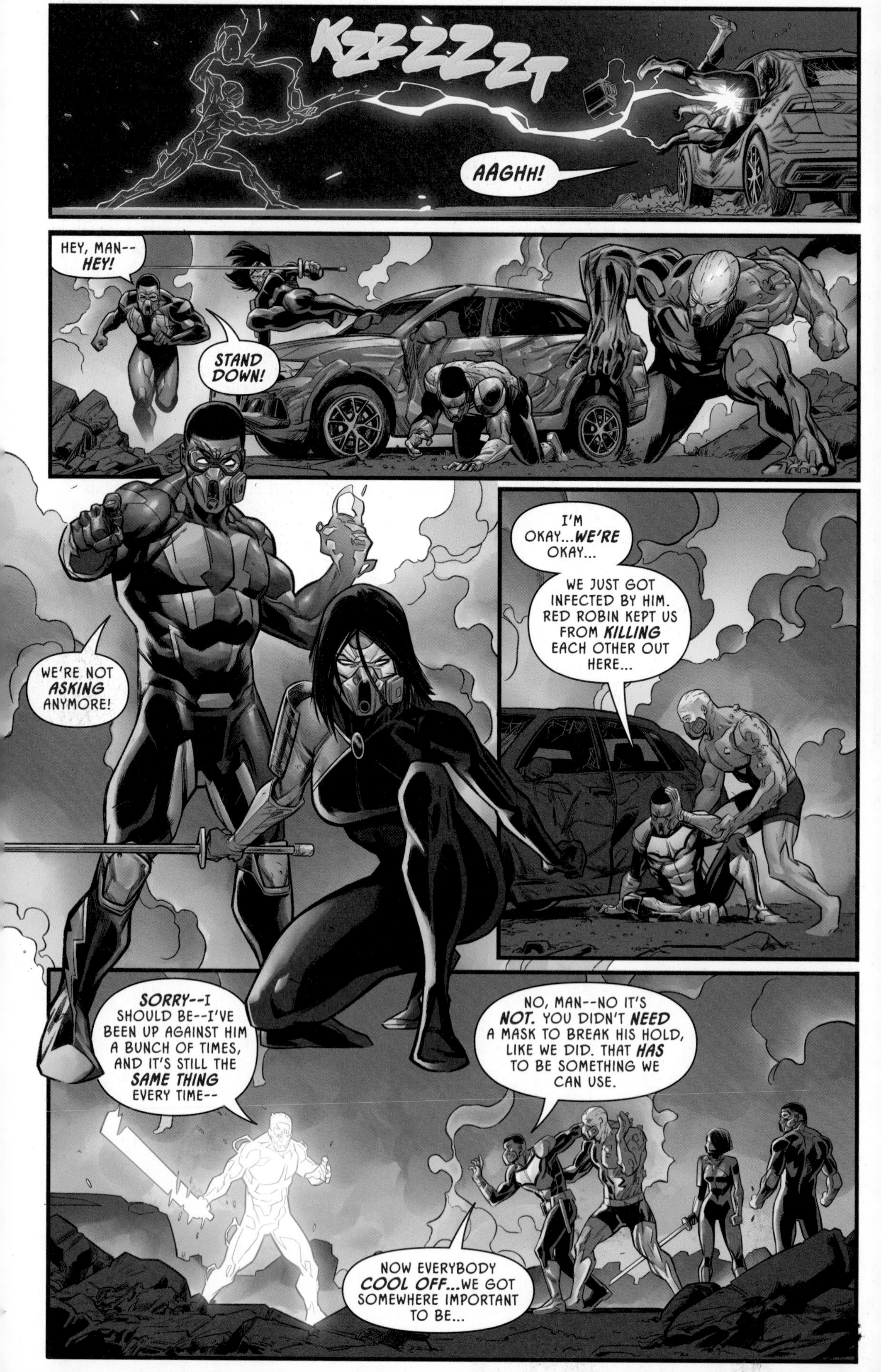
KZZZZZZT
AAGHH!
HEY, MAN-- HEY!
STAND DOWN!
WE'RE NOT ASKING ANYMORE!
I'M OKAY...WE'RE OKAY...
WE JUST GOT INFECTED BY HIM. RED ROBIN KEPT US FROM KILLING EACH OTHER OUT HERE...
SORRY--I SHOULD BE--I'VE BEEN UP AGAINST HIM A BUNCH OF TIMES, AND IT'S STILL THE SAME THING EVERY TIME--
NO, MAN--NO IT'S NOT. YOU DIDN'T NEED A MASK TO BREAK HIS HOLD, LIKE WE DID. THAT HAS TO BE SOMETHING WE CAN USE.
NOW EVERYBODY COOL OFF...WE GOT SOMEWHERE IMPORTANT TO BE...

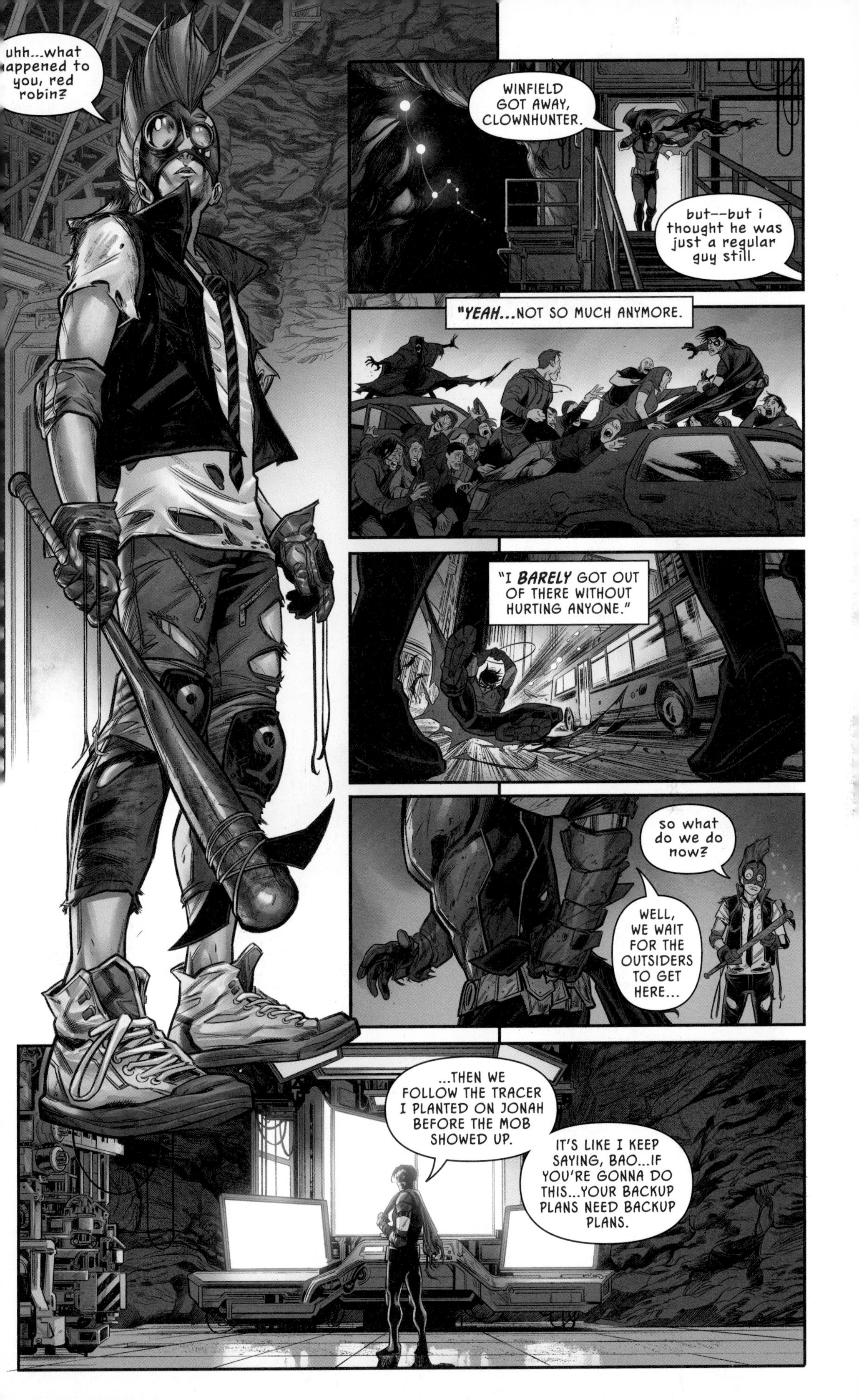
uhh...what
appened to
you, red
robin?
WINFIELD
GOT AWAY,
CLOWNHUNTER.
but--but i
thought he was
just a regular
guy still.
"YEAH...NOT SO MUCH ANYMORE.
"I BARELY GOT OUT
OF THERE WITHOUT
HURTING ANYONE."
so what
do we do
now?
WELL,
WE WAIT
FOR THE
OUTSIDERS
TO GET
HERE...
...THEN WE
FOLLOW THE TRACER
I PLANTED ON JONAH
BEFORE THE MOB
SHOWED UP.
IT'S LIKE I KEEP
SAYING, BAO...IF
YOU'RE GONNA DO
THIS...YOUR BACKUP
PLANS NEED BACKUP
PLANS.

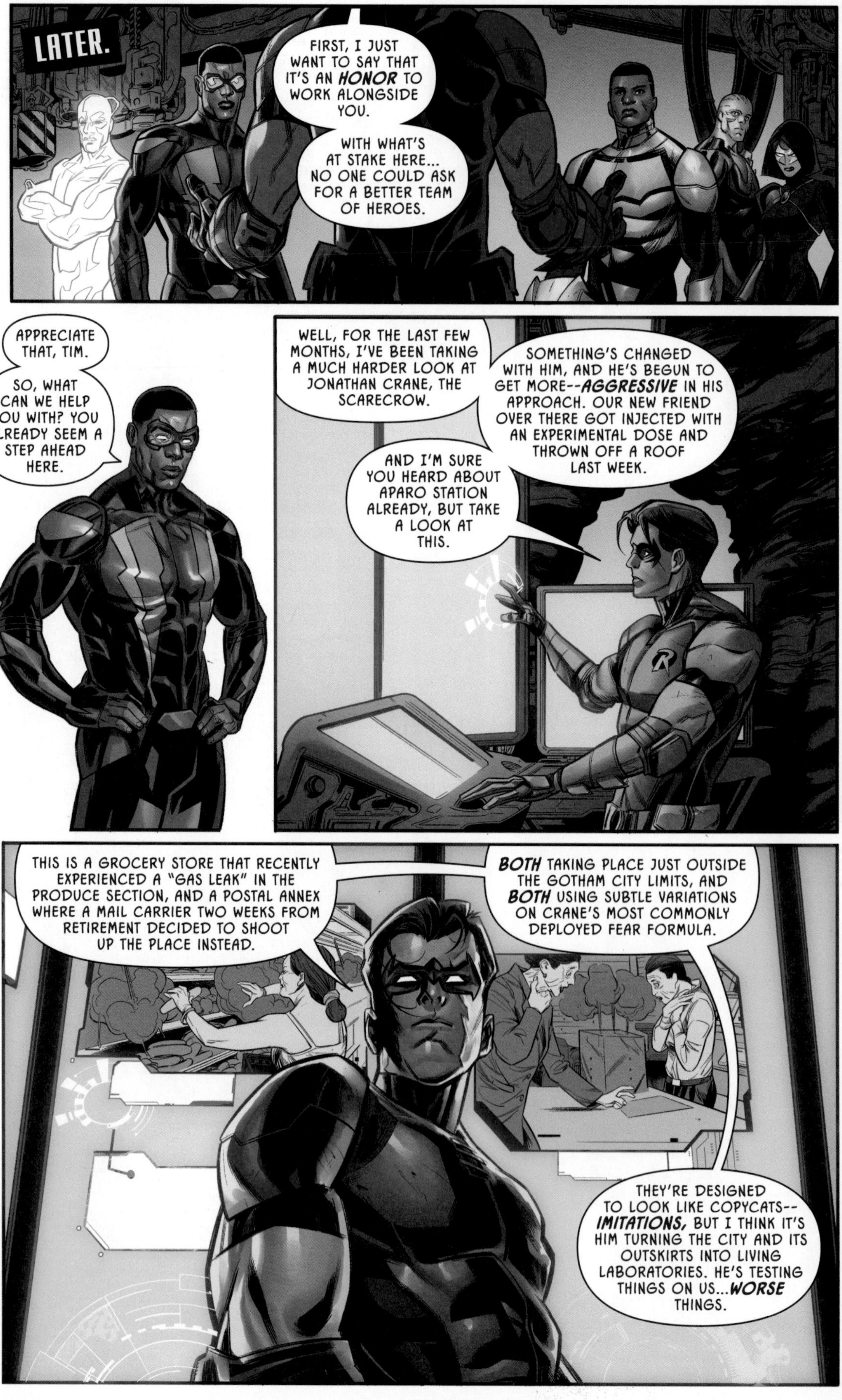
LATER.
FIRST, I JUST WANT TO SAY THAT IT'S AN HONOR TO WORK ALONGSIDE YOU.
WITH WHAT'S AT STAKE HERE... NO ONE COULD ASK FOR A BETTER TEAM OF HEROES.
APPRECIATE THAT, TIM.
SO, WHAT CAN WE HELP YOU WITH? YOU ALREADY SEEM A STEP AHEAD HERE.
WELL, FOR THE LAST FEW MONTHS, I'VE BEEN TAKING A MUCH HARDER LOOK AT JONATHAN CRANE, THE SCARECROW.
SOMETHING'S CHANGED WITH HIM, AND HE'S BEGUN TO GET MORE--AGGRESSIVE IN HIS APPROACH. OUR NEW FRIEND OVER THERE GOT INJECTED WITH AN EXPERIMENTAL DOSE AND THROWN OFF A ROOF LAST WEEK.
AND I'M SURE YOU HEARD ABOUT APARO STATION ALREADY, BUT TAKE A LOOK AT THIS.
THIS IS A GROCERY STORE THAT RECENTLY EXPERIENCED A "GAS LEAK" IN THE PRODUCE SECTION, AND A POSTAL ANNEX WHERE A MAIL CARRIER TWO WEEKS FROM RETIREMENT DECIDED TO SHOOT UP THE PLACE INSTEAD.
BOTH TAKING PLACE JUST OUTSIDE THE GOTHAM CITY LIMITS, AND BOTH USING SUBTLE VARIATIONS ON CRANE'S MOST COMMONLY DEPLOYED FEAR FORMULA.
THEY'RE DESIGNED TO LOOK LIKE COPYCATS--IMITATIONS, BUT I THINK IT'S HIM TURNING THE CITY AND ITS OUTSKIRTS INTO LIVING LABORATORIES. HE'S TESTING THINGS ON US...WORSE THINGS.

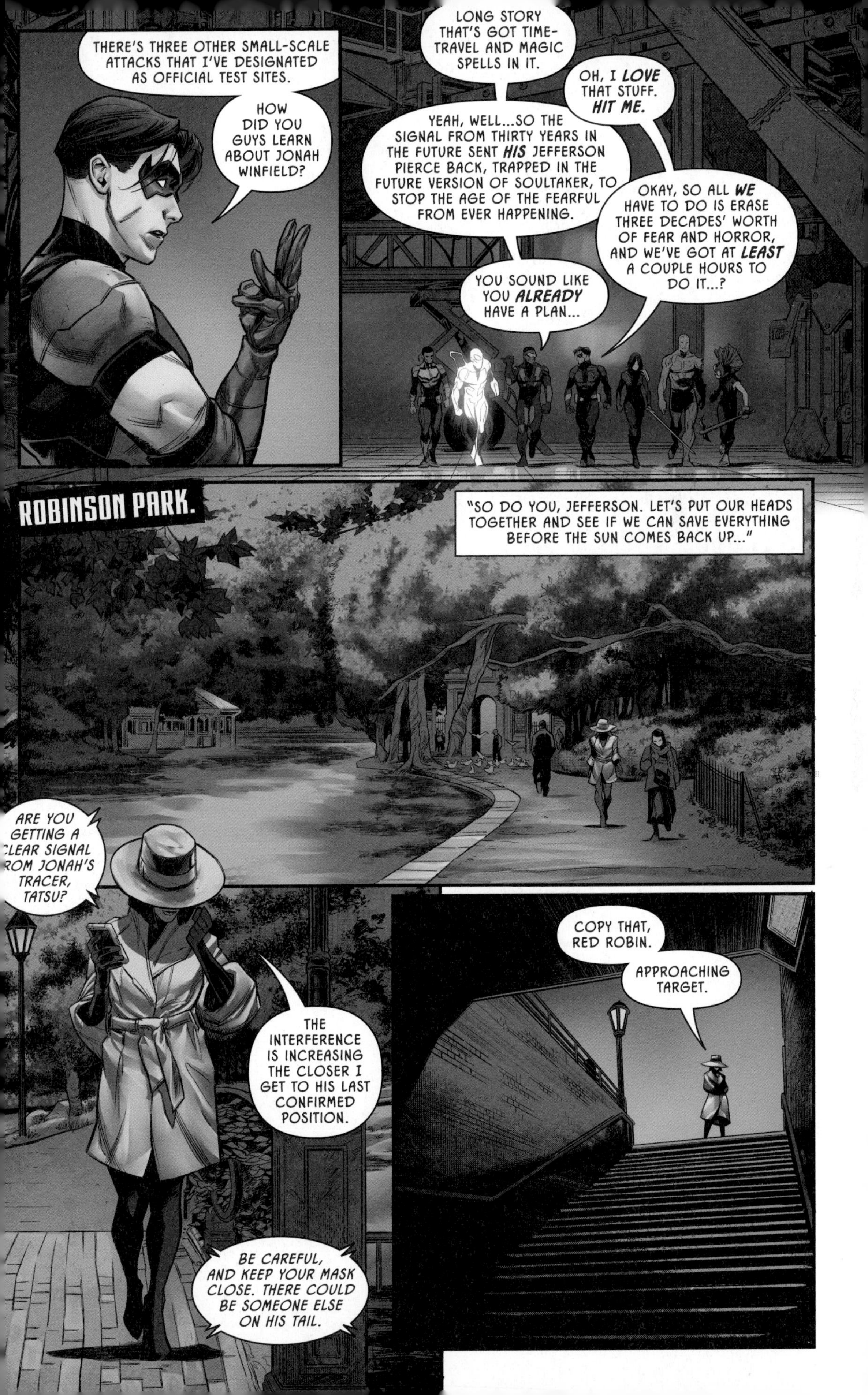
THERE'S THREE OTHER SMALL-SCALE ATTACKS THAT I'VE DESIGNATED AS OFFICIAL TEST SITES.
HOW DID YOU GUYS LEARN ABOUT JONAH WINFIELD?
LONG STORY THAT'S GOT TIME-TRAVEL AND MAGIC SPELLS IN IT.
OH, I LOVE THAT STUFF. HIT ME.
YEAH, WELL...SO THE SIGNAL FROM THIRTY YEARS IN THE FUTURE SENT HIS JEFFERSON PIERCE BACK, TRAPPED IN THE FUTURE VERSION OF SOULTAKER, TO STOP THE AGE OF THE FEARFUL FROM EVER HAPPENING.
OKAY, SO ALL WE HAVE TO DO IS ERASE THREE DECADES' WORTH OF FEAR AND HORROR, AND WE'VE GOT AT LEAST A COUPLE HOURS TO DO IT...?
YOU SOUND LIKE YOU ALREADY HAVE A PLAN...
ROBINSON PARK.
"SO DO YOU, JEFFERSON. LET'S PUT OUR HEADS TOGETHER AND SEE IF WE CAN SAVE EVERYTHING BEFORE THE SUN COMES BACK UP..."
ARE YOU GETTING A CLEAR SIGNAL FROM JONAH'S TRACER, TATSU?
THE INTERFERENCE IS INCREASING THE CLOSER I GET TO HIS LAST CONFIRMED POSITION.
BE CAREFUL, AND KEEP YOUR MASK CLOSE. THERE COULD BE SOMEONE ELSE ON HIS TAIL.
COPY THAT, RED ROBIN.
APPROACHING TARGET.

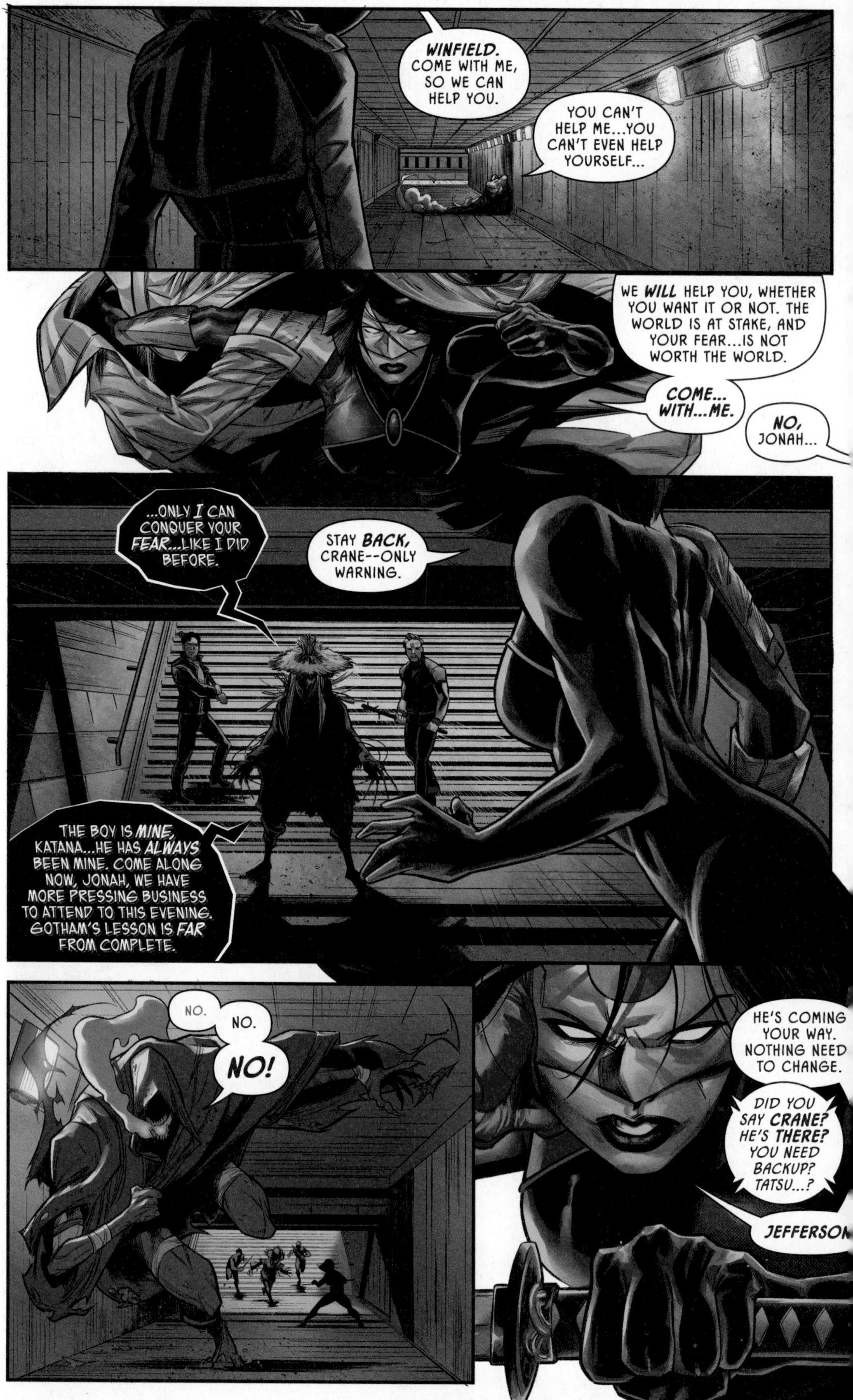
WINFIELD. COME WITH ME, SO WE CAN HELP YOU.
YOU CAN'T HELP ME...YOU CAN'T EVEN HELP YOURSELF...
WE WILL HELP YOU, WHETHER YOU WANT IT OR NOT. THE WORLD IS AT STAKE, AND YOUR FEAR...IS NOT WORTH THE WORLD.
COME... WITH...ME.
NO, JONAH...
...ONLY I CAN CONQUER YOUR FEAR...LIKE I DID BEFORE.
STAY BACK, CRANE--ONLY WARNING.
THE BOY IS MINE, KATANA...HE HAS ALWAYS BEEN MINE. COME ALONG NOW, JONAH, WE HAVE MORE PRESSING BUSINESS TO ATTEND TO THIS EVENING. GOTHAM'S LESSON IS FAR FROM COMPLETE.
NO.
NO.
NO!
HE'S COMING YOUR WAY. NOTHING NEED TO CHANGE.
DID YOU SAY CRANE? HE'S THERE? YOU NEED BACKUP? TATSU...?
JEFFERSON

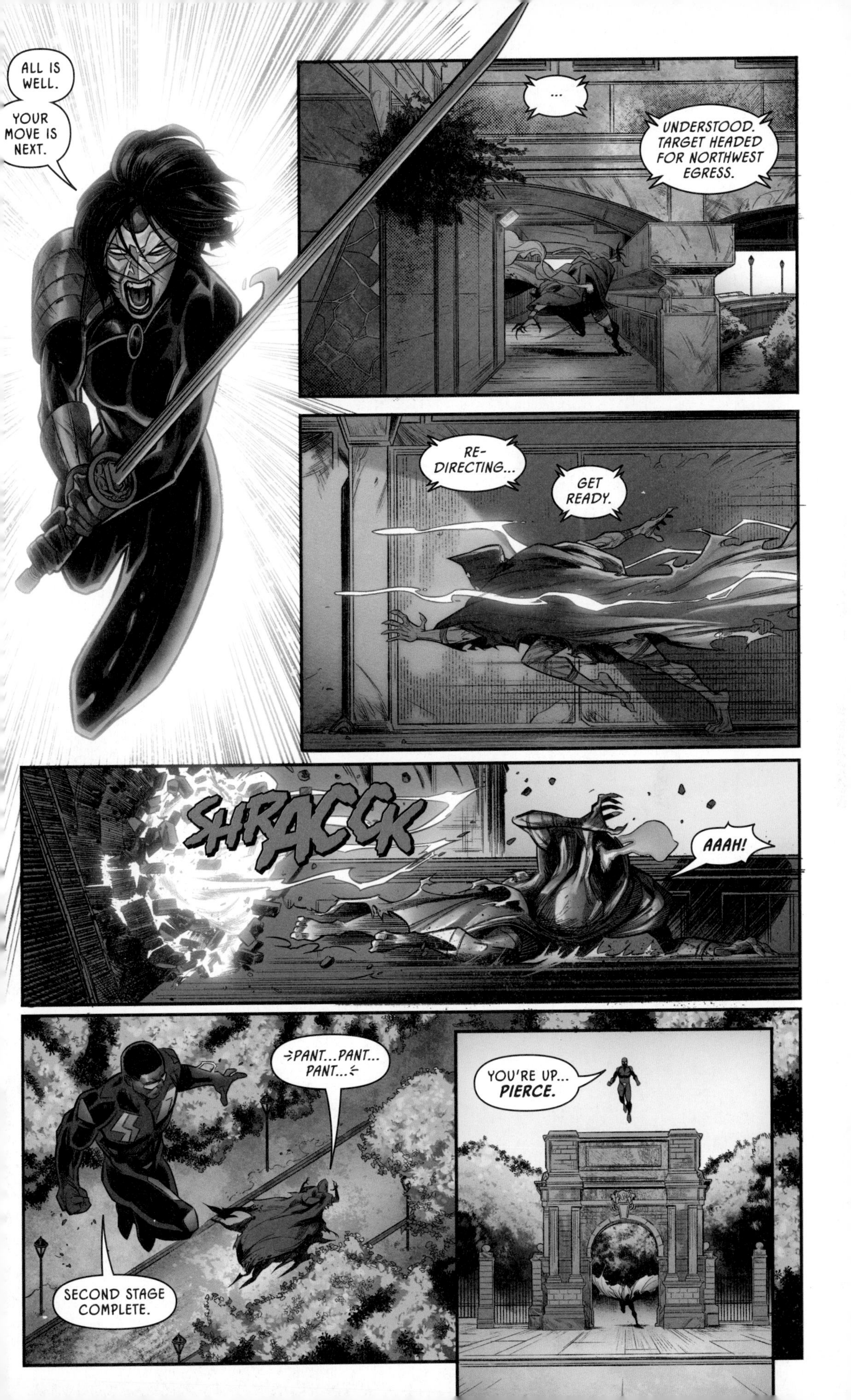
ALL IS WELL.
YOUR MOVE IS NEXT.
...
UNDERSTOOD. TARGET HEADED FOR NORTHWEST EGRESS.
RE-DIRECTING...
GET READY.
SHRACCK
AAAH!
PANT...PANT... PANT...
SECOND STAGE COMPLETE.
YOU'RE UP... PIERCE.

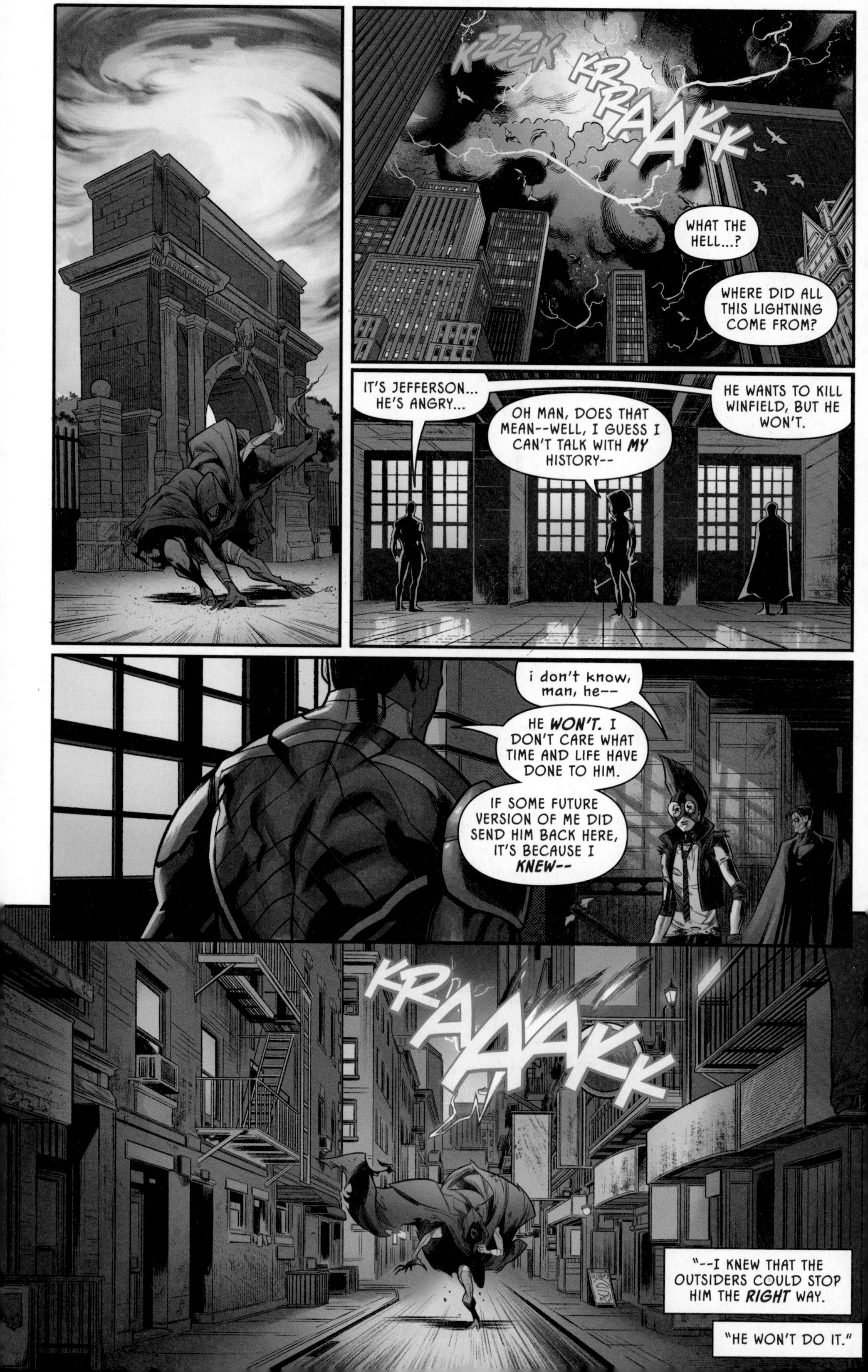
KZZZK
KRRAAKK
WHAT THE HELL...?
WHERE DID ALL THIS LIGHTNING COME FROM?
IT'S JEFFERSON... HE'S ANGRY...
OH MAN, DOES THAT MEAN--WELL, I GUESS I CAN'T TALK WITH MY HISTORY--
HE WANTS TO KILL WINFIELD, BUT HE WON'T.
i don't know, man, he--
HE WON'T. I DON'T CARE WHAT TIME AND LIFE HAVE DONE TO HIM.
IF SOME FUTURE VERSION OF ME DID SEND HIM BACK HERE, IT'S BECAUSE I KNEW--
KRAAAKK
"--I KNEW THAT THE OUTSIDERS COULD STOP HIM THE RIGHT WAY.
"HE WON'T DO IT."

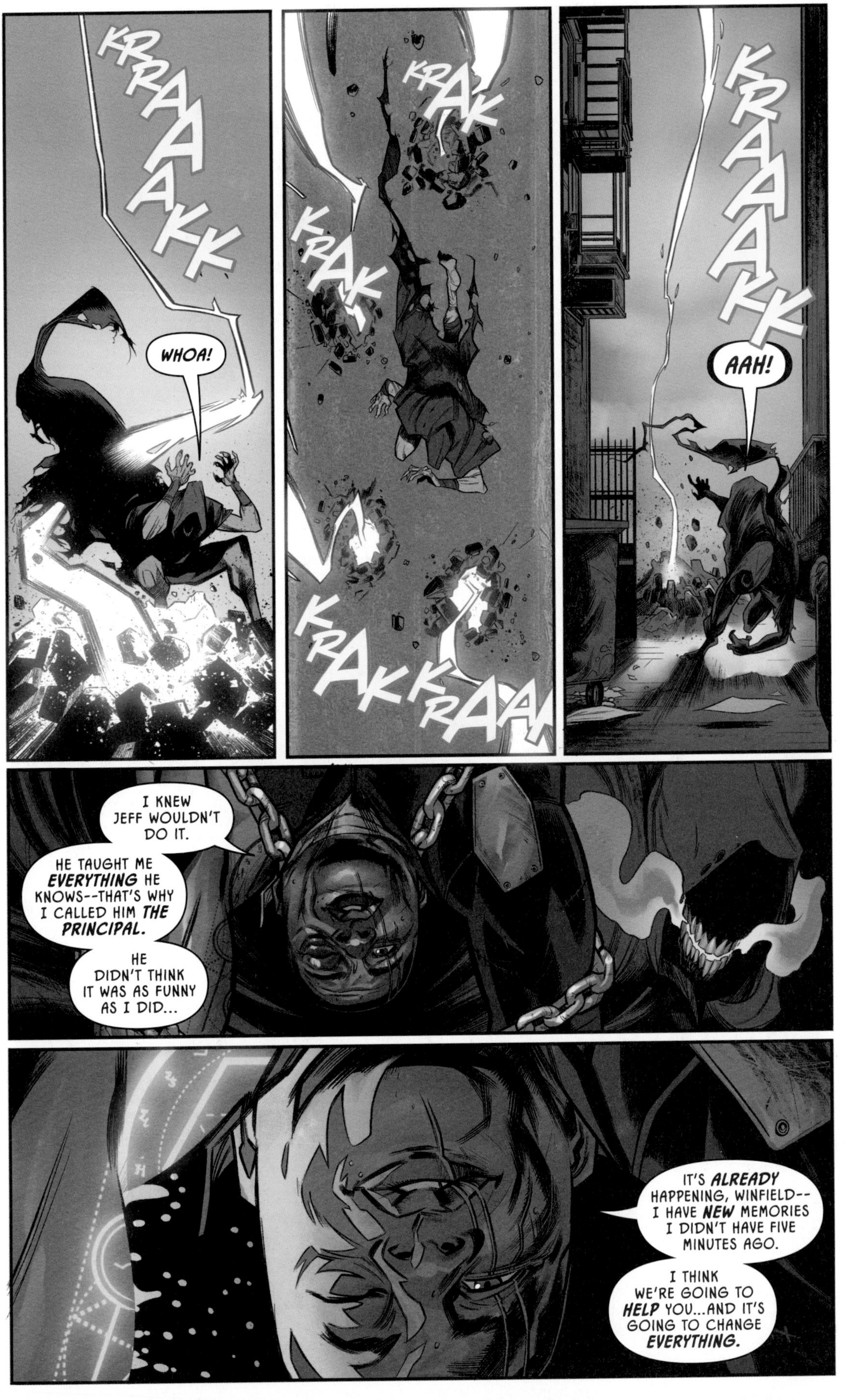
KRRAAAAKK
WHOA!
KRAK
KRAK
KRAK
KRAAA
KRAAAAKK
AAH!
I KNEW JEFF WOULDN'T DO IT.
HE TAUGHT ME EVERYTHING HE KNOWS--THAT'S WHY I CALLED HIM THE PRINCIPAL.
HE DIDN'T THINK IT WAS AS FUNNY AS I DID...
IT'S ALREADY HAPPENING, WINFIELD--I HAVE NEW MEMORIES I DIDN'T HAVE FIVE MINUTES AGO.
I THINK WE'RE GOING TO HELP YOU...AND IT'S GOING TO CHANGE EVERYTHING.

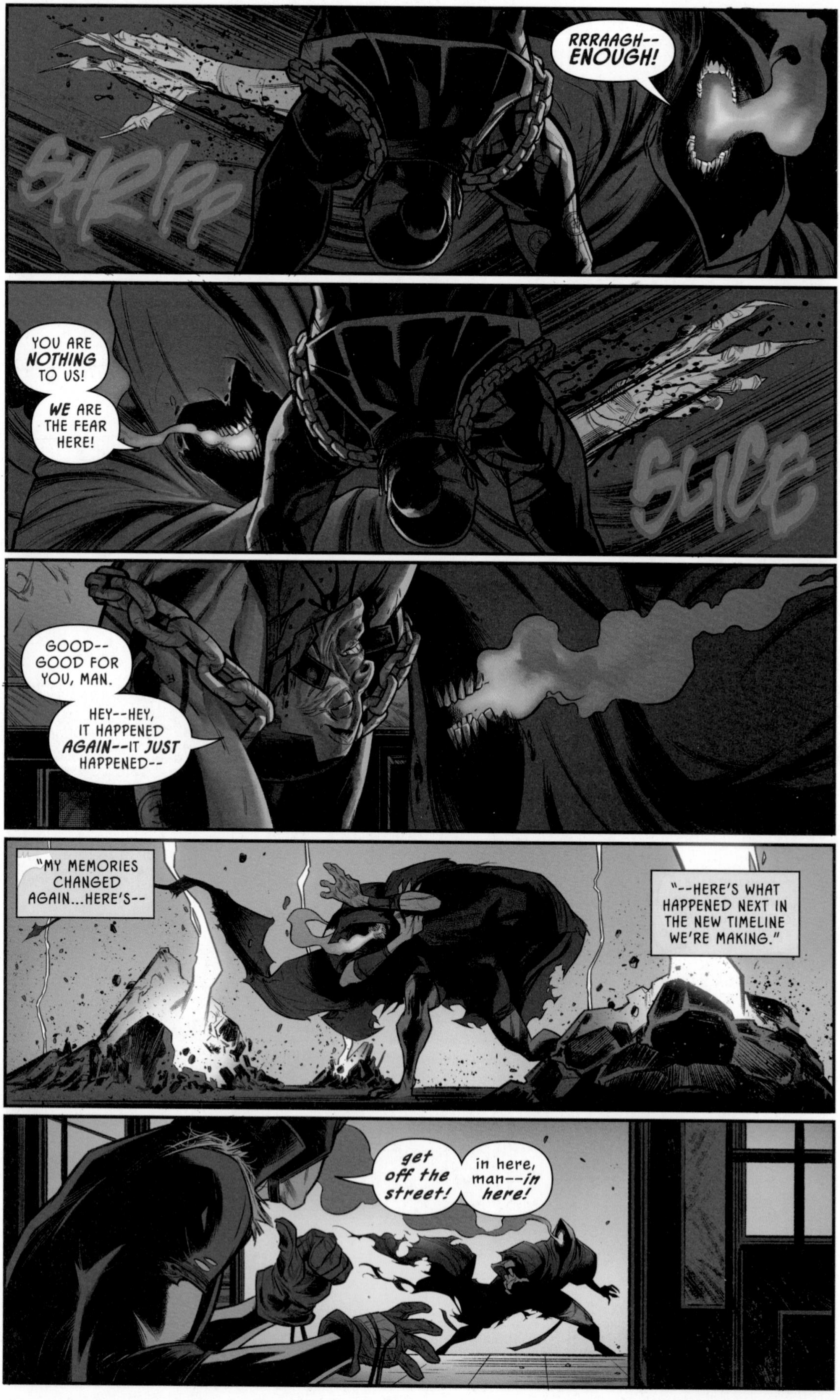
RRRAAGH--
ENOUGH!
SHRIPP
YOU ARE NOTHING TO US!
WE ARE THE FEAR HERE!
SLICE
GOOD--GOOD FOR YOU, MAN.
HEY--HEY, IT HAPPENED AGAIN--IT JUST HAPPENED--
"MY MEMORIES CHANGED AGAIN...HERE'S--
"--HERE'S WHAT HAPPENED NEXT IN THE NEW TIMELINE WE'RE MAKING."
get off the street!
in here, man--in here!

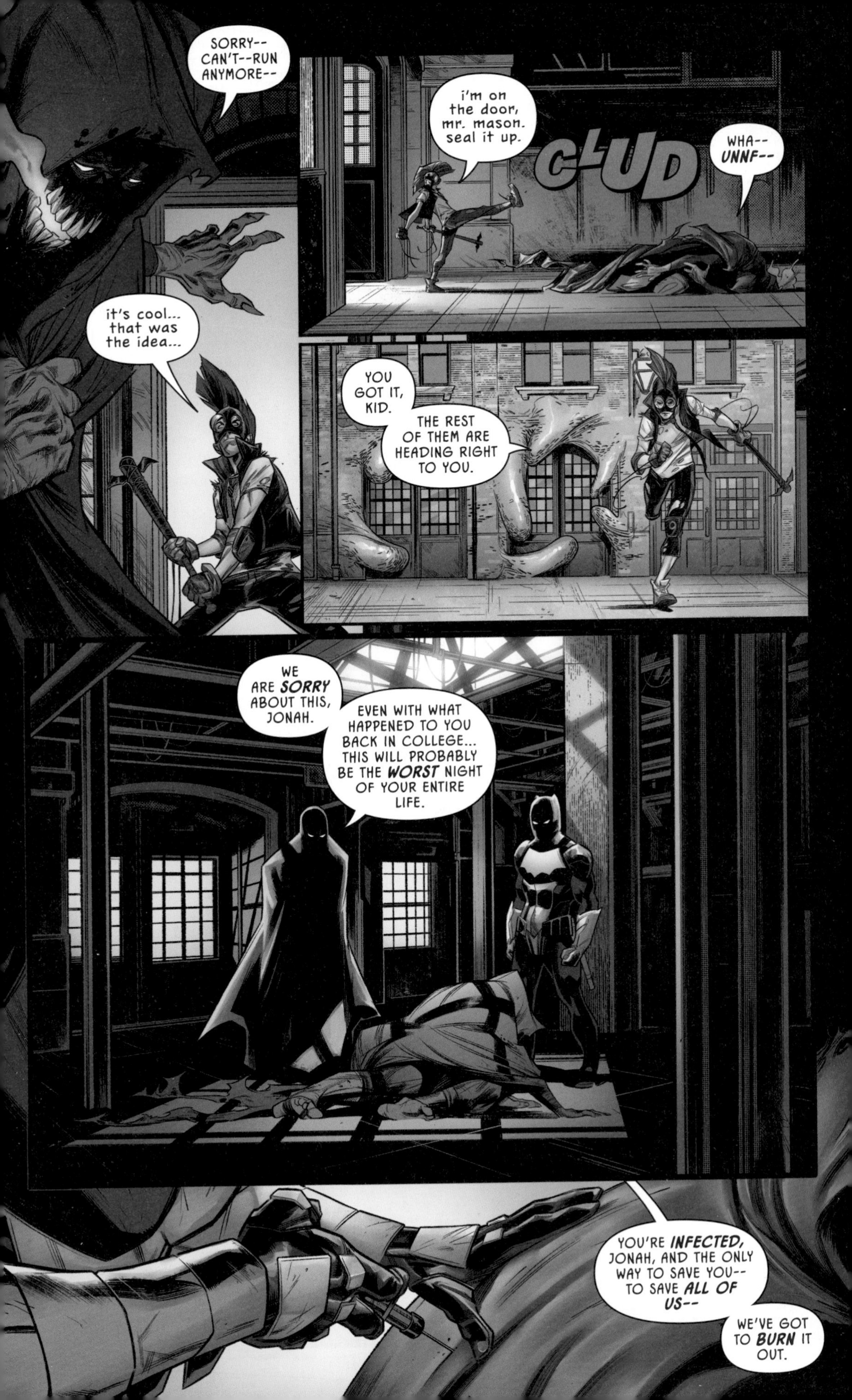
SORRY--
CAN'T--RUN
ANYMORE--
i'm on the door, mr. mason. seal it up.
CLUD
WHA--
UNNF--
it's cool... that was the idea...
YOU GOT IT, KID.
THE REST OF THEM ARE HEADING RIGHT TO YOU.
WE ARE SORRY ABOUT THIS, JONAH.
EVEN WITH WHAT HAPPENED TO YOU BACK IN COLLEGE... THIS WILL PROBABLY BE THE WORST NIGHT OF YOUR ENTIRE LIFE.
YOU'RE INFECTED, JONAH, AND THE ONLY WAY TO SAVE YOU-- TO SAVE ALL OF US--
WE'VE GOT TO BURN IT OUT.

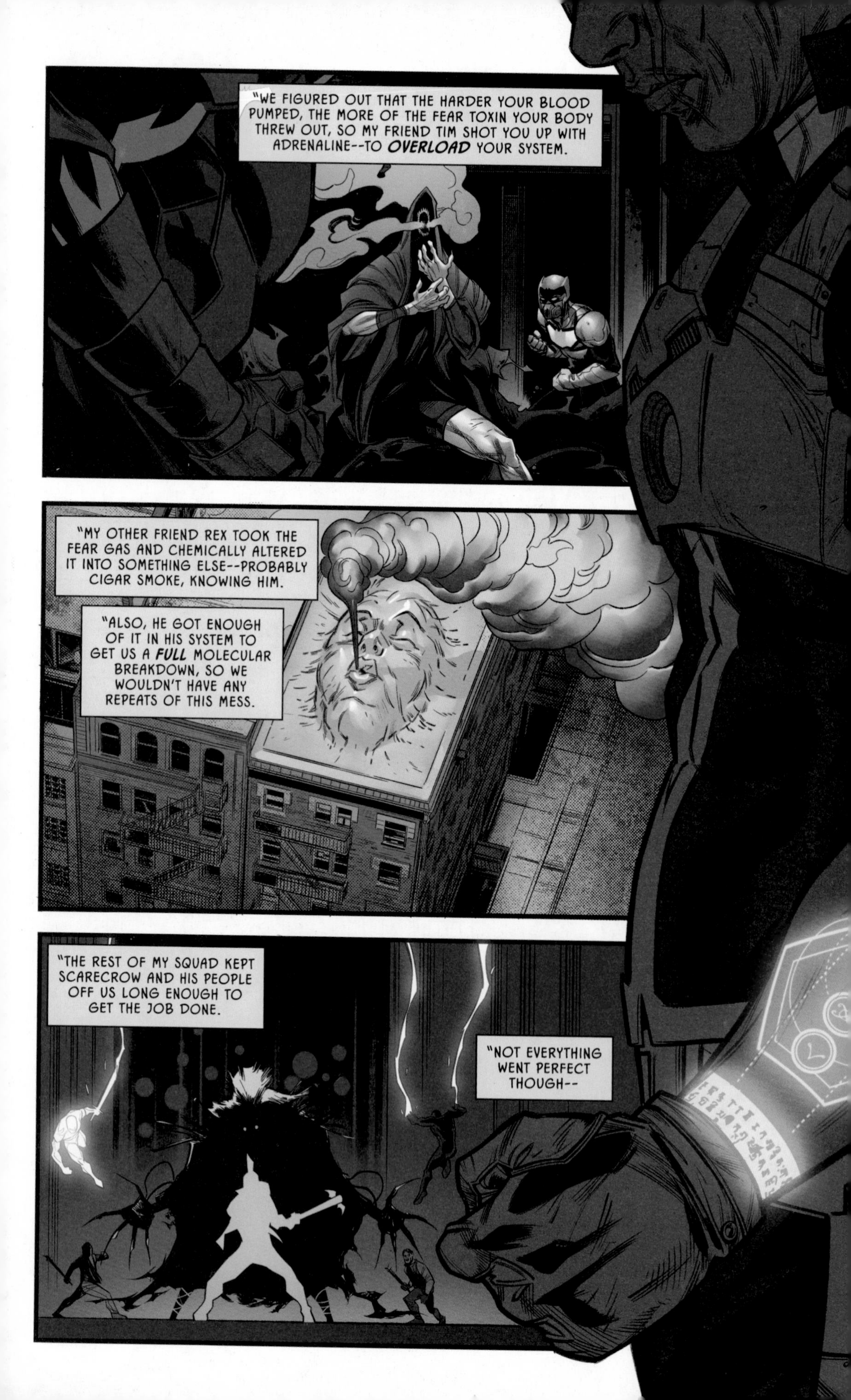
"WE FIGURED OUT THAT THE HARDER YOUR BLOOD PUMPED, THE MORE OF THE FEAR TOXIN YOUR BODY THREW OUT, SO MY FRIEND TIM SHOT YOU UP WITH ADRENALINE--TO OVERLOAD YOUR SYSTEM.
"MY OTHER FRIEND REX TOOK THE FEAR GAS AND CHEMICALLY ALTERED IT INTO SOMETHING ELSE--PROBABLY CIGAR SMOKE, KNOWING HIM.
"ALSO, HE GOT ENOUGH OF IT IN HIS SYSTEM TO GET US A FULL MOLECULAR BREAKDOWN, SO WE WOULDN'T HAVE ANY REPEATS OF THIS MESS.
"THE REST OF MY SQUAD KEPT SCARECROW AND HIS PEOPLE OFF US LONG ENOUGH TO GET THE JOB DONE.
"NOT EVERYTHING WENT PERFECT THOUGH--

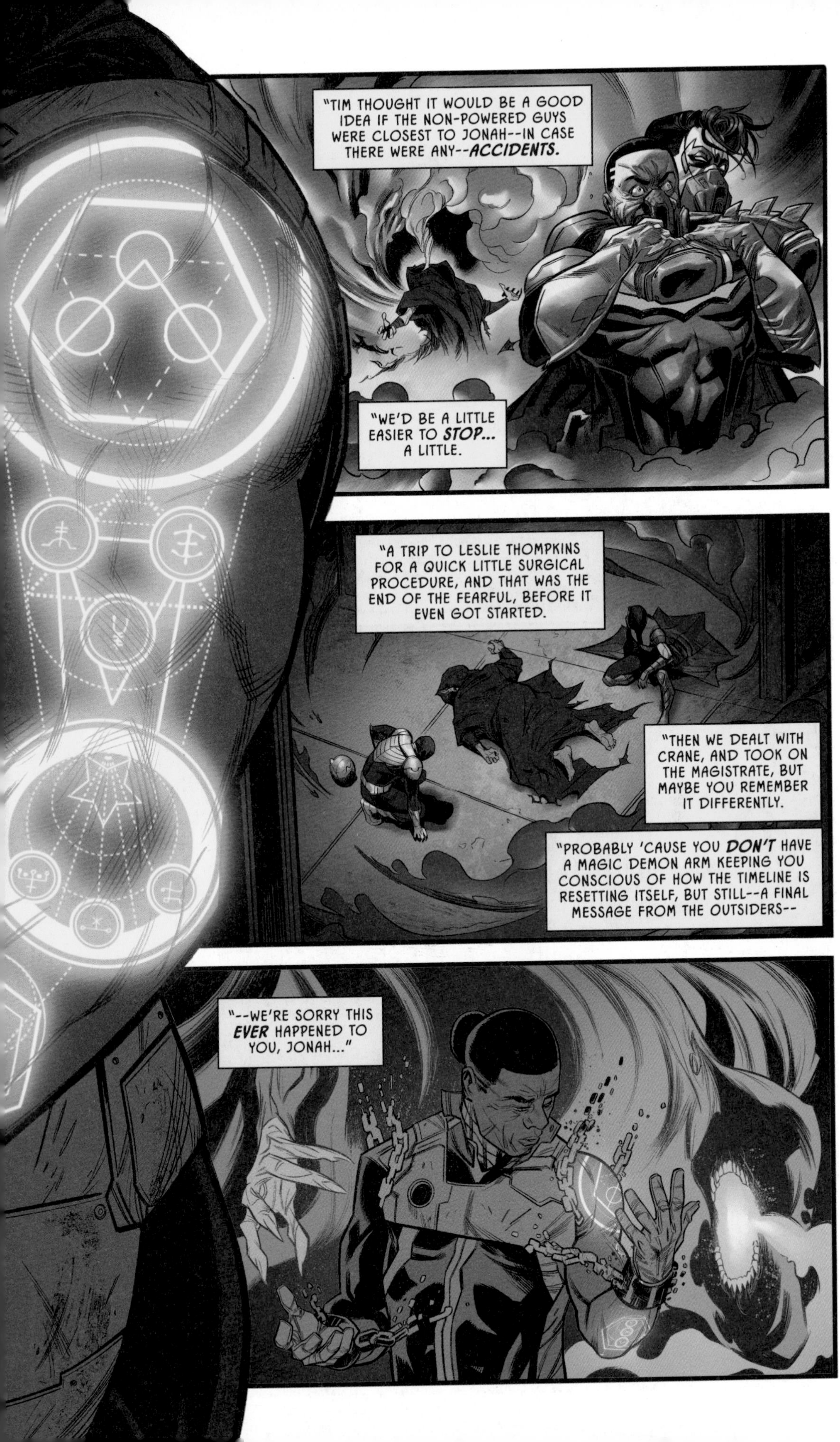
"TIM THOUGHT IT WOULD BE A GOOD IDEA IF THE NON-POWERED GUYS WERE CLOSEST TO JONAH--IN CASE THERE WERE ANY--ACCIDENTS.
"WE'D BE A LITTLE EASIER TO STOP... A LITTLE.
"A TRIP TO LESLIE THOMPKINS FOR A QUICK LITTLE SURGICAL PROCEDURE, AND THAT WAS THE END OF THE FEARFUL, BEFORE IT EVEN GOT STARTED.
"THEN WE DEALT WITH CRANE, AND TOOK ON THE MAGISTRATE, BUT MAYBE YOU REMEMBER IT DIFFERENTLY.
"PROBABLY 'CAUSE YOU DON'T HAVE A MAGIC DEMON ARM KEEPING YOU CONSCIOUS OF HOW THE TIMELINE IS RESETTING ITSELF, BUT STILL--A FINAL MESSAGE FROM THE OUTSIDERS--
"--WE'RE SORRY THIS EVER HAPPENED TO YOU, JONAH..."

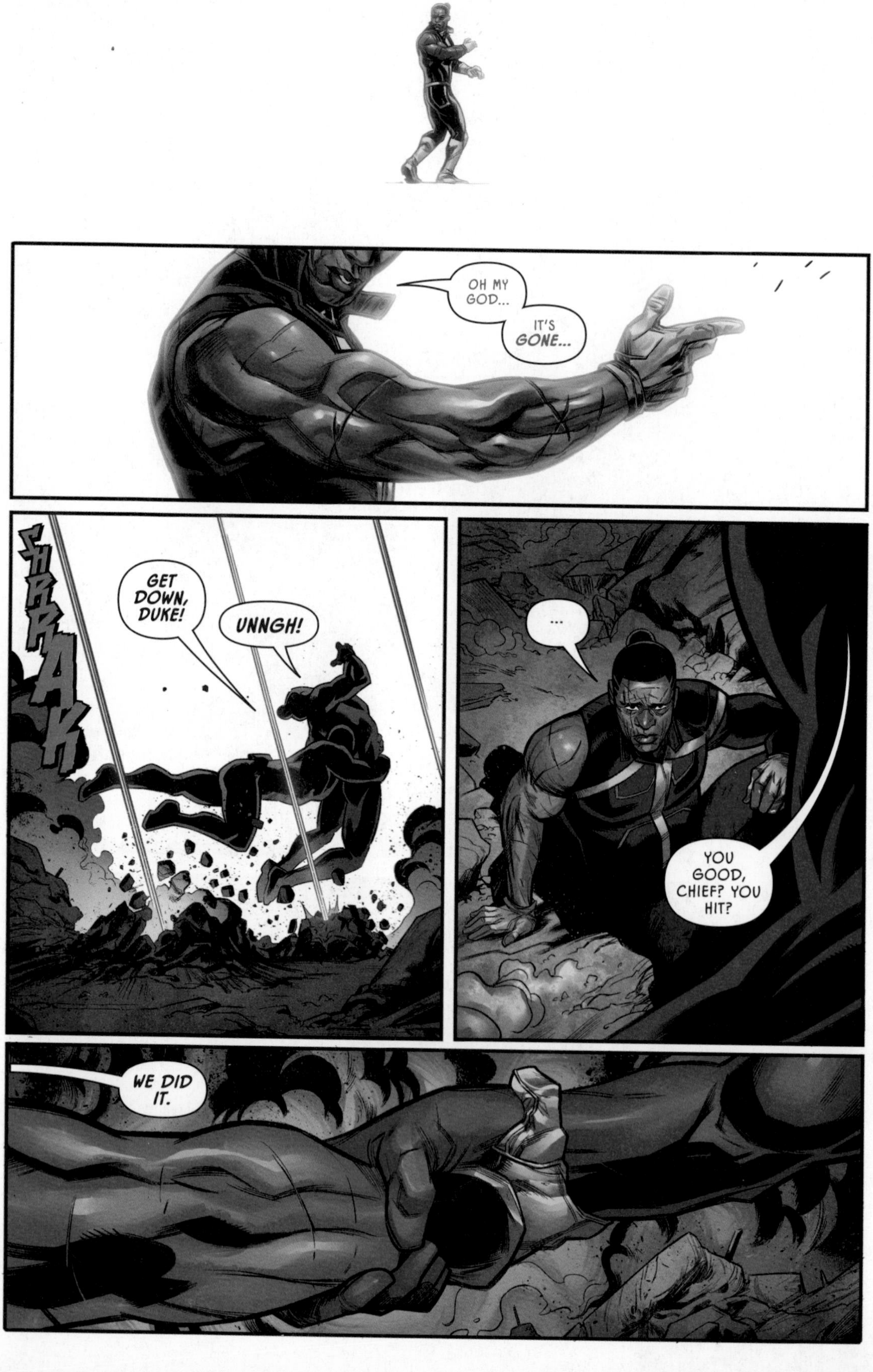

OH MY GOD...
IT'S GONE...
SHRRAK
GET DOWN, DUKE!
UNNGH!
...
YOU GOOD, CHIEF? YOU HIT?
WE DID IT.

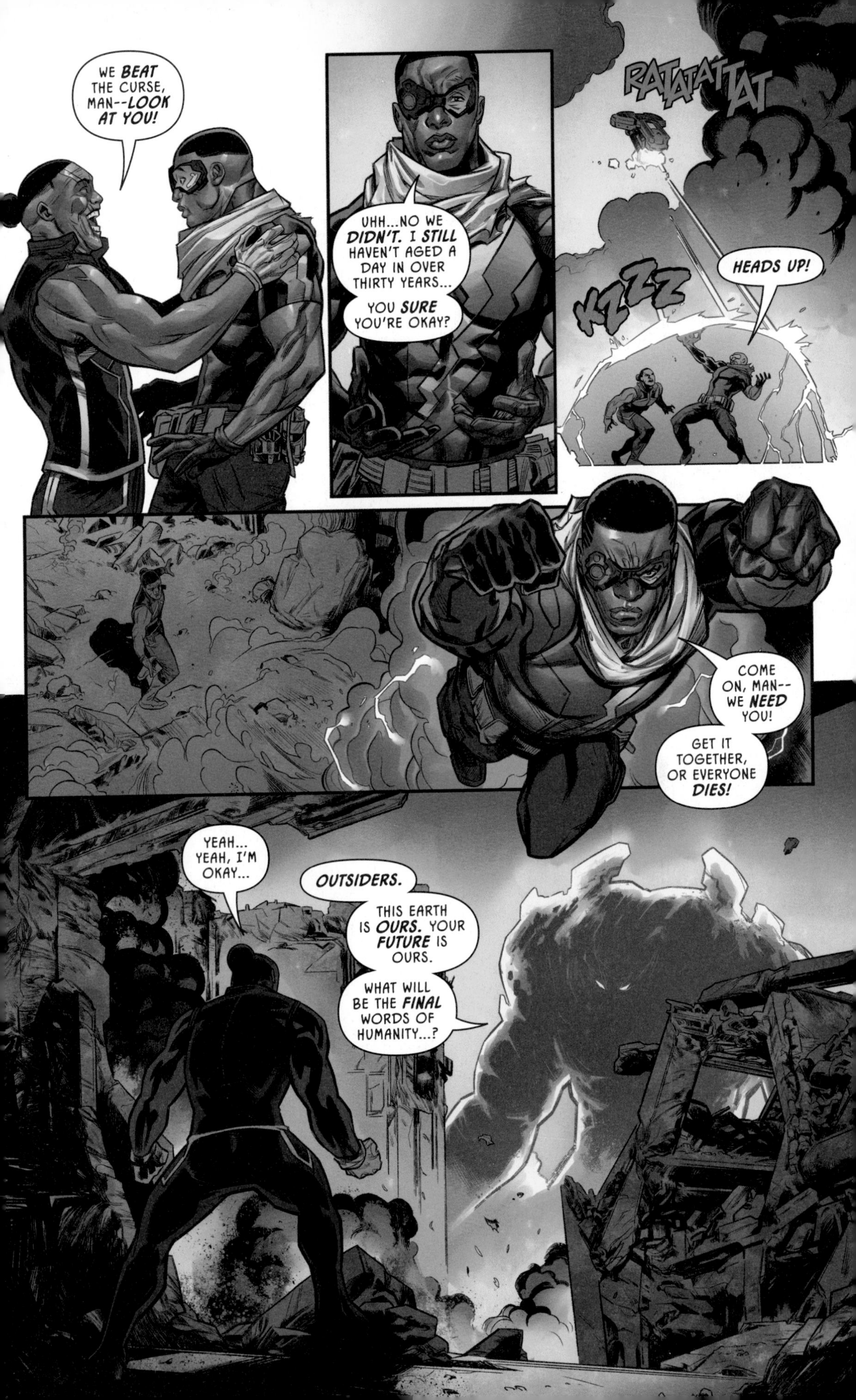
WE BEAT THE CURSE, MAN--LOOK AT YOU!
UHH...NO WE DIDN'T. I STILL HAVEN'T AGED A DAY IN OVER THIRTY YEARS...
YOU SURE YOU'RE OKAY?
RATATATTAT
KZZZ
HEADS UP!
COME ON, MAN--WE NEED YOU!
GET IT TOGETHER, OR EVERYONE DIES!
YEAH... YEAH, I'M OKAY...
OUTSIDERS.
THIS EARTH IS OURS. YOUR FUTURE IS OURS.
WHAT WILL BE THE FINAL WORDS OF HUMANITY...?

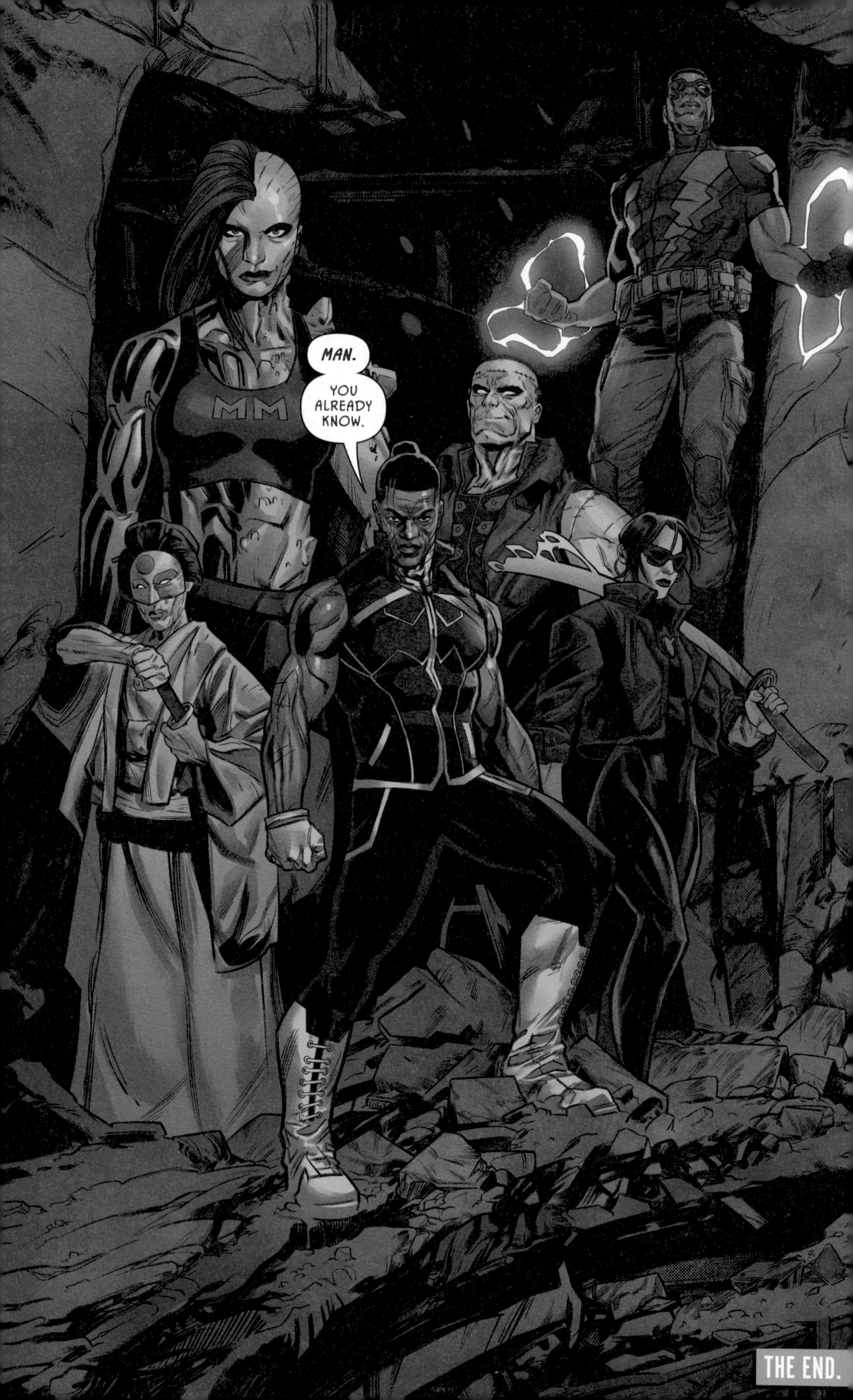
MAN.
YOU ALREADY KNOW.
THE END.

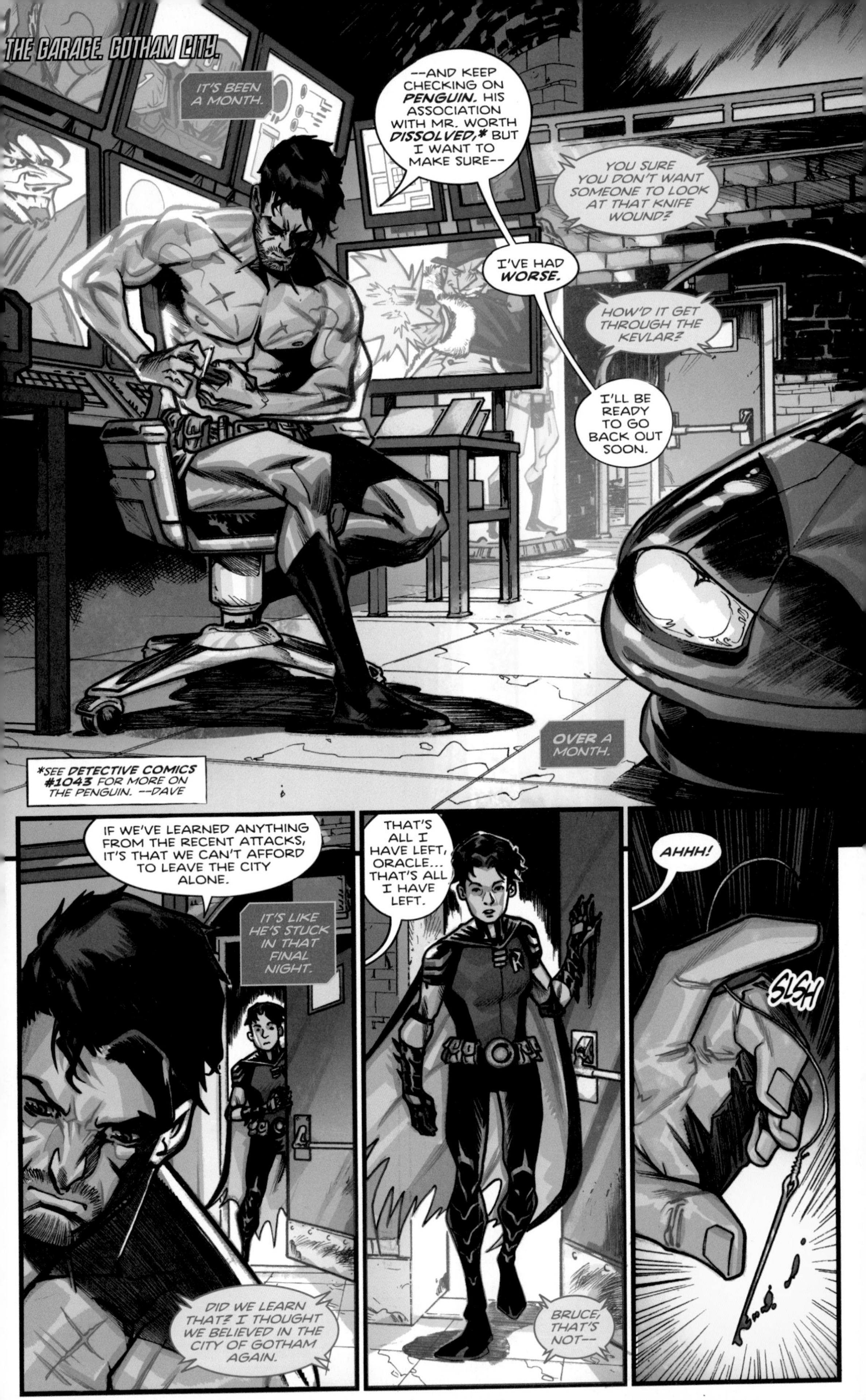
THE GARAGE. GOTHAM CITY.
IT'S BEEN A MONTH.
--AND KEEP CHECKING ON PENGUIN. HIS ASSOCIATION WITH MR. WORTH DISSOLVED,* BUT I WANT TO MAKE SURE--
YOU SURE YOU DON'T WANT SOMEONE TO LOOK AT THAT KNIFE WOUND?
I'VE HAD WORSE.
HOW'D IT GET THROUGH THE KEVLAR?
I'LL BE READY TO GO BACK OUT SOON.
OVER A MONTH.
*SEE DETECTIVE COMICS #1043 FOR MORE ON THE PENGUIN. --DAVE
IF WE'VE LEARNED ANYTHING FROM THE RECENT ATTACKS, IT'S THAT WE CAN'T AFFORD TO LEAVE THE CITY ALONE.
IT'S LIKE HE'S STUCK IN THAT FINAL NIGHT.
DID WE LEARN THAT? I THOUGHT WE BELIEVED IN THE CITY OF GOTHAM AGAIN.
THAT'S ALL I HAVE LEFT, ORACLE... THAT'S ALL I HAVE LEFT.
BRUCE, THAT'S NOT--
AHHH!
SLSH

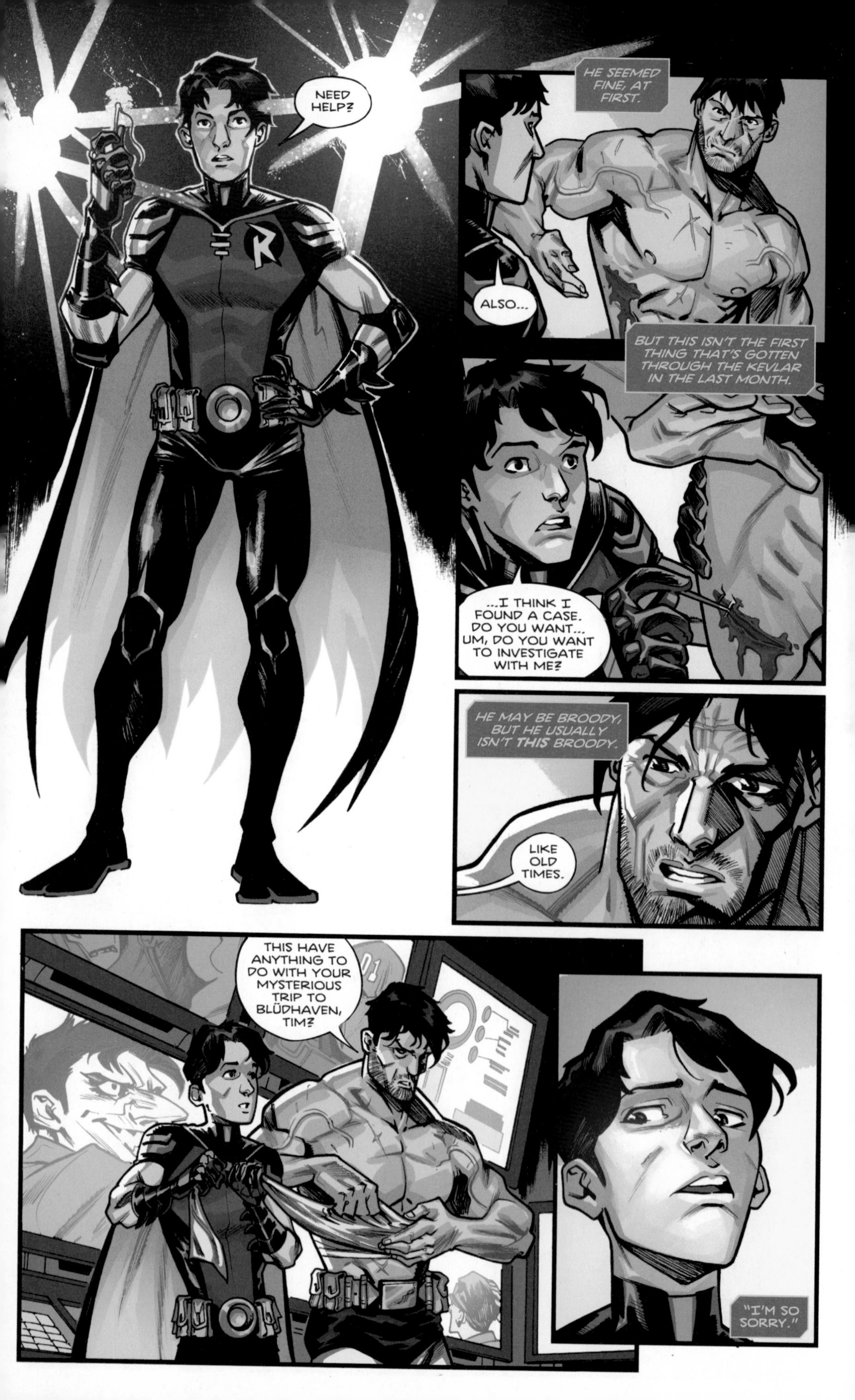
NEED HELP?
HE SEEMED FINE, AT FIRST.
ALSO...
BUT THIS ISN'T THE FIRST THING THAT'S GOTTEN THROUGH THE KEVLAR IN THE LAST MONTH.
...I THINK I FOUND A CASE. DO YOU WANT... UM, DO YOU WANT TO INVESTIGATE WITH ME?
HE MAY BE BROODY, BUT HE USUALLY ISN'T **THIS** BROODY.
LIKE OLD TIMES.
THIS HAVE ANYTHING TO DO WITH YOUR MYSTERIOUS TRIP TO BLÜDHAVEN, TIM?
"I'M SO SORRY."

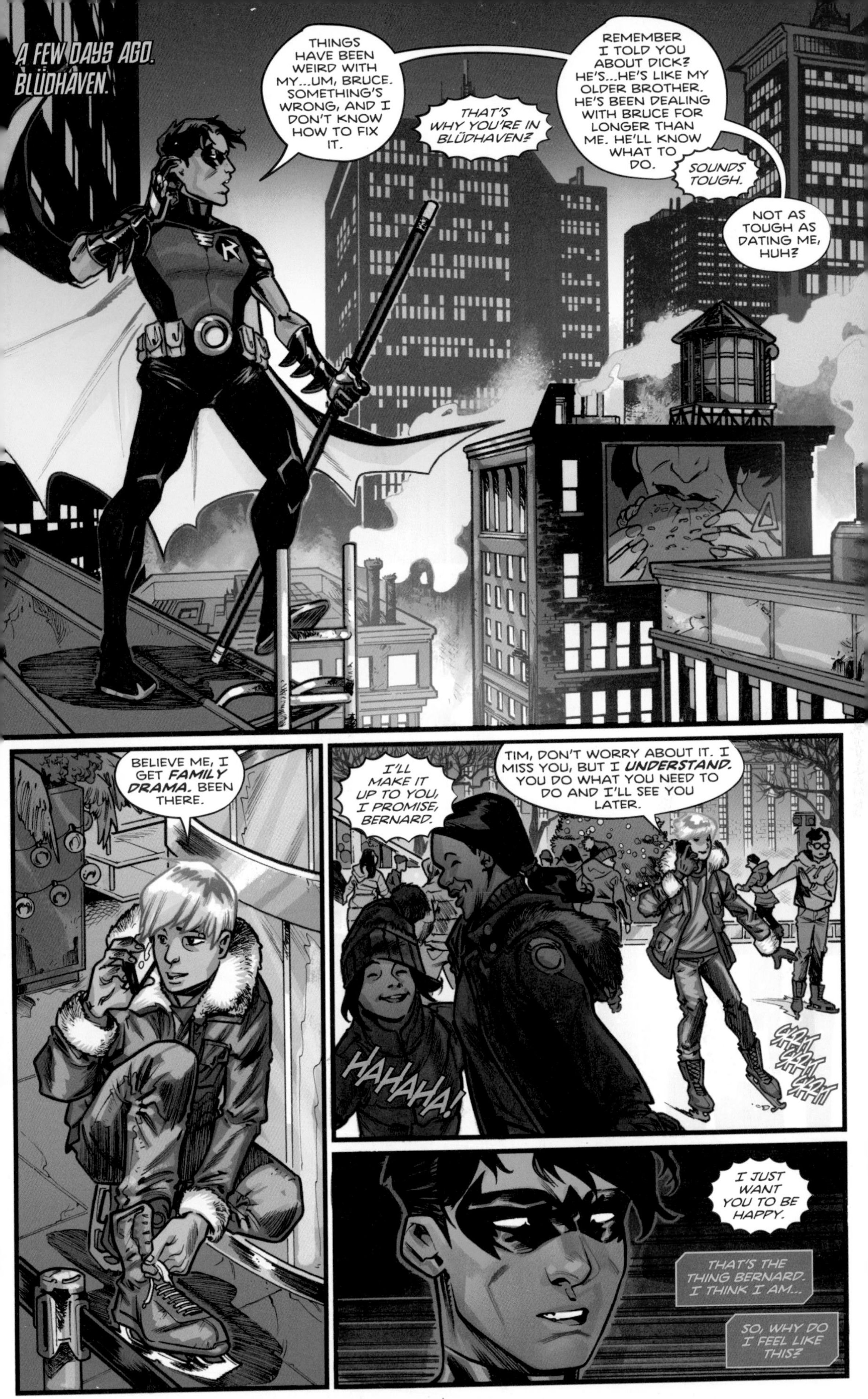
A FEW DAYS AGO. BLÜDHAVEN.
THINGS HAVE BEEN WEIRD WITH MY...UM, BRUCE. SOMETHING'S WRONG, AND I DON'T KNOW HOW TO FIX IT.
THAT'S WHY YOU'RE IN BLÜDHAVEN?
REMEMBER I TOLD YOU ABOUT DICK? HE'S...HE'S LIKE MY OLDER BROTHER. HE'S BEEN DEALING WITH BRUCE FOR LONGER THAN ME. HE'LL KNOW WHAT TO DO.
SOUNDS TOUGH.
NOT AS TOUGH AS DATING ME, HUH?
BELIEVE ME, I GET FAMILY DRAMA. BEEN THERE.
I'LL MAKE IT UP TO YOU, I PROMISE, BERNARD.
TIM, DON'T WORRY ABOUT IT. I MISS YOU, BUT I UNDERSTAND. YOU DO WHAT YOU NEED TO DO AND I'LL SEE YOU LATER.
HAHAHA!
I JUST WANT YOU TO BE HAPPY.
THAT'S THE THING BERNARD. I THINK I AM...
SO, WHY DO I FEEL LIKE THIS?

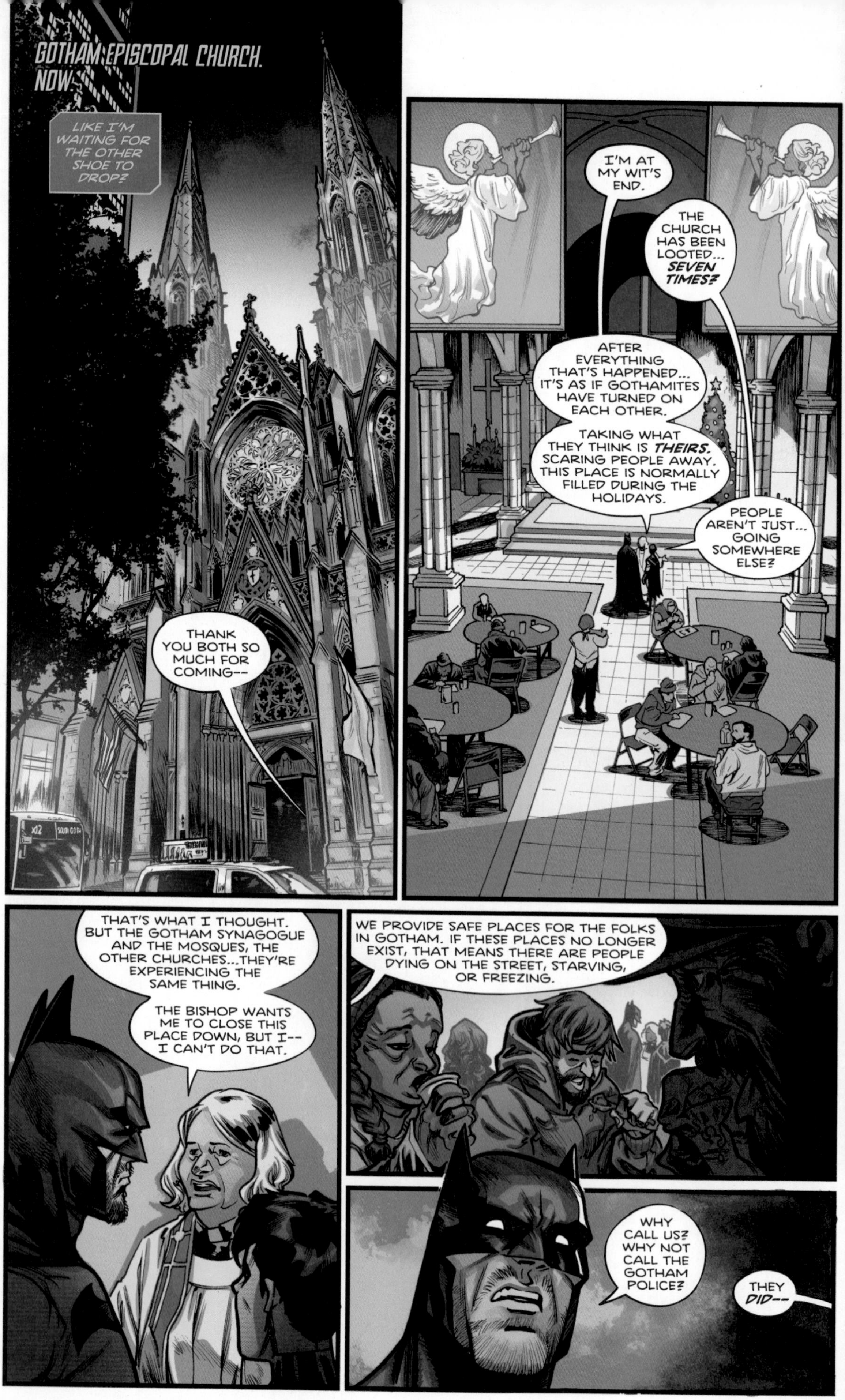
GOTHAM EPISCOPAL CHURCH. NOW.
LIKE I'M WAITING FOR THE OTHER SHOE TO DROP?
THANK YOU BOTH SO MUCH FOR COMING--
I'M AT MY WIT'S END.
THE CHURCH HAS BEEN LOOTED... SEVEN TIMES?
AFTER EVERYTHING THAT'S HAPPENED... IT'S AS IF GOTHAMITES HAVE TURNED ON EACH OTHER.
TAKING WHAT THEY THINK IS THEIRS. SCARING PEOPLE AWAY. THIS PLACE IS NORMALLY FILLED DURING THE HOLIDAYS.
PEOPLE AREN'T JUST... GOING SOMEWHERE ELSE?
THAT'S WHAT I THOUGHT. BUT THE GOTHAM SYNAGOGUE AND THE MOSQUES, THE OTHER CHURCHES...THEY'RE EXPERIENCING THE SAME THING.
THE BISHOP WANTS ME TO CLOSE THIS PLACE DOWN, BUT I-- I CAN'T DO THAT.
WE PROVIDE SAFE PLACES FOR THE FOLKS IN GOTHAM. IF THESE PLACES NO LONGER EXIST, THAT MEANS THERE ARE PEOPLE DYING ON THE STREET, STARVING, OR FREEZING.
WHY CALL US? WHY NOT CALL THE GOTHAM POLICE?
THEY DID--

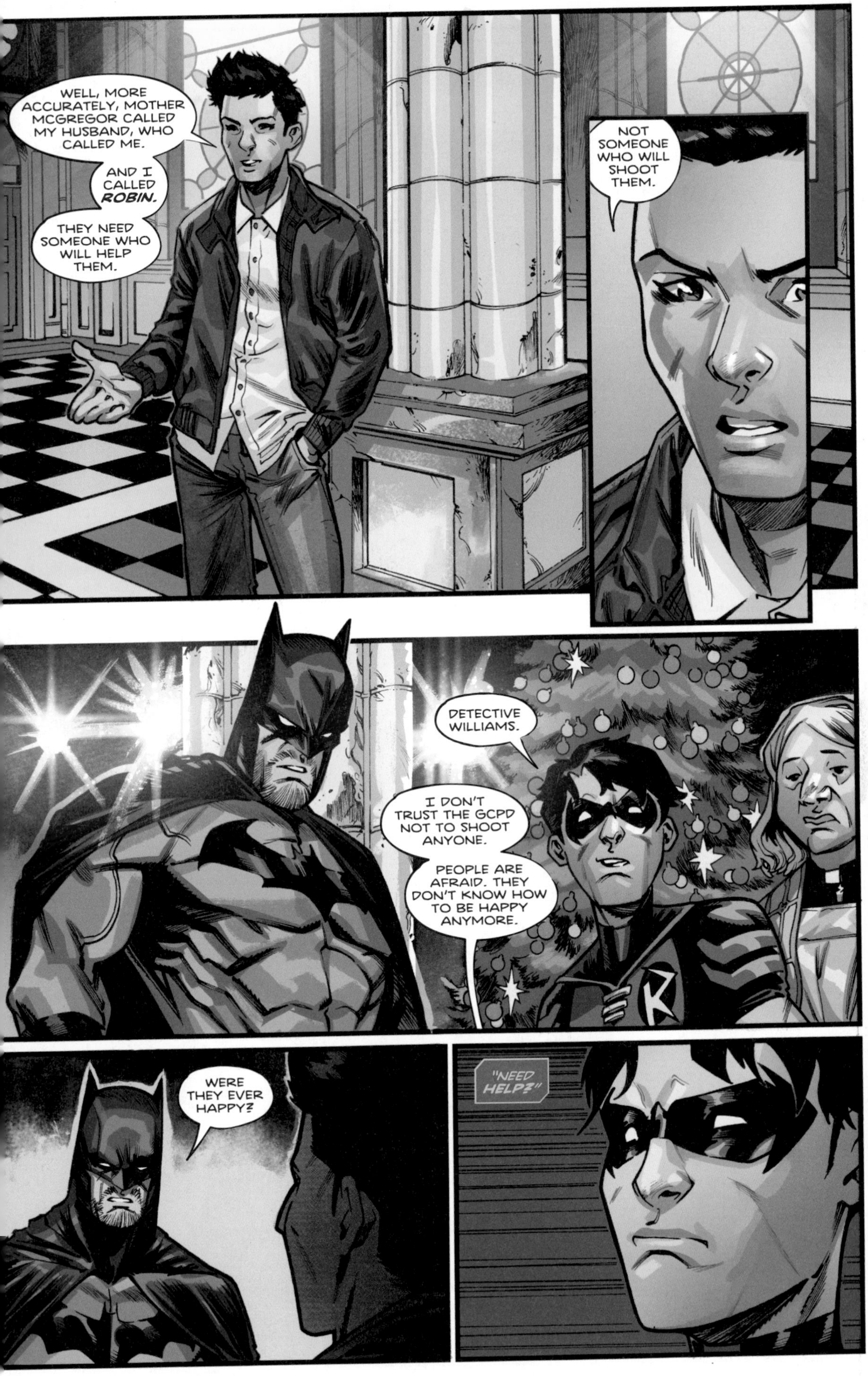
WELL, MORE ACCURATELY, MOTHER MCGREGOR CALLED MY HUSBAND, WHO CALLED ME.
AND I CALLED ROBIN.
THEY NEED SOMEONE WHO WILL HELP THEM.
NOT SOMEONE WHO WILL SHOOT THEM.
DETECTIVE WILLIAMS.
I DON'T TRUST THE GCPD NOT TO SHOOT ANYONE.
PEOPLE ARE AFRAID. THEY DON'T KNOW HOW TO BE HAPPY ANYMORE.
WERE THEY EVER HAPPY?
"NEED HELP?"

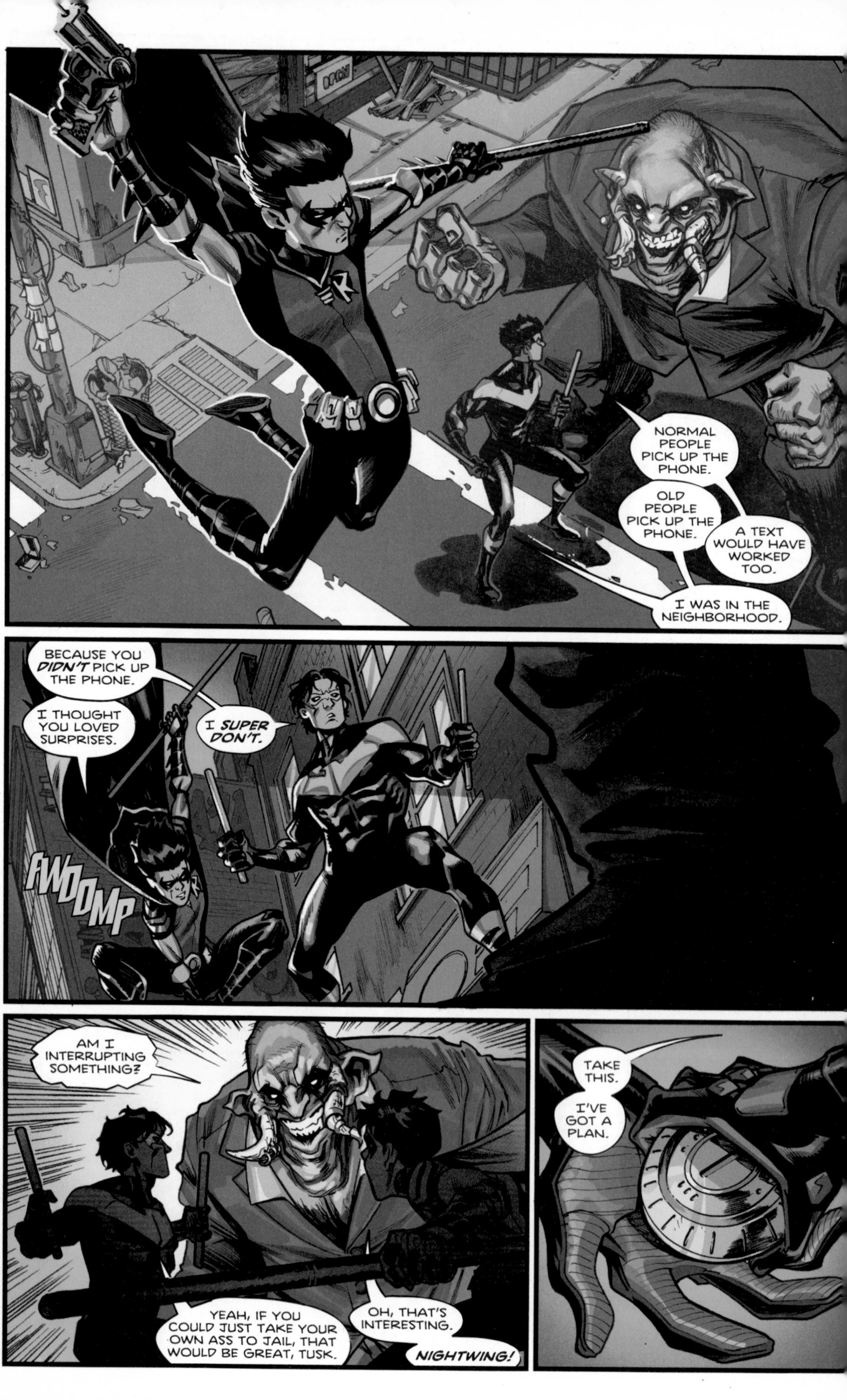
NORMAL PEOPLE PICK UP THE PHONE.
OLD PEOPLE PICK UP THE PHONE.
A TEXT WOULD HAVE WORKED TOO.
I WAS IN THE NEIGHBORHOOD.
BECAUSE YOU *DIDN'T* PICK UP THE PHONE.
I THOUGHT YOU LOVED SURPRISES.
I *SUPER DON'T.*
FWDOMP
AM I INTERRUPTING SOMETHING?
YEAH, IF YOU COULD JUST TAKE YOUR OWN ASS TO JAIL, THAT WOULD BE GREAT, TUSK.
OH, THAT'S INTERESTING.
NIGHTWING!
TAKE THIS.
I'VE GOT A PLAN.

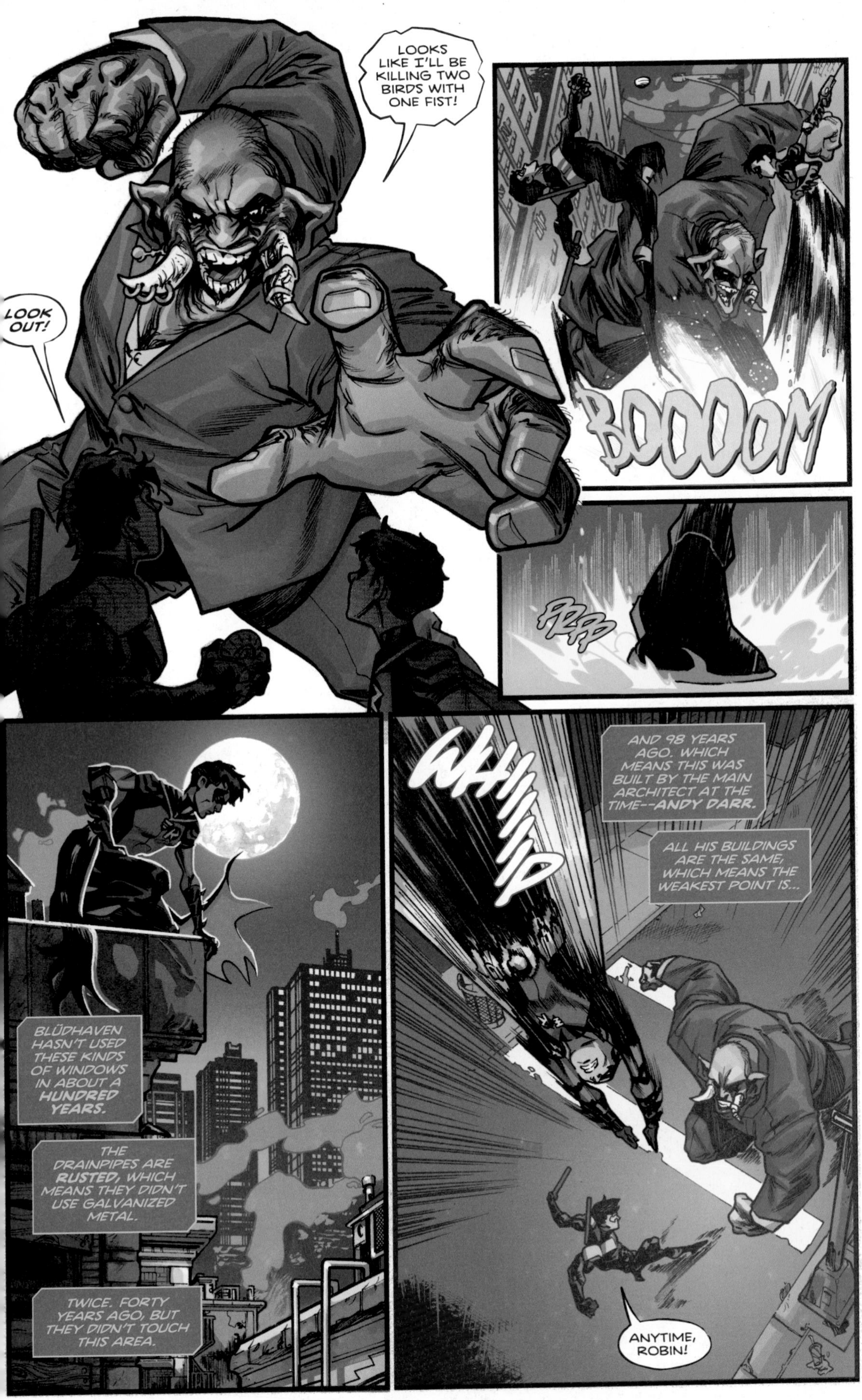
LOOKS LIKE I'LL BE KILLING TWO BIRDS WITH ONE FIST!
LOOK OUT!
BOOOOM
FRRR
BLÜDHAVEN HASN'T USED THESE KINDS OF WINDOWS IN ABOUT A HUNDRED YEARS.
THE DRAINPIPES ARE RUSTED, WHICH MEANS THEY DIDN'T USE GALVANIZED METAL.
TWICE. FORTY YEARS AGO, BUT THEY DIDN'T TOUCH THIS AREA.
AND 98 YEARS AGO. WHICH MEANS THIS WAS BUILT BY THE MAIN ARCHITECT AT THE TIME--ANDY DARR.
ALL HIS BUILDINGS ARE THE SAME, WHICH MEANS THE WEAKEST POINT IS...
ANYTIME, ROBIN!

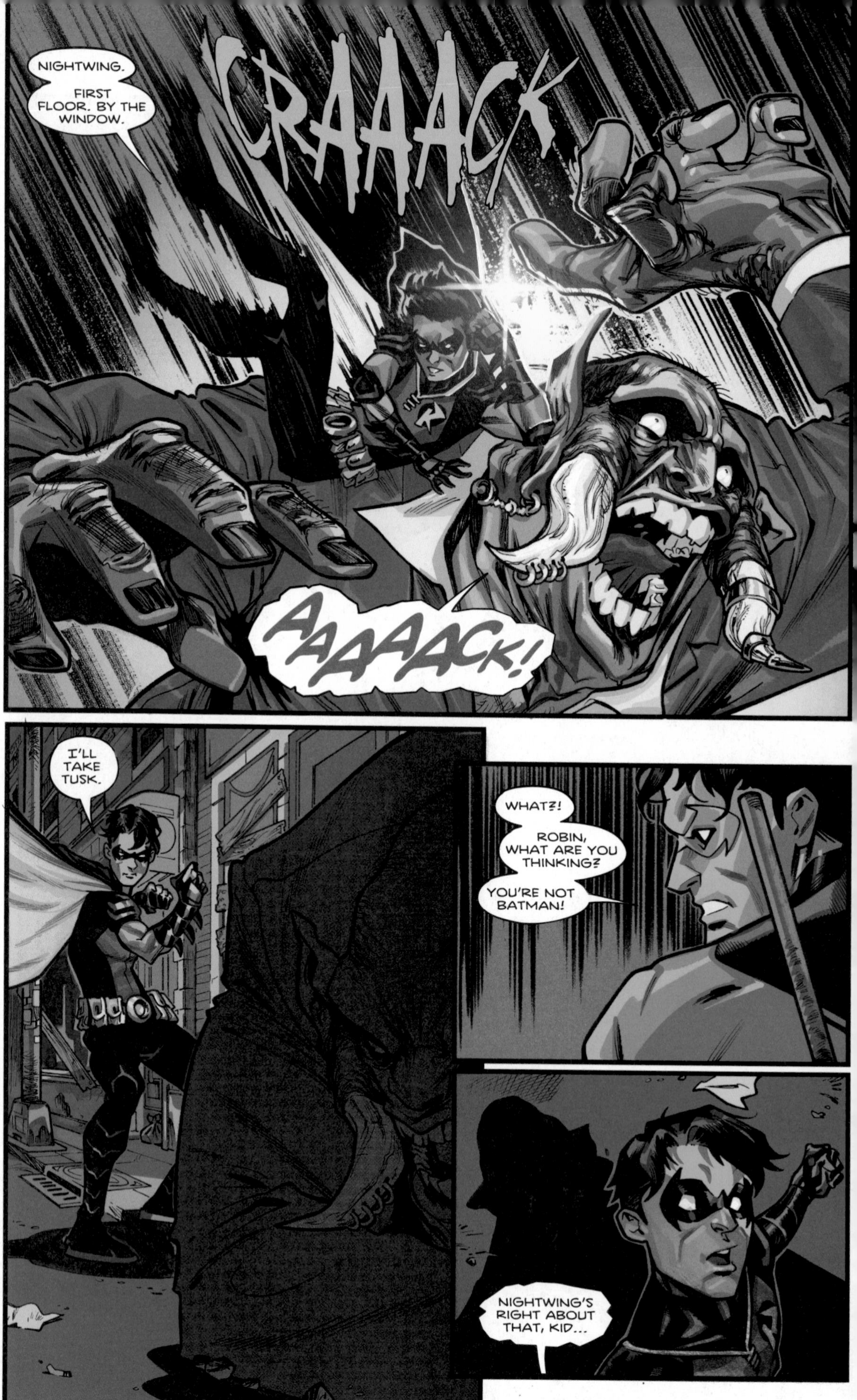
NIGHTWING.
FIRST FLOOR. BY THE WINDOW.
CRAAACK
AAAAACK!
I'LL TAKE TUSK.
WHAT?!
ROBIN, WHAT ARE YOU THINKING?
YOU'RE NOT BATMAN!
NIGHTWING'S RIGHT ABOUT THAT, KID...

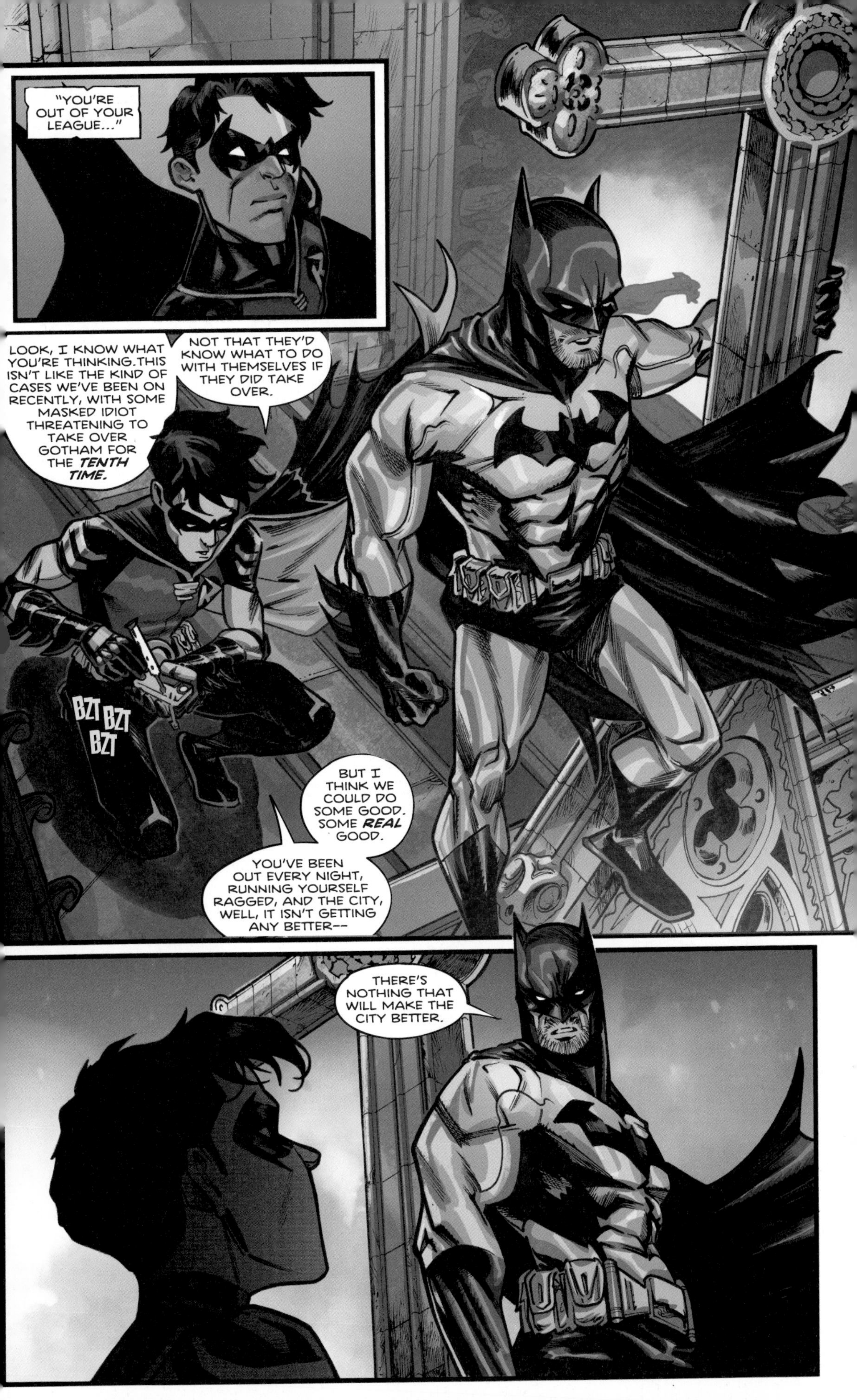
"YOU'RE OUT OF YOUR LEAGUE..."
LOOK, I KNOW WHAT YOU'RE THINKING.THIS ISN'T LIKE THE KIND OF CASES WE'VE BEEN ON RECENTLY, WITH SOME MASKED IDIOT THREATENING TO TAKE OVER GOTHAM FOR THE *TENTH TIME.*
NOT THAT THEY'D KNOW WHAT TO DO WITH THEMSELVES IF THEY DID TAKE OVER.
BZT BZT BZT
BUT I THINK WE COULD DO SOME GOOD. SOME *REAL* GOOD.
YOU'VE BEEN OUT EVERY NIGHT, RUNNING YOURSELF RAGGED, AND THE CITY, WELL, IT ISN'T GETTING ANY BETTER--
THERE'S NOTHING THAT WILL MAKE THE CITY BETTER.

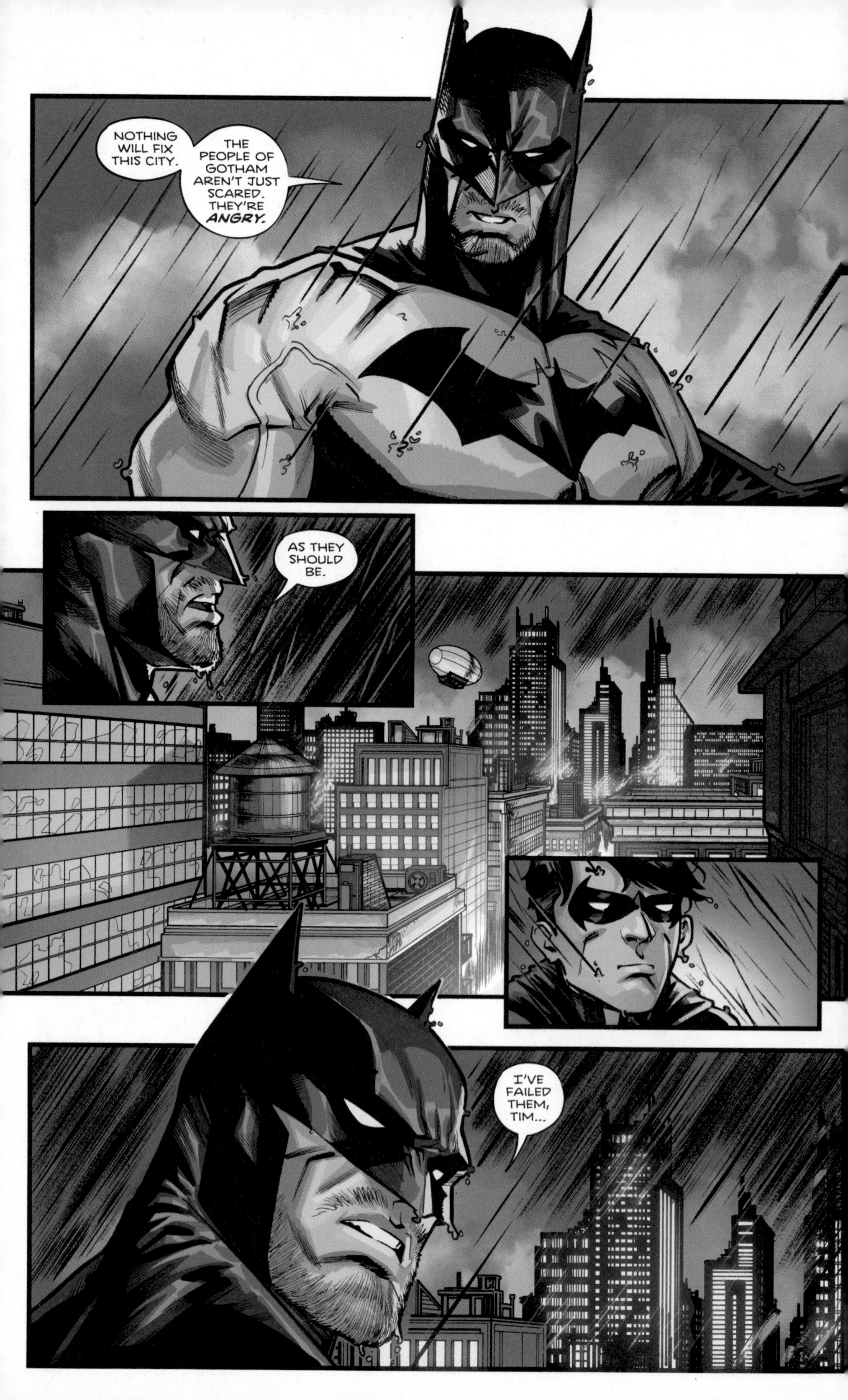
NOTHING WILL FIX THIS CITY.
THE PEOPLE OF GOTHAM AREN'T JUST SCARED. THEY'RE ANGRY.
AS THEY SHOULD BE.
I'VE FAILED THEM, TIM...

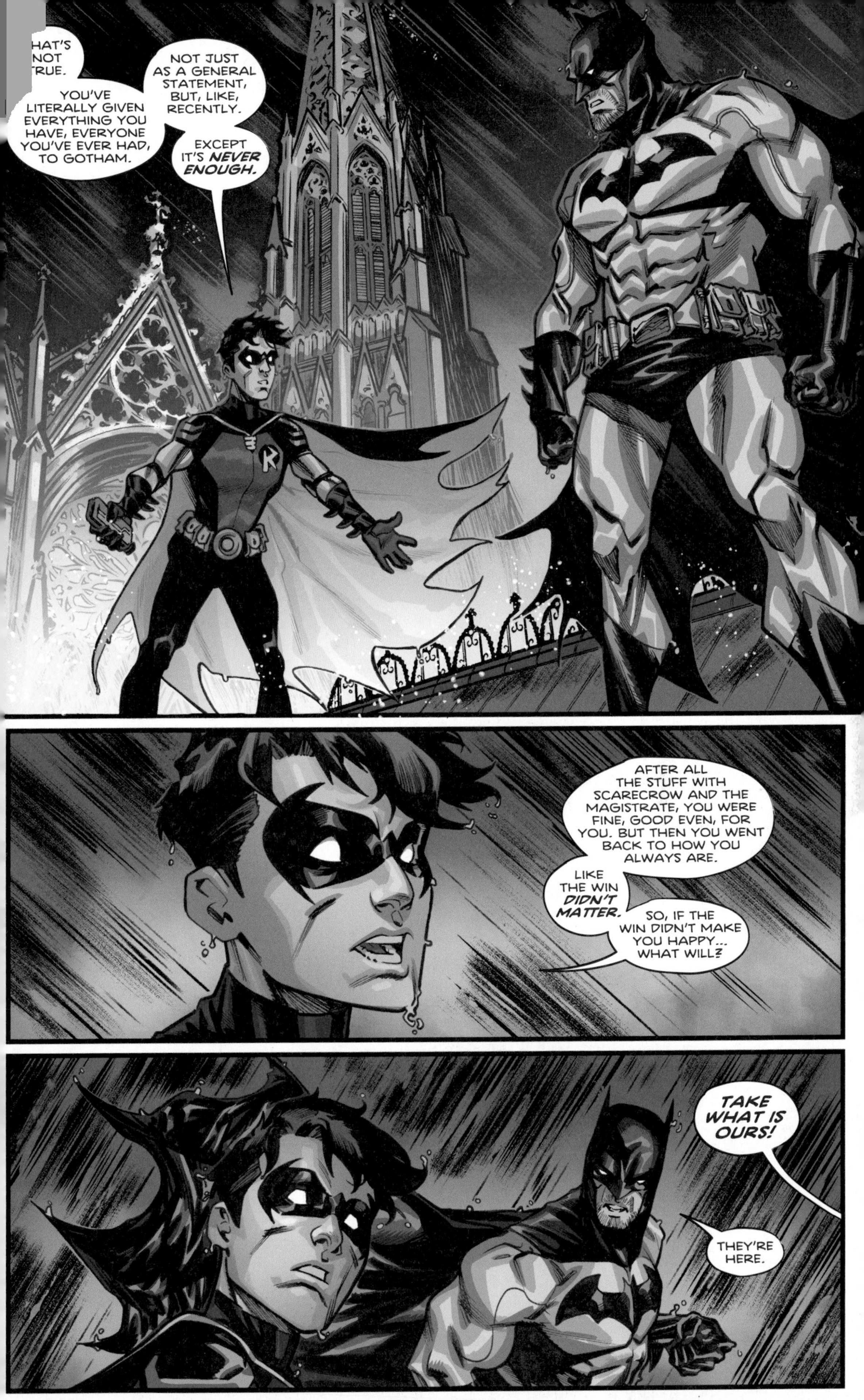

HAT'S NOT TRUE.
YOU'VE LITERALLY GIVEN EVERYTHING YOU HAVE, EVERYONE YOU'VE EVER HAD, TO GOTHAM.
NOT JUST AS A GENERAL STATEMENT, BUT, LIKE, RECENTLY.
EXCEPT IT'S NEVER ENOUGH.
AFTER ALL THE STUFF WITH SCARECROW AND THE MAGISTRATE, YOU WERE FINE, GOOD EVEN, FOR YOU. BUT THEN YOU WENT BACK TO HOW YOU ALWAYS ARE.
LIKE THE WIN DIDN'T MATTER.
SO, IF THE WIN DIDN'T MAKE YOU HAPPY... WHAT WILL?
TAKE WHAT IS OURS!
THEY'RE HERE.

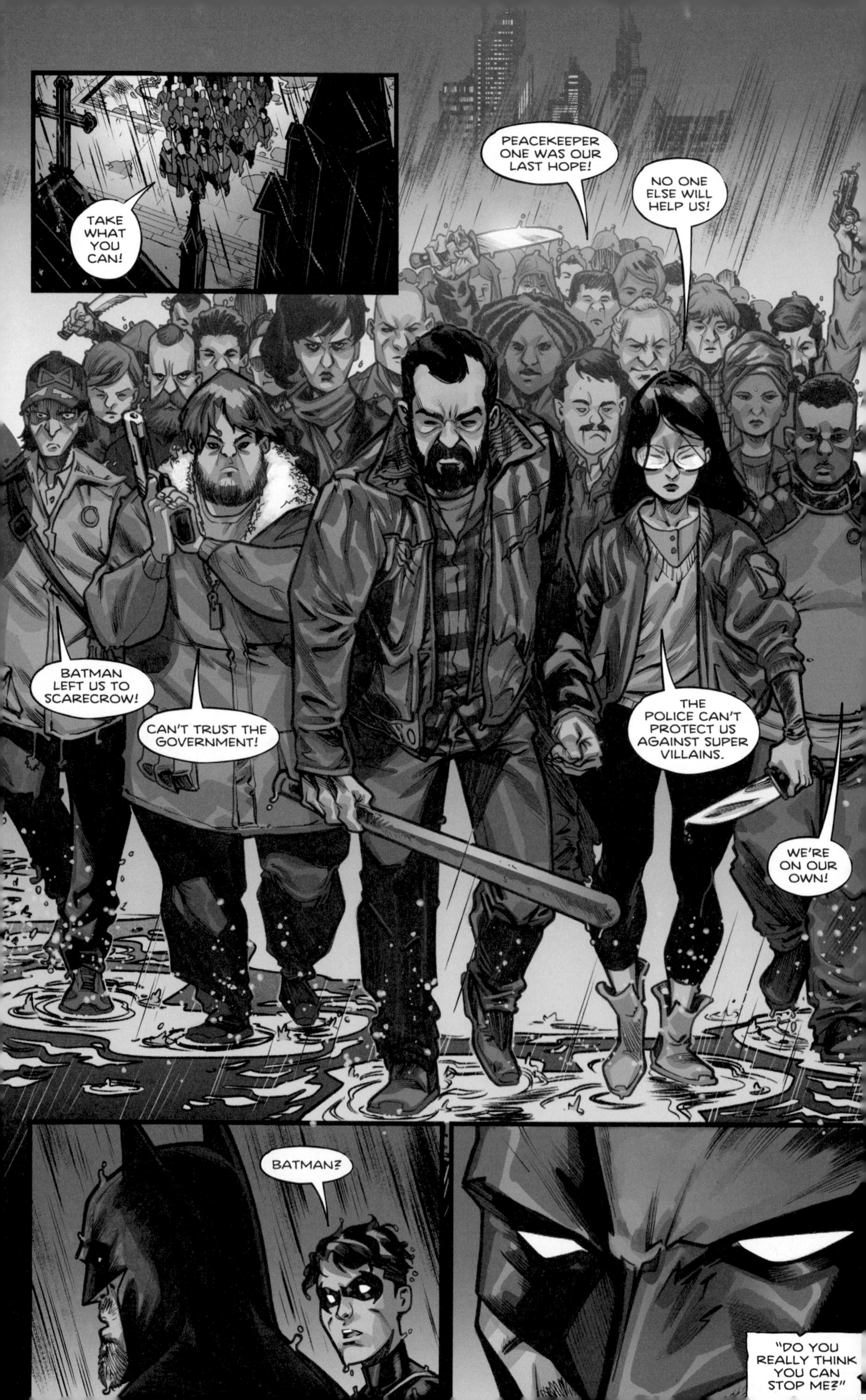
TAKE WHAT YOU CAN!
PEACEKEEPER ONE WAS OUR LAST HOPE!
NO ONE ELSE WILL HELP US!
BATMAN LEFT US TO SCARECROW!
CAN'T TRUST THE GOVERNMENT!
THE POLICE CAN'T PROTECT US AGAINST SUPER VILLAINS.
WE'RE ON OUR OWN!
BATMAN?
"DO YOU REALLY THINK YOU CAN STOP ME?"

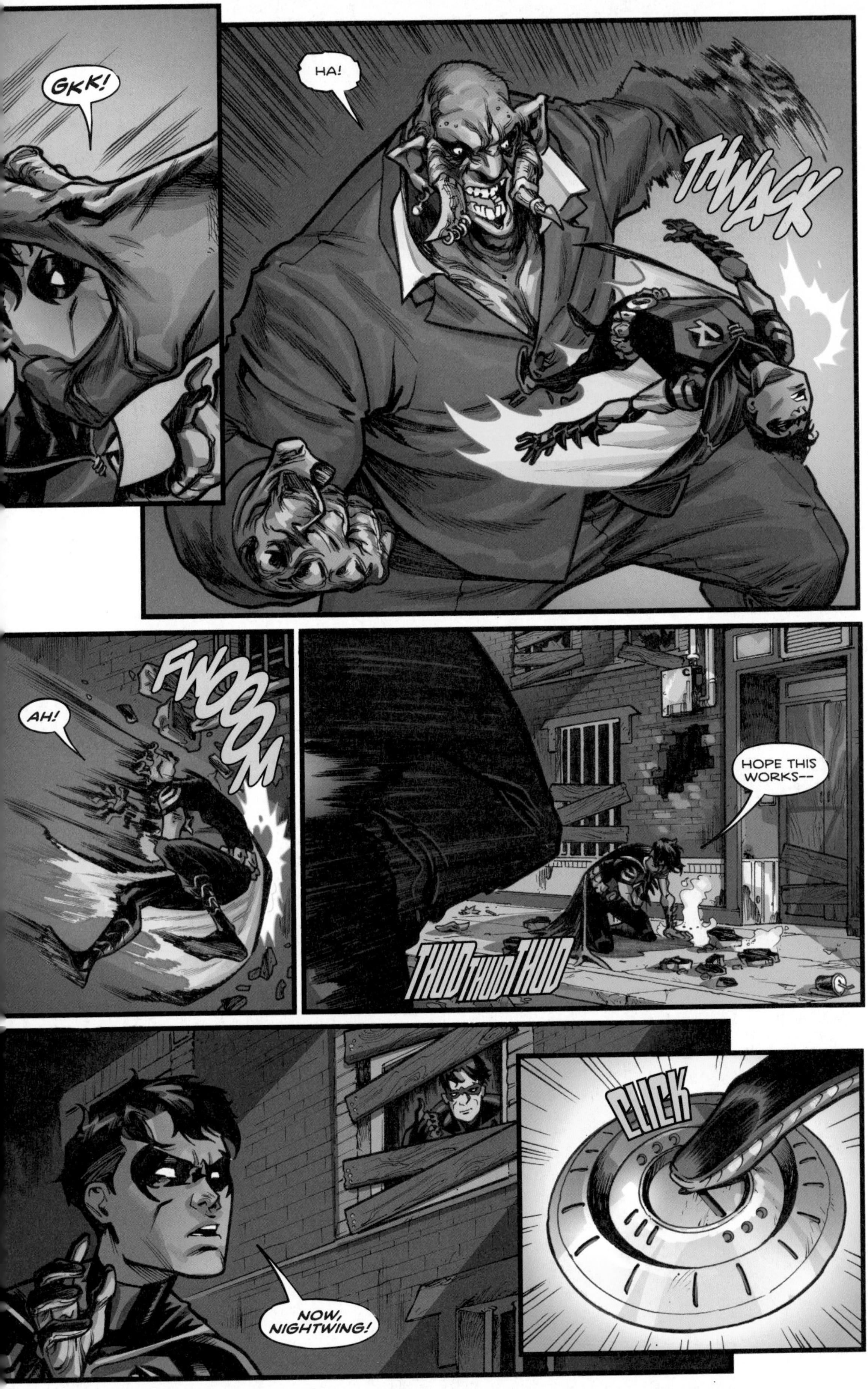
GKK!
HA!
THWACK
AH!
FWOOOM
HOPE THIS WORKS--
THUD THUD THUD
NOW, NIGHTWING!
CLICK

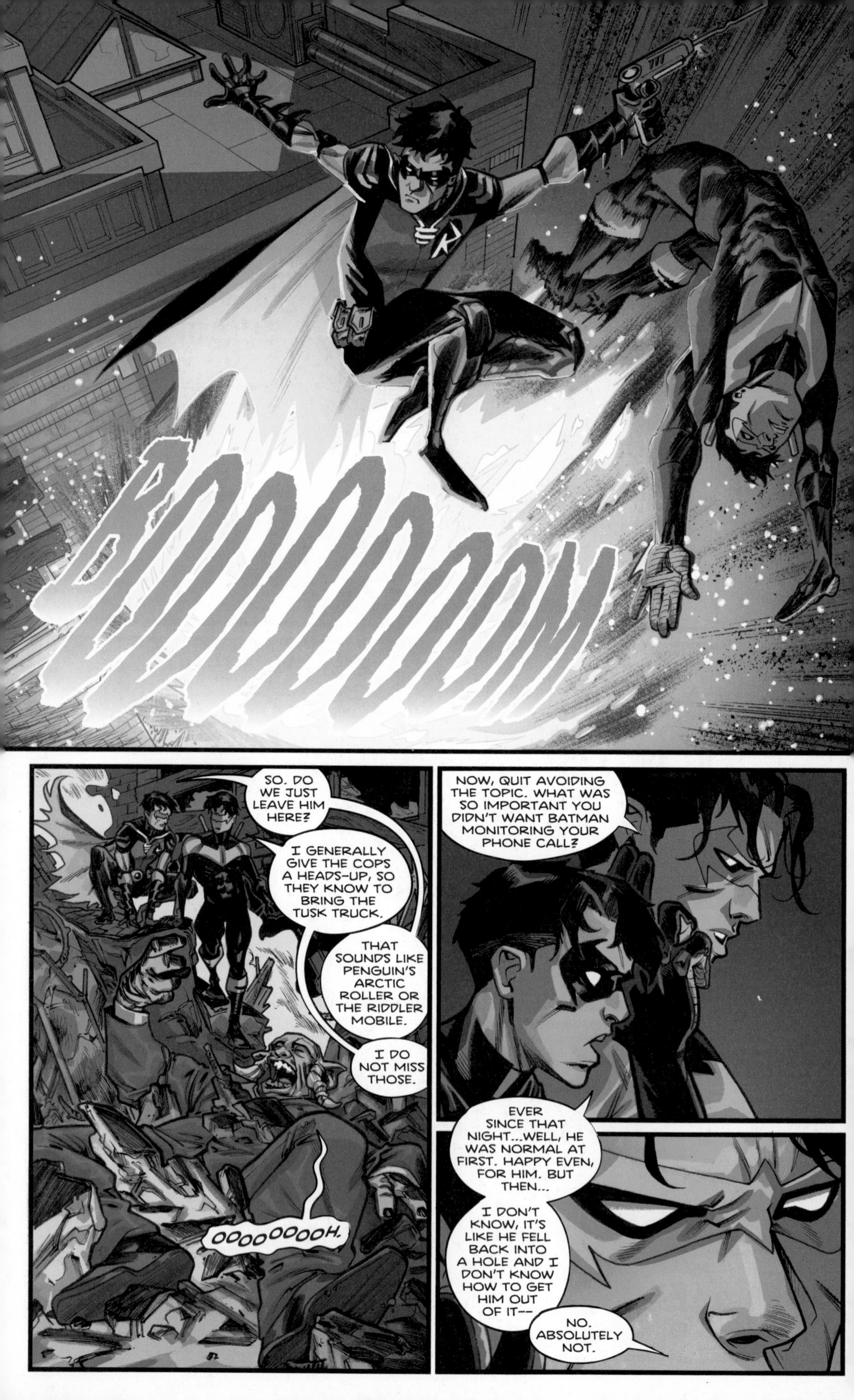
BOOOOOOM
SO. DO WE JUST LEAVE HIM HERE?
I GENERALLY GIVE THE COPS A HEADS-UP, SO THEY KNOW TO BRING THE TUSK TRUCK.
THAT SOUNDS LIKE PENGUIN'S ARCTIC ROLLER OR THE RIDDLER MOBILE.
I DO NOT MISS THOSE.
OOOOOOOOH.
NOW, QUIT AVOIDING THE TOPIC. WHAT WAS SO IMPORTANT YOU DIDN'T WANT BATMAN MONITORING YOUR PHONE CALL?
EVER SINCE THAT NIGHT...WELL, HE WAS NORMAL AT FIRST. HAPPY EVEN, FOR HIM. BUT THEN...
I DON'T KNOW, IT'S LIKE HE FELL BACK INTO A HOLE AND I DON'T KNOW HOW TO GET HIM OUT OF IT--
NO. ABSOLUTELY NOT.

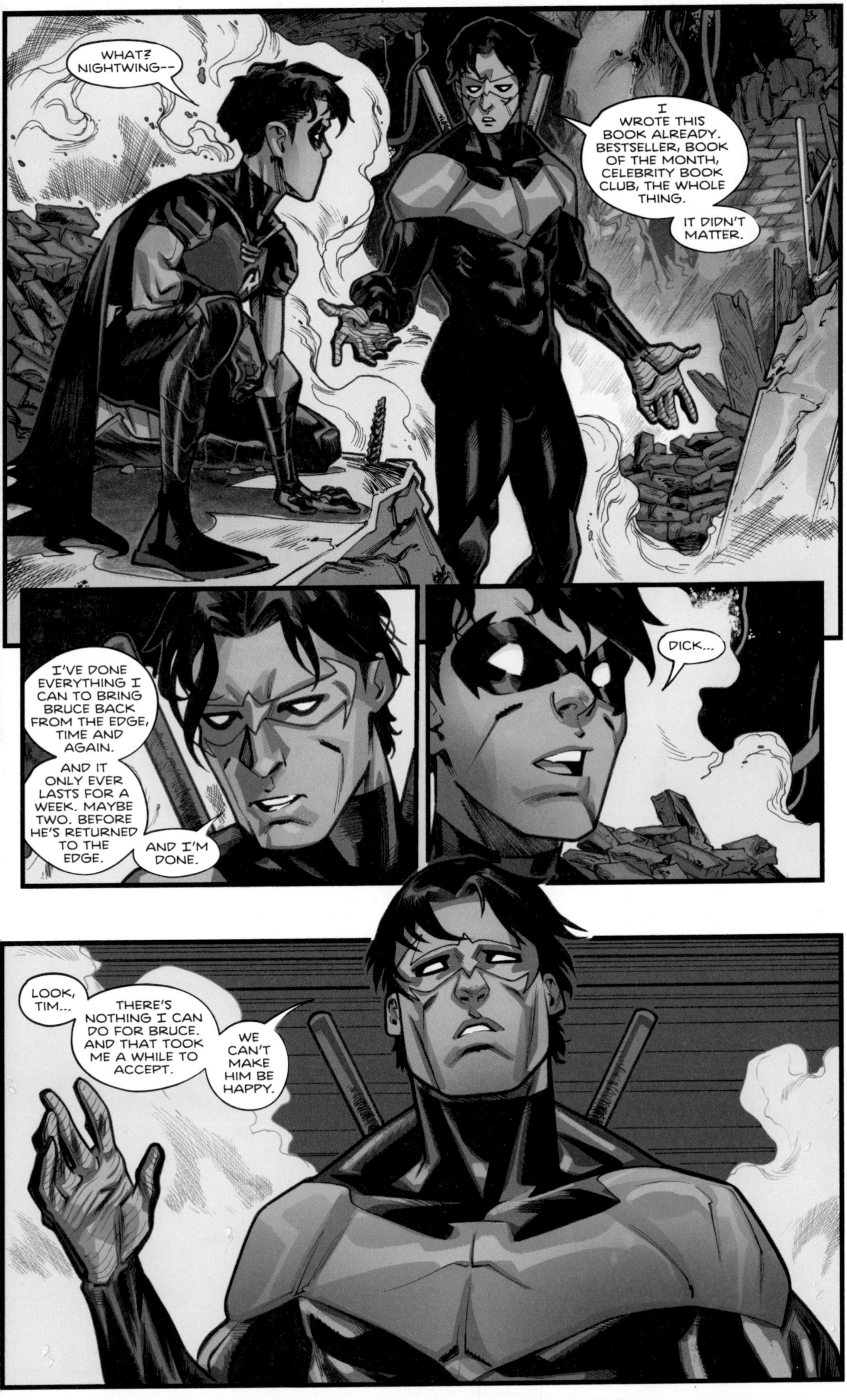
WHAT? NIGHTWING--
I WROTE THIS BOOK ALREADY. BESTSELLER, BOOK OF THE MONTH, CELEBRITY BOOK CLUB, THE WHOLE THING.
IT DIDN'T MATTER.
I'VE DONE EVERYTHING I CAN TO BRING BRUCE BACK FROM THE EDGE, TIME AND AGAIN.
AND IT ONLY EVER LASTS FOR A WEEK. MAYBE TWO. BEFORE HE'S RETURNED TO THE EDGE.
AND I'M DONE.
DICK...
LOOK, TIM...
THERE'S NOTHING I CAN DO FOR BRUCE. AND THAT TOOK ME A WHILE TO ACCEPT.
WE CAN'T MAKE HIM BE HAPPY.

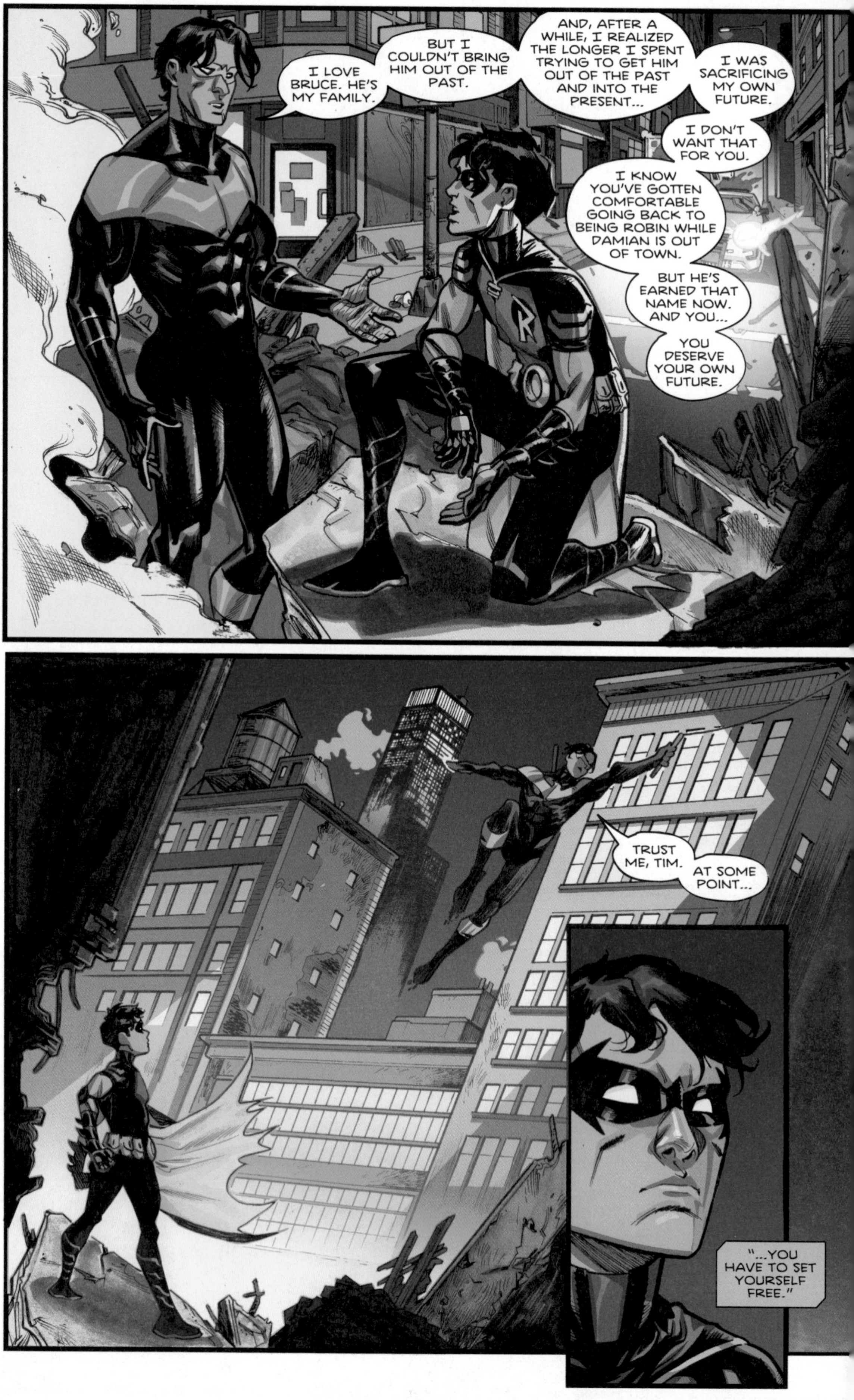

I LOVE BRUCE. HE'S MY FAMILY.
BUT I COULDN'T BRING HIM OUT OF THE PAST.
AND, AFTER A WHILE, I REALIZED THE LONGER I SPENT TRYING TO GET HIM OUT OF THE PAST AND INTO THE PRESENT...
I WAS SACRIFICING MY OWN FUTURE.
I DON'T WANT THAT FOR YOU.
I KNOW YOU'VE GOTTEN COMFORTABLE GOING BACK TO BEING ROBIN WHILE DAMIAN IS OUT OF TOWN.
BUT HE'S EARNED THAT NAME NOW. AND YOU...
YOU DESERVE YOUR OWN FUTURE.
TRUST ME, TIM.
AT SOME POINT...
"...YOU HAVE TO SET YOURSELF FREE."

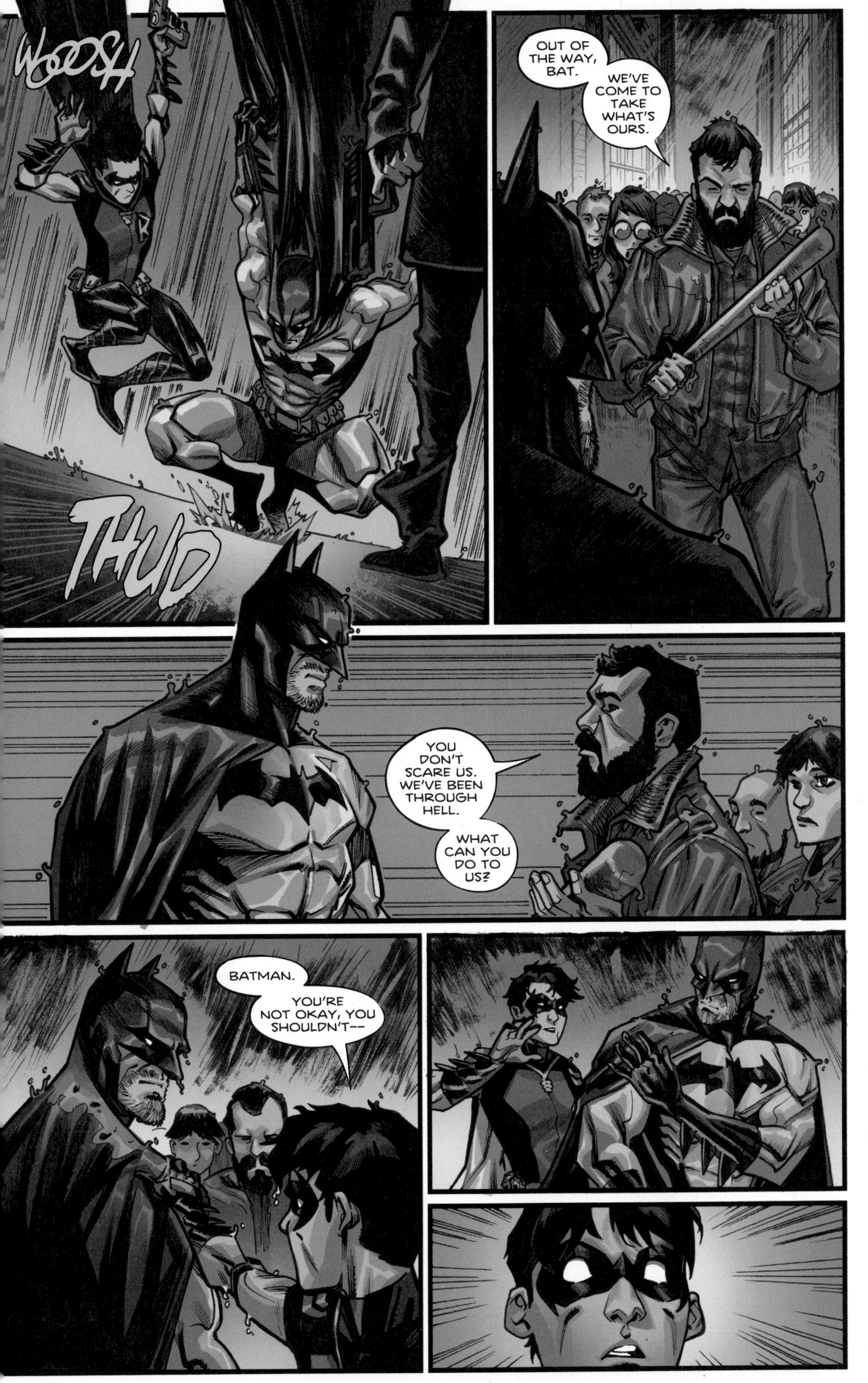
WOOSH
THUD
OUT OF THE WAY, BAT.
WE'VE COME TO TAKE WHAT'S OURS.
YOU DON'T SCARE US. WE'VE BEEN THROUGH HELL.
WHAT CAN YOU DO TO US?
BATMAN.
YOU'RE NOT OKAY, YOU SHOULDN'T--

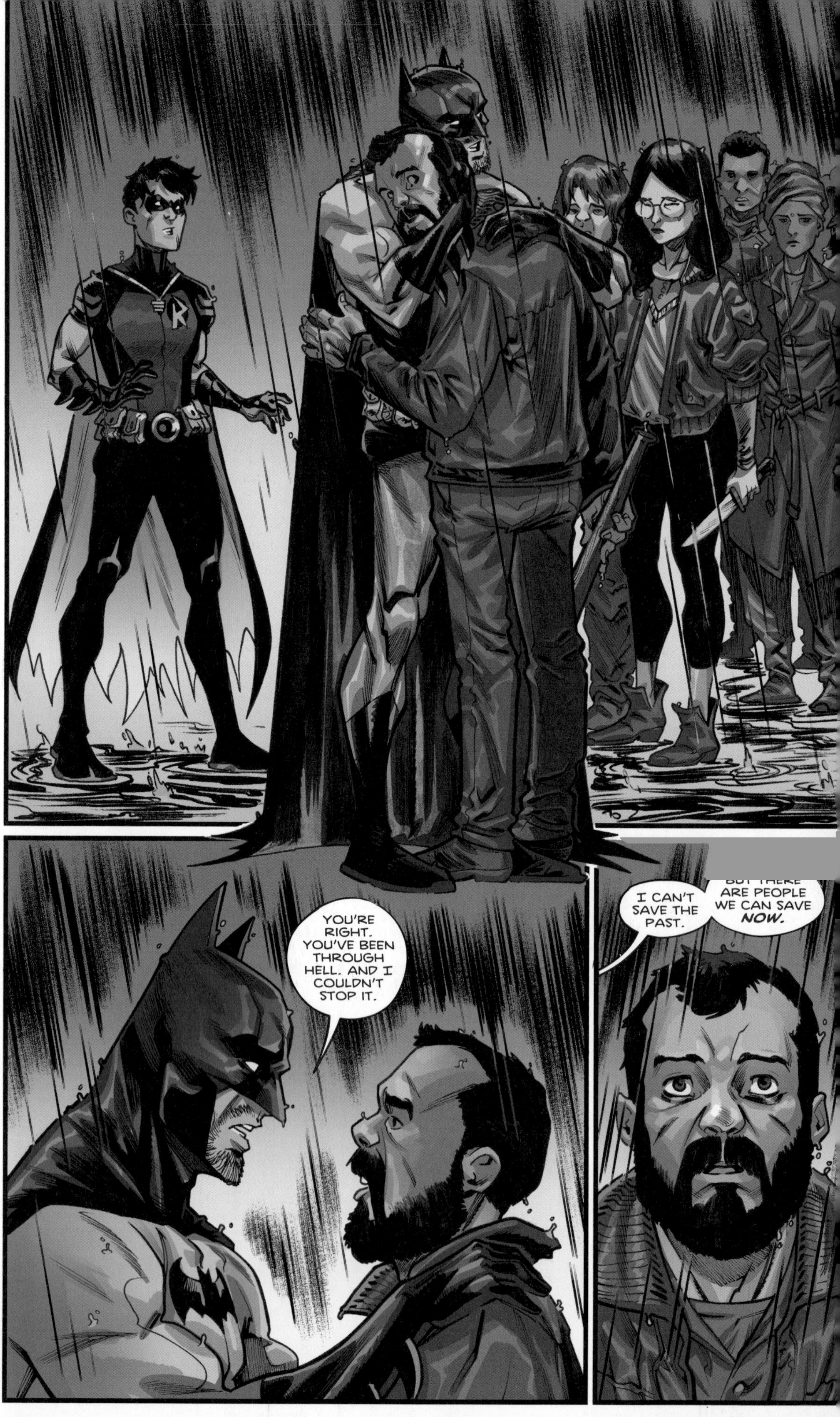
YOU'RE RIGHT. YOU'VE BEEN THROUGH HELL. AND I COULDN'T STOP IT.
I CAN'T SAVE THE PAST.
ARE PEOPLE WE CAN SAVE NOW.

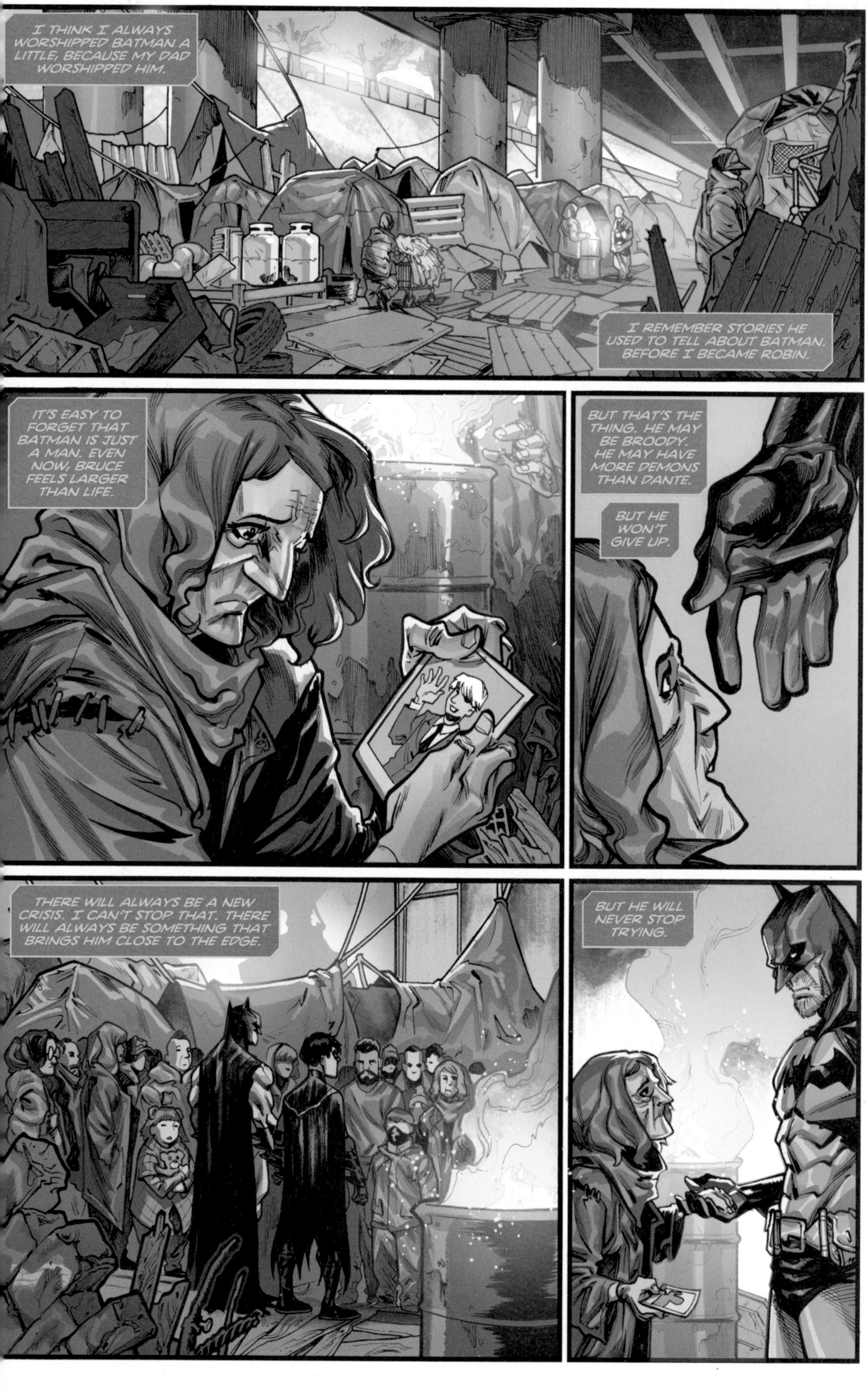
I THINK I ALWAYS WORSHIPPED BATMAN A LITTLE, BECAUSE MY DAD WORSHIPPED HIM.
I REMEMBER STORIES HE USED TO TELL ABOUT BATMAN. BEFORE I BECAME ROBIN.
IT'S EASY TO FORGET THAT BATMAN IS JUST A MAN. EVEN NOW, BRUCE FEELS LARGER THAN LIFE.
BUT THAT'S THE THING. HE MAY BE BROODY. HE MAY HAVE MORE DEMONS THAN DANTE.
BUT HE WON'T GIVE UP.
THERE WILL ALWAYS BE A NEW CRISIS. I CAN'T STOP THAT. THERE WILL ALWAYS BE SOMETHING THAT BRINGS HIM CLOSE TO THE EDGE.
BUT HE WILL NEVER STOP TRYING.

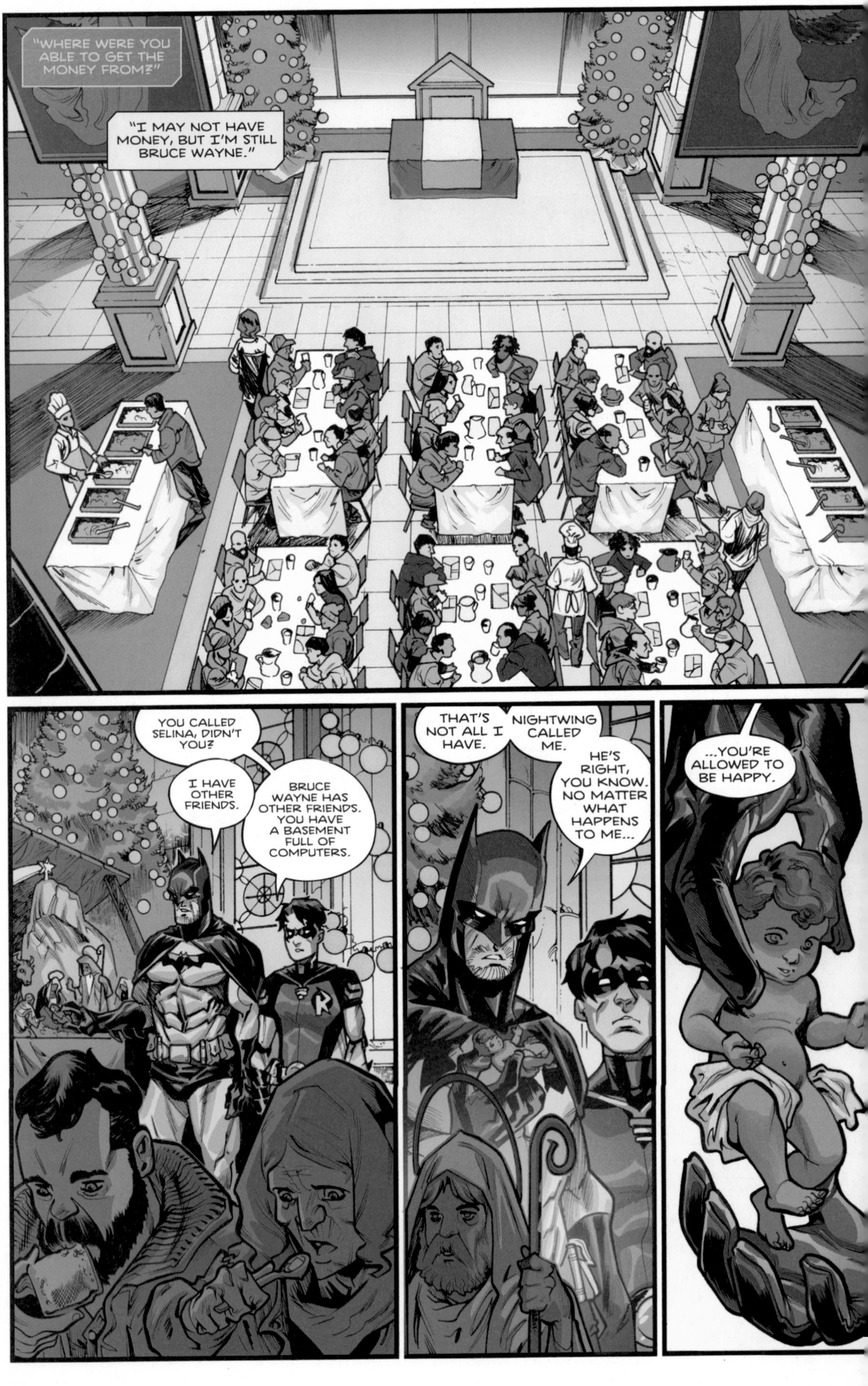
"WHERE WERE YOU ABLE TO GET THE MONEY FROM?"
"I MAY NOT HAVE MONEY, BUT I'M STILL BRUCE WAYNE."
YOU CALLED SELINA, DIDN'T YOU?
I HAVE OTHER FRIENDS.
BRUCE WAYNE HAS OTHER FRIENDS. YOU HAVE A BASEMENT FULL OF COMPUTERS.
THAT'S NOT ALL I HAVE.
NIGHTWING CALLED ME.
HE'S RIGHT, YOU KNOW. NO MATTER WHAT HAPPENS TO ME...
...YOU'RE ALLOWED TO BE HAPPY.

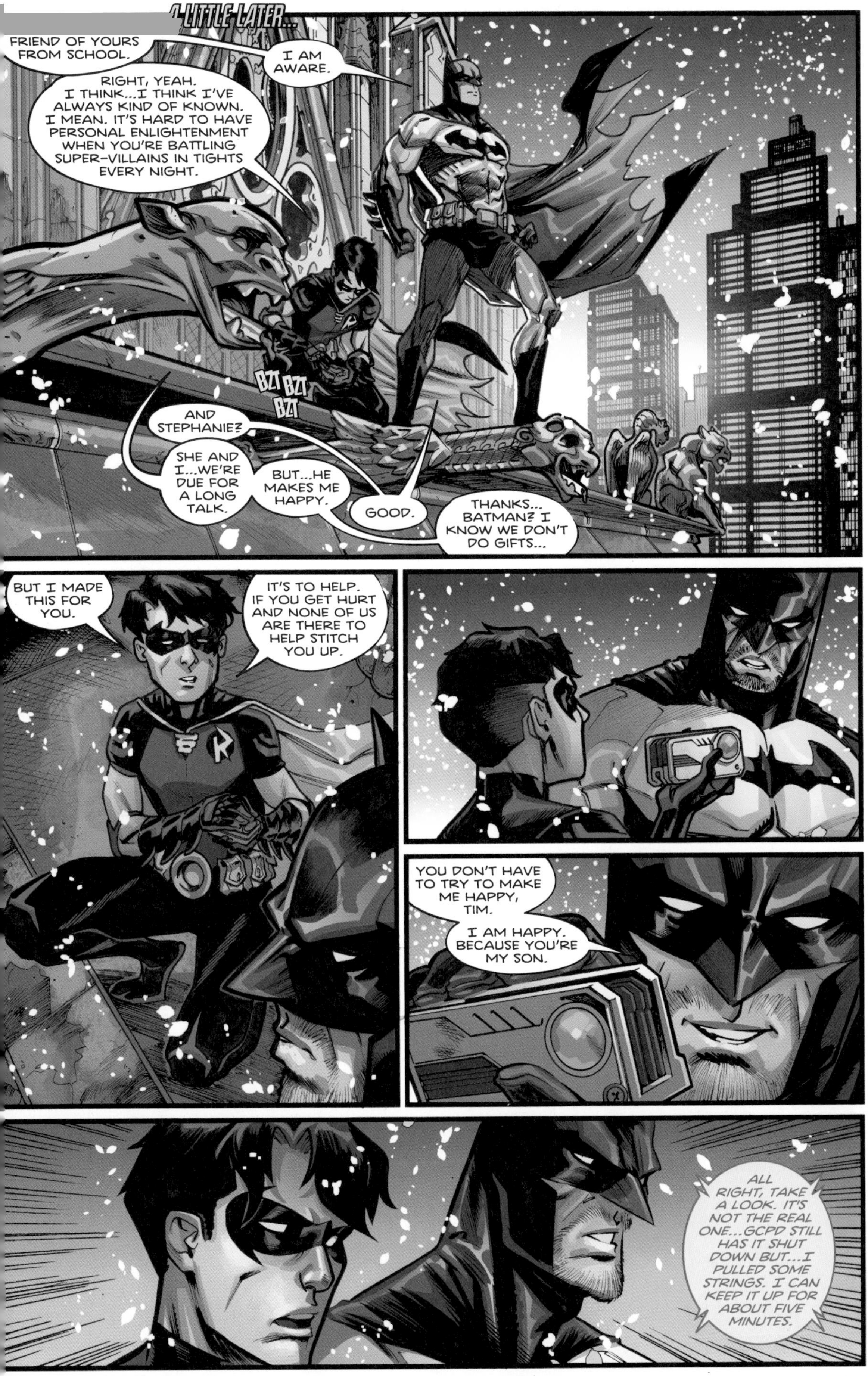
A LITTLE LATER...
FRIEND OF YOURS FROM SCHOOL.
I AM AWARE.
RIGHT, YEAH. I THINK...I THINK I'VE ALWAYS KIND OF KNOWN. I MEAN. IT'S HARD TO HAVE PERSONAL ENLIGHTENMENT WHEN YOU'RE BATTLING SUPER-VILLAINS IN TIGHTS EVERY NIGHT.
BZT BZT BZT
AND STEPHANIE?
SHE AND I...WE'RE DUE FOR A LONG TALK.
BUT...HE MAKES ME HAPPY.
GOOD.
THANKS... BATMAN? I KNOW WE DON'T DO GIFTS...
BUT I MADE THIS FOR YOU.
IT'S TO HELP. IF YOU GET HURT AND NONE OF US ARE THERE TO HELP STITCH YOU UP.
YOU DON'T HAVE TO TRY TO MAKE ME HAPPY, TIM.
I AM HAPPY. BECAUSE YOU'RE MY SON.
ALL RIGHT, TAKE A LOOK. IT'S NOT THE REAL ONE...GCPD STILL HAS IT SHUT DOWN BUT...I PULLED SOME STRINGS. I CAN KEEP IT UP FOR ABOUT FIVE MINUTES.

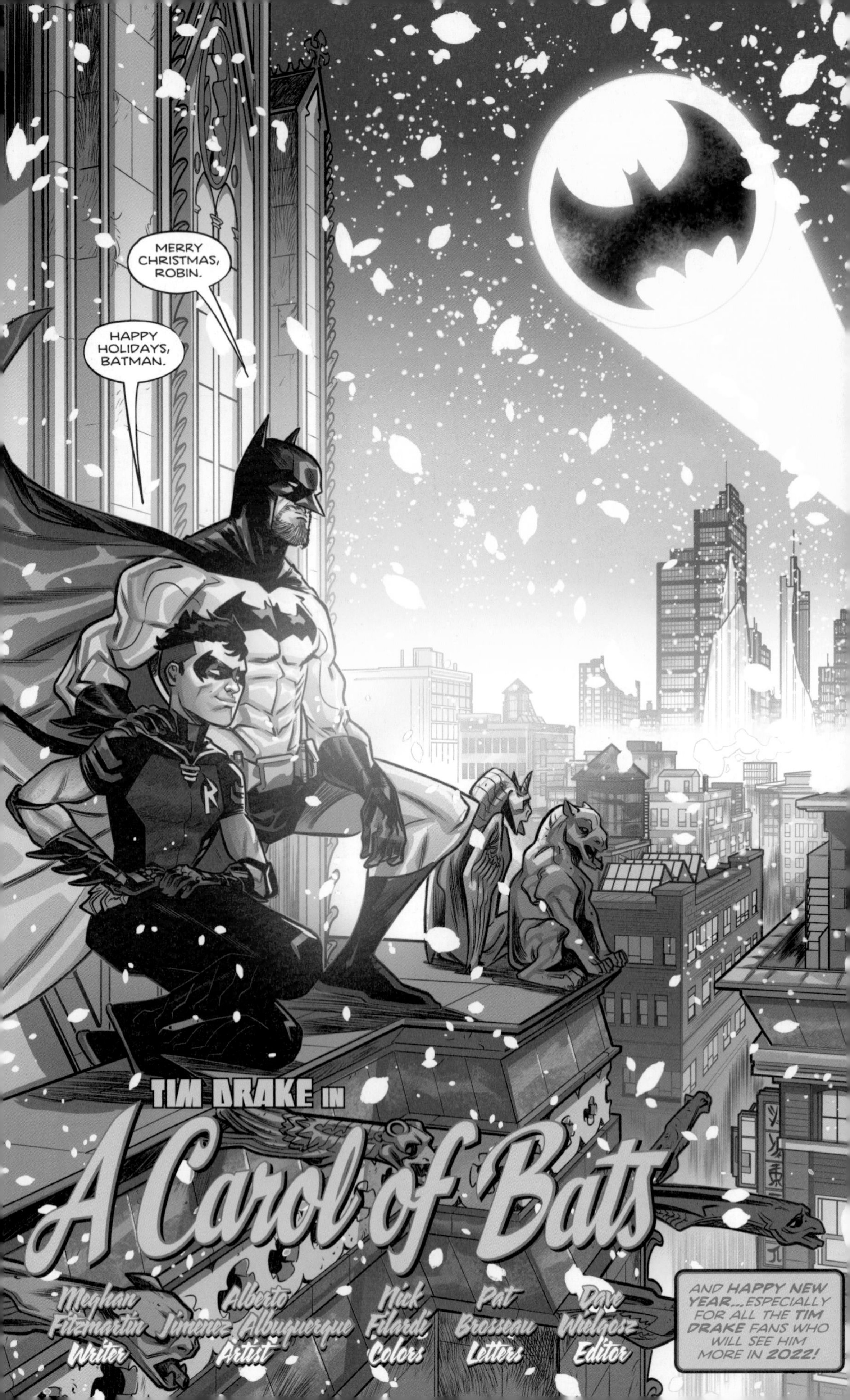

MERRY CHRISTMAS, ROBIN.
HAPPY HOLIDAYS, BATMAN.
TIM DRAKE IN
A Carol of Bats
Meghan Fitzmartin Writer
Alberto Jimenez Albuquerque Artist
Nick Filardi Colors
Pat Brosseau Letters
Dave Wielgosz Editor
AND HAPPY NEW YEAR...ESPECIALLY FOR ALL THE TIM DRAKE FANS WHO WILL SEE HIM MORE IN 2022!

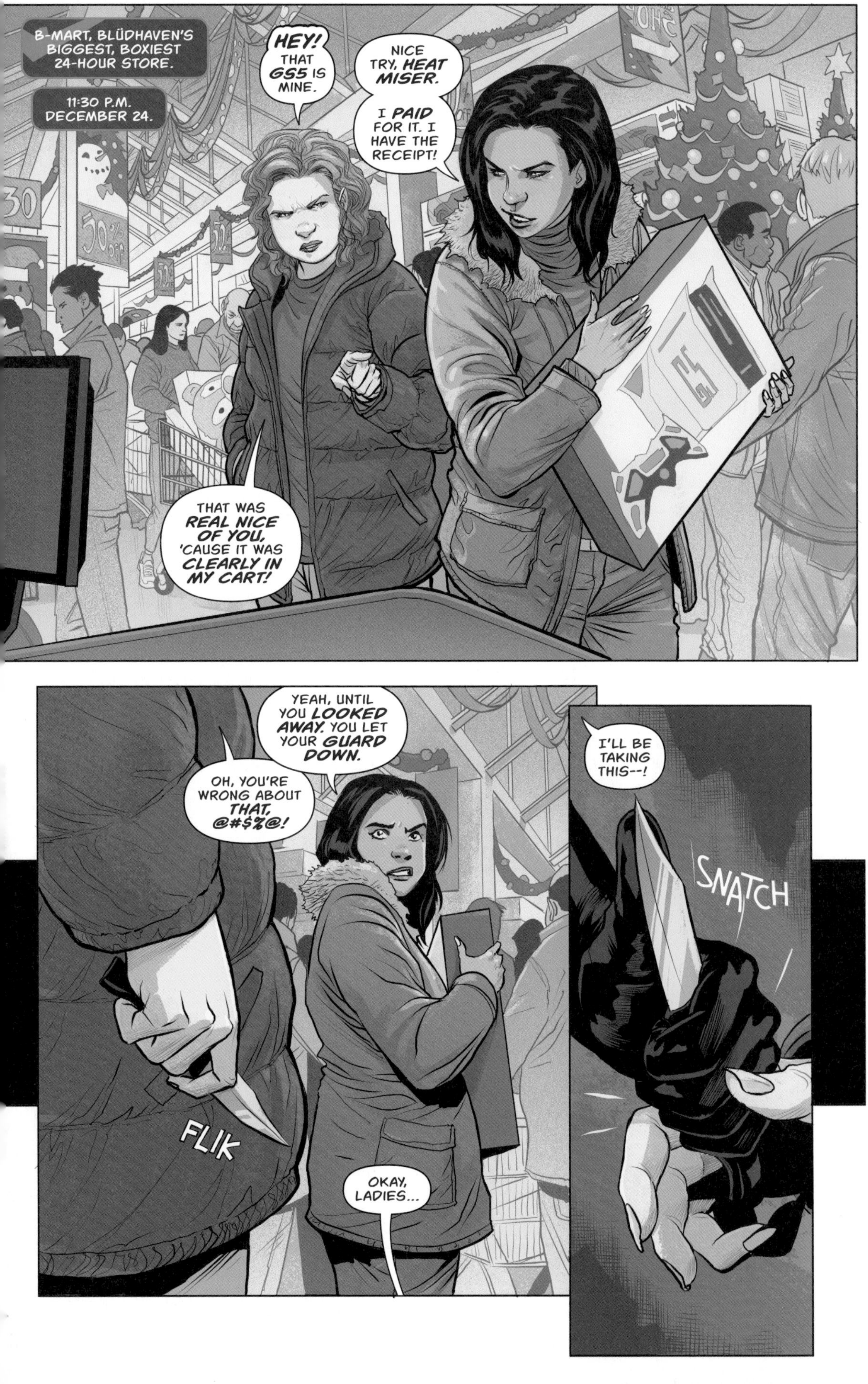
B-MART, BLÜDHAVEN'S BIGGEST, BOXIEST 24-HOUR STORE.
11:30 P.M. DECEMBER 24.
HEY! THAT GS5 IS MINE.
NICE TRY, HEAT MISER.
I PAID FOR IT. I HAVE THE RECEIPT!
THAT WAS REAL NICE OF YOU, 'CAUSE IT WAS CLEARLY IN MY CART!
YEAH, UNTIL YOU LOOKED AWAY. YOU LET YOUR GUARD DOWN.
OH, YOU'RE WRONG ABOUT THAT, @#$%@!
FLIK
OKAY, LADIES...
I'LL BE TAKING THIS--!
SNATCH

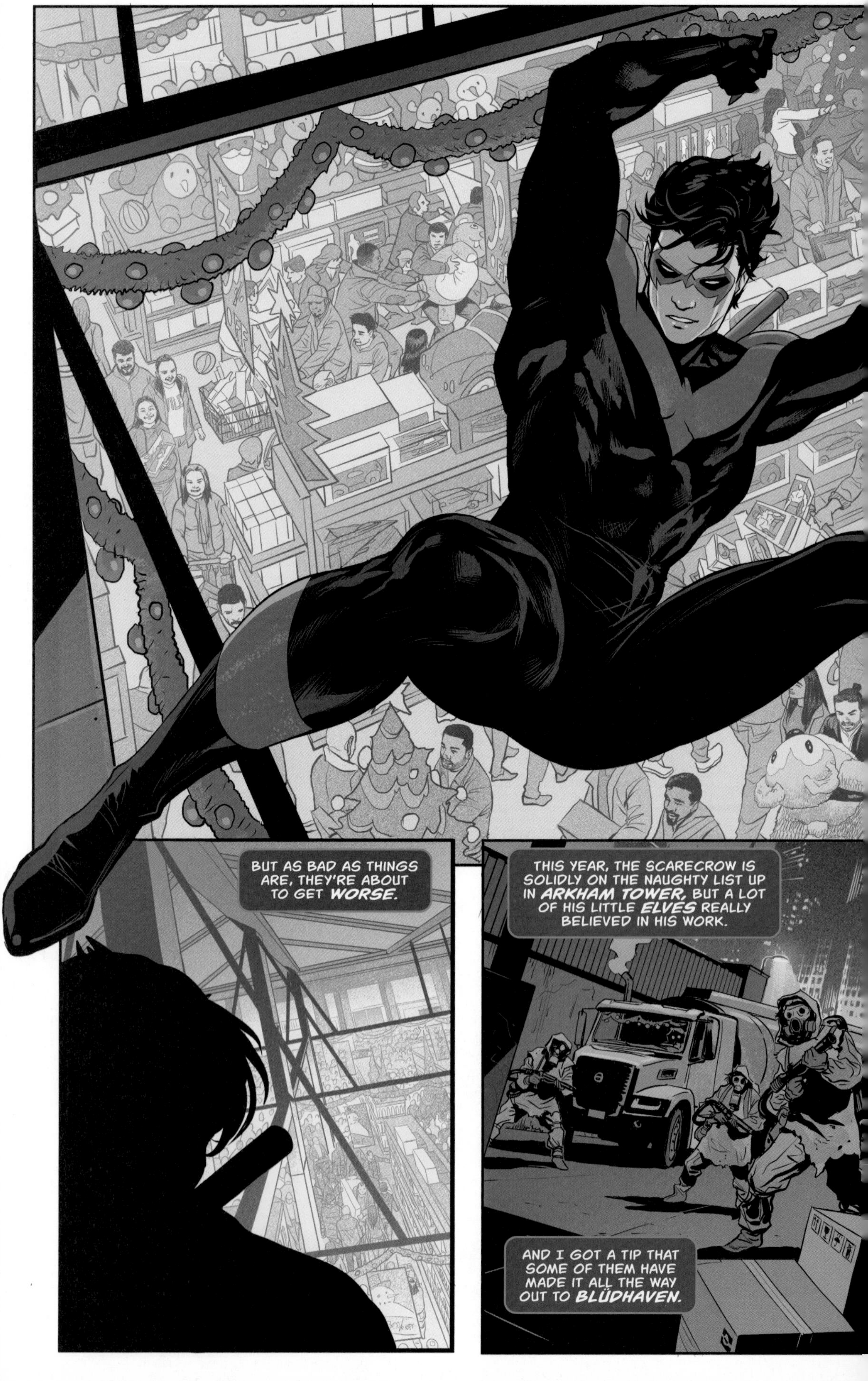
BUT AS BAD AS THINGS ARE, THEY'RE ABOUT TO GET WORSE.
THIS YEAR, THE SCARECROW IS SOLIDLY ON THE NAUGHTY LIST UP IN ARKHAM TOWER, BUT A LOT OF HIS LITTLE ELVES REALLY BELIEVED IN HIS WORK.
AND I GOT A TIP THAT SOME OF THEM HAVE MADE IT ALL THE WAY OUT TO BLÜDHAVEN.

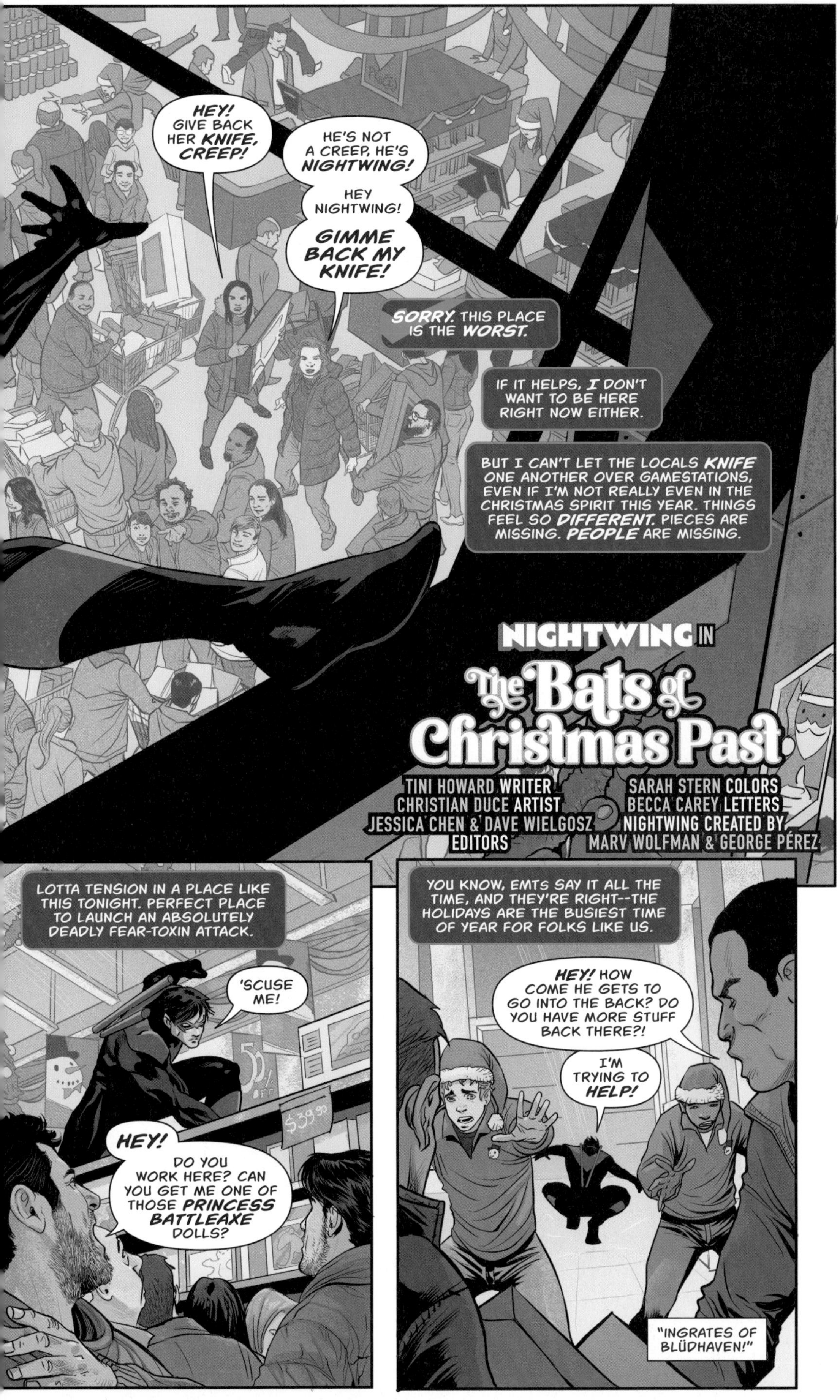
HEY! GIVE BACK HER KNIFE, CREEP!
HE'S NOT A CREEP, HE'S NIGHTWING!
HEY NIGHTWING!
GIMME BACK MY KNIFE!
SORRY. THIS PLACE IS THE WORST.
IF IT HELPS, I DON'T WANT TO BE HERE RIGHT NOW EITHER.
BUT I CAN'T LET THE LOCALS KNIFE ONE ANOTHER OVER GAMESTATIONS, EVEN IF I'M NOT REALLY EVEN IN THE CHRISTMAS SPIRIT THIS YEAR. THINGS FEEL SO DIFFERENT. PIECES ARE MISSING. PEOPLE ARE MISSING.
NIGHTWING IN
The Bats of Christmas Past
TINI HOWARD WRITER
CHRISTIAN DUCE ARTIST
JESSICA CHEN & DAVE WIELGOSZ EDITORS
SARAH STERN COLORS
BECCA CAREY LETTERS
NIGHTWING CREATED BY MARV WOLFMAN & GEORGE PÉREZ
LOTTA TENSION IN A PLACE LIKE THIS TONIGHT. PERFECT PLACE TO LAUNCH AN ABSOLUTELY DEADLY FEAR-TOXIN ATTACK.
'SCUSE ME!
$39.90
HEY!
DO YOU WORK HERE? CAN YOU GET ME ONE OF THOSE PRINCESS BATTLEAXE DOLLS?
YOU KNOW, EMTS SAY IT ALL THE TIME, AND THEY'RE RIGHT--THE HOLIDAYS ARE THE BUSIEST TIME OF YEAR FOR FOLKS LIKE US.
HEY! HOW COME HE GETS TO GO INTO THE BACK? DO YOU HAVE MORE STUFF BACK THERE?!
I'M TRYING TO HELP!
"INGRATES OF BLÜDHAVEN!"

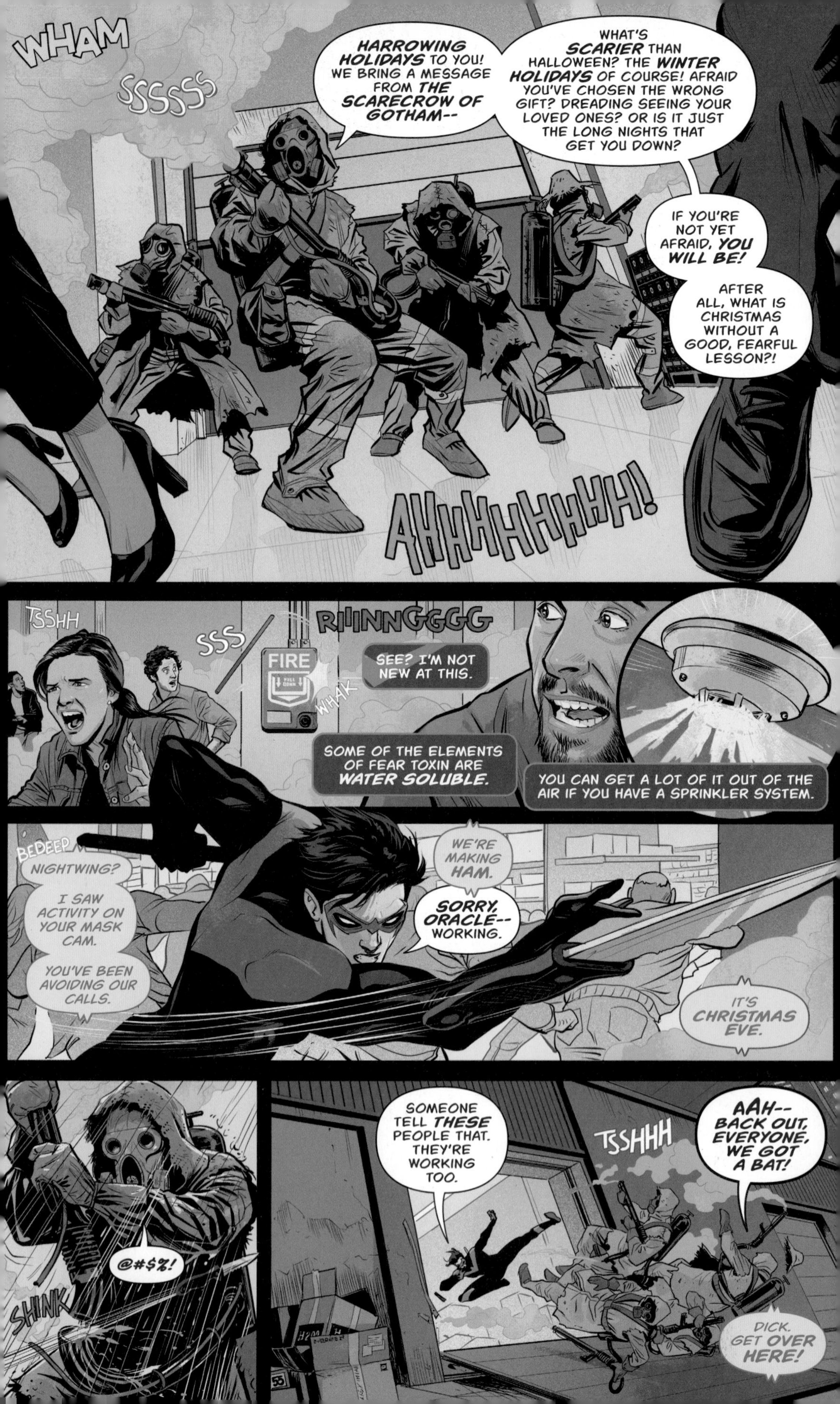
WHAM
SSSSSS
HARROWING HOLIDAYS TO YOU! WE BRING A MESSAGE FROM THE SCARECROW OF GOTHAM--
WHAT'S SCARIER THAN HALLOWEEN? THE WINTER HOLIDAYS OF COURSE! AFRAID YOU'VE CHOSEN THE WRONG GIFT? DREADING SEEING YOUR LOVED ONES? OR IS IT JUST THE LONG NIGHTS THAT GET YOU DOWN?
IF YOU'RE NOT YET AFRAID, YOU WILL BE!
AFTER ALL, WHAT IS CHRISTMAS WITHOUT A GOOD, FEARFUL LESSON?!
AHHHHHHHHH!
TSSHH
SSS
RIIINNGGGG
FIRE
WHAK
SEE? I'M NOT NEW AT THIS.
SOME OF THE ELEMENTS OF FEAR TOXIN ARE WATER SOLUBLE.
YOU CAN GET A LOT OF IT OUT OF THE AIR IF YOU HAVE A SPRINKLER SYSTEM.
BEDEEP
NIGHTWING?
I SAW ACTIVITY ON YOUR MASK CAM.
YOU'VE BEEN AVOIDING OUR CALLS.
WE'RE MAKING HAM.
SORRY, ORACLE-- WORKING.
IT'S CHRISTMAS EVE.
@#$%!
SHINK
SOMEONE TELL THESE PEOPLE THAT. THEY'RE WORKING TOO.
TSSHHH
AAH-- BACK OUT, EVERYONE, WE GOT A BAT!
DICK. GET OVER HERE!

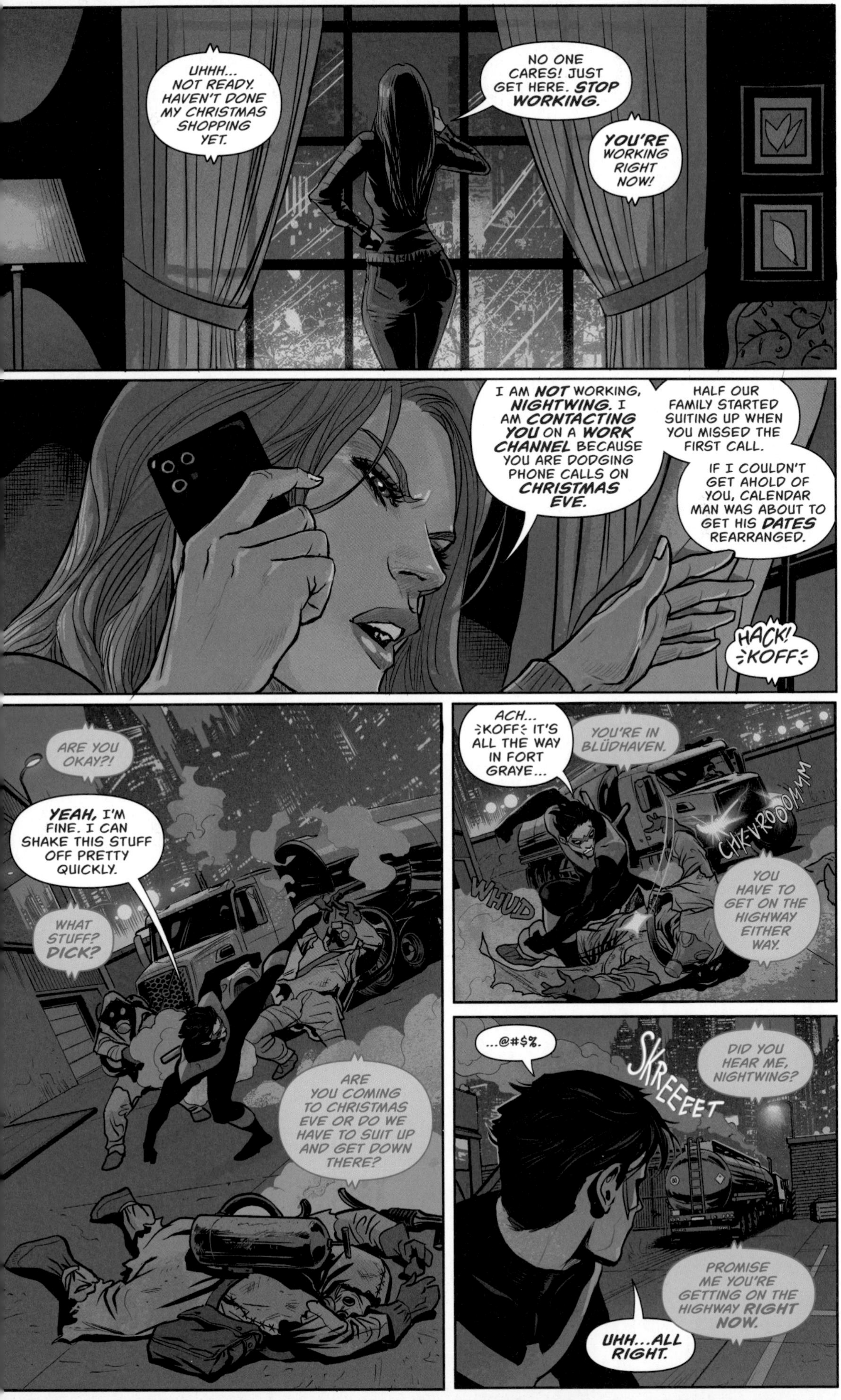
UHHH... NOT READY. HAVEN'T DONE MY CHRISTMAS SHOPPING YET.
NO ONE CARES! JUST GET HERE. STOP WORKING.
YOU'RE WORKING RIGHT NOW!
I AM NOT WORKING, NIGHTWING. I AM CONTACTING YOU ON A WORK CHANNEL BECAUSE YOU ARE DODGING PHONE CALLS ON CHRISTMAS EVE.
HALF OUR FAMILY STARTED SUITING UP WHEN YOU MISSED THE FIRST CALL.
IF I COULDN'T GET AHOLD OF YOU, CALENDAR MAN WAS ABOUT TO GET HIS DATES REARRANGED.
HACK! KOFF
ARE YOU OKAY?!
YEAH, I'M FINE. I CAN SHAKE THIS STUFF OFF PRETTY QUICKLY.
WHAT STUFF? DICK?
ARE YOU COMING TO CHRISTMAS EVE OR DO WE HAVE TO SUIT UP AND GET DOWN THERE?
ACH... KOFF IT'S ALL THE WAY IN FORT GRAYE...
YOU'RE IN BLÜDHAVEN.
CHK-VROOOMMM
WHUD
YOU HAVE TO GET ON THE HIGHWAY EITHER WAY.
...@#$%.
SKREEEEET
DID YOU HEAR ME, NIGHTWING?
PROMISE ME YOU'RE GETTING ON THE HIGHWAY RIGHT NOW.
UHH...ALL RIGHT.

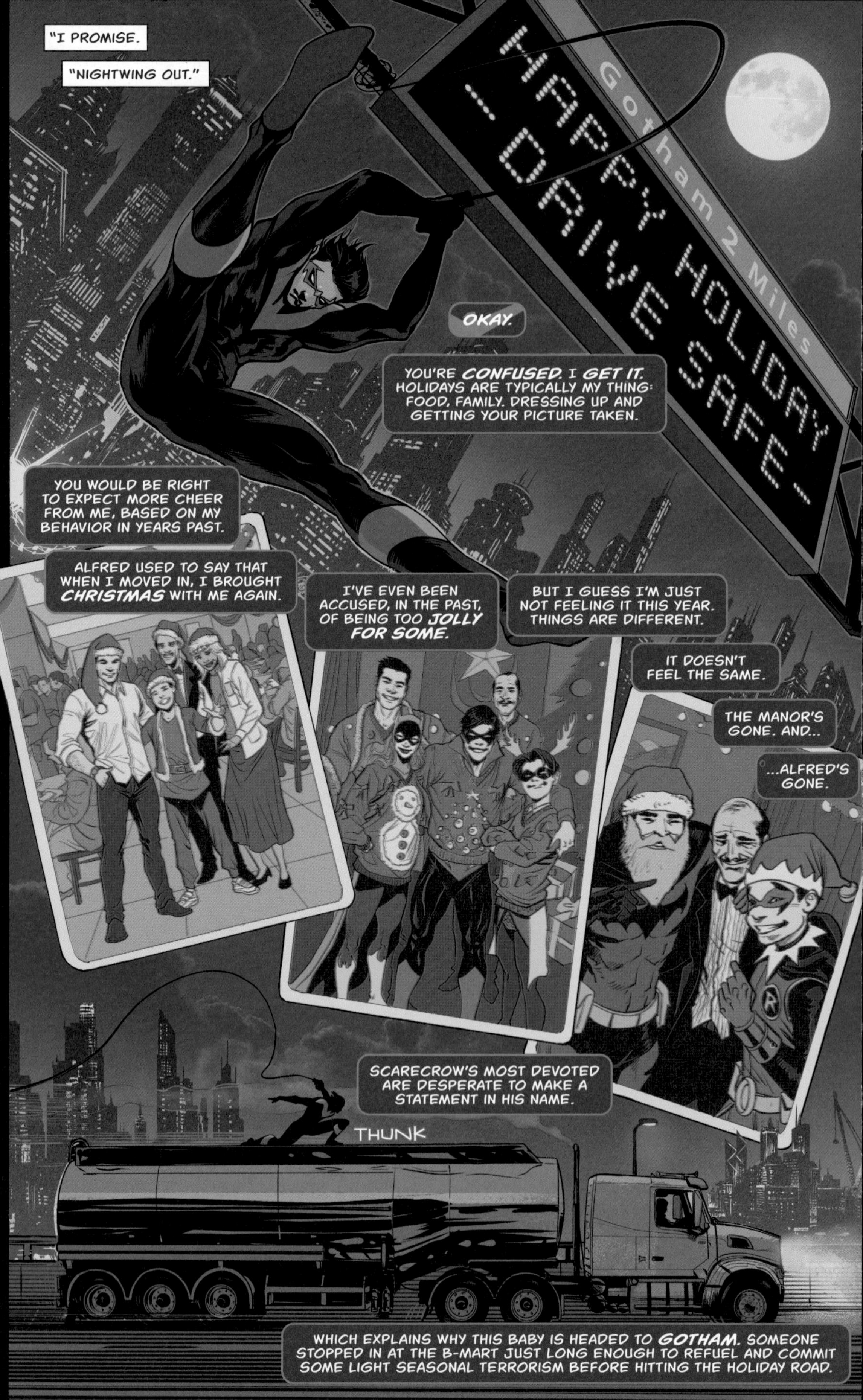
"I PROMISE.
"NIGHTWING OUT."
Gotham 2 Miles
HAPPY HOLIDAY - DRIVE SAFE -
OKAY.
YOU'RE CONFUSED. I GET IT. HOLIDAYS ARE TYPICALLY MY THING: FOOD, FAMILY. DRESSING UP AND GETTING YOUR PICTURE TAKEN.
YOU WOULD BE RIGHT TO EXPECT MORE CHEER FROM ME, BASED ON MY BEHAVIOR IN YEARS PAST.
ALFRED USED TO SAY THAT WHEN I MOVED IN, I BROUGHT CHRISTMAS WITH ME AGAIN.
I'VE EVEN BEEN ACCUSED, IN THE PAST, OF BEING TOO JOLLY FOR SOME.
BUT I GUESS I'M JUST NOT FEELING IT THIS YEAR. THINGS ARE DIFFERENT.
IT DOESN'T FEEL THE SAME.
THE MANOR'S GONE. AND...
...ALFRED'S GONE.
SCARECROW'S MOST DEVOTED ARE DESPERATE TO MAKE A STATEMENT IN HIS NAME.
THUNK
WHICH EXPLAINS WHY THIS BABY IS HEADED TO GOTHAM. SOMEONE STOPPED IN AT THE B-MART JUST LONG ENOUGH TO REFUEL AND COMMIT SOME LIGHT SEASONAL TERRORISM BEFORE HITTING THE HOLIDAY ROAD.

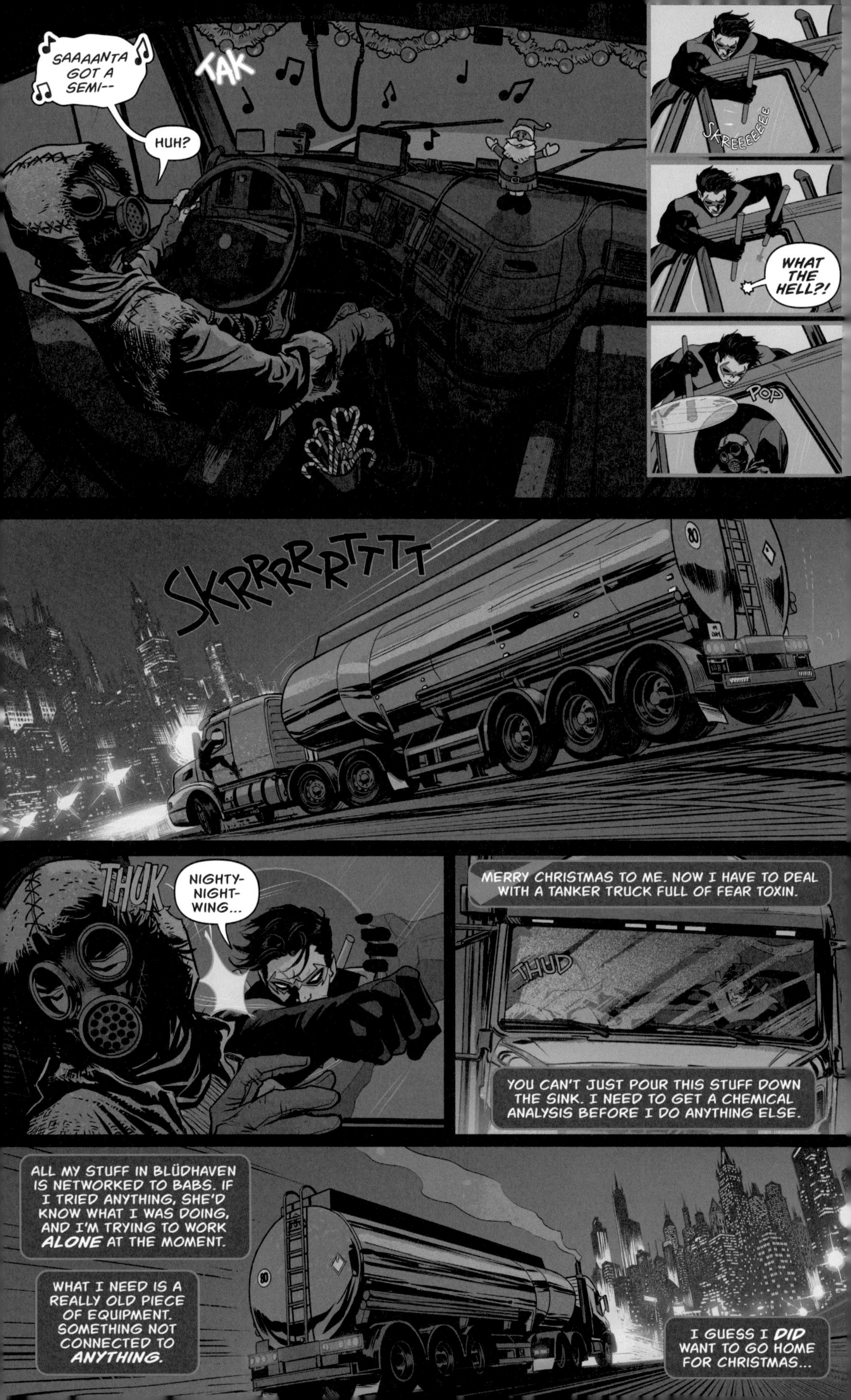
SAAAANTA GOT A SEMI--
TAK
HUH?
SKREEEEEEE
WHAT THE HELL?!
POP
SKRRRRTTTT
THUK
NIGHTY-NIGHT-WING...
MERRY CHRISTMAS TO ME. NOW I HAVE TO DEAL WITH A TANKER TRUCK FULL OF FEAR TOXIN.
THUD
YOU CAN'T JUST POUR THIS STUFF DOWN THE SINK. I NEED TO GET A CHEMICAL ANALYSIS BEFORE I DO ANYTHING ELSE.
ALL MY STUFF IN BLÜDHAVEN IS NETWORKED TO BABS. IF I TRIED ANYTHING, SHE'D KNOW WHAT I WAS DOING, AND I'M TRYING TO WORK *ALONE* AT THE MOMENT.
WHAT I NEED IS A REALLY OLD PIECE OF EQUIPMENT. SOMETHING NOT CONNECTED TO *ANYTHING*.
I GUESS I *DID* WANT TO GO HOME FOR CHRISTMAS...

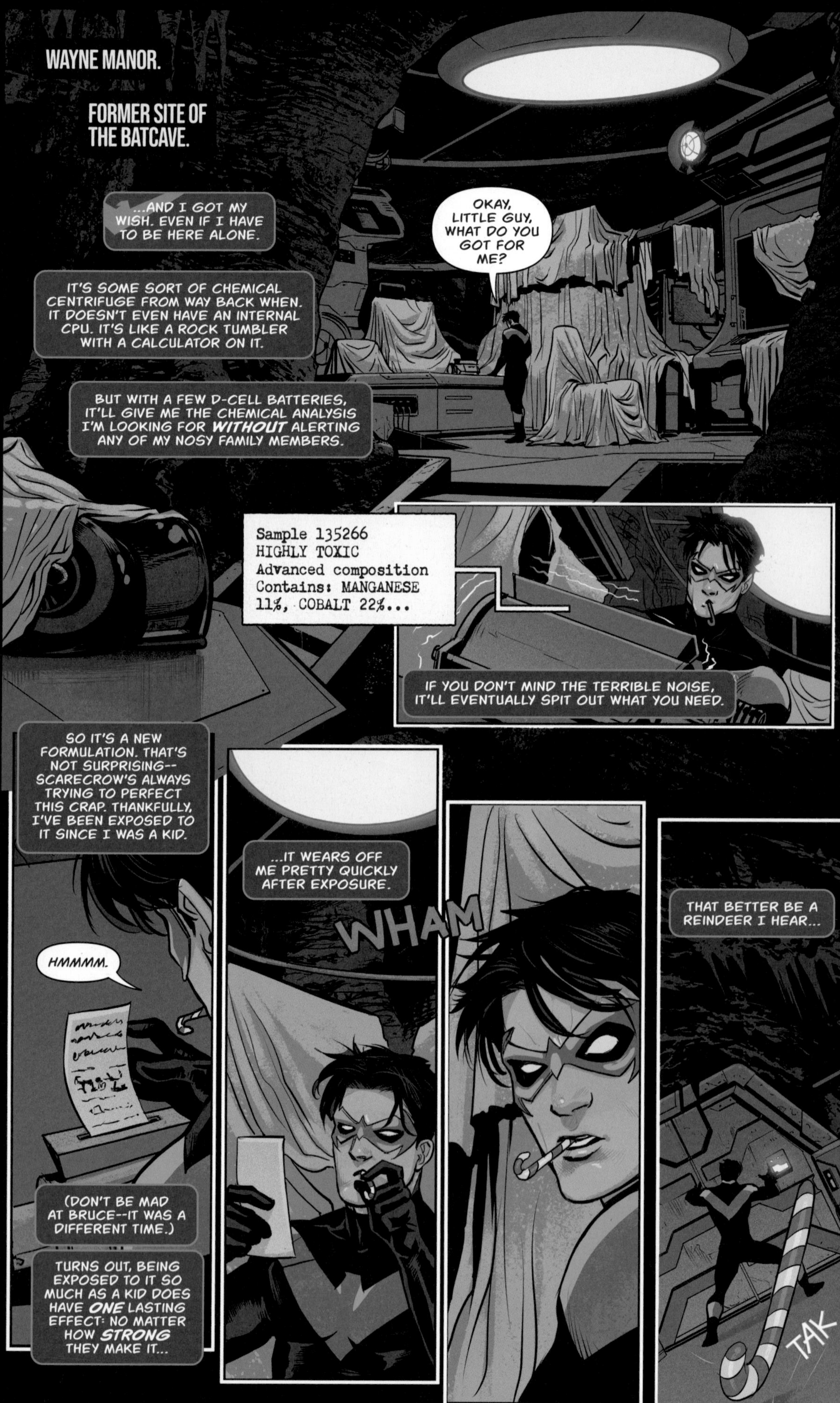
WAYNE MANOR.
FORMER SITE OF THE BATCAVE.
...AND I GOT MY WISH. EVEN IF I HAVE TO BE HERE ALONE.
OKAY, LITTLE GUY, WHAT DO YOU GOT FOR ME?
IT'S SOME SORT OF CHEMICAL CENTRIFUGE FROM WAY BACK WHEN. IT DOESN'T EVEN HAVE AN INTERNAL CPU. IT'S LIKE A ROCK TUMBLER WITH A CALCULATOR ON IT.
BUT WITH A FEW D-CELL BATTERIES, IT'LL GIVE ME THE CHEMICAL ANALYSIS I'M LOOKING FOR WITHOUT ALERTING ANY OF MY NOSY FAMILY MEMBERS.
Sample 135266
HIGHLY TOXIC
Advanced composition
Contains: MANGANESE
11%, COBALT 22%...
IF YOU DON'T MIND THE TERRIBLE NOISE, IT'LL EVENTUALLY SPIT OUT WHAT YOU NEED.
SO IT'S A NEW FORMULATION. THAT'S NOT SURPRISING--SCARECROW'S ALWAYS TRYING TO PERFECT THIS CRAP. THANKFULLY, I'VE BEEN EXPOSED TO IT SINCE I WAS A KID.
HMMMM.
(DON'T BE MAD AT BRUCE--IT WAS A DIFFERENT TIME.)
TURNS OUT, BEING EXPOSED TO IT SO MUCH AS A KID DOES HAVE ONE LASTING EFFECT: NO MATTER HOW STRONG THEY MAKE IT...
...IT WEARS OFF ME PRETTY QUICKLY AFTER EXPOSURE.
WHAM
THAT BETTER BE A REINDEER I HEAR...
TAK

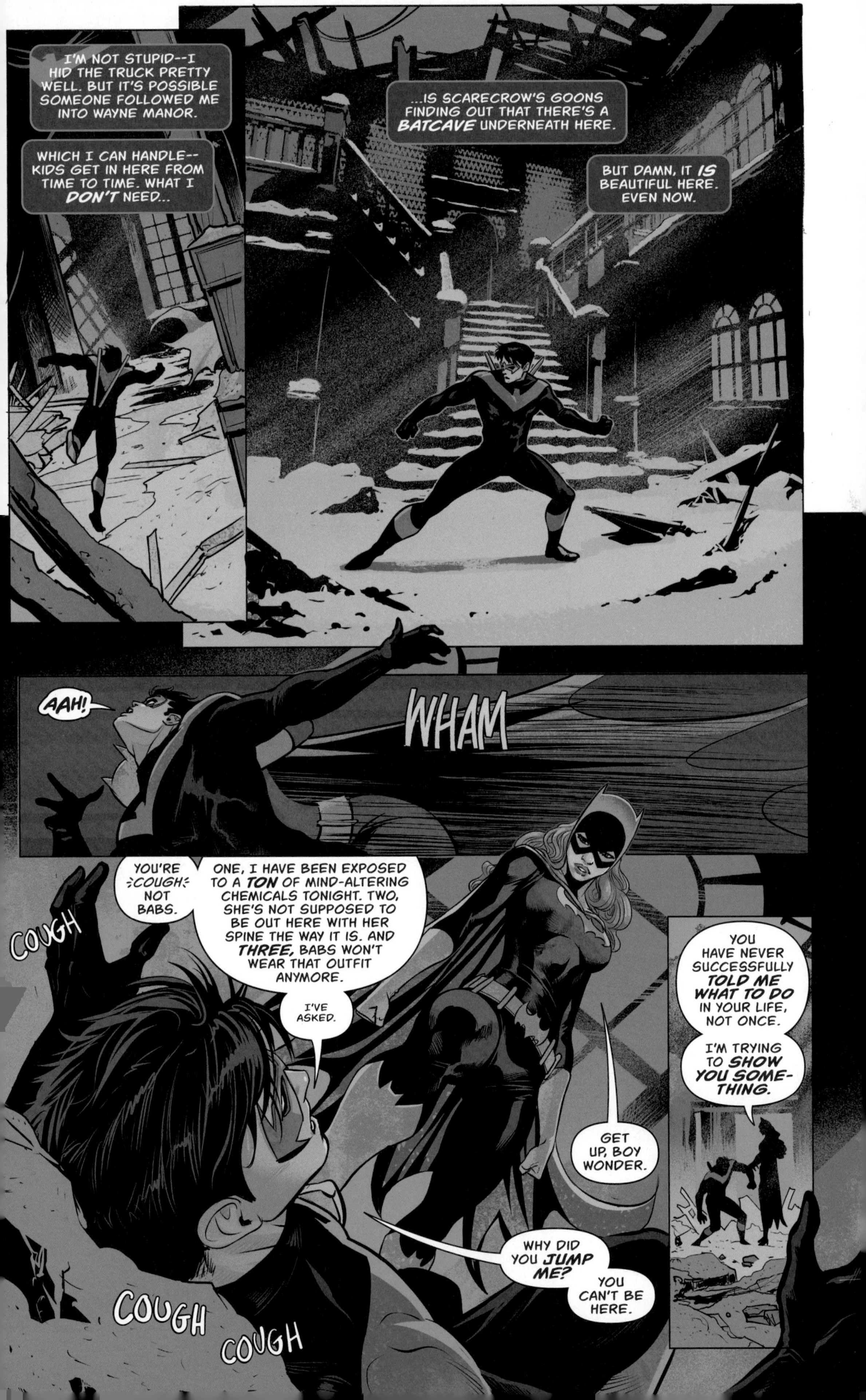

I'M NOT STUPID--I HID THE TRUCK PRETTY WELL. BUT IT'S POSSIBLE SOMEONE FOLLOWED ME INTO WAYNE MANOR.
WHICH I CAN HANDLE--KIDS GET IN HERE FROM TIME TO TIME. WHAT I DON'T NEED...
...IS SCARECROW'S GOONS FINDING OUT THAT THERE'S A BATCAVE UNDERNEATH HERE.
BUT DAMN, IT IS BEAUTIFUL HERE. EVEN NOW.
AAH!
WHAM
YOU'RE *COUGH* NOT BABS.
ONE, I HAVE BEEN EXPOSED TO A TON OF MIND-ALTERING CHEMICALS TONIGHT. TWO, SHE'S NOT SUPPOSED TO BE OUT HERE WITH HER SPINE THE WAY IT IS. AND THREE, BABS WON'T WEAR THAT OUTFIT ANYMORE.
I'VE ASKED.
COUGH
YOU HAVE NEVER SUCCESSFULLY TOLD ME WHAT TO DO IN YOUR LIFE, NOT ONCE.
I'M TRYING TO SHOW YOU SOMETHING.
GET UP, BOY WONDER.
WHY DID YOU JUMP ME?
YOU CAN'T BE HERE.
COUGH
COUGH

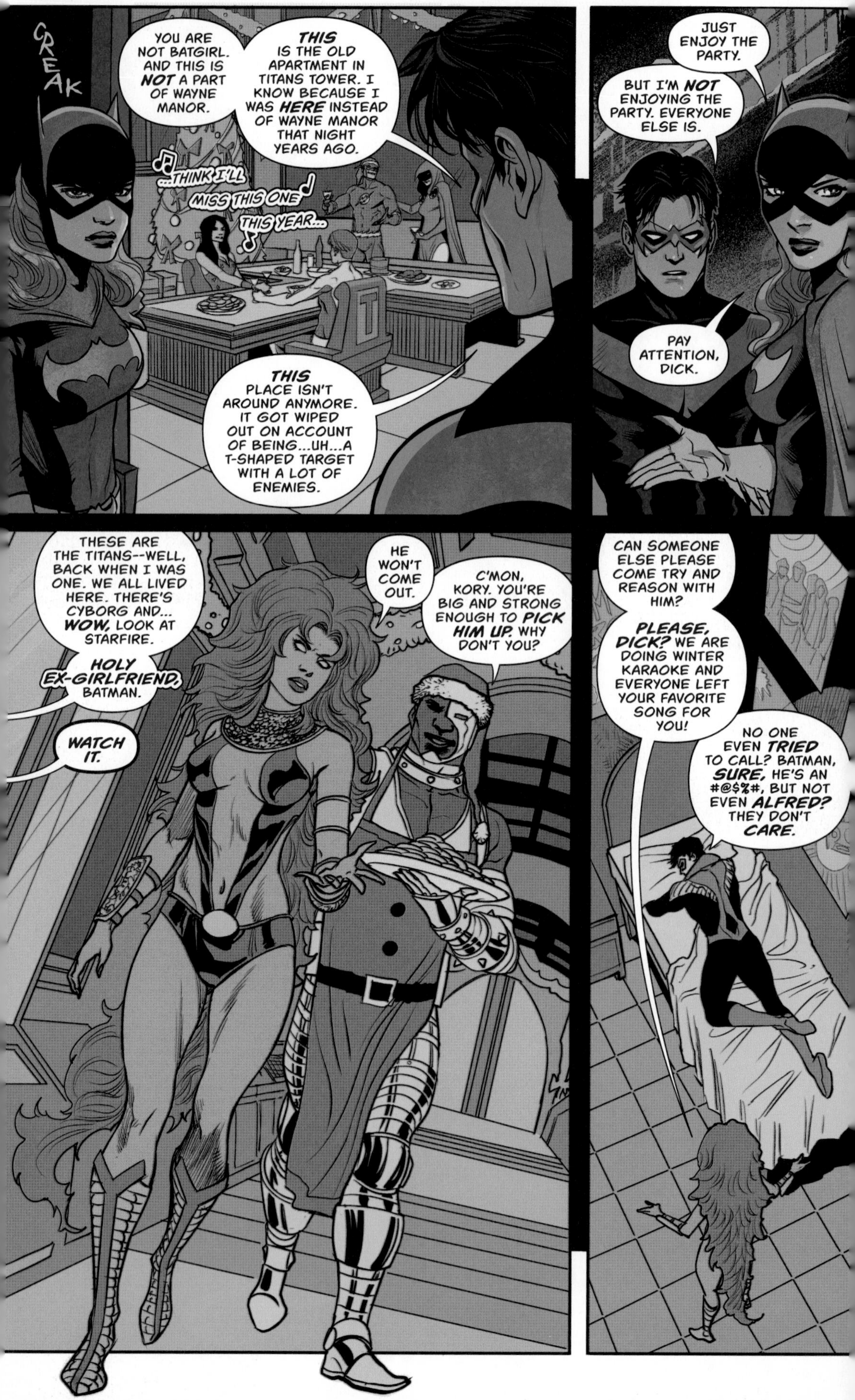
CREAK
YOU ARE NOT BATGIRL. AND THIS IS NOT A PART OF WAYNE MANOR.
THIS IS THE OLD APARTMENT IN TITANS TOWER. I KNOW BECAUSE I WAS HERE INSTEAD OF WAYNE MANOR THAT NIGHT YEARS AGO.
...THINK I'LL MISS THIS ONE THIS YEAR...
THIS PLACE ISN'T AROUND ANYMORE. IT GOT WIPED OUT ON ACCOUNT OF BEING...UH...A T-SHAPED TARGET WITH A LOT OF ENEMIES.
JUST ENJOY THE PARTY.
BUT I'M NOT ENJOYING THE PARTY. EVERYONE ELSE IS.
PAY ATTENTION, DICK.
THESE ARE THE TITANS--WELL, BACK WHEN I WAS ONE. WE ALL LIVED HERE. THERE'S CYBORG AND... WOW, LOOK AT STARFIRE.
HOLY EX-GIRLFRIEND, BATMAN.
WATCH IT.
HE WON'T COME OUT.
C'MON, KORY. YOU'RE BIG AND STRONG ENOUGH TO PICK HIM UP. WHY DON'T YOU?
CAN SOMEONE ELSE PLEASE COME TRY AND REASON WITH HIM?
PLEASE, DICK? WE ARE DOING WINTER KARAOKE AND EVERYONE LEFT YOUR FAVORITE SONG FOR YOU!
NO ONE EVEN TRIED TO CALL? BATMAN, SURE, HE'S AN #@$%#, BUT NOT EVEN ALFRED? THEY DON'T CARE.

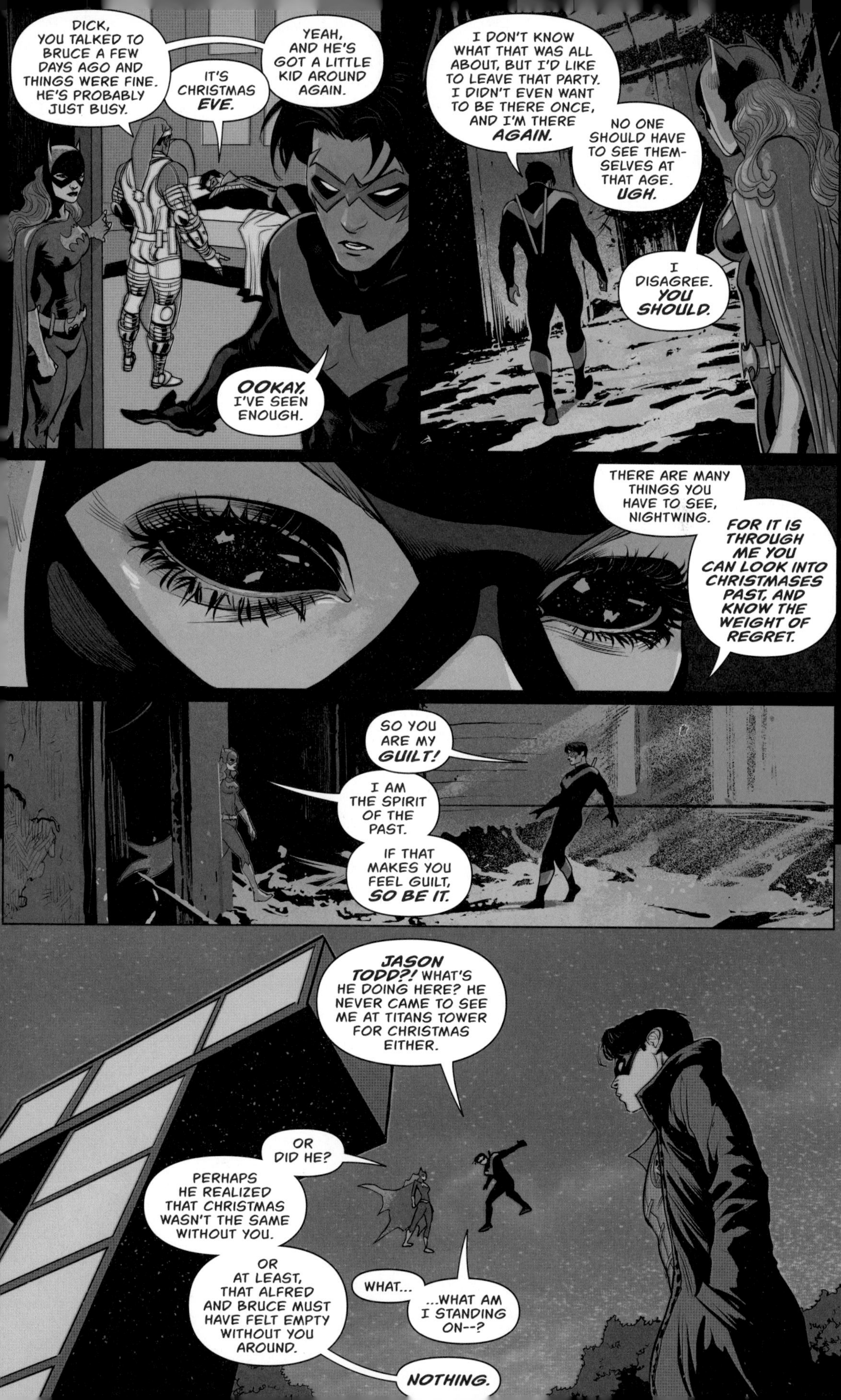

DICK, YOU TALKED TO BRUCE A FEW DAYS AGO AND THINGS WERE FINE. HE'S PROBABLY JUST BUSY.
IT'S CHRISTMAS EVE.
YEAH, AND HE'S GOT A LITTLE KID AROUND AGAIN.
OOKAY, I'VE SEEN ENOUGH.
I DON'T KNOW WHAT THAT WAS ALL ABOUT, BUT I'D LIKE TO LEAVE THAT PARTY. I DIDN'T EVEN WANT TO BE THERE ONCE, AND I'M THERE AGAIN.
NO ONE SHOULD HAVE TO SEE THEM-SELVES AT THAT AGE. UGH.
I DISAGREE. YOU SHOULD.
THERE ARE MANY THINGS YOU HAVE TO SEE, NIGHTWING.
FOR IT IS THROUGH ME YOU CAN LOOK INTO CHRISTMASES PAST, AND KNOW THE WEIGHT OF REGRET.
SO YOU ARE MY GUILT!
I AM THE SPIRIT OF THE PAST.
IF THAT MAKES YOU FEEL GUILT, SO BE IT.
JASON TODD?! WHAT'S HE DOING HERE? HE NEVER CAME TO SEE ME AT TITANS TOWER FOR CHRISTMAS EITHER.
OR DID HE?
PERHAPS HE REALIZED THAT CHRISTMAS WASN'T THE SAME WITHOUT YOU.
OR AT LEAST, THAT ALFRED AND BRUCE MUST HAVE FELT EMPTY WITHOUT YOU AROUND.
WHAT...
...WHAT AM I STANDING ON--?
NOTHING.

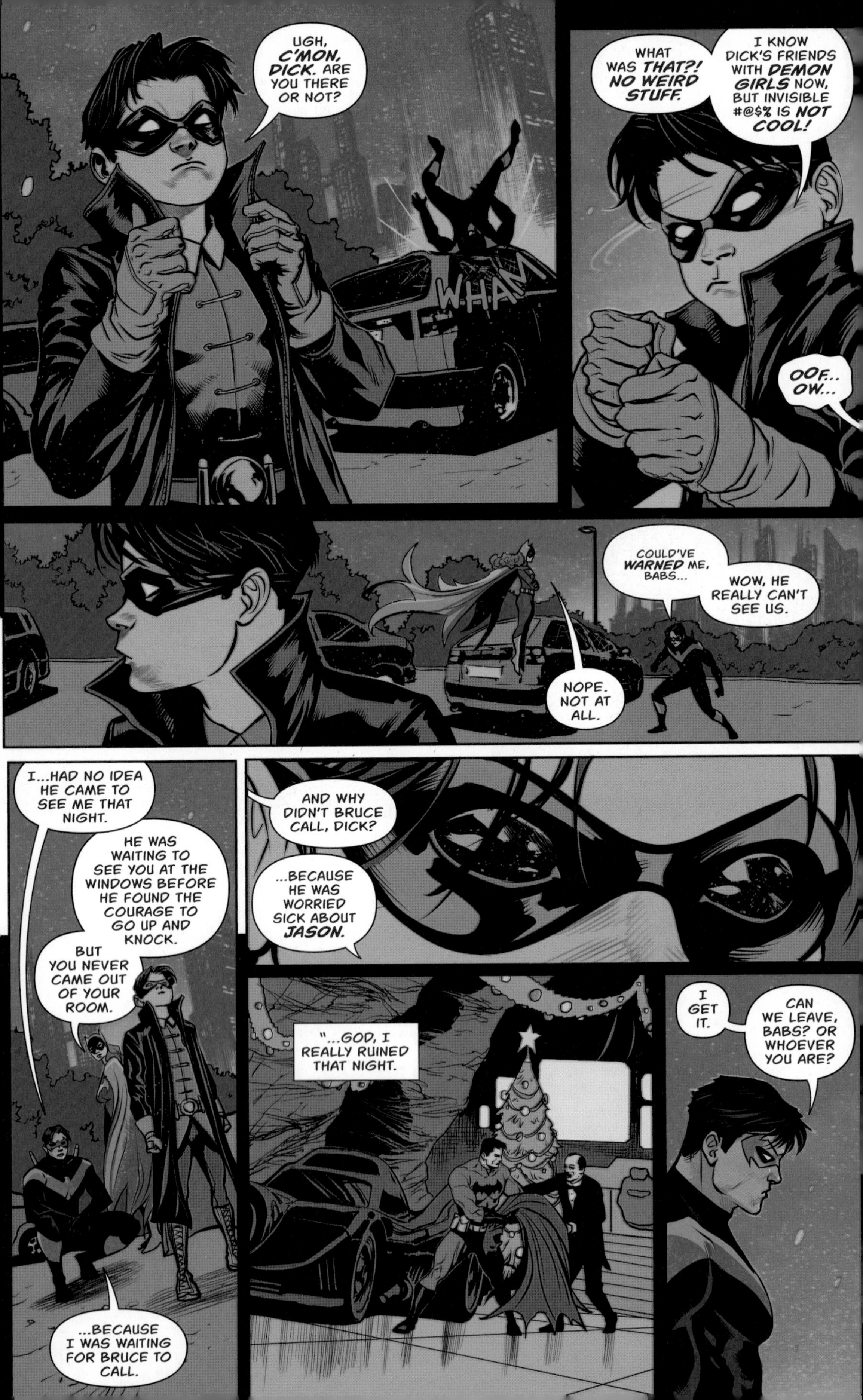
UGH, C'MON, DICK. ARE YOU THERE OR NOT?
WHAM
WHAT WAS THAT?! NO WEIRD STUFF.
I KNOW DICK'S FRIENDS WITH DEMON GIRLS NOW, BUT INVISIBLE #@$% IS NOT COOL!
OOF... OW...
COULD'VE WARNED ME, BABS...
WOW, HE REALLY CAN'T SEE US.
NOPE. NOT AT ALL.
I...HAD NO IDEA HE CAME TO SEE ME THAT NIGHT.
HE WAS WAITING TO SEE YOU AT THE WINDOWS BEFORE HE FOUND THE COURAGE TO GO UP AND KNOCK.
BUT YOU NEVER CAME OUT OF YOUR ROOM.
...BECAUSE I WAS WAITING FOR BRUCE TO CALL.
AND WHY DIDN'T BRUCE CALL, DICK?
...BECAUSE HE WAS WORRIED SICK ABOUT JASON.
"...GOD, I REALLY RUINED THAT NIGHT.
I GET IT.
CAN WE LEAVE, BABS? OR WHOEVER YOU ARE?

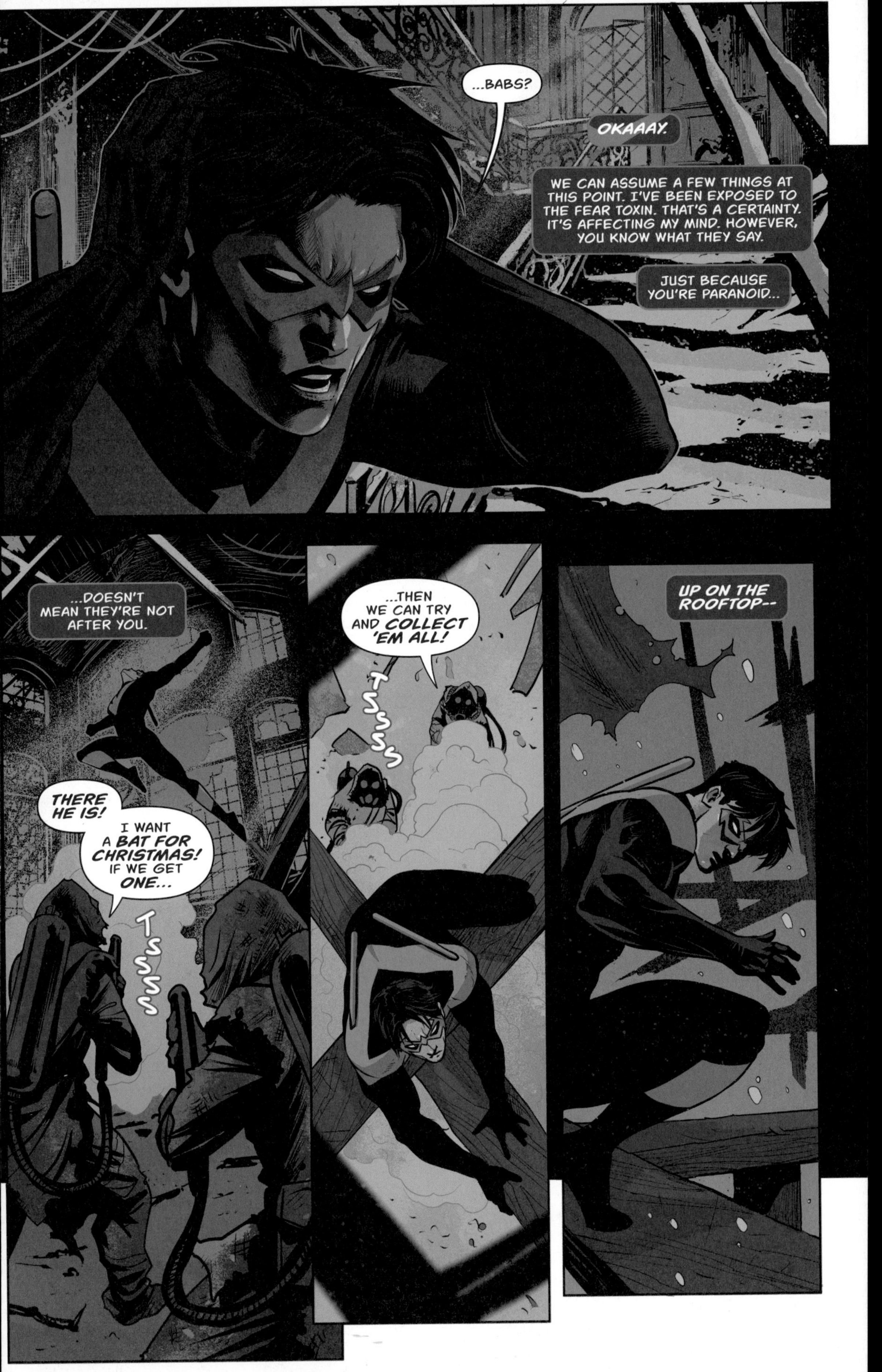
...BABS?
OKAAAY.
WE CAN ASSUME A FEW THINGS AT THIS POINT. I'VE BEEN EXPOSED TO THE FEAR TOXIN. THAT'S A CERTAINTY. IT'S AFFECTING MY MIND. HOWEVER, YOU KNOW WHAT THEY SAY.
JUST BECAUSE YOU'RE PARANOID...
...DOESN'T MEAN THEY'RE NOT AFTER YOU.
THERE HE IS!
I WANT A BAT FOR CHRISTMAS! IF WE GET ONE...
TSSSS
...THEN WE CAN TRY AND COLLECT 'EM ALL!
TSSSS
UP ON THE ROOFTOP--

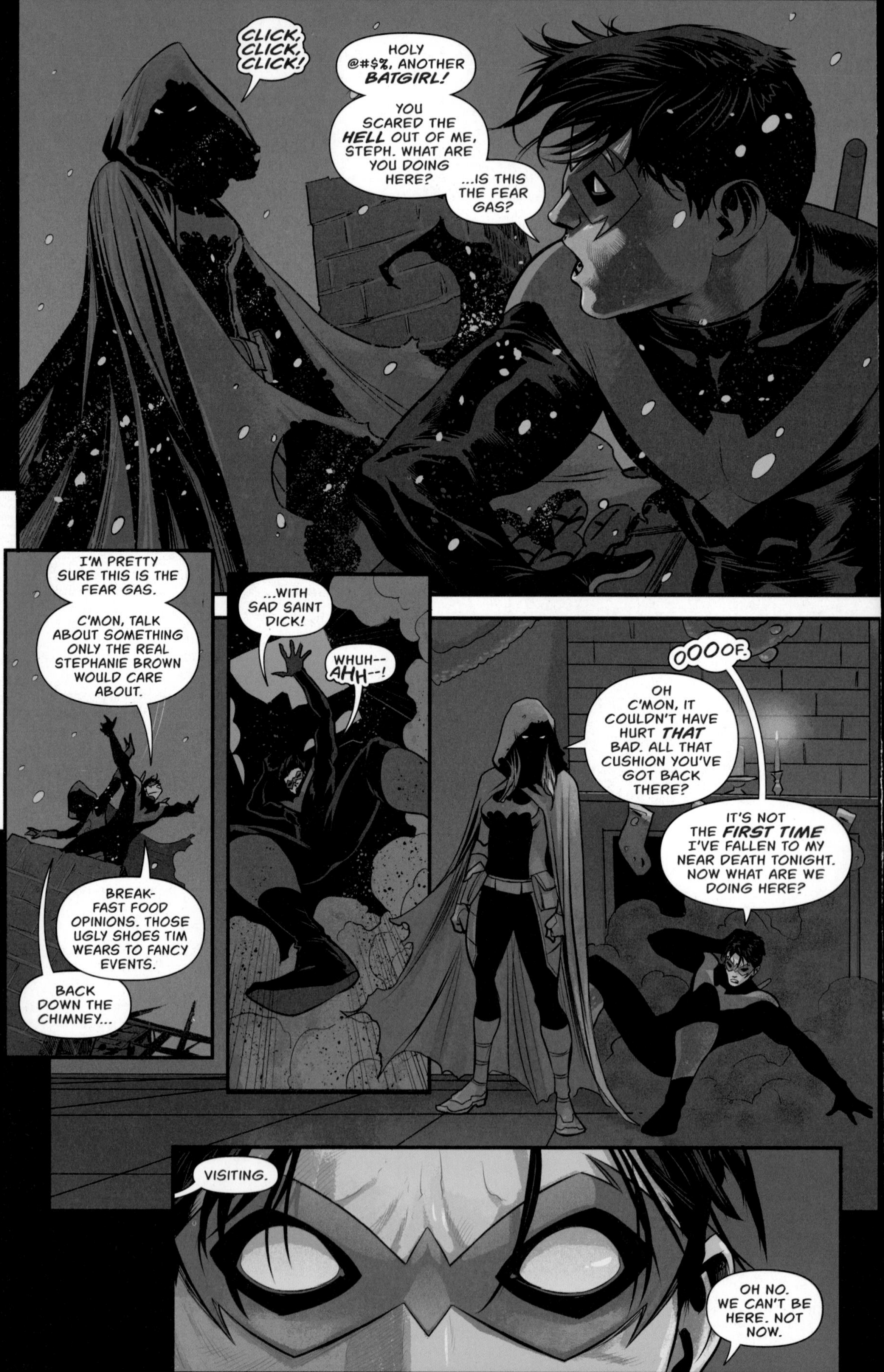
CLICK, CLICK, CLICK!
HOLY @#$%, ANOTHER BATGIRL!
YOU SCARED THE HELL OUT OF ME, STEPH. WHAT ARE YOU DOING HERE?
...IS THIS THE FEAR GAS?
I'M PRETTY SURE THIS IS THE FEAR GAS.
C'MON, TALK ABOUT SOMETHING ONLY THE REAL STEPHANIE BROWN WOULD CARE ABOUT.
BREAK-FAST FOOD OPINIONS. THOSE UGLY SHOES TIM WEARS TO FANCY EVENTS.
BACK DOWN THE CHIMNEY...
...WITH SAD SAINT DICK!
WHUH--AHH--!
OOOOF.
OH C'MON, IT COULDN'T HAVE HURT THAT BAD. ALL THAT CUSHION YOU'VE GOT BACK THERE?
IT'S NOT THE FIRST TIME I'VE FALLEN TO MY NEAR DEATH TONIGHT. NOW WHAT ARE WE DOING HERE?
VISITING.
OH NO. WE CAN'T BE HERE. NOT NOW.

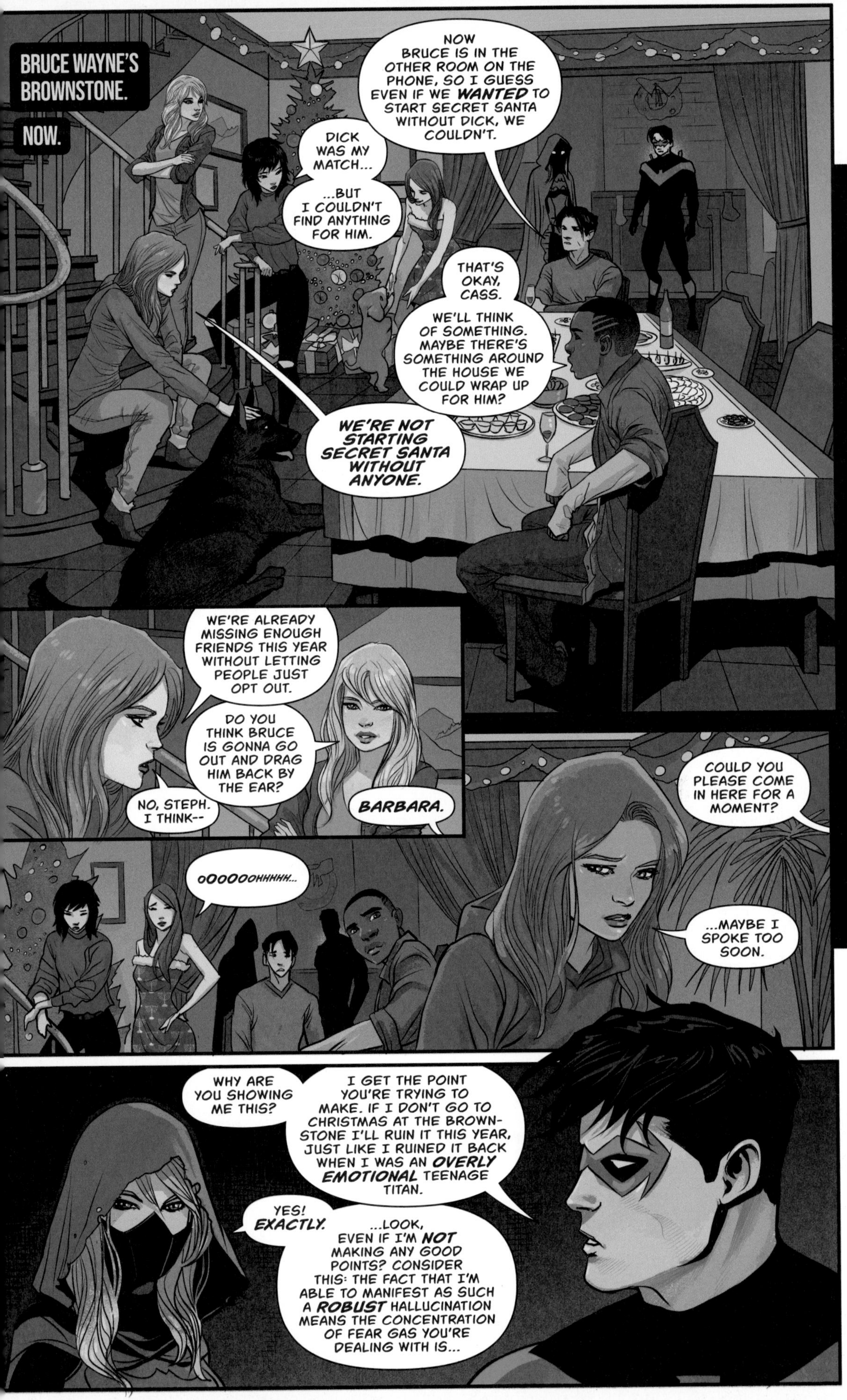
BRUCE WAYNE'S BROWNSTONE.
NOW.
NOW BRUCE IS IN THE OTHER ROOM ON THE PHONE, SO I GUESS EVEN IF WE *WANTED* TO START SECRET SANTA WITHOUT DICK, WE COULDN'T.
DICK WAS MY MATCH...
...BUT I COULDN'T FIND ANYTHING FOR HIM.
THAT'S OKAY, CASS.
WE'LL THINK OF SOMETHING. MAYBE THERE'S SOMETHING AROUND THE HOUSE WE COULD WRAP UP FOR HIM?
WE'RE NOT STARTING SECRET SANTA WITHOUT ANYONE.
WE'RE ALREADY MISSING ENOUGH FRIENDS THIS YEAR WITHOUT LETTING PEOPLE JUST OPT OUT.
DO YOU THINK BRUCE IS GONNA GO OUT AND DRAG HIM BACK BY THE EAR?
NO, STEPH. I THINK--
BARBARA.
COULD YOU PLEASE COME IN HERE FOR A MOMENT?
OOOOOOHHHHH...
...MAYBE I SPOKE TOO SOON.
WHY ARE YOU SHOWING ME THIS?
I GET THE POINT YOU'RE TRYING TO MAKE. IF I DON'T GO TO CHRISTMAS AT THE BROWN-STONE I'LL RUIN IT THIS YEAR, JUST LIKE I RUINED IT BACK WHEN I WAS AN *OVERLY EMOTIONAL* TEENAGE TITAN.
YES! *EXACTLY.*
...LOOK, EVEN IF I'M *NOT* MAKING ANY GOOD POINTS? CONSIDER THIS: THE FACT THAT I'M ABLE TO MANIFEST AS SUCH A *ROBUST* HALLUCINATION MEANS THE CONCENTRATION OF FEAR GAS YOU'RE DEALING WITH IS...

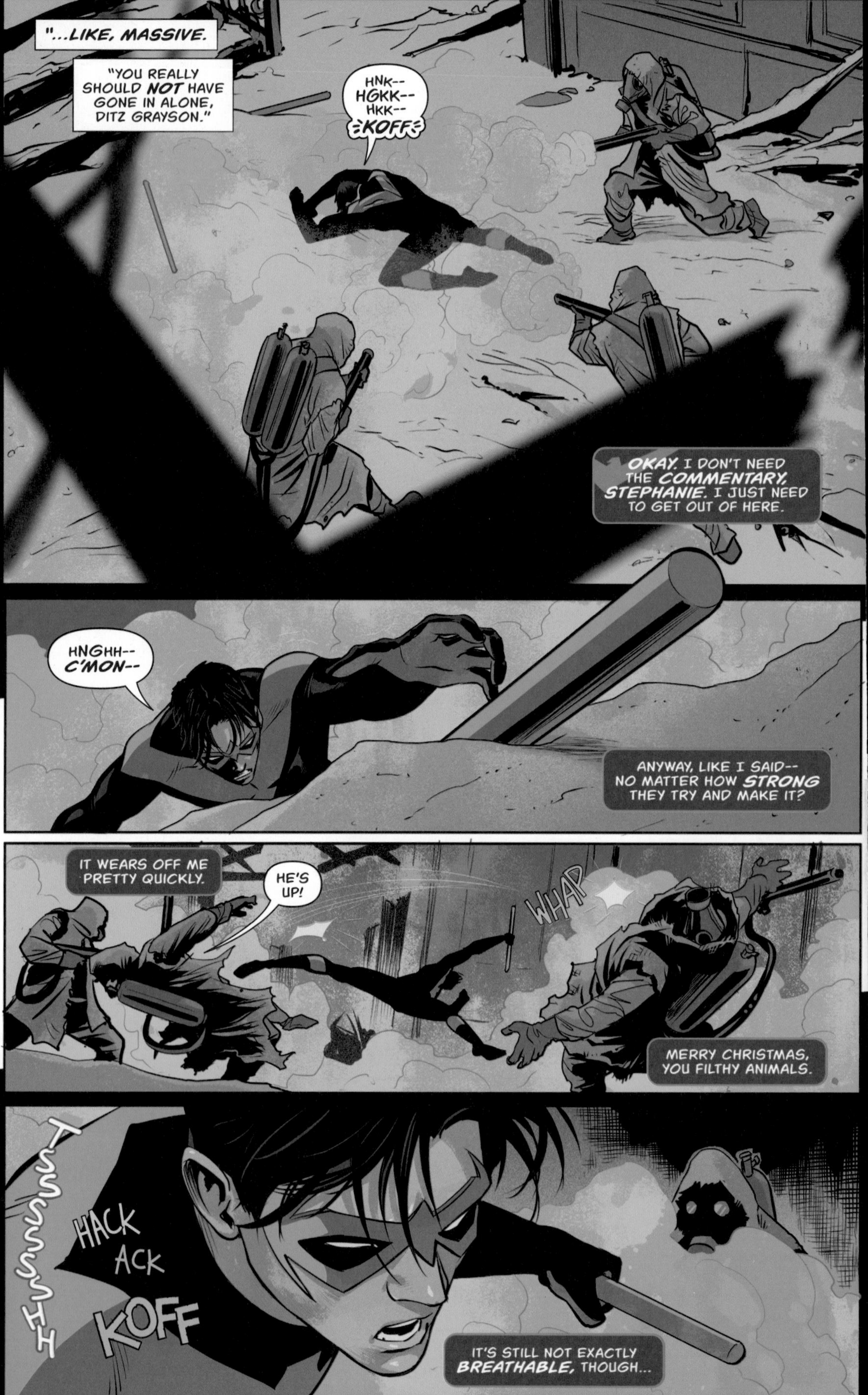
"...LIKE, MASSIVE.
"YOU REALLY SHOULD NOT HAVE GONE IN ALONE, DITZ GRAYSON."
HNK-- HGKK-- HKK-- KOFF
OKAY. I DON'T NEED THE COMMENTARY, STEPHANIE. I JUST NEED TO GET OUT OF HERE.
HNGHH-- C'MON--
ANYWAY, LIKE I SAID-- NO MATTER HOW STRONG THEY TRY AND MAKE IT?
IT WEARS OFF ME PRETTY QUICKLY.
HE'S UP!
WHAP
MERRY CHRISTMAS, YOU FILTHY ANIMALS.
TSSSSSHHH
HACK
ACK
KOFF
IT'S STILL NOT EXACTLY BREATHABLE, THOUGH...

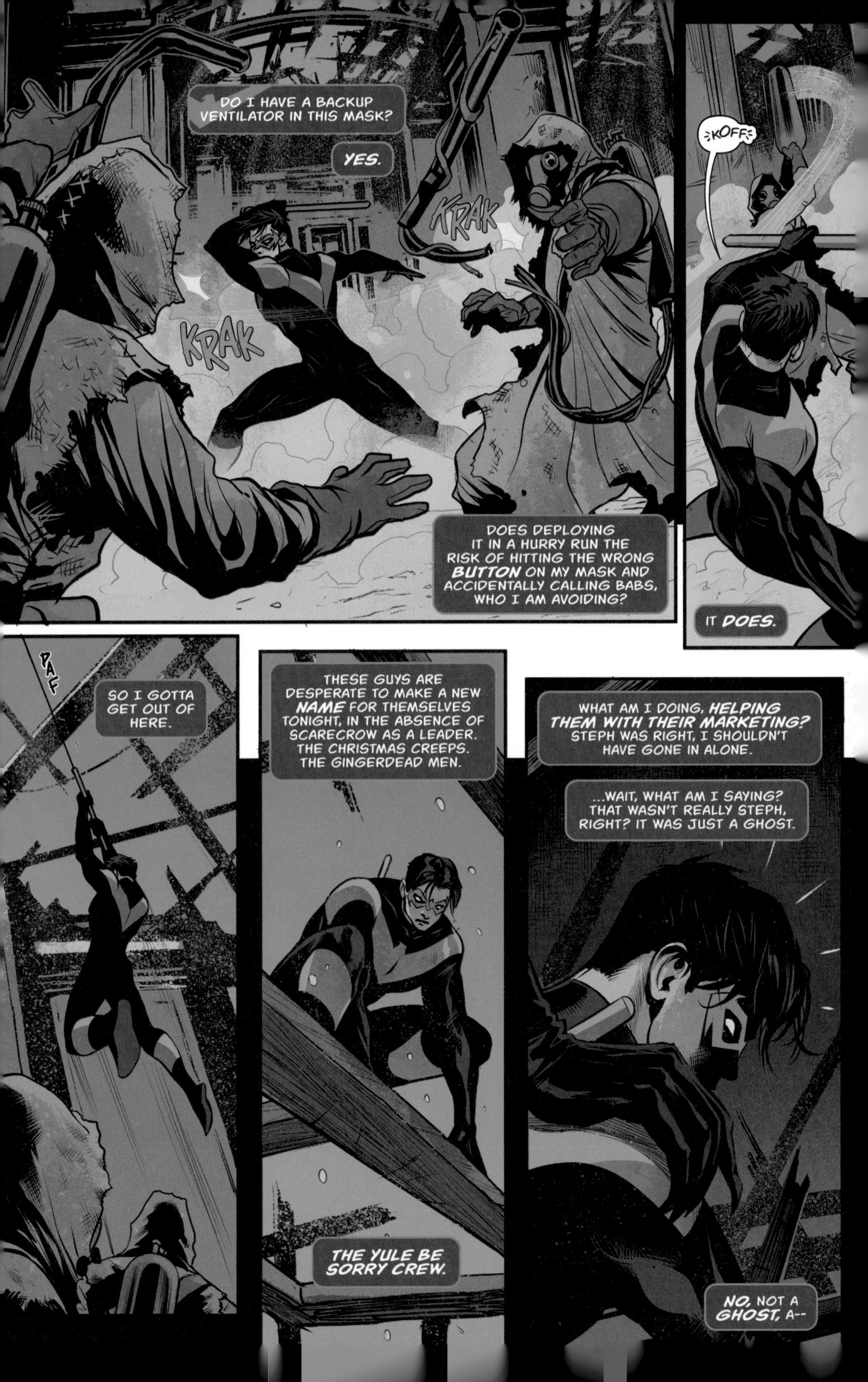

DO I HAVE A BACKUP VENTILATOR IN THIS MASK?
YES.
KRAK
KRAK
DOES DEPLOYING IT IN A HURRY RUN THE RISK OF HITTING THE WRONG BUTTON ON MY MASK AND ACCIDENTALLY CALLING BABS, WHO I AM AVOIDING?
KOFF
IT DOES.
PAF
SO I GOTTA GET OUT OF HERE.
THESE GUYS ARE DESPERATE TO MAKE A NEW NAME FOR THEMSELVES TONIGHT, IN THE ABSENCE OF SCARECROW AS A LEADER. THE CHRISTMAS CREEPS. THE GINGERDEAD MEN.
THE YULE BE SORRY CREW.
WHAT AM I DOING, HELPING THEM WITH THEIR MARKETING? STEPH WAS RIGHT, I SHOULDN'T HAVE GONE IN ALONE.
...WAIT, WHAT AM I SAYING? THAT WASN'T REALLY STEPH, RIGHT? IT WAS JUST A GHOST.
NO, NOT A GHOST, A--

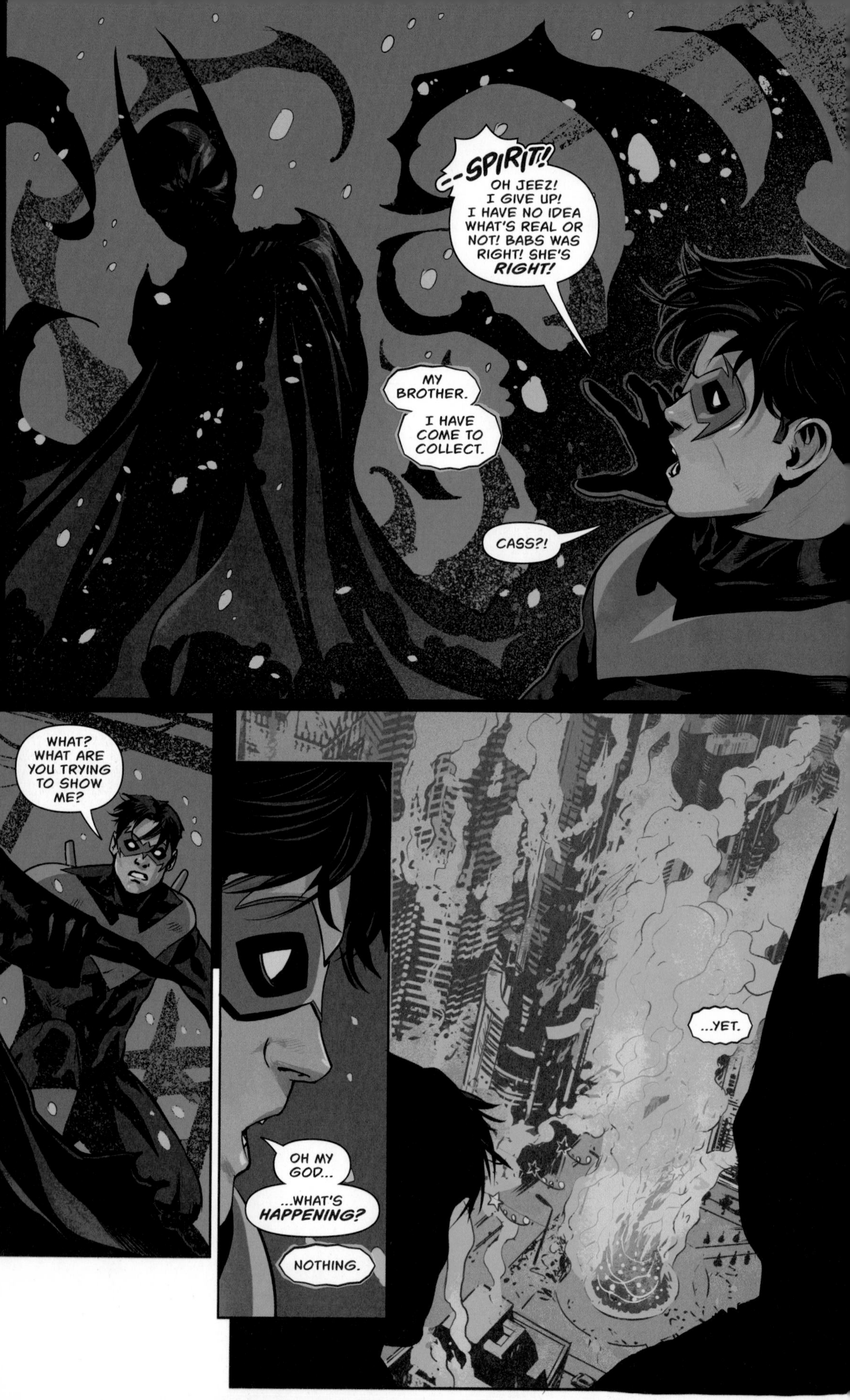
--SPIRIT!
OH JEEZ! I GIVE UP! I HAVE NO IDEA WHAT'S REAL OR NOT! BABS WAS RIGHT! SHE'S RIGHT!
MY BROTHER.
I HAVE COME TO COLLECT.
CASS?!
WHAT? WHAT ARE YOU TRYING TO SHOW ME?
OH MY GOD...
...WHAT'S HAPPENING?
NOTHING.
...YET.

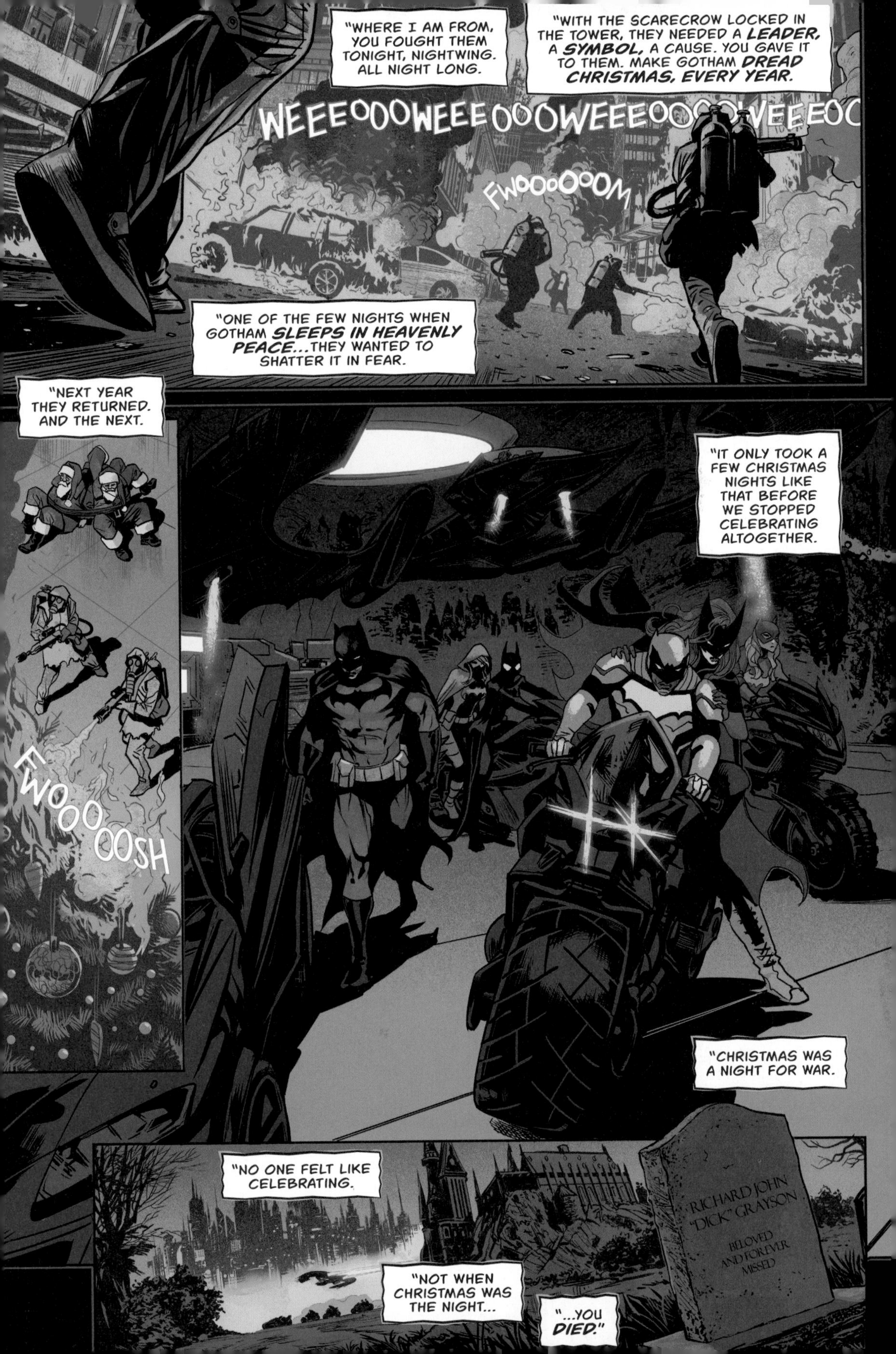
"WHERE I AM FROM, YOU FOUGHT THEM TONIGHT, NIGHTWING. ALL NIGHT LONG.
"WITH THE SCARECROW LOCKED IN THE TOWER, THEY NEEDED A LEADER, A SYMBOL, A CAUSE. YOU GAVE IT TO THEM. MAKE GOTHAM DREAD CHRISTMAS, EVERY YEAR.
WEEEOOOWEEEOOOWEEEOOOWEEEOO
FWOOOOOOM
"ONE OF THE FEW NIGHTS WHEN GOTHAM SLEEPS IN HEAVENLY PEACE...THEY WANTED TO SHATTER IT IN FEAR.
"NEXT YEAR THEY RETURNED. AND THE NEXT.
FWOOOOOSH
"IT ONLY TOOK A FEW CHRISTMAS NIGHTS LIKE THAT BEFORE WE STOPPED CELEBRATING ALTOGETHER.
"CHRISTMAS WAS A NIGHT FOR WAR.
"NO ONE FELT LIKE CELEBRATING.
RICHARD JOHN "DICK" GRAYSON
BELOVED AND FOREVER MISSED
"NOT WHEN CHRISTMAS WAS THE NIGHT...
"...YOU DIED."

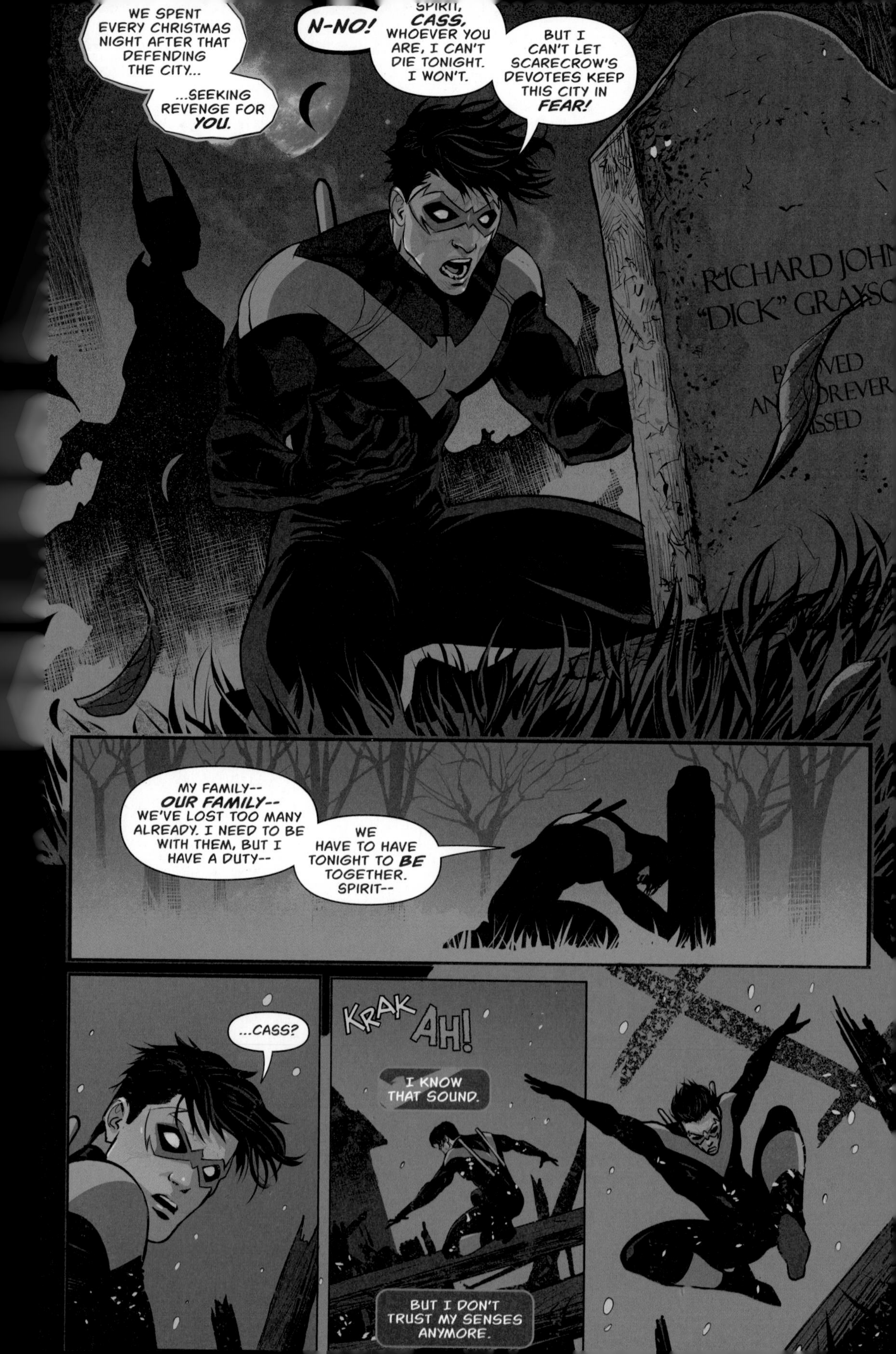
WE SPENT EVERY CHRISTMAS NIGHT AFTER THAT DEFENDING THE CITY...
...SEEKING REVENGE FOR YOU.
N-NO!
SPIRIT, CASS, WHOEVER YOU ARE, I CAN'T DIE TONIGHT. I WON'T.
BUT I CAN'T LET SCARECROW'S DEVOTEES KEEP THIS CITY IN FEAR!
RICHARD JOHN "DICK" GRAYSO
B OVED AN OREVER ISSED
MY FAMILY-- OUR FAMILY-- WE'VE LOST TOO MANY ALREADY. I NEED TO BE WITH THEM, BUT I HAVE A DUTY--
WE HAVE TO HAVE TONIGHT TO BE TOGETHER. SPIRIT--
...CASS?
KRAK
AH!
I KNOW THAT SOUND.
BUT I DON'T TRUST MY SENSES ANYMORE.

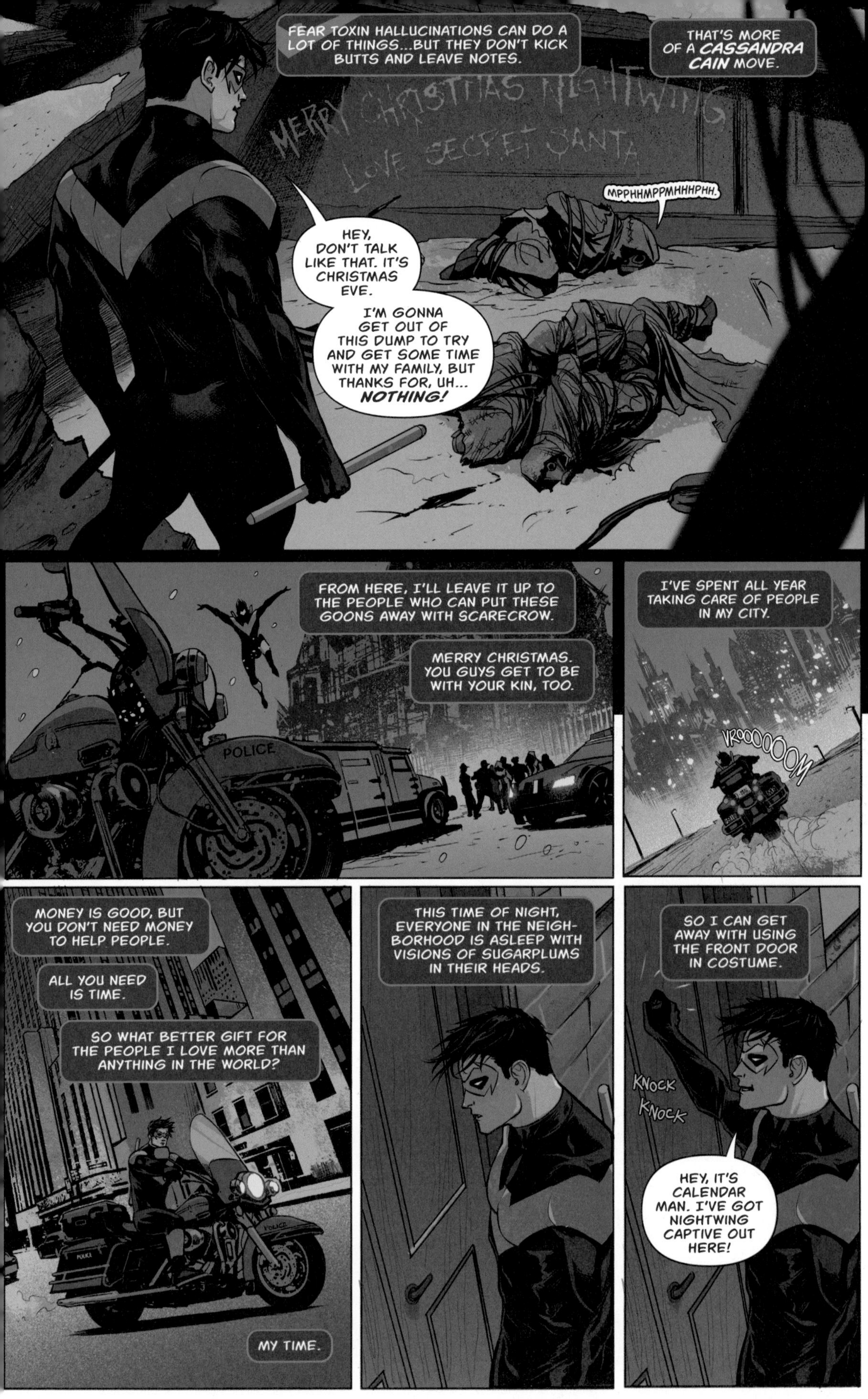
FEAR TOXIN HALLUCINATIONS CAN DO A LOT OF THINGS...BUT THEY DON'T KICK BUTTS AND LEAVE NOTES.
THAT'S MORE OF A *CASSANDRA CAIN* MOVE.
MERRY CHRISTMAS NIGHTWING
LOVE SECRET SANTA
MPPHHMPPMHHHPHH.
HEY, DON'T TALK LIKE THAT. IT'S CHRISTMAS EVE.
I'M GONNA GET OUT OF THIS DUMP TO TRY AND GET SOME TIME WITH MY FAMILY, BUT THANKS FOR, UH... ***NOTHING!***
FROM HERE, I'LL LEAVE IT UP TO THE PEOPLE WHO CAN PUT THESE GOONS AWAY WITH SCARECROW.
MERRY CHRISTMAS. YOU GUYS GET TO BE WITH YOUR KIN, TOO.
POLICE
I'VE SPENT ALL YEAR TAKING CARE OF PEOPLE IN MY CITY.
VROOOOOOM
MONEY IS GOOD, BUT YOU DON'T NEED MONEY TO HELP PEOPLE.
ALL YOU NEED IS TIME.
SO WHAT BETTER GIFT FOR THE PEOPLE I LOVE MORE THAN ANYTHING IN THE WORLD?
MY TIME.
THIS TIME OF NIGHT, EVERYONE IN THE NEIGH-BORHOOD IS ASLEEP WITH VISIONS OF SUGARPLUMS IN THEIR HEADS.
SO I CAN GET AWAY WITH USING THE FRONT DOOR IN COSTUME.
KNOCK
KNOCK
HEY, IT'S CALENDAR MAN. I'VE GOT NIGHTWING CAPTIVE OUT HERE!

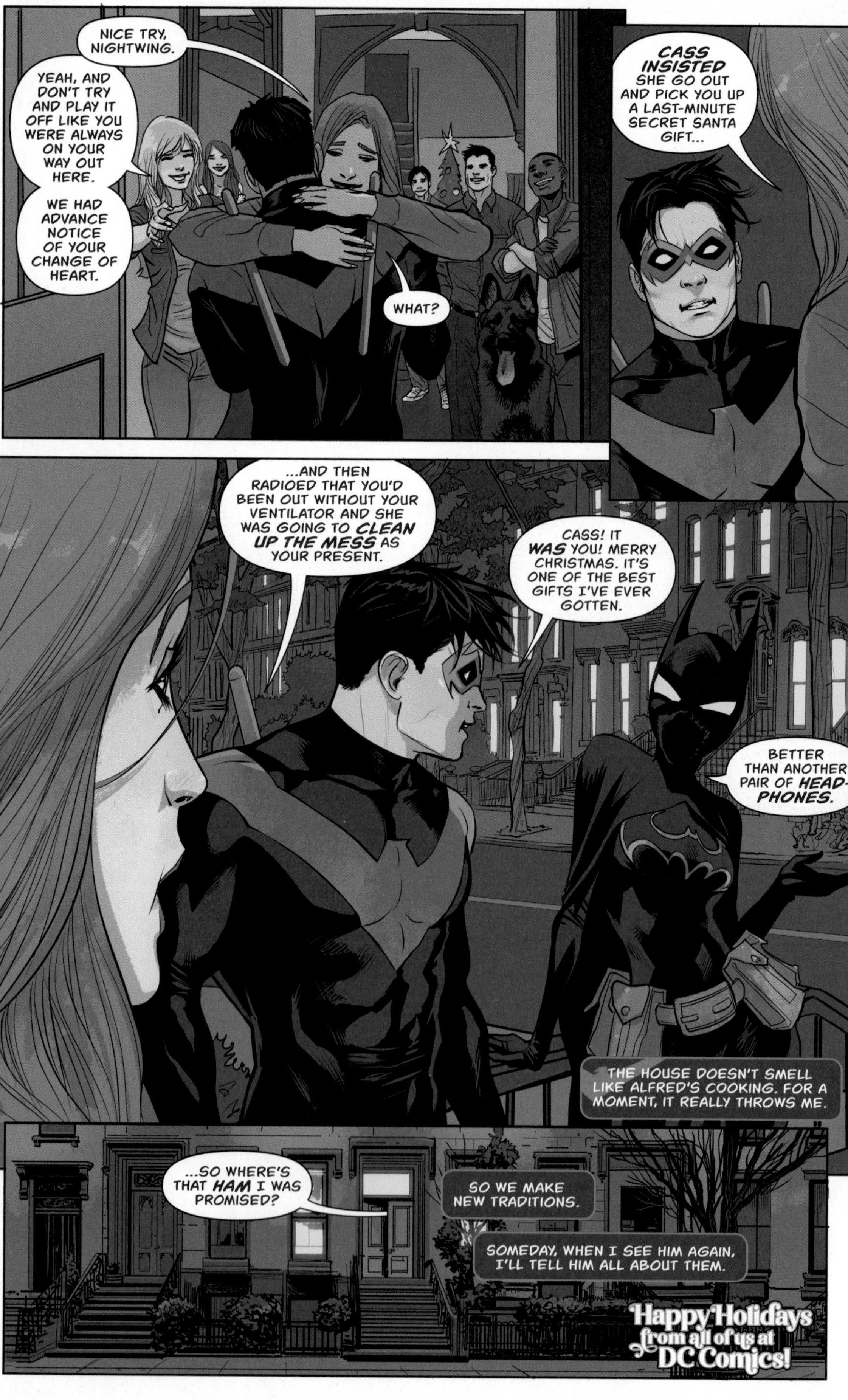
NICE TRY, NIGHTWING.
YEAH, AND DON'T TRY AND PLAY IT OFF LIKE YOU WERE ALWAYS ON YOUR WAY OUT HERE.
WE HAD ADVANCE NOTICE OF YOUR CHANGE OF HEART.
WHAT?
CASS INSISTED SHE GO OUT AND PICK YOU UP A LAST-MINUTE SECRET SANTA GIFT...
...AND THEN RADIOED THAT YOU'D BEEN OUT WITHOUT YOUR VENTILATOR AND SHE WAS GOING TO CLEAN UP THE MESS AS YOUR PRESENT.
CASS! IT WAS YOU! MERRY CHRISTMAS. IT'S ONE OF THE BEST GIFTS I'VE EVER GOTTEN.
BETTER THAN ANOTHER PAIR OF HEAD-PHONES.
THE HOUSE DOESN'T SMELL LIKE ALFRED'S COOKING. FOR A MOMENT, IT REALLY THROWS ME.
...SO WHERE'S THAT HAM I WAS PROMISED?
SO WE MAKE NEW TRADITIONS.
SOMEDAY, WHEN I SEE HIM AGAIN, I'LL TELL HIM ALL ABOUT THEM.
Happy Holidays from all of us at DC Comics!

BATMAN: URBAN LEGENDS

COVER GALLERY

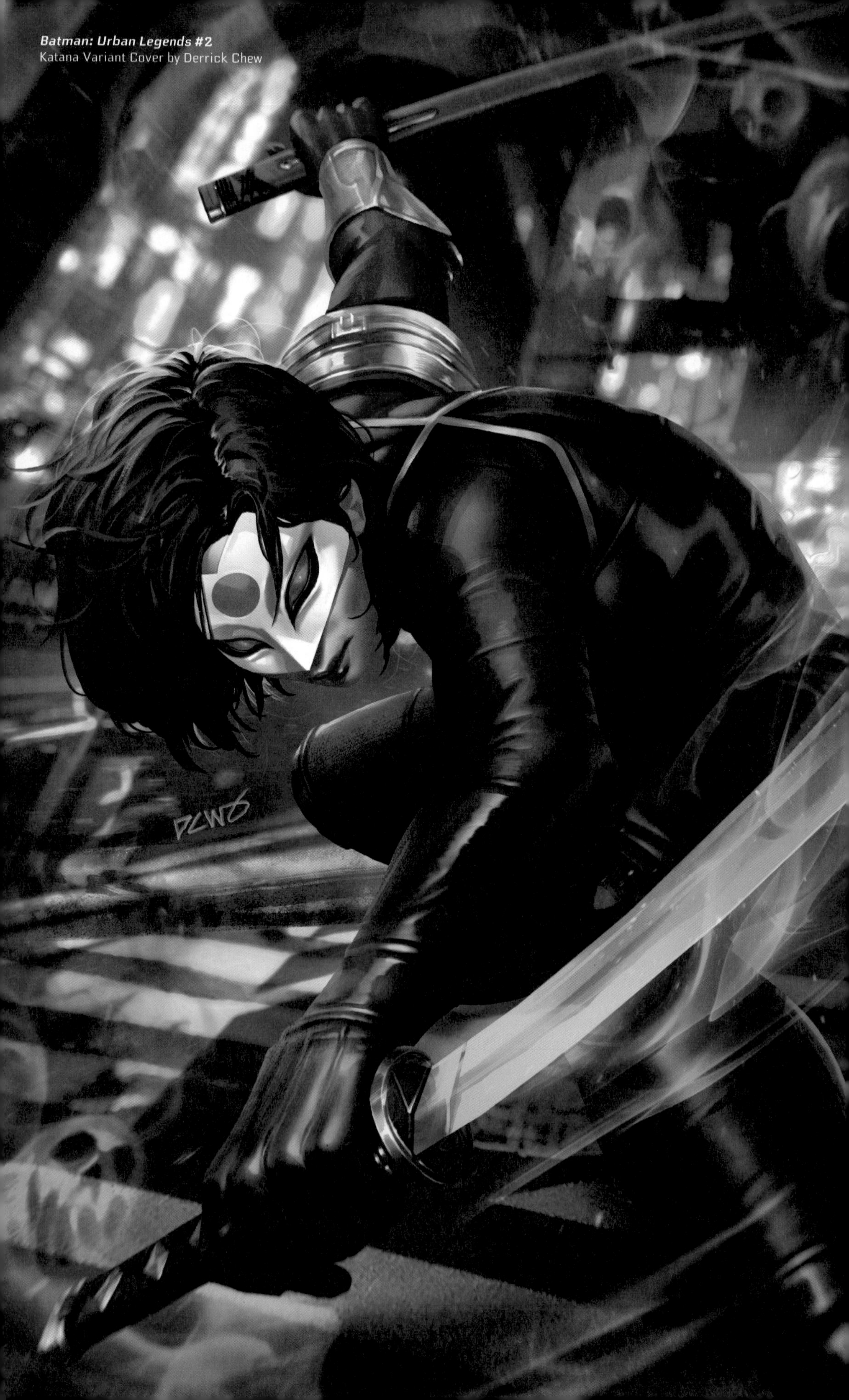

***Batman: Urban Legends* #2**
Katana Variant Cover by Derrick Chew

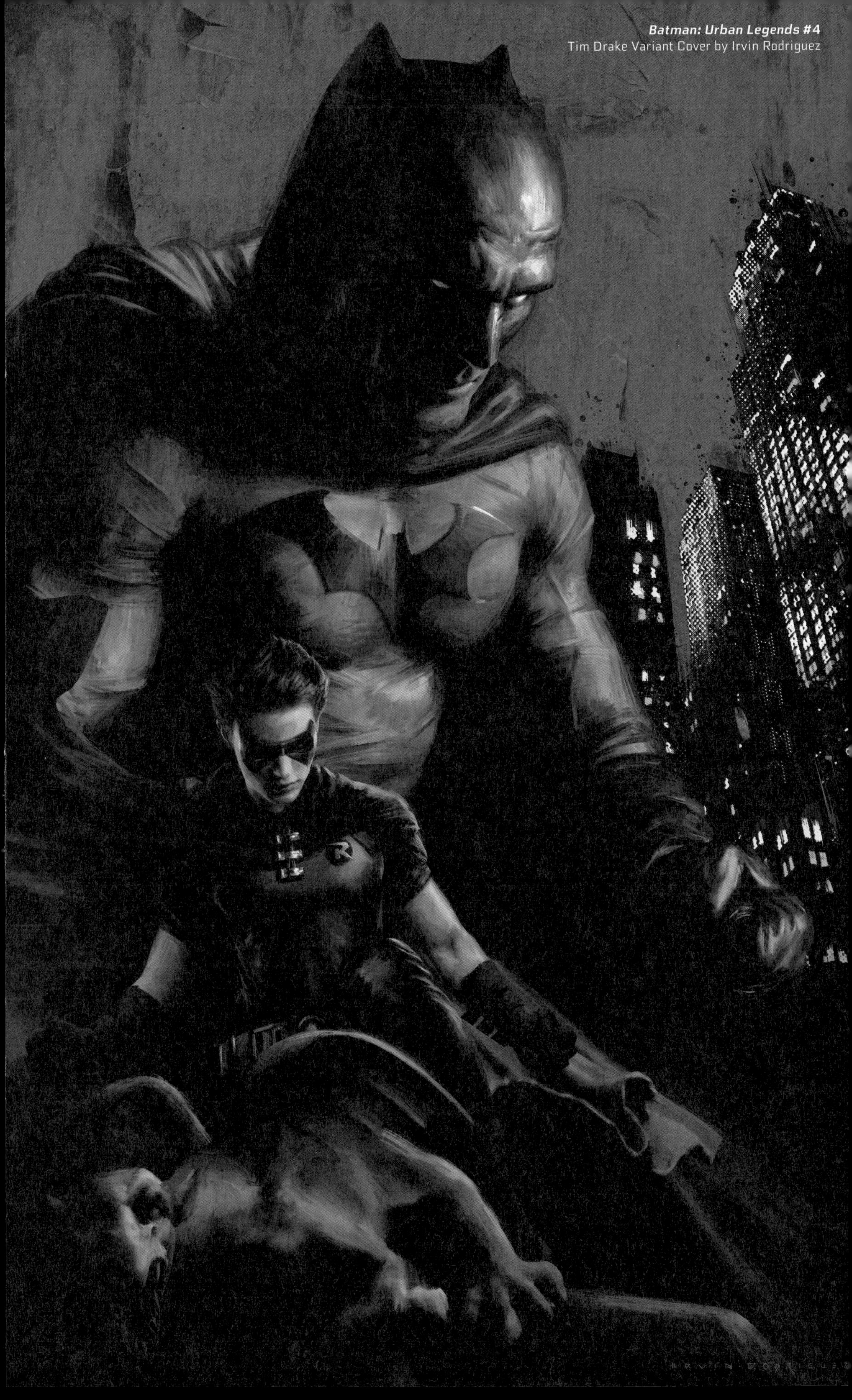

***Batman: Urban Legends* #4**
Tim Drake Variant Cover by Irvin Rodriguez

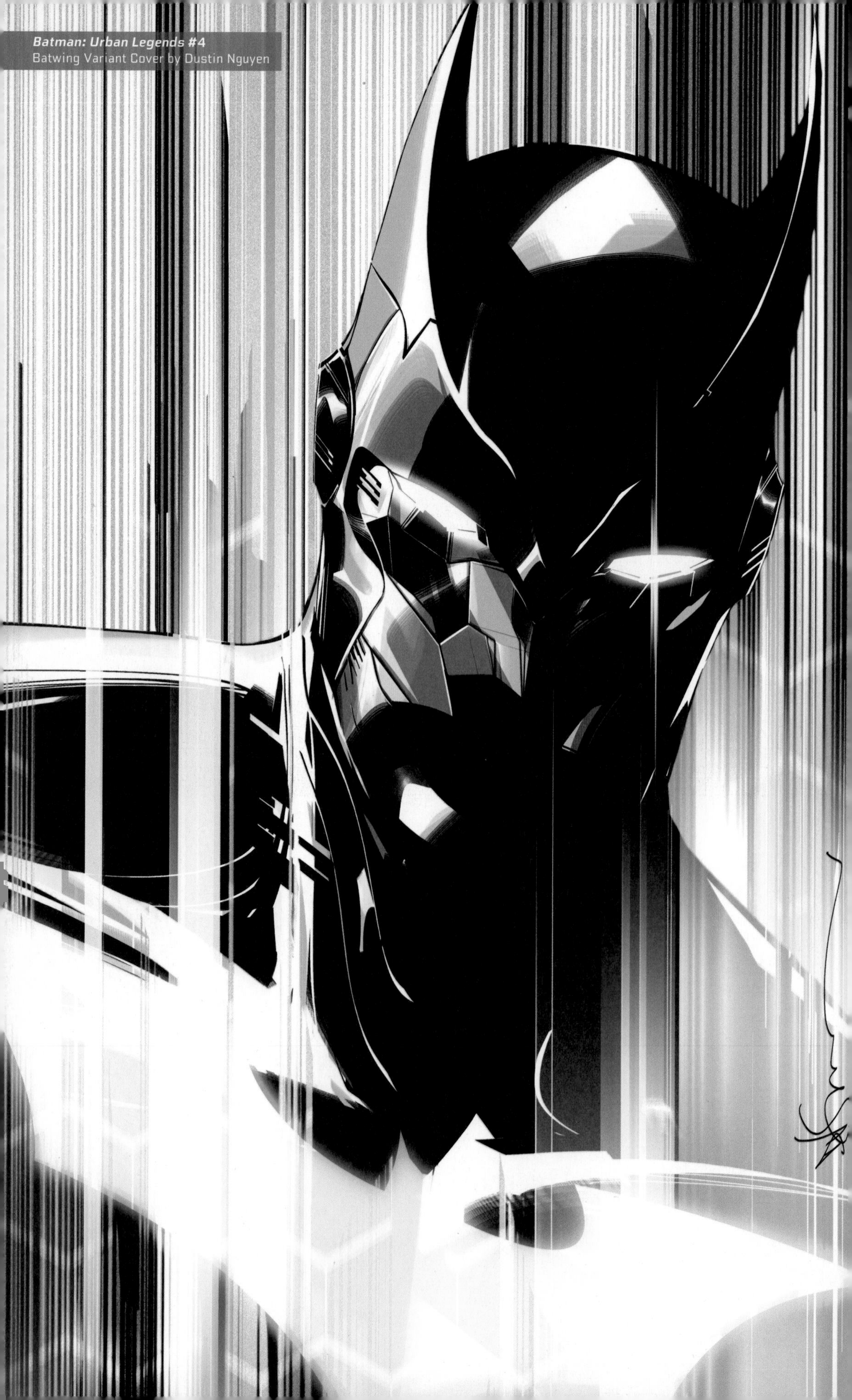

***Batman: Urban Legends* #4**
Batwing Variant Cover by Dustin Nguyen

***Batman: Urban Legends* #5**
Batgirls Variant Cover by Mimi Yoon

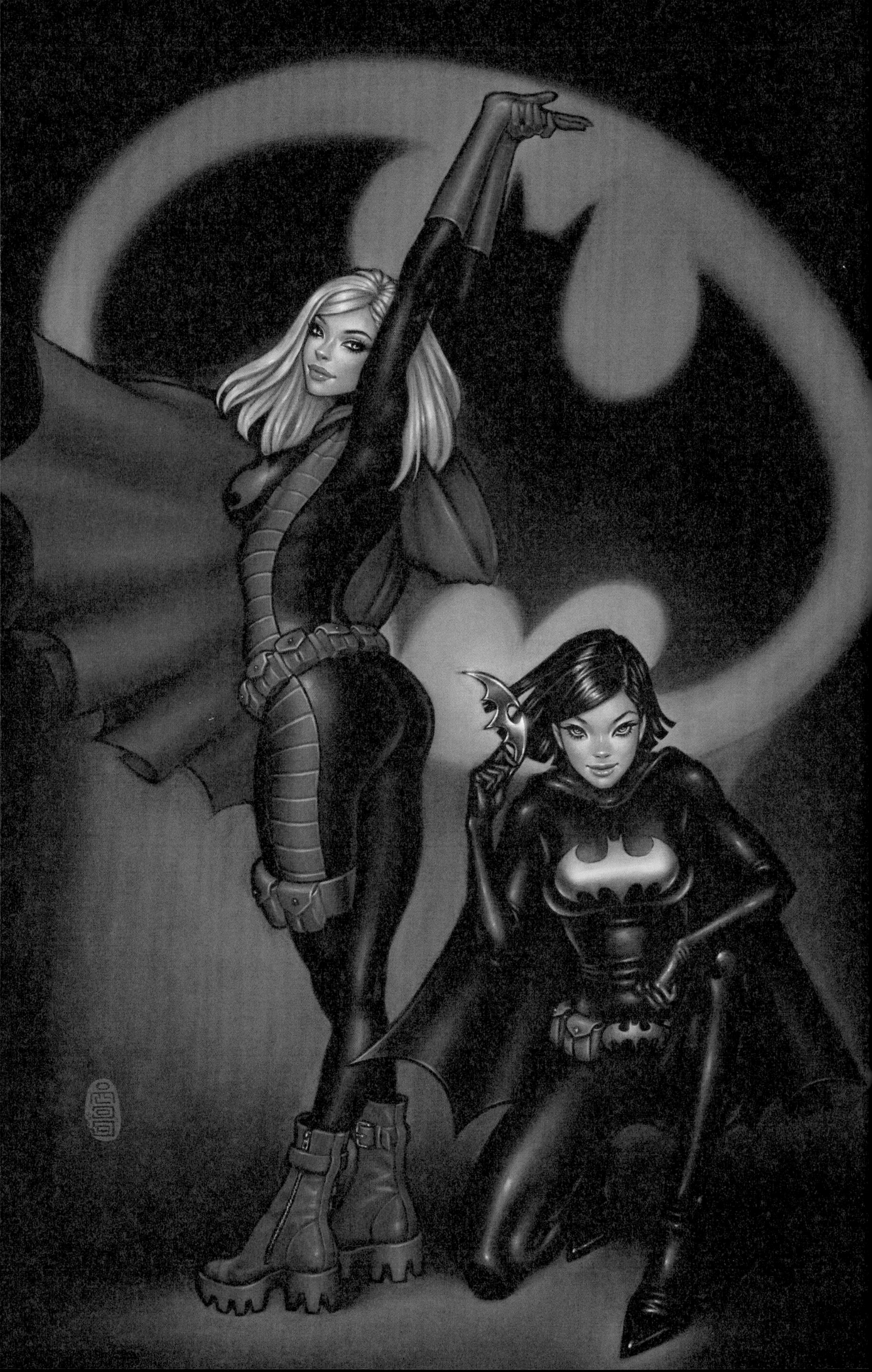

Batman: Urban Legends #9
Main Cover by Colleen Doran

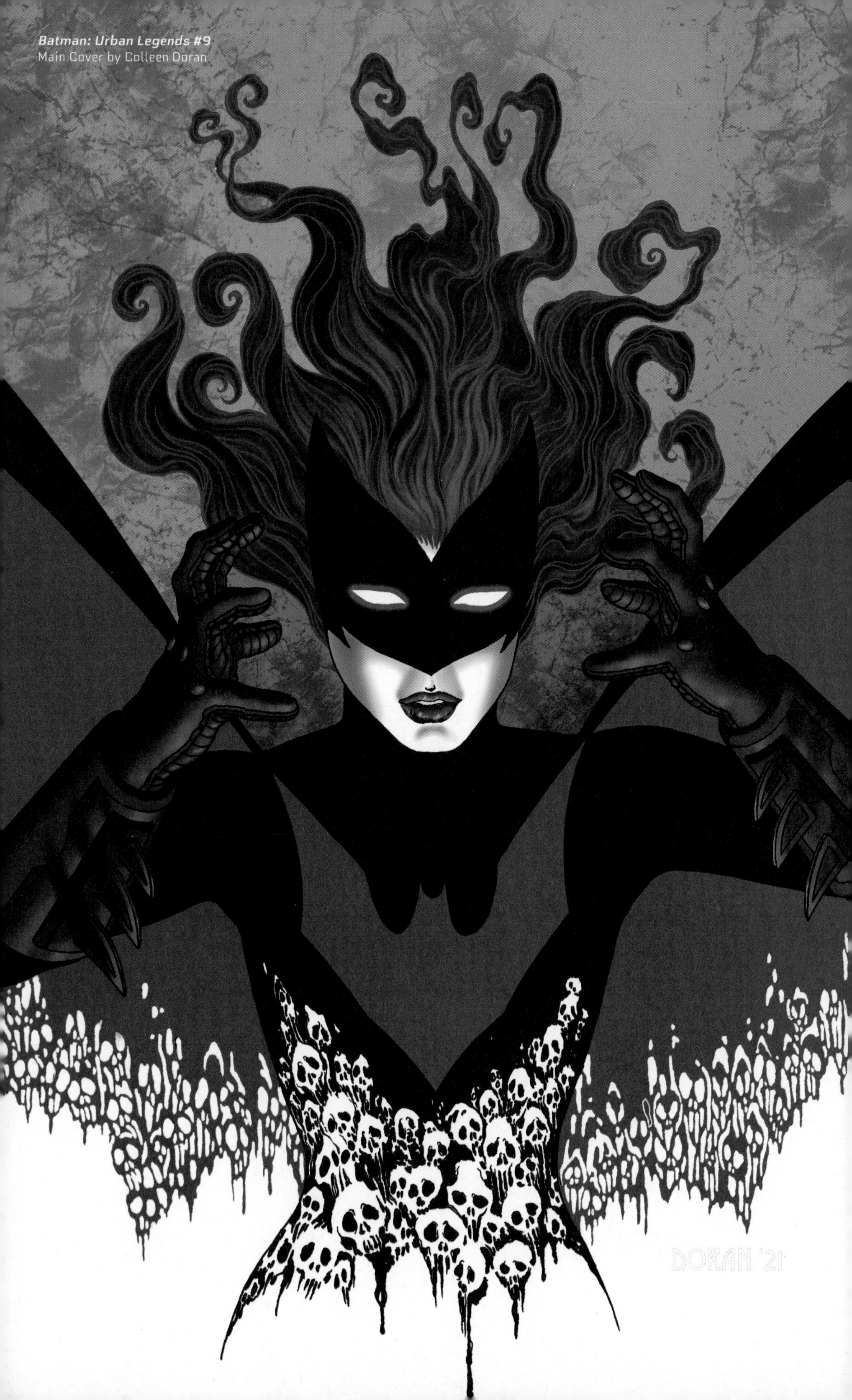
DORAN '21

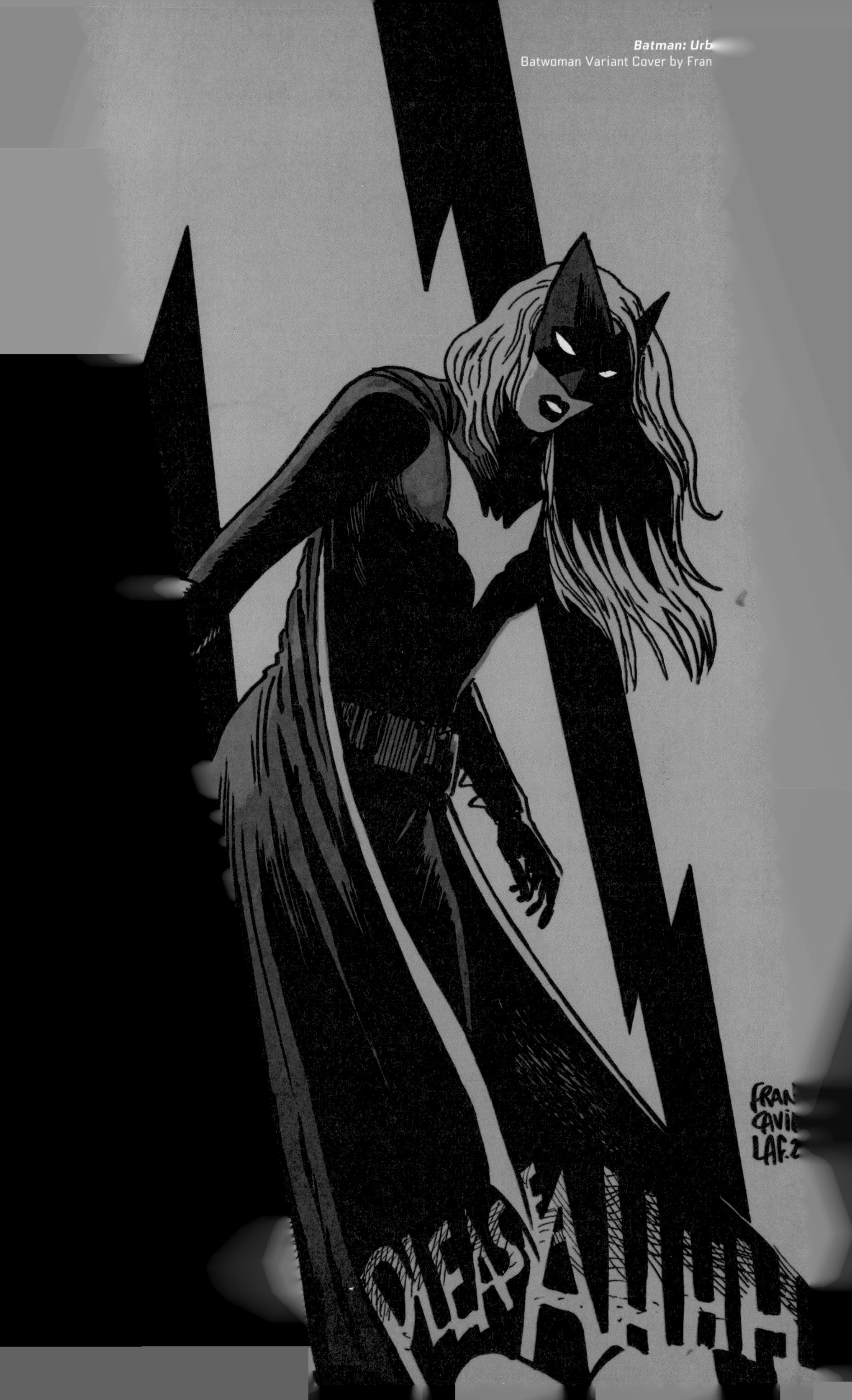

Batman: Urb
Batwoman Variant Cover by Fran

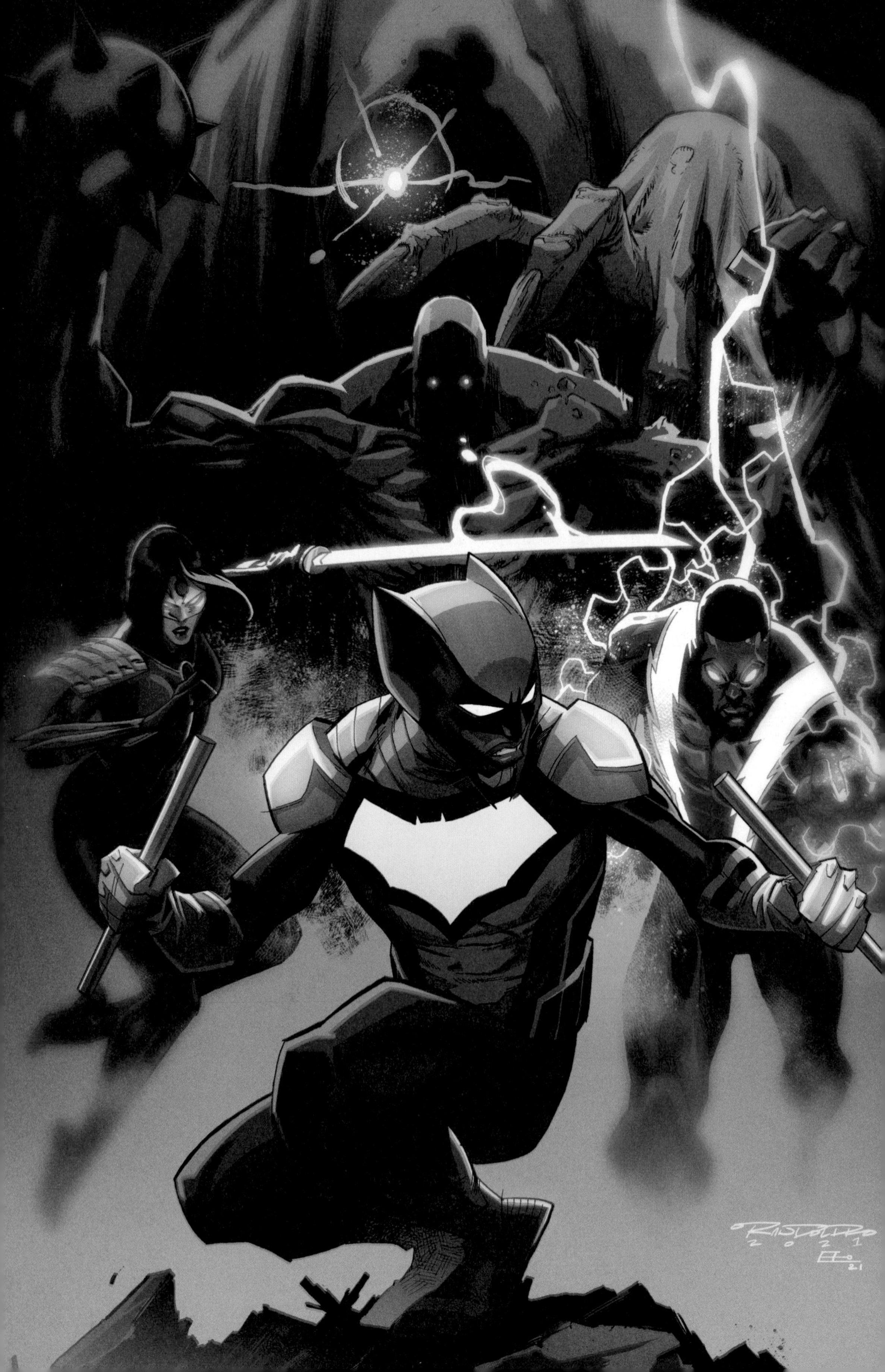

***Batman: Urban Legends* #9**
Outsiders Variant Cover by Khary Randolph & Emilio Lopez

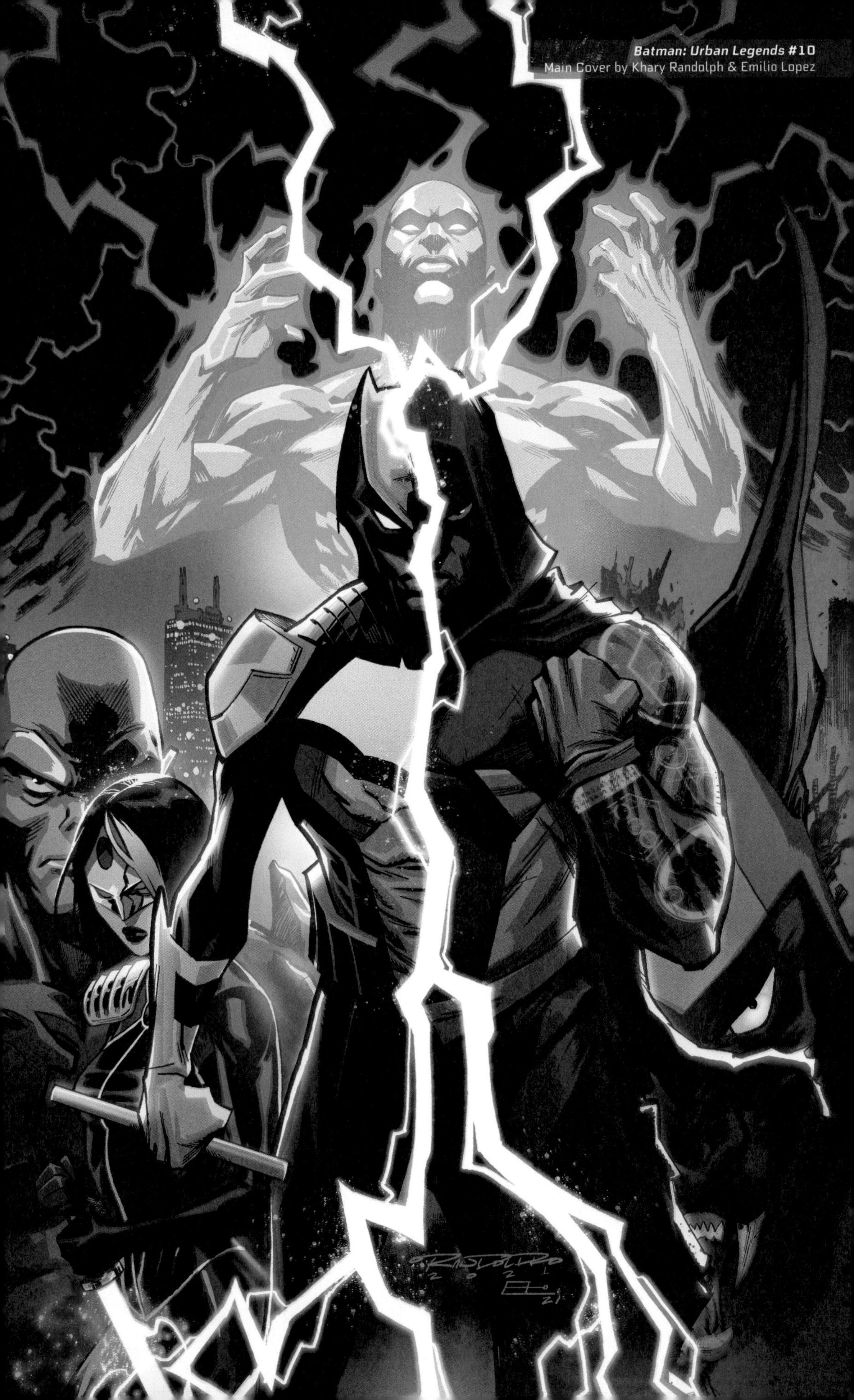

***Batman: Urban Legends* #10**
Main Cover by Khary Randolph & Emilio Lopez

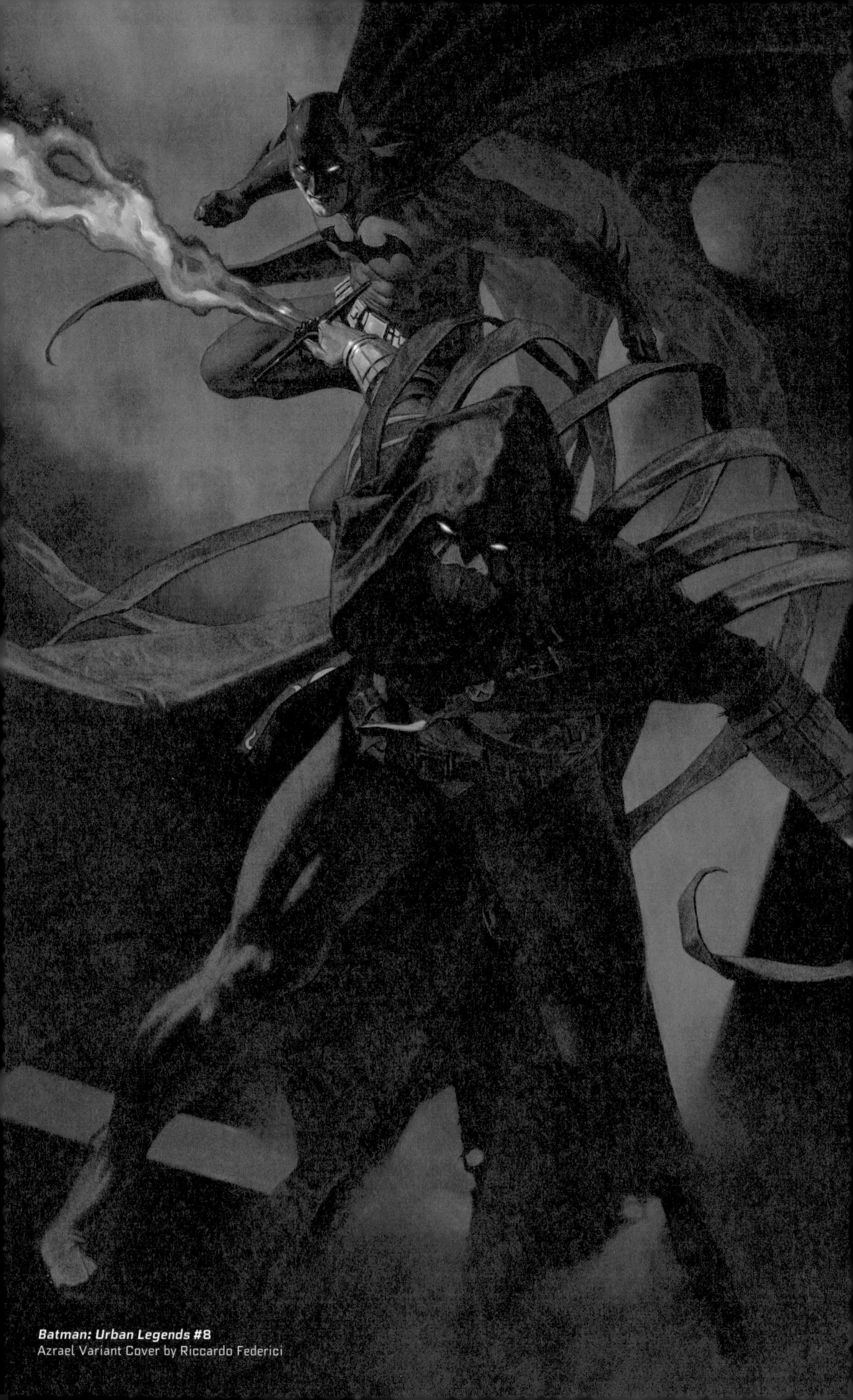

***Batman: Urban Legends* #8**
Azrael Variant Cover by Riccardo Federici

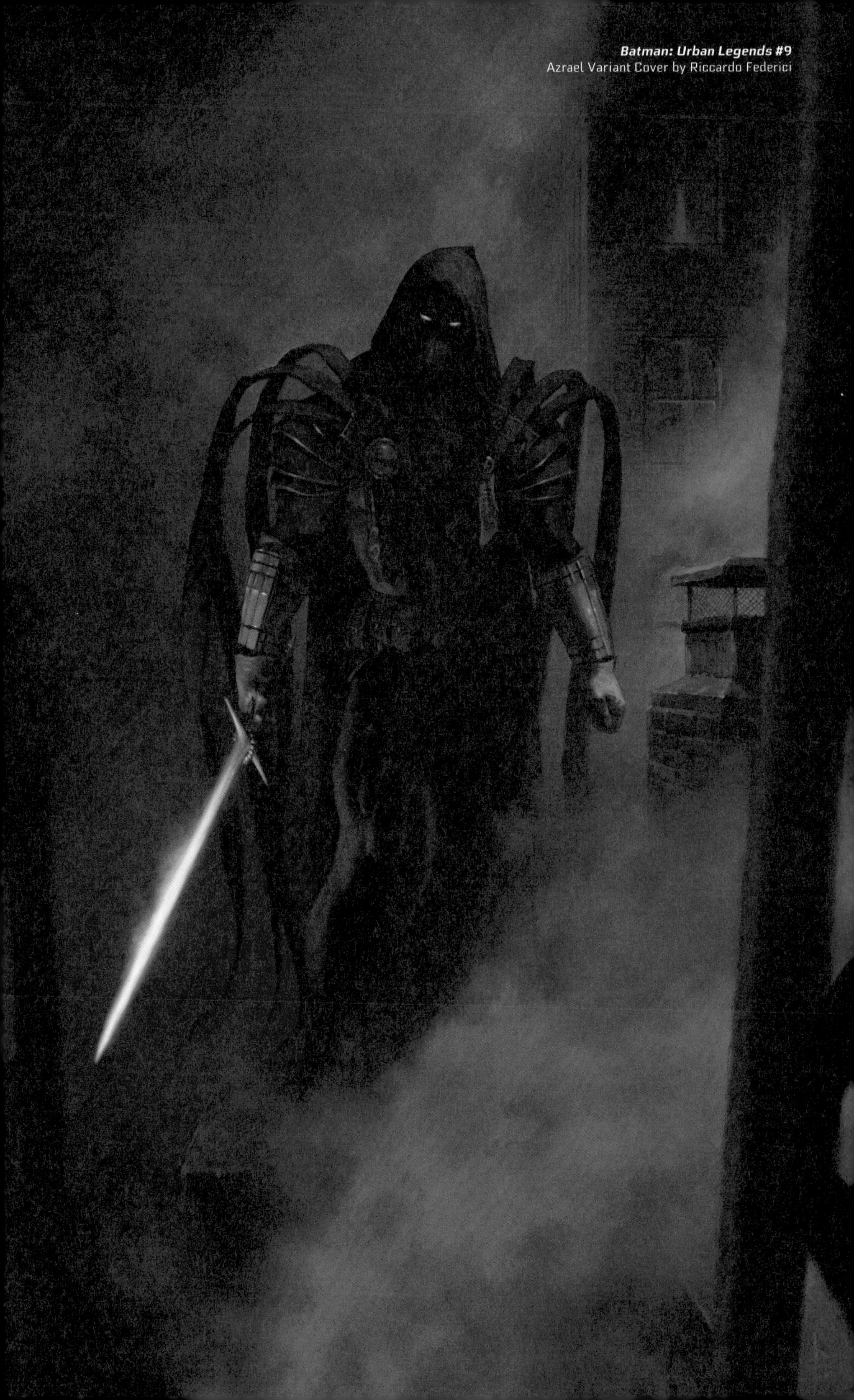

***Batman: Urban Legends* #9**
Azrael Variant Cover by Riccardo Federici

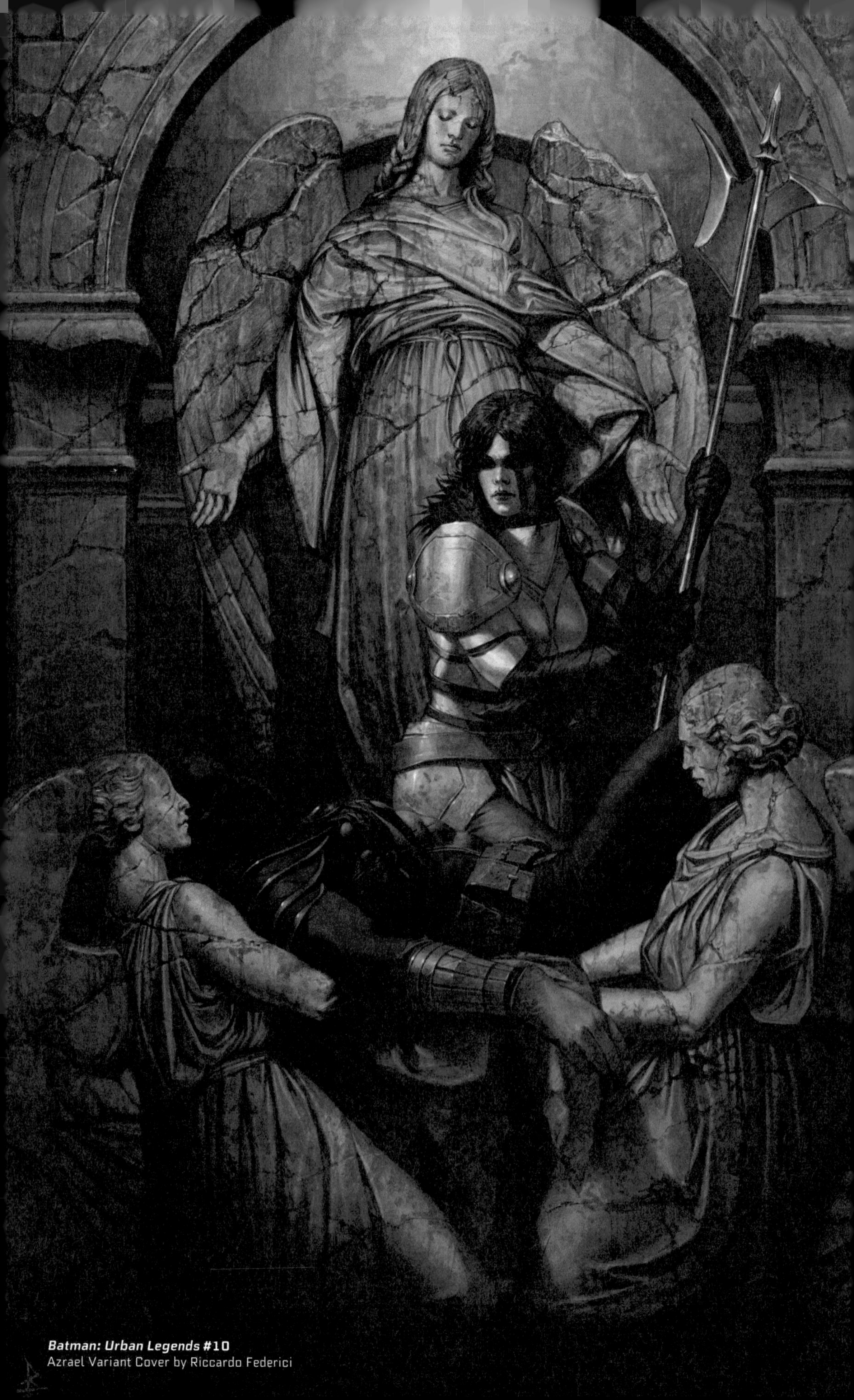

***Batman: Urban Legends* #10**
Azrael Variant Cover by Riccardo Federici

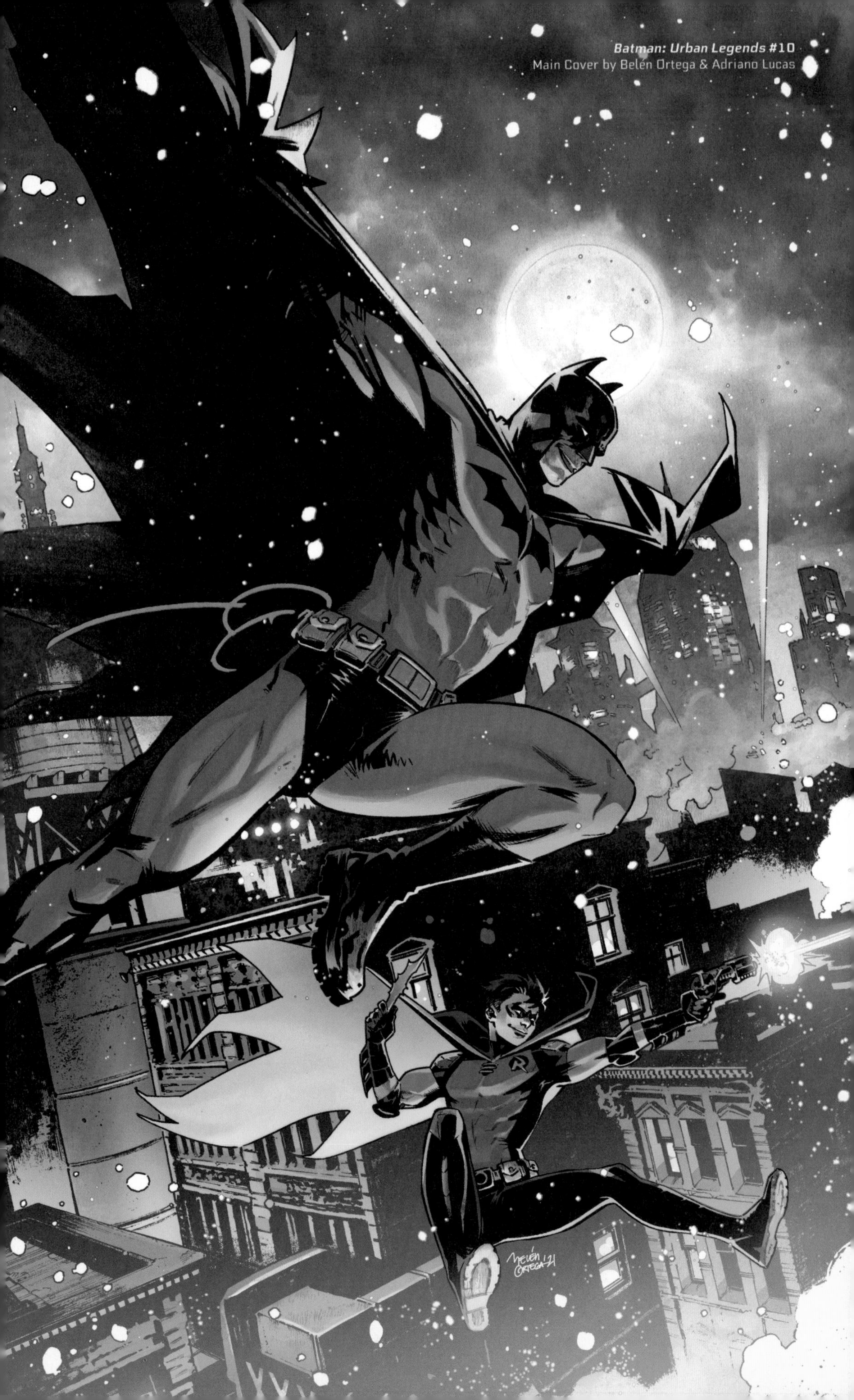

Belén Ortega '21

Batman: Urban Legends #10
Main Cover by Belén Ortega & Adriano Lucas

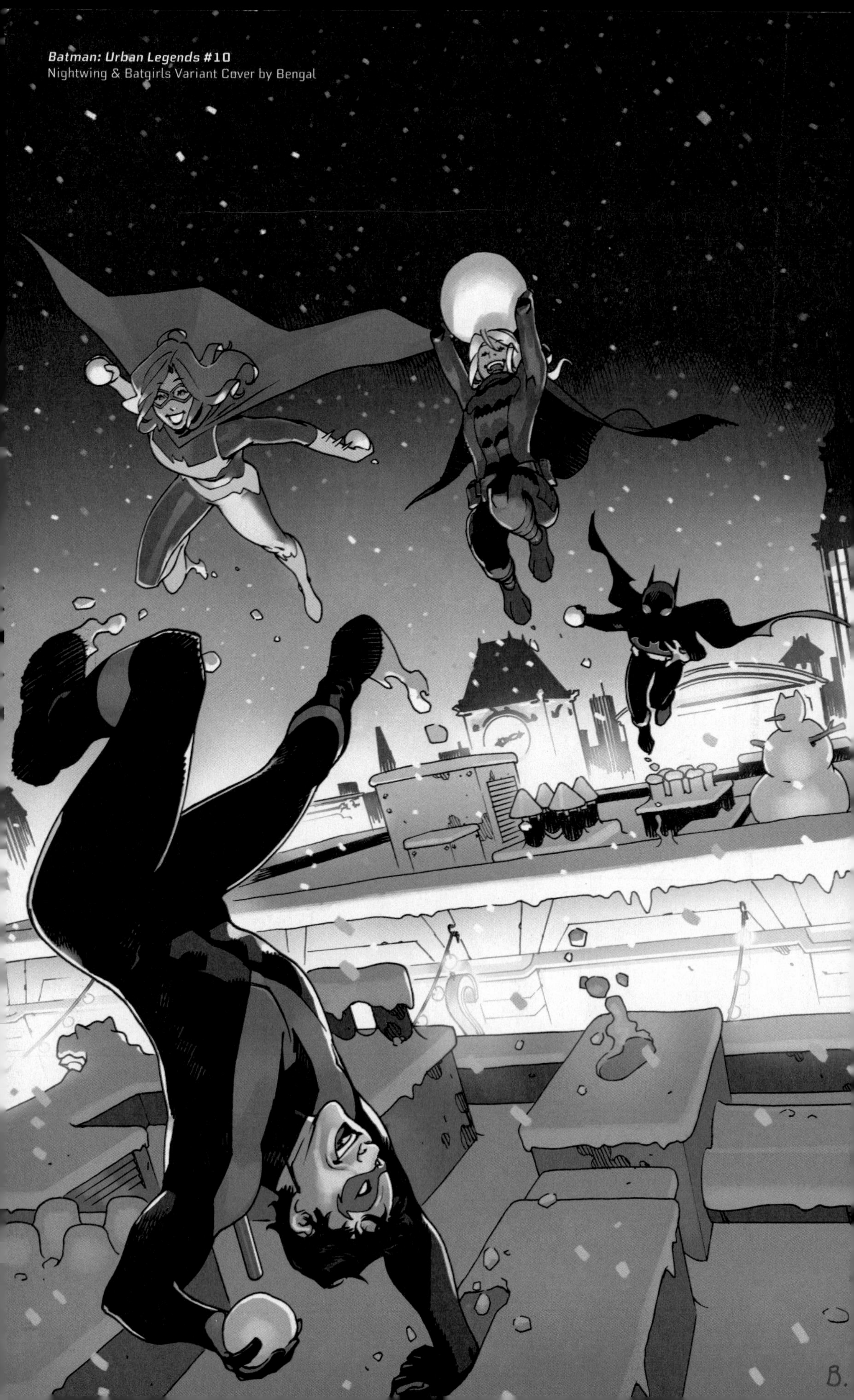

Batman: Urban Legends #10
Nightwing & Batgirls Variant Cover by Bengal